THE HISTORY OF ENGLAND

FROM THE ACCESSION OF JAMES THE SECOND

BY

LORD MACAULAY

EDITED BY

CHARLES HARDING FIRTH, M.A.

REGIUS PROFESSOR OF MODERN HISTORY IN THE
UNIVERSITY OF OXFORD

IN SIX VOLUMES

VOLUME V

MACMILLAN AND CO., LIMITED
ST. MARTIN'S STREET, LONDON

1914

THE HISTORY OF ENGLAND

VOLUME V

MACMILLAN AND CO., Limited
LONDON · BOMBAY · CALCUTTA
MELBOURNE

THE MACMILLAN COMPANY
NEW YORK · BOSTON · CHICAGO
DALLAS · SAN FRANCISCO

THE MACMILLAN CO. OF CANADA, Ltd.
TORONTO

CONTENTS OF THE FIFTH VOLUME

CHAPTER XVIII

CONTENTS

CHAPTER XIX

CHAPTER XX

CONTENTS

CHAPTER XXI

CONTENTS

LIST OF ILLUSTRATIONS

LIST OF ILLUSTRATIONS xiii

FULL PAGE PLATES IN COLOUR

HISTORY OF ENGLAND

CHAPTER XVIII

ON the nineteenth of October 1691, William arrived at Kensington from the Netherlands.[1] Three days later he opened the Parliament. The aspect of affairs was, on the whole, cheering. By land there had been gains and losses : but the balance was in favour of England. Against the fall of Mons might well be set off the taking of Athlone, the victory of Aghrim, the surrender of Limerick, and the pacification of Ireland. At sea there had been no great victory : but there had been a great display of power and of activity ; and, though many were dissatisfied because more had not been done, none could deny that there had been a change for the better. The ruin caused by the follies and vices of Torrington had been repaired: the fleet had been well equipped : the rations had been abundant and wholesome ; and the health of the crews had consequently been, for that age, wonderfully good. Russell, who commanded the naval forces of the allies, had in vain offered battle to the French. The white flag, which, in the preceding year, had ranged the Channel unresisted from the Land's End to the Straits of Dover, now, as soon as our topmasts were descried, abandoned the open sea, and retired into the depths of the harbour of Brest. The appearance of an English squadron in the estuary of the Shannon had decided the fate of the last fortress which had held out for King James ; and a fleet of merchantmen from the Levant, valued at four millions sterling, had, through dangers which had caused many sleepless nights to the underwriters of Lombard Street, been convoyed safe into the Thames.[2] The Lords and Commons listened with signs of satisfaction to a speech

Opening of the Parliament

[1] London Gazette, Oct. 22. 1691.

[2] Burnet, ii. 78, 79.; Burchett's Memoirs of Transactions at Sea ; Journal of the English and Dutch fleet, in a Letter from an Officer on board the Lennox, at Torbay, licensed August 21. 1691. The writer says : "We attribute our health, under God, to the extraordinary care taken in the well ordering of our provisions, both meat and drink."

in which the King congratulated them on the event of the war in Ireland, and expressed his confidence that they would continue to support him in the war with France. He told them that a great naval armament would be necessary, and that, in his opinion, the conflict by land could not be effectually maintained with less than sixty five thousand men.[1]

He was thanked in affectionate terms : the force which he asked was voted ; and large supplies were granted with little difficulty. But, **Debates on the salaries and fees of official men** when the Ways and Means were taken into consideration, symptoms of discontent began to appear. Eighteen months before, when the Commons had been employed in settling the Civil List, many members had shown a very natural disposition to complain of the amount of the salaries and fees received by official men. Keen speeches had been made, and, what was much less usual, had been printed : there had been much excitement out of doors : but nothing had been done. The subject was now revived. A report made by the Commissioners who had been appointed in the preceding year to examine the public accounts disclosed some facts which excited indignation, and others which raised grave suspicion. The House seemed fully determined to make an extensive reform ; and, in truth, nothing could have averted such a reform except the folly and violence of the reformers. That they should have been angry is indeed not strange. The enormous gains, direct and indirect, of the servants of the public went on increasing, while the gains of everybody else were diminishing. Rents were falling: trade was languishing : every man who lived either on what his ancestors had left him or on the fruits of his own industry was forced to retrench. The placeman alone throve amidst the general distress. " Look," cried the incensed squires, " at the Comptroller of the Customs. Ten years ago, he walked, and we rode. Our incomes have been curtailed : his salary has been doubled : we have sold our horses : he has bought them; and now we go on foot and are splashed by his coach and six." Lowther vainly endeavoured to stand up against the storm. He was heard with little favour by those country gentlemen who had not long before looked up to him as one of their leaders. He had left them : he had become a courtier : he had two good places, one in the Treasury, the other in the household. He had recently received from the King's own hand a gratuity of two thousand guineas.[2] It seemed perfectly natural that he should defend abuses by which he profited. The taunts and reproaches with which he was assailed were insupportable to his sensitive nature. He lost his head, almost fainted away on the floor of the House, and

[1] Lords' and Commons' Journals, Oct. 22. 1691.

[2] This appears from a letter written by Lowther, after he became Lord Lonsdale, to his son. A copy of this letter is among the Mackintosh MSS.

WILLIAM III

From a mezzotint by P. Schenck in the Sutherland Collection, dated 1691

talked about righting himself in another place.[1]   Unfortunately no member rose at this conjuncture to propose that the civil establishments of the kingdom should be carefully revised, that sinecures should be abolished, that exorbitant official incomes should be reduced, and that no servant of the State should be allowed to exact, under any pretence, anything beyond his known and lawful remuneration.   In this way it would have been possible to diminish the public burdens, and at the same time to increase the efficiency of every public department.   But, on this as on many other occasions, those who were loud in clamouring against the prevailing abuses were utterly destitute of the qualities necessary for the work of reform.   On the twelfth of December, some foolish man, whose name has not come down to us, moved that no person employed in any civil office, the Speaker, Judges, and Ambassadors excepted, should receive more than five hundred pounds a year ; and this motion was not only carried, but carried without one dissentient voice.[2]   Those who were most interested in opposing it doubtless saw that opposition would, at that moment, only irritate the majority, and reserved themselves for a more favourable time.   The more favourable time soon came.   No man of common sense could, when his blood had cooled, remember without shame that he had voted for a resolution which made no distinction between sinecurists and laborious public servants, between clerks employed in copying letters and ministers on whose wisdom and integrity the fate of the nation might depend.   The salary of the Doorkeeper of the Excise Office had been, by a scandalous job, raised to five hundred a year.   It ought to have been reduced to fifty.   On the other hand, the services of a Secretary of State who was well qualified for his post would have been cheap at five thousand.   If the resolution of the Commons had been carried into effect, both the salary which ought not to have exceeded fifty pounds, and the salary which might without impropriety have amounted to five thousand, would have been fixed at five hundred.   Such absurdity must have shocked even the roughest and plainest foxhunter in the House.   A reaction took place ; and when, after an interval of a few weeks, it was proposed to insert in a bill of supply a clause in conformity with the resolution of the twelfth of December, the Noes were loud : the Speaker was of opinion that they had it : the Ayes did not venture to dispute his

[1] See Commons' Journals, Dec. 3. 1691 ; and Grey's Debates.   It is to be regretted that the Report of the Commissioners of Accounts has not been preserved.   Lowther, in his letter to his son, alludes to the badgering of this day with great bitterness.   " What man," he asks, " that hath bread to eat, can endure, after having served with all the diligence and application mankind is capable of, and after having given satisfaction to the King from whom all officers of state derive their authoritie, after acting rightly by all men, to be baited by men who do it to all people in authoritie ? "

[2] Commons' Journals, Dec. 12. 1691.

THE USURPER'S HABIT: A CARICATURE AGAINST LEWIS XIV

Number 1267 in the British Museum Catalogue of Satirical Prints

opinion : the senseless plan which had been approved without a division was rejected without a division ; and the subject was not again mentioned.   Thus a grievance so scandalous that none of those who profited by it dared to defend it was perpetuated merely by the imbecility and intemperance of those who attacked it.[1]

Early in the Session the Treaty of Limerick became the subject of a grave and earnest discussion.   The Commons, in the exercise of that

Act excluding Papists from public trust in Ireland
supreme power which the English legislature possessed over all the dependencies of England, sent up to the Lords a bill providing that no person should sit in the Irish Parliament, should hold any Irish office, civil, military, or ecclesiastical, or should practise law or medicine in Ireland, till he had taken the Oaths of Allegiance and Supremacy, and subscribed the Declaration against Transubstantiation.   The Lords were not more inclined than the Commons to favour the Irish.   No peer was disposed to entrust Roman Catholics with political power.   Nay, it seems that no peer objected to the principle of the absurd and cruel rule which excluded Roman Catholics from the liberal professions.   But it was thought that this rule, though unobjectionable in principle, would, if adopted without some exceptions, be a breach of a positive compact.   Their Lordships called for the Treaty of Limerick, ordered it to be read at the table, and proceeded to consider whether the law framed by the Lower House was consistent with the engagements into which the government had entered.   One discrepancy was noticed.   It was stipulated, by the second civil article, that every person actually residing in any fortress occupied by an Irish garrison should be permitted, on taking the Oath of Allegiance, to resume any calling which he had exercised before the Revolution.   It would, beyond all doubt, have been a violation of this covenant to require that a lawyer or a physician, who had been within the walls of Limerick during the siege, and who was willing to take the Oath of Allegiance, should also take the Oath of Supremacy and subscribe the Declaration against Transubstantiation, before he could exercise his profession.   Holt was consulted, and was directed to prepare clauses in conformity with the terms of the capitulation.

The bill, as amended by the Chief Justice, was sent back to the Commons.   They at first rejected the amendment, and demanded a conference.   The conference was granted.   Rochester, in the Painted

---

[1] Commons' Journals, Feb. 15. 169$\frac{1}{2}$; Baden to the States General, $\frac{\text{Jan. 26.}}{\text{Feb. 5.}}$.   On the 8th of December 1797, Mr. John Nicholls, a reformer of much more zeal than wisdom, proposed, in the House of Commons, a resolution framed on the model of the resolution of the 12th of December 1691.   Mr. Pitt justly remarked that the precedent on which Mr. Nicholls relied was of no value, for that the gentlemen who passed the resolution of the 12th of December 1691 had, in a very short time, discovered and acknowledged their error.   The debate is much better given in the Morning Chronicle than in the Parliamentary History.

Chamber, delivered to the managers of the Lower House a copy of the Treaty of Limerick, and earnestly represented the importance of preserving the public faith inviolate. This appeal was one which no honest man, though inflamed by national and religious animosity, could resist. The Commons reconsidered the subject, and, after hearing the Treaty read, agreed, with some slight modifications, to what the Lords had proposed.[1]

The bill became a law. It attracted, at the time, little notice, but was, after the lapse of several generations, the subject of a very acrimonious controversy. Many of us can well remember how strongly the public mind was stirred, in the days of George the Third and George the Fourth, by the question whether Roman Catholics should be permitted to sit in Parliament. It may be doubted whether any dispute has produced stranger perversions of history. The whole past was falsified for the sake of the present. All the great events of three centuries long appeared to us distorted and discoloured by a mist sprung from our own theories and our own passions. Some friends of religious liberty, not content with the advantage which they possessed in the fair conflict of reason with reason, weakened their case by maintaining that the law which excluded Irish Roman Catholics from Parliament was inconsistent with the civil Treaty of Limerick. The first article of that Treaty, it was said, guaranteed to the Irish Roman Catholic such privileges in the exercise of his religion as he had enjoyed in the time of Charles the Second. In the time of Charles the Second no test excluded Roman Catholics from the Irish Parliament. Such a test could not therefore, it was argued, be imposed without a breach of public faith. In the year 1828, especially, this argument was put forward in the House of Commons as if it had been the main strength of a cause which stood in need of no such support. The champions of Protestant ascendency were well pleased to see the debate diverted from a political question about which they were in the wrong, to a historical question about which they were in the right. They had no difficulty in proving that the first article, as understood by all the contracting parties, meant only that the Roman Catholic worship should be tolerated as in time past. That article was drawn up by Ginkell; and, just before he drew it up, he had declared that he would rather try the chance of arms than consent that Irish Papists should be capable of holding civil and military offices, of exercising liberal professions, and of becoming members of municipal corporations. How is it possible to believe that he would, of his own accord, have promised that the House of Lords and the House of Commons should be open to men to whom he would not open a

---

[1] Stat. 3. W. & M. c. 2., Lords' Journals; Lords' Journals, 16 Nov. 1691; Commons' Journals, Dec. 1. 9. 5.

guild of skinners or a guild of cordwainers? How, again, is it possible to believe that the English Peers would, while professing the most punctilious respect for public faith, while lecturing the Commons on the duty of observing public faith, while taking counsel with the most learned and upright jurist of the age as to the best mode of maintaining public faith, have committed a flagrant violation of public faith, and that not a single lord should have been so honest or so factious as to protest against an act of monstrous perfidy aggravated by hypocrisy? Or, if we could believe this, how can we believe that no voice would have been raised in any part of the world against such wickedness; that the Court of Saint Germains and the Court of Versailles would have remained profoundly silent; that no Irish exile, no English malecontent, would have uttered a murmur; that not a word of invective or sarcasm on so inviting a subject would have been found in the whole compass of the Jacobite literature; and that it would have been reserved for politicians of the nineteenth century to discover that a treaty made in the seventeenth century had, a few weeks after it had been signed, been outrageously violated in the sight of all Europe.[1]

On the same day on which the Commons read for the first time the bill which subjected Ireland to the absolute dominion of the Protestant minority, they took into consideration another matter of high importance. Throughout the country, but especially in the capital, in the seaports, and in the manufacturing towns, the minds of men were greatly excited on the subject of the trade with the East Indies: a fierce paper war had during some time been raging; and several grave questions, both constitutional and commercial, had been raised, which the legislature only could decide.

Debates on the East India trade

It has often been repeated, and ought never to be forgotten, that our polity differs widely from those polities which have, during the last eighty years, been methodically constructed, digested into articles, and ratified by constituent assemblies. It grew up in a rude age. It is not to be found entire in any formal instrument. All along the line which separates the functions of the prince from those of the legislator there was long a disputed territory. Encroachments were

---

[1] The Irish Roman Catholics complained, and with but too much reason, that, at a later period, the Treaty of Limerick was violated; but those very complaints are admissions that the Statute 3 W. & M. c. 2. was not a violation of the Treaty. Thus the author of A Light to the Blind, speaking of the first article, says, "This article, in seven years after, was broken by a Parliament in Ireland summoned by the Prince of Orange, wherein a law was passed for banishing the Catholic bishops, dignitaries, and regular clergy." Surely he never would have written thus, if the article really had, only two months after it was signed, been broken by the English Parliament. The Abbé Mac Geoghegan, too, complains that the Treaty was violated some years after it was made. But, by so complaining, he admits that it was not violated by Stat. 3 W. & M. c. 2.

perpetually committed, and, if not very outrageous, were often tolerated. Trespass, merely as trespass, was commonly suffered to pass un-resented.   It was only when the trespass produced some positive damage that the aggrieved party stood on his right, and demanded that the frontier should be set out by metes and bounds, and that the land-marks should thenceforward be punctiliously respected.

Many of the points which had occasioned the most violent disputes between our Sovereigns and their Parliaments had been finally decided by the Bill of Rights.   But one question, scarcely less important than any of the questions which had been set at rest for ever, was still undetermined.   Indeed, that question was never, as far as can now be ascertained, even mentioned in the Convention.   The King had un-doubtedly, by the ancient laws of the realm, large powers for the regulation of trade : but the ablest judge would have found it difficult to say what was the precise extent of those powers.   It was universally acknow-ledged that it belonged to the King to prescribe weights and measures, and to coin money ; that no fair or market could be held without authority from him ; that no ship could unload in any bay or estuary which he had not declared to be a port.   In addition to his undoubted right to grant special commercial privileges to particular places, he long claimed a right to grant special commercial privileges to particular societies and to particular individuals ; and our ancestors, as usual, did not think it worth their while to dispute this claim, till it produced serious inconvenience.   At length, in the reign of Elizabeth, the power of creating monopolies began to be grossly abused ; and, as soon as it began to be grossly abused, it began to be questioned.   The Queen wisely declined a conflict with a House of Commons backed by the whole nation.   She frankly acknowledged that there was reason for com-plaint : she cancelled the patents which had excited the public clamours ; and her people, delighted by this concession, and by the gracious manner in which it had been made, did not require from her an express renunciation of the disputed prerogative.

The discontents which her wisdom had appeased were revived by the dishonest and pusillanimous policy which her successor called king-craft.   He readily granted oppressive patents of monopoly.   When he needed the help of his Parliament, he as readily annulled them.   As soon as the Parliament had ceased to sit, his Great Seal was put to instruments more odious than those which he had recently cancelled.   At length that excellent House of Commons which met in 1623 determined to apply a strong remedy to the evil.   The King was forced to give his assent to a law which declared monopolies established by royal authority to be null and void.   Some exceptions, however, were made, and, unfortunately, were not very clearly defined.   It was especially provided that every Society of Merchants which had been instituted for the purpose of carrying on any trade should retain all legal privileges.[1] The question whether a monopoly granted by the Crown to such a society were or were not a legal privilege was left unsettled, and continued to exercise, during many years, the ingenuity of lawyers.[2] The nation, however, relieved at once from a multitude of impositions and vexations which were painfully felt every day at every fireside, was in no humour to dispute the validity of the charters under which a few companies in London traded with distant parts of the world.

Of these companies by far the most important was that which had been, on the last day of the sixteenth century, incorporated by Queen Elizabeth under the name of the Governor and Company of Merchants of London trading to the East Indies.[3] When this celebrated body began to exist, the Mogul monarchy was at the zenith of power and glory. Akbar, the ablest and the best of the princes of the House of Tamerlane, had just been borne, full of years and honours, to a mausoleum surpassing in magnificence any that Europe could show. He had bequeathed to his posterity an empire containing more than twenty times the population, and yielding more than twenty times the revenue, of the England which, under our great Queen, held a foremost place among European powers. It is curious and interesting to consider how little the two countries, destined to be one day so closely connected, were then known to each other. The most enlightened Englishmen looked on India with ignorant admiration. The most enlightened natives of India were scarcely aware that England existed. Our ancestors had a dim notion of endless bazaars, swarming with buyers and sellers, and blazing with cloth of gold, with variegated silks, and with precious stones ; of treasuries where diamonds were piled in heaps, and sequins in mountains ; of palaces, compared with which Whitehall and Hampton Court were hovels ; of armies ten times as numerous as that which they had seen assembled at Tilbury to repel the Armada. On the other

---

[1] Stat. 21 Jac. I. c. 3.

[2] See particularly Two Letters by a Barrister concerning the East Indian Company (1676), and an Answer to the Two Letters published in the same year. See also the Judgment of Lord Jeffreys concerning the Great Case of Monopolies. This judgment was published in 1689, after the downfall of Jeffreys. It was thought necessary to apologise in the preface for printing anything that bore so odious a name. "To commend this argument," says the editor, "I'll not undertake, because of the author. But yet I may tell you what is told me, that it is worthy any gentleman's perusal." The language of Jeffreys is most offensive, sometimes scurrilous, sometimes basely adulatory : but his reasoning as to the mere point of law is certainly able, if not conclusive.

[3] I have left my account of the East India Company as it stood in 1855. It is unnecessary to say that it contains some expressions which would not have been used, if it had been written in 1858.

hand, it was probably not known to one of the statesmen in the Durbar of Agra that there was, near the setting sun, a great city of infidels, called London, where a woman reigned, and that she had given to an association of Frank merchants the exclusive privilege of freighting ships from her dominions to the Indian seas. That this association would one day rule all India, from the ocean to the everlasting snow, would reduce to profound obedience great provinces which had never submitted to Akbar's authority, would send Lieutenant Governors to preside in his capital, and would dole out a monthly pension to his heir, would have seemed to the wisest of European or of Oriental politicians as impossible as that inhabitants of our globe should found an empire in Venus or Jupiter.

Three generations passed away ; and still nothing indicated that the East India Company would ever become a great Asiatic potentate. The Mogul empire, though undermined by internal causes of decay, and tottering to its fall, still presented to distant nations the appearance of undiminished prosperity and vigour. Aurengzebe, who, in the same month in which Oliver Cromwell died, assumed the magnificent title of Conqueror of the World, continued to reign till Anne had been long on the English throne. He was the sovereign of a larger territory than had obeyed any of his predecessors. His name was great in the farthest regions of the West. Here he had been made by Dryden the hero of a tragedy which would alone suffice to show how little the English of that age knew about the vast empire which their grandchildren were to conquer and to govern. The poet's Mussulman princes make love in the style of Amadis, preach about the death of Socrates, and embellish their discourse with allusions to the mythological stories of Ovid. The Brahminical metempsychosis is represented as an article of the Mussulman creed ; and the Mussulman Sultanas burn themselves with their husbands after the Brahminical fashion. This drama, once rapturously applauded by crowded theatres, and known by heart to fine gentlemen and fine ladies, is now forgotten. But one noble passage still lives, and is repeated by thousands who know not whence it comes.[1]

Though nothing yet indicated the high political destiny of the East India Company, that body had a great sway in the City of London. The offices, built on a very small part of the ground which the present offices cover, had escaped the ravages of the fire. The India House of those days was an edifice of timber and plaster, rich with the quaint carving and latticework of the Elizabethan age. Above the windows

[1] Addison's Clarinda, in the week of which she kept a journal, read nothing but Aurengzebe : Spectator, 323. She dreamed that Mr. Froth lay at her feet, and called her Indamora. Her friend Miss Kitty repeated, without book, the eight best lines of the play ; those, no doubt, which begin, " Trust on, and think tomorrow will repay." There are not eight finer lines in Lucretius.

was a painting which represented a fleet of merchantmen tossing on the waves.   The whole was surmounted by a colossal wooden seaman, who, from between two dolphins, looked down on the crowds of Leadenhall Street.[1]   In this abode, narrow and humble indeed when compared with the vast labyrinth of passages and chambers which now bears the same name, the Company enjoyed, during the greater part of the reign of Charles the Second, a prosperity to which the history of trade scarcely furnishes any parallel, and which excited the wonder, the cupidity, and the envious animosity of the whole capital.   Wealth and luxury were then rapidly increasing.   The taste for the spices, the tissues, and the jewels of the East became stronger day by day.   Tea, which, at the time when Monk brought the army of Scotland to London, had been handed round to be stared at and just touched with the lips, as a great rarity from China, was, eight years later, a regular article of import, and was soon consumed in such quantities that financiers began to consider it as an important source of revenue.[2]   The progress which was making in the art of war had created an unprecedented demand for the ingredients of which gunpowder is compounded.   It was calculated that all Europe would hardly produce in a year saltpetre enough for the siege of one town fortified on the principles of Vauban.[3]   But for the supplies from India, it was said, the English government would be unable to equip a fleet without digging up the cellars of London in order to collect the nitrous particles from the walls.[4]   Before the Restoration scarcely one ship from the Thames had ever visited the Delta of the Ganges.   But, during the twenty three years which followed the Restoration, the value of the annual imports from that rich and populous district increased from eight thousand pounds to three hundred thousand.

The gains of the body which had the exclusive possession of this fast growing trade were almost incredible.   The capital which had been actually paid up did not exceed three hundred and seventy thousand pounds : but the Company could, without difficulty, borrow money at six per cent, and the borrowed money, thrown into the trade, produced, it was rumoured, thirty per cent.   The profits were such that, in 1676, every proprietor received as a bonus a quantity of stock equal to that which he held.   On the capital, thus doubled, were paid, during five

---

[1] A curious engraving of the India House of the seventeenth century will be found in the Gentleman's Magazine for December 1784.

[2] It is a curious fact, which I do not remember to have ever seen noticed, that tea came into fashion, and, after a short time, went out of fashion, at Paris, some years before the name appears to have been known in London.   Cardinal Mazarin and the Chancellor Seguier were great tea drinkers.   See the letters of Gui Patin to Charles Spon, dated March 10. and 22. 1648, and April 1. 1657.   Patin calls the taste for tea " l'impertinente nouveauté du siècle."

[3] See Davenant's Letter to Mulgrave.

[4] Answer to Two Letters concerning the East India Company, 1676.

THE EAST INDIA HOUSE IN LEADENHALL STREET

From an engraving in the British Museum

years, dividends amounting on an average to twenty per cent annually. There had been a time when a hundred pounds of the stock could be purchased for sixty. Even in 1664 the price in the market was only seventy. But in 1677 the price had risen to two hundred and forty five : in 1681 it was three hundred : it subsequently rose to three hundred and sixty; and it is said that some sales were effected at five hundred.[1]

The enormous gains of the Indian trade might perhaps have excited little murmuring if they had been distributed among numerous proprietors. But, while the value of the stock went on increasing, the number of stockholders went on diminishing. At the time when the prosperity of the Company reached the highest point, the management was entirely in the hands of a few merchants of enormous wealth. A proprietor then had a vote for every five hundred pounds of stock that stood in his name. It is asserted in the pamphlets of that age that five persons had a sixth part, and fourteen persons a third part of the votes.[2] More than one fortunate speculator was said to derive an annual income of ten thousand pounds from the monopoly ; and one great man was pointed out on the Royal Exchange as having, by judicious or lucky purchases of stock, created in no long time an estate of twenty thousand a year. This commercial grandee, who in wealth, and in the influence which attends wealth, vied with the greatest nobles of his time, was Sir Josiah Child. There were those who still remembered him an apprentice, sweeping one of the counting houses of the City. But from a humble position his abilities had raised him rapidly to opulence, power and fame. Before the Restoration he was highly considered in the mercantile world. Soon after that event he published his thoughts on the philosophy of trade. His speculations were not always sound : but they were the speculations of an ingenious and reflecting man. Into whatever errors he may occasionally have fallen as a theorist, it is certain that, as a practical man of business, he had few equals. Almost as soon as he became a member of the committee which directed the affairs of the Company, his ascendency was felt. Soon many of the most important posts, both in Leadenhall Street and in the factories of Bombay and Bengal, were filled by his kinsmen and creatures. His riches, though expended with ostentatious profusion, continued to increase and multiply. He obtained a baronetcy : he purchased a stately seat at Wanstead ; and there he laid out immense sums in excavating fishponds, and in planting whole square miles of barren land with walnut trees. He married his daughter to the eldest

---

[1] Anderson's Dictionary ; G. White's Account of the Trade to the East Indies, 1691 ; Treatise on the East India Trade, by Philopatris, 1681.

[2] Reasons for constituting a New East India Company in London, 1681 ; Some Remarks upon the Present State of the East India Company's Affairs, 1690.

THE TEA TABLE IN THE REIGN OF QUEEN ANNE

Number 1555 in the British Museum Catalogue of Satirical Prints

son of the Duke of Beaufort, and paid down with her a portion of fifty thousand pounds.[1]

But this wonderful prosperity was not uninterrupted. Towards the close of the reign of Charles the Second the Company began to be fiercely attacked from without, and to be at the same time distracted by internal dissensions. The profits of the Indian trade were so tempting that private adventurers had sometimes, in defiance of the royal charter, fitted out ships for the Eastern seas. But the competition of these interlopers did not become really formidable till the year 1680. The nation was then violently agitated by the dispute about the Exclusion Bill. Timid men were anticipating another civil war. The two great parties, newly named Whigs and Tories, were fiercely contending in every county and town of England; and the feud soon spread to every corner of the civilised world where Englishmen were to be found.

The Company was popularly considered as a Whig body. Among the members of the directing committee were some of the most vehement Exclusionists in the City. Indeed two of them, Sir Samuel Barnardistone and Thomas Papillon, drew on themselves a severe persecution by their zeal against Popery and arbitrary power.[2] Child had been originally brought into the direction by these men : he had long acted in concert with them ; and he was supposed to hold their political opinions. He had, during many years, stood high in the esteem of the chiefs of the parliamentary opposition, and had been especially obnoxious to the Duke of York.[3] The interlopers therefore determined to affect the character of loyal men, who were determined to stand by the throne against the insolent tribunes of the City. They spread, at all the factories in the East, reports that England was in confusion, that the sword had been drawn or would immediately be drawn, and that the Company was forward in the rebellion. These rumours, which, in truth, were not improbable, easily found credit among people separated from London by what was then a voyage of twelve months. Some servants of the Company who were in ill humour with their employers, and others who were zealous royalists, joined the private traders. At Bombay, the garrison and the great body of the English inhabitants declared that they would no longer obey a society which did not obey the King : they imprisoned the Deputy Governor ; and they proclaimed that they held the island for the Crown. At Saint Helena there was a rising. The insurgents took the name of King's men, and displayed the royal standard. They were, not without difficulty, put down ; and some of them were executed by martial law.[4]

[1] Evelyn, March 16. 168⅔.   [2] See the State Trials.
[3] Pepys's Diary, April 2. and May 10. 1669.
[4] Tench's Modest and Just Apology for the East India Company, 1690.

If the Company had still been a Whig Company when the news of these commotions reached England, it is probable that the government would have approved of the conduct of the mutineers, and that the

The English Fort of Bombay

The English Fort of Bombay towards ye water side

VIEWS OF THE ENGLISH FORT OF BOMBAY

From an engraving in Churchill's Voyages

charter on which the monopoly depended would have had the fate which about the same time befell so many other charters. But while the interlopers were, at a distance of many thousands of miles, making war on the Company in the name of the King, the Company and the

H. E. V   B

King had been reconciled. When the Oxford Parliament had been dissolved, when many signs indicated that a strong reaction in favour of prerogative was at hand, when all the corporations which had incurred the royal displeasure were beginning to tremble for their franchises, a rapid and complete revolution took place at the India House. Child, who was then Governor, or, in the modern phrase, Chairman, separated himself from his old friends, excluded them from the direction, and negotiated a treaty of peace and of close alliance with the Court.[1]   It is not improbable that the near connection into which he had just entered with the great Tory house of Beaufort may have had something to do with this change in his politics. Papillon, Barnardistone, and other Whig shareholders, sold their stock : their places in the committee were supplied by persons devoted to Child ; and he was thenceforth the autocrat of the Company. The treasures of the Company were absolutely at his disposal. The most important papers of the Company were kept, not in the muniment room of the office in Leadenhall Street, but in his desk at Wanstead. The boundless power which he exercised at the India House enabled him to become a favourite at Whitehall ; and the favour which he enjoyed at Whitehall confirmed his power at the India House. A present of ten thousand guineas was graciously received from him by Charles. Ten thousand more were accepted by James, who readily consented to become a holder of stock. All who could help or hurt at Court, ministers, mistresses, priests, were kept in good humour by presents of shawls and silks, birds' nests and atar of roses, bulses of diamonds and bags of guineas.[2]   Of what the Dictator expended no account was asked by his colleagues ; and in truth he seems to have deserved the confidence which they reposed in him. His bribes, distributed with judicious prodigality, speedily produced a large return. Just when the Court became all powerful in the State, he became all powerful at the Court. Jeffreys pronounced a decision in favour of the monopoly, and of the strongest acts which had been done in defence of the monopoly. James ordered his seal to be put to a new charter which confirmed and extended all the privileges bestowed on the Company by his predecessors. All captains of Indiamen received commissions from the Crown, and were permitted to hoist the royal ensigns.[3]   John Child, brother of Sir Josiah, and Governor of Bombay, was created a baronet by the style of Sir John Child of Surat : he was declared General of all the English forces in the East ; and he was

[1] Some Remarks on the Present State of the East India Company's Affairs, 1690 ; Hamilton's New Account of the East Indies.

[2] White's Account of the East India Trade, 1691 ; Pierce Butler's Tale, 1691.

[3] White's Account of the Trade to the East Indies, 1691 ; Hamilton's New Account of the East Indies ; Sir John Wyborne to Pepys from Bombay, Jan. 7. 168⅞.

authorised to assume the title of Excellency.   The Company, on the other hand, distinguished itself among many servile corporations by obsequious homage to the throne, and set to all the merchants of the kingdom the example of readily and even eagerly paying those customs which James, at the commencement of his reign, exacted without the authority of Parliament.[1]

It seemed that the private trade would now be utterly crushed, and that the monopoly, protected by the whole strength of the royal prerogative, would be more profitable than ever.   But unfortunately just at this moment a quarrel arose between the agents of the Company in India and the Mogul Government.   Where the fault lay is a question which was vehemently disputed at the time, and which it is now impossible to decide.   The interlopers threw all the blame on the Company. The Governor of Bombay, they affirmed, had always been grasping and violent : but his baronetcy and his military commission had completely turned his head.   The very natives who were employed about the factory had noticed the change, and had muttered, in their broken English, that there must be some strange curse attending the word Excellency ; for that, ever since the chief of the strangers was called Excellency, everything had gone to ruin.   Meanwhile, it was said, the brother in England had sanctioned all the unjust and impolitic acts of the brother in India, till at length insolence and rapine, disgraceful to the English nation and to the Christian religion, had roused the just resentment of the native authorities.   The Company warmly recriminated. The story told at the India House was that the quarrel was entirely the work of the interlopers, who were now designated not only as interlopers but as traitors.   They had, it was alleged, by flattery, by presents, and by false accusations, induced the viceroys of the Mogul to oppress and persecute the body which in Asia represented the English Crown.   And indeed this charge seems not to have been altogether without foundation. It is certain that one of the most pertinacious enemies of the Childs went up to the Court of Aurengzebe, took his station at the palace gate, stopped the Great King who was in the act of mounting on horseback, and, lifting a petition high in the air, demanded justice in the name of the common God of Christians and Mussulmans.[2]   Whether Aurengzebe paid much attention to the charges brought by infidel Franks against each other may be doubted.   But it is certain that a complete rupture took place between his deputies and the servants of the Company.   On the sea the ships of his subjects were seized by the English.   On land the English settlements were taken and plundered. The trade was suspended ; and, though great annual dividends were still paid in London, they were no longer paid out of annual profits.

[1] London Gazette, Feb. $\frac{16}{26}$. 168$\frac{4}{5}$.   [2] Hamilton's New Account of the East Indies.

Just at this conjuncture, while every Indiaman that arrived in the Thames was bringing unwelcome news from the East, all the politics of Sir Josiah were utterly confounded by the Revolution. He had flattered himself that he had secured the body of which he was the chief against the machinations of interlopers, by uniting it closely with the strongest government that had existed within his memory. That government had fallen ; and whatever had leaned on the ruined fabric began to totter. The bribes had been thrown away. The connections which had been the strength and boast of the corporation were now its weakness and its shame. The King who had been one of its members was an exile. The Judge by whom all its most exorbitant pretensions had been pronounced legitimate was a prisoner. All the old enemies of the Company, reinforced by those great Whig merchants whom Child had expelled from the direction, demanded justice and vengeance from the Whig House of Commons which had just placed William and Mary on the throne. No voice was louder in accusation than that of Papillon, who had, some years before, been more zealous for the charter than any man in London.[1] The Commons censured in severe terms the persons who had inflicted death by martial law at Saint Helena, and even resolved that some of those offenders should be excluded from the Act of Indemnity.[2] The great question, how the trade with the East should for the future be carried on, was referred to a Committee. The report was to have been made on the twenty-seventh of January 1690 ; but on that very day the Parliament ceased to exist.

The first two sessions of the succeeding Parliament were so short and so busy that little was said about India in either House. But, out of Parliament, all the arts both of controversy and of intrigue were employed on both sides. Almost as many pamphlets were published about the India trade as about the oaths. The despot of Leadenhall Street was libelled in prose and verse. Wretched puns were made on his name. He was compared to Cromwell, to the King of France, to Goliath of Gath, to the Devil. It was vehemently declared to be necessary that, in any Act which might be passed for the regulation of our traffic with the Eastern seas, Sir Josiah should be by name excluded from all trust.[3]

[1] Papillon was of course reproached with his inconsistency. Among the pamphlets of that time is one entitled, " A Treatise concerning the East India Trade, wrote at the Instance of Thomas Papillon, Esquire, and in his House, and printed in the year 1680, and now reprinted for the better Satisfaction of himself and others."

[2] Commons' Journals, June 8. 1689.

[3] Among the pamphlets in which Child is most fiercely attacked, are : Some Remarks on the Present State of the East India Company's Affairs, 1690 ; Pierce Butler's Tale, 1691 ; and White's Account of the Trade to the East Indies, 1691.

Sʳ Josiah Child Barᵗ

SIR JOSIAH CHILD

From an engraving in the Sutherland Collection

There were, however, great differences of opinion among those who agreed in hating Child and the body of which he was the head. The manufacturers of Spitalfields, of Norwich, of Yorkshire, and of Wiltshire, considered the trade with the Eastern seas as rather injurious than beneficial to the kingdom. The importation of Indian spices, indeed, was admitted to be harmless, and the importation of Indian saltpetre to be necessary. But the importation of silks and of Bengals, as shawls were then called, was pronounced to be a curse to the country. The effect of the growing taste for such frippery was that our gold and silver went abroad, and that much excellent English drapery lay in our warehouses till it was devoured by the moths. Those, it was said, were happy days for the inhabitants both of our pasture lands and of our manufacturing towns, when every gown, every waistcoat, every bed was made of materials which our own flocks had furnished to our own looms. Where were now the brave old hangings of arras which had adorned the walls of lordly mansions in the time of Elizabeth? And was it not a shame to see a gentleman, whose ancestors had worn nothing but stuffs made by English workmen out of English fleeces, flaunting in a calico shirt and a pair of silk stockings from Moorshedabad? Clamours such as these had, a few years before, extorted from Parliament the Act which required that the dead should be wrapped in woollen ; and some sanguine clothiers hoped that the legislature would, by excluding all Indian textures from our ports, impose the same necessity on the living.[1]

But this feeling was confined to a minority. The public was, indeed, inclined rather to overrate than to underrate the benefits which might be derived by England from the Indian trade. What was the most effectual mode of extending that trade was a question which excited general interest, and which was answered in very different ways.

A small party, consisting chiefly of merchants resident at Bristol and other provincial seaports, maintained that the best way to extend trade was to leave it free. They urged the well known arguments which prove that monopoly is injurious to commerce ; and, having fully established the general law, they asked why the commerce between England and India was to be considered as an exception to that law. Any trader ought, they said, to be permitted to send from any port in the kingdom a cargo to Surat or Canton as freely as he now sent a cargo to Hamburg or Lisbon.[2] In our time these doctrines may

[1] Discourse concerning the East India Trade, showing it to be unprofitable to the Kingdom, by Mr. Cary ; Pierce Butler's Tale, representing the State of the Wool Case, or the East India Trade truly stated, 1691. Several petitions to the same effect will be found in the Journals of the House of Commons.

[2] Reasons against establishing an East India Company with a Joint Stock, exclusive to all others, 1691.

probably be considered, not only as sound, but as trite and obvious. In the seventeenth century, however, they were thought paradoxical. It was then generally held to be an almost selfevident truth, that our trade with the countries lying beyond the Cape of Good Hope could be advantageously carried on only by means of a great Joint Stock Company. There was no analogy, it was said, between our European trade and our Indian trade. Our government had diplomatic relations with the European States. If necessary, a maritime force could easily be sent from hence to the mouth of the Elbe or of the Tagus. But the English Kings had no envoy at the Court of Agra or Pekin. There was seldom a single English man of war within ten thousand miles of the Bay of Bengal or of the Gulf of Siam. As our merchants could not, in those remote seas, be protected by their Sovereign, they must protect themselves, and must, for that end, exercise some of the rights of sovereignty. They must have forts, garrisons, and armed ships. They must have power to send and receive embassies, to make a treaty of alliance with one Asiatic prince, to wage war on another. It was evidently impossible that every merchant should have this power independently of the rest. The merchants trading to India must therefore be joined together in a corporation which could act as one man. In support of these arguments the example of the Dutch was cited, and was generally considered as decisive. For in that age the immense prosperity of Holland was everywhere regarded with admiration, not the less earnest because it was largely mingled with envy and hatred. In all that related to trade, her statesmen were considered as oracles, and her institutions as models.

The great majority, therefore, of those who assailed the Company assailed it, not because it traded on joint funds and possessed exclusive privileges, but because it was ruled by one man, and because his rule had been mischievous to the public, and beneficial only to himself and his creatures. The obvious remedy, it was said, for the evils which his maladministration had produced was to transfer the monopoly to a new corporation so constituted as to be in no danger of falling under the dominion either of a despot or of a narrow oligarchy. Many persons who were desirous to be members of such a corporation formed themselves into a society, signed an engagement, and entrusted the care of their interests to a committee which contained some of the chief traders of the City. This society, though it had, in the eye of the law, no personality, was early designated, in popular speech, as the New Company ; and the hostilities between the New Company and the Old Company soon caused almost as much excitement and anxiety, at least in that busy hive of which the Royal Exchange was the centre, as the hostilities between the Allies and the French King. The headquarters of the younger association were in Dowgate : the Skinners lent their stately hall ; and the meetings were held in a parlour renowned for the fragrance which exhaled from a magnificent wainscot of cedar.[1]

While the contention was hottest, important news arrived from India, and was announced in the London Gazette as in the highest degree satisfactory.   Peace had been concluded between the Great Mogul and the English.   That mighty potentate had not only withdrawn his troops from the factories, but had bestowed on the Company privileges such as it had never before enjoyed.   Soon, however, appeared a very different version of the story.   The enemies of Child had, before this time, accused him of systematically publishing false intelligence.   He had now, they said, outlied himself.   They had obtained a true copy of the Firman which had put an end to the war ; and they printed a translation of it. It appeared that Aurengzebe had contemptuously granted to the English, in consideration of their penitence and of a large tribute, his forgiveness for their past delinquency, had charged them to behave themselves better for the future, and had, in the tone of a master, laid on them his commands to remove the principal offender, Sir John Child, from power and trust.   The death of Sir John occurred so seasonably that these commands could not be obeyed.   But it was only too evident that the pacification which the rulers of the India House had represented as advantageous and honourable had really been effected on terms disgraceful to the English name.[2]

During the summer of 1691, the controversy which raged on this subject between the Leadenhall Street Company and the Dowgate Company kept the City in constant agitation.   In the autumn, the Parliament had no sooner met than both the contending parties presented petitions to the House of Commons.[3]   The petitions were immediately taken into serious consideration, and resolutions of grave importance were passed.   The first resolution was that the trade with the East Indies was beneficial to the kingdom : the second was that the trade with the East Indies would be best carried on by a joint stock company possessed of exclusive privileges.[4]   It was plain, therefore, that neither those manufacturers who wished to prohibit the trade, nor those merchants at the outports who wished to throw it open, had the smallest chance of attaining their objects.   The only question left was the question between the Old and the New Company.   Seventeen years elapsed before that question ceased to disturb both political and commercial circles.   It was fatal to the honour and power of one great

[1] The engagement was printed, and has been several times reprinted   As to Skinners' Hall, see Seymour's History of London, 1734.

[2] London Gazette, May 11. 1691 ; White's Account of the East India Trade.

[3] Commons' Journals, Oct. 28. 1691.   [4] Ibid. Oct. 29. 1691.

THE SKINNERS' HALL IN DOWGATE

From a water colour drawing in the British Museum, made in 1750

minister, and to the peace and prosperity of many private families. The tracts which the rival bodies put forth against each other were innumerable. If the drama of that age may be trusted, the feud between the India House and Skinners' Hall was sometimes as serious an impediment to the course of true love in London as the feud of the Capulets and Montagues had been at Verona.[1] Which of the two contending parties was the stronger it is not easy to say. The New Company was supported by the Whigs, the Old Company by the Tories. The New Company was popular : for it promised largely, and could not yet be accused of having broken its promises : it made no dividends, and therefore was not envied : it had no power to oppress, and had therefore been guilty of no oppression. The Old Company, though generally regarded with little favour by the public, had the immense advantage of being in possession, and of having only to stand on the defensive. The burden of framing a plan for the regulation of the India trade, and of proving that plan to be better than the plan hitherto followed, lay on the New Company. The Old Company had merely to find objections to every change that was proposed ; and such objections there was little difficulty in finding. The members of the New Company were ill provided with the means of purchasing support at Court and in Parliament. They had no corporate existence, no common treasury. If any of them gave a bribe, he gave it out of his own pocket, with little chance of being reimbursed. But the Old Company, though surrounded by dangers, still held its exclusive privileges, and still made its enormous profits. Its stock had indeed gone down greatly in value since the golden days of Charles the Second : but a hundred pounds still sold for a hundred and twenty two.[2] After a large dividend had been paid to the proprietors, a surplus remained amply sufficient, in those days, to corrupt half a cabinet ; and this surplus was absolutely at the disposal of one able, determined, and unscrupulous man, who maintained the fight with wonderful art and pertinacity.

The majority of the Commons wished to effect a compromise, to retain the Old Company, but to remodel it, and to incorporate with it the members of the New Company. With this view it was, after long and vehement debates and close divisions, resolved that the capital should be increased to a million and a half. In order to prevent a single person or a small junto from domineering over the whole society, it was determined that five thousand pounds of stock should be the

[1] Rowe, in the Biter, which was damned, and deserved to be so, introduced an old gentleman haranguing his daughter thus : " Thou hast been bred up like a virtuous and a sober maiden ; and wouldest thou take the part of a profane wretch who sold his stock out of the Old East India Company ? "

[2] Hop to the States General, $\frac{\text{Oct. 30.}}{\text{Nov. 9.}}$ 1691.

NICHOLAS ROWE

From a mezzotint by J. Faber, after a painting by M. Dahl

largest quantity that any single proprietor could hold, and that those who held more should be required to sell the overplus at any price not below par. In return for the exclusive privilege of trading to the Eastern seas, the Company was to be required to furnish annually five hundred tons of saltpetre to the Crown at a low price, and to export annually English manufactures to the value of two hundred thousand pounds.[1]

A bill founded on these resolutions was brought in, read twice, and committed, but was suffered to drop in consequence of the positive refusal of Child and his associates to accept the offered terms. He objected to every part of the plan ; and his objections are highly curious and amusing. The great monopolist took his stand on the principles of free trade. In a luminous and powerfully written paper he exposed the absurdity of the expedients which the House of Commons had devised. To limit the amount of stock which might stand in a single name would, he said, be most unreasonable. Surely a proprietor whose whole fortune was staked on the success of the Indian trade was far more likely to exert all his faculties vigorously for the promotion of that trade than a proprietor who had risked only what it would be no great disaster to lose. The demand that saltpetre should be furnished to the Crown for a fixed sum Child met by those arguments, familiar to our generation, which prove that prices should be left to settle themselves. To the demand that the Company should bind itself to export annually two hundred thousand pounds' worth of English manufactures he very properly replied that the Company would most gladly export two millions' worth if the market required such a supply, and that, if the market were overstocked, it would be mere folly to send good cloth half round the world to be eaten by white ants. It was never, he declared with much spirit, found politic to put trade into straitlaced bodices, which, instead of making it grow upright and thrive, must either kill it or force it awry.

The Commons, irritated by Child's obstinacy, presented an address requesting the King to dissolve the Old Company, and to grant a charter to a new Company on such terms as to His Majesty's wisdom might seem fit.[2] It is plainly implied in the terms of this address that the Commons thought the King constitutionally competent to grant an exclusive privilege of trading to the East Indies.

The King replied that the subject was most important, that he would consider it maturely, and that he would, at a future time, give the House a more precise answer.[3] In Parliament nothing more was

---

[1] Hop mentions the length and warmth of the debates ; Nov. $\frac{13}{23}$. 1691. See the Commons' Journals, Dec. 17. and 18.

[2] Commons' Journals, Feb. 4. and 6. 1691.   [3] Ibid. Feb. 11. 1691.

said on the subject during that session : but out of Parliament the war was fiercer than ever ; and the belligerents were by no means scrupulous about the means which they employed. The chief weapons of the New Company were libels : the chief weapons of the Old Company were bribes.

In the same week in which the bill for the regulation of the Indian trade was suffered to drop, another bill, which had produced great excitement and had called forth an almost unprecedented display of parliamentary ability, underwent the same fate.

During the eight years which preceded the Revolution, the Whigs had complained bitterly, and not more bitterly than justly, of the hard measure dealt out to persons accused of political offences. Was it not monstrous, they asked, that a culprit should be denied a sight of his indictment ? Often an unhappy prisoner had not known of what he was accused till he had held up his hand at the bar. The crime imputed to him might be plotting to shoot the King : it might be plotting to poison the King. The more innocent the defendant was, the less likely he was to guess the nature of the charge on which he was to be tried ; and how could he have evidence ready to rebut a charge the nature of which he could not guess ? The Crown had power to compel the attendance of witnesses. The prisoner had no such power. If witnesses voluntarily came forward to speak in his favour, they could not be sworn. Their testimony therefore made less impression on a jury than the testimony of the witnesses for the prosecution, whose veracity was guaranteed by the most solemn sanctions of law and of religion. The juries, carefully selected by Sheriffs whom the government had named, were men animated by the fiercest party spirit, men who had as little tenderness for an Exclusionist or a Dissenter as for a mad dog. The Crown was served by a band of able, experienced, and unprincipled lawyers, who could, by merely glancing over a brief, distinguish every weak and every strong point of a case, whose presence of mind never failed them, whose flow of speech was inexhaustible, and who had passed their lives in dressing up the worse reason so as to make it appear the better. Was it not horrible to see three or four of these shrewd, learned, and callous orators arrayed against one poor wretch who had never in his life uttered a word in public, who was ignorant of the legal definition of treason and of the first principles of the law of evidence, and whose intellect, unequal at best to a fencing match with professional gladiators, was confused by the near prospect of a cruel and ignominious death ? Such however was the rule ; and even for a man so much stupefied by sickness that he could not hold up his hand or make his voice heard, even for a poor old woman who understood nothing of what was passing except that she

Debates on the Bill for regulating trials in cases of high treason

was going to be roasted alive for doing an act of charity, no advocate was suffered to utter a word. That a State trial so conducted was little better than a judicial murder had been, during the proscription of the Whig party, a fundamental article of the Whig creed. The Tories, on the other hand, though they could not deny that there had been some hard cases, maintained that, on the whole, substantial justice had been done. Perhaps a few seditious persons who had gone very near to the frontier of treason, but had not actually passed that frontier, might have suffered as traitors. But was that a sufficient reason for enabling the chiefs of the Rye House Plot and of the Western Insurrection to elude, by mere chicanery, the punishment of their guilt? On what principle was the traitor to have chances of escape which were not allowed to the felon? The culprit who was accused of larceny was subject to all the same disadvantages which, in the case of regicides and rebels, were thought so unjust: yet nobody pitied him. Nobody thought it monstrous that he should not have time to study a copy of his indictment, that his witnesses should be examined without being sworn, that he should be left to defend himself, without the help of counsel, against the most crafty veteran of the Old Bailey bar. The Whigs, it seemed, reserved all their compassion for those crimes which subvert government and dissolve the whole frame of human society. Guy Faux was to be treated with an indulgence which was not to be extended to a shoplifter. Bradshaw was to have privileges which were refused to a boy who had robbed a henroost.

The Revolution produced, as was natural, some change in the sentiments of both the great parties. In the days when none but Roundheads and Nonconformists were accused of treason, even the most humane and upright Cavaliers were disposed to think that the laws which were the safeguards of the throne could hardly be too severe. But, as soon as loyal Tory gentlemen and venerable fathers of the Church were in danger of being called in question for corresponding with Saint Germains, a new light flashed on many understandings which had been unable to discover the smallest injustice in the proceedings against Algernon Sidney and Alice Lisle. It was no longer thought utterly absurd to maintain that some advantages which were withheld from a man accused of felony might reasonably be allowed to a man accused of treason. What probability was there that any sheriff would pack a jury, that any barrister would employ all the arts of sophistry and rhetoric, that any judge would strain law and misrepresent evidence, in order to convict an innocent person of burglary or sheepstealing? But on a trial for high treason a verdict of acquittal must always be considered as a defeat of the government; and there was but too much reason to fear that many sheriffs, barristers, and judges might be impelled by party spirit, or by some baser motive, to do anything which might save the government from the inconvenience and shame of a defeat. The cry of the whole body of Tories now was that the lives of good Englishmen who happened to be obnoxious to the ruling powers were not sufficiently protected ; and this cry was swelled by the voices of some lawyers who had distinguished themselves by the malignant zeal and dishonest ingenuity with which they had conducted State prosecutions in the days of Charles and James.

The feeling of the Whigs, though it had not, like the feeling of the Tories, undergone a complete change, was yet not quite what it had been. Some, who had thought it most unjust that Russell should have no counsel and that Cornish should have no copy of his indictment, now began to mutter that the times had changed ; that the dangers of the State were extreme ; that liberty, property, religion, national indepen-dence, were all at stake ; that many Englishmen were engaged in schemes of which the object was to make England the slave of France and of Rome ; and that it would be most unwise to relax, at such a moment, the laws against political offences. It was true that the injustice, with which, in the late reigns, State trials had been conducted, had given great scandal. But this injustice was to be ascribed to the bad kings and bad judges with whom the nation had been cursed. William was now on the throne : Holt was seated for life on the bench ; and William would never exact, nor would Holt ever perform, services so shameful and wicked as those for which the banished tyrant had rewarded Jeffreys with riches and titles. This language however was at first held but by few. The Whigs, as a party, seem to have felt that they could not honourably defend, in the season of their prosperity, what, in the time of their adversity, they had always designated as a crying grievance. A bill for regulating trials in cases of high treason was brought into the House of Commons, and was received with general applause. Treby had the courage to make some objections : but no division took place. The chief enactments were that no person should be convicted of high treason committed more than three years before the indictment was found ; that every person indicted for high treason should be allowed to avail himself of the assistance of counsel, and should be furnished, ten days before the trial, with a copy of the indict-ment, and with a list of the freeholders from among whom the jury was to be taken ; that his witnesses should be sworn, and that they should be cited by the same process by which the attendance of the witnesses against him was secured.

The Bill went to the Upper House, and came back with an impor-tant amendment. The Lords had long complained of the anomalous and iniquitous constitution of that tribunal which had jurisdiction over them in cases of life and death.   When a grand jury has found a bill of indictment against a temporal peer for any offence higher than a misdemeanour, the Crown appoints a Lord High Steward ; and in the Lord High Steward's Court the case is tried.   This Court was anciently composed in two very different ways.   It consisted, if Parliament happened to be sitting, of all the members of the Upper House.   When Parliament was not sitting, the Lord High Steward summoned any twelve or more peers at his discretion to form a jury.   The consequence was that a peer accused of high treason during a recess was tried by a jury which his prosecutors had packed.   The Lords now demanded that, during a recess as well as during a session, every peer accused of high treason should be tried by the whole body of the peerage.

The demand was resisted by the House of Commons with a vehemence and obstinacy which men of the present generation may find it difficult to understand.   The truth is that some invidious privileges of peerage which have since been abolished, and others which have since fallen into entire desuetude, were then in full force and were daily used. No gentleman who had had a dispute with a nobleman could think, without indignation, of the advantages enjoyed by the favoured caste.   If His Lordship were sued at law, his privilege enabled him to impede the course of justice.   If a rude word were spoken of him, such a word as he might himself utter with perfect impunity, he might vindicate his insulted dignity both by civil and criminal proceedings.   If a barrister, in the discharge of his duty to a client, spoke with severity of the conduct of a noble seducer, if an honest squire on the racecourse applied the proper epithets to the tricks of a noble swindler, the affronted patrician had only to complain to the proud and powerful body of which he was a member.   His brethren made his cause their own.   The offender was taken into custody by Black Rod, brought to the bar, flung into prison, and kept there till he was glad to obtain forgiveness by the most degrading submissions.   Nothing could therefore be more natural than that an attempt of the Peers to obtain any new advantage for their order should be regarded by the Commons with extreme jealousy. There is strong reason to suspect that some able Whig politicians, who thought it dangerous to relax, at that moment, the laws against political offences, but who could not, without incurring the charge of inconsistency, declare themselves adverse to any relaxation, had conceived a hope that they might, by fomenting the dispute about the Court of the Lord High Steward, defer for at least a year the passing of a bill which they disliked, and yet could not decently oppose.   If this really was their plan, it succeeded perfectly.   The Lower House rejected the amendment : the Upper House persisted : a free conference was held ; and the question was argued with great force and ingenuity on both sides.

The reasons in favour of the amendment are obvious, and indeed at first sight seem unanswerable. It was surely difficult to defend a system under which the Sovereign nominated a conclave of his own creatures to decide the fate of men whom he regarded as his mortal enemies. And could anything be more absurd than that a nobleman accused of high treason should be entitled to be tried by the whole body of his peers if his indictment happened to be brought into the House of Lords the minute before a prorogation, but that, if the indictment arrived a minute after the prorogation, he should be at the mercy of a small junto named by the very authority which prosecuted him? That anything could have been said on the other side seems strange : but those who managed the conference for the Commons were not ordinary men, and seem on this occasion to have put forth all their powers. Conspicuous among them was Charles Montague, who was rapidly rising to the highest rank among the orators of that age. To him the lead seems on this occasion to have been left ; and to his pen we owe an account of the discussion, which gives an excellent notion of his talents for debate. " We have framed,"—such was in substance his reasoning,—" we have framed a law which has in it nothing exclusive, a law which will be a blessing to every class, from the highest to the lowest. The new securities, which we propose to give to innocence oppressed by power, are common between the premier peer and the humblest day labourer. The clause which establishes a time of limitation for prosecutions protects us all alike. To every Englishman accused of the highest crime against the state, whatever be his rank, we give the privilege of seeing his indictment, the privilege of being defended by counsel, the privilege of having his witnesses summoned by a writ of subpœna and sworn on the Holy Gospels. Such is the bill which we sent up to Your Lordships ; and you return it to us with a clause of which the effect is to give certain advantages to your noble order at the expense of the ancient prerogatives of the Crown. Surely before we consent to take away from the King any power which his predecessors have possessed for ages, and to give it to Your Lordships, we ought to be satisfied that you are more likely to use it well than he. Something we must risk : somebody we must trust ; and since we are forced, much against our will, to institute what is necessarily an invidious comparison, we must own ourselves unable to discover any reason for believing that a prince is less to be trusted than an aristocracy. Is it reasonable, you ask, that you should be tried for your lives before a few members of your House, selected by the Crown? Is it reasonable, we ask in our turn, that you should have the privilege of being tried by all the members of your House, that is to say, by your brothers, your uncles, your first cousins, your second cousins, your fathers in law, your

H.E. V   c

brothers in law, your most intimate friends? You marry so much into each other's families, you live so much in each other's society, that there is scarcely a nobleman who is not connected by consanguinity or affinity with several others, and who is not on terms of friendship with several more. There have been great men whose death put a third or fourth part of the baronage of England into mourning. Nor is there much danger that even those peers who may be unconnected with an accused lord will be disposed to send him to the block if they can with decency say 'Not Guilty, upon my honour.' For the ignominious death of a single member of a small aristocratical body necessarily leaves a stain on the reputation of his fellows. If, indeed, your Lordships proposed that every one of your body should be compelled to attend and vote, the Crown might have some chance of obtaining justice against a guilty peer, however strongly connected. But you propose that attendance shall be voluntary. Is it possible to doubt what the consequence will be? All the prisoner's relations and friends will be in their places to vote for him. Good nature and the fear of making powerful enemies will keep away many who, if they voted at all, would be forced by conscience and honour to vote against him. The new system which you propose would therefore evidently be unfair to the Crown; and you do not show any reason for believing that the old system has been found in practice unfair to yourselves. We may confidently affirm that, even under a government less just and merciful than that under which we have the happiness to live, an innocent peer has little to fear from any set of peers that can be brought together in Westminster Hall to try him. How stands the fact? In what single case has a guiltless head fallen by the verdict of this packed jury? It would be easy to make out a long list of squires, merchants, lawyers, surgeons, yeomen, artisans, ploughmen, whose blood, barbarously shed during the late evil times, cries for vengeance to heaven. But what single member of your House, in our days, or in the days of our fathers, or in the days of our grandfathers, suffered death unjustly by sentence of the Court of the Lord High Steward? Hundreds of the common people were sent to the gallows by common juries for the Rye House Plot and the Western Insurrection. One peer, and one alone, my Lord Delamere, was brought at that time before the Court of the Lord High Steward; and he was acquitted. You say that the evidence against him was legally insufficient. Be it so. But so was the evidence against Sidney, against Cornish, against Alice Lisle; yet it sufficed to destroy them. You say that the peers before whom my Lord Delamere was brought were selected with shameless unfairness by King James and by Jeffreys. Be it so. But this only proves that, under the worst possible King, and under the worst possible High Steward, a lord tried by lords has a better chance for life than a commoner who puts himself on his country. We cannot, therefore, under the mild government which we now possess, feel much apprehension for the safety of any innocent peer. Would that we felt as little apprehension for the safety of that government! But it is notorious that the settlement with which our liberties are inseparably bound up is attacked at once by foreign and by domestic enemies. We cannot consent, at such a crisis, to relax the restraints which have, it may well be feared, already proved too feeble to prevent some men of high rank from plotting the ruin of their country. To sum up the whole, what is asked of us is that we will consent to transfer a certain power from their Majesties to your Lordships. Our answer is that, at this time, in our opinion, their Majesties have not too much power, and your Lordships have quite power enough."

These arguments, though eminently ingenious, and not without real force, failed to convince the Upper House. The Lords insisted that every peer should be entitled to be a Trier. The Commons were with difficulty induced to consent that the number of Triers should never be less than thirty six, and positively refused to make any further concession. The bill was therefore suffered to drop.[1]

It is certain that those who in the conference on this bill represented the Commons did not exaggerate the dangers to which the government was exposed. While the constitution of the Court which was to try peers for treason was under discussion, a treason planned with rare skill by a peer was all but carried into execution.

Marlborough had never ceased to assure the Court of Saint Germains that the great crime which he had committed was constantly present to his thoughts, and that he lived only for the purpose of repentance and reparation. Not only had he been himself converted: he had also converted the Princess Anne. In 1688, the Churchills had, with little difficulty, induced her to fly from her father's palace. In 1691, they, with as little difficulty, induced her to copy out and sign a letter expressing her deep concern for his misfortunes and her earnest wish to atone for her breach of duty.[2] At the same time Marlborough held out hopes that it might be in his power to effect the restoration of his old master in the best possible way, without the help of a single foreign soldier or sailor, by the votes of the English Lords and Commons, and by the support of the English army. We are not fully informed as to all the details of his plan. But

Plot formed by Marlborough against the government of William

---

[1] The history of this bill is to be collected from the bill itself, which is among the Archives of the Upper House, from the Journals of the two Houses during November and December 1690, and January 1691 ; particularly from the Commons' Journals of December 11. and January 13. and 25., and the Lords' Journals of January 20. and 28. See also Grey's Debates.

[2] The letter, dated December 1. 1691, is in the Life of James, ii. 477.

the outline is known to us from a most interesting paper written by James, of which one copy is in the Bodleian Library, and another among the archives of the French Foreign Office.

The jealousy with which the English regarded the Dutch was at this time intense. There had never been a hearty friendship between the nations. They were indeed near of kin to each other. They spoke two dialects of one widespread language. Both boasted of their political freedom. Both were attached to the reformed faith. Both were threatened by the same enemy, and could be safe only while they were united. Yet there was no cordial feeling between them. They would probably have loved each other more, if they had, in some respects, resembled each other less. They were the two great commercial nations, the two great maritime nations. In every sea their flags were found together, in the Baltic and in the Mediterranean, in the Gulf of Mexico and in the Straits of Malacca. Every where the merchant of London and the merchant of Amsterdam were trying to forestall each other and to undersell each other. In Europe the contest was not sanguinary. But too often, in barbarous countries, where there was no law but force, the competitors had met, burning with cupidity, burning with animosity, armed for battle, each suspecting the other of hostile designs, and each resolved to give the other no advantage. In such circumstances it is not strange that many violent and cruel acts should have been perpetrated. What had been done in those distant regions could seldom be exactly known in Europe. Everything was exaggerated and distorted by vague report and by national prejudice. Here it was the popular belief that the English were always blameless, and that every quarrel was to be ascribed to the avarice and inhumanity of the Dutch. Lamentable events which had taken place in the Spice Islands were brought on our stage. The Englishmen were all saints and heroes ; the Dutchmen all fiends in human shape, lying, robbing, ravishing, murdering, torturing. The angry passions indicated by these representations had more than once found vent in war. Thrice in the lifetime of one generation the two nations had contended, with equal courage and with various success, for the sovereignty of the Ocean. The tyranny of James, as it had reconciled Tories to Whigs, and Churchmen to Nonconformists, had also reconciled the English to the Dutch. While our ancestors were looking to the Hague for deliverance, the massacre of Amboyna and the great humiliation of Chatham had seemed to be forgotten. But since the Revolution the old feeling had revived. Though England and Holland were now closely bound together by treaty, they were as far as ever from being bound together by affection. Once, just after the battle of Beachy Head, our countrymen had seemed disposed to be just : but a violent reaction had speedily followed.

DUTCH MEN OF WAR

From an engraving by W. Hollar, dated 1647

Torrington, who deserved to be shot, became a popular favourite ; and the allies whom he had shamefully abandoned were accused of persecuting him without a cause.   The partiality shown by the King to the companions of his youth was the favourite theme of the sowers of sedition.   The most lucrative posts in his household, it was said, were held by Dutchmen : the House of Lords was fast filling with Dutchmen : the finest manors of the Crown were given to Dutchmen : the army was commanded by Dutchmen.   That it would have been wise in William to exhibit somewhat less obtrusively his laudable fondness for his native country, and to remunerate his early friends somewhat more sparingly, is perfectly true.   But it will not be easy to prove that, on any important occasion during his whole reign, he sacrificed the interests of our island to the interests of the United Provinces.   The English, however, were on this subject prone to fits of jealousy which made them quite incapable of listening to reason.   One of the sharpest of those fits came on in the autumn of 1691.   The antipathy to the Dutch was at that time strong in all classes, and nowhere stronger than in the Parliament and in the army.[1]

Of that antipathy Marlborough determined to avail himself for the purpose, as he assured James and James's adherents, of effecting a restoration.   The temper of both Houses was such that they might not improbably be induced by skilful management to present a joint address requesting that all foreigners might be dismissed from the service of their Majesties.   Marlborough undertook to move such an address in the Lords ; and there would have been no difficulty in finding some gentleman of great weight to make a similar motion in the Commons.

If the address should be carried, what could William do ?   Would he yield ?   Would he discard all his dearest, his oldest, his most trusty friends ?   It was hardly possible to believe that he would make so painful, so humiliating, a concession.   If he did not yield, there would be a rupture between him and the Parliament ; and the Parliament would be backed by the people.   Even a King reigning by a hereditary title might well shrink from such a contest with the Estates of the Realm.   But to a King whose title rested on a resolution of the Estates of the Realm such a contest must almost necessarily be fatal.   The last hope of William would be in the army.   The army Marlborough undertook to manage ; and it is highly probable that what he undertook he could have performed.   His courage, his abilities, his noble and winning

---

[1] Burnet, ii. 85.; and Burnet MS. Harl. 6584.   See also a memorial signed by Holmes, but consisting of intelligence furnished by Ferguson, among the extracts from the Nairne Papers, printed by Macpherson.   It bears date October 1691.   " The Prince of Orange," says Holmes, " is mortally hated by the English.   They see very fairly that he hath no love for them ; neither doth he confide in them, but all in his Dutch. . . . .   It's not doubted but the Parliament will not be for foreigners to ride them with a caveson."

Naues Bellicæ

Nauis Mercatoria Hollandica, per Indias Orientales

DUTCH EAST INDIA SHIPS

From an engraving by W. Hollar, dated 1647

manners, the splendid success which had attended him on every occasion on which he had been in command, had made him, in spite of his sordid vices, a favourite with his brethren in arms. They were proud of having one countryman who had shown that he wanted nothing but opportunity to vie with the ablest Marshal of France. The Dutch were even more disliked by the English troops than by the English nation generally. Had Marlborough therefore, after securing the cooperation of some distinguished officers, presented himself at the critical moment to those regiments which he had led to victory in Flanders and in Ireland, had he called on them to rally round him, to protect the Parliament, and to drive out the aliens, there is strong reason to think that the call would have been obeyed. He would then have had it in his power to fulfil the promises which he had so solemnly made to his old master.

Of all the schemes ever formed for the restoration of James or of his descendants, this scheme promised the fairest. That national pride, that hatred of arbitrary power, which had hitherto been on William's side, would now be turned against him. Hundreds of thousands, who would have put their lives in jeopardy to prevent a French army from imposing a government on the English, would have felt no disposition to prevent an English army from driving out the Dutch. Even the Whigs could scarcely, without renouncing their old doctrines, support a prince who obstinately refused to comply with the general wish of his people signified to him by his Parliament. The plot looked well. An active canvass was made. Many members of the House of Commons, who did not at all suspect that there was any ulterior design, promised to vote against the foreigners. Marlborough was indefatigable in inflaming the discontents of the army. His house was constantly filled with officers who heated each other into fury by talking against the Dutch. But, before the preparations were complete, a strange suspicion rose in the minds of some of the Jacobites. That the author of this bold and artful scheme wished to pull down the existing government there could be little doubt. But was it quite certain what government he meant to set up? Might he not depose William without restoring James? Was it not possible that a man so wise, so aspiring, and so wicked, might be meditating a double treason, such as would have been thought a masterpiece of statecraft by the great Italian politicians of the fifteenth century, such as Borgia would have envied, such as Machiavel would have extolled to the skies? What if this consummate dissembler should cheat both the rival kings? What if, when he found himself commander of the army and protector of the Parliament, he should proclaim Queen Anne? Was it not possible that the weary and harassed nation might gladly acquiesce in such a settlement? James was unpopular because he was a Papist influenced by Popish priests. William was unpopular

JOHN CHURCHILL, 1st DUKE OF MARLBOROUGH, K.G., 1650-1722.
From the painting in the National Portrait Gallery, after Sir Godfrey Kneller.

because he was a foreigner attached to foreign favourites. Anne was at once a Protestant and an Englishwoman. Under her government the country would be in no danger of being overrun either by Jesuits or by Dutchmen. That Marlborough had the strongest motives for placing her on the throne was evident. He could never, in the court of her father, be more than a repentant criminal, whose services were overpaid by a pardon. In her court the husband of her adored friend would be what Pepin Heristal and Charles Martel had been to the Chilperics and Childeberts. He would be the chief director of the civil and military government. He would wield the whole power of England. He would hold the balance of Europe. Great kings and commonwealths would bid against each other for his favour, and exhaust their treasuries in the vain hope of satiating his avarice. The presumption was, therefore, that, if he had the English crown in his hands, he would put it on the head of the Princess. What evidence there was to confirm this presumption is not known : but it is certain that something took place which convinced some of the most devoted friends of the exiled family that he was meditating a second perfidy, surpassing even the feat which he had performed at Salisbury. They were afraid that if, at that moment, they succeeded in getting rid of William, the situation of James would be more hopeless than ever. So fully were they persuaded of the duplicity of their accomplice, that they not only refused to proceed further in the execution of the plan which he had formed, but disclosed his whole scheme to Portland.

Marlborough's plot disclosed by the Jacobites

William seems to have been alarmed and provoked by this intelligence to a degree very unusual with him. In general he was indulgent, nay, wilfully blind, to the baseness of the English statesmen whom he employed. He suspected, indeed he knew, that some of his servants were in correspondence with his competitor ; and yet he did not punish them, did not disgrace them, did not even frown on them. He thought meanly, and he had but too good reason for thinking meanly, of the whole of that breed of public men which the Restoration had formed and had bequeathed to the Revolution. He knew them too well to complain because he did not find in them veracity, fidelity, consistency, disinterestedness. The very utmost that he expected from them was that they would serve him as far as they could serve him without serious danger to themselves. If he learned that, while sitting in his council and enriched by his bounty, they were trying to make for themselves at Saint Germains an interest which might be of use to them in the event of a counterrevolution, he was more inclined to bestow on them the contemptuous commendation which was bestowed of old on the worldly wisdom of the unjust steward than to call them to a severe account. But the crime of Marlborough was of a very different kind.

His treason was not that of a fainthearted man desirous to keep a retreat open for himself in every event, but that of a man of dauntless courage, profound policy, and measureless ambition. William was not prone to fear; but, if there was any thing on earth that he feared, it was Marlborough. To treat the criminal as he deserved was indeed impossible: for those by whom his designs had been made known to the government would never have consented to appear against him in the witness box. But to permit him to retain high command in that army which he was then engaged in seducing would have been madness.

Late in the evening of the ninth of January the Queen had a painful explanation with the Princess Anne. Early the next morning Marlborough was informed that their Majesties had no further occasion for his services, and that he must not presume to appear in the royal presence. He had been loaded with honours, and with what he loved better, riches. All was at once taken away.

1692.
Disgrace
of Marl-
borough

The real history of these events was known to very few. Evelyn, who had in general excellent sources of information, believed that the corruption and extortion of which Marlborough was notoriously guilty had roused the royal indignation. The Dutch ministers could only tell the States General that six different stories were spread abroad by Marlborough's enemies. Some said that he had indiscreetly suffered an important military secret to escape him; some that he had spoken disrespectfully of their Majesties; some that he had done ill offices between the Queen and the Princess; some that he had been forming cabals in the army; some that he had carried on an unauthorised correspondence with the Danish government about the general politics of Europe; and some that he had been trafficking with the agents of the Court of Saint Germains.[1] His friends contradicted every one of these tales, and affirmed that his only crime was his dislike of the foreigners who were lording it over his countrymen, and that he had fallen a victim to the machinations of Portland, whom he was known to dislike, and whom he had not very politely described as a wooden fellow. The mystery, which from the first overhung the story of Marlborough's disgrace, was darkened, after the lapse of fifty years, by the shameless mendacity of his widow. The concise narrative of James dispels that mystery, and makes it clear, not only why Marlborough was disgraced, but also how several of the reports about the cause of his disgrace originated.[2]

Various
reports
touching
the cause
of Marl-
borough's
disgrace

---

[1] Evelyn's Diary, Jan. 24.; Hop to States General, $\frac{\text{Jan. 22.}}{\text{Feb. 1.}}$ 169½; Baden to States General, Feb. $\frac{18}{28}$.

[2] The words of James are these; they were written in November 1692 :—

"Mes amis, l'année passée, avoient dessein de me rappeler par le Parlement. La manière étoit concertée; et Milord Churchill devoit proposer dans le Parlement de chasser tous les

QUEEN MARY II

From a mezzotint by P. Schenck in the Sutherland Collection, dated 1691

Though William assigned to the public no reason for exercising his undoubted prerogative by dismissing his servant, Anne had been informed of the truth; and it had been left to her to judge whether an officer who had been guilty of a foul treason was a fit inmate of the palace. Three weeks passed. Lady Marlborough still retained her post and her apartments at Whitehall. Her husband still resided with her; and still the King and Queen gave no sign of displeasure. At length the haughty and vindictive Countess, emboldened by their patience, determined to brave them face to face, and accompanied her mistress one evening to the drawingroom at

Rupture between Mary and Anne

étrangers tant des conseils et de l'armée que du royaume. Si le Prince d'Orange avoit consenti à cette proposition, ils l'auroient eu entre leurs mains. S'il l'avoit refusée, il auroit fait déclarer le Parlement contre lui; et en même temps Milord Churchill devoit se déclarer avec l'armée pour le Parlement; et la flotte devoit faire de même; et l'on devoit me rappeler. L'on avoit déjà commencé d'agir dans ce projet; et on avoit gagné un gros parti, quand quelques fidèles sujets indiscrets, croyant me servir, et s'imaginant que ce que Milord Churchill faisoit n'étoit pas pour moi, mais pour la Princesse de Danemarck, eurent l'imprudence de découvrir le tout à Benthing, et détournèrent ainsi le coup."

A translation of this most remarkable passage, which at once solves many interesting and perplexing problems, was published eighty years ago by Macpherson. But, strange to say, it attracted no notice, and has never, as far as I know, been mentioned by any biographer of Marlborough.

The narrative of James requires no confirmation; but it is strongly confirmed by the Burnet MS. Harl. 6584. "Marleburrough," Burnet wrote in September 1693, "set himself to decry the King's conduct and to lessen him in all his discourses, and to possess the English with an aversion to the Dutch, who, as he pretended, had a much larger share of the King's favour and confidence than they,"—the English I suppose,—"had. This was a point on which the English, who are too apt to despise all other nations, and to overvalue themselves, were easily enough inflamed. So it grew to be the universal subject of discourse, and was the constant entertainment at Marleburrough's, where there was a constant randivous of the English officers." About the dismission of Marlborough, Burnet wrote at the same time: "The King said to myself upon it that he had very good reason to believe that he had made his peace with King James, and was engaged in a correspondence with France. It is certain he was doing all he could to set on a faction in the army and the nation against the Dutch."

It is curious to compare this plain tale, told while the facts were recent, with the shuffling narrative which Burnet prepared for the public eye many years later, when Marlborough was closely united to the Whigs, and was rendering great and splendid services to the country. Burnet, ii. 90.

The Duchess of Marlborough, in her Vindication, had the effrontery to declare that she "could never learn what cause the King assigned for his displeasure." She suggests that Young's forgery may have been the cause. Now she must have known that Young's forgery was not committed till some months after her husband's disgrace. She was indeed lamentably deficient in memory, a faculty which is proverbially said to be necessary to persons of the class to which she belonged. Her own volume convicts her of falsehood. She gives a letter from Mary to Anne, in which Mary says, "I need not repeat the cause my Lord Marlborough has given the King to do what he has done." These words plainly imply that Anne had been apprised of the cause. If she had not been apprised of the cause, would she not have said so in her answer? But we have her answer; and it contains not a word on the subject. She was then apprised of the cause; and is it possible to believe that she kept it a secret from her adored Mrs. Freeman?

Kensington. This was too much even for the gentle Mary. She would indeed have expressed her indignation before the crowd which surrounded the card tables, had she not remembered that her sister was in a state which entitles women to peculiar indulgence. Nothing was said that night; but on the following day a letter from the Queen was delivered to the Princess. Mary declared that she was unwilling to give pain to a sister whom she loved, and in whom she could easily pass over any ordinary fault: but this was a serious matter. Lady Marlborough must be dismissed. While she lived at Whitehall her Lord would live there. Was it proper that a man in his situation should be suffered to make the palace of his injured master his home? Yet so unwilling was His Majesty to deal severely with the worst offenders, that even this had been borne, and might have been borne longer, had not Anne brought the Countess to defy the King and Queen in their own presence chamber. " It was unkind," Mary wrote, " in a sister : it would have been uncivil in an equal ; and I need not say that I have more to claim." The Princess, in her answer, did not attempt to exculpate or excuse Marlborough, but expressed a firm conviction that his wife was innocent, and implored the Queen not to insist on so heart-rending a separation. "There is no misery," Anne wrote, "that I cannot resolve to suffer rather than the thoughts of parting from her."

The Princess sent for her uncle Rochester, and implored him to carry her letter to Kensington and to be her advocate there. Rochester declined the office of messenger, and, though he tried to restore harmony between his kinswomen, was by no means disposed to plead the cause of the Churchills. He had indeed long seen with extreme uneasiness the absolute dominion exercised over his younger niece by that un-principled pair. Anne's expostulation was sent to the Queen by a servant. The only reply was a message from the Lord Chamberlain, Dorset, commanding Lady Marlborough to leave the palace. Mrs. Morley would not be separated from Mrs. Freeman. As to Mr. Morley, all places where he could have his three courses and his three bottles were alike to him. The Princess and her whole family therefore retired to Sion House, a villa belonging to the Duke of Somerset, and situated on the margin of the Thames. In London she occupied Berkeley House, which stood in Piccadilly, on the site now covered by Devonshire House.[1] Her income was secured by Act of Parliament : but no punishment which it was in the power of the Crown to inflict on her was spared. Her guard of honour was taken away. The foreign ministers ceased to wait upon her. When she went to Bath, the Secretary of State wrote

---

[1] My account of these transactions I have been forced to take from the narrative of the Duchess of Marlborough, a narrative which is to be read with constant suspicion, except when, as is often the case, she relates some instance of her own malignity and insolence.

to request the Mayor of that city not to receive her with the ceremonial with which royal visitors were usually welcomed. When she attended divine service at St. James's Church, she found that the rector had been forbidden to show her the customary marks of respect, to bow to her from his pulpit, and to send a copy of his text to be laid on her cushion. Even the bellman of Piccadilly, it was said, perhaps falsely, was ordered not to chant her praises in his doggrel verse under the windows of Berkeley House.[1]

That Anne was in the wrong is clear; but it is not equally clear that the King and Queen were in the right. They should have either dissembled their displeasure, or openly declared the true reasons for it. Unfortunately, they let every body see the punishment, and they let scarcely any body know the provocation. They should have remembered that, in the absence of information about the cause of a quarrel, the public is naturally inclined to side with the weaker party, and that this inclination is likely to be peculiarly strong when a sister is, without any apparent reason, harshly treated by a sister. They should have remembered, too, that they were exposing to attack what was unfortunately the one vulnerable part of Mary's character. A cruel fate had put enmity between her and her father. Her detractors pronounced her utterly destitute of natural affection; and even her eulogists, when they spoke of the way in which she had discharged the duties of the filial relation, were forced to speak in a subdued and apologetic tone. Nothing therefore could be more unfortunate than that she should a second time appear unmindful of the ties of consanguinity. She was now at open war with both the two persons who were nearest to her in blood. Many, who thought that her conduct towards her parent was justified by the extreme danger which had threatened her country and her religion, were unable to defend her conduct towards her sister. While Mary, who was really guilty in this matter of nothing worse than imprudence, was regarded by the world as an oppressor, Anne, who was as culpable as her small faculties enabled her to be, assumed the interesting character of a meek, resigned, sufferer. In those private letters, indeed, to which the name of Morley was subscribed, the Princess expressed the sentiments of a fury in the style of a fishwoman, railed savagely at the whole Dutch nation, and called her brother in law sometimes the abortion, sometimes the monster, sometimes Caliban.[2] But the nation heard

---

[1] The Duchess of Marlborough's Vindication; Dartmouth's Note on Burnet, ii. 92.; Verses of the Night Bellman of Piccadilly and my Lord Nottingham's Order thereupon, 1691. There is a bitter lampoon on Lady Marlborough of the same date, entitled the Universal Health, a true Union to the Queen and Princess.

[2] It must not be supposed that Anne was a reader of Shakspeare. She had, no doubt, often seen the Enchanted Island. That miserable *rifacimento* of the Tempest was then a favourite with the town, on account of the machinery and the decorations.

THE SOUTH-WEST VIEW OF SION=ABBY, IN THE COUNTY OF MIDDLESEX.

SION ABBEY

From Buck's Antiquities of England

nothing of her language and saw nothing of her deportment but what was decorous and submissive. The truth seems to have been that the rancorous and coarseminded Countess gave the tone to her Highness's confidential correspondence, while the graceful, serene, and politic Earl was suffered to prescribe the course which was to be taken before the public eye. During a short time the Queen was generally blamed. But the charm of her temper and manners was irresistible ; and in a few months she regained the popularity which she had lost.[1]

It was a most fortunate circumstance for Marlborough that, just at the very time when all London was talking about his disgrace, and trying **Fuller's plot** to guess at the cause of the King's sudden anger against one who had always seemed to be a favourite, an accusation of treason was brought by William Fuller against many persons of high consideration, was strictly investigated, and was proved to be false and malicious. The consequence was that the public, which rarely discriminates nicely, could not, at that moment, be easily brought to believe in the reality of any Jacobite conspiracy.

That Fuller's plot is less celebrated than the Popish plot is the fault rather of the historians than of Fuller, who did all that man could do to secure an eminent place among villains. Every person well read in history must have observed that depravity has its temporary modes, which come in and go out like modes of dress and upholstery. It may be doubted whether, in our country, any man ever, before the year 1678, invented and related on oath a circumstantial history, altogether fictitious, of a treasonable plot, for the purpose of making himself important by destroying men who had given him no provocation. But in the year 1678 this execrable crime became the fashion, and continued to be so during the twenty years which followed. Preachers designated it as our peculiar national sin, and prophesied that it would draw on us some awful national judgment. Legislators proposed new punishments of terrible severity for this new atrocity.[2] It was not however found necessary to resort to those punishments. The fashion changed ; and during the last century and a half there has perhaps not been a single instance of this particular kind of wickedness.

The explanation is simple. Oates was the founder of a school. His success proved that no romance is too wild to be received with faith by understandings which fear and hatred have disordered. His slanders were monstrous : but they were well timed : he spoke to a people made credulous by their passions ; and thus, by impudent and cruel lying, he raised himself in a week from beggary and obscurity

[1] Burnet MS. Harl. 6584.

[2] The history of an abortive attempt to legislate on this subject will be found in the Commons' Journals of 169$\frac{2}{3}$.

OLD DEVONSHIRE HOUSE, FORMERLY BERKELEY HOUSE

From a drawing in the British Museum

to luxury, renown, and power.   He had once eked out the small tithes of a miserable vicarage by stealing the pigs and fowls of his parishioners.[1]   He was now lodged in a palace : he was followed by admiring crowds : he had at his mercy the estates and lives of Howards and Herberts.   A crowd of imitators instantly appeared.   It seemed that much more might be got, and that much less was risked, by testifying to an imaginary conspiracy than by robbing on the highway or clipping the coin.   Accordingly the Bedloes, Dangerfields, Dugdales, Turberviles, made haste to transfer their industry to an employment at once more profitable and less perilous than any to which they were accustomed.   Till the dissolution of the Oxford Parliament, Popish plots were the chief manufacture.   Then, during seven years, Whig plots were the only plots which paid.   After the Revolution, Jacobite plots came in : but the public had become cautious ; and, though the new false witnesses were in no respect less artful than their predecessors, they found much less encouragement.   The history of the first great check given to the practices of this abandoned race of men well deserves to be circumstantially related.

In 1689, and in the beginning of 1690, William Fuller had rendered to the government service such as the best governments sometimes require, and such as none but the worst men ever perform.   His useful treachery had been rewarded by his employers, as was meet, with money and with contempt.   Their liberality enabled him to live during some months like a fine gentleman.   He called himself a Colonel, hired servants, clothed them in gorgeous liveries, bought fine horses, lodged in Pall Mall, and showed his brazen forehead, overtopped by a wig worth fifty guineas, in the antechambers of the palace and in the stage box at the theatre.   He even gave himself the airs of a favourite of royalty, and, as if he thought that William could not live without him, followed His Majesty first to Ireland, and then to the Congress of Princes at the Hague.   The vagabond afterwards boasted that, at the Hague, he appeared with a retinue fit for an ambassador, that he gave ten guineas a week for an apartment, and that the worst waistcoat which he condescended to wear was of silver stuff at forty shillings the yard.   Such profusion, of course, brought him to poverty.   Soon after his return to England he took refuge from the bailiffs in Axe Yard, a place lying within the verge of Whitehall.   His fortunes were desperate : he owed great sums : on the government he had no claim : his past services had been overpaid : no future service was to be expected from him : having appeared in the witness box as evidence for the Crown, he could no longer be of any use as a spy on the Jacobites ; and by all men of virtue and honour, to whatever party they might belong, he was abhorred and shunned.

[1] North's Examen.

Just at this time, when he was in the frame of mind in which men are open to the worst temptations, he fell in with the worst of tempters, in truth, with the Devil in human shape. Oates had obtained his liberty, his pardon, and a pension which made him a much richer man than nineteen twentieths of the members of that profession of which he was the disgrace. But he was still unsatisfied. He complained that he had now less than three hundred a year. In the golden days of the Plot he had been allowed three times as much, had been sumptuously lodged in the palace, had dined on plate, and had been clothed in silk. He clamoured for an increase of his stipend. Nay, he was even impudent enough to aspire to ecclesiastical preferment, and thought it hard that, while so many mitres were distributed, he could not get a deanery, a prebend, or even a rectory. He missed no opportunity of urging his pretensions. He haunted the public offices and the lobbies of the Houses of Parliament. He might be seen and heard every day, hurrying, as fast as his uneven legs would carry him, between Charing Cross and Westminster Hall, puffing with haste and self importance, chattering about what he had done for the good cause, and reviling, in the style of the boatmen on the river, all the statesmen and divines whom he suspected of doing him ill offices at Court, and keeping him back from a bishopric. When he found that there was no hope for him in the Established Church, he turned to the Baptists. They, at first, received him very coldly; but he gave such touching accounts of the wonderful work of grace which had been wrought in his soul, and vowed so solemnly, before Jehovah and the holy angels, to be thenceforth a burning and shining light, that it was difficult for simple and well meaning people to think him altogether insincere. He mourned, he said, like a turtle. On one Lord's day he thought he should have died of grief at being shut out from fellowship with the saints. He was at length admitted to communion : but, before he had been a year among his new friends, they discovered his true character, and solemnly cast him out as a hypocrite. Thenceforth he became the mortal enemy of the leading Baptists, and persecuted them with the same treachery, the same mendacity, the same effrontery, the same black malice, which had, many years before, wrought the destruction of more celebrated victims. Those who had lately been edified by his account of his blessed experiences stood aghast to hear him crying out that he would be revenged, that revenge was God's own sweet morsel, that the wretches who had excommunicated him should be ruined, that they should be forced to fly their country, that they should be stripped to the last shilling. His designs were at length frustrated by a righteous decree of the Court of Chancery, a decree which would have left a deep stain on the character of an ordinary man, but which makes no perceptible addition to the infamy of Titus Oates.[1]   Through all changes, however, he was surrounded by a small knot of hotheaded and foulmouthed agitators, who, abhorred and despised by every respectable Whig, yet called themselves Whigs, and thought themselves injured because they were not rewarded for scurrility and slander with the best places under the Crown.

In 1691, Titus, in order to be near the focal point of political intrigue and faction, had taken a house within the precinct of White-hall.   To this house Fuller, who lived hard by, found admission.   The evil work, which had been begun in him, when he was still a child, by the memoirs of Dangerfield, was now completed by the conversation of Oates.   The Salamanca Doctor was, as a witness, no longer formidable ; but he was impelled, partly by the savage malignity which he felt towards all whom he considered as his enemies, and partly by mere monkeylike restlessness and love of mischief, to do, through the instrumentality of others, what he could no longer do in person.   In Fuller he had found the corrupt heart, the ready tongue, and the unabashed front, which are the first qualifications for the office of a false accuser. A friendship, if that word may be so used, sprang up between the pair. Oates opened his house and even his purse to Fuller.   The veteran sinner, both directly and through the agency of his dependents, intimated to the novice that nothing made a man so important as the discovering of a plot, and that these were. times when a young fellow who would stick at nothing and fear nobody might do wonders.   The Revolution, —such was the language constantly held by Titus and his parasites,— had produced little good.   The brisk boys of Shaftesbury had not been recompensed according to their merits.   Even the Doctor,—such was the ingratitude of men,—was looked on coldly at the new Court.   Tory rogues sate at the council board, and were admitted to the royal closet. It would be a noble feat to bring their necks to the block.   Above all, it would be delightful to see Nottingham's long solemn face on Tower Hill.   For the hatred with which these bad men regarded Nottingham had no bounds, and was probably excited less by his political opinions, in which there was doubtless much to condemn, than by his moral character, in which the closest scrutiny will detect little that is not deserving of approbation.   Oates, with the authority which experience and success entitle a preceptor to assume, read his pupil a lecture on the art of bearing false witness.   "You ought," he said, with many oaths and curses, "to have made more, much more, out of what you heard and saw at Saint Germains.   Never was there a finer foundation for a plot.   But you are a fool : you are a coxcomb : I could beat you : I would not have done so.   I used to go to Charles and tell him his

[1] North's Examen ; Ward's London Spy ; Crosby's English Baptists, vol. iii. chap. 2.

own. I called Lauderdale names to his face. I made King, Ministers, Lords, Commons, afraid of me. But you young men have no spirit." Fuller was greatly edified by these exhortations. It was, however, hinted to him by some of his associates that, if he meant to take up the trade of swearing away lives, he would do well not to show himself so often at coffeehouses in the company of Titus. " The Doctor," said one of the gang, "is an excellent person, and has done great things in his time : but many people are prejudiced against him ; and, if you are really going to discover a plot, the less you are seen with him the better." Fuller accordingly ceased to appear in Oates's train at public places, but still continued to receive his great master's instructions in private.

To do Fuller justice, he seems not to have taken up the trade of a false witness till he could no longer support himself by begging or swindling. He lived for a time on the charity of the Queen. He then levied contributions by pretending to be one of the noble family of Sidney. He wheedled Tillotson out of some money, and requited the good Archbishop's kindness by passing himself off as His Grace's favourite nephew. But in the autumn of 1691 all these shifts were exhausted. After lying in several spunging houses, Fuller was at length lodged in the King's Bench prison, and he now thought it time to announce that he had discovered a plot.[1]

He addressed himself first to Tillotson and Portland : but both Tillotson and Portland soon perceived that he was lying. What he said was, however, reported to the King, who, as might have been expected, treated the information and the informer with cold contempt. All that remained was to try whether a flame could be raised in the Parliament.

Soon after the Houses met, Fuller petitioned the Commons to hear what he had to say, and promised to make wonderful disclosures. He was brought from his prison to the bar of the House ; and he there repeated a long romance. James, he said, had delegated the regal authority to six commissioners, of whom Halifax was first. More than fifty lords and gentlemen had signed an address to the French King, imploring him to make a great effort for the restoration of the House of Stuart. Fuller declared that he had seen this address, and recounted many of the names appended to it. Some members made severe remarks on the improbability of the story and on the character of the witness. He is, it was said, one of the greatest rogues on the face of the earth ; and he tells such things as could scarcely be credited if they were told by an angel from heaven. Fuller audaciously pledged himself to bring proofs which would satisfy the most incredulous. He was, he averred, in communication with some agents of James. Those persons were ready to make reparation to their country. Their testimony would be decisive ;

---

[1] The history of this part of Fuller's life I have taken from his own narrative.

for they were in possession of documentary evidence which would confound the guilty. They held back only because they saw some of the traitors high in office and near the royal person, and were afraid of incurring the enmity of men so powerful and so wicked. Fuller ended by asking for a sum of money, and by assuring the Commons that he would lay it out to good account.[1] Had his impudent request been granted, he would probably have paid his debts, obtained his liberty, and absconded : but the House very wisely insisted on seeing his witnesses first. He then began to shuffle. The gentlemen were on the Continent, and could not come over without passports. Passports were delivered to him : but he complained that they were insufficient. At length the Commons, fully determined to get at the truth, presented an address requesting the King to send Fuller a blank safe conduct in the largest terms.[2] The safe conduct was sent. Six weeks passed, and nothing was heard of the witnesses. The friends of the lords and gentlemen who had been accused represented strongly that the House ought not to separate for the summer without coming to some decision on charges so grave. Fuller was ordered to attend. He pleaded sickness, and asserted, not for the first time, that the Jacobites had poisoned him. But all his plans were confounded by the laudable promptitude and vigour with which the Commons acted. A Committee was sent to his bedside, with orders to ascertain whether he really had any witnesses, and where those witnesses resided. The members who were deputed for this purpose went to the King's Bench prison, and found him suffering under a disorder, produced, in all probability, by some emetic which he had swallowed for the purpose of deceiving them. In answer to their questions, he said that two of his witnesses, Delaval and Hayes, were in England, and were lodged at the house of a Roman Catholic apothecary in Holborn. The Commons, as soon as the Committee had reported, sent some members to the house which he had indicated. That house and all the neighbouring houses were searched. Delaval and Hayes were not to be found ; nor had anybody in the vicinity ever seen such men or heard of them. The House, therefore, on the last day of the session, just before Black Rod knocked at the door, unanimously resolved that William Fuller was a cheat and a false accuser; that he had insulted the Government and the Parliament ; that he had calumniated honourable men ; and that an address should be carried up to the throne, requesting that he might be prosecuted for his villany.[3] He was consequently tried, convicted, and sentenced to fine, imprisonment, and the pillory. The exposure, more terrible than death to a mind not lost to

[1] Commons' Journals, Dec. 2. and 9. 1691.; Grey's Debates.
[2] Commons' Journals, Jan. 4. 169½ ; Grey's Debates.
[3] Commons' Journals, Feb. 22, 23, and 24. 169½.

all sense of shame, he underwent with a hardihood worthy of his two favourite models, Dangerfield and Oates. He had the impudence to persist, year after year, in affirming that he had fallen a victim to the machinations of the late King, who had spent six thousand pounds in order to ruin him. Delaval and Hayes—so this fable ran—had been instructed by James in person. They had, in obedience to his orders, induced Fuller to pledge his word for their appearance, and had then absented themselves, and left him exposed to the resentment of the House of Commons.[1] The story had the reception which it deserved ; and Fuller sank into an obscurity from which he twice or thrice, at long intervals, again emerged for a moment into infamy.

On the twenty-fourth of February 1692, about an hour after the Commons had voted Fuller an impostor, they were summoned to the chamber of the Lords. The King thanked the Houses for their loyalty and liberality, informed them that he must soon set out for the Continent, and commanded them to adjourn themselves. He gave his assent on that day to many bills, public and private : but when the title of one bill, which had passed the Lower House without a single division and the Upper House without a single protest, had been read by the Clerk of the Crown, the Clerk of the Parliaments answered, according to the ancient form, that the King and the Queen would consider of the matter. Those words had very rarely been pronounced before the accession of William. They have been pronounced only once since his death. But by him the power of putting a Veto on laws which had been passed by the Estates of the Realm was used on several important occasions. His detractors truly asserted that he rejected a greater number of important bills than all the Kings of the House of Stuart put together, and most absurdly inferred that the sense of the Estates of the Realm was much less respected by him than by his uncles and his grandfather. A judicious student of history will have no difficulty in discovering why William repeatedly exercised a prerogative to which his predecessors very seldom had recourse, and which his successors have suffered to fall into utter desuetude.

His predecessors passed laws easily because they broke laws easily. Charles the First gave his assent to the Petition of Right, and immediately violated every clause of that great statute. Charles the Second gave his assent to an Act which provided that a Parliament should be held at least once in three years: but when he died the country had been near four years without a Parliament. The laws which abolished the Court of High Commission, the laws which instituted the Sacramental Test, were passed without the smallest difficulty: but they did

Close of the session: bill for ascertaining the salaries of the Judges rejected

[1] Fuller's Original Letters of the late King James and others to his greatest Friends in England.

not prevent James the Second from reestablishing the Court of High Commission, and from filling the Privy Council, the public offices, the courts of justice, and the municipal corporations with persons who had never taken the Test. Nothing could be more natural than that a King should not think it worth while to refuse his assent to a statute with which he could dispense whenever he thought fit.

The situation of William was very different. He could not, like those who had ruled before him, pass an Act in the spring and violate it in the summer. He had, by assenting to the Bill of Rights, solemnly renounced the dispensing power; and he was restrained, by prudence as well as by conscience and honour, from breaking the compact under which he held his crown. A law might be personally offensive to him: it might appear to him to be pernicious to his people: but, as soon as he had passed it, it was, in his eyes, a sacred thing. He had therefore a motive, which preceding Kings had not, for pausing before he passed such a law. They gave their word readily, because they had no scruple about breaking it. He gave his word slowly, because he never failed to keep it.

But his situation, though it differed widely from that of the princes of the House of Stuart, was not precisely that of the princes of the House of Brunswick. A prince of the House of Brunswick is guided, as to the use of every royal prerogative, by the advice of a responsible ministry; and this ministry must be taken from the party which predominates in the two Houses, or, at least, in the Lower House. It is hardly possible to conceive circumstances in which a Sovereign so situated can refuse to assent to a bill which has been approved by both branches of the legislature. Such a refusal would necessarily imply one of two things, that the Sovereign acted in opposition to the advice of the ministry, or that the ministry was at issue, on a question of vital importance, with a majority both of the Commons and of the Lords. On either supposition the country would be in a most critical state, in a state which, if long continued, must end in a revolution. But in the earlier part of the reign of William there was no ministry. The heads of the executive departments had not been appointed exclusively from either party. Some were zealous Whigs, others zealous Tories. The most enlightened statesmen did not hold it to be unconstitutional that the King should exercise his highest prerogatives on the most important occasions without any other guidance than that of his own judgment. His refusal, therefore, to assent to a bill which had passed both Houses indicated, not, as a similar refusal would now indicate, that the whole machinery of government was in a state of fearful disorder, but merely that there was a difference of opinion between him and the two other branches of the legislature as to the expediency of a particular law.

Such a difference of opinion might exist, and, as we shall hereafter see, actually did exist, at a time when he was, not merely on friendly, but on most affectionate terms with the Estates of the Realm.

The circumstances under which he used his Veto for the first time have never yet been correctly stated. A well meant but unskilful attempt had been made to complete a reform which the Bill of Rights had left imperfect. That great law had deprived the Crown of the power of arbitrarily removing the Judges, but had not made them entirely independent. They were remunerated partly by fees and partly by salaries. Over the fees the King had no control: but the salaries he had full power to reduce or to withhold. That William had ever abused this power was not pretended: but it was undoubtedly a power which no prince ought to possess; and this was the sense of both Houses. A bill was therefore brought in by which a salary of a thousand a year was strictly secured to each of the twelve Judges. Thus far all was well. But unfortunately the salaries were made a charge on the hereditary revenue. No such proposition would now be entertained by the House of Commons, without the royal consent previously signified by a Privy Councillor. But this wholesome rule had not then been established ; and William could defend the proprietary rights of the Crown only by putting his negative on the bill. At the time there was, as far as can now be ascertained, no outcry. Even the Jacobite libellers were almost silent. It was not till the provisions of the bill had been forgotten, and till nothing but its title was remembered, that William was accused of having been influenced by a wish to keep the judges in a state of dependence.[1]

[1] Burnet (ii. 86.). Burnet had evidently forgotten what the bill contained. Ralph knew nothing about it but what he had learned from Burnet. I have scarcely seen any allusion to the subject in any of the numerous Jacobite lampoons of that day. But there is a remarkable passage in a pamphlet which appeared towards the close of William's reign, and which is entitled The Art of Governing by Parties. The writer says, "We still want an Act to ascertain some fund for the salaries of the judges ; and there was a bill, since the Revolution, past both Houses of Parliament to this purpose: but whether it was for being any way defective or otherwise that His Majesty refused to assent to it, I cannot remember. But I know the reason satisfied me at that time. And I make no doubt but he'll consent to any good bill of this nature whenever 'tis offered." These words convinced me that the bill was open to some grave objection which did not appear in the title, and which no historian had noticed. I found among the archives of the House of Lords the original parchment, endorsed with the words "Le Roy et La Royne s'aviseront ;" and it was clear at the first glance what the objection was.

There is a hiatus in that part of Narcissus Luttrell's Diary which relates to this matter. "The King," he wrote, "passed ten public bills and thirty-four private ones, and rejected that of the ——"

As to the present practice of the House of Commons in such cases, see Hatsell's valuable work, ii. 356. I quote the edition of 1818. Hatsell says that many bills which affect the interest of the Crown may be brought in without any signification of the royal consent, and that it is enough if the consent be signified on the second reading, or even later ; but that, in a proceeding which affects the hereditary revenue, the consent must be signified in the earliest stage.

The Houses broke up ; and the King prepared to set out for the Continent.   Before his departure he made some changes in his house-

Ministerial changes in England

hold and in several departments of the government, changes, however, which did not indicate a very decided preference for either of the great political parties.   Rochester was sworn of the Council.   It is probable that he had earned this mark of royal favour by taking the Queen's side in the unhappy dispute between her and her sister.   Pembroke took charge of the Privy Seal, and was succeeded at the Board of Admiralty by Charles Lord Cornwallis, a moderate Tory : Lowther accepted a seat at the same board, and was succeeded at the Treasury by Sir Edward Seymour.   Many Tory country gentlemen, who had looked on Seymour as their leader in the war against placemen and Dutchmen, were moved to indignation by learning that he had become a courtier.   They remembered that he had voted for a Regency, that he had taken the oaths with no good grace, and that he had spoken with little respect of the Sovereign whom he was now ready to serve for the sake of emoluments hardly worthy of the acceptance of a man of his wealth and parliamentary interest. It was strange that the haughtiest of human beings should be the meanest, that one who seemed to reverence nothing on earth but himself should abase himself for the sake of quarter day.   About such reflections he troubled himself very little.   He found, however, that there was one disagreeable circumstance connected with his new office. At the Board of Treasury he must sit below the Chancellor of the Exchequer.   The First Lord, Godolphin, was a peer of the realm ; and his right to precedence, according to the rules of the heralds, could not be questioned.   But everybody knew who was the first of English commoners.   What was Richard Hampden that he should take place of a Seymour, of the head of the Seymours ?   With much difficulty, the dispute was compromised.   Many concessions were made to Sir Edward's punctilious pride.   He was sworn of the Council.   He was appointed one of the Cabinet.   The King took him by the hand and presented him to the Queen.   " I bring you," said William, " a gentleman who will in my absence be a valuable friend."   In this way Sir Edward was so much soothed and flattered that he ceased to insist on his right to thrust himself between the First Lord and the Chancellor of the Exchequer.

In the same Commission of Treasury in which the name of Seymour appeared, appeared also the name of a much younger politician, who had, during the late session, raised himself to high distinction in the House of Commons, Charles Montague.   This appointment gave great satisfaction to the Whigs, in whose esteem Montague now stood higher than their veteran chiefs Sacheverell and Powle, and was indeed second to Somers alone.

The Right Honoᵇˡᵉ Charles Mountague One of the Lords Commissioners of the Treasury &c.

G. Kneller Eques pinx.   L. Smith fec: & excud.

CHARLES MONTAGUE

From a mezzotint by J. Smith, after a painting by Sir G. Kneller

Sidney delivered up the seals which he had held during more than a year, and was appointed Lord Lieutenant of Ireland. Some months elapsed before the place which he had quitted was filled up ; and during this interval the whole business which had ordinarily been divided between two Secretaries of State was transacted by Nottingham.[1]

While these arrangements were in progress, events had taken place in a distant part of the island, which were not, till after the lapse of many months, known in the best informed circles of London, but which gradually obtained a fearful notoriety, and which, after the lapse of more than a hundred and sixty years, are never mentioned without horror.

Ministerial changes in Scotland

Soon after the Estates of Scotland had separated in the autumn of 1690, a change was made in the administration of that kingdom. William was not satisfied with the way in which he had been represented in the Parliament House. He thought that the rabbled curates had been hardly treated. He had very reluctantly suffered the law which abolished patronage to be touched with his sceptre. But what especially displeased him was that the Acts which established a new ecclesiastical polity had not been accompanied by an Act granting liberty of conscience to those who were attached to the old ecclesiastical polity. He had directed his Commissioner Melville to obtain for the Episcopalians of Scotland an indulgence similar to that which Dissenters enjoyed in England.[2] But the Presbyterian preachers were loud and vehement against lenity to Amalekites. Melville, with useful talents, and perhaps with fair intentions, had neither large views nor an intrepid spirit. He shrank from uttering a word so hateful to the theological demagogues of his country as Toleration. By obsequiously humouring their prejudices he quelled the clamour which was rising at Edinburgh ; but the effect of his timid caution was that a far more formidable clamour soon rose in the south of the island against the bigotry of the schismatics who domineered in the north, and against the pusillanimity of the government which had not dared to withstand that bigotry. On this subject the High Churchman and the Low Churchman were of one mind, or rather the Low Churchman was the more angry of the two. A man like South, who had during many years been predicting that, if ever the Puritans ceased to be oppressed, they would become oppressors, was at heart not ill pleased to see his prophecy fulfilled. But in a man like Burnet, the great object of whose life had been to mitigate the animosity which the ministers of the Anglican Church felt towards

---

[1] The history of these ministerial arrangements I have taken chiefly from the London Gazette of March 3. and March 7. 1694, and from Narcissus Luttrell's Diary for that month. Two or three slight touches are from contemporary pamphlets.

[2] William to Melville, May 22. 1690.

the Presbyterians, the intolerant conduct of the Presbyterians could awaken no feeling but indignation, shame, and grief. There was, therefore, at the English Court nobody to speak a good word for Melville. It was impossible that in such circumstances he should remain at the head of the Scottish administration. He was, however, gently let down from his high position. He continued during more than a year to be Secretary of State: but another Secretary was appointed, who was to reside near the King, and to have the chief direction of affairs. The new Prime Minister for Scotland was the able, eloquent, and accomplished Sir John Dalrymple. His father, the Lord President of the Court of Session, had lately been raised to the peerage by the title of Viscount Stair: and Sir John Dalrymple was consequently, according to the ancient usage of Scotland, designated as the Master of Stair. In a few months Melville resigned his secretaryship, and accepted an office of some dignity and emolument, but of no political importance.[1]

The Lowlands of Scotland were, during the year which followed the parliamentary session of 1690, as quiet as they had ever been within the memory of man: but the state of the Highlands caused much anxiety to the government. The civil war in that wild region, after it had ceased to flame, had continued during some time to smoulder. At length, early in the year 1691, the rebel chiefs informed the Court of Saint Germains that, pressed as they were on every side, they could hold out no longer without succour from France. James had sent them a small quantity of meal, brandy, and tobacco, and had frankly told them that he could do nothing more. Money was so scarce among them that six hundred pounds sterling would have been a most acceptable addition to their funds: but even such a sum he was unable to spare. He could scarcely, in such circumstances, expect them to defend his cause against a government which had a regular army and a large revenue. He therefore informed them that he should not take it ill of them if they made their peace with the new dynasty, provided always that they were prepared to rise in insurrection as soon as he should call on them to do so.[2]

Meanwhile it had been determined at Kensington, in spite of the opposition of the Master of Stair, to try the plan which Tarbet had recommended two years before, and which, if it had been tried when he recommended it, would probably have prevented much bloodshed and confusion. It was resolved that twelve or fifteen thousand pounds

State of the Highlands

---

[1] See the preface to the Leven and Melville Papers. I have given what I believe to be a true explanation of Burnet's hostility to Melville. Melville's descendant, who has deserved well of all students of history by the diligence and fidelity with which he has performed his editorial duties, thinks that Burnet's judgment was blinded by zeal for Prelacy and hatred of Presbyterianism. This accusation will surprise and amuse English High Churchmen.

[2] Life of James, ii. 468, 469.

should be laid out in quieting the Highlands. This was a mass of treasure which to an inhabitant of Appin or Lochaber seemed almost fabulous, and which indeed bore a greater proportion to the income of Keppoch or Glengarry than fifteen hundred thousand pounds bore to the income of Lord Bedford or Lord Devonshire. The sum was ample ; but the King was not fortunate in the choice of an agent.[1]

John Earl of Breadalbane, the head of a younger branch of the great house of Campbell, ranked high among the petty princes of the mountains. He could bring seventeen hundred claymores into the field ; and, ten years before the Revolution, he had actually marched into the Lowlands with this great force for the purpose of supporting the prelatical tyranny.[2] In those days he had affected zeal for monarchy and episcopacy : but in truth he cared for no government and no religion. He seems to have united two different sets of vices, the growth of two different regions, and of two different stages in the progress of society. In his castle among the hills he had learned the barbarian pride and ferocity of a Highland chief. In the Council Chamber at Edinburgh he had contracted the deep taint of treachery and corruption. After the Revolution he had, like too many of his fellow nobles, joined and betrayed every party in turn, had sworn fealty to William and Mary, and had plotted against them. To trace all the turns and doublings of his course, during the year 1689 and the earlier part of 1690, would be wearisome.[3] That course became somewhat less tortuous when the battle of the Boyne had cowed the spirit of the Jacobites. It now seemed probable that the Earl would be a loyal subject of their Majesties, till some great disaster should befall them. Nobody who knew him could trust him : but few Scottish statesmen could then be trusted; and yet Scottish statesmen must be employed. His position and connections marked him out as a man who might, if he would, do much towards the work of quieting the Highlands ; and his interest seemed to be a guarantee for his zeal. He had, as he declared with every appearance of truth, strong personal reasons for wishing to see tranquillity restored. His domains were so situated that, while the civil war lasted, his vassals could not tend their herds or sow their oats in peace. His lands were daily ravaged: his cattle were daily driven away: one of his houses had been burnt down. It was probable, therefore, that he would do his best to put an end to hostilities.[4]

Breadalbane employed to negotiate with the rebel clans

---

[1] Burnet, ii. 88. ; Master of Stair to Breadalbane, Dec. 2. 1691.   [2] Burnet, i. 418.

[3] Crawford to Melville, July 23. 1689; The Master of Stair to Melville, Aug. 16. 1689; Cardross to Melville, Sept. 9. 1689; Balcarras's Memoirs ; Annandale's Confession, Aug. 14. 1690.

[4] Breadalbane to Melville, Sept. 17. 1690.

JOHN, FIRST EARL OF BREADALBANE

From a painting by Sir J. B. Medina amongst the Breadalbane Family Pictures at Langton

He was accordingly commissioned to treat with the Jacobite chiefs, and was entrusted with the money which was to be distributed among them. He invited them to a conference at his residence in Glenorchy. They came : but the treaty went on very slowly. Every head of a tribe asked for a larger share of the English gold than was to be obtained. Breadalbane was suspected of intending to cheat both the King and the clans. The dispute between the rebels and the government was complicated with another dispute still more embarrassing. The Camerons and Macdonalds were really at war, not with William, but with Mac Callum More ; and no arrangement to which Mac Callum More was not a party could really produce tranquillity. A grave question therefore arose, whether the money entrusted to Breadalbane should be paid directly to the discontented chiefs, or should be employed to satisfy the claims which Argyle had upon them. The shrewdness of Lochiel and the arrogant pretensions of Glengarry contributed to protract the discussions. But no Celtic potentate was so impracticable as Macdonald of Glencoe, known among the mountains by the hereditary appellation of Mac Ian.[1]

Mac Ian dwelt in the mouth of a ravine situated not far from the southern shore of Lochleven, an arm of the sea which deeply indents the western coast of Scotland, and separates Argyleshire from Invernesshire. Near his house were two or three small hamlets inhabited by his tribe. The whole population which he governed was not supposed to exceed two hundred souls. In the neighbourhood of the little cluster of villages was some copsewood and some pasture land : but a little further up the defile no sign of population or of fruitfulness was to be seen. In the Gaelic tongue, Glencoe signifies the Glen of Weeping : and in truth that pass is the most dreary and melancholy of all the Scottish passes, the very Valley of the Shadow of Death. Mists and storms brood over it through the greater part of the finest summer ; and even on those rare days when the sun is bright, and when there is no cloud in the sky, the impression made by the landscape is sad and awful. The path lies along a stream which issues from the most sullen and gloomy of mountain pools. Huge precipices of naked stone frown on both sides. Even in July the streaks of snow may often be discerned in the rifts near the summits. All down the sides of the crags heaps of ruin mark the headlong paths of the torrents. Mile after mile the traveller looks in vain for the smoke of one hut, or for one human form wrapped in a plaid, and listens in vain for the bark of a shepherd's dog, or the bleat of a lamb. Mile after mile the only sound that indicates life is the faint cry of a bird

Glencoe

---

[1] The Master of Stair to Hamilton, Aug. $\frac{17}{27}$. 1691 ; Hill to Melville, June 26. 1691 ; The Master of Stair to Breadalbane, Aug. 24. 1691.

GLENCOE.

From a water-colour drawing by G. F. Robson, in the Sutherland Collection.

of prey from some storm beaten pinnacle of rock. The progress of civilisation, which has turned so many wastes into fields yellow with harvests or gay with apple blossoms, has only made Glencoe more desolate. All the science and industry of a peaceful age can extract nothing valuable from that wilderness : but, in an age of violence and rapine, the wilderness itself was valued on account of the shelter which it afforded to the plunderer and his plunder. Nothing could be more natural than that the clan to which this rugged desert belonged should have been noted for predatory habits. For, among the Highlanders generally, to rob was thought at least as honourable an employment as to cultivate the soil ; and, of all the Highlanders, the Macdonalds of Glencoe had the least productive soil, and the most convenient and secure den of robbers. Successive governments had tried to punish this wild race : but no large force had ever been employed for that purpose ; and a small force was easily resisted or eluded by men familiar with every recess and every outlet of the natural fortress in which they had been born and bred. The people of Glencoe would probably have been less troublesome neighbours if they had lived among their own kindred. But they were an outpost of the Clan Donald, separated from every other branch of their own family, and almost surrounded by the domains of the hostile race of Diarmid.[1] They were impelled by hereditary enmity, as well as by want, to live at the expense of the tribe of Campbell. Breadalbane's property had suffered greatly from their depredations ; and he was not of a temper to forgive such injuries. When, therefore, the Chief of Glencoe made his appearance at the congress in Glenorchy, he was ungraciously received. The Earl, who ordinarily bore himself with the solemn dignity of a Castilian grandee, forgot, in his resentment, his wonted gravity, forgot his public character, forgot the laws of hospitality, and, with angry reproaches and menaces, demanded reparation for the herds which had been driven from his lands by Mac Ian's followers. Mac Ian was seriously apprehensive of some personal outrage, and was glad to get safe back to his own glen.[2] His pride had been wounded ; and the promptings of interest concurred with those of pride. As the head of a people who lived by pillage, he had strong reasons for wishing that the country might continue to be in a perturbed state. He had little chance of

[1] " The real truth is, they were a branch of the Macdonalds (who were a brave courageous people always), seated among the Campbells, who (I mean the Glencoe men) are all Papists, if they have any religion, were always counted a people much given to rapine and plunder, or sorners as we call it, and much of a piece with your highwaymen in England. Several governments desired to bring them to justice : but their country was inaccessible to small parties." See An impartial Account of some of the Transactions in Scotland concerning the Earl of Breadalbane, Viscount and Master of Stair, Glenco Men, &c., London, 1695.

[2] Report of the Commissioners, signed at Holyrood, June 20. 1695.

H. E. V   E

receiving one guinea of the money which was to be distributed among the malecontents.   For his share of that money would scarcely meet Breadalbane's demands for compensation ; and there could be little doubt that, whoever might be unpaid, Breadalbane would take care to pay himself.   Mac Ian therefore did his best to dissuade his allies from accepting terms from which he could himself expect no benefit ; and his influence was not small.   His own vassals, indeed, were few in number : but he came of the best blood of the Highlands : he kept up a close connection with his more powerful kinsmen ; nor did they like him the less because he was a robber ; for he never robbed them ; and that robbery, merely as robbery, was a wicked and dis-graceful act, had never entered into the mind of any Celtic chief.   Mac Ian was therefore held in high esteem by the confederates.   His age was venerable : his aspect was majestic ; and he possessed in large measure those intellectual qualities which, in rude societies, give men an ascendency over their fellows.   Breadalbane found himself, at every step of the negotiation, thwarted by the arts of his old enemy, and abhorred the name of Glencoe more and more every day.[1]

But the government did not trust solely to Breadalbane's diplomatic skill.   The authorities at Edinburgh put forth a proclamation exhorting the clans to submit to King William and Queen Mary, and offering pardon to every rebel who, on or before the thirty-first of December 1691, should swear to live peaceably under the government of their Majesties.   It was announced that those who should hold out after that day would be treated as enemies and traitors.[2]   Warlike preparations were made, which showed that the threat was meant in earnest.   The Highlanders were alarmed, and, though the pecuniary terms had not been satisfactorily settled, thought it prudent to give the pledge which was demanded of them.   No chief, indeed, was willing to set the example of submission.   Glengarry blustered, and pretended to fortify his house.[3]   " I will not," said Lochiel, " break the ice.   That is a point of honour with me.   But my tacksmen and people may use their free-dom."[4]   His tacksmen and people understood him, and repaired by hundreds to the Sheriff to take the oaths.   The Macdonalds of Sleat, Clanronald, Keppoch, and even Glengarry, imitated the Camerons ; and the chiefs, after trying to outstay each other as long as they durst, imitated their vassals.

The thirty-first of December arrived ; and still the Macdonalds of Glencoe had not come in.   The punctilious pride of Mac Ian was doubtless gratified by the thought that he had continued to defy the

[1] Gallienus Redivivus ; Burnet, ii. 88. ; Report of the Commission of 1695.
[2] Report of the Glencoe Commission, 1695.   [3] Hill to Melville, May 15. 1691.
[4] Hill to Melville, June 3. 1691.

government after the boastful Glengarry, the ferocious Keppoch, the magnanimous Lochiel had yielded : but he bought his gratification dear.

At length, on the thirty-first of December, he repaired to Fort William, accompanied by his principal vassals, and offered to take the oaths. To his dismay, he found that there was in the fort no person competent to administer them. Colonel Hill, the Governor, was not a magistrate ; nor was there any magistrate nearer than Inverary. Mac Ian, now fully sensible of the folly of which he had been guilty in postponing to the very last moment an act on which his life and his estate depended, set off for Inverary in great distress. He carried with him a letter from Hill to the Sheriff of Argyleshire, Sir Colin Campbell of Ardkinglass, a respectable gentleman, who, in the late reign, had suffered severely for his Whig principles. In this letter the Colonel expressed a goodnatured hope that, even out of season, a lost sheep, and so fine a lost sheep, would be gladly received. Mac Ian made all the haste in his power, and did not stop even at his own house, though it lay nigh to the road. But in that age a journey through Argyleshire in the depth of winter was necessarily slow. The old man's progress up steep mountains and along boggy valleys was obstructed by snow storms ; and it was not till the sixth of January that he presented himself before the Sheriff at Inverary. The Sheriff hesitated. His power, he said, was limited by the terms of the proclamation ; and he did not see how he could swear a rebel who had not submitted within the prescribed time. Mac Ian begged earnestly and with tears that he might be sworn. His people, he said, would follow his example. If any of them proved refractory, he would himself send the recusant to prison, or ship him off for Flanders. His entreaties and Hill's letter overcame Sir Colin's scruples. The oath was administered ; and a certificate was transmitted to the Council at Edinburgh, setting forth the special circumstances which had induced the Sheriff to do what he knew not to be strictly regular.[1]

The news that Mac Ian had not submitted within the prescribed time was received with cruel joy by three powerful Scotchmen who were then at the English Court. Breadalbane had gone up to London at Christmas in order to give an account of his stewardship. There he met his kinsman Argyle. Argyle was, in personal qualities, one of the most insignificant of the long line of nobles who have borne that great name. He was the descendant of eminent men, and the parent of eminent men. He was the grandson of one of the ablest of Scottish

_____

[1] Burnet, ii. 8, 9.; Report of the Glencoe Commission. The authorities quoted in this part of the Report were the depositions of Hill, of Campbell of Ardkinglass, and of Mac Ian's two sons

politicians; the son of one of the bravest and most truehearted of Scottish patriots; the father of one Mac Callum More renowned as a warrior and as an orator, as the model of every courtly grace, and as the judicious patron of arts and letters, and of another Mac Callum More distinguished by talents for business and command, and by skill in the exact sciences. Both of such an ancestry and of such a progeny Argyle was unworthy. He had even been guilty of the crime, common enough among Scottish politicians, but in him singularly disgraceful, of tampering with the agents of James while professing loyalty to William. Still Argyle had the importance inseparable from high rank, vast domains, extensive feudal rights, and almost boundless patriarchal authority. To him, as to his cousin Breadalbane, the intelligence that the tribe of Glencoe was out of the protection of the law was most gratifying; and the Master of Stair more than sympathised with them both.

The feeling of Argyle and Breadalbane is perfectly intelligible. They were the heads of a great clan; and they had an opportunity of destroying a neighbouring clan with which they were at deadly feud. Breadalbane had received peculiar provocation. His estate had been repeatedly devastated; and he had just been thwarted in a negotiation of high moment. Unhappily there was scarcely any excess of ferocity for which a precedent could not be found in Celtic tradition. Among all warlike barbarians revenge is esteemed the most sacred of duties and the most exquisite of pleasures; and so it had long been esteemed among the Highlanders. The history of the clans abounds with frightful tales, some perhaps fabulous or exaggerated, some certainly true, of vindictive massacres and assassinations. The Macdonalds of Glengarry, for example, having been affronted by the people of a parish near Inverness, surrounded the parish church on a Sunday, shut the doors, and burned the whole congregation alive. While the flames were raging, the hereditary musician of the murderers mocked the shrieks of the perishing crowd with the notes of his bagpipe.[1] A band of Macgregors, having cut off the head of an enemy, laid it, the mouth filled with bread and cheese, on his sister's table, and had the satisfaction of seeing her go mad with horror at the sight. They then carried the ghastly trophy in triumph to their chief. The whole clan met under the roof of an ancient church. Every one in turn laid his hand on the dead man's scalp, and vowed to defend the slayers.[2] The inhabitants of Eigg seized some Macleods, bound them hand and foot, and turned them adrift in a boat to be swallowed up by the waves, or to perish of hunger. The Macleods retaliated by driving the population of Eigg

[1] Johnson's Tour to the Hebrides.

[2] Proclamation of the Privy Council of Scotland, Feb. 4. 1589. I give this reference on the authority of Sir Walter Scott. See the preface to the Legend of Montrose.

ARCHIBALD, FIRST DUKE OF ARGYLE

From a mezzotint by R. Cooper, after a painting by W. Aikman

into a cavern, lighting a fire at the entrance, and suffocating the whole race, men, women, and children.[1]   It is much less strange that the two great Earls of the house of Campbell, animated by the passions of Highland chieftains, should have planned a Highland revenge, than that they should have found an accomplice, and something more than an accomplice, in the Master of Stair.

The Master of Stair was one of the first men of his time, a jurist, a statesman, a fine scholar, an eloquent orator.   His polished manners and lively conversation were the delight of aristocratical societies ; and none who met him in such societies would have thought it possible that he could bear the chief part in any atrocious crime.   His political principles were lax, yet not more lax than those of most Scotch politicians of that age.   Cruelty had never been imputed to him.   Those who most disliked him did him the justice to own that, where his schemes of policy were not concerned, he was a very goodnatured man.[2]   There is not the slightest reason to believe that he gained a single pound Scots by the act which has covered his name with infamy.   He had no personal reason to wish the Glencoe men any ill.   There had been no feud between them and his family.   His property lay in a district where their tartan was never seen.   Yet he hated them with a hatred as fierce and implacable as if they had laid waste his fields, burned his mansion, murdered his child in the cradle.

To what cause are we to ascribe so strange an antipathy ?   This question perplexed the Master's contemporaries ; and any answer which may now be offered ought to be offered with diffidence.[3]   The most probable conjecture is that he was actuated by an inordinate, an unscrupulous, a remorseless zeal for what seemed to him to be the interest of the state.   This explanation may startle those who have not considered how large a proportion of the blackest crimes recorded in history is to be ascribed to ill regulated public spirit.   We daily see men do for their party, for their sect, for their country, for their favourite schemes of political and social reform, what they would not do to enrich or to avenge themselves.   At a temptation directly addressed to our private cupidity or to our private animosity, whatever virtue we have takes the alarm.   But virtue itself may contribute to the fall of him who imagines that it is in his power, by violating some general rule of morality, to confer an important benefit on a church, on a commonwealth, on mankind.   He

---

[1] Johnson's Tour to the Hebrides.   [2] Lockhart's Memoirs.

[3] " What under heaven was the Master's byass in this matter? I can imagine none."— Impartial Account, 1695.   " Nor can any man of candour and ingenuity imagine that the Earl of Stair, who had neither estate, friendship nor enmity in that country, nor so much as knowledge of these persons, and who was never noted for cruelty in his temper, should have thirsted after the blood of these wretches."—Complete History of Europe, 1707.

SIR JOHN DALRYMPLE, MASTER, AFTERWARDS FIRST EARL OF STAIR

From a painting by Sir G. Kneller

silences the remonstrances of conscience, and hardens his heart against the most touching spectacles of misery, by repeating to himself that his intentions are pure, that his objects are noble, that he is doing a little evil for the sake of a great good. By degrees he comes altogether to forget the turpitude of the means in the excellence of the end, and at length perpetrates without one internal twinge acts which would shock a buccaneer. There is no reason to believe that Dominic would, for the best archbishopric in Christendom, have incited ferocious marauders to plunder and slaughter a peaceful and industrious population, that Everard Digby would, for a dukedom, have blown a large assembly of people into the air, or that Robespierre would have murdered for hire one of the thousands whom he murdered from philanthropy.

The Master of Stair seems to have proposed to himself a truly great and good end, the pacification and civilisation of the Highlands. He was, by the acknowledgment of those who most hated him, a man of large views. He justly thought it monstrous that a third part of Scotland should be in a state scarcely less savage than New Guinea, that letters of fire and sword should, through a third part of Scotland, be, century after century, a species of legal process, and that no attempt should be made to apply a radical remedy to such evils. The independence affected by a crowd of petty sovereigns, the contumacious resistance which they were in the habit of offering to the authority of the Crown and of the Court of Session, their wars, their robberies, their fireraisings, their practice of exacting black mail from people more peaceable and more useful than themselves, naturally excited the disgust and indignation of an enlightened and politic gownsman, who was, both by the constitution of his mind and by the habits of his profession, a lover of law and order. His object was no less than a complete dissolution and reconstruction of society in the Highlands, such a dissolution and reconstruction as, two generations later, followed the battle of Culloden. In his view the clans, as they existed, were the plagues of the kingdom; and of all the clans the worst was that which inhabited Glencoe. He had, it is said, been particularly struck by a frightful instance of the lawlessness and ferocity of those marauders. One of them, who had been concerned in some act of violence or rapine, had given information against his companions. He had been bound to a tree and murdered. The old chief had given the first stab; and scores of dirks had then been plunged into the wretch's body.[1] By the mountaineers

---

[1] Dalrymple, in his Memoirs, relates this story, without referring to any authority. His authority probably was family tradition. That reports were current in 1692 of horrible crimes committed by the Macdonalds of Glencoe is certain from the Burnet MS. Harl. 6584. "They had indeed been guilty of many black murthers," were Burnet's words, written in 1693. He afterwards softened down this expression.

such an act was probably regarded as a legitimate exercise of patriarchal jurisdiction.   To the Master of Stair it seemed that people among whom such things were done and were approved ought to be treated like a pack of wolves, snared by any device, and slaughtered without mercy.   He was well read in history, and doubtless knew how great rulers had, in his own and other countries, dealt with such banditti.   He doubtless knew with what energy and what severity James the Fifth had put down the mosstroopers of the border, how the chief of Henderland had been hung over the gate of the castle in which he had prepared a banquet for the King ; how John Armstrong and his thirty six horsemen, when they came forth to welcome their sovereign, had scarcely been allowed time to say a single prayer before they were all tied up and turned off.   Nor probably was the Secretary ignorant of the means by which Sixtus the Fifth had cleared the ecclesiastical state of outlaws. The eulogists of that great pontiff tell us that there was one formidable gang which could not be dislodged from a stronghold among the Apennines.   Beasts of burden were therefore loaded with poisoned food and wine, and sent by a road which ran close to the fastness.   The robbers sallied forth, seized the prey, feasted, and died ; and the pious old Pope exulted greatly when he heard that the corpses of thirty ruffians, who had been the terror of many peaceful villages, had been found lying among the mules and packages.   The plans of the Master of Stair were conceived in the spirit of James and of Sixtus ; and the rebellion of the mountaineers furnished what seemed to be an excellent opportunity for carrying those plans into effect.   Mere rebellion, indeed, he could have easily pardoned.   On Jacobites, as Jacobites, he never showed any inclination to bear hard.   He hated the Highlanders, not as enemies of this or that dynasty, but as enemies of law, of industry, and of trade.   In his private correspondence he applied to them the short and terrible form of words in which the implacable Roman pronounced the doom of Carthage.   His project was no less than this, that the whole hill country from sea to sea, and the neighbouring islands, should be wasted with fire and sword, that the Camerons, the Macleans, and all the branches of the race of Macdonald, should be rooted out. He therefore looked with no friendly eye on schemes of reconciliation, and, while others were hoping that a little money would set everything right, hinted very intelligibly his opinion that whatever money was to be laid out on the clans would be best laid out in the form of bullets and bayonets.   To the last moment he continued to flatter himself that the rebels would be obstinate, and would thus furnish him with a plea for accomplishing that great social revolution on which his heart was set.[1]

[1] That the plan originally framed by the Master of Stair was such as I have represented it, is clear from parts of his letters which are quoted in the Report of 1695, and from his letters to

The letter is still extant in which he directed the commander of the forces in Scotland how to act if the Jacobite chiefs should not come in before the end of December. There is something strangely terrible in the calmness and conciseness with which the instructions are given. "Your troops will destroy entirely the country of Lochaber, Lochiel's lands, Keppoch's, Glengarry's and Glencoe's. Your power shall be large enough. I hope the soldiers will not trouble the government with prisoners."[1]

This despatch had scarcely been sent off when news arrived in London that the rebel chiefs, after holding out long, had at last appeared before the Sheriffs and taken the oaths. Lochiel, the most eminent man among them, had not only declared that he would live and die a true subject to King William, but had announced his intention of visiting England, in the hope of being permitted to kiss His Majesty's hand. In London it was announced exultingly that all the clans had submitted; and the announcement was generally thought most satisfactory.[2] But the Master of Stair was bitterly disappointed. The Highlands were then to continue to be what they had been, the shame and curse of Scotland. A golden opportunity of subjecting them to the law had been suffered to escape, and might never return. If only the Macdonalds would have stood out, nay, if an example could but have been made of the two worst Macdonalds, Keppoch and Glencoe, it would have been something. But it seemed that even Keppoch and Glencoe, marauders who in any well governed country would have been hanged thirty years before, were safe.[3] While the Master was brooding over thoughts like these, Argyle brought him some comfort. The report that Mac Ian had taken the oaths within the prescribed time was erroneous. The Secretary was consoled. One clan, then, was at the mercy of the government, and that clan the most lawless of all. One great act of justice, nay of charity, might be performed. One terrible and memorable example might be made.[4]

Yet there was a difficulty. Mac Ian had taken the oaths. He had taken them, indeed, too late to be entitled to plead the letter of the royal promise: but the fact that he had taken them was one which

Breadalbane of October 27., December 2., and December 3. 1691. Of these letters to Breadalbane the last two are in Dalrymple's Appendix. The first is in the Appendix to the first volume of Mr. Burton's valuable History of Scotland. "It appeared," says Burnet (ii. 157.), "that a black design was laid, not only to cut off the men of Glencoe, but a great many more clans, reckoned to be in all above six thousand persons."

[1] This letter is in the Report of 1695.   [2] London Gazette, January 14. and 18. 169½.

[3] "I could have wished the Macdonalds had not divided; and I am sorry that Keppoch and Mackian of Glenco are safe."—Letter of the Master of Stair to Levingstone, Jan. 9. 169½, quoted in the Report of 1695.

[4] Letter of the Master of Stair to Levingstone, Jan. 11. 169½, quoted in the Report of 1695.

evidently ought to have been brought under consideration before his fate was decided. By a dark intrigue, of which the history is but imperfectly known, but which was, in all probability, directed by the Master of Stair, the evidence of Mac Ian's tardy submission was suppressed. The certificate which the Sheriff of Argyleshire had transmitted to the Council at Edinburgh was never laid before the Board, but was privately submitted to some persons high in office, and particularly to Lord President Stair, the father of the Secretary. These persons pronounced the certificate irregular, and, indeed, absolutely null ; and it was cancelled.

Meanwhile the Master of Stair was forming, in concert with Breadalbane and Argyle, a plan for the destruction of the people of Glencoe. It was necessary to take the King's pleasure, not, indeed, as to the details of what was to be done, but as to the question whether Mac Ian and his people should or should not be treated as rebels out of the pale of the ordinary law. The Master of Stair found no difficulty in the royal closet. William had, in all probability, never heard the Glencoe men mentioned except as banditti. He knew that they had not come in by the prescribed day. That they had come in after that day he did not know. If he paid any attention to the matter, he must have thought that so fair an opportunity of putting an end to the devastations and depredations from which a quiet and industrious population had suffered so much ought not to be lost.

An order was laid before him for signature. He signed it, but, if Burnet may be trusted, did not read it. Whoever has seen anything of public business knows that princes and ministers daily sign, and indeed must sign, documents which they have not read ; and of all documents a document relating to a small tribe of mountaineers, living in a wilderness not set down in any map, was least likely to interest a Sovereign whose mind was full of schemes on which the fate of Europe might depend.[1] But, even on the supposition that he read the order to which he affixed his name, there seems to be no reason for blaming him. That order, directed to the Commander of the Forces in Scotland, runs thus : " As for Mac Ian of Glencoe and that tribe, if they can be well distinguished from the other Highlanders, it will be proper, for the vindication of public justice, to extirpate that set of thieves." These words naturally bear a sense perfectly innocent, and would, but for the horrible event which followed, have been universally understood in that sense. It is undoubtedly one of the first duties of every government to

[1] Burnet, ii. 89. Burnet, in 1693, wrote thus about William :—" He suffers matters to run till there is a great heap of papers ; and then he signs them as much too fast as he was before too slow in despatching them." Burnet MS. Harl. 6584. There is no sign either of procrastination or of undue haste in William's correspondence with Heinsius. The truth is that the King understood Continental politics thoroughly, and gave his whole mind to them. To English business he attended less, and to Scotch business least of all.

extirpate gangs of thieves.   This does not mean that every thief ought
to be treacherously assassinated in his sleep, or even that every thief
ought to be put to death after a fair trial, but that every gang, as
a gang, ought to be completely broken up, and that whatever severity
is indispensably necessary for that end ought to be used.   It is in
this sense that we praise the Marquess of Hastings for extirpating
the Pindarees, and Lord William Bentinck for extirpating the Thugs.
If the King had read and weighed the words which were submitted to
him by his Secretary, he would probably have understood them to
mean that Glencoe was to be occupied by troops, that resistance, if
resistance were attempted, was to be put down with a strong hand,
that severe punishment was to be inflicted on those leading members of
the clan who could be proved to have been guilty of great crimes, that
some active young freebooters, who were more used to handle the
broad sword than the plough, and who did not seem likely to settle
down into quiet labourers, were to be sent to the army in the Low
Countries, that others were to be transported to the American plantations, and that those Macdonalds who were suffered to remain in their
native valley were to be disarmed and required to give hostages for
good behaviour.   A plan very nearly resembling this had, we know,
actually been the subject of much discussion in the political circles of
Edinburgh.[1]   There can be little doubt that William would have
deserved well of his people if he had, in this manner, extirpated, not
only the tribe of Mac Ian, but every Highland tribe whose calling was
to steal cattle and burn houses.

The extirpation planned by the Master of Stair was of a different
kind.   His design was to butcher the whole race of thieves, the whole
damnable race.   Such was the language in which his hatred vented
itself.   He studied the geography of the wild country which surrounded
Glencoe, and made his arrangements with infernal skill.   If possible
the blow must be quick, and crushing, and altogether unexpected.   But
if Mac Ian should apprehend danger, and should attempt to take
refuge in the territories of his neighbours, he must find every road
barred.   The pass of Rannoch must be secured.   The Laird of Weem,
who was powerful in Strath Tay, must be told that, if he harbours the
outlaws, he does so at his peril.   Breadalbane promised to cut off the
retreat of the fugitives on one side, Mac Callum More on another.
It was fortunate, the Secretary wrote, that it was winter.   This was the
time to maul the wretches.   The nights were so long, the mountain
tops so cold and stormy, that even the hardiest men could not long
bear exposure to the open air without a roof or a spark of fire.   That
the women and the children could find shelter in the desert was quite

[1] Impartial Account, 1695.

impossible. While he wrote thus, no thought that he was committing a great wickedness crossed his mind. He was happy in the approbation of his own conscience. Duty, justice, nay charity and mercy, were the names under which he disguised his cruelty; nor is it by any means improbable that the disguise imposed upon himself.[1]

Hill, who commanded the forces assembled at Fort William, was not entrusted with the execution of the design. He seems to have been a humane man ; he was much distressed when he learned that the government was determined on severity; and it was probably thought that his heart might fail him in the most critical moment. He was directed to put a strong detachment under the orders of his second in command, Lieutenant Colonel Hamilton. To Hamilton a significant hint was conveyed that he had now an excellent opportunity of establishing his character in the estimation of those who were at the head of affairs. Of the troops entrusted to him a large proportion were Campbells, and belonged to a regiment lately raised by Argyle, and called by Argyle's name. It was probably thought that, on such an occasion, humanity might prove too strong for the mere habit of military obedience, and that little reliance could be placed on hearts which had not been ulcerated by a feud such as had long raged between the people of Mac Ian and the people of Mac Callum More.

Had Hamilton marched openly against the Glencoe men and put them to the edge of the sword, the act would probably not have wanted apologists, and most certainly would not have wanted precedents. But the Master of Stair had strongly recommended a different mode of proceeding. If the least alarm were given, the nest of robbers would be found empty ; and to hunt them down in so wild a region would, even with all the help that Breadalbane and Argyle could give, be a long and difficult business. " Better," he wrote, " not meddle with them than meddle to no purpose. When the thing is resolved, let it be secret and sudden." [2] He was obeyed ; and it was determined that the Glencoe men should perish, not by military execution, but by the most dastardly and perfidious form of assassination.

On the first of February a hundred and twenty soldiers of Argyle's regiment, commanded by a captain named Campbell and a lieutenant named Lindsay, marched to Glencoe. Captain Campbell was commonly called in Scotland Glenlyon, from the pass in which his property lay. He had every qualification for the service on which he was employed, an unblushing forehead, a smooth lying tongue, and a heart of adamant. He was also one of the few Campbells who were likely to be trusted

[1] See his letters quoted in the Report of 1695, and in the Memoirs of the Massacre of Glencoe.

[2] Report of 1695.

and welcomed by the Macdonalds : for his niece was married to Alexander, the second son of Mac Ian.

The sight of the red coats approaching caused some anxiety among the population of the valley. John, the eldest son of the Chief, came, accompanied by twenty clansmen, to meet the strangers, and asked what this visit meant. Lieutenant Lindsay answered that the soldiers came as friends, and wanted nothing but quarters. They were kindly received, and were lodged under the thatched roofs of the little community. Glenlyon and several of his men were taken into the house of a tacksman who was named, from the cluster of cabins over which he exercised authority, Inverriggen. Lindsay was accommodated nearer to the abode of the old chief. Auchintriater, one of the principal men of the clan, who governed the small hamlet of Auchnaion, found room there for a party commanded by a serjeant named Barbour. Provisions were liberally supplied. There was no want of beef, which had probably fattened in distant pastures; nor was any payment demanded : for in hospitality, as in thievery, the Gaelic marauders rivalled the Bedouins. During twelve days the soldiers lived familiarly with the people of the glen. Old Mac Ian, who had before felt many misgivings as to the relation in which he stood to the government, seems to have been pleased with the visit. The officers passed much of their time with him and his family. The long evenings were cheerfully spent by the peat fire with the help of some packs of cards which had found their way to that remote corner of the world, and of some French brandy which was probably part of James's farewell gift to his Highland supporters. Glenlyon appeared to be warmly attached to his niece and her husband Alexander. Every day he came to their house to take his morning draught. Meanwhile he observed with minute attention all the avenues by which, when the signal for the slaughter should be given, the Macdonalds might attempt to escape to the hills ; and he reported the result of his observations to Hamilton.

Hamilton fixed five o'clock in the morning of the thirteenth of February for the deed. He hoped that, before that time, he should reach Glencoe with four hundred men, and should have stopped all the earths in which the old fox and his two cubs,—so Mac Ian and his sons were nicknamed by the murderers,—could take refuge. But, at five precisely, whether Hamilton had arrived or not, Glenlyon was to fall on, and to slay every Macdonald under seventy.

The night was rough. Hamilton and his troops made slow progress, and were long after their time. While they were contending with the wind and snow, Glenlyon was supping and playing at cards with those whom he meant to butcher before daybreak. He and Lieutenant

Lindsay had engaged themselves to dine with the old Chief on the morrow.

Late in the evening a vague suspicion that some evil was intended crossed the mind of the Chief's eldest son. The soldiers were evidently in a restless state; and some of them uttered strange exclamations.

CAPTAIN CAMPBELL OF GLENLYON

From a plate in the possession of Messrs. James MacLehose and Sons

Two men, it is said, were overheard whispering. " I do not like this job," one of them muttered: "I should be glad to fight the Macdonalds. But to kill men in their beds—" " We must do as we are bid," answered another voice. "If there is any thing wrong, our officers must answer for it." John Macdonald was so uneasy that, soon after midnight, he went to Glenlyon's quarters. Glenlyon and his men were all up, and seemed to be getting their arms ready for action. John, much alarmed, asked what these preparations meant. Glenlyon was profuse of friendly assurances. "Some of Glengarry's people have been harrying the country. We are getting ready to march against them. You are quite safe. Do you think that, if you were in any danger, I should not have given a hint to your brother Sandy and his wife?" John's suspicions were quieted. He returned to his house, and lay down to rest.

It was five in the morning. Hamilton and his men were still some miles off; and the avenues which they were to have secured were open. But the orders which Glenlyon had received were precise; and he began to execute them at the little village where he was himself quartered. His host Inverriggen and nine other Macdonalds were dragged out of their beds, bound hand and foot, and murdered. A boy twelve years old clung round the Captain's legs, and begged hard for life. He would do anything: he would go any where: he would follow Glenlyon round the world. Even Glenlyon, it is said, showed signs of relenting: but a ruffian named Drummond shot the child dead.

At Auchnaion the tacksman Auchintriater was up early that morning, and was sitting with eight of his family round the fire, when a volley of musketry laid him and seven of his companions dead or dying on the floor. His brother, who alone had escaped unhurt, called to Serjeant Barbour, who commanded the slayers, and asked as a favour to be allowed to die in the open air. "Well," said the Serjeant, "I will do you that favour for the sake of your meat which I have eaten." The mountaineer, bold, athletic, and favoured by the darkness, came forth, rushed on the soldiers who were about to level their pieces at him, flung his plaid over their faces, and was gone in a moment.

Meanwhile Lindsay had knocked at the door of the old Chief and had asked for admission in friendly language. The door was opened. Mac Ian, while putting on his clothes and calling to his servants to bring some refreshment for his visitors, was shot through the head. Two of his attendants were slain with him. His wife was already up and dressed in such finery as the princesses of the rude Highland glens were accustomed to wear. The assassins pulled off her clothes and trinkets. The rings were not easily taken from her fingers: but a soldier tore them away with his teeth. She died on the following day.

The statesman, to whom chiefly this great crime is to be ascribed, had planned it with consummate ability: but the execution was complete in nothing but in guilt and infamy. A succession of blunders saved three fourths of the Glencoe men from the fate of their chief. All the moral qualities which fit men to bear a part in a massacre Hamilton and Glenlyon possessed in perfection. But neither seems to have had much professional skill. Hamilton had arranged his plan without making allowance for bad weather, and this at a season when, in the Highlands, the weather was very likely to be bad. The consequence was that the fox earths, as he called them, were not stopped in time. Glenlyon and his men committed the error of despatching their hosts with firearms instead of using the cold steel. The peal and flash of gun after gun gave notice, from three different parts of the valley at once, that murder was doing. From fifty cottages the half naked peasantry fled under cover of the night to the recesses of their pathless glen. Even the sons of Mac Ian, who had been especially marked out for destruction, contrived to escape. They were roused from sleep by faithful servants. John, who, by the death of his father, had become the patriarch of the tribe, quitted his dwelling just as twenty soldiers with fixed bayonets marched up to it. It was broad day long before Hamilton arrived. He found the work not even half performed. About thirty corpses lay wallowing in blood on the dunghills before the doors. One or two women were seen among the number, and a yet more fearful and piteous sight, a little hand, which had been lopped in the tumult of the butchery from some infant. One aged Macdonald was found alive. He was probably too infirm to fly, and, as he was above seventy, was not included in the orders under which Glenlyon had acted. Hamilton murdered the old man in cold blood. The deserted hamlets were then set on fire ; and the troops departed, driving away with them many sheep and goats, nine hundred kine, and two hundred of the small shaggy ponies of the Highlands.

It is said, and may but too easily be believed, that the sufferings of the fugitives were terrible. How many old men, how many women with babes in their arms, sank down and slept their last sleep in the snow ; how many, having crawled, spent with toil and hunger, into nooks among the precipices, died in those dark holes, and were picked to the bone by the mountain ravens, can never be known. But it is probable that those who perished by cold, weariness, and want were not less numerous than those who were slain by the assassins. When the troops had retired, the Macdonalds crept out of the caverns of Glencoe, ventured back to the spot where the huts had formerly stood, collected the scorched corpses from among the smoking ruins, and performed some rude rites of sepulture. The tradition runs that the hereditary bard of the tribe took his seat on a rock which overhung the place of slaughter, and poured forth a long lament over his mur-dered brethren and his desolate home. Eighty years later that sad dirge was still repeated by the population of the valley.[1]

[1] Deposition of Ronald Macdonald in the Report of 1695 ; Letters from the Mountains, May 17. 1773. I quote Mrs. Grant's authority only for what she herself heard and saw. Her

The survivors might well apprehend that they had escaped the shot and the sword only to perish by famine. The whole domain was a waste. Houses, barns, furniture, implements of husbandry, herds, flocks, horses, were gone. Many months must elapse before the clan would be able to raise on its own ground the means of supporting even the most miserable existence.[1]

It may be thought strange that these events should not have been instantly followed by a burst of execration from every part of the civilised world. The fact, however, is that years elapsed before the public indignation was thoroughly awakened, and that months elapsed before the blackest part of the story found credit even among the enemies of the government. That the massacre should not have been mentioned in the London Gazettes, in the Monthly Mercuries, which were scarcely less courtly than the Gazettes, or in pamphlets licensed by official censors, is perfectly intelligible. But that no allusion to it should be found in private journals and letters, written by persons free from all restraint, may seem extraordinary. There is not a word on the subject in Evelyn's Diary. In Narcissus Luttrell's Diary is a remarkable entry made five weeks after the butchery. The letters from Scotland, he says, described that kingdom as perfectly tranquil, except that there was still some grumbling about ecclesiastical questions. The Dutch ministers regularly reported all the Scotch news to their government. They thought it worth while, about this time, to mention that a collier had been taken by a privateer near Berwick, that the Edinburgh mail had been robbed, that a whale, with a tongue seventeen feet long and seven feet broad, had been stranded near Aberdeen. But it is not hinted in any of their despatches that there was any rumour of any extraordinary occurrence in the Highlands. Reports that some of the Macdonalds had been slain did indeed, in about three weeks, travel through Edinburgh up to London. But these reports were vague and contradictory ; and the very worst of them was far from coming up to the horrible truth. The Whig version of the story was that the old robber Mac Ian had laid an ambuscade

account of the massacre was written apparently without the assistance of books, and is grossly incorrect.   Indeed she makes a mistake of two years as to the date.

[1] I have taken the account of the Massacre of Glencoe chiefly from the Report of 1695, and from the Gallienus Redivivus. An unlearned, and indeed a learned, reader may be at a loss to guess why the Jacobites should have selected so strange a title for a pamphlet on the massacre of Glencoe. The explanation will be found in a letter of the Emperor Gallienus, preserved by Trebellius Pollio in the Life of Ingenuus. Ingenuus had raised a rebellion in Mœsia. He was defeated and killed. Gallienus ordered the whole province to be laid waste, and wrote to one of his lieutenants in language to which that of the Master of Stair bore but too much resemblance. "Non mihi satisfacies si tantum armatos occideris, quos et fors belli interimere potuisset. Perimendus est omnis sexus virilis. Occidendus est quicunque maledixit. Occidendus est quicunque male voluit. Lacera. Occide. Concide."

for the soldiers, that he had been caught in his own snare, and that he and some of his clan had fallen sword in hand. The Jacobite version, written at Edinburgh on the twenty-third of March, appeared in the Paris Gazette of the seventh of April. Glenlyon, it was said, had been sent with a detachment from Argyle's regiment, under cover of darkness, to surprise the inhabitants of Glencoe, and had killed thirty six men and boys and four women.[1] In this there was nothing very strange or shocking. A night attack on a gang of freebooters occupying a strong natural fortress may be a perfectly legitimate military operation ; and, in the obscurity and confusion of such an attack, the most humane man may be so unfortunate as to shoot a woman or a child. The circumstances which give a peculiar character to the slaughter of Glencoe, the breach of faith, the breach of hospitality, the twelve days of feigned friendship and conviviality, of morning calls, of social meals, of healthdrinking, of cardplaying, were not mentioned by the Edinburgh correspondent of the Paris Gazette ; and we may therefore confidently infer that those circumstances were as yet unknown even to inquisitive and busy malecontents residing in the Scottish capital within a hundred miles of the spot where the deed had been done. In the south of the island, the matter produced, as far as can now be judged, scarcely any sensation. To the Londoner of those days Appin was what Caffraria or Borneo is to us. He was not more moved by hearing that some Highland thieves had been surprised and killed than we are by hearing that a band of Amakosah cattle stealers has been cut off, or that a bark full of Malay pirates has been sunk. He took it for granted that nothing had been done in Glencoe beyond what was doing in many other glens. There might have been violence; but it had been in a land of violence. There had been a night brawl, one of a hundred night brawls, between the Macdonalds and the Campbells; and the Campbells had knocked the Macdonalds on the head.

By slow degrees the whole came out. From a letter written at Edinburgh before the end of April, it appears that the true story was already current among the Jacobites of that city. In the summer Argyle's regiment was quartered in the south of England, and some of the men made strange confessions, over their ale, about what they had been forced to do in the preceding winter. The nonjurors soon got hold of the clue, and followed it resolutely : their secret presses went to work ; and at length, near a year after the crime had been committed, it was published to the world.[2] But the world was long incredulous.

---

[1] What I have called the Whig version of the story is given, as well as the Jacobite version, in the Paris Gazette of April 7. 1692.

[2] I believe that the circumstances which give so peculiar a character of atrocity to the Massacre of Glencoe were first published in print by Charles Leslie in the Appendix to his answer to King. The date of Leslie's answer is 1692. But it must be remembered that the date of 1692 was then used down to what we should call the 25th of March 1693. Leslie's book

The habitual mendacity of the Jacobite libellers had brought on them an appropriate punishment. Now, when, for the first time, they told the truth, they were supposed to be romancing. They complained bitterly that the story, though perfectly authentic, was regarded by the public as a factious lie.[1] So late as the year 1695, Hickes, in a tract in which he endeavoured to defend his darling tale of the Theban legion against the unanswerable argument drawn from the silence of historians, remarked that it might well be doubted whether any historian would make mention of the massacre of Glencoe. There were in England, he said, many thousands of well educated men who had never heard of that massacre, or who regarded it as a mere fable.[2]

Nevertheless the punishment of some of the guilty began very early. Hill, who indeed can scarcely be called guilty, was much disturbed. Breadalbane, hardened as he was, felt the stings of conscience or the dread of retribution. A few days after the Macdonalds had returned to their old dwellingplace, his steward visited the ruins of the house of Glencoe, and endeavoured to persuade the sons of the murdered chief to sign a paper declaring that they held the Earl guiltless of the blood which had been shed. They were assured that, if they would do this, all His Lordship's great influence should be employed to obtain for them from the Crown a free pardon and a remission of all forfeitures.[3] Glenlyon did his best to assume an air of unconcern. He made his appearance in the most fashionable coffeehouse at Edinburgh, and talked loudly and selfcomplacently about the important service in which he had been engaged among the mountains. Some of his soldiers, however, who observed him closely, whispered that all this bravery was put on. He was not the man that he had been before that night. The form of his countenance was changed. In all places, at all hours, whether he waked or slept, Glencoe was ever before him.[4]

But, whatever apprehensions might disturb Breadalbane, whatever spectres might haunt Glenlyon, the Master of Stair had neither fear nor remorse. He was indeed mortified : but he was mortified only by the blunders of Hamilton and by the escape of so many of the damnable breed. "Do right, and fear nobody;" such is the language of his letters. "Can there be a more sacred duty than to rid the country of thieving? The only thing that I regret is that any got away."[5]

On the sixth of March, William, entirely ignorant, in all probability, **William goes to the Continent** of the details of the crime which has cast a dark shade over his glory, had set out for the continent, leaving the Queen his vicegerent in England.[6]

contains some remarks on a sermon by Tillotson which was not printed till November 1692. The Gallienus Redivivus speedily followed.

[1] Gallienus Redivivus.   [2] Hickes on Burnet and Tillotson, 1695.   [3] Report of 1695.

[4] Gallienus Redivivus.   [5] Report of 1695.   [6] London Gazette, Mar. 7. 169½.

He would perhaps have postponed his departure if he had been aware that the French Government had, during some time, been making

FRANÇOIS LE TELLIER, MARQUIS DE LOUVOIS

From an engraving by J. Hainzelman, after a painting by F. Voet

great preparations for a descent on our island.[1]   An event had taken place which had changed the policy of the Court of Versailles.   Louvois

---

[1] Burnet (ii. 93.) says that the King was not at this time informed of the intentions of the French Government.   Ralph contradicts Burnet with great asperity.   But that Burnet was in the

was no more.   He had been at the head of the military administration of his country during a quarter of a century ; he had borne a chief part **Death of Louvois** in the direction of two wars which had enlarged the French territory, and had filled the world with the renown of the French arms, and he had lived to see the beginning of a third war which tasked his great powers to the utmost.   Between him and the celebrated captains who carried his plans into execution there was little harmony.   His imperious temper and his confidence in himself impelled him to interfere too much with the conduct of troops in the field, even when those troops were commanded by Condé, by Turenne, or by Luxemburg.   But he was the greatest Adjutant General, the greatest Quartermaster General, the greatest Commissary General, that Europe had seen.   He may indeed be said to have made a revolution in the art of disciplining, distributing, equipping, and provisioning armies.   In spite, however, of his abilities and of his services, he had become odious to Lewis and to her who governed Lewis.   On the last occasion on which the King and the minister transacted business together, the ill humour on both sides broke violently forth.   The servant, in his vexation, dashed his portfolio on the ground.   The master, forgetting, what he seldom forgot, that a king should be a gentleman, lifted his cane.   Fortunately his wife was present.   She, with her usual prudence, caught his arm.   She then got Louvois out of the room, and exhorted him to come back the next day as if nothing had happened.   The next day he came, but with death in his face.   The King, though full of resentment, was touched with pity, and advised Louvois to go home and take care of himself.   That evening the great minister died.[1]

Louvois had constantly opposed all plans for the invasion of England.   His death was therefore regarded at Saint Germains as a fortunate event.[2]   It was however necessary to look sad, and to send a gentleman to Versailles with some words of condolence.   The messenger found the gorgeous circle of courtiers assembled round their master on the terrace above the orangery.   "Sir," said Lewis, in a tone so easy and cheerful that it filled all the bystanders with amazement, "present my compliments and thanks to the King and Queen of England, and tell them that neither my affairs nor theirs will go on the worse for what has happened."   These words were doubtless meant to intimate that the influence of Louvois had not been exerted in favour of the House of

right is proved beyond dispute by William's correspondence with Heinsius.   So late as $\frac{\text{April 24.}}{\text{May 4.}}$ William wrote thus : " Je ne puis vous dissimuler que je commence à apprehender une descente en Angleterre, quoique je n'aye pu le croire d'abord : mais les avis sont si multipliés de tous les côtés, et accompagnés de tant de particularités, qu'il n'est plus guère possible d'en douter."   I quote from the French translation among the Mackintosh MSS.

[1] Burnet, ii. 95. and Onslow's note ; Mémoires de Saint Simon ; Journal de Dangeau.

[2] Life of James, ii. 411, 412.

Stuart.[1]　One compliment, however, a compliment which cost France dear, Lewis thought it right to pay to the memory of his ablest servant.

FRANÇOIS LE TELLIER, MARQUIS DE BARBESIEUX
From an engraving in the Sutherland Collection

The Marquess of Barbesieux, son of Louvois, was placed, in his twenty-fifth year, at the head of the war department.　The young man was by

[1] Mémoires de Dangeau ; Mémoires de Saint Simon.　Saint Simon was on the terrace, and, young as he was, observed this singular scene with an eye which nothing escaped.

no means deficient in abilities, and had been, during some years, employed in business of grave importance.   But his passions were strong : his judgment was not ripe ; and his sudden elevation turned his head. His manners gave general disgust.   Old officers complained that he kept them long in his antechamber while he was amusing himself with his spaniels and his flatterers.   Those who were admitted to his presence went away disgusted by his rudeness and arrogance.   As was natural at his age, he valued power chiefly as the means of procuring pleasure. Millions of crowns were expended on the luxurious villa where he loved to forget the cares of office in gay conversation, delicate cookery, and foaming Champagne.   He often pleaded an attack of fever as an excuse for not making his appearance at the proper hour in the royal closet, when in truth he had been playing truant among his boon companions and mistresses.   "The French King," said William, "has an odd taste.   He chooses an old woman for his mistress, and a young man for his minister."[1]

There can be little doubt that Louvois, by pursuing that course which had made him odious to the inmates of Saint Germains, had deserved well of his country.   He was not maddened by Jacobite enthusiasm.   He well knew that exiles are the worst of all advisers. He had excellent information : he had excellent judgment : he calculated the chances ; and he saw that a descent was likely to fail, and to fail disastrously and disgracefully.   James might well be impatient to try the experiment, though the odds should be ten to one against him. He might gain ; and he could not lose.   His folly and obstinacy had left him nothing to risk.   His food, his drink, his lodging, his clothes, he owed to charity.   Nothing could be more natural than that, for the very smallest chance of recovering the three kingdoms which he had thrown away, he should be willing to stake what was not his own, the honour of the French arms, the grandeur and the safety of the French monarchy.   To a French statesman such a wager might well appear in a different light.   But Louvois was gone.   His master yielded to the importunity of James, and determined to send an expedition against England.[2]

The scheme was, in some respects, well concerted.   It was resolved that a camp should be formed on the coast of Normandy, and that in The French this camp all the Irish regiments which were in the French government service should be assembled under their countryman Sarsfield. determines to send an With them were to be joined about ten thousand French expedition troops.   The whole army was to be commanded by Marshal against England Bellefonds.

[1] Mémoires de Saint Simon , Burnet, ii. 95. ; Guardian, No. 48.   See the excellent letter of Lewis to the Archbishop of Rheims, which is quoted by Voltaire in the Siècle de Louis XIV.

[2] In the Nairne Papers printed by Macpherson are two memorials from James urging Lewis to invade England.   Both were written in January 1692.

A noble fleet of about eighty ships of the line was to convoy this force to the shores of England. In the dockyards both of Britanny

BERNARDIN GIGAULT, MARQUIS DE BELLEFONDS, MARSHAL OF FRANCE

From an engraving in the Sutherland Collection

and of Provence immense preparations were made. Four and forty men of war, some of which were among the finest that had ever been built, were assembled in the harbour of Brest under Tourville. The

Count of Estrees, with thirty five more, was to sail from Toulon. Ushant was fixed for the place of rendezvous. The very day was named. In order that there might be no want either of seamen or of vessels for the intended expedition, all maritime trade, all privateering, was, for a time, interdicted by a royal mandate.[1] Three hundred transports were collected near the spot where the troops were to embark. It was hoped that all would be ready early in the spring, before the English ships were half rigged or half manned, and before a single Dutch man of war was in the Channel.[2]

James had indeed persuaded himself that, even if the English fleet should fall in with him, it would not oppose him. He imagined that

James believes that the English fleet is friendly to him

he was personally a favourite with the mariners of all ranks. His emissaries had been busy among the naval officers, and had found some who remembered him with kindness, and others who were out of humour with the men now in power. All the wild talk of a class of people not distinguished by taciturnity or discretion was reported to him with exaggeration, till he was deluded into a belief that he had more friends than enemies on board of the vessels which guarded our coasts. Yet he should have known that a rough sailor, who thought himself ill used by the Admiralty, might, after the third bottle, when drawn on by artful companions, express his regret for the good old times, curse the new government, and curse himself for being such a fool as to fight for that government, and yet might be by no means prepared to go over to the French on the day of battle. Of the malecontent officers, who, as James believed, were impatient to desert, the great majority had probably given no pledge of their attachment to him except an idle word hiccoughed out when they were drunk, and forgotten when they were sober. One of those from whom he expected support, Rear Admiral Carter, had indeed heard and perfectly understood what the Jacobite agents had to say, had given them fair words, and had reported the whole to the Queen and her ministers.[3]

But the chief dependence of James was on Russell. That false, arrogant, and wayward politician was to command the Channel Fleet.

Conduct of Russell

He had never ceased to assure the Jacobite emissaries that he was bent on effecting a Restoration. Those emissaries fully reckoned, if not on his entire cooperation, yet at least on his connivance; and there could be no doubt that, with his connivance, a French fleet might easily convey an army to our shores. James flattered himself that, as soon as he had landed, he should be master

[1] London Gazette, Feb. 15. 169½.

[2] Mémoires de Berwick ; Burnet, ii. 92. ; Life of James, ii. 478, 491.

[3] History of the late Conspiracy, 1693.

COUNT D'ESTRÉES

From an engraving by J. Audran, after a painting by N. Largillière

of the island.   But in truth, when the voyage had ended, the difficulties
of his enterprise would have been only beginning.   Two years before
he had received a lesson by which he should have profited.   He had
then deceived himself and others into the belief that the English were
regretting him, were pining for him, were eager to rise in arms by tens
of thousands to welcome him.   William was then, as now, at a distance.
Then, as now, the administration was entrusted to a woman.   There
were then fewer regular troops in England than now.   Torrington had
then done as much to injure the government which he served as
Russell could now do.   The French fleet had then, after riding, during
several weeks, victorious and dominant in the Channel, landed some
troops on the southern coast.   The immediate effect had been that
whole counties, without distinction of Tory or Whig, Churchman or
Dissenter, had risen up, as one man, to repel the foreigners, and that
the Jacobite party, which had, a few days before, seemed to be half the
nation, had crouched down in silent terror, and had made itself so small
that it had, during some time, been invisible.   What reason was there
for believing that the multitudes who had, in 1690, at the first lighting
of the beacons, snatched up firelocks, pikes, scythes, to defend their
native soil against the French, would now welcome the French as allies ?
And of the army by which James was now to be accompanied the
French formed the least odious part.   More than half of that army was
to consist of Irish Papists ; and the feeling, compounded of hatred and
scorn, with which the Irish Papists had long been regarded by the
English Protestants, had by recent events been stimulated to a vehemence before unknown.   The hereditary slaves, it was said, had been
for a moment free ; and that moment had sufficed to prove that they
knew neither how to use nor how to defend their freedom.   During
their short ascendency they had done nothing but slay, and burn, and
pillage, and demolish, and attaint, and confiscate.   In three years they
had committed such waste on their native land as thirty years of English
intelligence and industry would scarcely repair.   They would have maintained their independence against the world, if they had been as ready
to fight as they were to steal.   But they had retreated ignominiously
from the walls of Londonderry.   They had fled like deer before the
yeomanry of Enniskillen.   The Prince whom they now presumed to
think that they could place, by force of arms, on the English throne,
had himself, on the morning after the rout of the Boyne, reproached
them with their cowardice, and told them that he would never again
trust to their soldiership.   On this subject Englishmen were of one
mind.   Tories, Nonjurors, even Roman Catholics, were as loud as
Whigs in reviling the ill fated race.   It is, therefore, not difficult to
guess what effect would have been produced by the appearance on our

soil of enemies whom, on their own soil, we had vanquished and trampled down.

James, however, in spite of the recent and severe teaching of experience, believed whatever his correspondents in England told him; and they told him that the whole nation was impatiently expecting him, that both the West and the North were ready to rise, that he would proceed from the place of landing to Whitehall with as little opposition as he had encountered when, in old times, he made a progress through his kingdom, escorted, by long cavalcades of gentlemen, from one lordly mansion to another. Ferguson distinguished himself by the confidence with which he predicted a complete and bloodless victory. He and his printer, he was absurd enough to write, would be the two first men in the realm to take horse for His Majesty. Many other agents were busy, up and down the country, during the winter and the early part of the spring. It does not appear that they had much success in the counties south of Trent. But in the north, particularly in Lancashire, where the Roman Catholics were more numerous and more powerful than in any other part of the kingdom, and where there seems to have been, even among the Protestant gentry, more than the ordinary proportion of bigoted Jacobites, some preparations for an insurrection were made. Arms were privately bought: officers were appointed: yeomen, small farmers, grooms, huntsmen, were induced to enlist. Those who gave in their names were distributed into eight regiments of cavalry and dragoons, and were directed to hold themselves in readiness to mount at the first signal.[1]

One of the circumstances which filled James, at this time, with vain hopes, was that his wife was pregnant and near her delivery. He flattered himself that malice itself would be ashamed to repeat any longer the story of the warming pan, and that multitudes whom that story had deceived would instantly return to their allegiance. He took, on this occasion, all those precautions which, four years before, he had foolishly and perversely forborne to take. He contrived to transmit to England letters summoning many Protestant women of quality to assist at the expected birth; and he promised, in the name of his dear brother the Most Christian King, that they should be free to come and go in safety. Had some of those witnesses been invited to Saint James's on the morning of the tenth of June 1688, the House of Stuart might, perhaps, now be reigning in our island. But it is easier to keep a crown than to regain one. It might be true that a calumnious fable had done much to bring about the Revolution. But it by no means followed that the most complete

A daughter born to James

[1] Life of James, ii. 479. 524. Memorials furnished by Ferguson to Holmes in the Nairne Papers.

refutation of that fable would bring about a Restoration.   Not a single lady crossed the sea in obedience to James's call.   His Queen was safely delivered of a daughter; but this event produced no perceptible effect on the state of public feeling in England.[1]

Meanwhile the preparations for his expedition were going on fast. He was on the point of setting out for the place of embarkation before **Prepara-** the English government was at all aware of the danger **tions made** which was impending.   It had been long known indeed **in England** **to repel** that many thousands of Irish were assembled in Normandy: **invasion** but it was supposed that they had been assembled merely that they might be mustered and drilled before they were sent to Flanders, Piedmont, and Catalonia.[2]   Now, however, intelligence, arriving from many quarters, left no doubt that an invasion would be almost immediately attempted.   Vigorous preparations for defence were made. The equipping and manning of the ships was urged forward with vigour.   The regular troops were drawn together between London and the Channel.   A great camp was formed on the down which overlooks Portsmouth.   The militia all over the kingdom was called out.   Two Westminster regiments and six City regiments, making up a force of thirteen thousand fighting men, were arrayed in Hyde Park, and passed in review before the Queen.   The trainbands of Kent, Sussex, and Surrey marched down to the coast.   Watchmen were posted by the beacons.   Some nonjurors were imprisoned, some disarmed, some held to bail.   The house of the Earl of Huntingdon, a noted Jacobite, was searched.   He had had time to burn his papers and to hide his arms: but his stables presented a most suspicious appearance.   Horses enough to mount a whole troop of cavalry were at the mangers; and this circumstance, though not legally sufficient to support a charge of treason, was thought sufficient, at such a conjuncture, to justify the Privy Council in sending him to the Tower.[3]

Meanwhile James had gone down to his army, which was encamped round the basin of La Hogue, on the northern coast of the peninsula **James goes** known by the name of the Cotentin.   Before he quitted Saint **down to** Germains, he held a Chapter of the Garter for the purpose **his army at** **La Hogue** of admitting his son into the order.   Two noblemen were honoured with the same distinction, Powis, who, among his brother exiles, was now called a Duke, and Melfort, who had returned from Rome, and was again James's Prime Minister.[4]   Even at this moment, when it was of the greatest importance to conciliate the sons of the Church of England, none but sons of the Church of Rome were thought

[1] Life of James, ii. 474.   [2] See the Monthly Mercuries of the spring of 1692.
[3] Narcissus Luttrell's Diary for April and May 1692; London Gazette, May 9. and 12.
[4] Sheridan MS.; Life of James, ii. 492.

Chez N. Bonnart, rue S. Jaques, a l'aigle avec privil.

Louise Marie Stuart, Princesse d'Angleterre.
Fille de Jaques II. Roy d'Angleterre, et de Marie Eleonor d'Este.
Née à S.t Germain en Laye le 28. juin 1692.

PRINCESS LOUISE MARIE STUART

From an engraving in the Sutherland Collection

worthy of any mark of royal favour. Powis indeed might be thought
to have a fair claim to the Garter. He was an eminent member of the
English aristocracy; and his countrymen disliked him as little as they
disliked any conspicuous Papist. But Melfort was not even an Englishman: he had never held office in England: he had never sate in
the English Parliament; and he had therefore no pretensions to a
decoration peculiarly English. He was moreover hated by all the
contending factions of all the three kingdoms. Royal letters counter-
signed by him had been sent both to the Convention at Westminster
and to the Convention at Edinburgh; and, both at Westminster and at
Edinburgh, the sight of his odious name and handwriting had made
the most zealous friends of hereditary right hang down their heads
in shame. It seems strange that even James should have chosen, at
such a conjuncture, to proclaim to the world that the men whom
his people most abhorred were the men whom he most delighted to
honour.

Still more strange seems the Declaration in which he announced
his intentions to his subjects. Of all the State papers which were put
James's forth even by him it was the most elaborately and ostenta-
Declaration tiously injudicious. When it had disgusted and exasperated
all good Englishmen of all parties, the Papists at Saint Germains
pretended that it had been drawn up by a stanch Protestant, Edward
Herbert, who had been Chief Justice of the Common Pleas before
the Revolution, and who now bore the empty title of Chancellor.[1]
But it is certain that Herbert was never consulted about any matter of
importance, and that the Declaration was the work of Melfort and
of Melfort alone.[2] In truth, those qualities of head and heart which had
made Melfort the favourite of his master shone forth in every sentence.
Not a word was to be found indicating that three years of banishment
had made the King wiser, that he had repented of a single error, that he
took to himself even the smallest part of the blame of that revolution
which had dethroned him, or that he purposed to follow a course in any
respect differing from that which had already been fatal to him. All
the charges which had been brought against him he pronounced to be
utterly unfounded. Wicked men had put forth calumnies. Weak men
had believed those calumnies. He alone had been faultless. He held
out no hope that he would consent to any restriction of that vast dispensing power to which he had formerly laid claim, that he would not
again, in defiance of the plainest statutes, fill the Privy Council, the
bench of justice, the public offices, the army, the navy, with Papists, that
he would not reestablish the High Commission, that he would not

[1] Life of James, ii. 488.
[2] James told Sheridan that the Declaration was written by Melfort. Sheridan MS.

THEOPHILUS HASTINGS, SEVENTH EARL OF HUNTINGDON

From a mezzotint by R. Williams, after a painting by Sir G. Kneller

G

appoint a new set of regulators to remodel all the constituent bodies of the kingdom. He did indeed condescend to say that he would maintain the legal rights of the Church of England : but he had said this before ; and all men knew what those words meant in his mouth. Instead of assuring his people of his forgiveness, hc menaced them with a butchery more terrible than any that our island had ever seen. He published a long list of persons who had no mercy to expect. Among these were Ormond, Caermarthen, Nottingham, Tillotson and Burnet. After the roll of those who were proscribed by name, came a series of categories. First stood all the crowd of rustics who had been rude to James when he was stopped at Sheerness in his flight. These poor ignorant wretches, some hundreds in number, were reserved for another bloody circuit. Then His Majesty, in open defiance of the law of the land, proceeded to doom to death a multitude of persons who were guilty only of having acted under William since William had been king in fact, and who were therefore under the protection of a well known statute of Henry the Seventh. But to James statutes were still what they had always been. He denounced vengeance against all persons who had in any manner borne a part in the punishment of any Jacobite conspirator, judges, counsel, witnesses, grand jurymen, petty jurymen, sheriffs and under-sheriffs, constables and turnkeys, in short, all the ministers of justice from Holt down to Ketch. Then he threatened with the gallows all spies and all informers who had divulged to the usurpers the designs of the Court of Saint Germains. All justices of the peace who should not declare for their rightful Sovereign the moment that they heard of his landing, all gaolers who should not instantly set political prisoners at liberty, were to be left to the extreme rigour of the law. No exception was made in favour of a justice or of a gaoler who might be within a hundred yards of one of William's regiments, and a hundred miles from the nearest place where there was a single Jacobite in arms.

It might have been expected that James, after thus declaring that he could hold out no hope of mercy to large classes of his subjects, would at least have offered a general pardon to the rest. But he pardoned nobody. He did indeed promise that any offender who was not in any of the categories of proscription, and who should by any eminent service merit indulgence, should have a special pardon passed under the Great Seal. But, with this exception, all the offenders, hundreds of thousands in number, were merely informed that, if they did no act or thing in opposition to the King's restoration, they might hope to be, at a convenient time, included in a general Act of Indemnity.

The agents of James speedily dispersed his Declaration over every part of the kingdom, and by doing so rendered a great service to William. The general cry was that the banished oppressor had at least given Englishmen fair warning, and that, if, after such a warning, they welcomed him home, they would have no pretence for complaining, though every county town should be polluted by an assize Effect produced by James's Declaration resembling that which Jeffreys had held at Taunton. That some hundreds of people,—the Jacobites put the number so low as five hundred,—were to be hanged without pity was certain ; and nobody who had concurred in the Revolution, nobody who had fought for the new government by sea or land, no soldier who had borne a part in the conquest of Ireland, no Devonshire ploughman or Cornish miner who had taken arms to defend his wife and children against Tourville, could be certain that he should not be hanged. It was easy to understand why James, instead of proclaiming a general amnesty, offered special pardons under his Great Seal. Every such pardon must be paid for. There was not a priest in the royal household who would not make his fortune. How abject too, how spiteful, must be the nature of a man who, engaged in the most momentous of all undertakings, and aspiring to the noblest of all prizes, could not refrain from proclaiming that he thirsted for the blood of a multitude of poor fishermen, because, more than three years before, they had pulled him about and called him Hatchetface ![1] If, at the very moment when he had the strongest motives for trying to conciliate his people by the show of clemency, he could not bring himself to hold towards them any language but that of an implacable enemy, what was to be expected from him when he should be again their master? So savage was his nature that, in a situation in which all other tyrants have resorted to blandishments and fair promises, he could utter nothing but reproaches and threats. The only words in his Declaration which had any show of graciousness were those in which he promised to send away the foreign troops as soon as his authority was reestablished ; and many said that those words, when examined, would be found full of sinister meaning. He held out no hope that he would send away Popish troops who were his own subjects. His intentions were manifest. The French might go : but the Irish would remain. The people of England were to be kept down by these thrice subjugated barbarians. No doubt a Rapparee who had run away at Newton Butler and the Boyne might find courage enough to guard the scaffolds on which his conquerors were to die, and to lay waste our country as he had laid waste his own.

The Queen and her ministers, instead of attempting to suppress James's manifesto, very wisely reprinted it, and sent it forth licensed by

[1] That the Declaration made the impression which I have described, is acknowledged in the Life of James, ii. 489. "They thought," says the biographer, "His Majesty's resentment descended too low to except the Feversham Mob, that five hundred men were excluded, and no man realy pardon'd except he should merit it by some service, and then the Pardons being to pass the Seals look'd as if it were to bring mony into the pocket of some favorits "

the Secretary of State, and interspersed with remarks by a shrewd and severe commentator. It was refuted in many keen pamphlets : it was turned into doggrel rhymes ; and it was left undefended even by the boldest and most acrimonious libellers among the nonjurors.[1]

Indeed, some of the nonjurors were so much alarmed by observing the effect which this manifesto produced, that they affected to treat it as spurious, and published as their master's genuine Declaration a paper full of gracious professions and promises. They made him offer a free pardon to all his people with the exception of four great criminals. They made him hold out hopes of great remissions of taxation. They made him pledge his word that he would entrust the whole ecclesiastical administration to the nonjuring bishops. But this forgery imposed on nobody, and was important only as showing that even the Jacobites were ashamed of the prince whom they were labouring to restore.[2]

No man read the Declaration with more surprise and anger than Russell. Bad as he was, he was much under the influence of two feelings, which, though they cannot be called virtuous, have some affinity to virtue, and are respectable when compared with mere selfish cupidity. Professional spirit and party spirit were strong in him. He might be false to his sovereigns, but not to his flag ; and, even in becoming a Jacobite, he had not ceased to be a Whig. In truth, he was a Jacobite only because he was the most intolerant and acrimonious of Whigs. He thought himself and his faction ungratefully neglected by William, and was for a time too much blinded by resentment to perceive that it would be mere madness in the old Roundheads, the old Exclusionists, to punish William by recalling James. The near prospect of an invasion, and the Declaration in which Englishmen were plainly told what they had to expect if that invasion should be successful, produced, it should seem, a sudden change in Russell's feelings ; and that change he distinctly avowed. " I wish," he said to Lloyd, " to serve King James. The thing might be done, if it were not his own fault. But he takes the

[1] A Letter to a Friend concerning a French Invasion to restore the late King James to his Throne, and what may be expected from him should he be successful in it, 1692 ; a second Letter to a Friend concerning a French Invasion, in which the Declaration lately dispersed under the Title of His Majesty's most gracious Declaration to all his loving Subjects, commanding their Assistance against the P. of O. and his Adherents, is entirely and exactly published according to the Dispersed Copies, with some short Observations upon it, 1692 ; The Pretences of the French Invasion examined, 1692 ; Reflections on the late King James's Declaration, 1692. The two Letters to a Friend were written, I believe, by Lloyd Bishop of Saint Asaph. Sheridan says, " The King's Declaration pleas'd none, and was turn'd into ridicule burlesque lines in England." I do not believe that a defence of this unfortunate Declaration is to be found in any Jacobite tract. A virulent Jacobite writer, in a reply to Dr. Welwood, printed in 1693, says, " As for the Declaration that was printed last year, . . . I assure you that it was as much misliked by many, almost all, of the King's friends, as it can be exposed by his enemies."

[2] Narcissus Luttrell's Diary, April 1692.

wrong way with us. Let him forget all the past: let him grant a general pardon; and then I will see what I can do for him." Lloyd hinted something about the honours and rewards designed for Russell himself.

From a broadside in the Sutherland Collection

But the Admiral, with a spirit worthy of a better man, cut him short. "I do not wish to hear anything on that subject. My solicitude is for the public. And do not think that I will let the French triumph over us in our own sea.   Understand this, that if I meet them I fight them, aye, though His Majesty himself should be on board."

This conversation was truly reported to James : but it does not appear to have alarmed him.   He was, indeed, possessed with a belief that Russell, even if willing, would not be able to induce the officers and sailors of the English navy to fight against their old King, who was also their old Admiral.

The hopes which James felt he and his favourite Melfort succeeded in imparting to Lewis and to Lewis's ministers.[1]   But for those hopes, indeed, it is probable that all thoughts of invading England in the course of that year would have been laid aside.   For the extensive plan which had been formed in the winter had, in the course of the spring, been disconcerted by a succession of accidents such as are beyond the control of human wisdom.   The time fixed for the assembling of all the maritime forces of France at Ushant had long elapsed ; and not a single sail had appeared at the place of rendezvous.   The Atlantic squadron was still detained by bad weather in the port of Brest.   The Mediterranean squadron, opposed by a strong west wind, was vainly struggling to pass the pillars of Hercules.   Two fine vessels had gone to pieces on the rocks of Ceuta.[2]   Meanwhile the admiralties of the allied powers had been active.   Before the end of April the English fleet was ready to sail.   Three noble ships, just launched from our dockyards, appeared for the first time on the water.[3]   William had been hastening the maritime preparations of the United Provinces ; and his exertions had been successful.   On the twenty-ninth of April a fine squadron from the Texel appeared in the Downs.   Soon came the North Holland squadron, the Meuse squadron, the Zealand squadron.[4]   The whole force of the con-

The English and Dutch fleets join federate powers was assembled at Saint Helen's in the second week of May, more than ninety sail of the line, manned by between thirty and forty thousand of the finest seamen of the two great maritime nations.   Russell had the chief command.   He was assisted by Sir Ralph Delaval, Sir John Ashby, Sir Cloudesley Shovel, Rear Admiral Carter, and Rear Admiral Rooke.   Of the Dutch officers Van Almonde was highest in rank.

No mightier armament had ever appeared in the British Channel. There was little reason for apprehension that such a force could be **Temper of the English fleet** defeated in a fair conflict.   Nevertheless there was great uneasiness in London.   It was known that there was a Jacobite party in the navy.   Alarming rumours had worked their way round from France.   It was said that the enemy reckoned on the cooperation

[1] Sheridan MS. ; Mémoires de Dangeau.

[2] London Gazette, May 12. 16. 1692 ; Gazette de Paris, May $\frac{2}{11}$. 1692.

[3] London Gaz., April 28. 1692.   [4] London Gazette, May 2. 5. 12. 16.

of some of those officers on whose fidelity, in this crisis, the safety of the
State might depend.   Russell, as far as can now be discovered, was still
unsuspected.   But others, who were probably less criminal, had been
more indiscreet.   At all the coffee houses admirals and captains were

SIR CLOUDESLEY SHOVELL

From a mezzotint by Bernard Lens, after a painting by M. Dahl

mentioned by name as traitors who ought to be instantly cashiered, if
not shot.   It was even confidently affirmed that some of the guilty had
been put under arrest, and others turned out of the service.   The Queen
and her counsellors were in a great strait.   It was not easy to say
whether the danger of trusting the suspected persons or the danger of

removing them were the greater.   Mary, with many painful misgivings, resolved,—and the event proved that she resolved wisely,—to treat the evil reports as calumnious, to make a solemn appeal to the honour of the accused gentlemen, and then to trust the safety of her kingdom to their national and professional spirit.

On the fifteenth of May a great assembly of officers was convoked at Saint Helen's on board of the Britannia, a fine threedecker, from which Russell's flag was flying.   The Admiral told them that he had received a despatch which he was charged to read to them.   It was from Nottingham.   The Queen, the Secretary wrote, had been informed that stories deeply affecting the character of the navy were in circulation.   It had even been affirmed that she had found herself under the necessity of dismissing many officers.   But Her Majesty was determined to believe nothing against those brave servants of the State.   The gentlemen who had been so foully slandered might be assured that she placed entire reliance on them.   This letter was admirably calculated to work on those to whom it was addressed.   Very few of them probably had been guilty of any worse offence than rash and angry talk over their wine.   They were as yet only grumblers.   If they had fancied that they were marked men, they might in selfdefence have become traitors. They became enthusiastically loyal as soon as they were assured that the Queen reposed entire confidence in their loyalty.   They eagerly signed an address in which they entreated her to believe that they would, with the utmost resolution and alacrity, venture their lives in defence of her rights, of English freedom, and of the Protestant religion, against all foreign and Popish invaders.   " God," they added, " preserve your person, direct your counsels, and prosper your arms ; and let all your people say Amen."[1]

The sincerity of these professions was soon brought to the test. A few hours after the meeting on board of the Britannia the masts of Tourville's squadron were seen from the cliffs of Portland.   One messenger galloped with the news from Weymouth to London, and roused Whitehall at three in the morning.   Another took the coast road, and carried the intelligence to Russell.   All was ready ; and on the morning of the seventeenth of May the allied fleet stood out to sea.[2]

Tourville had with him only his own squadron, consisting of forty four ships of the line.   But he had received positive orders to protect **Battle of** the descent on England, and not to decline a battle.   Though **La Hogue** these orders had been given before it was known at Versailles that the Dutch and English fleets had joined, he was not disposed to take on himself the responsibility of disobedience.   He still remembered

[1] London Gazette, May 16. 1692 ; Burchett.
[2] Narcissus Luttrell's Diary ; London Gazette, May 19. 1692.

with bitterness the reprimand which his extreme caution had drawn upon him after the fight of Beachy Head. He would not again be told that he was a timid and unenterprising commander, that he had no courage but the vulgar courage of a common sailor. He was also persuaded that the odds against him were rather apparent than real. He believed, on the authority of James and Melfort, that the English seamen, from the flag officers down to the cabin boys, were Jacobites. Those who fought would fight with half a heart; and there would probably be numerous desertions at the most critical moment. Animated by such hopes he sailed from Brest, steered first towards the north east, came in sight of the coast of Dorsetshire, and then struck across the Channel towards La Hogue, where the army which he was to convoy to England had already begun to embark on board of the transports. He was within a few leagues of Barfleur when, before sunrise, on the morning of the nineteenth of May, he saw the great armament of the allies stretching along the eastern horizon. He determined to bear down on them. By eight the two lines of battle were formed; but it was eleven before the firing began. It soon became plain that the English, from the Admiral downwards, were resolved to do their duty. Russell had visited all his ships, and exhorted all his crews. "If your commanders play false," he said, "overboard with them, and with myself the first." There was no defection. There was no slackness. Carter was the first who broke the French line. He was struck by a splinter of one of his own yardarms, and fell dying on the deck. He would not be carried below. He would not let go his sword. "Fight the ship," were his last words: "fight the ship as long as she can swim." The battle lasted till four in the afternoon. The roar of the guns was distinctly heard more than twenty miles off by the army which was encamped on the coast of Normandy. During the earlier part of the day the wind was favourable to the French: they were opposed to only half of the allied fleet; and against that half they maintained the conflict with their usual courage and with more than their usual seamanship. After a hard and doubtful fight of five hours, Tourville thought that enough had been done to maintain the honour of the white flag, and began to draw off. But by this time the wind had veered, and was with the allies. They were now able to avail themselves of their great superiority of force. They came on fast. The retreat of the French became a flight. Tourville fought his own ship desperately. She was named, in allusion to Lewis's favourite emblem, the Royal Sun, and was widely renowned as the finest vessel in the world. It was reported among the English sailors that she was adorned with an image of the Great King, and that he appeared there, as he appeared in the Place of Victories, with vanquished nations in

A TRUE DRAUGHT OF THE LATE ENGAGEMENT

From an engraving in

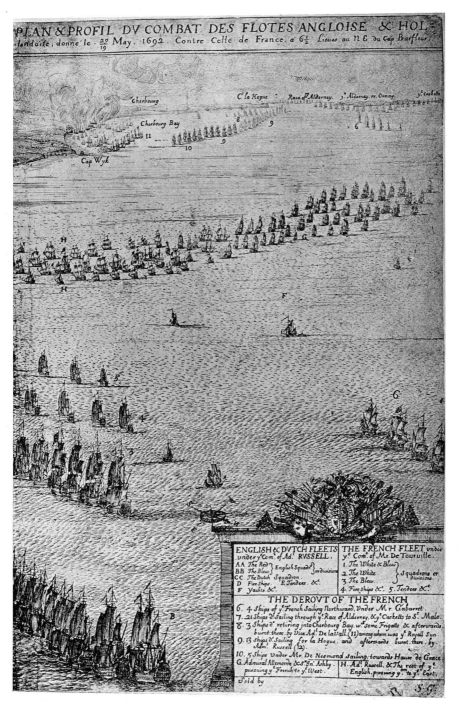

BETWEEN THE ENGLISH AND THE FRENCH FLEETS

the Sutherland Collection

chains beneath his feet.   The gallant ship, surrounded by enemies, lay like a great fortress on the sea, scattering death on every side from her hundred and four portholes.   She was so formidably manned that all attempts to board her failed.   Long after sunset, she got clear of her assailants, and, with all her scuppers spouting blood, made for the coast of Normandy.   She had suffered so much that Tourville hastily removed his flag to a ship of ninety guns which was named the Ambitious.   By this time his fleet was scattered far over the sea.   About twenty of his smallest ships made their escape by a road which was too perilous for any courage but the courage of despair.   In the double darkness of night and of a thick sea fog, they ran, with all their sails spread, through the boiling waves and treacherous rocks of the Race of Alderney, and, by a strange good fortune, arrived without a single disaster at Saint Maloes.   The pursuers did not venture to follow the fugitives into that terrible strait, the place of innumerable shipwrecks.[1]

Those French vessels which were too bulky to venture into the Race of Alderney fled to the havens of the Cotentin.   The Royal Sun and two other threedeckers reached Cherburg in safety.   The Ambitious, with twelve other ships, all firstrates or secondrates, took refuge in the Bay of La Hogue, close to the head quarters of the army of James.

The three ships which had fled to Cherburg were closely chased by an English squadron under the command of Delaval.   He found them hauled up into shoal water where no large man of war could get at them.   He therefore determined to attack them with his fireships and boats.   The service was gallantly and successfully performed.   In a short time the Royal Sun and her two consorts were burned to ashes.   Part of the crews escaped to the shore ; and part fell into the hands of the English.[2]

Meanwhile Russell with the greater part of his victorious fleet had blockaded the Bay of La Hogue.   Here, as at Cherburg, the French men of war had been drawn up into shallow water.   They were close to the camp of the army which was destined for the invasion of England. Six of them were moored under a fort named Lisset.   The rest lay under the guns of another fort named Saint Vaast, where James had fixed his head quarters, and where the British flag, variegated by the crosses of Saint George and Saint Andrew, hung by the side of the White flag of France.   Marshal Bellefonds had planted several batteries

---

[1] Russell's Letter to Nottingham, May 20. 1692, in the London Gazette of May 23. ; Particulars of Another Letter from the Fleet published by authority ; Burchett ; Burnet, ii. 93. ; Life of James, ii. 493, 494. ; Narcissus Luttrell's Diary ; Mémoires de Berwick. See also the contemporary ballad on the battle, one of the best specimens of English street poetry, and the Advice to a Painter, 1692.

[2] See Delaval's Letter to Nottingham, dated Cherburg, May 22. 1692, in the London Gazette of May 26.

which, it was thought, would deter the boldest enemy from approaching either Fort Lisset or Fort Saint Vaast. James, however, who knew something of English seamen, was not perfectly at ease, and proposed to send strong bodies of soldiers on board of the ships. But Tourville would not consent to put such a slur on his profession.

Russell meanwhile was preparing for an attack. On the afternoon of the twenty-third of May all was ready. A flotilla consisting of sloops, of fireships, and of two hundred boats, was entrusted to the command of Rooke. The whole armament was in the highest spirits. The rowers, flushed by success, and animated by the thought that they were going to fight under the eyes of the French and Irish troops who had been assembled for the purpose of subjugating England, pulled manfully and with loud huzzas towards the six huge wooden castles which lay close to Fort Lisset. The French, though an eminently brave people, have always been more liable to sudden panics than their phlegmatic neighbours the English and Germans. On this day there was a panic both in the fleet and in the army. Tourville ordered his sailors to man their boats, and would have led them to encounter the enemy in the bay. But his example and his exhortations were vain. His boats turned round and fled in confusion. The ships were abandoned. The cannonade from Fort Lisset was so feeble and ill directed that it did no execution. The regiments on the beach, after wasting a few musket shots, drew off. The English boarded the men of war, set them on fire, and having performed this great service without the loss of a single life, retreated at a late hour with the retreating tide. The bay was in a blaze during the night; and now and then a loud explosion announced that the flames had reached a powder room or a tier of loaded guns. At eight the next morning the tide came back strong; and with the tide came back Rooke and his two hundred boats. The enemy made a faint attempt to defend the vessels which were near Fort Saint Vaast. During a few minutes the batteries did some execution among the crews of our skiffs: but the struggle was soon over. The French poured fast out of their ships on one side: the English poured in as fast on the other, and, with loud shouts, turned the captured guns against the shore. The batteries were speedily silenced. James and Melfort, Bellefonds and Tourville, looked on in helpless despondency while the second conflagration proceeded. The conquerors, leaving the ships of war in flames, made their way into an inner basin where many transports lay. Eight of these vessels were set on fire. Several were taken in tow. The rest would have been either destroyed or carried off, had not the sea again begun to ebb. It was impossible to do more; and the victorious flotilla slowly retired, insulting the hostile camp with a thundering chant of " God save the King."

Thus ended, at noon on the twenty-fourth of May, the great conflict which had raged during five days over a wide extent of sea and shore. One English fireship had perished in its calling. Sixteen French men of war, all noble vessels, and eight of them threedeckers, had been sunk or burned down to the wateredge. The battle is called, from the place where it terminated, the battle of La Hogue.[1]

The news was received in London with boundless exultation. In the fight on the open sea, indeed, the numerical superiority of the allies

Rejoicings in England had been so great that they had little reason to boast of their success. But the courage and skill with which the crews of the English boats had, in a French harbour, in sight of a French army, and under the fire of French batteries, destroyed a fine French fleet, amply justified the pride with which our fathers pronounced the name of La Hogue. That we may fully enter into their feelings, we must remember that this was the first great check that had ever been given to the arms of Lewis the Fourteenth, and the first great victory that the English had gained over the French since the day of Agincourt. The stain left on our fame by the shameful defeat of Beachy Head was effaced. This time the glory was all our own. The Dutch had indeed done their duty, as they have always done it in maritime war, whether fighting on our side or against us, whether victorious or vanquished. But the English had borne the brunt of the fight. Russell who commanded in chief was an Englishman. Delaval who directed the attack on Cherburg was an Englishman. Rooke who led the flotilla into the Bay of La Hogue was an Englishman. The only two officers of note who had fallen, Admiral Carter and Captain Hastings of the Sandwich, were Englishmen. Yet the pleasure with which the good news was received here must not be ascribed solely or chiefly to national pride. The island was safe. The pleasant pastures, cornfields and commons of Hampshire and Surrey would not be the seat of war. The houses and gardens, the kitchens and dairies, the cellars and plate chests, the wives and daughters of our gentry and clergy would not be at the mercy of Irish Rapparees, who had sacked the dwellings and skinned the cattle of the Englishry of Leinster, or of French dragoons accustomed to live at free quarter on the Protestants of Auvergne. Whigs and Tories joined in thanking God for this great deliverance; and the most respectable nonjurors could not but be glad at heart that the rightful King was not to be brought back by an army of foreigners.

[1] London Gaz., May 26. 1692; Burchett's Memoirs of Transactions at Sea; Baden to the States General, $\frac{May\ 24.}{June\ 3.}$; Life of James, ii. 494.; Russell's Letters in the Commons' Journals of Nov. 28. 1692; An Account of the Great Victory, 1692; Monthly Mercuries for June and July 1692; Paris Gazette, $\frac{May\ 28.}{June\ 7.}$; Van Almonde's despatch to the States General, dated $\frac{May\ 24.}{June\ 3.}$ 1692. The French official account will be found in the Monthly Mercury for July. A report drawn up by Foucault, Intendant of the province of Normandy, will be found in M. Capefigue's Louis XIV.

DUTCH CARICATURE ON THE BATTLE OF LA HOGUE

Number 1281 in the British Museum Catalogue of Satirical Prints

The public joy was therefore all but universal. During several days
the bells of London pealed without ceasing. Flags were flying on all
the steeples. Rows of candles were in all the windows. Bonfires were
at all the corners of the streets.[1] The sense which the government
entertained of the services of the navy was promptly, judiciously, and
gracefully manifested. Sidney and Portland were sent to meet the fleet
at Portsmouth, and were accompanied by Rochester, as the representative of the Tories. The three Lords took down with them thirty seven
thousand pounds in coin, which they were to distribute as a donative
among the sailors.[2] Gold medals were given to the officers.[3] The
remains of Hastings and Carter were brought on shore with every mark
of honour. Carter was buried at Portsmouth, with a great display of
military pomp.[4] The corpse of Hastings was carried up to London,
and laid, with unusual solemnity, under the pavement of Saint James's
Church. The footguards with reversed arms escorted the hearse. Four
royal state carriages, each drawn by six horses, were in the procession :
a crowd of men of quality in mourning cloaks filled the pews ; and the
Bishop of Lincoln preached the funeral sermon.[5] While such marks of
respect were paid to the slain, the wounded were not neglected. Fifty
surgeons, plentifully supplied with instruments, bandages, and drugs,
were sent down in all haste from London to Portsmouth.[6] It is not
easy for us to form a notion of the difficulty which there then was
in providing at short notice commodious shelter and skilful attendance
for hundreds of maimed and lacerated men. At present every county,
every large town, can boast of some spacious palace in which the
poorest labourer who has fractured a limb may find an excellent bed,
an able medical attendant, a careful nurse, medicines of the best quality,
and nourishment such as an invalid requires. But there was not then,
in the whole realm, a single infirmary supported by voluntary con-
tribution. Even in the capital the only edifices open to the wounded
were the two ancient hospitals of Saint Thomas and Saint Bartholomew.
The Queen gave orders that in both these hospitals arrangements
should be made at the public charge for the reception of patients from
the fleet.[7] At the same time it was announced that a noble and lasting

---

[1] An Account of the late Great Victory, 1692 ; Monthly Mercury for June ; Baden to the
States General $\frac{\text{May 24}}{\text{June 3.}}$; Narcissus Luttrell's Diary.

[2] London Gazette, June 2. 1692 ; Monthly Mercury ; Baden to the States General, June $\frac{14}{24}$. ;
Narcissus Luttrell's Diary.

[3] Narcissus Luttrell's Diary ; Monthly Mercury.

[4] London Gazette, June 9. ; Baden to the States General, June $\frac{7}{17}$.

[5] Baden to the States General, June $\frac{9}{13}$.

[6] Baden to the States General, $\frac{\text{May 24.}}{\text{June 3.}}$; Narcissus Luttrell's Diary.

[7] An Account of the late Great Victory, 1692 ; Narcissus Luttrell's Diary.

WILLIAM AND MARY POTTERY.

Reproduced by permission of Dr. Glaisher, F.R.S., from his collection, on loan in the
Fitzwilliam Museum, Cambridge.

THE CRIER OF VERSAILLES

Number 1270 in the British Museum Catalogue of Satirical Prints

memorial of the gratitude which England felt for the courage and patriotism of her sailors would soon rise on a site eminently appropriate. Among the suburban residences of our kings, that which stood at Greenwich had long held a distinguished place. Charles the Second liked the situation, and determined to rebuild the house and to improve the gardens. Soon after his Restoration, he began to erect, on a spot almost washed by the Thames at high tide, a mansion of vast extent and cost. Behind the palace were planted long avenues of trees which, when William reigned, were scarcely more than saplings, but which have now covered with their massy shade the summer rambles of several generations. On the slope which has long been the scene of the holiday sports of the Londoners, were constructed flights of terraces, of which the vestiges may still be discerned. The Queen now publicly declared, in her husband's name, that the building commenced by Charles should be completed, and should be a retreat for seamen disabled in the service of their country.[1]

One of the happiest effects produced by the good news was the calming of the public mind. During about a month the nation had been hourly expecting an invasion and a rising, and had consequently been in an irritable and suspicious mood. In many parts of England a nonjuror could not show himself without great risk of being insulted. A report that arms were hidden in a house sufficed to bring a furious mob to the door. The mansion of one Jacobite gentleman in Kent had been attacked, and, after a fight in which several shots were fired, had been stormed and pulled down.[2] Yet such riots were by no means the worst symptoms of the fever which had inflamed the whole society. The exposure of Fuller, in February, had, as it seemed, put an end to the practices of that vile tribe of which Oates was the patriarch. During some weeks, indeed, the world was disposed to be unreasonably incredulous about plots. But in April there was a reaction. The French and Irish were coming. There was but too much reason to believe that there were traitors in the island. Whoever pretended that he could point out those traitors was sure to be heard with attention ; and there was not wanting a false witness to avail himself of the golden opportunity.

This false witness was named Robert Young. His history was in his own lifetime so fully investigated, and so much of his correspondence
Young's plot has been preserved, that the whole man is before us. His character is indeed a curious study. His birthplace was a subject of dispute among three nations. The English pronounced him Irish. The Irish, not being ambitious of the honour of having him for a countryman, affirmed that he was born in Scotland. Wherever he may

[1] Baden to the States General, June $\frac{7}{17}$. 1692.   [2] Narcissus Luttrell's Diary.

THE ROYAL HOSPITAL AT GREENWICH

From an engraving by Sutton Nicholls

have been born, it is impossible to doubt where he was bred: for his phraseology is precisely that of the Teagues who were, in his time, favourite characters on our stage. He called himself a priest of the Established Church : but he was in truth only a deacon ; and his deacon's orders he had obtained by producing forged certificates of his learning and moral character. Long before the Revolution he held curacies in various parts of Ireland ; but he did not remain many days in any spot. He was driven from one place by the scandal which was the effect of his lawless amours. He rode away from another place on a borrowed horse, which he never returned. He settled in a third parish, and was taken up for bigamy. Some letters which he wrote on this occasion from the gaol of Cavan have been preserved. He assured each of his wives, with the most frightful imprecations, that she alone was the object of his love ; and he thus succeeded in inducing one of them to support him in prison, and the other to save his life by forswearing herself at the assizes. The only specimens which remain to us of his method of imparting religious instruction are to be found in these epistles. He compares himself to David, the man after God's own heart, who had been guilty both of adultery and murder. He declares that he repents : he prays for the forgiveness of the Almighty, and then entreats his dear honey, for Christ's sake, to perjure herself. Having narrowly escaped the gallows, he wandered during several years about Ireland and England, begging, stealing, cheating, personating, forging, and lay in many prisons under many names. In 1684 he was convicted at Bury of having fraudulently counterfeited Sancroft's signature, and was sentenced to the pillory and to imprisonment. From his dungeon he wrote to implore the Primate's mercy. The letter may still be read with all the original bad grammar and bad spelling.[1] The writer acknowledged his guilt, wished that his eyes were a fountain of water, and declared that he should never know peace till he had received episcopal absolution. He very cunningly tried to ingratiate himself with the Archbishop, by professing a mortal hatred of Dissenters. But, as all this contrition and all this orthodoxy produced no effect, the penitent, after swearing bitterly to be revenged on Sancroft, betook himself to another device. The Western Insurrection had just broken out. The magistrates all over the country were but too ready to listen to any accusation that might be brought against Whigs and Nonconformists. Young declared on oath that, to his knowledge, a design had been formed in Suffolk against the life of King James, and named a peer, several gentlemen, and ten Presbyterian ministers, as parties to the plot. Some of the accused were brought to trial ; and Young appeared

---

[1] I give one short sentence as a specimen : " O fie that ever it should be said that a clergyman have committed such durty actions ! "

in the witness box : but the story which he told was proved by overwhelming evidence to be false.   Soon after the Revolution he was
again convicted of forgery, pilloried for the fourth or fifth time, and
sent to Newgate.   While he lay there, he determined to try whether

MEDALS COMMEMORATING THE BATTLE OF LA HOGUE

he should be more fortunate as an accuser of Jacobites than he had
been as an accuser of Puritans.   He first addressed himself to Tillotson.
There was a horrible plot against their Majesties, a plot as deep as
hell ; and some of the first men in England were concerned in it.
Tillotson, though he placed little confidence in information coming

from such a source, thought that the oath which he had taken as a Privy Councillor made it his duty to mention the subject to William. William, after his fashion, treated the matter very lightly. " I am confident," he said, " that this is a villany ; and I will have nobody disturbed on such grounds." After this rebuff, Young remained some time quiet. But when William was on the Continent, and when the nation was agitated by the apprehension of a French invasion and of a Jacobite insurrection, a false accuser might hope to obtain a favourable audience. The mere oath of a man who was well known to the turnkeys of twenty gaols was not likely to injure any body. But Young was master of a weapon which is, of all weapons, the most formidable to innocence. He had lived during some years by counterfeiting hands, and had at length attained such consummate skill in that bad art that even experienced clerks who were conversant with manuscript could scarcely, after the most minute comparison, discover any difference between his imitations and the originals. He had succeeded in making a collection of papers written by men of note who were suspected of disaffection. Some autographs he had stolen; and some he had obtained by writing in feigned names to ask after the characters of servants or curates. He now drew up a paper purporting to be an Association for the Restoration of the banished King. This document set forth that the subscribers bound themselves in the presence of God to take arms for His Majesty, and to seize on the Prince of Orange, dead or alive. To the Association Young appended the names of Marlborough, of Cornbury, of Salisbury, of Sancroft, and of Sprat, Bishop of Rochester and Dean of Westminster.

The next thing to be done was to put the paper into some hiding place in the house of one of the persons whose signatures had been counterfeited. As Young could not quit Newgate, he was forced to employ a subordinate agent for this purpose. He selected a wretch named Blackhead, who had formerly been convicted of perjury and sentenced to have his ears clipped. The selection was not happy; for Blackhead had none of the qualities which the trade of a false witness requires except wickedness. There was nothing plausible about him. His voice was harsh. Treachery was written in all the lines of his yellow face. He had no invention, no presence of mind, and could do little more than repeat by rote the lies taught him by others.

This man, instructed by his accomplice, repaired to Sprat's palace at Bromley, introduced himself there as the confidential servant of an imaginary Doctor of Divinity, delivered to the Bishop, on bended knee, a letter ingeniously manufactured by Young, and received, with the semblance of profound reverence, the episcopal benediction. The servants made the stranger welcome. He was taken to the cellar, drank their master's health, and entreated them to let him see the house.   They could not venture to show any of the private apartments. Blackhead, therefore, after begging importunately, but in vain, to be suffered to have one look at the study, was forced to content himself with dropping the Association into a flowerpot which stood in a parlour near the kitchen.

Every thing having been thus prepared, Young informed the ministers that he could tell them something of the highest importance to the welfare of the State, and earnestly begged to be heard.   His request reached them on perhaps the most anxious day of an anxious month. Tourville had just stood out to sea.   The army of James was embarking. London was agitated by reports about the disaffection of the naval officers.   The Queen was deliberating whether she should cashier those who were suspected, or try the effect of an appeal to their honour and patriotism.   At such a moment the ministers could not refuse to listen to any person who professed himself able to give them valuable information.   Young and his accomplice were brought before the Privy Council.   They there accused Marlborough, Cornbury, Salisbury, Sancroft, and Sprat of high treason.   These great men, Young said, had invited James to invade England, and had promised to join him.   The eloquent and ingenious Bishop of Rochester had undertaken to draw up a Declaration which would inflame the nation against the government of King William.   The conspirators were bound together by a written instrument.   That instrument, signed by their own hands, would be found at Bromley if careful search was made.   Young particularly requested that the messengers might be ordered to examine the Bishop's flowerpots.

The ministers were seriously alarmed.   The story was circumstantial; and part of it was probable.   Marlborough's dealings with Saint Germains were well known to Caermarthen, to Nottingham, and to Sidney.   Cornbury was a tool of Marlborough, and was the son of a nonjuror and of a notorious plotter.   Salisbury was a Papist.   Sancroft had, not many months before, been, with too much show of reason, suspected of inviting the French to invade England.   Of all the accused persons Sprat was the most unlikely to be concerned in any hazardous design.   He had neither enthusiasm nor constancy.   Both his ambition and his party spirit had always been effectually kept in order by his love of ease and his anxiety for his own safety.   He had been guilty of some criminal compliances in the hope of gaining the favour of James, had sate in the High Commission, had concurred in several iniquitous decrees pronounced by that court, and had, with trembling hands and faltering voice, read the Declaration of Indulgence in the choir of the Abbey.   But there he had stopped.   As soon as it began to be whispered that the civil and religious constitution of England would speedily be vindicated by extraordinary means, he had resigned the powers which he had during two years exercised in defiance of law, and had hastened to make his peace with his clerical brethren. He had in the Convention voted for a Regency : but he had taken the oaths without hesitation : he had borne a conspicuous part in the coronation of the new Sovereigns ; and by his skilful hand had been added to the Form of Prayer used on the fifth of November those sentences in which the Church expresses her gratitude for the second great deliverance wrought on that day.[1]   Such a man, possessed of a plentiful income, of a seat in the House of Lords, of one agreeable mansion among the elms of Bromley, and of another in the cloisters of Westminster, was very unlikely to run the risk of martyrdom. He was not, indeed, on perfectly good terms with the government. For the feeling, which, next to solicitude for his own comfort and repose, seems to have had the greatest influence on his public conduct, was his dislike of the Puritans, a dislike which sprang, not from bigotry, but from Epicureanism. Their austerity was a reproach to his slothful and luxurious life : their phraseology shocked his fastidious taste ; and, where they were concerned, his ordinary good nature forsook him. Loathing the nonconformists as he did, he was not likely to be very zealous for a prince whom the nonconformists regarded as their protector. But Sprat's faults afforded ample security that he would never, from spleen against William, engage in any plot to bring back James. Why Young should have assigned the most perilous part in an enterprise full of peril to a man singularly pliant, cautious, and selfindulgent, it is difficult to say.

The first step which the ministers took was to send Marlborough to the Tower. He was by far the most formidable of all the accused persons ; and that he had held a traitorous correspondence with Saint Germains was a fact which, whether Young were perjured or not, the Queen and her chief advisers knew to be true. One of the Clerks of the Council and several messengers were sent down to Bromley with a warrant from Nottingham. Sprat was taken into custody. All the apartments in which it could reasonably be supposed that he would have hidden an important document were searched, the library, the diningroom, the drawingroom, the bedchamber, and the adjacent closets. His papers were strictly examined. Much good prose was found, and probably some bad verse, but no treason. The messengers pried into every flowerpot that they could find, but to no purpose. It never occurred to them to look into the room in which Blackhead had hidden the Association : for that room was near the offices occupied by the servants, and was little used by the Bishop and his family. The officers returned to London with their prisoner, but without the document which, if it had been found, might have been fatal to him.

[1] Gutch, Collectanea Curiosa.

Late at night he was brought to Westminster, and was suffered to sleep at his deanery. All his bookcases and drawers were examined; and sentinels were posted at the door of his bedchamber, but with strict orders to behave civilly and not to disturb the family.

On the following day he was brought before the Council. The examination was conducted by Nottingham with great humanity and courtesy. The Bishop, conscious of entire innocence, behaved with temper and firmness. He made no complaints. " I submit," he said, " to the necessities of State at such a time of jealousy and danger as this." He was asked whether he had drawn up a Declaration for King James, whether he had held any correspondence with France, whether he had signed any treasonable association, and whether he knew of any such association. To all these questions he, with perfect truth, answered in the negative, on the word of a Christian and a Bishop. He was taken back to his deanery. He remained there in easy confinement during ten days, and then, as nothing tending to criminate him had been discovered, was suffered to return to Bromley.

Meanwhile the false accusers had been devising a new scheme. Blackhead paid another visit to Bromley, and contrived to take the forged Association out of the place in which he had hid it, and to bring it back to Young. One of Young's two wives then carried it to the Secretary's Office, and told a lie, invented by her husband, to explain how a paper of such importance had come into her hands. But it was not now so easy to frighten the ministers as it had been a few days before. The battle of La Hogue had put an end to all apprehensions of invasion. Nottingham, therefore, instead of sending down a warrant to Bromley, merely wrote to beg that Sprat would call on him at Whitehall. The summons was promptly obeyed, and the accused prelate was brought face to face with Blackhead before the Council. Then the truth came out fast. The Bishop remembered the villanous look and voice of the man who had knelt to ask the episcopal blessing. The Bishop's secretary confirmed his master's assertions. The false witness soon lost his presence of mind. His cheeks, always sallow, grew frightfully livid. His voice, generally loud and coarse, sank into a whisper. The Privy Councillors saw his confusion, and crossexamined him sharply. For a time he answered their questions by repeatedly stammering out his original lie in the original words. At last he found that he had no way of extricating himself but by owning his guilt. He acknowledged that he had given an untrue account of his visit to Bromley; and, after much prevarication, he related how he had hidden the Association, and how he had removed it from its hiding place, and confessed that he had been set on by Young.

The two accomplices were then confronted. Young, with unabashed forehead, denied every thing. He knew nothing about the flowerpots. " If so," cried Nottingham and Sidney together, " why did you give such particular directions that the flowerpots at Bromley should be searched ? " " I never gave any directions about the flowerpots," said Young. Then the whole council broke forth. " How dare you say so ? We all remember it." Still the knave stood up erect, and exclaimed, with an impudence which Oates might have envied, " This hiding is all a trick got up between the Bishop and Blackhead. The Bishop has taken Blackhead off ; and they are both trying to stifle the plot." This was too much. There was a smile and a lifting up of hands all round the board. " Man," cried Caermarthen, " wouldst thou have us believe that the Bishop contrived to have this paper put where it was ten to one that our messengers had found it, and where, if they had found it, it might have hanged him ? "

The false accusers were removed in custody. The Bishop, after warmly thanking the ministers for their fair and honourable conduct, took his leave of them. In the antechamber he found a crowd of people staring at Young, while Young sate, enduring the stare with the serene fortitude of a man who had looked down on far greater multi- tudes from half the pillories in England. " Young," said Sprat, " your conscience must tell you that you have cruelly wronged me. For your own sake I am sorry that you persist in denying what your associate has confessed." " Confessed ! " cried Young : " no, all is not confessed yet ; and that you shall find to your sorrow. There is such a thing as impeachment, my Lord. When Parliament sits you shall hear more of me." " God give you repentance," answered the Bishop. " For, depend upon it, you are in much more danger of being damned than I of being impeached." [1]

Forty eight hours after the detection of this execrable fraud, Marl- borough was admitted to bail. Young and Blackhead had done him an inestimable service. That he was concerned in a plot quite as criminal as that which they had falsely imputed to him, and that the government was in possession of moral proofs of his guilt, is now certain. But his contemporaries had not, as we have, the evidence of his perfidy before them. They knew that he had been accused of an offence of which he was innocent, that perjury and forgery had been employed to ruin him, and that, in consequence of these machinations, he had passed some weeks in the Tower. There was in the public mind a very natural confusion between his disgrace and his imprison- ment. He had been imprisoned without sufficient cause. Might it

---

[1] My account of this plot is chiefly taken from Sprat's Relation of the late Wicked Con- trivance of Stephen Blackhead and Robert Young, 1692. There are very few better narratives in the language.

not, in the absence of all information, be reasonably presumed that he had been disgraced without sufficient cause? It was certain that a vile calumny, destitute of all foundation, had caused him to be treated as a criminal in May. Was it not probable, then, that calumny might have deprived him of his master's favour in January?

Young's resources were not yet exhausted. As soon as he had been carried back from Whitehall to Newgate, he set himself to construct a new plot, and to find a new accomplice. He addressed himself to a man named Holland, who was in the lowest state of poverty. Never, said Young, was there such a golden opportunity. A bold, shrewd, fellow might easily earn five hundred pounds. To Holland five hundred pounds seemed fabulous wealth. What, he asked, was he to do for it? Nothing, he was told, but to speak the truth, that was to say, substantial truth, a little disguised and coloured. There really was a plot; and this would have been proved if Blackhead had not been bought off. His desertion had made it necessary to call in the help of fiction. "You must swear that you and I were in a back room upstairs at the Lobster in Southwark. Some men came to meet us there. They gave a password before they were admitted. They were all in white camlet cloaks. They signed the Association in our presence. Then they paid each his shilling and went away. And you must be ready to identify my Lord Marlborough and the Bishop of Rochester as two of these men." "How can I identify them?" said Holland, "I never saw them." "You must contrive to see them," answered the tempter, "as soon as you can. The Bishop will be at the Abbey. Any body about the court will point out my Lord Marlborough." Holland immediately went to Whitehall, and repeated this conversation to Nottingham. The unlucky imitator of Oates was prosecuted, by order of the government, for perjury, subornation of perjury, and forgery. He was convicted and imprisoned, was again set in the pillory, and underwent, in addition to the exposure, about which he cared little, such a pelting as had seldom been known.[1] After his punishment, he was, during some years, lost in the crowd of pilferers, ringdroppers, and sharpers who infested the capital. At length, in the year 1700, he emerged from his obscurity, and excited a momentary interest. The newspapers announced that Robert Young, Clerk, once so famous, had been taken up for coining, then that he had been found guilty, then that the dead warrant had come down, and finally that the reverend gentleman had been hanged at Tyburn, and had greatly edified a large assembly of spectators by his penitence.[2]

[1] Baden to the States General, Feb. $\frac{4}{14}$. 1693.
[2] Postman, April 13 and 20. 1700; Postboy, April 18.; Flying Post, April 20.

CHAPTER XIX

WHILE England was agitated, first by the dread of an invasion, and then by joy at the deliverance wrought for her by the valour of her

Foreign policy of William

seamen, important events were taking place on the Continent. On the sixth of March the King had arrived at the Hague, and had proceeded to make his arrangements for the approaching campaign.[1]

The prospect which lay before him was gloomy. The coalition of which he was the author and the chief had, during some months, been in constant danger of dissolution. By what strenuous exertions, by what ingenious expedients, by what blandishments, by what bribes, he succeeded in preventing his allies from throwing themselves, one by one, at the feet of France, can be but imperfectly known. The fullest and most authentic record of the labours and sacrifices by which he kept together, during eight years, a crowd of fainthearted and treacherous potentates, negligent of the common interest and jealous of each other, is to be found in his correspondence with Heinsius. In that correspondence William is all himself. He had, in the course of his eventful life, to sustain some high parts for which he was not eminently qualified; and, in those parts, his success was imperfect. As sovereign of England, he showed abilities and virtues which entitle him to honourable mention in history : but his deficiencies were great. He was to the last a stranger among us, cold, reserved, never in good spirits, never at his ease. His kingdom was a place of exile. His finest palaces were prisons. He was always counting the days which must elapse before he should again see the land of his birth, the clipped trees, the wings of the innumerable windmills, the nests of the storks on the tall gables, and the long lines of painted villas reflected in the sleeping canals. He took no pains to hide the preference which he felt for his native soil and for his early friends; and therefore, though he rendered great services to our country, he did not reign in our hearts. As a general in the field, again, he showed rare courage and capacity : but, from whatever cause, he was,

[1] London Gazette, March 14. 169½.

VIEW OF THE HAGUE, SHOWING THE CANAL FROM DELFT

From an engraving by T. Scheurleer in the Sutherland Collection

as a tactician, inferior to some of his contemporaries, who, in general powers of mind, were far inferior to him. The business for which he was preeminently fitted was diplomacy, in the highest sense of the word. It may be doubted whether he has ever had a superior in the art of conducting those great negotiations on which the welfare of the commonwealth of nations depends. His skill in this department of politics was never more severely tasked or more signally proved than during the latter part of 1691 and the early part of 1692.

One of his chief difficulties was caused by the sullen and menacing demeanour of the Northern powers. Denmark and Sweden had at one

The Northern powers

time seemed disposed to join the coalition : but they had early become cold, and were fast becoming hostile. From France they flattered themselves that they had little to fear. It was not very probable that her armies would cross the Elbe, or that her fleets would force a passage through the Sound. But the naval strength of England and Holland united might well excite apprehension at Stockholm and Copenhagen. Soon arose vexatious questions of maritime right, questions such as, in almost every extensive war of modern times, have arisen between belligerents and neutrals. The Scandinavian princes complained that the legitimate trade between the Baltic and France was tyrannically interrupted. Though they had not in general been on very friendly terms with each other, they began to draw close together, intrigued at every petty German court, and tried to form what William called a Third Party in Europe. The King of Sweden, who, as Duke of Pomerania, was bound to send three thousand men for the defence of the Empire, sent, instead of them, his advice that the allies would make peace on the best terms which they could get.[1]   The King of Denmark seized a great number of Dutch merchantships, and collected in Holstein an army which caused no small uneasiness to his neighbours. " I fear," William wrote, in an hour of deep dejection, to Heinsius, " I fear that the object of this Third Party is a peace which will bring in its train the slavery of Europe. The day will come when Sweden and her confederates will know too late how great an error they have committed. They are farther, no doubt, than we from the danger; and therefore it is that they are thus bent on working our ruin and their own. That France will now consent to reasonable terms is not to be expected ; and it were better to fall sword in hand than to submit to whatever she may dictate." [2]

While the King was thus disquieted by the conduct of the northern powers, ominous signs began to appear in a very different quarter. It

[1] The Swedes came, it is true, but not till the campaign was over. London Gazette, Sept. 10. 1691.

[2] William to Heinsius, March $\frac{14}{24}$. 1692.

Christianus V. D.G. Rex Daniæ Norvegiæ Vandaloru Gothoruq &c &c &c.

Dav. Loggan fecit

CHRISTIAN V, KING OF DENMARK

From a mezzotint by D. Loggan

had, from the first, been no easy matter to induce sovereigns who hated, and who in their own dominions, persecuted, the Protestant religion, to

The Pope

countenance the revolution which had saved that religion from a great peril. But happily the example and the authority of the Vatican had overcome their scruples. Innocent the Eleventh and Alexander the Eighth had regarded William with ill concealed partiality. He was not indeed their friend; but he was their enemy's enemy; and James had been, and, if restored, must again be, their enemy's vassal. To the heretic nephew therefore they gave their effective support, to the orthodox uncle only compliments and benedictions. But Alexander the Eighth had occupied the papal throne little more than fifteen months. His successor, Antonio Pignatelli, who took the name of Innocent the Twelfth, was impatient to be reconciled to Lewis. Lewis was now sensible that he had committed a great error when he had roused against him at once the spirit of Protestantism and the spirit of Popery. He permitted the French Bishops to submit themselves to the Holy See. The dispute, which had, at one time, seemed likely to end in a great Gallican schism, was accommodated; and there was reason to believe that the influence of the head of the Church would be exerted for the purpose of severing the ties which bound so many Catholic princes to the Calvinist who had usurped the British throne.

Meanwhile the coalition, which the Third Party on one side and the Pope on the other were trying to dissolve, was in no small danger of

Conduct of the allies

falling to pieces from mere rottenness. Two of the allied powers, and two only, were hearty in the common cause; England, drawing after her the other British kingdoms, and Holland, drawing after her the other Batavian commonwealths. England and Holland were indeed torn by internal factions, and were separated from each other by mutual jealousies and antipathies : but both were fully resolved not to submit to French domination ; and both were ready to bear their share, and more than their share, of the charges of the contest. Most of the members of the confederacy were not nations, but men, an Emperor, a King, Electors, Dukes, Landgraves ; and of these men there was scarcely one whose whole soul was in the struggle, scarcely one who did not hang back, who did not find some excuse for omitting to fulfil his engagements, who did not expect to be hired to defend his own rights and interests against the common enemy. But the war was the war of the people of England and of the people of Holland. Had it not been so, the burdens which it made necessary would not have been borne by either England or Holland during a single year. When William said that he would rather die sword in hand than humble himself before France, he expressed what was felt, not by himself alone, but by two great communities of which he was the first magistrate.

POPE INNOCENT XII

From a mezzotint by J. Gole

With those two communities, unhappily, other states had little sympathy.
Indeed those two communities were regarded by other states as rich,
plaindealing, generous dupes are regarded by needy sharpers. England
and Holland were wealthy; and they were zealous. Their wealth
excited the cupidity of the whole alliance; and to that wealth their zeal
was the key. They were persecuted with sordid importunity by all
their confederates, from Cæsar, who, in the pride of his solitary dignity,
would not honour King William with the title of Majesty, down to the
smallest Margrave who could see his whole principality from the cracked
windows of the mean and ruinous old house which he called his palace.
It was not enough that England and Holland furnished much more than
their contingents to the war by land, and bore unassisted the whole
charge of the war by sea. They were beset by a crowd of illustrious
mendicants, some rude, some obsequious, but all indefatigable and
insatiable. One prince came mumping to them annually with a lamentable story about his distresses. A more sturdy beggar threatened to join
the Third Party, and to make a separate peace with France, if his demands
were not granted. Every Sovereign too had his ministers and favourites;
and these ministers and favourites were perpetually hinting that France
was willing to pay them for detaching their masters from the coalition,
and that it would be prudent in England and Holland to outbid France.

Yet the embarrassment caused by the rapacity of the allied courts
was scarcely greater than the embarrassment caused by their ambition
and their pride. This prince had set his heart on some childish distinction, a title or a cross, and would do nothing for the common cause
till his wishes were accomplished. That prince chose to fancy that he
had been slighted, and would not stir till reparation had been made to
him. The Duke of Brunswick Lunenburg would not furnish a battalion
for the defence of Germany unless he was made an Elector.[1] The
Elector of Brandenburg declared that he was as hostile as he had ever
been to France : but he had been ill used by the Spanish government;
and he therefore would not suffer his soldiers to be employed in the
defence of the Spanish Netherlands. He was willing to bear his share
of the war : but it must be in his own way : he must have the command
of a distinct army ; and he must be stationed between the Rhine and
the Meuse.[2] The Elector of Saxony complained that bad winter
quarters had been assigned to his troops : he therefore recalled them
just when they should have been preparing to take the field, but very
coolly offered to send them back if England and Holland would give
him four hundred thousand rixdollars.[3]

It might have been expected that at least the two chiefs of the
House of Austria would have put forth, at this conjuncture, all their

[1] William to Heinsius, Feb. $\frac{2}{12}$. 1692.   [2] Ibid. Jan. $\frac{12}{22}$. 1692.   [3] Ibid. Jan. $\frac{18}{28}$. 1692.

strength against the rival House of Bourbon. Unfortunately they could not be induced to exert themselves vigorously even for their own preservation. They were deeply interested in keeping the The French out of Italy. Yet they could with difficulty be Emperor prevailed upon to lend the smallest assistance to the Duke of Savoy.

MEDALS COMMEMORATING THE LEAGUE AGAINST THE TURKS

They seemed to think it the business of England and Holland to defend the passes of the Alps, and to prevent the armies of Lewis from overflowing Lombardy. To the Emperor indeed the war against France

MEDALS COMMEMORATING THE TREATY OF CARLOWITZ

was a secondary object. His first object was the war against Turkey. He was dull and bigoted. His mind misgave him that the war against France was, in some sense, a war against the Catholic religion; and the war against Turkey was a crusade. His recent campaign on the Danube had been successful. He might easily have concluded an honourable peace with the Porte, and have turned his arms westward.

But he had conceived the hope that he might extend his hereditary dominions at the expense of the Infidels.   Visions of a triumphant entry into Constantinople and of a Te Deum in Saint Sophia's had risen in his brain.   He not only employed in the East a force more than sufficient to have defended Piedmont and reconquered Lorraine ; but he seemed to think that England and Holland were bound to reward him largely for neglecting their interests and pursuing his own.[1]

Spain already was what she has continued to be down to our own time.   Of the Spain which had domineered over the land and the ocean, over the Old and the New World, of the Spain which had, in the short space of twelve years, led captive a Pope and a King of France, a Sovereign of Mexico and a Sovereign of Peru, of the Spain which had sent an army to the walls of Paris and had equipped a mighty fleet to invade England, nothing remained but an arrogance which had once excited terror and hatred, but which could now excite only derision.   In extent, indeed, the dominions of the Catholic King exceeded those of Rome when Rome was at the zenith of power.   But the huge mass lay torpid and helpless, and could be insulted or despoiled with impunity.   The whole administration, military and naval, financial and colonial, was utterly disorganized.   Charles was a fit representative of his kingdom, impotent physically, intellectually, and morally, sunk in ignorance, listlessness, and superstition, yet swollen with a notion of his own dignity, and quick to imagine and to resent affronts.   So wretched had his education been that, when he was told of the fall of Mons, the most important fortress in his vast empire, he asked whether Mons was in England.[2]   Among the ministers who were raised up and pulled down by his sickly caprice, was none capable of applying a remedy to the distempers of the State.   In truth to brace anew the nerves of that paralysed body would have been a hard task even for Ximenes.   No servant of the Spanish Crown occupied a more important post, and none was more unfit for an important post, than the Marquess of Gastanaga.   He was Governor of the Netherlands ; and in the Netherlands it seemed probable that the fate of Christendom would be decided. He had discharged his trust as every public trust was then discharged in every part of that vast monarchy on which it was boastfully said that the sun never set.   Fertile and rich as was the country which he ruled, he threw on England and Holland the whole charge of defending it. He expected that arms, ammunition, waggons, provisions, every thing, would be furnished by the heretics.   It had never occurred to him that it was his business, and not theirs, to put Mons in a condition to stand a siege.   The public voice loudly accused him of having sold that cele-

Spain

[1] Burnet, ii. 82, 83. ; Correspondence of William and Heinsius, passim.
[2] Mémoires de Torcy.

brated stronghold to France.   But it is probable that he was guilty of
nothing worse than the haughty apathy and sluggishness characteristic
of his nation.

ERNEST AUGUSTUS, DUKE OF BRUNSWICK LUNEBURG

From a mezzotint by J. Faber, after a painting by Sir G. Kneller

Such was the state of the coalition of which William was the
head.   There were moments when he felt himself overwhelmed, when
his spirits sank, when his patience was wearied out, and when his

constitutional irritability broke forth. " I cannot," he wrote, " offer a
suggestion without being met by a demand for a subsidy."[1]   " I have
William   refused point blank," he wrote on another occasion, when he
succeeds in
preventing   had been importuned for money: " it is impossible that the
the dissolu-
tion of the   States General and England can bear the charge of the army
coalition   on the Rhine, of the army in Piedmont, and of the whole
defence of Flanders, to say nothing of the immense cost of the naval
war.   If our allies can do nothing for themselves, the sooner the alliance
goes to pieces the better."[2]   But, after every short fit of despondency
and ill humour, he called up all the force of his mind, and put a strong
curb on his temper.   Weak, mean, false, selfish, as too many of the
confederates were, it was only by their help that he could accomplish
what he had from his youth up considered as his mission.   If they
abandoned him, France would be dominant without a rival in Europe.
Well as they deserved to be punished, he would not, to punish them,
acquiesce in the subjugation of the whole civilised world.   He set himself therefore to surmount some difficulties and to evade others.   The
Scandinavian powers he conciliated by waiving, reluctantly indeed, and
not without a hard internal struggle, some of his maritime rights.[3]   At
Rome his influence, though indirectly exercised, balanced that of the
Pope himself.   Lewis and James found that they had not a friend at
the Vatican except Innocent ; and Innocent, whose nature was gentle
and irresolute, shrank from taking a course directly opposed to the
sentiments of all who surrounded him.   In private conversations with
Jacobite agents he declared himself devoted to the interest of the
House of Stuart : but in his public acts he observed a strict neutrality.
He sent twenty thousand crowns to Saint Germains : but he excused
himself to the enemies of France by protesting that this was not a
subsidy for any political purpose, but merely an alms to be distributed
among poor British Catholics.   He permitted prayers for the good
cause to be read in the English College at Rome : but he insisted that
those prayers should be drawn up in general terms, and that no name
should be mentioned.   It was in vain that the ministers of the Houses
of Stuart and Bourbon adjured him to take a more decided course.
" God knows," he exclaimed on one occasion, " that I would gladly
shed my blood to restore the King of England.   But what can I do ?
If I stir, I am told that I am favouring the French, and helping them
to set up an universal monarchy.   I am not like the old Popes.   Kings
will not listen to me as they listened to my predecessors.   There is
no religion now, nothing but wicked, worldly, policy.   The Prince of
Orange is master.   He governs us all.   He has got such a hold on the

[1] William to Heinsius, $\frac{Oct. 28.}{Nov. 8.}$ 1691.   [2] Ibid. Jan. $\frac{18}{29}$. 1692.
[3] His letters to Heinsius are full of this subject.

George Lewis D.G. Elector of Brunswick & of the Holy
Roman Empire, & Son to the most Illustrious Princess Sophia
Born 28 May 1666.

GEORGE LEWIS, ELECTOR OF BRUNSWICK, AFTERWARDS GEORGE I

From a mezzotint by J. Smith, after a painting by J. Hirseman

Emperor and on the King of Spain that neither of them dares to displease him. God help us! He alone can help us." And, as the old man spoke, he beat the table with his hand in an agony of impotent grief and indignation.[1]

To keep the German princes steady was no easy task: but it was accomplished. Money was distributed among them, much less indeed than they asked, but much more than they had any decent pretence for asking. With the Elector of Saxony a composition was made. He had, together with a strong appetite for subsidies, a great desire to be a member of the most select and illustrious orders of knighthood. It seems that, instead of the four hundred thousand rixdollars which he had demanded, he consented to accept one hundred thousand and the Garter.[2] His prime minister Schœning, the most covetous and perfidious of mankind, was secured, it was hoped, by a pension.[3] For the Duke of Brunswick Lunenburg, William, not without difficulty, procured the long desired title of Elector of Hanover. By such means as these the breaches which had divided the coalition were so skilfully repaired that it appeared still to present a firm front to the enemy.

William had complained bitterly to the Spanish Court of the incapacity and inertness of Gastanaga; and that government, helpless and drowsy as it was, could not be altogether insensible to the dangers which threatened Flanders and Brabant. Gastanaga was recalled; and William was invited to take upon himself the government of the Low Countries, with powers not less than regal. Philip the Second would not easily have believed that, within a century after his death, his greatgrandson would implore the greatgrandson of William the Silent to exercise the authority of a sovereign at Brussels.[4]

New arrangements for the government of the Spanish Netherlands

The offer was in one sense tempting: but William was too wise to accept it. He knew that the population of the Spanish Netherlands was firmly attached to the Church of Rome. Every act of a Protestant

---

[1] See the Letters from Rome among the Nairne Papers. Those in 1692 are from Lytcott; those in 1693 from Cardinal Howard; those in 1694 from Bishop Ellis; those in 1695 from Lord Perth. They all tell the same story.

[2] William's correspondence with Heinsius; London Gazette, Feb. 4. 1691. In a pasquinade published in 1693, and entitled "La Foire d'Ausbourg, Ballet Allégorique," the Elector of Saxony is introduced saying:

> "Moy, je diray naïvement
> Qu'une jartière d'Angleterre
> Feroit tout mon empressement;
> Et je ne vois rien sur la terre
> Ou je trouve plus d'agrément."

[3] William's correspondence with Heinsius. There is a curious account of Schœning in the Memoirs of Count Dohna.

[4] Burnet, ii. 84.

VIEW OF HANOVER

From an engraving by C. Merian

ruler was certain to be regarded with suspicion by the clergy and people of those countries. Already Gastanaga, mortified by his disgrace, had written to inform the Court of Rome that changes were in contemplation which would make Ghent and Antwerp as heretical as Amsterdam and London.[1] It had doubtless also occurred to William that if, by governing mildly and justly, and by showing a decent respect for the ceremonies and the ministers of the Roman Catholic religion, he should succeed in obtaining the confidence of the Belgians, he would inevitably raise against himself a storm of obloquy in our island. He knew by experience what it was to govern two nations strongly attached to two different Churches. A large party among the Episcopalians of England could not forgive him for having consented to the establishment of the presbyterian polity in Scotland. A large party among the Presbyterians of Scotland blamed him for maintaining the episcopal polity in England. If he now took under his protection masses, processions, graven images, friaries, nunneries, and, worst of all, Jesuit pulpits, Jesuit confessionals, and Jesuit colleges, what could he expect but that England and Scotland would join in one cry of reprobation? He therefore refused to accept the government of the Low Countries, and proposed that it should be entrusted to the Elector of Bavaria. The Elector of Bavaria was, after the Emperor, the most powerful of the Roman Catholic potentates of Germany. He was young, brave, and ambitious of military distinction. The Spanish Court was willing to appoint him ; and he was desirous to be appointed : but much delay was caused by an absurd difficulty. The Elector thought it beneath him to ask for what he wished to have. The formalists of the Cabinet of Madrid thought it beneath the dignity of the Catholic King to give what had not been asked. Mediation was necessary, and was at last successful. But much time was lost ; and the spring was far advanced before the new Governor of the Netherlands entered on his functions.[2]

William had saved the coalition from the danger of perishing by disunion. But by no remonstrance, by no entreaty, by no bribe, could **Lewis takes the field** he prevail on his allies to be early in the field. They ought to have profited by the severe lesson which had been given them in the preceding year. But again every one of them lingered, and wondered why the rest were lingering ; and again he who singly wielded the whole power of France was found, as his haughty motto had long boasted, a match for a multitude of adversaries.[3] His enemies, while

[1] Narcissus Luttrell's Diary.

[2] Monthly Mercuries of January and April 1693 ; Burnet, ii. 84. In the Burnet MS. Harl. 6584, is a warm eulogy on the Elector of Bavaria. When the MS. was written, he was allied with England against France. In the History, which was prepared for publication when he was allied with France against England, the eulogy is omitted.

[3] " Nec pluribus impar."

Et trahit, et terret, servat, frænátque, domátque.
Cives, Odrysios, propria, régna, Budam.
Relligione, manu, studiis, victricibus armis.
Patris, Avi, Proavum, Cæsaris, atque Suis.

MAXIMILIAN EMMANUEL, ELECTOR OF BAVARIA

From an engraving by C. G. Amling

still unready, learned with dismay that he had taken the field in person at the head of his nobility. On no occasion had that gallant aristocracy appeared with more splendour in his train. A single circumstance may suffice to give a notion of the pomp and luxury of his camp. Among the musketeers of his household rode, for the first time, a stripling of seventeen, who soon afterwards succeeded to the title of Duke of Saint Simon, and to whom we owe those inestimable memoirs which have preserved, for the delight and instruction of many lands and of many generations, the vivid picture of a France which has long passed away. Though the boy's family was at that time very hard pressed for money, he travelled with thirty five horses and sumpter mules. The princesses of the blood, each surrounded by a group of highborn and graceful ladies, accompanied the King ; and the smiles of so many charming women inspired the throng of vain and voluptuous but high-spirited gentlemen with more than common courage. In the brilliant crowd which surrounded the French Augustus appeared the French Virgil, the graceful, the tender, the melodious Racine. He had, in conformity with the prevailing fashion, become devout, and had given up writing for the theatre. He now, having determined to apply himself vigorously to the discharge of the duties which belonged to him as historiographer of France, came to see the great events which it was his office to record.[1] In the neighbourhood of Mons, Lewis entertained the ladies with the most magnificent review that had ever been seen in modern Europe. A hundred and twenty thousand of the finest troops in the world were drawn up in a line eight miles long. It may be doubted whether such an array was ever brought together under the Roman eagles. The show began early in the morning, and was not over when the long summer day closed. Racine left the ground, astonished, deafened, dazzled, and tired to death. In a private letter he ventured to give utterance to an amiable wish which he probably took good care not to whisper in the courtly circle : " Would to heaven that all these poor fellows were in their cottages again with their wives and their little ones ! "[2]

After this superb pageant Lewis announced his intention of attacking Namur. In five days he was under the walls of that city, at the **Siege of Namur** head of more than thirty thousand men. Twenty thousand peasants, pressed in those parts of the Netherlands which the French occupied, were compelled to act as pioneers. Luxemburg, with eighty thousand men, occupied a strong position on the road between Namur and Brussels, and was prepared to give battle to any

---

[1] Mémoires de Saint Simon ; Dangeau ; Racine's Letters, and Narrative entitled Relation de ce qui s'est passé au Siège de Namur ; Monthly Mercury, May 1692.

[2] Mémoires de Saint Simon ; Racine to Boileau, May 21. 1692.

Du Theatre Francois l'honneur & la merveille
J'ai su resusciter Sophocle dans mes Vers,
Et sans me perdre dans les airs,
Voler aussi haut que Corneille. Boileau.

Vertue sculp: Lond:

JEAN RACINE

From an engraving by G. Vertue

force which might attempt to raise the siege.[1] This partition of duties
excited no surprise. It had long been known that the Great Monarch
loved sieges, and that he did not love battles. He professed to think
that the real test of military skill was a siege. The event of an
encounter between two armies on an open plain was, in his opinion,
often determined by chance : but only science could prevail against
ravelins and bastions which science had constructed. His detractors
sneeringly pronounced it fortunate that the department of the military
art which His Majesty considered as the noblest was one in which it
was seldom necessary for him to expose to serious risk a life invaluable
to his people.

Namur, situated at the confluence of the Sambre and the Meuse,
was one of the great fortresses of Europe. The town lay in the plain,
and had no strength except what was derived from art. But art and
nature had combined to fortify that renowned citadel which, from the
summit of a lofty rock, looks down on a boundless expanse of cornfields, woods and meadows, watered by two fine rivers. The people of
the city and of the surrounding region were proud of their impregnable
castle. Their boast was that never, in all the wars which had devastated the Netherlands, had skill or valour been able to penetrate those
walls. The neighbouring fastnesses, famed throughout the world for
their strength, Antwerp and Ostend, Ypres, Lisle, and Tournay, Mons
and Valenciennes, Cambray and Charleroy, Limburg and Luxemburg,
had opened their gates to conquerors : but never once had the flag been
pulled down from the battlements of Namur. That nothing might be
wanting to the interest of the siege, the two great masters of the art of
fortification were opposed to each other. Vauban had during many
years been regarded as the first of engineers : but a formidable rival
had lately arisen, Menno, Baron of Cohorn, the ablest officer in the
service of the States General. The defences of Namur had been recently
strengthened and repaired under Cohorn's superintendence ; and he was
now within the walls. Vauban was in the camp of Lewis. It might
therefore be expected that both the attack and the defence would be
conducted with consummate ability.

By this time the allied armies had assembled : but it was too late.[2]
William hastened towards Namur. He menaced the French works,
first from the west, then from the north, then from the east. But
between him and the lines of circumvallation lay the army of Luxemburg, turning as he turned, and always so strongly posted that to attack
it would have been the height of imprudence. Meanwhile the besiegers,
directed by the skill of Vauban and animated by the presence of Lewis,

---

[1] Monthly Mercury for June ; William to Heinsius, $\frac{\text{May 26.}}{\text{June 5.}}$ 1692.
[2] William to Heinsius, $\frac{\text{May 26.}}{\text{June 5.}}$ 1692.

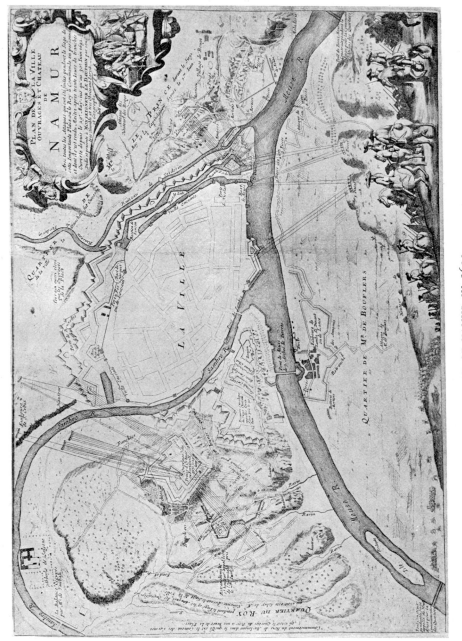

PLAN OF NAMUR IN 1692

From the Sutherland Collection

made rapid progress. There were indeed many difficulties to be surmounted and many hardships to be endured. The weather was stormy ;
and, on the eighth of June, the feast of Saint Medard, who holds in the
French Calendar the same inauspicious place which in our Calendar
belongs to Saint Swithin, the rain fell in torrents. The Sambre rose
and covered many square miles on which the harvest was green. The
Mehaigne whirled down its bridges to the Meuse. All the roads became
swamps. The trenches were so deep in water and mire that it was the
business of three days to move a gun from one battery to another. The
six thousand waggons which had accompanied the French army were
useless. It was necessary that gunpowder, bullets, corn, hay, should be
carried from place to place on the backs of the war horses. Nothing
but the authority of Lewis could, in such circumstances, have maintained
order and inspired cheerfulness. His soldiers, in truth, showed much
more reverence for him than for what their religion had made sacred.
They cursed Saint Medard heartily, and broke or burned every image
of him that could be found. But for their King there was nothing that
they were not ready to do and to bear. In spite of every obstacle they
constantly gained ground. Cohorn was severely wounded while defending
with desperate resolution a fort which he had himself constructed, and
of which he was proud. His place could not be supplied. The governor
was a feeble man whom Gastanaga had appointed, and whom William
had recently advised the Elector of Bavaria to remove. The spirit of
the garrison gave way. The town surrendered on the eighth day of the
siege, the citadel about three weeks later.[1]

The history of the fall of Namur in 1692 bears a close resemblance
to the history of the fall of Mons in 1691. Both in 1691 and in 1692,
Lewis, the sole and absolute master of the resources of his kingdom, was
able to open the campaign, before William, the captain of a coalition,
had brought together his dispersed forces. In both years the advantage
of having the first move decided the event of the game. At Namur, as
at Mons, Lewis, assisted by Vauban, conducted the siege : Luxemburg
covered it : William vainly tried to raise it, and, with deep mortification,
assisted as a spectator at the victory of his enemy.

In one respect however the fate of the two fortresses was very
different. Mons was delivered up by its own inhabitants. Namur
might perhaps have been saved if the garrison had been as zealous and
determined as the population. Strange to say, in this place, so long
subject to a foreign rule, there was found a patriotism resembling that

---

[1] Monthly Mercuries of June and July 1692 ; London Gazettes of June ; Gazette de Paris ;
Mémoires de Saint Simon ; Journal de Dangeau ; William to Heinsius, $\frac{\text{May 30.}}{\text{June 9.}}$, June $\frac{2}{12}$. June $\frac{11}{21}$. ;
Vernon's Letters to Colt, printed in Tindal's History ; Racine's Narrative and Letters to Boileau
of June 15. and 24.

Messire Sebastien le Prestre de Vauban
cheualier Seigneur de Basoges et Autres lieux Lieutenant General des
Armées du Roy Commissaire General des Fortiffications, Gouverneur de
la Citadelle de Lisle

SEBASTIAN DE VAUBAN, AFTERWARDS MARSHAL OF FRANCE

From a mezzotint by E. Bernard, after a painting by De Troy

of the little Greek commonwealths. There is no reason to believe that the burghers cared about the balance of power, or had any preference for James or for William, for the Most Christian King or for the Most Catholic King. But every citizen considered his own honour as bound up with the honour of the maiden fortress. It is true that the French did not abuse their victory. No outrage was committed : the privileges of the municipality were respected ; the magistrates were not changed. Yet the people could not see a conqueror enter their hitherto un-conquered castle without tears of rage and shame. Even the bare-footed Carmelites, who had renounced all pleasures, all property, all society, all domestic affection, whose days were all fast days, who passed month after month without uttering a word, were strangely moved. It was in vain that Lewis attempted to sooth them by marks of respect and by munificent bounty. Whenever they met a French uniform they turned their heads away with a look which showed that a life of prayer, of abstinence, and of silence had left one earthly feeling still unsubdued.[1]

This was perhaps the moment at which the arrogance of Lewis reached the highest point. He had achieved the last and the most splendid military exploit of his life. His confederated foes, English, Dutch and German, had, in their own despite, swelled his triumph, and had been witnesses of the glory which made their hearts sick. His exultation was boundless. The inscriptions on the medals which he struck to commemorate his success, the letters by which he enjoined the prelates of his kingdom to sing the Te Deum, were boastful and sarcastic. His people, a people among whose many fine qualities moderation in prosperity cannot be reckoned, seemed for a time to be drunk with pride. Even Boileau, hurried along by the prevailing enthusiasm, forgot the good sense and good taste to which he owed his reputation. He fancied himself a lyric poet, and gave vent to his feelings in a hundred and sixty lines of frigid bombast about Alcides, Mars, Bacchus, Ceres, the lyre of Orpheus, the Thracian oaks, and the Permessian nymphs. He wondered whether Namur had, like Troy, been built by Apollo and Neptune. He asked what power could subdue a city stronger than that before which the Greeks lay ten years ; and he returned answer to himself that such a miracle could be wrought only by Jupiter or by Lewis. The feather in the hat of Lewis was the loadstar of victory. To Lewis all things must yield, princes, nations, winds, waters. In conclusion the poet addressed himself to the banded enemies of France, and tauntingly bade them carry back to their homes the tidings that Namur had been taken in their sight. Before many months had elapsed both the boastful king and the boastful poet were

[1] Mémoires de Saint Simon.

taught that it is prudent as well as graceful to be modest in the hour of victory.

One mortification Lewis had suffered even in the midst of his prosperity. While he lay before Namur, he heard the sounds of rejoicing from the distant camp of the allies. Three peals of thunder from

LEWIS XIV AT THE SIEGE OF NAMUR
From an engraving in the Cabinet des Estampes

a hundred and forty pieces of cannon were answered by three volleys from sixty thousand muskets. It was soon known that these salutes were fired on account of the battle of La Hogue. The French King exerted himself to appear serene. "They make a strange noise," he said, "about the burning of a few ships." In truth he was much disturbed, and the more so because a report had reached the Low Countries that there had been a sea fight, and that his fleet had been victorious. His good humour however was soon restored by the brilliant success of those operations which were under his own immediate direction. When

Lewis returns to Versailles the siege was over, he left Luxemburg in command of the army, and returned to Versailles. At Versailles the unfortunate Tourville presented himself, and was graciously received. As soon as he appeared in the circle, the King welcomed him in a loud voice. " I am perfectly satisfied with you and with my sailors. We have been beaten, it is true : but your honour and that of the nation are unsullied."[1]

Though Lewis had quitted the Netherlands, the eyes of all Europe were still fixed on that region. The armies there had been strengthened by reinforcements drawn from many quarters. Everywhere else the military operations of the year were languid and without interest. The Grand Vizier and Lewis of Baden did little more than watch each other on the Danube. Marshal Noailles and the Duke of Medina Sidonia did little more than watch each other under the Pyrenees. On the Upper Rhine, and along the frontier of Piedmont, an indecisive predatory war was carried on, by which the soldiers suffered little and the cultivators of the soil much. But all men looked, with anxious expectation of some great event, to the frontier of Brabant, where William was opposed to Luxemburg.

Luxemburg, now in his sixty-sixth year, had risen, by slow degrees, and by the deaths of several great men, to the first place among the

Luxemburg generals of his time. He was of that noble house of Montmorency which united many mythical and many historical titles to glory, which boasted that it sprang from the first Frank who was baptised into the name of Christ in the fifth century, and which had, since the eleventh century, given to France a long and splendid succession of Constables and Marshals. In valour and abilities Luxemburg was not inferior to any of his illustrious race. But, highly descended and highly gifted as he was, he had with difficulty surmounted the obstacles which impeded him in the road to fame. If he owed much to the bounty of nature and fortune, he had suffered still more from their spite. His features were frightfully harsh : his stature was diminutive : a huge and pointed hump rose on his back. His constitution was feeble and sickly. Cruel imputations had been thrown on his morals. He had been accused of trafficking with sorcerers and with compounders of poison, had languished long in a dungeon, and had at length regained his liberty without entirely regaining his

[1] London Gazette, May 30. 1692 ; Mémoires de Saint Simon ; Journal de Dangeau ; Boyer's History of William III. 1702.

honour.[1]   He had always been disliked both by Louvois and by Lewis. Yet the war against the European coalition had lasted but a very short time when both the minister and the King felt that the general who was personally odious to them was necessary to the state.   Condé and Turenne were no more ; and Luxemburg was without dispute the first soldier that France still possessed.   In vigilance, diligence, and perseverance he was deficient.   He seemed to reserve his great qualities for great emergencies.   It was on a pitched field of battle that he was all himself.   His glance was rapid and unerring.   His judgment was clearest and surest when responsibility pressed heaviest on him, and when difficulties gathered thickest around him.   To his skill, energy, and presence

MEDAL COMMEMORATING THE CAPTURE OF NAMUR BY LEWIS XIV

of mind his country owed some glorious days.   But, though eminently successful in battles, he was not eminently successful in campaigns. He gained immense renown at William's expense ; and yet there was, as respected the objects of the war, little to choose between the two commanders.   Luxemburg was repeatedly victorious : but he had not the art of improving a victory.   William was repeatedly defeated : but of all generals he was the best qualified to repair a defeat.

In the month of July William's headquarters were at Lambeque. About six miles off, at Steinkirk, Luxemburg had encamped with the main body of his army ; and about six miles further off lay a

[1] Mémoires de Saint Simon ; Voltaire, Siècle de Louis XIV.   Voltaire speaks with a contempt which is probably just of the account of this affair in the Causes Célèbres.   See also the Letters of Madame de Sévigné during the months of January and February 1680.   In several English lampoons Luxemburg is nicknamed Æsop, from his deformity, and called a wizard, in allusion to his dealings with La Voisin.   In one Jacobite allegory he is the necromancer Grandorsio.   In Narcissus Luttrell's Diary for June 1692 he is called a conjuror.   I have seen two or three English caricatures of Luxemburg's figure.

considerable force commanded by the Marquess of Boufflers, one of the best officers in the service of Lewis.

The country between Lambeque and Steinkirk was intersected by innumerable hedges and ditches ; and neither army could approach the other without passing through several long and narrow defiles. Luxemburg had therefore little reason to apprehend that he should be attacked in his entrenchments; and he felt assured that he should have ample notice before any attack was made : for he had succeeded in corrupting an adventurer named Millevoix, who was chief musician and private secretary of the Elector of Bavaria. This man regularly sent to the French headquarters authentic information touching the designs of the allies.

The Marshal, confident in the strength of his position and in the accuracy of his intelligence, lived in his tent as he was accustomed to live in his hotel at Paris. He was at once a valetudinarian and a voluptuary ; and, in both characters, he loved his ease. He scarcely ever mounted his horse. Light conversation and cards occupied most of his hours. His table was luxurious ; and, when he had sate down to supper, it was a service of danger to disturb him. Some scoffers remarked that in his military dispositions he was not guided exclusively by military reasons, that he generally contrived to entrench himself in some place where the veal and the poultry were remarkably good, and that he was always solicitous to keep open such communications with the sea as might ensure him, from September to April, a regular supply of Sandwich oysters. If there were any agreeable women in the neighbourhood of his camp, they were generally to be found at his banquets. It may easily be supposed that, under such a commander, the young princes and nobles of France vied with one another in splendour and gallantry.[1]

While he was amusing himself after his wonted fashion, the confederate princes discovered that their counsels were betrayed. A **Battle of Steinkirk** peasant picked up a letter which had been dropped, and carried it to the Elector of Bavaria. It contained full proofs of the guilt of Millevoix. William conceived a hope that he might be able to take his enemies in the snare which they had laid for him. The perfidious secretary was summoned to the royal presence and taxed with his crime. A pen was put into his hand : a pistol was held to his breast; and he was commanded to write on pain of instant death. His letter, dictated by William, was conveyed to the French camp. It apprised Luxemburg that the allies meant to send out a strong foraging party on the next day. In order to protect this party from molestation, some battalions of infantry, accompanied by artillery, would march by

[1] Mémoires de Saint Simon ; Mémoires de Villars ; Racine to Boileau, May 21. 1692.

Francois de Montmorency   Duc de Luxembourg et de Piney,
Pair, Maréchal, premier Baron et premier Chréten   de France, Souverain de Luxe et d'Aigremot,Chevalier
des Ordres du Roy, Capitaine de la premiere et plus   ancienne, Compagnie françoise des Gardes de son Corps,
Gouverneur et Lieutenant qual pour Sa Majesté en la   Province de Normandie, commandant l'Armée en Flandre.

FRANÇOIS DE MONTMORENCY, DUKE DE LUXEMBOURG

From an engraving by Vermeulen, after a painting by H. Rigaud

night to occupy the defiles which lay between the armies. The Marshal read, believed, and went to rest, while William urged forward the preparations for a general assault on the French lines.

The whole allied army was under arms while it was still dark. In the grey of the morning, Luxemburg was awakened by scouts, who brought tidings that the enemy was advancing in great force. He at first treated the news very lightly. His correspondent, it seemed, had been, as usual, diligent and exact. The Prince of Orange had sent out a detachment to protect his foragers, and this detachment had been magnified by fear into a great host. But one alarming report followed another fast. All the passes, it was said, were choked with multi-tudes of foot, horse, and artillery, under the banners of England and of Spain, of the United Provinces and of the Empire ; and every column was moving towards Steinkirk. At length the Marshal rose, got on horseback, and rode out to see what was doing.

By this time the vanguard of the allies was close to his outposts. About half a mile in advance of his army was encamped a brigade named from the province of Bourbonnais. These troops had to bear the first brunt of the onset. Amazed and panickstricken, they were swept away in a moment, and ran for their lives, leaving their tents and seven pieces of cannon to the assailants.

Thus far William's plans had been completely successful : but now fortune began to turn against him. He had been misinformed as to the nature of the ground which lay between the station of the brigade of Bourbonnais and the main encampment of the enemy. He had expected that he should be able to push forward without a moment's pause, that he should find the French army in a state of wild disorder, and that his victory would be easy and complete. But his progress was obstructed by several fences and ditches : there was a short delay ; and a short delay sufficed to frustrate his design. Luxemburg was the very man for such a conjuncture. He had committed great faults : he had kept careless guard : he had trusted implicitly to information which had proved false : he had neglected information which had proved true : one of his divisions was flying in confusion : the other divisions were unprepared for action. That crisis would have paralysed the faculties of an ordinary captain : it only braced and stimulated those of Luxemburg. His mind, nay his sickly and distorted body, seemed to derive health and vigour from disaster and dismay. In a short time he had disposed every thing. The French army was in battle order. Conspicuous in that great array were the household troops of Lewis, the most renowned body of fighting men in Europe ; and at their head appeared, glittering in lace and embroidery hastily thrown on and half fastened, a crowd of young princes and lords who

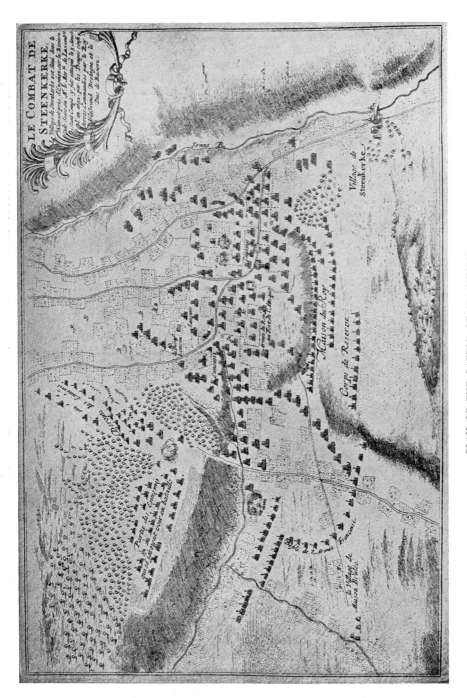

PLAN OF THE BATTLE OF STEINKIRK

From an engraving in the Sutherland Collection

had just been roused by the trumpet from their couches or their revels, and who had hastened to look death in the face with the gay and festive intrepidity characteristic of French gentlemen.   Highest in rank among these highborn warriors was a lad of sixteen, Philip Duke of Chartres, son of the Duke of Orleans, and nephew of the King of France.   It was with difficulty and by importunate solicitation that the gallant boy had extorted Luxemburg's permission to be where the fire was hottest.   Two other youths of royal blood, Lewis Duke of Bourbon, and Armand Prince of Conti, showed a spirit worthy of their descent.   With them was a descendant of one of the bastards of Henry the Fourth, Lewis Duke of Vendome, a man sunk in indolence and in the foulest vice, yet capable of exhibiting on a great occasion the qualities of a great soldier.   Berwick, who was beginning to earn for himself an honourable name in arms, was there ; and at his side rode Sarsfield, whose courage and ability earned, on that day, the esteem of the whole French army.[1]   Meanwhile Luxemburg had sent off a pressing message to summon Boufflers.   But the message was needless.   Boufflers had heard the firing, and, like a brave and intelligent captain, was already hastening towards the point from which the sound came.

Though the assailants had lost all the advantage which belongs to a surprise, they came on manfully.   In front of the battle were the British commanded by Count Solmes.   The division which was to lead the way was Mackay's.   He was to have been supported, according to William's plan, by a strong body of foot and horse.   Though most of Mackay's men had never before been under fire, their behaviour gave promise of Blenheim and Ramilies.   They first encountered the Swiss, who held a distinguished place in the French army.   The fight was so close and desperate that the muzzles of the muskets crossed.   The Swiss were driven back with fearful slaughter.   More than eighteen hundred of them appear from the French returns to have been killed or wounded. Luxemburg afterwards said that he had never in his life seen so furious a struggle.   He collected in haste the opinion of the generals who surrounded him.   All thought that the emergency was one which could be met by no common means.   The King's household must charge the English.   The Marshal gave the word ; and the household, headed by the princes of the blood, came on, flinging their muskets back on their shoulders.   "Sword in hand," was the cry through all the ranks of that terrible brigade : "sword in hand.   No firing.   Do it with the cold steel."   After a long and bloody contest, the English were borne down. They never ceased to repeat that, if Solmes had done his duty by them, they would have beaten even the household.   But Solmes gave them no

[1] See the honourable mention of Sarsfield in Luxemburg's despatch.

FRANÇOIS LOUIS DE BOURBON, PRINCE DE CONTI

From a mezzotint by C. Weigel

effective support. He pushed forward some cavalry which, from the nature of the ground, could do little or nothing. His infantry he would not suffer to stir. They could do no good, he said ; and he would not send them to be slaughtered. Ormond was eager to hasten to the assistance of his countrymen, but was not permitted. Mackay sent a pressing message to represent that he and his men were left to certain destruction : but all was vain. " God's will be done," said the brave veteran. He died as he had lived, like a good Christian and a good soldier. With him fell Douglas and Lanier, two generals distinguished among the conquerors of Ireland. Mountjoy too was among the slain. After languishing three years in the Bastille, he had just been exchanged for Richard Hamilton, and, having been converted to Whiggism by wrongs more powerful than all the arguments of Locke and Sidney, had instantly hastened to join William's camp as a volunteer.[1] Five fine regiments were entirely cut to pieces. No part of this devoted band would have escaped but for the courage and conduct of Auver-querque, who came to the rescue in the moment of extremity with two fresh battalions. The gallant manner in which he brought off the remains of Mackay's division was long remembered and talked of with grateful admiration by the British camp fires. The ground where the conflict had raged was piled with corpses ; and those who buried the slain remarked that almost all the wounds had been given in close fighting by the sword or the bayonet.

It was said that William so far forgot his wonted stoicism as to utter a passionate exclamation at the way in which the English regiments had been sacrificed. Soon, however, he recovered his equanimity, and determined to fall back. It was high time : for the French army was every moment becoming stronger, as the regiments commanded by Boufflers came up in rapid succession. The allied army returned to Lambeque unpursued and in unbroken order.[2]

[1] Narcissus Luttrell, April 28. 1692.

[2] London Gazette, Aug. 4. 8. 11. 1692 ; Gazette de Paris, Aug. 9. 16. ; Voltaire, Siècle de Louis XIV. ; Burnet, ii. 97. ; Mémoires de Berwick ; Dykvelt's Letter to the States General dated August 4. 1692. See also the very interesting debate which took place in the House of Commons on Nov. 21. 1692. An English translation of Luxemburg's elaborate and artful despatch will be found in the Monthly Mercury for September 1692. The original has recently been printed in the new edition of Dangeau. Lewis pronounced it the best despatch that he had ever seen. The editor of the Monthly Mercury maintains that it was manufactured at Paris. " To think otherwise," he says, " is mere folly ; as if Luxemburg could be at so much leisure to write such a long letter, more like a pedant than a general, or rather the monitor of a school, giving an account to his master how the rest of the boys behaved themselves." In the Monthly Mercury will be found also the French official list of killed and wounded. Of all the accounts of the battle that which seems to me the best is in the Memoirs of Feuquières. It is illustrated by a map. Feuquières divides his praise and blame very fairly between the generals. The tradi-tions of the English mess tables have been preserved by Sterne, who was brought up at the knees

A Paris chez I. Mariette rue St. Jacques aux Colonnes d'Hercule.

Loüis Joseph Duc de Vandosme,
Generalissime des Armées de France,
Fils de Loüis Duc de Vandosme est né le j.er juillet 1654.

LOUIS JOSEPH, DUKE DE VENDOME

From an engraving by Mariette in the Sutherland Collection

The French owned that they had about seven thousand men killed and wounded. The loss of the allies had been little, if at all, greater. The relative strength of the armies was what it had been on the preceding day ; and they continued to occupy their old positions. But the moral effect of the battle was great. The splendour of William's fame grew pale. Even his admirers were forced to own that, in the field, he was not a match for Luxemburg. In France the news was received with transports of joy and pride. The Court, the Capital, even the peasantry of the remotest provinces, gloried in the impetuous valour which had been displayed by so many youths, the heirs of illustrious names. It was exultingly and fondly repeated all over the kingdom that the young Duke of Chartres could not by any remonstrances be kept out of danger, that a ball had passed through his coat, that he had been wounded in the shoulder. The people lined the roads to see the princes and nobles who returned from Steinkirk. The jewellers devised Steinkirk buckles : the perfumers sold Steinkirk powder. But the name of the field of battle was peculiarly given to a new species of collar. Lace neckcloths were then worn by men of fashion ; and it had been usual to arrange them with great care. But at the terrible moment when the brigade of Bourbonnais was flying before the onset of the allies, there was no time for foppery ; and the finest gentlemen of the Court came spurring to the front of the line of battle with their rich cravats in disorder. It therefore became a fashion among the beauties of Paris to wear round their necks kerchiefs of the finest lace studiously disarranged ; and these kerchiefs were called Steinkirks.[1]

In the camp of the allies all was disunion and discontent. National jealousies and animosities raged without restraint or disguise. The resentment of the English was loudly expressed. Solmes, though he was said by those who knew him well to have some valuable qualities, was not a man likely to conciliate soldiers who were prejudiced against him as a foreigner. His demeanour was arrogant, his temper ungovernable. Even before the unfortunate day of Steinkirk the English officers did not willingly communicate with him, and the private men murmured at his harshness. But after the battle the outcry against him became furious. He was accused, perhaps unjustly, of having said with unfeeling levity, while the English regiments were contending desperately against great odds, that he was curious to see how the bulldogs would come off.

of old soldiers of William. " ' There was Cutts's,' continued the Corporal, clapping the forefinger of his right hand upon the thumb of his left, and counting round his hand ; ' there was Cutts's, Mackay's, Angus's, Graham's and Leven's, all cut to pieces ; and so had the English Lifeguards too, had it not been for some regiments on the right, who marched up boldly to their relief, and received the enemy's fire in their faces, before any one of their own platoons discharged a musket. They'll go to heaven for it,' added Trim."

[1] Voltaire, Siècle de Louis XIV.

Would anybody, it was asked, now pretend that it was on account of his superior skill and experience that he had been put over the heads of so many English officers? It was the fashion to say that those officers had never seen war on a large scale. But surely the merest

FRENCH MEDALS COMMEMORATING THE BATTLE OF STEINKIRK

novice was competent to do all that Solmes had done, to misunderstand orders, to send cavalry on duty which none but infantry could perform, and to look on at safe distance while brave men were cut to pieces. It was too much to be at once insulted and sacrificed, excluded from the honours of war, yet pushed on all its extreme dangers, sneered at as raw recruits, and then left to cope unsupported with the finest body of veterans in the world.   Such were the complaints of the English army ; and they were echoed by the English nation.

Fortunately about this time a discovery was made which furnished both the camp at Lambeque and the coffeehouses of London with a subject of conversation much less agreeable to the Jacobites than the disaster of Steinkirk.

A plot against the life of William had been, during some months, maturing in the French War Office.   It should seem that Louvois **Conspiracy** had originally sketched the design, and had bequeathed it, **of Grandval** still rude, to his son and successor Barbesieux.   By Barbesieux the plan was perfected.   The execution was entrusted to an officer named Grandval.   Grandval was undoubtedly brave, and full of zeal for his country and his religion.   He was indeed flighty and half witted, but not on that account the less dangerous.   Indeed a flighty and half witted man is the very instrument generally preferred by cunning politicians when very hazardous work is to be done.   No shrewd calculator would, for any bribe, however enormous, have exposed himself to the fate of Chatel, of Ravaillac, or of Gerarts.[1]

Grandval secured, as he conceived, the assistance of two adventurers, Dumont, a Walloon, and Leefdale, a Dutchman.   In April, soon after William had arrived in the Low Countries, the murderers were directed to repair to their posts.   Dumont was then in Westphalia.   Grandval and Leefdale were at Paris.   Uden in North Brabant was fixed as the place where the three were to meet, and whence they were to proceed together to the headquarters of the allies.   Before Grandval left Paris he paid a visit to Saint Germains, and was presented to James and to Mary of Modena.   "I have been informed," said James, "of the business. If you and your companions do me this service, you shall never want."

After this audience Grandval set out on his journey.   He had not the faintest suspicion that he had been betrayed both by the accomplice who accompanied him and by the accomplice whom he was going to meet.   Dumont and Leefdale were not enthusiasts.   They cared nothing for the restoration of James, the grandeur of Lewis, or the ascendency of the Church of Rome.   It was plain to every man of common sense that, whether the design succeeded or failed, the reward of the assassins would probably be to be disowned, with affected abhorrence, by the Courts of Versailles and Saint Germains, and to be torn with redhot pincers, smeared with melted lead, and dismembered by horses.   To vulgar natures the prospect of such a martyrdom was not alluring.   Both these men, therefore, had, almost at the same time, though, as far as appears,

[1] Langhorne, the chief lay agent of the Jesuits in England, always, as he owned to Tillotson, selected tools on this principle.   Burnet, i. 230.

without any concert, conveyed to William, through different channels, warnings that his life was in danger. Dumont had acknowledged every thing to the Duke of Zell, one of the confederate princes. Leefdale had transmitted full intelligence through his relations who resided in Holland. Meanwhile Morel, a Swiss Protestant of great learning who was then in France, wrote to inform Burnet that the weak and hotheaded Grandval had been heard to talk boastfully of the event which would soon astonish the world, and had confidently predicted that the Prince of Orange would not live to the end of the next month.

These cautions were not neglected. From the moment at which Grandval entered the Netherlands, his steps were among snares. His movements were watched : his words were noted : he was arrested, examined, confronted with his accomplices, and sent to the camp of the allies. About a week after the battle of Steinkirk he was brought before a Court Martial. Ginkell, who had been rewarded for his great services in Ireland with the title of Earl of Athlone, presided; and Talmash was among the judges. Mackay and Lanier had been named members of the board : but they were no more ; and their places were filled by younger officers.

The duty of the Court Martial was very simple : for the prisoner attempted no defence. His conscience had, it should seem, been suddenly awakened. He admitted, with expressions of remorse, the truth of all the charges, made a minute, and apparently an ingenuous confession, and owned that he had deserved death. He was sentenced to be hanged, drawn, and quartered, and underwent his punishment with great fortitude and with a show of piety. He left behind him a few lines, in which he declared that he was about to lose his life for having too faithfully obeyed the injunctions of Barbesieux.

His confession was immediately published in several languages, and was read with very various and very strong emotions. That it was genuine could not be doubted : for it was warranted by the signatures of some of the most distinguished military men living. That it was prompted by the hope of pardon could hardly be supposed : for William had taken pains to discourage that hope. Still less could it be supposed that the prisoner had uttered untruths in order to avoid the torture. For, though it was the universal practice in the Netherlands to put convicted assassins to the rack in order to wring out from them the names of their employers and associates, William had given orders that, on this occasion, the rack should not be used or even named. It should be added, that the Court did not interrogate the prisoner closely, but suffered him to tell his story in his own way. It is therefore reasonable to believe that his narrative is substantially true ; and no part of it has a stronger air of truth than his account of the audience with which James had honoured him at Saint Germains.

In our island the sensation produced by the news was great. The Whigs loudly called both James and Lewis assassins. How, it was asked, was it possible, without outraging common sense, to put an innocent meaning on the words which Grandval declared that he had heard from the lips of the banished King of England? And who that knew the Court of Versailles would believe that Barbesieux, a youth, a mere novice in politics, and rather a clerk than a minister, would have dared to do what he had done without taking his master's pleasure? Very charitable and very ignorant persons might perhaps indulge a hope that Lewis had not been an accessory before the fact. But that he was an accessory after the fact no human being could doubt. He must have

MEDAL COMMEMORATING THE EXECUTION OF GRANDVAL

seen the proceedings of the Court Martial, the evidence, the confession. If he really abhorred assassination as honest men abhor it, would not Barbesieux have been driven with ignominy from the Royal presence, and flung into the Bastille? Yet Barbesieux was still at the War Office; and it was not pretended that he had been punished even by a word or a frown. It was plain, then, that both Kings were partakers in the guilt of Grandval. And, if it were asked how two princes who made a high profession of religion could have fallen into such wickedness, the answer was that they had learned their religion from the Jesuits. In reply to these reproaches the English Jacobites said very little; and the French government said nothing at all.[1]

---

[1] I have taken the history of Grandval's plot chiefly from Grandval's own confession. I have not mentioned Madame de Maintenon, because Grandval, in his confession, did not mention her. The accusation brought against her rests solely on the authority of Dumont. See also a True account of the horrid Conspiracy against the Life of His most Sacred Majesty William III. 1692; Reflections upon the late horrid Conspiracy contrived by some of the French Court to murder

The campaign in the Netherlands ended without any other event deserving to be recorded. On the eighteenth of October William arrived in England. Late in the evening of the twentieth he reached Kensington, having traversed the whole length of the capital. His reception was cordial : the crowd was great : the acclamations were loud : and all the windows along his route, from Aldgate to Piccadilly, were lighted up.[1]

Return of William to England

But, notwithstanding these favourable symptoms, the nation was disappointed and discontented. The war had been unsuccessful by land. By sea a great advantage had been gained, but had not been improved. The general expectation had been that the victory of May would be followed by a descent on the coast of France, that Saint Maloes would be bombarded, that the last remains of Tourville's squadron would be destroyed, and that the arsenals of Brest and Rochefort would be laid in ruins. This expectation was, no doubt, unreasonable. It did not follow, because Rooke and his seamen had silenced the batteries hastily thrown up by Bellefonds, that it would be safe to expose ships to the fire of regular fortresses. The government, however, was not less sanguine than the nation. Great preparations were made. The allied fleet, having been speedily refitted at Portsmouth, stood out again to sea. Rooke was sent to examine the soundings and the currents along the shore of Britanny.[2] Transports were collected at Saint Helen's. Fourteen thousand troops were assembled at Portsdown under the command of Meinhart Schomberg, who had been rewarded for his father's services and his own with the highest rank in the Irish peerage, and was now Duke of Leinster. Under him were Ruvigny, who, for his good service at Aghrim, had been created Earl of Galway, La Melloniere and Cambon with their gallant bands of refugees, and Argyle with the regiment which bore his name, and which, as it began to be faintly rumoured, had last winter done something strange and horrible in a wild country of rocks and snow, never yet explored by any Englishman.

Naval maladministration

On the twenty-sixth of July the troops were all on board. The transports sailed, and in a few hours joined the naval armament in the neighbourhood of Portland. On the twenty-eighth a general council of war was held. All the naval commanders, with Russell at their head, declared that it would be madness to carry their ships within the range of the guns of Saint Maloes, and that the town must be reduced to straits by land before the men of war in the harbour could, with any

His Majesty in Flanders, 1692 ; Burnet, ii. 92. ; Vernon's letters from the camp to Colt, published by Tindal ; the London Gazette, Aug. 11. The Paris Gazette contains not one word on the subject,—a most significant silence.

[1] London Gazette, Oct. 20. 24. 1692.   [2] See his report in Burchett.

MEINHART SCHOMBERG, DUKE OF LEINSTER

From an engraving by J. Smith, after a painting by Sir G. Kneller

chance of success, be attacked from the sea. The military men declared with equal unanimity that the land forces could effect nothing against the town without the co-operation of the fleet. It was then considered whether it would be advisable to make an attempt on Brest or Rochefort. Russell and the other flag officers, among whom were Rooke, Shovel, Van Almonde, and Evertsen, pronounced that the summer was too far spent for either enterprise.[1] We must suppose that an opinion in which so many distinguished admirals, both English and Dutch, concurred, however strange it may seem to us, was in conformity with what were then the established principles of the art of maritime war. But why all these questions could not have been fully discussed a week earlier, why fourteen thousand troops should have been shipped and sent to sea, before it had been considered what they were to do, or whether it would be possible for them to do any thing, we may reasonably wonder. The armament returned to Saint Helen's, to the astonishment and disgust of the whole nation.[2] The ministers blamed the commanders : the commanders blamed the ministers. The reproaches exchanged between Nottingham and Russell were loud and angry. Nottingham, upright, industrious, versed in civil business, and eloquent in parliamentary debate, was deficient in the qualities of a war minister, and was not at all aware of his deficiencies. Between him and the whole body of professional sailors there was a feud of long standing. He had, some time before the Revolution, been a Lord of the Admiralty; and his own opinion was that he had then acquired a profound knowledge of maritime affairs. This opinion however he had very much to himself. Men who had passed half their lives on the waves, and who had been in battles, storms, and shipwrecks, were impatient of his somewhat pompous lectures and reprimands, and pronounced him a mere pedant, who, with all his book learning, was ignorant of what every cabin boy knew. Russell had always been froward, arrogant, and mutinous; and now prosperity and glory brought out his vices in full strength. With the government which he had saved he took all the liberties of an insolent servant who believes himself to be necessary, treated the orders of his superiors with contemptuous levity, resented reproof, however gentle, as an outrage, furnished no plan of his own, and showed a sullen determination to execute no plan furnished by any body else. To Nottingham he had a strong and very natural antipathy. They were indeed an ill matched pair. Nottingham was a Tory : Russell was a Whig. Nottingham

[1] London Gazette, July 28. 1692. See the resolutions of the Council of War in Burchett. In a letter to Nottingham, dated July 10., Russell says, "Six weeks will near conclude what we call summer." Lords' Journals, Dec. 19. 1692.

[2] Monthly Mercury, Aug. and Sept. 1692.

was a speculative seaman, confident in his theories : Russell was a practical seaman, proud of his achievements. The strength of Nottingham lay in speech : the strength of Russell lay in action. Nottingham's demeanour was decorous even to formality: Russell was passionate and rude. Lastly, Nottingham was an honest man ; and Russell was a villain. They now became mortal enemies. The Admiral sneered at the Secretary's ignorance of naval affairs : the Secretary accused the Admiral of sacrificing the public interests to mere wayward humour ; and both were in the right.[1]

While they were wrangling, the merchants of all the ports in the kingdom were clamouring against the naval administration. The victory of which the nation was so proud was, in the City, pronounced to have been a positive disaster. During some months before the battle all the maritime strength of the enemy had been collected in two great masses, one in the Mediterranean and one in the Atlantic. There had consequently been little privateering ; and the voyage to New England or Jamaica had been almost as safe as in time of peace. Since the battle, the remains of the force which had lately been collected under Tourville were dispersed over the ocean. Even the passage from England to Ireland was insecure. Every week it was announced that twenty, thirty, fifty vessels belonging to London or Bristol had been taken by the French. More than a hundred prizes were carried during that autumn into Saint Maloes alone. It would have been far better, in the opinion of the shipowners and of the underwriters, that the Royal Sun had still been afloat with her thousand fighting men on board than that she should be lying a heap of ashes on the beach at Cherburg, while her crew, distributed among twenty brigantines, prowled for booty over the sea between Cape Finisterre and Cape Clear.[2]

The privateers of Dunkirk had long been celebrated ; and among them, John Bart, humbly born, and scarcely able to sign his name, but eminently brave and active, had attained an undisputed preeminence. In the country of Anson and Hawke, of Howe and Rodney, of Duncan, Saint Vincent, and Nelson, the name of the most daring and skilful corsair would have little chance of being remembered. But France, among whose many unquestioned titles to glory very few are derived from naval war, still ranks Bart among her great men. In the autumn of 1692 this enterprising freebooter was the terror of all the English and Dutch merchants who traded with the Baltic. He took and destroyed

[1] Evelyn's Diary, July 25. 1692 ; Burnet, ii. 94, 95., and Lord Dartmouth's Note. The history of the quarrel between Russell and Nottingham will be best learned from the Parliamentary Journals and Debates of the Session of 169⅔.

[2] Commons' Journals, Nov. 19. 1692 ; Burnet, ii. 95. ; Grey's Debates, Nov. 21. 1692 ; Paris Gazettes of August and September ; Narcissus Luttrell's Diary.

vessels close to the eastern coast of our island. He even ventured to land in Northumberland, and burned many houses before the trainbands could be collected to oppose him. The prizes which he carried back into his native port were estimated at about a hundred thousand pounds sterling.[1] About the same time a younger adventurer, destined to equal or surpass Bart, Du Guay Trouin, was entrusted with the command of a small armed vessel. The intrepid boy,—for he was not yet twenty years old,—entered the estuary of the Shannon, sacked a mansion in the county of Clare, and did not reimbark till a detachment from the garrison of Limerick marched against him.[2]

While our trade was interrupted and our shores menaced by these rovers, some calamities which no human prudence could have averted

Earthquake at Port Royal increased the public ill humour. An earthquake of terrible violence laid waste in less than three minutes the flourishing colony of Jamaica. Whole plantations changed their place. Whole villages were swallowed up. Port Royal, the fairest and wealthiest city which the English had yet built in the New World, renowned for its quays, for its warehouses, and for its stately streets, which were said to rival Cheapside, was turned into a mass of ruins. Fifteen hundred of the inhabitants were buried under their own dwellings. The effect of this disaster was severely felt by many of the great mercantile houses of London and Bristol.[3]

A still heavier calamity was the failure of the harvest. The summer had been wet all over Western Europe. Those heavy rains

Distress in England which had impeded the exertions of the French pioneers in the trenches of Namur had been fatal to the crops. Old men remembered no such year since 1648. No fruit ripened. The price of the quarter of wheat doubled. The evil was aggravated by the state of our silver coin, which had been clipped to such an extent that the words pound and shilling had ceased to have a fixed meaning. Compared with France indeed England might well be esteemed prosperous. Here the public burdens were heavy : there they were crushing. Here the labouring man was forced to husband his coarse barley loaf : but there it not seldom happened that the wretched peasant was found dead on the earth with halfchewed grass in his mouth. Our ancestors found some consolation in thinking that they were gradually wearing out the strength of their formidable enemy, and that his resources were likely to be drained sooner than theirs. Still there was much suffering

---

[1] See Bart's Letters of Nobility, and the Paris Gazettes of the autumn of 1692.

[2] Mémoires de Du Guay Trouin.

[3] London Gazette, Aug. 11. 1692 ; Evelyn's Diary, Aug. 10. ; Monthly Mercury for September ; A Full Account of the late dreadful Earthquake at Port Royal in Jamaica, licensed Sept. 9. 1692.

Le sieur Jean Baert, Capitaine de Vaisseaux
de Roy, annoblit par sa Majesté, et fait cheualier de l'Ordre de S. Louis, Natif de la Ville de Dunquerk.

JEAN BART

From an engraving in the Cabinet des Estampes

and much repining. In some counties mobs attacked the granaries. The necessity of retrenchment was felt by families of every rank. An idle man of wit and pleasure, who little thought that his buffoonery would ever be cited to illustrate the history of his times, complained that, in this year, wine ceased to be put on many hospitable tables where he had been accustomed to see it, and that its place was supplied by punch.[1]

A symptom of public distress much more alarming than the substitution of brandy and lemons for claret was the increase of crime.

Increase of crime During the autumn of 1692 and the following winter, the capital was kept in constant terror by housebreakers. One gang, thirteen strong, entered the mansion of the Duke of Ormond in Saint James's Square, and all but succeeded in carrying off his magnificent plate and jewels. Another gang made an attempt on Lambeth Palace.[2] When stately abodes, guarded by numerous servants, were in such danger, it may easily be believed that no shopkeeper's till or stock could be safe. From Bow to Hyde Park, from Thames Street to Bloomsbury, there was no parish in which some quiet dwelling had not been sacked by burglars.[3] Meanwhile the great roads were made almost impassable by freebooters who formed themselves into troops larger than had before been known. There was a sworn fraternity of twenty footpads which met at an alehouse in Southwark.[4] But the most formidable band of plunderers consisted of two and twenty horsemen.[5] It should seem that, at this time, a journey of fifty miles through the wealthiest and most populous shires of England was as dangerous as a pilgrimage across the deserts of Arabia. The Oxford stage coach was pillaged in broad day after a bloody fight.[6] A waggon laden with fifteen thousand pounds of public money was stopped and ransacked. As this operation took some time, all the travellers who came to the spot while the thieves were busy were seized and guarded. When the booty had been secured, the prisoners were suffered to depart on foot, but their horses, sixteen or eighteen in number, were shot or hamstringed, to prevent pursuit.[7] The Portsmouth mail was robbed twice in one week by men well armed and mounted.[8] Some jovial Essex squires, while riding after a hare, were themselves chased

[1] Evelyn's Diary, June 25. Oct. 1. 1690; Narcissus Luttrell's Diary, June 1692, May 1693; Monthly Mercury, April, May, and June 1693; Tom Brown's Description of a Country Life, 1692.

[2] Narcissus Luttrell's Diary, Nov. 1692.

[3] See, for example, the London Gazette of Jan. 12. 169¾.

[4] Narcissus Luttrell's Diary, Dec. 1692.   [5] Ibid. Jan. 1693.   [6] Ibid. July 1692.

[7] Evelyn's Diary, Nov. 20. 1692; Narcissus Luttrell's Diary; London Gazette, Nov. 24.; Hop to the Greffier of the States General, Nov. 18/28.

[8] London Gazette, Dec. 19. 1692.

THE
GOLDEN Farmer's
Laſt FAREWEEL

Who was arraigned and found Guilty of wilfull Murther, and likewiſe many notorious Robberies; for which he received a due Sentance of Death, and was accordingly Executed on the 22d. of December, 1690 in Fleetſtreet.

To the Tune of The Rich Merchant-man.   Licenſed according to Order.

Unto you all this day,
 my Faults I do declare,
Alas! I have not long to stay,
 I muſt for Death prepare
A moſt notorious Wretch,
 I many years have been,
For which I now at length muſt ſtretch,
 a juſt Reward for Sin:
No Tongue, nor Pen can tell
 what Sorrows I conceive;
Your Golden Farmer's laſt Farewell,
 unto the World I leave.

A Gang of Robbers then
 my ſelf did entertain;
Notorious hardy Highway-men,
 who did like Ruffians reign:
We'd rob, we'd laugh, and joke,
 and revel night and day;
But now the knot of us is broke,
 'tis I that leads the way:
No Tongue nor Pen can tell
 what Sorrows I conceive,
Your Golden Farmer's laſt Farewell
 unto the World I leave.

We Houſes did beſet,
 and robb'd them night and day,
Making all Fiſh that came to Net,
 for ſtill we clear'd the way;
Five hundred Pounds and more,
 in Money, Gold, and Plate,
From the right Owner we have bore,
 but now my wretched State,
No Tongue nor Pen can tell, &c.

We always gagg'd and bound
 moſt of the Family,
That we might ſearch untill we found
 their hidden Treaſury;
Which if we could not find,
 a Piſtol cock'd ſtreightway,
Preſented at their Breaſt, to make
 them ſhew us where it lay:
No Tongue nor Pen can tell, &c.

I having run my Race,
 I now at laſt do ſee,
That in much ſhame and ſad diſgrace,
 my Life will ended be:
I took Delight to rob,
 and rifle rich and poor,
But now at laſt, my Friend Old Mob,
 I ne'er ſhall ſee thee more:
No Tongue nor Pen can tell;
 what Sorrows I conceive;
Your Golden Farmer's laſt Farewell,
 unto the World I leave.

The Bloud which I have ſpilt,
 now on my Conſcience lies,
The heavy dreadfull thought of Guilt
 my Senſes do's ſurprize;
The thoughts of Death I fear,
 although a juſt Reward,
As knowing that I muſt appear,
 before the living Lord,
No Tongue nor Pen can tell, &c.

I ſolemnly declare,
 who am to Juſtice brought,
All kind of wicked Sins that are,
 I eagerly have wrought;
No Villains are more rife,
 than thoſe which I have bred;
And thus a moſt perfidious Life
 I in this World have led:
No Tongue nor Pen can tell, &c.

Long have I liv'd you ſee,
 by this unlawful Trade,
And at the length am brought to be
 a juſt Example made:
Good God my Sins forgive,
 whoſe Laws I did offend,
for here I may no longer live,
 my Life is at an end:
No Tongue nor Pen can tell;
 what Sorrows I conceive;
Your Golden Farmer's laſt Farewell,
 unto the World I leave.

Printed for P. Brooksby, J. Deacon, J. Blare, and J. Back.

THE GOLDEN FARMER'S LAST FAREWELL

From the Bagford Ballads

and run down by nine hunters of a different sort, and were heartily glad to find themselves at home again, though with empty pockets.[1]

The friends of the government asserted that the marauders were all Jacobites ; and indeed there were some appearances which gave colour to the assertion. For example, fifteen butchers, going on a market day to buy beasts at Thame, were stopped by a large gang, and compelled first to deliver their moneybags, and then to drink King James's health in brandy.[2] The thieves, however, to do them justice, showed, in the exercise of their calling, no decided preference for any political party. Some of them fell in with Marlborough near Saint Albans, and, notwithstanding his known hostility to the Court and his recent imprisonment, compelled him to deliver up five hundred guineas, which he doubtless never ceased to regret to the last moment of his long career of prosperity and glory.[3]

When William, on his return from the Continent, learned to what an extent these outrages had been carried, he expressed great indignation, and announced his resolution to put down the malefactors with a strong hand. A veteran robber was induced to turn informer, and to lay before the King a list of the chief highwaymen, and a full account of their habits and of their favourite haunts. It was said that this list contained not less than eighty names.[4] Strong parties of cavalry were sent out to protect the roads ; and this precaution, which would, in ordinary circumstances, have caused much murmuring, seems to have been generally approved. A fine regiment, now called the Second Dragoon Guards, which had distinguished itself by activity and success in the irregular war against the Irish Rapparees, was selected to guard several of the great avenues of the capital. Blackheath, Barnet, Hounslow, became places of arms.[5] In a few weeks the roads were as safe as usual. The executions were numerous : for, till the evil had been suppressed, the King resolutely refused to listen to any solicitations for mercy.[6] Among those who suffered was James Whitney, the most celebrated captain of banditti in the kingdom. He had been, during some months, the terror of all who travelled from London either northward or westward, and was at length with difficulty secured after a desperate conflict in which one soldier was killed and several wounded.[7]

---

[1] Narcissus Luttrell's Diary, Dec. 1692.   [2] Ibid. Nov. 1692.   [3] Ibid. August 1692.

[4] Hop to the Greffier of the States General, $\frac{\text{Dec. 23.}}{\text{Jan. 2.}}$ 169$\frac{2}{3}$. The Dutch despatches of this year are filled with stories of robberies.

[5] Hop, $\frac{\text{Dec. 23.}}{\text{Jan. 2.}}$ 169$\frac{2}{3}$; Historical Records or the Queen's Bays, published by authority ; Narcissus Luttrell's Diary, Nov. 15.

[6] Narcissus Luttrell's Diary, Dec. 22.

[7] Ibid. Dec. 1692 ; Hop, Jan. $\frac{8}{15}$. Hop calls Whitney, "den befaamsten roover in Engelandt."

The True Effigies of James Whitney, the Notorious Highwayman

JAMES WHITNEY

From an engraving in the British Museum

The London Gazette announced that the famous highwayman had been taken, and invited all persons who had been robbed by him to repair to Newgate and to see whether they could identify him. To identify him should have been easy : for he had a wound in the face, and had lost a thumb.[1] He, however, in the hope of perplexing the witnesses for the Crown, expended a hundred pounds in procuring a sumptuous embroidered suit against the day of trial. This ingenious device was frustrated by his hardhearted keepers. He was put to the bar in his ordinary clothes, convicted, and sentenced to death.[2] He had previously tried to ransom himself by offering to raise a fine troop of cavalry, all highwaymen, for service in Flanders : but his offer had been rejected.[3] He had one resource still left. He declared that he was privy to a treasonable plot. Some Jacobite lords had promised him immense rewards if he would, at the head of his gang, fall upon the King at a stag hunt in Windsor Forest. There was nothing intrinsically improbable in Whitney's story. Indeed a design very similar to that which he imputed to the malecontents was, only three years later, actually formed by some of them, and was all but carried into execution. But it was far better that a few bad men should go unpunished than that all honest men should live in fear of being falsely accused by felons sentenced to the gallows. Chief Justice Holt advised the King to let the law take its course. William, never much inclined to give credit to stories about conspiracies, assented. The Captain, as he was called, was hanged in Smithfield, and made a most penitent end.[4]

Meanwhile, in the midst of discontent, distress, and disorder, had begun a session of Parliament singularly eventful, a session from which **Meeting of Parliament** dates a new era in the history of English finance, a session in which some grave constitutional questions, not yet entirely set at rest, were for the first time debated.

It is much to be lamented that any account of this session which can be framed out of the scanty and dispersed materials now accessible **State of parties** must leave many things obscure. The relations of the parliamentary factions were, during this year, in a singularly complicated state. Each of the two Houses was divided and subdivided by several lines. To omit minor distinctions, there was the great line which separated the Whig party from the Tory party; and there was the great line which separated the official men and their friends and dependents, who were sometimes called the Court party, from those who were sometimes nicknamed the Grumbletonians and sometimes

---

[1] London Gazette, January 2. 169$\frac{2}{3}$.

[2] Narcissus Luttrell's Diary, Jan. 169$\frac{2}{3}$.   [3] Ibid. Dec. 1692.

[4] Ibid. January and February; Hop, $\frac{\text{Jan. 31.}}{\text{Feb. 10.}}$ and Feb. $\frac{2}{13}$. 1693; Letter to Secretary Trenchard, 1694 ; New Court Contrivances, or More Sham Plots still, 1693.

honoured with the appellation of the Country party. And these two great lines were intersecting lines. For of the servants of the Crown and of their adherents about one half were Whigs and one half Tories. It is also to be remembered that there was, quite distinct from the feud between Whigs and Tories, quite distinct also from the feud between those who were in and those who were out, a feud between the Lords as Lords and the Commons as Commons. The spirit both of the hereditary and of the elective chamber had been thoroughly roused in the preceding session by the dispute about the Court of the Lord High Steward ; and they met in a pugnacious mood.

The speech which the King made at the opening of the session was skilfully framed for the purpose of conciliating the Houses. He came, he told them, to ask for their advice and assistance. He *The King's* congratulated them on the victory of La Hogue. He acknow- *speech* ledged with much concern that the operations of the allies had been less successful by land than by sea; but he warmly declared that, both by land and by sea, the valour of his English subjects had been preeminently conspicuous. The distress of his people, he said, was his own : his interest was inseparable from theirs : it was painful to him to call on them to make sacrifices : but from sacrifices which were necessary to the safety of the English nation and of the Protestant religion no good Englishman and no good Protestant would shrink.[1]

The Commons thanked the King in cordial terms for his gracious speech.[2] But the Lords were in a bad humour. Two of their body, Marlborough and Huntingdon, had, during the recess, when *Question of* an invasion and an insurrection were hourly expected, been *privilege* sent to the Tower, and were still under recognisances. Had *raised by* a country gentleman or a merchant been taken up and held to bail on *the Lords* even slighter grounds at so alarming a crisis, the Lords would assuredly not have interfered. But they were easily moved to anger by anything that looked like an indignity offered to their own order. They not only crossexamined with great severity Aaron Smith, the Solicitor of the Treasury, whose character, to say the truth, entitled him to little indulgence, but passed, by thirty five votes to twenty eight, a resolution implying a censure on the Judges of the King's Bench, men certainly not inferior in probity, and very far superior in legal learning, to any peer of the realm. The King thought it prudent to sooth the wounded pride of the nobility by ordering the recognisances to be cancelled ; and with this concession the House was satisfied, to the great vexation of the Jacobites, who had hoped that the quarrel would be prosecuted to some fatal issue, and who, finding themselves disappointed, vented

[1] Lords' and Commons' Journals, Nov. 4., Jan. 1692.
[2] Commons' Journals, Nov. 10. 1692.

their spleen by railing at the tameness of the degenerate barons of England.[1]

Both Houses held long and earnest deliberations on the state of the nation. The King, when he requested their advice, had, perhaps, not foreseen that his words would be construed into an invitation to scrutinise every part of the administration, and to offer suggestions touching matters which parliaments have generally thought it expedient to leave entirely to the Crown. Some of the discontented peers proposed that a Committee, chosen partly by the Lords and partly by the Commons, should be authorised to enquire into the whole management of public affairs. But it was generally apprehended that such a Committee would become a second and more powerful Privy Council, independent of the Crown, and unknown to the constitution. The motion was therefore rejected by forty eight votes to thirty six. On this occasion the ministers, with scarcely an exception, voted in the majority. A protest was signed by eighteen of the minority, among whom were the bitterest Whigs and the bitterest Tories in the whole peerage.[2]

Debates on the state of the nation

The Houses enquired, each for itself, into the causes of the public calamities. The Commons resolved themselves into a Grand Committee to consider of the advice to be given to the King. From the concise abstracts and fragments which have come down to us it seems that, in this Committee, which continued to sit many days, the debates wandered over a vast space. One member spoke of the prevalence of highway robbery : another deplored the quarrel between the Queen and the Princess, and proposed that two or three gentlemen should be deputed to wait on Her Majesty and try to make matters up. A third described the machinations of the Jacobites in the preceding spring. It was notorious, he said, that preparations had been made for a rising, and that arms and horses had been collected ; yet not a single traitor had been brought to justice.[3]

The events of the war by land and sea furnished matter for several earnest debates. Many members complained of the preference given to aliens over Englishmen. The whole battle of Steinkirk was fought over again ; and severe reflections were thrown on Solmes. " Let English soldiers be commanded by none but English generals," was the almost universal cry. Seymour, who had once been distinguished by his hatred of foreigners, but who, since he had been at the Board of Treasury, had

---

[1] See the Lords' Journals from Nov. 7. to Nov. 18. 1692 ; Burnet, ii. 102. Tindal's account of these proceedings was taken from letters addressed by Warre, Under Secretary of State, to Colt, Envoy at Hanover. Letter to Mr. Secretary Trenchard, 1694.

[2] Lords' Journals, Dec. 7. ; Tindal, from the Colt Papers ; Burnet, ii. 105.

[3] Grey's Debates, Nov. 21. and 23. 1692.

Henry Comte de Naſsau D'Auverquerk Feld Marshab
des Armees de L.H.P. Les Estats Generaux des Provinces Vnies. &c.

G. Kneller S.R. Imp. & Ang. Eques Aur. pinx.   I. Smith fec.   Sold by I. Smith at ÿ Lyon & Crown in Ruſsel Street Covent Garden

HENRI DE NASSAU D'AUVERQUERQUE
From a mezzotint by J. Smith, after a painting by Sir G. Kneller

H.E. V   M

reconsidered his opinions, asked where English generals were to be found. "I have no love for foreigners as foreigners : but we have no choice. Men are not born generals : nay, a man may be a very valuable captain or major, and not be equal to the conduct of an army. Nothing but experience will form great commanders : very few of our country-men have that experience ; and therefore we must for the present employ strangers." Lowther followed on the same side. "We have had a long peace ; and the consequence is that we have not a sufficient supply of officers fit for high commands. The parks and the camp at Hounslow were very poor military schools, when compared with the fields of battle and the lines of contravallation in which the great com-manders of the continental nations have learned their art." In reply to these arguments an orator on the other side was so absurd as to declare that he could point out ten Englishmen who, if they were in the French service, would be made Marshals. Four or five colonels who had been at Steinkirk took part in the debate. It was said of them that they showed as much modesty in speech as they had shown courage in action ; and, from the very imperfect report which has come down to us, the compliment seems to have been not undeserved. They did not join in the vulgar cry against the Dutch. They spoke well of the foreign officers generally, and did full justice to the valour and conduct with which Auverquerque had rescued the shattered remains of Mackay's division from what seemed certain destruction. But in defence of Solmes not a word was said. His severity, his haughty manners, and, above all, the indifference with which he had looked on while the English, borne down by overwhelming numbers, were fighting hand to hand with the French household troops, had made him so odious that many members were prepared to vote for an address requesting that he might be removed, and that his place might be filled by Talmash, who, since the disgrace of Marlborough, was universally allowed to be the best officer in the army. But Talmash's friends judiciously interfered. "I have," said one of them, "a true regard for that gentleman ; and I implore you not to do him an injury under the notion of doing him a kindness. Consider that you are usurping what is peculiarly the King's prerogative. You are turning officers out and putting officers in." The debate ended without any vote of censure on Solmes. But a hope was expressed, in language not very parliamentary, that what had been said in the Committee would be reported to the King, and that His Majesty would not disregard the general wish of the representatives of his people.[1]

The Commons next proceeded to enquire into the naval administra-tion, and very soon came to a quarrel with the Lords on that subject.

[1] Grey's Debates, Nov. 21. 1692 ; Colt Papers in Tindal.

LIEUTENANT-GENERAL THOMAS TALMASH

From an engraving by J. Houbraken, after a painting by Sir G. Kneller

That there had been mismanagement somewhere was but too evident. It was hardly possible to acquit both Russell and Nottingham ; and each House stood by its own member.   The Commons had, at the opening of the session, unanimously passed a vote of thanks to Russell for his conduct at La Hogue.   They now, in the Grand Committee of Advice, took into consideration the miscarriages which had followed the battle.   A motion was made so vaguely worded that it could hardly be said to mean any thing.   It was understood however to imply a censure on Nottingham, and was therefore strongly opposed by his friends.   On the division the Ayes were a hundred and sixty five, the Noes a hundred and sixty four.[1]

On the very next day Nottingham appealed to the Lords.   He told his story with all the skill of a practised orator, and with all the authority which belongs to unblemished integrity.   He then laid on the table a great mass of papers, which he requested the House to read and consider.   The Peers seem to have examined the papers seriously and diligently.   The result of the examination was by no means favourable to Russell.   Yet it was thought unjust to condemn him unheard ; and it was difficult to devise any way in which their Lordships could hear him.   At last it was resolved to send the papers down to the Commons with a message which imported that, in the opinion of the Upper House, there was a case against the Admiral which he ought to be called upon to answer.   With the papers was sent an abstract of the contents.[2]

The message was not very respectfully received.   Russell had, at that moment, a popularity which he little deserved, but which will not seem strange to us when we remember that the public knew nothing of his treasons, and knew that he was the only living Englishman who had won a great battle.   The abstract of the papers was read by the clerk. Russell then spoke with great applause ; and his friends pressed for an immediate decision.   Sir Christopher Musgrave very justly observed that it was impossible to pronounce judgment on such a pile of despatches without perusing them : but this objection was overruled.   The Whigs regarded the accused member as one of themselves : many of the Tories were dazzled by the splendour of his recent victory ; and neither Whigs nor Tories were disposed to show any deference for the authority of the Peers.   The House, without reading the papers, passed an unanimous resolution expressing warm approbation of Russell's whole conduct. The temper of the assembly was such that some ardent Whigs thought that they might now venture to propose a vote of censure on Nottingham by name.   But the attempt failed.   " I am ready," said Lowther,—and he doubtless expressed what many felt,—" I am ready to support any

---

[1] Tindal, Colt Papers ; Commons' Journals, Jan. 11. 169⅔.

Colt Papers in Tindal ; Lords' Journals from Dec. 6. to Dec. 19. 1692, inclusive.

motion that may do honour to the Admiral : but I cannot join in an attack on the Secretary of State. For, to my knowledge, their Majesties have no more zealous, laborious, or faithful servant than my Lord Nottingham." Finch exerted all his mellifluous eloquence in defence of his brother, and contrived, without directly opposing himself to the prevailing sentiment, to insinuate that Russell's conduct had not been faultless. The vote of censure on Nottingham was not pressed. But the vote which pronounced Russell's conduct to have been deserving of all praise was communicated to the Lords ; and the papers which they had sent down were very unceremoniously returned.[1] The Lords, much offended, demanded a free conference. It was granted ; and the managers of the two Houses met in the Painted Chamber. Rochester, in the name of his brethren, expressed a wish to be informed of the grounds on which the Admiral had been declared faultless. To this appeal the gentlemen who stood on the other side of the table answered only that they had not been authorised to give any explanation, but that they would report to those who had sent them what had been said.[2]

By this time the Commons were thoroughly tired of the enquiry into the conduct of the war. The members had got rid of much of the ill humour which they had brought up with them from their country seats by the simple process of talking it away. Burnet hints that those arts of which Caermarthen and Trevor were the great masters were employed for the purpose of averting votes which would have seriously embarrassed the government. But, though it is not improbable that a few noisy pretenders to patriotism may have been quieted with bags of guineas, it would be absurd to suppose that the House generally was influenced in this manner. Whoever has seen anything of such assemblies knows that the spirit with which they enter on long enquiries very soon flags, and that their resentment, if not kept alive by injudicious opposition, cools fast. In a short time every body was sick of the Grand Committee of Advice. The debates had been tedious and desultory. The resolutions which had been carried were for the most part merely childish. The King was to be humbly advised to employ men of ability and integrity. He was to be humbly advised to employ men who would stand by him against James. The patience of the House was wearied out by long discussions ending in the pompous promulgation of truisms like these. At last the explosion came. One of the grumblers called the attention of the Grand Committee to the alarming fact that two Dutchmen were employed in the Ordnance department, and moved that the King should be requested to dismiss

[1] As to the proceedings of this day in the House of Commons, see the Journals, Dec. 20., and the letter of Robert Wilmot, M.P. for Derby, to his colleague Anchitel Grey, in Grey's Debates.

[2] Commons' Journals, Jan. 4. 169⅔.

them. The motion was received with disdainful mockery. It was remarked that the military men especially were loud in the expression of contempt. "Do we seriously think of going to the King and telling him that, as he has condescended to ask our advice at this momentous crisis, we humbly advise him to turn a Dutch storekeeper out of the Tower? Really, if we have no more important suggestion to carry up to the throne, we may as well go to our dinners." The members generally were of the same mind. The chairman was voted out of the chair, and was not directed to ask leave to sit again. The Grand Committee ceased to exist. The resolutions which it had passed were formally reported to the House. One of them was rejected : the others were suffered to drop; and the Commons, after considering during several weeks what advice they should give to the King, ended by giving him no advice at all.[1]

The temper of the Lords was different. From many circumstances it appears that there was no place where the Dutch were, at this time, so much hated as in the Upper House. The dislike with which an Englishman of the middle class regarded the King's foreign friends was merely national. The preferment which they had obtained was preferment which he would have had no chance of obtaining if they had never existed. But to an English peer they were objects of personal jealousy. They stood between him and Majesty. They intercepted from him the rays of royal favour. The preference given to them wounded him both in his interests and in his pride. His chance of a Garter or of a troop of Life Guards was much smaller since they had become his competitors. He might have been Master of the Horse but for Auverquerque, Master of the Robes but for Zulestein, Groom of the Stole but for Bentinck.[2] The ill humour of the aristocracy was inflamed by Marlborough, who, at this time, affected the character of a patriot persecuted for standing up against the Dutch in defence of the interests of his native land, and who did not foresee that a day would come when he would be accused of sacrificing the interests of his native land to gratify the Dutch. The Peers determined to present an address requesting William not to place his English troops under the command of a foreign general. They took up very seriously that question which had moved the House of Commons to laughter, and solemnly counselled their Sovereign not to employ foreigners in his magazines. At Marlborough's suggestion they urged the King to insist that the youngest English general should take precedence of the oldest general in the

[1] Colt Papers in Tindal ; Commons' Journals, Dec. 16. 1692, Jan. 11. 169⅔ ; Burnet, ii. 104.

[2] The peculiar antipathy of the English nobles to the Dutch favourites is mentioned in a highly interesting note written by Renaudot in 1698, and preserved among the Archives of the French Foreign Office.

service of the States General. It was, they said, derogatory to the dignity of the Crown, that an officer who held a commission from His Majesty should ever be commanded by an officer who held a similar commission from a republic. To this advice, evidently dictated by an ignoble malevolence to Holland, William, who troubled himself little about votes of the Upper House which were not backed by the Lower, returned, as might have been expected, a very short and dry answer.[1]

While the enquiry into the conduct of the war was pending, the Commons resumed the consideration of an important subject which had occupied much of their attention in the preceding year. **Bill for the** The Bill for the Regulation of Trials in cases of High **Regulation** Treason was again brought in, but was strongly opposed by **of Trials in cases of** the official men, both Whigs and Tories. Somers, now **Treason** Attorney General, strongly recommended delay. That the law, as it stood, was open to grave objections, was not denied : but it was contended that the proposed reform would, at that moment, produce more harm than good. Nobody would assert that, under the existing government, the lives of innocent subjects were in any danger. Nobody would deny that the government itself was in great danger. Was it the part of wise men to increase the perils of that which was already in serious peril, for the purpose of giving new security to that which was already perfectly secure? Those who held this language were twitted with their inconsistency, and asked why they had not ventured to oppose the bill in the preceding session. They answered very plausibly that the events which had taken place during the recess had taught an important lesson to all who were capable of learning. The country had been threatened at once with invasion and insurrection. No rational man doubted that many traitors had made preparations for joining the French, and had collected arms, ammunition, and horses for that purpose. Yet, though there was abundant moral evidence against these enemies of their country, it had not been possible to find legal evidence against a single one of them. The law of treason might, in theory, be harsh, and had undoubtedly, in times past, been grossly abused. But a statesman, who troubled himself less about theory than about practice, and less about times past than about the time present, would pronounce that law not too stringent but too lax, and would, while the commonwealth remained in extreme jeopardy, refuse to consent to any further relaxation. In spite of all opposition, however, the principle of the bill was approved by one hundred and seventy one votes to one hundred and fifty two. But in the committee it was moved and carried that the new rules of procedure should not come into operation till after the end of the war with France. When the

[1] Colt Papers in Tindal ; Lords' Journals, Nov. 28. and 29. 1692, Feb. 18. and 24. 169⅔.

report was brought up the House divided on this amendment, and ratified it by a hundred and forty five votes to a hundred and twenty five.   The bill was consequently suffered to drop.[1]   Had it gone up to the Peers it would in all probability have been lost after causing another quarrel between the Houses.   For the Peers were fully determined that no such bill should pass, unless it contained a clause altering the constitution of the Lord High Steward's Court ; and a clause altering the constitution of the Lord High Steward's Court would have been less likely than ever to find favour with the Commons.   For in the course of this session an event took place which proved that the great were only too well protected by the law as it stood, and which well deserves to be recorded as a striking illustration of the state of manners and morals in that age.

Of all the actors who were then on the English stage the most graceful was William Mountford.   He had every physical qualification **Case of Lord** for his calling, a noble figure, a handsome face, a melodious **Mohun**   voice.   It was not easy to say whether he succeeded better in heroic or in ludicrous parts.   He was allowed to be both the best Alexander and the best Sir Courtly Nice that ever trod the boards. Queen Mary, whose knowledge was very superficial, but who had naturally a quick perception of what was excellent in art, admired him greatly.   He was a dramatist as well as a player, and has left us one comedy which is not contemptible.[2]

The most popular actress of the time was Anne Bracegirdle.   There were on the stage many women of more faultless beauty, but none whose features and deportment had such power to fascinate the senses and the hearts of men.   The sight of her bright black eyes and of her rich brown cheek sufficed to put the most turbulent audience into good humour.   It was said of her that in the crowded theatre she had as many lovers as she had male spectators.   Yet no lover, however rich, however high in rank, had prevailed on her to be his mistress.   Those who are acquainted with the parts which she was in the habit of playing, and with the epilogues which it was her especial business to recite, will not easily give her credit for any extraordinary measure of virtue or of delicacy.   She seems to have been a cold, vain, and interested coquette, who perfectly understood how much the influence of her charms was increased by the fame of a severity which cost her nothing, and who could venture to flirt with a succession of admirers, in the just confidence that no flame which she might kindle in them would thaw her own ice.[3]

[1] Grey's Debates, Nov. 18. 1692 ; Commons' Journals, Nov. 18., Dec. 1. 1692.

[2] See Cibber's Apology, and Mountford's Greenwich Park.

[3] See Cibber's Apology, Tom Brown's Works, and indeed the works of every man of wit and pleasure about town.

The Indian Queen

J. Smith ex. *W. Vincent sc.*

MRS. BRACEGIRDLE AS THE INDIAN QUEEN

From a mezzotint by J. Smith

Among those who pursued her with an insane desire was a profligate captain in the army named Hill. With Hill was closely bound in a league of debauchery and violence Charles Lord Mohun, a young noble-man whose life was one long revel and brawl. Hill, finding that the beautiful brunette was invincible, took it into his head that he was rejected for a more favoured rival, and that this rival was the brilliant Mountford. The jealous lover swore over his wine at a tavern that he would stab the villain. " And I," said Mohun, " will stand by my friend." From the tavern the pair went, with some soldiers whose services Hill had secured, to Drury Lane, where the lady was to sup. They lay some time in wait for her. As soon as she appeared in the street she was seized and hurried to a coach. She screamed for help : her mother clung round her : the whole neighbourhood rose ; and she was rescued. Hill and Mohun went away vowing vengeance. They swaggered sword in hand during two hours about the streets near Mountford's dwelling. The watch requested them to put up their weapons. But when the young lord announced that he was a peer, and bade the constables touch him if they dared, they let him pass. So strong was privilege then ; and so weak was law. Messengers were sent to warn Mountford of his danger : but unhappily they missed him. He came. A short altercation took place between him and Mohun ; and, while they were wrangling, Hill ran the unfortunate actor through the body, and fled.

The grand jury of Middlesex, consisting of gentlemen of note, found a bill of murder against Hill and Mohun. Hill escaped. Mohun was taken. His mother threw herself at William's feet, but in vain. " It was a cruel act," said the King : "I shall leave it to the law." The trial came on in the Court of the Lord High Steward ; and, as Parliament happened to be sitting, the culprit had the advantage of being judged by the whole body of the peerage. There was then no lawyer in the Upper House. It therefore became necessary, for the first time since Buckhurst had pronounced sentence on Essex and Southampton, that a peer who had never made jurisprudence his special study should preside over that grave tribunal. Caermarthen, who, as President of the Council, took precedence of all the nobility, was appointed Lord High Steward. A full report of the proceedings has come down to us. No person, who carefully examines that report, and attends to the opinion unanimously given by the Judges, in answer to a question which Nottingham drew up, and in which the facts established by the evidence are stated with perfect fairness, can doubt that the crime of murder was fully brought home to the prisoner. Such was the opinion of the King who was present during the trial ; and such was the almost unanimous opinion of the public. Had the issue been tried by Holt and twelve plain men

CHARLES, THIRD LORD MOHUN

From a mezzotint by J. Faber, after a painting by Sir G. Kneller

at the Old Bailey, there can be no doubt that a verdict of Guilty would have been returned.   The Peers, however, by sixty nine votes to fourteen, acquitted their accused brother.   One great nobleman was so brutal and stupid as to say, " After all the fellow was but a player ; and players are rogues."   All the newsletters, all the coffeehouse orators, complained that the blood of the poor was shed with impunity by the great.   Wits remarked that the only fair thing about the trial was the show of ladies in the galleries.   Letters and journals are still extant in which men of all shades of opinion, Whigs, Tories, Nonjurors, condemn the partiality of the tribunal.   It was not to be expected that, while the memory of this scandal was fresh in the public mind, the Commons would be induced to give any new advantage to accused peers.[1]

The Commons had, in the meantime, resumed the consideration of another highly important matter, the state of the trade with India. **Debates on the India trade** They had, towards the close of the preceding session, requested the King to dissolve the old Company and to constitute a new Company on such terms as he should think fit ; and he had promised to take their request into his serious consideration.   He now sent a message to inform them that it was out of his power to do what they had asked.   He had referred the charter of the old Company to the Judges, and the Judges had pronounced that, under the provisions of that charter, the old Company could not be dissolved without three years' notice, and must retain during those three years the exclusive privilege of trading to the East Indies.   He added that, being sincerely desirous to gratify the Commons, and finding himself unable to do so in the way which they had pointed out, he had tried to prevail on the old Company to agree to a compromise : but that body stood obstinately on its extreme rights ; and his endeavours had been frustrated.[2]

This message reopened the whole question.   The two factions which divided the City were instantly on the alert.   The debates in the House were long and warm.   Petitions against the old Company were laid on the table.   Satirical handbills against the new Company were distributed in the lobby.   At length, after much discussion, it was resolved to present an address requesting the King to give the notice which the Judges had pronounced necessary.   He promised to bear the subject in mind, and to do his best to promote the welfare of the

---

[1] The chief source of information about this case is the report of the trial, which will be found in the Collection of State Trials.   See Evelyn's Diary, February 4. 169⅔.   I have taken some circumstances from Narcissus Luttrell's Diary, from a letter to Sancroft, which is among the Tanner MSS. in the Bodleian Library, and from two letters addressed by Brewer to Wharton, which are also in the Bodleian Library.

[2] Commons' Journals, Nov. 14. 1692.

kingdom. With this answer the House was satisfied ; and the subject was not again mentioned till the next session.[1]

THE DUEL BETWEEN LORD MOHUN AND THE DUKE OF HAMILTON

From a mezzotint in the Sutherland Collection

The debates of the Commons on the conduct of the war, on the law of treason, and on the trade with India, occupied much time, and

[1] Commons' Journals of the Session, particularly of Nov. 17., Dec. 10., Feb. 25., March 3.; Colt Papers in Tindal.

produced no important result. But meanwhile real business was doing in the Committee of Supply and in the Committee of Ways and Means.

Supply   In the Committee of Supply the estimates passed rapidly. A few members declared it to be their opinion that England ought to withdraw her troops from the Continent, to carry on the war with vigour by sea, and to keep up only such an army as might be sufficient to repel any invader who might elude the vigilance of her fleets. But this doctrine, which speedily became and long continued to be the badge of one of the great parties in the state, was as yet professed only by a small minority which did not venture to call for a division.[1]

In the Committee of Ways and Means, it was determined that a great part of the charge of the year should be defrayed by means of an

Ways and Means: Land Tax   impost, which, though old in substance, was new in form. From a very early period to the middle of the seventeenth century, our Parliaments had provided for the extraordinary necessities of the government chiefly by granting subsidies. A subsidy was raised by an impost on the people of the realm in respect of their reputed estates. Landed property was the chief subject of taxation, and was assessed nominally at four shillings in the pound. But the assessment was made in such a way that it not only did not rise in proportion to the rise in the value of land or to the fall in the value of the precious metals, but went on constantly sinking, till at length the rate was in truth less than twopence in the pound. In the time of Charles the First a real tax of four shillings in the pound on land would probably have yielded near a million and a half: but a subsidy amounted to little more than fifty thousand pounds.[2]

The financiers of the Long Parliament devised a more efficient mode of taxing estates. The sum which was to be raised was fixed. It was then distributed among the counties in proportion to their supposed wealth, and was levied within each county by a rate. The revenue derived from these assessments in the time of the Commonwealth varied from thirty-five thousand pounds to a hundred and twenty thousand pounds a month.

After the Restoration the legislature seemed for a time inclined to revert, in finance as in other things, to the ancient practice. Subsidies were once or twice granted to Charles the Second. But it soon appeared that the old system was much less convenient than the new system. The Cavaliers condescended to take a lesson in the art of taxation from the Roundheads; and, during the interval between the Restoration and

---

[1] Commons' Journals, Dec. 10.; Tindal, Colt Papers.

[2] See Coke's Institutes, part iv. chapter 1. In 1566 a subsidy was 120,000*l.*; in 1598, 78,000*l.*; when Coke wrote his Institutes, about the end of the reign of James I., 70,000*l.* Clarendon tells us that, in 1640, twelve subsidies were estimated at about 600,000*l.*

the Revolution, extraordinary calls were occasionally met by assessments resembling the assessments of the Commonwealth. After the Revolution, the war with France made it necessary to have recourse annually to this abundant source of revenue. In 1689, in 1690, and in 1691, great sums had been raised on the land. At length, in 1692, it was determined to draw supplies from real property more largely than ever. The Commons resolved that a new and more accurate valuation of estates should be made over the whole realm, and that on the rental thus ascertained a pound rate should be paid to the government.

Such was the origin of the existing land tax. The valuation made in 1692 has remained unaltered down to our own time. According to that valuation, one shilling in the pound on the rental of the kingdom amounted, in round numbers, to half a million. During a hundred and six years, a land tax bill was annually presented to Parliament, and was annually passed, though not always without murmurs from the country gentlemen. The rate was, in time of war, four shillings in the pound. In time of peace, before the reign of George the Third, only two or three shillings were usually granted; and, during a short part of the prudent and gentle administration of Walpole, the government asked for only one shilling. But, after the disastrous year in which England drew the sword against her American colonies, the rate was never less than four shillings. At length, in the year 1798, the Parliament relieved itself from the trouble of passing a new Act every spring. The land tax, at four shillings in the pound, was made permanent; and those who were subject to it were permitted to redeem it. A great part has been redeemed; and at present little more than a fiftieth of the ordinary revenue required in time of peace is raised by that impost which was once regarded as the most productive of all the resources of the State.[1]

The land tax was fixed, for the year 1693, at four shillings in the pound, and consequently brought about two millions into the Treasury. That sum, small as it may seem to a generation which has expended a hundred and twenty millions in twelve months, was such as had never before been raised here in one year by direct taxation. It seemed immense both to Englishmen and to foreigners. Lewis, who found it almost impossible to wring by cruel exactions from the beggared peasantry of France the means of supporting the greatest army and the most gorgeous court that had existed in Europe since the downfall of the Roman empire, broke out, it is said, into an exclamation of angry surprise when he learned that the Commons of England had, from dread and hatred of his power, unanimously determined to lay on themselves, in a year of scarcity and of commercial embarrassment, a burden such as neither they nor their fathers had ever before borne. " My little

[1] See the old Land Tax Acts, and the debates on the Land Tax Redemption Bill of 1798.

cousin of Orange," he said, " seems to be firm in the saddle." He afterwards added, " No matter : the last piece of gold will win." This however was a consideration from which, if he had been well informed about the resources of England, he would not have derived much comfort. Kensington was certainly a mere hovel when compared to his superb Versailles. The display of jewels, plumes, and lace, led horses and gilded coaches, which daily surrounded him, far outshone the splendour which, even on great public occasions, our princes were in the habit of displaying. But the condition of the majority of the people of England was, beyond all doubt, such as the majority of the people of France might well have envied. In truth what was called severe distress here would have been called unexampled prosperity there.

The land tax was not imposed without a quarrel between the Houses. The Commons appointed commissioners to make the assessment. These commissioners were the principal gentlemen of every county, and were named in the bill. The Lords thought this arrangement inconsistent with the dignity of the peerage. They therefore inserted a clause providing that their estates should be valued by twenty of their own order. The Lower House indignantly rejected this amendment, and demanded an instant conference. After some delay, which increased the ill humour of the Commons, the conference took place. The bill was returned to the Peers with a very concise and haughty intimation that they must not presume to alter laws relating to money. A strong party among the Lords was obstinate. Mulgrave spoke at great length, and with great eloquence, against the pretensions of the plebeians. He told his brethren that, if they gave way, they would abdicate that authority which had belonged to the baronage of England ever since the foundation of the monarchy, and that they would have nothing left of their old greatness except their coronets and ermines. Burnet says that this speech was the finest that he ever heard in Parliament ; and Burnet was undoubtedly a good judge of speaking, and was neither partial to Mulgrave nor zealous for the privileges of the aristocracy. The orator, however, though he charmed his hearers, did not succeed in convincing them. Most of them shrank from a conflict in which they would have had against them the Commons united as one man, and the King, who, in case of necessity, would undoubtedly have created fifty peers rather than have suffered the land tax bill to be lost. Two strong protests, however, signed, the first by twenty seven, the second by twenty one dissentients, show how obstinately many nobles were prepared to contend at all hazards for the dignity of their caste. Another conference was held ; and Rochester announced that the Lords, for the sake of the public interest, waived what they must nevertheless assert to be their clear right, and would not insist on their amendment.[1] The bill passed, and was followed by bills for laying additional duties on imports, and for taxing the dividends of joint stock companies.

Still, however, the estimated revenue was not equal to the estimated expenditure. The year 1692 had bequeathed a large deficit to the year 1693; and it seemed probable that the charge for 1693 would exceed by about five hundred thousand pounds the charge for 1692. More than two millions had been voted for the army and ordnance, near two millions for the navy.[2] Only eight years before fourteen hundred thousand pounds had defrayed the whole annual charge of government. More than four times that sum was now required. Taxation, both direct and indirect, had been carried to an unprecedented point : yet the income of the state still fell short of the outlay by about a million. It was necessary to devise something. Something was devised, something of which the effects are felt to this day in every part of the globe.

There was indeed nothing strange or mysterious in the expedient to which the government had recourse. It was an expedient familiar, during two centuries, to the financiers of the Continent, and could hardly fail to occur to any English statesman who compared the void in the Exchequer with the overflow in the money market.

During the interval between the Restoration and the Revolution the riches of the nation had been rapidly increasing. Thousands of busy men found every Christmas that, after the expenses of the year's housekeeping had been defrayed out of the year's income, a surplus remained ; and how that surplus was to be employed was a question of some difficulty. In our time, to invest such a surplus, at something more than three per cent, on the best security that has ever been known in the world, is the work of a few minutes. But, in the seventeenth century, a lawyer, a physician, a retired merchant, who had saved some thousands and who wished to place them safely and profitably, was often greatly embarrassed. Three generations earlier, a man who had accumulated wealth in a trade or a profession generally purchased real property or lent his savings on mortgage. But the number of acres in the kingdom had remained the same ; and the value of those acres, though it had greatly increased, had by no means increased so fast as the quantity of capital which was

Origin of the national debt

[1] Lords' Journals, Jan. 16, 17, 18, 19, 20. ; Commons' Journals, Jan. 17, 18. 20. 1692 ; Tindal, from the Colt Papers ; Burnet, ii. 104, 105. Burnet has used an incorrect expression, which Tindal, Ralph, and others have copied. He says that the question was whether the Lords should tax themselves. The Lords did not claim any right to alter the amount of taxation laid on them by the bill as it came up to them. They only demanded that their estates should be valued, not by the ordinary commissioners, but by special commissioners of higher rank.

[2] Commons' Journals, Dec. $\frac{2}{13}$. 1692.

seeking for employment. Many too wished to put their money where they could find it at an hour's notice, and looked about for some species of property which could be more readily transferred than a house or a field. A capitalist might lend on bottomry or on personal security : but, if he did so, he ran a great risk of losing interest and principal. There were a few joint stock companies, among which the East India Company held the foremost place : but the demand for the stock of such companies was far greater than the supply. Indeed the cry for a new East India Company was chiefly raised by persons who had found difficulty in placing their savings at interest on good security. So great was that difficulty that the practice of hoarding was common. We are told that the father of Pope the poet, who retired from business in the City about the time of the Revolution, carried to a retreat in the country a strong box containing near twenty thousand pounds, and took out from time to time what was required for household expenses ; and it is highly probable that this was not a solitary case. At present the quantity of coin which is hoarded by private persons is so small that it would, if brought forth, make no perceptible addition to the circulation. But, in the earlier part of the reign of William the Third, all the greatest writers on currency were of opinion that a very considerable mass of gold and silver was hidden in secret drawers and behind wainscots.

The natural effect of this state of things was that a crowd of projectors, ingenious and absurd, honest and knavish, employed themselves in devising new schemes for the employment of redundant capital. It was about the year 1688 that the word stockjobber was first heard in London. In the short space of four years a crowd of companies, every one of which confidently held out to subscribers the hope of immense gains, sprang into existence; the Insurance Company, the Paper Company, the Lutestring Company, the Pearl Fishery Company, the Glass Bottle Company, the Alum Company, the Blythe Coal Company, the Swordblade Company. There was a Tapestry Company, which would soon furnish pretty hangings for all the parlours of the middle class and for all the bedchambers of the higher. There was a Copper Company, which proposed to explore the mines of England, and held out a hope that they would prove not less valuable than those of Potosi. There was a Diving Company, which undertook to bring up precious effects from shipwrecked vessels, and which announced that it had laid in a stock of wonderful machines resembling complete suits of armour. In front of the helmet was a huge glass eye like that of Polyphemus ; and out of the crest went a pipe through which the air was to be admitted. The whole process was exhibited on the Thames. Fine gentlemen and fine ladies were invited to the show, were hospitably

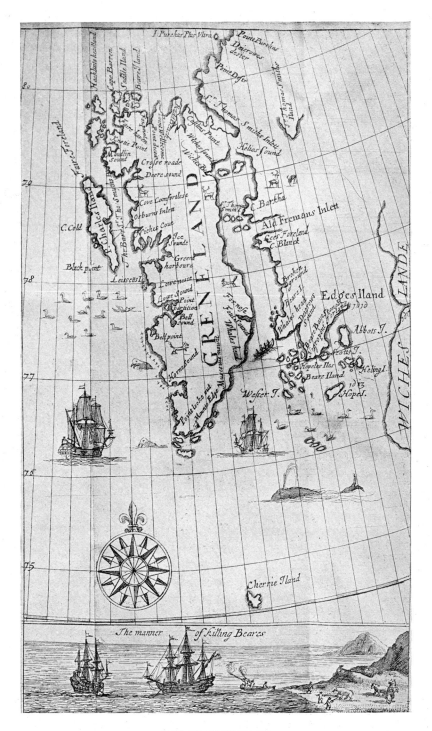

MAP OF GREENLAND

From an engraving in Churchill's Voyages, 1704

regaled, and were delighted by seeing the divers in their panoply descend into the river, and return laden with old iron and ship's tackle. There was a Greenland Fishing Company, which could not fail to drive the Dutch whalers and herring busses out of the Northern Ocean. There was a Tanning Company, which promised to furnish leather superior to the best that was brought from Turkey or Russia. There was a society which undertook the office of giving gentlemen a liberal education on low terms, and which assumed the sounding name of the Royal Academies Company. In a pompous advertisement it was announced that the directors of the Royal Academies Company had engaged the best masters in every branch of knowledge, and were about to issue twenty thousand tickets at twenty shillings each. There was to be a lottery : two thousand prizes were to be drawn ; and the fortunate holders of the prizes were to be taught, at the charge of the Company, Latin, Greek, Hebrew, French, Spanish, conic sections, trigonometry, heraldry, japanning, fortification, bookkeeping, and the art of playing the theorbo. Some of these companies took large mansions and printed their advertisements in gilded letters. Others, less ostentatious, were content with ink, and met at coffeehouses in the neighbourhood of the Royal Exchange. Jonathan's and Garraway's were in a constant ferment with brokers, buyers, sellers, meetings of directors, meetings of proprietors. Time bargains soon came into fashion. Extensive combinations were formed, and monstrous fables were circulated, for the purpose of raising or depressing the price of shares. Our country witnessed for the first time those phænomena with which a long experience has made us familiar. A mania of which the symptoms were essentially the same with those of the mania of 1720, of the mania of 1825, of the mania of 1845, seized the public mind. An impatience to be rich, a contempt for those slow but sure gains which are the proper reward of industry, patience, and thrift, spread through society. The spirit of the cogging dicers of Whitefriars took possession of the grave Senators of the City, Wardens of Trades, Deputies, Aldermen. It was much easier and much more lucrative to put forth a lying prospectus announcing a new stock, to persuade ignorant people that the dividends could not fall short of twenty per cent, and to part with five thousand pounds of this imaginary wealth for ten thousand solid guineas, than to load a ship with a well chosen cargo for Virginia or the Levant. Every day some new bubble was puffed into existence, rose buoyant, shone bright, burst, and was forgotten.[1]

[1] For this account of the origin of stockjobbing in the City of London I am chiefly indebted to a most curious periodical paper, entitled, "Collection for the Improvement of Husbandry and Trade, by J. Houghton, F.R.S." It is in fact a weekly history of the commercial speculations of that time. I have looked through the files of several years. In No. 33., March 17. 169⅔,

SCENES ILLUSTRATING THE GREENLAND TRADE

From an engraving in Churchill's Voyages, 1704

The new form which covetousness had taken furnished the comic poets and satirists with an excellent subject; nor was that subject the less welcome to them because some of the most unscrupulous and most successful of the new race of gamesters were men in sad coloured clothes and lank hair, men who called cards the Devil's books, men who thought it a sin and a scandal to win or lose twopence over a backgammon board. It was in the last drama of Shadwell that the hypocrisy and knavery of these speculators was, for the first time, exposed to public ridicule. He died in November 1692, just before his Stockjobbers came on the stage; and the epilogue was spoken by an actor dressed in deep mourning. The best scene is that in which four or five stern Nonconformists, clad in the full Puritan costume, after discussing the prospects of the Mousetrap Company and the Fleakilling Company, examine the question whether the godly may lawfully hold stock in a Company for bringing over Chinese ropedancers. "Considerable men have shares," says one austere person in cropped hair and bands; "but verily I question whether it be lawful or not." These doubts are removed by a stout old Roundhead colonel who had fought at Marston Moor, and who reminds his weaker brother that the saints need not themselves see the ropedancing, and that, in all probability, there will be no ropedancing to see. "The thing," he says, "is like to take. The shares will sell well; and then we shall not care whether the dancers come over or no." It is important to observe that this scene was exhibited and applauded before one farthing of the national debt had been contracted. So ill informed were the numerous writers who, at a later period, ascribed to the national debt the existence of stockjobbing and of all the immoralities connected with stockjobbing. The truth is that society had, in the natural course of its growth, reached a point at which it was inevitable that there should be stockjobbing whether there were a national debt or not, and inevitable also that, if there were a long and costly war, there should be a national debt.

How indeed was it possible that a debt should not have been contracted, when one party was impelled by the strongest motives to borrow, and another was impelled by equally strong motives to lend? A moment had arrived at which the government found it impossible, without exciting the most formidable discontents, to raise by taxation the supplies necessary to defend the liberty and independence of the nation; and, at that very moment, numerous capitalists were looking round them in

Houghton says, "The buying and selling of Actions is one of the great trades now on foot. I find a great many do not understand the affair." On June 13. and June 22. 1694, he traces the whole progress of stockjobbing. On July 13. of the same year he makes the first mention of time bargains. Whoever is desirous to know more about the companies mentioned in the text may consult Houghton's Collection, and a pamphlet entitled Angliæ Tutamen, published in 1695.

vain for some good mode of investing their savings, and, for want of such a mode, were keeping their wealth locked up, or were lavishing it on absurd projects.   Riches sufficient to equip a navy which would sweep

THOMAS SHADWELL

From the painting in the National Portrait Gallery by an unknown artist

the German Ocean and the Atlantic of French privateers, riches sufficient to maintain an army which might retake Namur and avenge the disaster of Steinkirk, were lying idle, or were passing away from the owners into the hands of sharpers. A statesman might well think that some part of the wealth which was daily buried or squandered might, with advantage to the proprietor, to the taxpayer, and to the State, be attracted into the Treasury. Why meet the extraordinary charge of a year of war by seizing the chairs, the tables, the beds of hardworking families, by compelling one country gentleman to cut down his trees before they were ready for the axe, another to let the cottages on his land fall to ruin, a third to take away his hopeful son from the University, when Change Alley was swarming with people who did not know what to do with their money and who were pressing everybody to borrow it?

It was often asserted at a later period by Tories, who hated the national debt most of all things, and who hated Burnet most of all men, that Burnet was the person who first advised the government to contract a national debt. But this assertion is proved by no trustworthy evidence, and seems to be disproved by the Bishop's silence. Of all men he was the least likely to conceal the fact that an important fiscal revolution had been his work. Nor was the Board of Treasury at that time one which much needed, or was likely much to regard, the counsels of a divine. At that Board sate Godolphin, the most prudent and experienced, and Montague, the most daring and inventive of financiers. Neither of these eminent men could be ignorant that it had long been the practice of the neighbouring states to spread over many years of peace the excessive taxation which was made necessary by one year of war. In Italy this practice had existed through several generations. France had, during the war which began in 1672 and ended in 1679, borrowed not less than thirty millions of our money. Sir William Temple, in his interesting work on the Batavian federation, had told his countrymen that, when he was ambassador at the Hague, the single province of Holland, then ruled by the frugal and prudent De Witt, owed about five millions sterling, for which interest at four per cent was always ready to the day, and that, when any part of the principal was paid off, the public creditor received his money with tears, well knowing that he could find no other investment equally secure. The wonder is not that England should have at length imitated the example both of her enemies and of her allies, but that the fourth year of her arduous and exhausting struggle against Lewis should have been drawing to a close before she resorted to an expedient so obvious.

On the fifteenth of December 1692 the House of Commons resolved itself into a Committee of Ways and Means. Somers took the chair. Montague proposed to raise a million by way of loan : the proposition was approved ; and it was ordered that a bill should be brought in. The details of the scheme were much discussed and modified ; but the principle appears to have been popular with all parties. The moneyed men were glad to have a good opportunity of investing what they had hoarded. The landed men, hard pressed by the load of taxation, were ready to consent to any thing for the sake of present ease. No member ventured to divide the House. On the twentieth of January the bill was read a third time, carried up to the Lords by Somers, and passed by them without any amendment.[1]

By this memorable law new duties were imposed on beer and other liquors. These duties were to be kept in the Exchequer separate from all other receipts, and were to form a fund on the credit of which a million was to be raised by life annuities. As the annuitants dropped off, their annuities were to be divided among the survivors, till the number of survivors was reduced to seven. After that time, whatever fell in was to go to the public. It was therefore certain that the eighteenth century would be far advanced before the debt would be finally extinguished; and, in fact, long after King George the Third was on the throne, a few aged men were receiving large incomes from the State, in return for a little money which had been advanced to King William on their account when they were children.[2] The rate of interest was to be ten per cent till the year 1700, and after that year seven per cent. The advantages offered to the public creditor by this scheme may seem great, but were not more than sufficient to compensate him for the risk which he ran. It was not impossible that there might be a counterrevolution; and it was certain that if there were a counterrevolution, those who had lent money to William would lose both interest and principal.

Such was the origin of that debt which has since become the greatest prodigy that ever perplexed the sagacity and confounded the pride of statesmen and philosophers. At every stage in the growth of that debt the nation has set up the same cry of anguish and despair. At every stage in the growth of that debt it has been seriously asserted by wise men that bankruptcy and ruin were at hand. Yet still the debt went on growing; and still bankruptcy and ruin were as remote as ever. When the great contest with Lewis the Fourteenth was finally terminated by the Peace of Utrecht, the nation owed about fifty millions; and that debt was considered, not merely by the rude multitude, not merely by foxhunting squires and coffeehouse orators, but by acute and profound thinkers, as an incumbrance which would permanently cripple the body politic. Nevertheless trade flourished: wealth increased: the nation

---

[1] Commons' Journals; Stat. 4 W. & M. c. 3.

[2] William Duncombe, whose name is well known to curious students of literary history, and who, in conjunction with his son John, translated Horace's works, died in 1769, having been seventy seven years an annuitant under the Act of 1692. A hundred pounds had been subscribed in William Duncombe's name when he was three years old; and, for this small sum, he received thousands upon thousands. Literary Anecdotes of the Eighteenth Century, viii. 265.

became richer and richer. Then came the war of the Austrian Succession ; and the debt rose to eighty millions. Pamphleteers, historians, and orators pronounced that now, at all events, our case was desperate.[1] Yet the signs of increasing prosperity, signs which could neither be counterfeited nor concealed, ought to have satisfied observant and reflecting men that a debt of eighty millions was less to the England which was governed by Pelham than a debt of fifty millions had been to the England which was governed by Oxford. Soon war again broke forth ; and, under the energetic and prodigal administration of the first William Pitt, the debt rapidly swelled to a hundred and forty millions. As soon as the first intoxication of victory was over, men of theory and men of business almost unanimously pronounced that the fatal day had now really arrived. The only statesman, indeed, active or speculative, who was too wise to share in the general delusion was Edmund Burke. David Hume, undoubtedly one of the most profound political economists of his time, declared that our madness had exceeded the madness of the Crusaders. Richard Cœur de Lion and Saint Lewis had not gone in the face of arithmetical demonstration. It was impossible to prove by figures that the road to Paradise did not lie through the Holy Land : but it was possible to prove by figures that the road to national ruin was through the national debt. It was idle, however, now to talk about the road : we had done with the road : we had reached the goal : all was over : all the revenues of the island north of Trent and west of Reading were mortgaged. Better for us to have been conquered by Prussia or Austria than to be saddled with the interest of a hundred and forty millions.[2] And yet this great philosopher,—for such he was,—had only to open his eyes, and to see improvement all around him, cities increasing, cultivation extending, marts too small for the crowd of buyers and sellers, harbours insufficient to contain the shipping, artificial rivers joining the chief inland seats of industry to the chief seaports, streets better lighted, houses better furnished, richer wares exposed to sale in statelier shops, swifter carriages rolling along smoother roads. He had, indeed, only to compare the Edinburgh of his boyhood with the Edinburgh of his old age. His prediction remains to posterity, a memorable instance of the weakness from which the strongest minds are not exempt. Adam Smith saw a little, and but a little further. He admitted that, immense as the pressure was, the nation did actually sustain it and thrive under it in a way which nobody could have foreseen. But he

[1] Smollett's Complete History of England from the Descent of Julius Cæsar to the Treaty of Aix la Chapelle, 1748, containing the Transactions of one thousand eight hundred and three years, was published at this time. The work ends with a vehement philippic against the government ; and that philippic ends with the tremendous words, "the national debt accumulated to the enormous sum of eighty millions sterling."

[2] See a very remarkable note in Hume's History of England, Appendix III.

warned his countrymen not to repeat so hazardous an experiment. The limit had been reached. Even a small increase might be fatal.[1] Not less gloomy was the view which George Grenville, a minister eminently diligent and practical, took of our financial situation. The nation must, he conceived, sink under a debt of a hundred and forty millions, unless a portion of the load were borne by the American colonies. The attempt to lay a portion of the load on the American colonies produced another war. That war left us with an additional hundred millions of debt, and without the colonies whose help had been represented as indispensable. Again England was given over; and again the strange patient persisted in becoming stronger and more blooming in spite of all the diagnostics and prognostics of State physicians. As she had been visibly more prosperous with a debt of one hundred and forty millions than with a debt of fifty millions, so she was visibly more prosperous with a debt of two hundred and forty millions than with a debt of one hundred and forty millions. Soon however the wars which sprang from the French Revolution, and which far exceeded in cost any that the world had ever seen, tasked the powers of public credit to the utmost. When the world was again at rest the funded debt of England amounted to eight hundred millions. If the most enlightened man had been told, in 1792, that, in 1815, the interest on eight hundred millions would be duly paid to the day at the Bank, he would have been as hard of belief as if he had been told that the government would be in possession of the lamp of Aladdin or of the purse of Fortunatus. It was in truth a gigantic, a fabulous, debt; and we can hardly wonder that the cry of despair should have been louder than ever. But again that cry was found to have been as unreasonable as ever. After a few years of exhaustion, England recovered herself. Yet like Addison's valetudinarian, who continued to whimper that he was dying of consumption till he became so fat that he was shamed into silence, she went on complaining that she was sunk in poverty till her wealth showed itself by tokens which made her complaints ridiculous. The beggared, the bankrupt, society not only proved able to meet all its obligations, but, while meeting those obligations, grew richer and richer so fast that the growth could almost be discerned by the eye. In every county, we saw wastes recently turned into gardens: in every city, we saw new streets, and squares, and markets, more brilliant lamps, more abundant supplies of water: in the suburbs of every great seat of industry, we saw villas multiplying fast, each embosomed in its gay little paradise of lilacs and roses. While shallow politicians were repeating that the energies of the people were borne down by the weight of the public burdens, the first journey was performed by steam on a railway. Soon the island

[1] Wealth of Nations, book v. chap. iii.

was intersected by railways. A sum exceeding the whole amount of
the national debt at the end of the American war was, in a few years,
voluntarily expended by this ruined people on viaducts, tunnels, embank-
ments, bridges, stations, engines. Meanwhile taxation was almost
constantly becoming lighter and lighter : yet still the Exchequer was
full. It may be now affirmed without fear of contradiction that we find
it as easy to pay the interest of eight hundred millions as our ancestors
found it, a century ago, to pay the interest of eighty millions.

It can hardly be doubted that there must have been some great
fallacy in the notions of those who uttered and of those who believed
that long succession of confident predictions, so signally falsified by a
long succession of indisputable facts. To point out that fallacy is the
office rather of the political economist than of the historian. Here it is
sufficient to say that ne prophets of evil were under a double delusion.
They erroneously imagined that there was an exact analogy between
the case of an individual who is in debt to another individual and the
case of a society which is in debt to a part of itself ; and this analogy
led them into endless mistakes about the effect of the system of funding. They were under an error not less serious touching the resources
of the country. They made no allowance for the effect produced by
the incessant progress of every experimental science, and by the incessant efforts of every man to get on in life. They saw that the debt
grew ; and they forgot that other things grew as well as the debt.

A long experience justifies us in believing that England may, in
the twentieth century, be better able to pay a debt of sixteen hundred
millions than she is at the present time to bear her present load. But be
this as it may, those who so confidently predicted that she must sink,
first under a debt of fifty millions, then under a debt of eighty millions,
then under a debt of a hundred and forty millions, then under a debt
of two hundred and forty millions, and lastly under a debt of eight
hundred millions, were beyond all doubt under a twofold mistake. They
greatly overrated the pressure of the burden : they greatly underrated
the strength by which the burden was to be borne.[1]

It may be desirable to add a few words touching the way in which
the system of funding has affected the interests of the great common-

[1] I have said that Burke, alone among his contemporaries, was superior to the vulgar error in
which men so eminent as David Hume and Adam Smith shared. I will quote, in illustration of
my meaning, a few weighty words from the Observations on the Late State of the Nation written
by Burke in 1769. " An enlightened reader laughs at the inconsistent chimera of our author
(George Grenville), of a people universally luxurious, and at the same time oppressed with taxes
and declining in trade. For my part, I cannot look on these duties as the author does. He sees
nothing but the burden. I can perceive the burden as well as he : but I cannot avoid con-
templating also the strength that supports it. From thence I draw the most comfortable assurances
of the future vigour and the ample resources of this great misrepresented country."

wealth of nations. If it be true that whatever gives to intelligence an advantage over brute force, and to honesty an advantage over dishonesty, has a tendency to promote the happiness and virtue of our race, it can scarcely be denied that, in the largest view, the effect of this system has been salutary. For it is manifest that all credit depends on two things, on the power of a debtor to pay debts, and on his inclination to pay them. The power of a society to pay debts is proportioned to the progress which that society has made in industry, in commerce, and in all the arts and sciences which flourish under the benignant influence of freedom and of equal law. The inclination of a society to pay debts is proportioned to the degree in which that society respects the obligations of plighted faith. Of the strength which consists in extent of territory and in number of fighting men, a rude despot who knows no law but his own childish fancies and headstrong passions, or a convention of socialists which proclaims all property to be robbery, may have more than falls to the lot of the best and wisest government. But the strength which is derived from the confidence of capitalists such a despot, such a convention, never can possess. That strength,—and it is a strength which has decided the event of more than one great conflict,—flies, by the law of its nature, from barbarism and fraud, from tyranny and anarchy, to follow civilisation and virtue, liberty and order.

While the bill which first created the funded debt of **Parliamentary Reform** England was passing, with general approbation, through the regular stages, the two Houses discussed, for the first time, the great question of Parliamentary Reform.

It is to be observed that the object of the reformers of that generation was merely to make the representative body a more faithful interpreter of the sense of the constituent body. It seems scarcely to have occurred to any of them that the constituent body might be an unfaithful interpreter of the sense of the nation. It is true that those disproportions in the structure of the constituent body, which, at length, in our own days, raised an irresistible storm of public indignation, were far less numerous and far less offensive in the seventeenth century than they had become in the nineteenth. Most of the boroughs which were disfranchised in 1832 were, if not positively, yet relatively, much more important places in the reign of William the Third than in the reign of William the Fourth. Of the populous and wealthy manufacturing towns, seaports, and watering places, to which the franchise was given in the reign of William the Fourth, some were, in the reign of William the Third, small hamlets, where a few ploughmen or fishermen lived under thatched roofs : some were fields covered with harvests, or moors abandoned to grouse. With the exception of Leeds and Manchester, there was not, at the time of the Revolution, a single town of five thousand inhabitants which did not send two representatives to the House of Commons. Even then, however, there was no want of startling anomalies. Looe, East and West, which contained not half the population or half the wealth of the smallest of the hundred parishes of London, returned as many members as London.[1] Old Sarum, a deserted ruin which the traveller feared to enter at night lest he should find robbers lurking there, had as much weight in the legislature as Devonshire or Yorkshire.[2] Some eminent individuals of both parties, Clarendon, for example, among the Tories, and Pollexfen among the Whigs, condemned this system. Yet both parties were, for very different reasons, unwilling to alter it. It was protected by the prejudices of one faction, and by the interests of the other. Nothing could be more repugnant to the genius of Toryism than the thought of destroying at a blow institutions which had stood through ages, for the purpose of building something more symmetrical out of the ruins. It was remembered too that Cromwell had tried to correct the deformities of the representative system ; and deformities which Cromwell had tried to correct were certain to be regarded as beauties by most of those gentlemen who were zealous for the Church and the Crown. The Whigs, on the other hand, could not but know that they were much more likely to lose than to gain by a change in this part of our polity. It would indeed be a great mistake to imagine that a law transferring political power from small to large constituent bodies would have operated in 1692 as it operated in 1832. In 1832 the effect of the transfer was to increase the power of the town population. In 1692 the effect would have been to make the power of the rural population irresistible. Of the one hundred and forty three members taken away in 1832 from small boroughs more than half were given to large and flourishing towns. But in 1692 there was hardly one large and flourishing town which had not already as many members as it could, with any show of reason, claim. Almost all therefore that was taken from the small boroughs must have been given to the counties ; and there can be no doubt that whatever tended to raise the counties and to depress the towns must on the whole have tended to raise the Tories and to depress the Whigs. From the commencement of our civil troubles the towns had been on the side of freedom and progress, the country gentlemen and the country clergymen on the side of authority and prescription. If therefore a reform bill, disfranchising many of the smallest constituent bodies and giving additional members to many of the largest constituent bodies, had become law soon after the Revolution, there can be little doubt that a decided majority of the House of Commons would have consisted of rustic baronets and squires, high Churchmen, high

[1] Wesley was struck with this anomaly in 1745. See his Journal.   [2] Pepys, June 10. 1668.

A Stratford　*Prospect of Old Sarum Aug 1. 1723.*　*B. the Icening Street.*
Stukeley de

VIEW OF OLD SARUM

From an engraving in Stukeley's Itinerarium Curiosum, 1723

Tories, and half Jacobites. With such a House of Commons it is almost certain that there would have been a persecution of the Dissenters: it is not easy to understand how there could have been a peaceful union with Scotland; and it is not improbable that there would have been a restoration of the Stuarts. Those parts of our constitution therefore which, in recent times, politicians of the liberal school have generally considered as blemishes, were, five generations ago, regarded with complacency by the men who were most zealous for civil and religious freedom.

But, while Whigs and Tories agreed in wishing to maintain the existing rights of election, both Whigs and Tories were forced to admit that the relation between the elector and the representative was not what it ought to be. Before the civil wars the House of Commons had enjoyed the fullest confidence of the nation. A House of Commons, distrusted, despised, hated by the Commons, was a thing unknown. The very words would, to Sir Peter Wentworth or Sir Edward Coke, have sounded like a contradiction in terms. But by degrees a change took place. The Parliament elected in 1661, during that fit of joy and fondness which followed the return of the royal family, represented, not the deliberate sense, but the momentary caprice of the nation. Many of the members were men who, a few months earlier or a few months later, would have had no chance of obtaining seats, men of broken fortunes and of dissolute habits, men whose only claim to public confidence was the ferocious hatred which they bore to rebels and Puritans. The people, as soon as they had become sober, saw with dismay, to what an assembly they had, during their intoxication, confided the care of their property, their liberty, and their religion. And the choice, made in a moment of frantic enthusiasm, might prove to be a choice for life. As the law then stood, it depended entirely on the King's pleasure whether, during his reign, the electors should have an opportunity of repairing their error. Eighteen years passed away. A new generation grew up. To the fervid loyalty with which Charles had been welcomed back from exile succeeded discontent and disaffection. The general cry was that the kingdom was misgoverned, degraded, given up as a prey to worthless men and more worthless women, that our navy had been found unequal to a contest with Holland, that our independence had been bartered for the gold of France, that our consciences were in danger of being again subjected to the yoke of Rome. The people had become Roundheads: but the body which alone was authorised to speak in the name of the people was still a body of Cavaliers. It is true that the King occasionally found even that House of Commons unmanageable. From the first it had contained not a few true Englishmen; others had been introduced into it as vacancies were made by death; and even the majority, courtly as it was, could not but feel some sympathy with the nation. A country party grew up and became formidable. But that party constantly found its exertions frustrated by systematic corruption. That some members of the legislature received direct bribes was with good reason suspected, but could not be proved. That the patronage of the Crown was employed on an extensive scale for the purpose of influencing votes was matter of notoriety. A large proportion of those who gave away the public money in supplies received part of that money back in salaries; and thus was formed a mercenary band on which the Court might, in almost any extremity, confidently rely.

The servility of this Parliament had left a deep impression on the public mind. It was the general opinion that England ought to be protected against all risk of being ever again represented, during a long course of years, by men who had forfeited her confidence, and who were retained by a fee to vote against her wishes and interests. The subject was mentioned in the Convention ; and some members wished to deal with it while the throne was still vacant. The cry for reform had ever since been becoming more and more importunate. The people, heavily pressed by taxes, were naturally disposed to regard those who lived on the taxes with little favour. The war, it was generally acknowledged, was just and necessary ; and war could not be carried on without large expenditure. But the larger the expenditure which was required for the defence of the nation, the more important it was that nothing should be squandered. The immense gains of official men moved envy and indignation. Here a gentleman was paid to do nothing. There many gentlemen were paid to do what would be better done by one. The coach, the liveries, the lace cravat, and the diamond buckles of the placeman were naturally seen with an evil eye by those who rose up early and lay down late in order to furnish him with the means of indulging in splendour and luxury. Such abuses it was the especial business of a House of Commons to correct. What then had the existing House of Commons done in the way of correction? Absolutely nothing. In 1690, indeed, while the Civil List was settling, some sharp speeches had been made. In 1691, when the Ways and Means were under consideration, a resolution had been passed so absurdly framed that it had proved utterly abortive. The nuisance continued, and would continue while it was a source of profit to those whose duty was to abate it. Who could expect faithful and vigilant stewardship from stewards who had a direct interest in encouraging the waste which they were employed to check? The House swarmed with placemen of all kinds, Lords of the Treasury, Lords of the Admiralty, Commissioners of Customs, Commissioners of Excise, Commissioners of Prizes, Tellers, Auditors, Receivers, Paymasters, Officers of the Mint,

Officers of the household, Colonels of regiments, Captains of men of war, Governors of forts. We send up to Westminster, it was said, one of our neighbours, an independent gentleman, in the full confidence that his feelings and interests are in perfect accordance with ours. We look to him to relieve us from every burden except those burdens without which the public service cannot be carried on, and which therefore, galling as they are, we patiently and resolutely bear. But, before he has been a session in Parliament, we learn that he is a Clerk of the Green Cloth or a Yeoman of the Removing Wardrobe, with a comfortable salary. Nay, we sometimes learn that he has obtained one of those places in the Exchequer of which the emoluments rise and fall with the taxes which we pay. It would be strange indeed if our interests were safe in the keeping of a man whose gains consist in a percentage on our losses. The evil would be greatly diminished if we had frequent opportunities of considering whether the powers of our agent ought to be renewed or revoked. But, as the law stands, it is not impossible that he may hold those powers twenty or thirty years. While he lives, and while either the King or the Queen lives, it is not likely that we shall ever again exercise our elective franchise, unless there should be a dispute between the Court and the Parliament. The more profuse and obsequious a Parliament is, the less likely it is to give offence to the Court. The worse our representatives, therefore, the longer we are likely to be cursed with them.

The outcry was loud. Odious nicknames were given to the Parliament. Sometimes it was the Officers' Parliament : sometimes it was the Standing Parliament, and was pronounced to be a greater nuisance than even a standing army.

Two specifics for the distempers of the State were strongly recommended, and divided the public favour. One was a law excluding placemen from the House of Commons. The other was a law limiting the duration of Parliaments to three years. In general the Tory reformers preferred a Place Bill, and the Whig reformers a Triennial Bill : but not a few zealous men of both parties were for trying both remedies.

Before Christmas a Place Bill was laid on the table of the Commons. That bill has been vehemently praised by writers who never saw it, The Place and who merely guessed at what it contained. But no person Bill who takes the trouble to study the original parchment, which, embrowned with the dust of a hundred and sixty years, reposes among the archives of the House of Lords, will find much matter for eulogy.

About the manner in which such a bill should have been framed there will, in our time, be little difference of opinion among enlightened Englishmen. They will agree in thinking that it would be most pernicious to open the House of Commons to all placemen, and not less pernicious to close that House against all placemen. To draw with precision the line between those who ought to be admitted and those who ought to be excluded would be a task requiring much time, thought, and knowledge of details. But the general principles which ought to guide us are obvious. The multitude of subordinate functionaries ought to be excluded. A few functionaries, who are at the head or near the head of the great departments of the administration, ought to be admitted.

The subordinate functionaries ought to be excluded, because their admission would at once lower the character of Parliament and destroy the efficiency of every public office. They are now excluded ; and the consequence is that the State possesses a valuable body of servants who remain unchanged while cabinet after cabinet is formed and dissolved, who instruct minister after minister in his duties, and with whom it is the most sacred point of honour to give true information, sincere advice, and strenuous assistance to their superior for the time being. To the experience, the ability, and the fidelity of this class of men is to be attributed the ease and safety with which the direction of affairs has been many times, within our own memory, transferred from Tories to Whigs and from Whigs to Tories. But no such class would have existed if persons who received salaries from the Crown had been suffered to sit without restriction in the House of Commons. Those commissionerships, assistant secretaryships, chief clerkships, which are now held for life by persons who stand aloof from the strife of parties, would have been bestowed on members of Parliament who were serviceable to the government as voluble speakers or steady voters. As often as the ministry was changed, all this crowd of retainers would have been ejected from office, and would have been succeeded by another set of members of Parliament who would probably have been ejected in their turn before they had half learned their business. Servility and corruption in the legislature, ignorance and incapacity in all the departments of the executive administration, would have been the inevitable effects of such a system.

Still more noxious, if possible, would be the effects of a system under which all the servants of the Crown, without exception, should be excluded from the House of Commons. Aristotle has, in that treatise on government which is perhaps the most judicious and instructive of all his writings, left us a warning against a class of laws artfully framed to delude the vulgar, democratic in seeming, but the very opposite of democratic in effect.[1] Had he had an opportunity of studying the history of the English constitution, he might easily have enlarged his list of such laws. That men who are in the service and pay of the Crown ought not

[1] See the Politics, iv. 13.

to sit in an assembly specially charged with the duty of guarding the rights and interests of the community against all aggression on the part of the Crown is a plausible and a popular doctrine. Yet it is certain that if those who, five generations ago, held that doctrine, had been able to mould the constitution according to their wishes, the effect would have been the depression of that branch of the legislature which springs from the people and is accountable to the people, and the ascendency of the monarchical and aristocratical elements of our polity. The government would have been entirely in patrician hands. The House of Lords, constantly drawing to itself the first abilities in the realm, would have become the most august of senates, while the House of Commons would have sunk almost to the rank of a vestry. From time to time undoubtedly men of commanding genius and of aspiring temper would have made their appearance among the representatives of the counties and boroughs. But every such man would have considered the elective chamber merely as a lobby through which he must pass to the hereditary chamber. The first object of his ambition would have been that coronet without which he could not be powerful in the state. As soon as he had shown that he could be a formidable enemy and a valuable friend to the government, he would have made haste to quit what would then have been in every sense the Lower House for what would then have been in every sense the Upper. The conflict between Walpole and Pulteney, the conflict between Pitt and Fox, would have been transferred from the popular to the aristocratic part of the legislature. On every great question, foreign, domestic, or colonial, the debates of the nobles would have been impatiently expected and eagerly devoured. The report of the proceedings of an assembly containing no person empowered to speak in the name of the government, no person who had ever been in high political trust, would have been thrown aside with contempt. Even the control of the purse of the nation must have passed, not perhaps in form, but in substance, to that body in which would have been found every man who was qualified to bring forward a budget or explain an estimate. The country would have been governed by Peers; and the chief business of the Commons would have been to wrangle about bills for the inclosing of moors and the lighting of towns.

These considerations were altogether overlooked in 1692. Nobody thought of drawing a line between the few functionaries who ought to be allowed to sit in the House of Commons and the crowd of functionaries who ought to be shut out. The only line which the legislators of that day took pains to draw was between themselves and their successors. Their own interest they guarded with a care of which it seems strange that they should not have been ashamed. Every one of them was allowed to keep the places which he had got, and to get as many more places as he could before the next dissolution of Parliament, an event which might not happen for many years.   But a member who should be chosen after the first of February 1693 was not to be permitted to accept any place whatever.[1]

In the House of Commons the bill went through all the stages rapidly and without a single division.   But in the Lords the contest was sharp and obstinate.   Several amendments were proposed in committee ; but all were rejected.   The motion that the bill should pass was supported by Mulgrave in a lively and poignant speech, which has been preserved, and which proves that his reputation for eloquence was not unmerited.   The Lords who took the other side did not, it should seem, venture to deny that there was an evil which required a remedy : but they maintained that the proposed remedy would only aggravate the evil.   The patriotic representatives of the people had devised a reform which might perhaps benefit the next generation : but they had carefully reserved to themselves the privilege of plundering the present generation.   If this bill passed, it was clear that, while the existing Parliament lasted, the number of placemen in the House of Commons would be little, if at all, diminished ; and, if this bill passed, it was highly probable that the existing Parliament would last till both King William and Queen Mary were dead.   For as, under this bill, Their Majesties would be able to exercise a much greater influence over the existing Parliament than over any future Parliament, they would naturally wish to put off a dissolution as long as possible.   The complaint of the electors of England was that now, in 1692, they were unfairly represented.   It was not redress, but mockery, to tell them that their children should be fairly represented in 1710 or 1720.   The relief ought to be immediate ; and the way to give immediate relief was to limit the duration of Parliaments, and to begin with that Parliament which, in the opinion of the country, had already held power too long.

The forces were so evenly balanced that a very slight accident might have turned the scale.   When the question was put that the bill do pass, eighty two peers were present.   Of these forty two were for the bill, and forty against it.   Proxies were then called.   There were only two proxies for the bill : there were seven against it : but of the seven three were questioned, and were with difficulty admitted.   The result was that the bill was lost by three votes.

The majority appears to have been composed of moderate Whigs and moderate Tories.   Twenty of the minority protested, and among them were the most violent and intolerant members of both parties, such as Warrington, who had narrowly escaped the block for conspiring against James, and Ailesbury, who afterwards narrowly escaped the block for

---

[1] The bill will be found among the archives of the House of Lords.

conspiring against William.   Marlborough, who, since his imprisonment, had gone all lengths in opposition to the government, not only put his own name to the protest, but made the Prince of Denmark sign what it was altogether beyond the faculties of His Royal Highness to comprehend.[1]

It is a remarkable circumstance that neither Caermarthen, the first in power as well as in abilities of the Tory ministers, nor Shrewsbury, the most distinguished of those Whigs who were then on bad terms with the Court, was present on this important occasion.   Their absence was in all probability the effect of design ; for both of them were in the House no long time before and no long time after the division.

A few days later Shrewsbury laid on the table of the Lords a bill for limiting the duration of Parliaments.   By this bill it was provided
The Trien- that the Parliament then sitting should cease to exist on
nial Bill   the first of January 1694, and that no future Parliament should last longer than three years.

Among the Lords there seems to have been almost perfect unanimity on this subject.   William in vain endeavoured to induce those peers in whom he placed the greatest confidence to support his prerogative. Some of them thought the proposed change salutary : others hoped to quiet the public mind by a liberal concession ; and others had held such language when they were opposing the Place Bill that they could not, without gross inconsistency, oppose the Triennial Bill.   The whole House too bore a grudge to the other House, and had a pleasure in putting the other House in a most disagreeable dilemma.   Burnet, Pembroke, nay, even Caermarthen, who was very little in the habit of siding with the people against the throne, supported Shrewsbury.   " My Lord," said the King to Caermarthen, with bitter displeasure, " you will live to repent the part which you are taking in this matter." [2]   The warning was disregarded ; and the bill, having passed the Lords smoothly and rapidly, was carried with great solemnity by two judges to the Commons.

Of what took place in the Commons we have but very meagre accounts : but from those accounts it is clear that the Whigs, as a body,
1693   supported the bill, and that the opposition came chiefly from
     Tories.   Old Titus, who had been a politician in the days of the Commonwealth, entertained the House with a speech after the pattern which had been fashionable in those days.   Parliaments, he said, resembled the manna which God bestowed on the chosen people.   They were excellent while they were fresh : but, if kept too

[1] Lords' Journals, Jan. 3. 169⅔.

[2] Introduction to the Copies and Extracts of some Letters written to and from the Earl of Danby, now Duke of Leeds, published by His Grace's Direction, 1710.

long, they became noisome; and foul worms were engendered by the corruption of that which had been sweeter than honey. Several of the leading Whigs spoke on the same side. Seymour, Finch, and Tredenham, all stanch Tories, were vehement against the bill; and even Sir John Lowther on this point dissented from his friend and patron Caermarthen. Some Tory orators appealed to a feeling which was strong in the House, and which had, since the Revolution, prevented many laws from passing. Whatever, they said, comes from the Peers is to be received with suspicion; and the present bill is of such a nature that, even if it were in itself good, it ought to be at once rejected merely because it has been brought down from them. If their Lordships were to send us the most judicious of all money bills, should we not kick it to the door? Yet to send us a money bill would hardly be a grosser affront than to send us such a bill as this. They have taken an initiative which, by every rule of parliamentary courtesy, ought to have been left to us. They have sate in judgment on us, convicted us, condemned us to dissolution, and fixed the first of January for the execution. Are we to submit patiently to so degrading a sentence, a sentence too passed by men who have not so conducted themselves as to have acquired any right to censure others? Have they ever made any sacrifice of their own interest, of their own dignity, to the general welfare? Have not excellent bills been lost because we would not consent to insert in them clauses conferring new privileges on the nobility? And, now that their Lordships are bent on obtaining popularity, do they propose to purchase it by relinquishing even the smallest of their own oppressive privileges? No: they seek to propitiate the multitude by a sacrifice which will cost themselves nothing, but which will cost us and will cost the Crown dear. In such circumstances it is our duty to repel the insult which has been offered to us, and, by doing so, to vindicate the lawful prerogative of the King.

Such topics as these were doubtless well qualified to inflame the passions of the House of Commons. The near prospect of a dissolution could not be very agreeable to a member whose election was likely to be contested. He must go through all the miseries of a canvass, must shake hands with crowds of freeholders or freemen, must ask after their wives and children, must hire conveyances for outvoters, must open alehouses, must provide mountains of beef, must set rivers of ale running, and might perhaps, after all the drudgery and all the expense, after being lampooned, hustled, pelted, find himself at the bottom of the poll, see his antagonists chaired, and sink half ruined into obscurity. All this evil he was now invited to bring on himself, and invited by men whose own seats in the legislature were permanent, who gave up neither dignity nor quiet, neither power nor money, but gained the praise of patriotism by forcing him to abdicate a high station, to undergo harassing labour and anxiety, to mortgage his cornfields and to hew down his woods. There was naturally much irritation, more probably than is indicated by the divisions. For the constituent bodies were generally delighted with the bill ; and many members who disliked it were afraid to oppose it. The House yielded to the pressure of public opinion, but not without a pang and a struggle. The discussions in the committee seem to have been acrimonious. Such sharp words passed between Seymour and one of the Whig members that it was necessary to put the Speaker in the chair and the mace on the table for the purpose of restoring order. One amendment was made. The respite which the Lords had granted to the existing Parliament was extended from the first of January to Lady Day, in order that there might be time for another session. The third reading was carried by two hundred votes to a hundred and sixty one. The Lords agreed to the bill as amended ; and nothing was wanting but the royal assent. Whether that assent would or would not be given was a question which remained in suspense till the last day of the session.[1]

One strange inconsistency in the conduct of the reformers of that generation deserves notice. It never occurred to any one of those who were zealous for the Triennial Bill that every argument which could be urged in favour of that bill was an argument against the rules which had been framed in old times for the purpose of keeping parliamentary deliberations and divisions strictly secret. It is quite natural that a government which withholds political privileges from the commonalty should withhold also political information. But nothing can be more irrational than to give power, and not to give the knowledge without which there is the greatest risk that power will be abused. What could be more absurd than to call constituent bodies frequently together that they might decide whether their representative had done his duty by them, and yet strictly to interdict them from learning, on trustworthy authority, what he had said or how he had voted ? The absurdity however appears to have passed altogether unchallenged. It is highly probable that among the two hundred members of the House of Commons who voted for the third reading of the Triennial Bill there was not one who would have hesitated about sending to New-gate any person who had dared to publish a report of the debate on that bill, or a list of the Ayes and the Noes. The truth is that the secrecy of parliamentary debates, a secrecy which would now be thought a grievance more intolerable than the Shipmoney or the Star Chamber, was then inseparably associated, even in the most honest and intelligent

[1] Commons' Journals ; Grey's Debates. The bill itself is among the archives of the House of Lords.

minds, with constitutional freedom. A few old men still living could remember times when a gentleman who was known at Whitehall to have let fall a sharp word against a court favourite would have been brought before the Privy Council and sent to the Tower. Those times were gone, never to return. There was no longer any danger that the King would oppress the members of the legislature; and there was much danger that the members of the legislature might oppress the people. Nevertheless the words, Privilege of Parliament, those words which the stern senators of the preceding generation had murmured when a tyrant filled their chamber with his guards, those words which a hundred thousand Londoners had shouted in his ears when he ventured for the last time within the walls of their city, still retained a magical influence over all who loved liberty. It was long before even the most enlightened men became sensible that the precautions which had been originally devised for the purpose of protecting patriots against the displeasure of the Court now served only to protect sycophants against the displeasure of the nation.

It is also to be observed that few of those who showed at this time the greatest desire to increase the political power of the people were as yet prepared to emancipate the press from the control of the government. The Licensing Act, which had passed, as a matter of course, in 1685, expired in 1693, and was renewed, not however without an opposition, which, though feeble when compared with the magnitude of the object in dispute, proved that the public mind was beginning dimly to perceive how closely civil freedom and freedom of conscience are connected with freedom of discussion.

The first parliamentary discussion on the liberty of the press

On the history of the Licensing Act no preceding writer has thought it worth while to expend any care or labour. Yet surely the events which led to the establishment of the liberty of the press in England, and in all the countries peopled by the English race, may be thought to have as much interest for the present generation as any of those battles and sieges of which the most minute details have been carefully recorded.

During the first three years of William's reign scarcely a voice seems to have been raised against the restrictions which the law imposed on literature. Those restrictions were in perfect harmony with the theory of government held by the Tories, and were not, in practice, galling to the Whigs. Sir Roger Lestrange, who had been licenser under the last two Kings of the House of Stuart, and who had shown as little tenderness to Exclusionists and Presbyterians in that character as in his other character of Observator, was turned out of office at the Revolution, and was succeeded by a Scotch gentleman, who, on account of his passion for rare books, and his habit of attending all sales of libraries, was known in the shops and coffeehouses near Saint Paul's by the name of Catalogue Fraser. Fraser was a zealous Whig. By Whig authors and publishers he was extolled as a most impartial and humane man. But the conduct which obtained their applause drew on him the abuse of the Tories, and was not altogether pleasing to his official superior Nottingham.[1] No serious difference however seems to have arisen till the year 1692. In that year an honest old clergyman named Walker, who had, in the time of the civil war, been intimately acquainted with Doctor John Gauden, wrote a book which convinced all sensible and dispassionate readers that Gauden, and not Charles the First, was the author of the Icon Basilike. This book Fraser suffered to be printed. If he had authorised the publication of a work in which the Gospel of Saint John or the Epistle to the Romans had been represented as spurious, the indignation of the High Church party could hardly have been greater. The question was not literary, but religious. Doubt was impiety. The Blessed Martyr was an inspired penman, his Icon a supplementary revelation. One grave divine indeed had gone so far as to propose that lessons taken out of the inestimable little volume should be read in the churches.[2] Fraser found it necessary to resign his place ; and Nottingham appointed a gentleman of good blood and scanty fortune, named Edmund Bohun. This change of men produced an immediate and total change of system : for Bohun was as strong a Tory as a conscientious man who had taken the oaths could possibly be. He had been conspicuous as a persecutor of non-conformists and a champion of the doctrine of passive obedience. He had edited Filmer's absurd treatise on the origin of government, and had written an answer to the paper which Algernon Sidney had delivered to the Sheriffs on Tower Hill. Nor did Bohun admit that, in swearing allegiance to William and Mary, he had done anything inconsistent with his old creed. For he had succeeded in convincing himself that they reigned by right of conquest, and that it was the duty of an Englishman to serve them as faithfully as Daniel had served Darius, or as Nehemiah had served Artaxerxes. This doctrine, whatever peace it might bring to his own conscience, found little favour with any party. The Whigs loathed it as servile : the Jacobites loathed it as revolutionary. Great numbers of Tories had doubtless submitted to William on the ground that he was, rightfully or wrongfully, King in possession : but very few of them were disposed to allow that his possession had originated in conquest. Indeed the plea which had satisfied the weak and narrow mind of Bohun was a mere fiction, and, had it been a truth, would have been a truth not to be uttered by Englishmen without agonies of shame

---

[1] Dunton's Life and Errors ; Autobiography of Edmund Bohun, privately printed in 1853. This autobiography is, in the highest degree, curious and interesting.

[2] Vox Cleri, 1689.

and mortification.[1]　He however clung to his favourite whimsy with a tenacity which the general disapprobation only made more intense. His old friends, the steadfast adherents of indefeasible hereditary right, grew cold and reserved.　He asked Sancroft's blessing, and got only a sharp word and a black look.　He asked Ken's blessing; and Ken, though not much in the habit of transgressing the rules of Christian charity and courtesy, murmured something about a little scribbler. Thus cast out by one faction, Bohun was not received by any other. He formed indeed a class apart : for he was at once a zealous Filmerite and a zealous Williamite.　He held that pure monarchy, not limited by any law or contract, was the form of government which had been divinely ordained.　But he held that William was now the absolute monarch, who might annul the Great Charter, abolish trial by jury, or impose taxes by royal proclamation, without forfeiting the right to be implicitly obeyed by Christian men.　As to the rest, Bohun was a man of some acuteness and learning, contracted understanding, and unpopular manners.　He had no sooner entered on his functions than all Paternoster Row and Little Britain were in a ferment.　The Whigs had, under Fraser's administration, enjoyed almost as entire a liberty as if there had been no censorship.　They were now as severely treated as in the days of Lestrange.　A History of the Bloody Assizes was about to be published, and was expected to have as great a run as the Pilgrim's Progress.　But the new licenser refused his Imprimatur.　The book, he said, represented rebels and schismatics as heroes and martyrs ; and he would not sanction it for its weight in gold.　A charge delivered by Lord Warrington to the grand jury of Cheshire was not permitted to appear, because His Lordship had spoken contemptuously of divine right and passive obedience.　Julian Johnson found that, if he wished to promulgate his notions of government, he must again have recourse, as in the evil times of King James, to a secret press.[2]　Such restraint as this, coming after several years of unbounded freedom, naturally produced violent exasperation.　Some Whigs began to think that the censorship itself was a grievance : all Whigs agreed in pronouncing the new censor unfit for his post, and were prepared to join in an effort to get rid of him.

Of the transactions which terminated in Bohun's dismission, and which produced the first parliamentary struggle for the liberty of

---

[1] Bohun was the author of the History of the Desertion, published immediately after the Revolution.　In that work he propounded his favourite theory.　" For my part," he says, " I am amazed to see men scruple the submitting to the present King : for, if ever man had a just cause of war, he had ; and that creates a right to the thing gained by it.　The King by withdrawing and disbanding his army yielded him the throne ; and if he had, without any more ceremony, ascended it, he had done no more than all other princes do on the like occasions."

[2] Character of Edmund Bohun, 1692.

unlicensed printing, we have accounts written by Bohun himself and by others : but there are strong reasons for believing that in none of those accounts is the whole truth to be found. It may perhaps not be impossible, even at this distance of time, to put together dispersed fragments of evidence in such a manner as to produce an authentic narrative which would have astonished the unfortunate licenser himself.

There was then about town a man of good family, of some reading, and of some small literary talent, named Charles Blount.[1]   In politics he belonged to the extreme section of the Whig party.   In the days of the Exclusion Bill he had been one of Shaftesbury's brisk boys, and had, under the signature of Junius Brutus, magnified the virtues and public services of Titus Oates, and exhorted the Protestants to take signal vengeance on the Papists for the fire of London and for the murder of Godfrey.[2]   As to the theological questions which were in issue between Protestants and Papists, Blount was perfectly impartial. He was an infidel, and the head of a small school of infidels who were troubled with a morbid desire to make converts.   He translated from the Latin translation part of the Life of Apollonius of Tyana, and appended to it notes of which the flippant profaneness called forth the severe censure of an unbeliever of a very different order, the illustrious Bayle.[3]   Blount also attacked Christianity in several original treatises, or rather in several treatises purporting to be original ; for he was the most audacious of literary thieves, and transcribed, without acknowledgment, whole pages from authors who had preceded him.   His delight was to worry the priests by asking them how light existed before the sun was made, how Paradise could be bounded by Pison, Gihon, Hiddekel, and Euphrates, how serpents moved before they were condemned to crawl, and where Eve found thread to stitch her figleaves. To his speculations on these subjects he gave the lofty name of the Oracles of Reason ; and indeed whatever he said or wrote was considered as oracular by his disciples.   Of those disciples the most noted was a bad writer named Gildon, who lived to pester another generation with doggrel and slander, and whose memory is still preserved, not by his own voluminous works, but by two or three lines in which his stupidity and venality have been contemptuously mentioned by Pope.[4]

[1] Dryden, in his Life of Lucian, speaks in too high terms of Blount's abilities. But Dryden's judgment was biassed ; for Blount's first work was a pamphlet in defence of the Conquest of Granada.

[2] See his Appeal from the Country to the City for the Preservation of His Majesty's Person, Liberty, Property, and the Protestant Religion.

[3] See the article on Apollonius in Bayle's Dictionary.   I say that Blount made his translation from the Latin ; for his works contain abundant proofs that he was not competent to translate from the Greek.

[4] See Gildon's edition of Blount's Works, 1695.

Little as either the intellectual or the moral character of Blount may seem to deserve respect, it is in a great measure to him that we must attribute the emancipation of the English press. Between him and the licensers there was a feud of long standing. Before the Revolution one of his heterodox treatises had been grievously mutilated by Lestrange, and at last suppressed by orders from Lestrange's superior the Bishop of London.[1] Bohun was a scarcely less severe critic than Lestrange. Blount therefore began to make war on the censorship and the censor. The hostilities were commenced by a tract which came forth without any license, and which was entitled A Just Vindication of Learning and of the Liberty of the Press, by Philopatris.[2] Whoever reads this piece, and is not aware that Blount was one of the most unscrupulous plagiaries that ever lived, will be surprised to find, mingled with the poor thoughts and poor words of a thirdrate pamphleteer, passages so elevated in sentiment and style that they would be worthy of the greatest name in letters. The truth is that the Just Vindication consists chiefly of garbled extracts from the Areopagitica of Milton. That noble discourse had been neglected by the generation to which it was addressed, had sunk into oblivion, and was at the mercy of every pilferer. The literary workmanship of Blount resembled the architectural workmanship of those barbarians who used the Coliseum and the Theatre of Pompey as quarries, built hovels out of Ionian friezes and propped cowhouses on pillars of lazulite. Blount concluded, as Milton had concluded, by recommending that the law should be so framed as to permit any book to be printed without a license, provided that the name of the author or publisher were registered.[3] The Just Vindication was well received. The blow was speedily followed up. There still remained in the Areopagitica many fine passages which Blount had not used in his first pamphlet. Out of these passages he constructed a second pamphlet entitled Reasons for the Liberty of Unlicensed Printing.[4] To these Reasons he appended a postscript entitled A Just and

[1] Wood's Athenæ Oxonienses, under the name Henry Blount (Charles Blount's father); Lestrange's Observator, No. 290.

[2] This piece was reprinted by Gildon in 1695 among Blount's Works.

[3] That the plagiarism of Blount should have been detected by few of his contemporaries is not wonderful. But it is wonderful that in the Biographia Britannica his Just Vindication should be warmly extolled, without the slightest hint that every thing good in it is stolen. The Areopagitica is not the only work which he pillaged on this occasion. He took a splendid passage from Bacon without acknowledgment.

[4] I unhesitatingly attribute this pamphlet to Blount, though it was not reprinted among his works by Gildon. If Blount did not actually write it, he must certainly have superintended the writing. That two men of letters, acting without concert, should bring out within a very short time two treatises on the same subject, one made out of one half of the Areopagitica and the other made out of the other half, is incredible. Why Gildon did not choose to reprint the second pamphlet will appear hereafter.

True Character of Edmund Bohun. This Character was written with extreme bitterness. Passages were quoted from the licenser's writings to prove that he held the doctrines of passive obedience and non-resistance. He was accused of using his power systematically for the purpose of favouring the enemies and silencing the friends of the Sovereigns whose bread he ate ; and it was asserted that he was the friend and the pupil of his predecessor Sir Roger.

The Just and True Character of Bohun could not be publicly sold ; but it was widely circulated. While it was passing from hand to hand, and while the Whigs were every where exclaiming against the new censor as a second Lestrange, he was requested to authorise the publication of an anonymous work entitled King William and Queen Mary Conquerors.[1] He readily and indeed eagerly complied. For there was between the doctrines which he had long professed and the doctrines which were propounded in this treatise a coincidence so exact that many suspected him of being the author ; nor was this suspicion weakened by a passage in which a compliment was paid to his political writings. But the real author was that very Blount who was, at that very time, labouring to inflame the public both against the Licensing Act and the licenser. Blount's motives may easily be divined. His own opinions were diametrically opposed to those which, on this occasion, he put forward in the most offensive manner. It is therefore impossible to doubt that his object was to ensnare and to ruin Bohun. It was a base and wicked scheme. But it cannot be denied that the trap was laid and baited with much skill. The republican succeeded in personating a high Tory. The atheist succeeded in personating a high Churchman. The pamphlet concluded with a devout prayer that the God of light and love would open the understanding and govern the will of Englishmen, so that they might see the things which belonged to their peace. The censor was in raptures. In every page he found his own thoughts expressed more plainly than he had ever expressed them. Never before, in his opinion, had the true claim of their Majesties to obedience been so clearly stated. Every Jacobite who read this admirable tract must inevitably be converted. The nonjurors would flock to take the oaths. The nation, so long divided, would at length be united. From these pleasing dreams Bohun was awakened by learning, a few hours after the appearance of the discourse which had charmed him, that the titlepage had set all London in a flame, and that the odious words, King William and Queen Mary Conquerors, had moved the indignation of multitudes who had never read further. Only four days after the publication he heard that the House of Commons had taken the matter up, that the book had been called by some members a rascally book, and that, as the author

[1] Bohun's Autobiography.

was unknown, the Serjeant at Arms was in search of the licenser.[1] Bohun's mind had never been strong ; and he was entirely unnerved and bewildered by the fury and suddenness of the storm which had burst upon him. He went to the House. Most of the members whom he met in the passages and lobbies frowned on him. When he was put to the bar, and, after three profound obeisances, ventured to lift his head and look round him, he could read his doom in the angry and contemptuous looks which were cast on him from every side. He hesitated, blundered, contradicted himself, called the Speaker My Lord, and, by his confused way of speaking, raised a tempest of rude laughter which confused him still more. As soon as he had withdrawn, it was unanimously resolved that the obnoxious treatise should be burned in Palace Yard by the common hangman. It was also resolved, without a division, that the King should be requested to remove Bohun from the office of licenser. The poor man, ready to faint with grief and fear, was conducted by the officers of the House to a place of confinement.[2]

But scarcely was he in his prison when a large body of members clamorously demanded a more important victim. Burnet had, shortly after he became Bishop of Salisbury, addressed to the clergy of his diocese a Pastoral Letter, exhorting them to take the oaths. In one paragraph of this letter he had held language bearing some resemblance to that of the pamphlet which had just been sentenced to the flames. There were indeed distinctions which a judicious and impartial tribunal would not have failed to notice. But the tribunal before which Burnet was arraigned was neither judicious nor impartial. His faults had made him many enemies, and his virtues many more. The discontented Whigs complained that he leaned towards the Court, the High Churchmen that he leaned towards the Dissenters ; nor can it be supposed that a man of so much boldness and so little tact, a man so indiscreetly frank and so restlessly active, had passed through life without crossing the schemes and wounding the feelings of some whose opinions agreed with his. He was regarded with peculiar malevolence by Howe. Howe had never, even while he was in office, been in the habit of restraining his bitter and petulant tongue ; and he had recently been turned out of office in a way which had made him ungovernably ferocious. The history of his dismission is not accurately known : but there was no doubt that something had happened which had cruelly galled his temper. If rumour could be trusted, he had fancied that Mary was in love with him, and had availed himself of an opportunity which offered itself while he was in attendance on her as Vice Chamberlain to make some advances which had justly moved her indignation.

[1] Bohun's Autobiography ; Commons' Journals, Jan. 20. 169⅔.
[2] Bohun's Autobiography ; Commons' Journals, Jan. 20, 21. 169⅔.

Soon after he was discarded, he was prosecuted for having, in a fit of passion, beaten one of his servants savagely within the verge of the palace. He had pleaded guilty, and had been pardoned : but from this time he showed, on every occasion, the most rancorous personal hatred of his royal mistress, of her husband, and of all who were favoured by either. It was known that the Queen frequently consulted Burnet ; and Howe was possessed with the belief that her severity was to be imputed to Burnet's influence.[1] Now was the time to be revenged. In a long and elaborate speech the spiteful Whig,—for such he still affected to be,—represented Burnet as a Tory of the worst class. "There should be a law," he said, "making it penal for the clergy to introduce politics into their discourses. Formerly they sought to enslave us by crying up the divine and indefeasible right of the hereditary prince. Now they try to arrive at the same result by telling us that we are a conquered people." It was moved that the Bishop should be impeached. To this motion there was an unanswerable objection, which the Speaker pointed out. The Pastoral Letter had been written in 1689, and was therefore covered by the Act of Grace which had been passed in 1690. Yet a member was not ashamed to say, "No matter : impeach him ; and force him to plead the Act." Few, however, were disposed to take a course so unworthy of a House of Commons. Some wag cried out, "Burn it ; burn it ;" and this bad pun ran along the benches, and was received with shouts of laughter. It was moved that the Pastoral Letter should be burned by the common hangman. A long and vehement debate followed. For Burnet was a man warmly loved as well as warmly hated. The great majority of the Whigs stood firmly by him ; and his goodnature and generosity had made him friends even among the Tories. The contest lasted two days. Montague and Finch, men of widely different opinions, appear to have been foremost among the Bishop's champions. An attempt to get rid of the subject by moving the previous question failed. At length the main question was put ; and the Pastoral Letter was condemned to the flames by a small majority in a full house. The Ayes were a hundred and sixty two ; the Noes a hundred and fifty five.[2] The general opinion, at least of the capital, seems to have been that Burnet was cruelly treated.[3]

He was not naturally a man of fine feelings ; and the life which he had led had not tended to make them finer. He had been during many years a mark for theological and political animosity. Grave doctors

[1] Oldmixon ; Narcissus Luttrell's Diary, Nov. and Dec. 1692 ; Burnet, ii. 334. ; Bohun's Autobiography.

[2] Grey's Debates ; Commons' Journals, Jan. 21. 23. 169$\frac{2}{3}$; Bohun's Autobiography ; Kennet's Life and Reign of King William and Queen Mary.

[3] " Most men pitying the Bishop."—Bohun's Autobiography.

had anathematised him : ribald poets had lampooned him : princes and ministers had laid snares for his life : he had been long a wanderer and an exile, in constant peril of being kidnapped, struck in the boots, hanged, quartered. Yet none of these things had ever moved him. His selfconceit had been proof against ridicule, and his dauntless temper against danger. But on this occasion his fortitude seems to have failed him. To be stigmatized by the popular branch of the legislature as a teacher of doctrines so servile that they disgusted even Tories, to be joined in one sentence of condemnation with the editor of Filmer, was too much. How deeply Burnet was wounded appeared many years later, when, after his death, his History of his Life and Times was given to the world. In that work he is ordinarily garrulous even to minuteness about all that concerns himself, and sometimes relates with amusing ingenuousness his own mistakes and the censures which those mistakes brought upon him. But about the ignominious judgment passed by the House of Commons on his Pastoral Letter he has preserved a most significant silence.[1]

The plot which ruined Bohun, though it did no honour to those who contrived it, produced important and salutary effects. Before the conduct of the unlucky licenser had been brought under the consideration of Parliament, the Commons had resolved, without any division, and, as far as appears, without any discussion, that the Act which subjected literature to a censorship should be continued. But the question had now assumed a new aspect ; and the continuation of the Act was no longer regarded as a matter of course. A feeling in favour of the liberty of the press, a feeling not yet, it is true, of wide extent or formidable intensity, began to show itself. The existing system, it was said, was prejudicial both to commerce and to learning. Could it be expected that any capitalist would advance the funds necessary for a great literary undertaking, or that any scholar would expend years of toil and research on such an undertaking, while it was possible that, at the last moment, the caprice, the malice, the folly of one man might frustrate the whole design ? And was it certain that the law which so grievously restricted both the freedom of trade and the freedom of thought had really added to the security of the State ? Had not recent experience proved that the licenser might himself be an enemy of their Majesties, or, worse still,

---

[1] The vote of the Commons is mentioned with much feeling in the memoirs which Burnet wrote at the time. "It look'd," he says, "somewhat extraordinary that I, who perhaps was the greatest assertor of publick liberty, from my first setting out, of any writer of the age, should be soe severely treated as an enemy to it. But the truth was the Toryes never liked me, and the Whiggs hated me because I went not into their notions and passions. But even this, and worse things that may happen to me shall not, I hope, be able to make me depart from moderate principles and the just asserting the liberty of mankind."—Burnet MS. Harl. 6584.

an absurd and perverse friend ; that he might suppress a book of which it would be for their interest that every house in the country should have a copy, and that he might readily give his sanction to a libel which tended to make them hateful to their people, and which deserved to be torn and burned by the hand of Ketch ?   Had the government gained much by establishing a literary police which prevented Englishmen from having the History of the Bloody Circuit, and allowed them, by way of compensation, to read tracts which represented King William and Queen Mary as conquerors ?

In that age persons who were not specially interested in a public bill very seldom petitioned Parliament against it or for it.   The only petitions therefore which were at this conjuncture presented to the two Houses against the censorship came from booksellers, bookbinders, and printers.[1] But the opinion which these classes expressed was certainly not confined to them.

The law which was about to expire had lasted eight years.   It was renewed for only two years.   It appears, from an entry in the Journals of the Commons which unfortunately is defective, that a division took place on an amendment about the nature of which we are left entirely in the dark.   The votes were ninety nine to eighty.   In the Lords it was proposed, according to the suggestion offered fifty years before by Milton and stolen from him by Blount, to exempt from the authority of the licenser every book which bore the name of an author or publisher. This amendment was rejected ; and the bill passed, but not without a protest signed by eleven peers, who declared that they could not think it for the public interest to subject all learning and true information to the arbitrary will and pleasure of a mercenary and perhaps ignorant licenser.   Among those who protested were Halifax, Shrewsbury, and Mulgrave, three noblemen belonging to different political parties, but all distinguished by their literary attainments.   It is to be lamented that the signatures of Tillotson and Burnet, who were both present on that day, should be wanting.   Dorset was absent.[2]

Blount, by whose exertions and machinations the opposition to the censorship had been raised, did not live to see that opposition successful. Though not a very young man, he was possessed by an insane passion for the sister of his deceased wife.   Having long laboured in vain to convince the object of his love that she might lawfully marry him, he at last, whether from weariness of life, or in the hope of touching her heart, inflicted on himself a wound of which, after languishing long, he died.   He has often been mentioned as a blasphemer and selfmurderer. But the important service which, by means doubtless most immoral

---

[1] Commons' Journals, Feb. 27. 169⅔ ; Lords' Journals, Mar. 4.
[2] Lords' Journals, March 8. 169⅔.

and dishonourable, he rendered to his country, has passed almost unnoticed.[1]

Late in this busy and eventful session the attention of the Houses was called to the condition of Ireland. The government of that kingdom had, during the six months which followed the surrender of State of Limerick, been in an unsettled state. It was not till those Ireland Irish troops who adhered to Sarsfield had sailed for France, and till those who had made their election to remain at home had been disbanded, that William at length put forth a proclamation solemnly announcing the termination of the civil war. From the hostility of the aboriginal inhabitants, destitute as they now were of chiefs, of arms, and of organisation, nothing was to be apprehended beyond occasional robberies and murders. But the warcry of the Irishry had scarcely died away when the murmurs of the Englishry began to be heard. Coningsby was during some months at the head of the administration. He soon made himself in the highest degree odious to the dominant caste. He was an unprincipled man : he was insatiable of riches ; and he was in a situation in which riches were easily to be obtained by an unprincipled man. Immense sums of money, immense quantities of military stores, had been sent over from England. Immense confiscations were taking place in Ireland. The rapacious governor had daily opportunities of embezzling and extorting ; and of those opportunities he availed himself without scruple or shame. This however was not, in the estimation of the colonists, his greatest offence. They might have pardoned his covetousness : but they could not pardon the clemency which he showed to their vanquished and enslaved enemies. His clemency indeed amounted merely to this, that he loved money more than he hated Papists, and that he was not unwilling to sell for a high price a scanty measure of justice to some of the oppressed class. Unhappily, to the ruling minority, sore from recent conflict and drunk with recent victory, the subjugated majority was as a drove of cattle, or rather as a pack of wolves. Man acknowledges in the inferior animals no right

---

[1] In the article on Blount in the Biographia Britannica he is extolled as having borne a principal share in the emancipation of the press. But the writer was very imperfectly informed as to the facts.

It is strange that the circumstances of Blount's death should be so uncertain. That he died of a wound inflicted by his own hand, and that he languished long, are undisputed facts. The common story was that he shot himself ; and Narcissus Luttrell, at the time, made an entry to this effect in his Diary. On the other hand, Pope, who had the very best opportunities of obtaining accurate information, asserts that Blount, "being in love with a near kinswoman of his, and rejected, gave himself a stab in the arm, as pretending to kill himself, of the consequence of which he really died."—Note on the Epilogue to the Satires, Dialogue I. Warburton, who had lived, first with the heroes of the Dunciad, and then with the most eminent men of letters of his time, ought to have known the truth ; and Warburton, by his silence, confirms Pope's assertion. Gildon's rhapsody about the death of his friend will suit either story equally.

inconsistent with his own convenience ; and as man deals with the inferior animals the Cromwellian thought himself at liberty to deal with the Roman Catholic. Coningsby therefore drew on himself a greater storm of obloquy by his few good acts than by his many bad acts. The clamour against him was so violent that he was removed ; and Sidney went over, with the full power and dignity of Lord Lieutenant, to hold a Parliament at Dublin.[1]

But the easy temper and graceful manners of Sidney failed to produce a conciliatory effect. He does not indeed appear to have been greedy of unlawful gain. But he did not restrain with a sufficiently firm hand the crowd of subordinate functionaries whom Coningsby's example and protection had encouraged to plunder the public and to sell their good offices to suitors. Nor was the new Viceroy of a temper to bear

---

[1] The charges brought against Coningsby will be found in the Journals of the two Houses of the English Parliament. Those charges were, after the lapse of a quarter of a century, versified by Prior, whom Coningsby had treated with great insolence and harshness. I will quote a few stanzas. It will be seen that the poet condescended to imitate the style of the street ballads.

> " Of Nero, tyrant, petty king,
> Who heretofore did reign
> In famed Hibernia, I will sing,
> And in a ditty plain.
>
> .   .   .   .   .   .
>
> " The articles recorded stand
> Against this peerless peer ;
> Search but the archives of the land,
> You'll find them written there."

The story of Gaffney is then related. Coningsby's peculations are described thus :

> " Vast quantities of stores did he
> Embezzle and purloin ;
> Of the King's stores he kept a key,
> Converting them to coin.
>
> " The forfeited estates also,
> Both real and personal,
> Did with the stores together go.
> Fierce Cerberus swallow'd all."

The last charge is the favour shown the Roman Catholics :

> " Nero, without the least disguise,
> The Papists at all times
> Still favour'd, and their robberies
> Look'd on as trivial crimes.
>
> " The Protestants whom they did rob
> During his government,
> Were forced with patience, like good Job,
> To rest themselves content.
>
> " For he did basely them refuse
> All legal remedy ;
> The Romans still he well did use,
> Still screen'd their roguery."

hard on the feeble remains of the native aristocracy. He therefore speedily became an object of suspicion and aversion to the Anglosaxon

JOHN, LORD CONINGSBY, AND HIS DAUGHTERS

From an engraving by G. Vertue

settlers. His first act was to send out the writs for a general election. The Roman Catholics had been excluded from every municipal corporation :

but no law had yet deprived them of the county franchise. It is probable however that not a single Roman Catholic freeholder ventured to approach the hustings. The members chosen were, with scarcely an exception, men animated by the spirit of Enniskillen and Londonderry, a spirit eminently heroic in times of distress and peril, but too often cruel and imperious in the season of prosperity and power. They detested the civil treaty of Limerick, and were indignant when they learned that the Lord Lieutenant fully expected from them a parliamentary ratification of that odious contract, a contract which gave a licence to the idolatry of the mass, and which prevented good Protestants from ruining their Popish neighbours by bringing civil actions for injuries done during the war.[1]

On the fifth of October 1692 the Parliament met at Dublin in Chichester House. It was very differently composed from the assembly which had borne the same title in 1689. Scarcely one peer, not one member of the House of Commons, who had sate at the King's Inns, was to be seen. To the crowd of O's and Macs, descendants of the old princes of the island, had succeeded men whose names indicated a Saxon origin. A single O, an apostate from the faith of his fathers, and three Macs, evidently emigrants from Scotland, and probably Presbyterians, had seats in the assembly.

The Parliament, thus composed, had then less than the powers of the Assembly of Jamaica or of the Assembly of Virginia. Not only was the legislature which sate at Dublin subject to the absolute control of the legislature which sate at Westminster: but a law passed in the fifteenth century, during the administration of the Lord Deputy Poynings, and called by his name, had provided that no bill which had not been considered and approved by the Privy Council of England should be brought into either House in Ireland, and that every bill so considered and approved should be either passed without amendment or rejected.[2]

The session opened with a solemn recognition of the paramount authority of the mother country. The Commons ordered their clerk to read to them the English Act which required them to take the Oath of Supremacy and to subscribe the Declaration against Transubstantiation. Having heard the Act read, they immediately proceeded to obey it. Addresses were then voted which expressed the warmest gratitude and attachment to the King. Two members, who had been untrue to the Protestant and English interest during the troubles, were expelled. Supplies, liberal when compared with the resources of a country devastated by years of predatory war, were voted with eagerness.

[1] An Account of the Sessions of Parliament in Ireland, 1692, London, 1693.
[2] This Act is 10 H. 7. c. 4. It was explained by another Act, 3 & 4 P. & M. c. 4.

SIR HENRY CAPEL

From an engraving by Edwards, after a painting by Sir P. Lely

But the bill for confirming the Act of Settlement was thought to be too favourable to the native gentry, and, as it could not be amended, was with little ceremony rejected.   A Committee of the whole House resolved that the unjustifiable indulgence with which the Irish had been treated since the battle of the Boyne was one of the chief causes of the misery of the kingdom.   A Committee of Grievances sate daily till eleven in the evening ; and the proceedings of this inquest greatly alarmed the Castle.   Many instances of gross venality and knavery on the part of men high in office were brought to light, and many instances also of what was then thought a criminal lenity towards the subject nation.   This Papist had been allowed to enlist in the army : that Papist had been allowed to keep a gun : a third had too good a horse : a fourth had been protected against Protestants who wished to bring actions against him for wrongs committed during the years of confusion.   The Lord Lieutenant, having obtained nearly as much money as he could expect, determined to put an end to these unpleasant inquiries.   He knew, however, that if he quarrelled with the Parliament for treating either peculators or Papists with severity, he should have little support in England.   He therefore looked out for a pretext, and was fortunate enough to find one.   The Commons had passed a vote which might with some plausibility be represented as inconsistent with the Poynings statute.   Any thing which looked like a violation of that great fundamental law was likely to excite strong disapprobation on the other side of Saint George's Channel.   The Viceroy saw his advantage, and availed himself of it.   He went to the chamber of the Lords at Chichester House, sent for the Commons, reprimanded them in strong language, charged them with undutifully and ungratefully encroaching on the rights of the mother country, and put an end to the session.[1]

Those whom he had lectured withdrew full of resentment.   The imputation which he had thrown on them was unjust.   They had a strong feeling of love and reverence for the land from which they sprang, and looked with confidence for redress to the supreme Parliament.   Several of them went to London for the purpose of vindicating themselves and of accusing the Lord Lieutenant.   They were favoured

[1] The history of this session I have taken from the Journals of the Irish Lords and Commons, from the narratives laid in writing before the English Lords and Commons by members of the Parliament of Ireland, and from a pamphlet entitled a Short Account of the Sessions of Parliament in Ireland, 1692, London, 1693.   Burnet seems to me to have taken a correct view of the dispute ; ii. 118.   "The English in Ireland thought the government favoured the Irish too much : some said this was the effect of bribery, whereas others thought it was necessary to keep them safe from the prosecutions of the English, who hated them, and were much sharpened against them. . . .   There were also great complaints of an ill administration, chiefly in the revenue, in the pay of the army, and in the embezzling of stores."

VIEW OF MOOR PARK

From a sketch by J. Hassell in 1822

with a long and attentive audience, both by the Lords and by the Commons, and were requested to put the substance of what had been said into writing. The humble language of the petitioners, and their protestations that they had never intended to violate the Poynings statute, or to dispute the paramount authority of England, effaced the impression which Sidney's accusations had made. Both Houses addressed the King on the state of Ireland. They censured no delinquent by name : but they expressed an opinion that there had been gross mal-administration, that the public had been plundered, and that the Roman Catholics had been treated with unjustifiable tenderness. William in reply promised that what was amiss should be corrected. His friend Sidney was soon recalled, and consoled for the loss of the viceregal dignity with the lucrative place of Master of the Ordnance. The government of Ireland was for a time entrusted to Lords Justices, among whom Sir Henry Capel, a zealous Whig, very little disposed to show indulgence to Papists, had the foremost place.

The prorogation drew nigh ; and still the fate of the Triennial Bill was uncertain. Some of the ablest ministers thought the bill a good one ; and, even had they thought it a bad one, they would probably have tried to dissuade their master from rejecting it. It was impossible, however, to remove from his mind the impression that a concession on this point would seriously impair his authority. Not relying on the judgment of his ordinary advisers, he sent Portland to ask the opinion of Sir William Temple. Temple had made a retreat for himself at a place called Moor Park, in the neighbourhood of Farnham. The country round his dwelling was almost a wilderness. His amusement during some years had been to create in the waste what those Dutch burgomasters, among whom he had passed some of the best years of his life, would have considered as a paradise. His hermitage had been occasionally honoured by the presence of the King, who had from a boy known and esteemed the author of the Triple Alliance, and who was well pleased to find, among the heath and furze of the wilds of Surrey, a spot which seemed to be part of Holland, a straight canal, a terrace, rows of clipped trees, and rectangular beds of flowers and potherbs.

The King refuses to pass the Triennial Bill

Portland now repaired to this secluded abode and consulted the oracle. Temple was decidedly of opinion that the bill ought to pass. He was apprehensive that the reasons which led him to form this opinion might not be fully and correctly reported to the King by Portland, who was indeed as brave a soldier and as trusty a friend as ever lived, whose natural abilities were not inconsiderable, and who, in some departments of business, had great experience, but who was very imperfectly acquainted with the history and constitution of England. As the

SIR WILLIAM TEMPLE, 1628-1699.

From the painting by Sir Peter Lely, in the National Portrait Gallery.

state of Sir William's health made it impossible for him to go himself to Kensington, he determined to send his secretary thither. The secretary was a poor scholar of four or five and twenty, under whose plain garb and ungainly deportment were concealed some of the choicest gifts that have ever been bestowed on any of the children of men, rare powers of observation, brilliant wit, grotesque invention, humour of the most austere flavour, yet exquisitely delicious, eloquence singularly pure, manly, and perspicuous. This young man was named Jonathan Swift. He was born in Ireland, but would have thought himself insulted if he had been called an Irishman. He was of unmixed English blood, and, through life, regarded the aboriginal population of the island in which he first drew breath as an alien and a servile caste. He had in the late reign kept terms at the University of Dublin, but had been distinguished there only by his irregularities, and had with difficulty obtained his degree. At the time of the Revolution, he had, with many thousands of his fellow colonists, taken refuge in the mother country from the violence of Tyrconnel, and had been so fortunate as to obtain shelter at Moor Park.[1] For that shelter, however, he had to pay a heavy price. He was thought to be sufficiently remunerated for his services with twenty pounds a year and his board. He dined at the second table. Sometimes, indeed, when better company was not to be had, he was honoured by being invited to play at cards with his patron ; and on such occasions Sir William was so generous as to give his antagonist a little silver to begin with.[2] The humble student would not have dared to raise his eyes to a lady of family : but, when he had become a clergyman, he began, after the fashion of the clergymen of that generation, to make love to a pretty waitingmaid who was the chief ornament of the servants' hall, and whose name is inseparably associated with his in a sad and mysterious history.

Swift many years later confessed some part of what he felt when he found himself on his way to Court. His spirit had been bowed down, and might seem to have been broken, by calamities and humiliations. The language which he was in the habit of holding to his patron, as far as we can judge from the specimens which still remain, was that of a lacquey, or rather of a beggar.[3] A sharp word or a cold look of the master sufficed to make the servant miserable during several days.[4] But this tameness was merely the tameness with which a tiger, caught, caged, and starved, submits to the keeper who brings him food. The humble menial was at heart the haughtiest, the most aspiring, the most vindictive, the most despotic of men. And now at length a great, a boundless prospect was opening

[1] As to Swift's extraction and early life, see the Anecdotes written by himself.
[2] Journal to Stella, Letter liii.   [3] See Swift's Letter to Temple of Oct. 6. 1694.
[4] Journal to Stella, Letter xix.

before him.   To William he was already slightly known.   At Moor Park
the King had sometimes, when his host was confined by gout to an easy

JONATHAN SWIFT

From the painting by C. Jervas in the National Portrait Gallery

chair, been attended by the secretary about the grounds.   His majesty
had condescended to teach his companion the Dutch way of cutting

and eating asparagus, and had graciously asked whether Mr. Swift would like to have a captain's commission in a cavalry regiment. But now for the first time the young man was to stand in the royal presence as a counsellor. He was admitted into the closet, delivered a letter from Temple, and explained and enforced the arguments which that

ESTHER JOHNSON (STELLA)

From a portrait in the possession of Sir F. R. Falkiner

letter contained, concisely, but doubtless with clearness and ability. There was, he said, no reason to think that short Parliaments would be more disposed than long Parliaments to encroach on the just prerogatives of the Crown. In fact the Parliament which had, in the preceding generation, waged war against a king, led him captive, sent him to the prison, to the bar, to the scaffold, was known in our annals as emphatically the Long Parliament. Never would such disasters have befallen the monarchy but for the fatal law which secured that assembly from dissolution.[1]   In this reasoning there was, it must be owned, a flaw which a man less shrewd than William might easily detect.   That one restriction of the royal prerogative had been mischievous did not prove that another restriction would be salutary.   It by no means followed, because one sovereign had been ruined by being unable to get rid of a hostile Parliament, that another sovereign might not be ruined by being forced to part with a friendly Parliament.   To the great mortification of the ambassador, his arguments failed to shake the King's resolution.   On the fourteenth of March the Commons were summoned to the Upper House : the title of the Triennial Bill was read ; and it was announced, after the ancient form, that the King and Queen would take the matter into their consideration.   The Parliament was then prorogued.

Soon after the prorogation William set out for the Continent.   It was necessary that, before his departure, he should make some important

Ministerial arrangements

changes.   He was resolved not to discard Nottingham, on whose integrity, a virtue rare among English statesmen, he placed a well founded reliance.   Yet, if Nottingham remained Secretary of State, it was impossible to employ Russell at sea.   Russell, though much mortified, was induced to accept a lucrative place in the household; and two naval officers of great note in their profession, Killegrew and Delaval, were placed at the Board of Admiralty and entrusted with the command of the Channel Fleet.[2]   These arrangements caused much murmuring among the Whigs : for Killegrew and Delaval were certainly Tories, and were by many suspected of being Jacobites.   But other promotions which took place at the same time proved that the King wished to bear himself evenly between the hostile factions.   Nottingham had, during a year, been the sole Secretary of State.   He was now joined with a colleague in whose society he must have felt himself very ill at ease, John Trenchard.   Trenchard belonged to the extreme section of the Whig party.   He was a Taunton man, animated by that spirit which had, during two generations, peculiarly distinguished Taunton.   He had, in the days of Popeburnings and of Protestant flails, been one of the renowned Green Riband Club : he had been an active member of several stormy Parliaments : he had brought in the first Exclusion Bill : he had been deeply concerned in the plots formed by the chiefs of the opposition : he had fled to the Continent : he had been long an exile ; and he had been excepted by name from the general pardon of 1686.   Though his life had been passed in turmoil, his temper was naturally calm : but he was closely connected with a set of men whose passions were far fiercer than his

[1] Swift's Anecdotes.   [2] London Gazette, March 27. 1693

SIR JOHN TRENCHARD Kn.t

Chief Justice of Chester and Principal Secretary of State to their Majestys King William & Queen Mary

James Watson fecit.

SIR JOHN TRENCHARD

From a mezzotint by James Watson

own. He had married the sister of Hugh Speke, one of the falsest and most malignant of the libellers who brought disgrace on the cause of constitutional freedom. Aaron Smith, the solicitor of the Treasury, a man in whom the fanatic and the pettifogger were strangely united, possessed too much influence over the new Secretary, with whom he had, ten years before, discussed plans of rebellion at the Rose. Why Trenchard was selected in preference to many men of higher rank and greater ability for a post of the first dignity and importance, it is difficult to say. It seems however that, though he bore the title and drew the salary of Secretary of State, he was not trusted with any of the graver secrets of State, and that he was little more than a superintendent of police, charged to look after the printers of unlicensed books, the pastors of nonjuring congregations, and the haunters of treason taverns.[1]

Another Whig of far higher character was called at the same time to a far higher place in the administration. The Great Seal had now been four years in commission. Since Maynard's retirement, the constitution of the Court of Chancery had commanded little respect. Trevor, who was the First Commissioner, wanted neither parts nor learning: but his integrity was with good reason suspected ; and the duties, which, as Speaker of the House of Commons, he had to perform during four or five months in the busiest part of every year, made it impossible for him to be an efficient judge in equity. The suitors complained that they had to wait a most unreasonable time for judgment, and that, when, after long delay, a judgment had been pronounced, it was very likely to be reversed on appeal. Meanwhile there was no minister of justice, no great functionary to whom it especially belonged to advise the King as to the appointment of Judges, of Counsel for the Crown, of Justices of the Peace.[2] It was known that William was sensible of the inconvenience of this state of things ; and, during several months, there had been flying rumours that a Lord Keeper or a Lord Chancellor would soon be appointed.[3] The name most frequently mentioned was that of Nottingham. But the reasons which had prevented him from accepting the great Seal in 1689 had, since that year, rather gained than lost strength. William at length fixed his choice on Somers.

Somers was only in his forty-second year ; and five years had not elapsed since, on the great day of the trial of the Bishops, his powers had first been made known to the world. From that time his fame had been steadily and rapidly rising. Neither in forensic nor in parliamentary eloquence had he any superior. The consistency of his public

---

[1] Burnet, ii. 108., and Speaker Onslow's Note ; Sprat's True Account of the Horrid Conspiracy ; Letter to Trenchard, 1694.

[2] Burnet, ii. 107.

[3] These rumours are more than once mentioned in Narcissus Luttrell's Diary.

The Right Honble Sr John Sommers Kn^t
LORD KEEPER of the GREAT SEAL of ENGLAND, And one
of their Maties most Honble Privy Council. 1693.

SIR JOHN SOMERS AS LORD KEEPER

From an engraving by R. White, after a painting by Sir G. Kneller

conduct had gained for him the entire confidence of the Whigs ; and the urbanity of his manners had conciliated the Tories.   It was not without great reluctance that he consented to quit an assembly over which he exercised an immense influence for an assembly where it would be necessary for him to sit in silence.   He had been but a short time in great practice.   His savings were small.   Not having the means of supporting a hereditary title, he must, if he accepted the high dignity which was offered to him, preside during some years in the Upper House without taking part in the debates.   The opinion of others, however, was that he would be more useful as head of the law than even as head of the Whig party in the Commons.   He was sent for to Kensington, and called into the Council Chamber.   Caermarthen spoke in the name of the King.   " Sir John," he said, " it is necessary for the public service that you should take this charge upon you ; and I have it in command from His Majesty to say that he can admit of no excuse."   Somers submitted.   The seal was delivered to him, with a patent which entitled him to a pension of two thousand a year from the day on which he should quit his office ; and he was immediately sworn in a Privy Councillor and Lord Keeper.[1]

The King goes to Holland   The Gazette which announced these changes in the administration, announced also the King's departure.   He set out for Holland on the twenty fourth of March.

He left orders that the Estates of Scotland should, after a recess of more than two years and a half, be again called together.   Hamilton, **A session of Parliament in Scotland** who had lived many months in retirement, had, since the fall of Melville, been reconciled to the Court, and now consented to quit his retreat, and to occupy Holyrood House as Lord High Commissioner.   It was necessary that one of the Secretaries of State for Scotland should be in attendance on the King.   The Master of Stair had therefore gone to the Continent.   His colleague, Johnstone, was chief manager for the Crown at Edinburgh, and was charged to correspond regularly with Carstairs, who never quitted William.[2]

It might naturally have been expected that the session would be turbulent.   The Parliament was that very Parliament which had, in 1689, passed, by overwhelming majorities, all the most violent resolutions which Montgomery and his club could frame, which had refused supplies, which had proscribed the ministers of the Crown, which had closed the Courts of Justice, which had seemed bent on turning Scotland into an oligarchical republic.   In 1690 the Estates had been in a better temper.   Yet, even in 1690, they had, when the ecclesiastical polity of the realm was under consideration, paid little deference to what was

[1] London Gazette, March 27. 1693 ; Narcissus Luttrell's Diary.
[2] Burnet, ii. 123. ; Carstairs Papers.

well known to be the royal wish. They had abolished patronage : they had sanctioned the rabbling of the episcopal clergy : they had refused to pass a Toleration Act. It seemed likely that they would still be found unmanageable when questions touching religion came before them; and such questions it was unfortunately necessary to bring forward. William had, during the recess, attempted to persuade the General Assembly of the Church to receive into communion such of the old curates as should subscribe the Confession of Faith and should submit to the government of Synods. But the attempt had failed ; and the Assembly had consequently been dissolved by the representative of the King. Unhappily, the Act which established the Presbyterian polity had not defined the extent of the power which was to be exercised by the Sovereign over the Spiritual Courts. No sooner therefore had the dissolution been announced than the Moderator requested permission to speak. He was told that he was now merely a private person. As a private person he requested a hearing, and protested, in the name of his brethren, against the royal mandate. The right, he said, of the officers of the Church to meet and deliberate touching her interests was derived from her Divine Head, and was not dependent on the pleasure of the temporal magistrate. His brethren stood up, and by an approving murmur signified their concurrence in what their President had said. Before they retired they fixed a day for their next meeting.[1] It was indeed a very distant day ; and when it came neither minister nor elder attended : for even the boldest members shrank from a complete rupture with the civil power. But, though there was not open war between the Church and the Government, they were estranged from each other, jealous of each other, and afraid of each other. No progress had been made towards a reconciliation when the Estates met ; and which side the Estates would take might well be doubted.

But the proceedings of this strange Parliament, in almost every one of its sessions, falsified all the predictions of politicians. It had once been the most unmanageable of senates. It was now the most obsequious. Yet the old men had again met in the old hall. There were all the most noisy agitators of the club, with the exception of Montgomery, who was dying of want and of a broken heart in a garret far from his native land. There were the canting Ross and the perfidious Annandale. There was Sir Patrick Hume, lately created a peer, and henceforth to be called Lord Polwarth, but still as eloquent as when his interminable declamations and dissertations ruined the expedition of Argyle. Nevertheless, the whole spirit of the assembly had undergone

---

[1] Register of the Actings or Proceedings of the General Assembly of the Church of Scotland, held at Edinburgh, Jan. 15. 1692, collected and extracted from the Records by the Clerk thereof. This interesting record was printed for the first time in 1852.

a change. The members listened with profound respect to the royal letter, and returned an answer in reverential and affectionate language. An extraordinary aid of a hundred and fourteen thousand pounds sterling was granted to the Crown. Severe laws were enacted against the Jacobites. The legislation on ecclesiastical matters was as Erastian as William himself could have desired. An Act was passed requiring all ministers of the Established Church to swear fealty to their Majesties, and directing the General Assembly to receive into communion those Episcopalian ministers, not yet deprived, who should declare that they conformed to the Presbyterian doctrine and discipline.[1] Nay, the Estates carried adulation so far as to make it their humble request to the King that he would be pleased to confer a Scotch peerage on his favourite Portland. This was indeed their chief petition. They did not ask for redress of a single grievance. They contented themselves with hinting in general terms that there were abuses which required correction, and with referring the King for fuller information to his own Ministers, the Lord High Commissioner and the Secretary of State.[2]

There was one subject on which it may seem strange that even the most servile of Scottish Parliaments should have kept silence. More than a year had elapsed since the massacre of Glencoe; and it might have been expected that the whole assembly, peers, commissioners of shires, commissioners of burghs, would with one voice have demanded a strict investigation into that great crime. It is certain, however, that no motion for investigation was made. The state of the Gaelic clans was indeed taken into consideration. A law was passed for the more effectual suppressing of depredations and outrages beyond the Highland line; and in that law was inserted a special proviso reserving to Mac Callum More his hereditary jurisdiction. But it does not appear, either from the public records of the proceedings of the Estates, or from those private letters in which Johnstone regularly gave Carstairs an account of what had passed, that any speaker made any allusion to the fate of Mac Ian and Mac Ian's tribe.[3] The only explanation of this extra-

---

[1] Act. Parl. Scot., June 12. 1693.   [2] Ibid. June 15. 1693.

[3] The editor of the Carstairs Papers was evidently very desirous, from whatever motive, to disguise this most certain and obvious truth. He therefore, with gross dishonesty, prefixed to some of Johnstone's letters descriptions which may possibly impose on careless readers. For example, Johnstone wrote to Carstairs on the 18th of April, before it was known that the session would be a quiet one, "All arts have been used and will be used to embroil matters." The editor's account of the contents of this letter is as follows: "Arts used to embroil matters with reference to the affair of Glencoe." Again, Johnstone, in a letter written some weeks later, complained that the liberality and obsequiousness of the Estates had not been duly appreciated. "Nothing," he says, "is to be done to gratify the Parliament, I mean that they would have reckoned a gratification." The editor's account of the contents of this letter is as follows: "Complains that the Parliament is not to be gratified by an inquiry into the massacre of Glencoe"

ordinary silence seems to be that the public men who were assembled in the capital of Scotland knew little and cared little about the fate of a thieving tribe of Celts. The injured clan, bowed down by fear of the allpowerful Campbells, and little accustomed to resort to the constituted authorities of the kingdom for protection or redress, presented no petition to the Estates. The story of the butchery had been told at coffeehouses, but had been told in different ways. Very recently, one or two books, in which the facts were but too truly related, had come forth from the secret presses of London. But those books were not publicly exposed to sale. They bore the name of no responsible author. The Jacobite writers were, as a class, savagely malignant and utterly regardless of truth. Since the Macdonalds did not complain, a prudent man might naturally be unwilling to incur the displeasure of the King, of the ministers, and of the most powerful family in Scotland, by bringing forward an accusation grounded on nothing but reports wandering from mouth to mouth, or pamphlets which no licenser had approved, to which no author had put his name, and which no bookseller ventured to place in his shopwindow. But whether this be or be not the true solution, it is certain that the Estates separated quietly after a session of two months, during which, as far as can now be discovered, the name of Glencoe was not once uttered in the Parliament House.

CHAPTER XX

IT is now time to relate the events which, since the battle of La Hogue, had taken place at Saint Germains.

James, after seeing the fleet which was to have convoyed him back to his kingdom burned down to the wateredge, had returned, in no good humour, to his abode near Paris. Misfortune generally made him devout after his own fashion; and he now starved himself and flogged himself till his spiritual guides were forced to interfere.[1]

State of the Court of Saint Germains

It is difficult to conceive a duller place than Saint Germains was when he held his court there; and yet there was scarcely in all Europe a residence more enviably situated than that which the generous Lewis had assigned to his suppliants. The woods were magnificent, the air clear and salubrious, the prospects extensive and cheerful. No charm of rural life was wanting; and the towers of the greatest city of the Continent were visible in the distance. The royal apartments were richly adorned with tapestry and marquetry, vases of silver and mirrors in gilded frames. A pension of more than forty thousand pounds sterling was annually paid to James from the French Treasury. He had a guard of honour composed of some of the finest soldiers in Europe. If he wished to amuse himself with field sports, he had at his command an establishment far more sumptuous than that which had belonged to him when he was at the head of a kingdom, an army of huntsmen and fowlers, a vast arsenal of guns, spears, buglehorns, and tents, miles of network, staghounds, foxhounds, harriers, packs for the boar and packs for the wolf, gerfalcons for the heron and haggards for the wild duck. His presence chamber and his antechamber were in outward show as splendid as when he was at Whitehall. He was still surrounded by blue ribands and white staves. But over the mansion and the domain brooded a constant gloom, the effect, partly of bitter regrets and of deferred hopes, but chiefly of the abject superstition which had taken complete possession of his own mind, and which was affected by all

[1] Life of James, ii. 497.

THE PALACE OF ST. GERMAINS EN LAYE

From an engraving by Mariette

those who aspired to his favour.   His palace wore the aspect of a monastery.   There were three places of worship within the spacious pile.   Thirty or forty ecclesiastics were lodged in the building ; and their apartments were eyed with envy by noblemen and gentlemen who had followed the fortunes of their Sovereign, and who thought it hard that, when there was so much room under his roof, they should be forced to sleep in the garrets of the neighbouring town.   Among the murmurers was the brilliant Anthony Hamilton.   He has left us a sketch of the life of Saint Germains, a slight sketch indeed, but not unworthy of the artist to whom we owe the most highly finished and vividly coloured picture of the English Court in the days when the English Court was gayest.   He complains that existence was one round of religious exercises ; that, in order to live in peace, it was necessary to pass half the day in devotion or in the outward show of devotion ; that, if he tried to dissipate his melancholy by breathing the fresh air of that noble terrace which looks down on the valley of the Seine, he was driven away by the clamour of a Jesuit who had got hold of some unfortunate Protestant loyalists from England, and was proving to them that no heretic could go to heaven.   In general, Hamilton said, men suffering under a common calamity have a strong fellow feeling, and are disposed to render good offices to each other.   But it was not so at Saint Germains.   There all was discord, jealousy, bitterness of spirit.   Malignity was concealed under the show of friendship and of piety.   All the saints of the royal household were praying for each other and backbiting each other from morning to night.   Here and there in the throng of hypocrites might be remarked a man too high-spirited to dissemble.   But such a man, however advantageously he might have made himself known elsewhere, was certain to be treated with disdain by the inmates of that sullen abode.[1]

Such was the Court of James, as described by a Roman Catholic. Yet, however disagreeable that Court may have been to a Roman Catholic, it was infinitely more disagreeable to a Protestant.   For the Protestant had to endure, in addition to all the dulness of which the Roman Catholic complained, a crowd of vexations from which the Roman Catholic was free.   In every competition between a Protestant and a Roman Catholic the Roman Catholic was preferred.   In every quarrel between a Protestant and a Roman Catholic the Roman Catholic was supposed to be in the right.   While the ambitious Protestant looked in vain for promotion, while the dissipated Protestant looked in vain for amusement, the serious Protestant looked in vain for spiritual instruction and consolation.   James might, no doubt, easily have obtained per-mission for those members of the Church of England who had sacrificed

[1] Hamilton's Zeneyde.

every thing in his cause to meet privately in some modest oratory, and to receive the eucharistic bread and wine from the hands of one of their own clergy : but he did not wish his residence to be defiled by such impious rites. Doctor Dennis Granville, who had quitted the richest deanery, the richest archdeaconry, and one of the richest livings in England, rather than take the oaths, gave mortal offence by asking leave to read prayers to the exiles of his own communion. His request was refused ; and he was so grossly insulted by his master's chaplains and their retainers that he was forced to quit Saint Germains. Lest some other Anglican doctor should be equally importunate, James wrote to inform his agents in England that he wished no Protestant divine to come out to him.[1] Indeed the nonjuring clergy were at least as much sneered at and as much railed at in his palace as in his nephew's. If any heretic had a claim to be mentioned with respect at Saint Germains, it was surely Sancroft. Yet it was reported that the bigots who were assembled there never spoke of him but with aversion and disgust. The sacrifice of the first place in the Church, of the first place in the peerage, of the mansion at Lambeth and the mansion at Croydon, of immense patronage, and of a revenue of more than five thousand a year, was thought but a poor atonement for the great crime of having modestly remonstrated against the unconstitutional Declaration of Indulgence. Sancroft was pronounced to be just such a traitor and just such a penitent as Judas Iscariot. The old hypocrite had, it was said, while affecting reverence and love for his master, given the fatal signal to his master's enemies. When the mischief had been done and could not be repaired, the conscience of the sinner had begun to torture him. He had, like his prototype, blamed himself and bemoaned himself. He had, like his prototype, flung down his wealth at the feet of those whose instrument he had been. The best thing that he could now do was to make the parallel complete by hanging himself.[2]

James seems to have thought that the strongest proof of kindness which he could give to heretics who had resigned wealth, country, family, for his sake, was to suffer them to be beset, on their dying beds, by his priests. If some sick man, helpless in body and in mind, and deafened by the din of bad logic and bad rhetoric, suffered a wafer to be thrust into his mouth, a great work of grace was triumphantly announced to the Court ; and the neophyte was buried with all the pomp of religion.

[1] A View of the Court of St. Germains from the Year 1690 to 1695, 1696 ; Ratio Ultima, 1697. In the Nairne Papers is a letter in which the nonjuring bishops are ordered to send a Protestant divine to Saint Germains. This letter was speedily followed by another letter revoking the order. Both letters will be found in Macpherson's collection. They both bear date Oct. 16. 1693. I suppose that the first letter was dated according to the New Style, and the letter of revocation according to the Old Style.

[2] Ratio Ultima, 1697 ; History of the late Parliament, 1699.

But if a royalist, of the highest rank and most stainless character, died professing firm attachment to the Church of England, a hole was dug in the fields ; and, at dead of night, he was flung into it, and covered up like a mass of carrion.   Such were the obsequies of the Earl of Dunfermline, who had served the House of Stuart with the hazard of his life and to the utter ruin of his fortunes, who had fought at Killiecrankie, and who had, after the victory, lifted from the earth the still breathing remains of Dundee.   While living Dunfermline had been treated with contumely.   The Scottish officers who had long served under him had in vain entreated that, when they were formed into a company, he might still be their commander.   His religion had been thought a fatal disqualification.   A worthless adventurer, whose only recommendation was that he was a Papist, was preferred.   Dunfermline continued, during a short time, to make his appearance in the circle which surrounded the Prince whom he had served too well : but it was to no purpose.   The bigots who ruled the Court refused to the ruined and expatriated Protestant Lord the means of subsistence : he died of a broken heart ; and they refused him even a grave.[1]

The insults daily offered at Saint Germains to the Protestant religion produced a great effect in England.   The Whigs triumphantly asked

Feeling of the Jacobites. Compounders and Noncompounders

whether it were not clear that the old tyrant was utterly incorrigible ; and many even of the nonjurors observed his proceedings with shame, disgust, and alarm.[2]   The Jacobite party had, from the first, been divided into two sections, which, three or four years after the Revolution, began to be known as the Compounders and the Noncompounders.   The Compounders were those who wished for a restoration, but for a restoration accompanied by a general amnesty, and by guarantees for the security of the civil and ecclesiastical constitution of the realm.   The Noncompounders thought it downright Whiggery, downright rebellion, to take advantage of His Majesty's unfortunate situation for the purpose of imposing on him any condition.   The plain duty of his subjects was to bring him back. What traitors he would punish and what traitors he would spare, what laws he would observe and with what laws he would dispense, were questions to be decided by himself alone.   If he decided them wrongly, he must answer for his fault to heaven, and not to his people.

[1] View of the Court of Saint Germains from 1690 to 1695.   That Dunfermline was grossly ill used is acknowledged even in the Jacobite Memoirs of Dundee, 1714.

[2] So early as the year 1690, that conclave of the leading Jacobites which gave Preston his instructions made a strong representation to James on this subject.   "He must overrule the bigotry of Saint Germains, and dispose their minds to think of those methods that are more likely to gain the nation.   For there is one silly thing or another daily done there, that comes to our notice here, which prolongs what they so passionately desire."   See also a Short and True Relation of Intrigues transacted both at Home and Abroad to restore the late King James, 1694.

GRANVILLE DECANUS DUNELMENSIS DIONYSIUS

ÆTAT SUÆ 54

Beaupouille pinxit

G. F. Edelinck sculp.

Impensis Thomæ Harquet

Rotomagensis hospitis sui anno Dom. 1693.

Serenissimum Dominum
Jacobum Secundum Magnæ
Britaniæ Regem secutus est
in Galliam Anno 1688.

Propter fidelitatem suam
Domino Regi Principe
Arausiacensi Coronam
Angliæ Vsurpante, depriva-
tus fuit Anno 1691.

DENNIS GRANVILLE, DEAN OF DURHAM

From an engraving by G. Edelinck, after a painting by Beaupoille

The pure Noncompounders were chiefly to be found among the Roman Catholics, who, very naturally, were not solicitous to obtain any security for a religion which they thought heretical, or for a polity from the benefits of which they were excluded. There were also some Protestant nonjurors, such as Kettlewell and Hickes, who resolutely followed the theory of Filmer to all the extreme consequences to which it led. But, though Kettlewell tried to convince his countrymen that monarchical government had been ordained by God, not as a means of making them happy here, but as a cross which it was their duty to take up and bear in the hope of being recompensed for their patience hereafter, and though Hickes assured them that there was not a single Compounder in the whole Theban legion, very few churchmen were inclined to run the risk of the gallows merely for the purpose of reestablishing the High Commission and the Dispensing Power.

The Compounders formed the main strength of the Jacobite party in England : but the Noncompounders had hitherto had undivided sway at Saint Germains.   No Protestant, no moderate Roman Catholic, no man who dared to hint that any law could bind the royal prerogative, could hope for the smallest mark of favour from the banished King. The priests and the apostate Melfort, the avowed enemy of the Protestant religion and of civil liberty, of Parliaments, of trial by jury and of the Habeas Corpus Act, were in exclusive possession of the royal ear.   Herbert was called Chancellor, walked before the other officers of state, wore a black robe embroidered with gold, and carried a seal : but he was a member of the Church of England ; and therefore he was not suffered to sit at the Council Board.[1]

The truth is that the faults of James's head and heart were incurable. In his view there could be between him and his subjects no reciprocity of obligation.   Their duty was to risk property, liberty, life, in order to replace him on the throne, and then to bear patiently whatever he chose to inflict upon them.   They could no more pretend to merit before him than before God.   When they had done all, they were still unprofitable servants.   The highest praise due to the royalist who shed his blood on the field of battle, or on the scaffold for hereditary monarchy, was simply that he was not a traitor.   After all the severe discipline which the deposed King had undergone, he was still as much bent on plundering and abasing the Church of England as on the day when he told the kneeling fellows of Magdalene to get out of his sight, or on the day

[1] View of the Court of Saint Germains. The account given in this View is confirmed by a remarkable paper, which is among the Nairne MSS. Some of the heads of the Jacobite party in England made a representation to James, one article of which is as follows : " They beg that Your Majesty would be pleased to admit of the Chancellor of England into your Council ; your enemies take advantage of his not being in it." James's answer is evasive. " The King will be, on all occasions, ready to express the just value and esteem he has for his Lord Chancellor."

Jacobus Secundus Dei Gratia Angliæ
Scotiæ Franciæ et Hiberniæ Rex &

N. De Largillierre Pinxit   I. Smith fecit   Cum Privilegio Regis   Sold by Alex. Browne at the Blew Balleony in little Queen Street

JAMES II

From a mezzotint by J. Smith, after a painting by N. de Largillière

when he sent the Bishops to the Tower. He was in the habit of declaring that he would rather die without seeing his country again than stoop to capitulate with those whom he ought to command.[1] In the Declaration of April 1692 the whole man appears without disguise, full of his own imaginary rights, unable to understand how any body but himself can have any rights, dull, obstinate, and cruel. Another paper, which he drew up about the same time, shows, if possible, still more clearly, how little he had profited by a sharp experience. In that paper he set forth the plan according to which he intended to govern when he should be restored. He laid it down as a rule that one Commissioner of the Treasury, one of the two Secretaries of State, the Secretary at War, the majority of the Great Officers of the Household, the majority of the Lords of the Bedchamber, the majority of the officers of the army, should always be Roman Catholics.[2]

It was to no purpose that the most eminent Compounders sent from London letter after letter filled with judicious counsel and earnest supplication. It was to no purpose that they demonstrated in the plainest manner the impossibility of establishing Popish ascendency in a country where at least forty nine fiftieths of the population and much more than forty nine fiftieths of the wealth and the intelligence were Protestant. It was to no purpose that they informed their master that the Declaration of April 1692 had been read with exultation by his enemies and with deep affliction by his friends ; that it had been printed and circulated by the usurpers ; that it had done more than all the libels of the Whigs to inflame the nation against him ; and that it had furnished those naval officers who had promised him support with a plausible pretext for breaking faith with him, and for destroying the fleet which was to have convoyed him back to his kingdom. He continued to be deaf to the remonstrances of his best friends in England till those remonstrances began to be echoed at Versailles. All the information which Lewis and his ministers were able to obtain touching the state of our island satisfied them that James would never be restored unless he could bring himself to make large concessions to his subjects. It was therefore intimated to him, kindly and courteously, but seriously, that he would do well to change his counsels and his counsellors. France could not continue the war for the purpose of forcing a Sovereign on an unwilling nation. She was crushed by public burdens. Her trade and industry languished. Her harvest and her vintage had failed. The peasantry were starving. The faint murmurs of the provincial Estates began to be heard. There was a limit to the amount of the sacrifices which the most absolute

[1] A Short and True Relation of Intrigues, 1694.

[2] See the paper headed " For my Son the Prince of Wales. 1692." It is printed at the end of the Life of James.

prince could demand from those whom he ruled. However desirous the Most Christian King might be to uphold the cause of hereditary monarchy and of pure religion all over the world, his first duty was to his own kingdom ; and, unless a counterrevolution speedily took place in England, his duty to his own kingdom might impose on him the painful necessity of treating with the Prince of Orange. It would therefore be wise in James to do without delay whatever he could honourably and conscientiously do to win back the hearts of his people.

Thus pressed, James unwillingly yielded. He consented to give a share in the management of his affairs to one of the most distinguished of the Compounders, Charles Earl of Middleton.

Change of ministry at Saint Germains: Middleton

Middleton's family and his peerage were Scotch. But he was closely connected with some of the noblest houses of England : he had resided long in England : he had been appointed by Charles the Second one of the English Secretaries of State, and had been entrusted by James with the lead of the English House of Commons. His abilities and acquirements were considerable : his temper was easy and generous : his manners were popular ; and his conduct had generally been consistent and honourable. He had, when Popery was in the ascendant, resolutely refused to purchase the royal favour by apostasy. Roman Catholic ecclesiastics had been sent to convert him ; and the town had been much amused by the dexterity with which the layman baffled the divines. A priest undertook to demonstrate the doctrine of transubstantiation, and made the approaches in the usual form. " Your Lordship believes in the Trinity ? " " Who told you so ? " said Middleton. " Not believe in the Trinity ! " cried the priest in amazement. " Nay," said Middleton : " prove your religion to be true if you can : but do not catechise me about mine." As it was plain that the Secretary was not a disputant whom it was easy to take at an advantage, the controversy ended almost as soon as it began.[1] When fortune changed, Middleton adhered to the cause of hereditary monarchy with a steadfastness which was the more respectable because he would have had no difficulty in making his peace with the new government. His sentiments were so well known that, when the kingdom was agitated by apprehensions of an invasion and an insurrection, he was arrested and sent to the Tower : but no evidence on which he could be convicted of treason was discovered ; and, when the dangerous crisis was past, he was set at liberty. It should seem indeed that, during the three years which followed the Revolution, he was by no means an active plotter. He saw that a Restoration could be effected only with the general assent of the nation, and that the nation would never assent to a

[1] Burnet, i. 683.

Restoration without securities against Popery and arbitrary power. He therefore conceived that, while his banished master obstinately refused to give such securities, it would be worse than idle to conspire against the existing government.

Such was the man whom James, in consequence of strong representations from Versailles, now invited to join him in France. The great body of Compounders learned with delight that they were at length to be represented in the Council at Saint Germains by one of their favourite leaders. Some noblemen and gentlemen, who, though they had not approved of the deposition of James, had been so much disgusted by his perverse and absurd conduct that they had long avoided all connection with him, now began to hope that he had seen his error. They had refused to have any thing to do with Melfort : but they communicated freely with Middleton. The new minister conferred also with the four traitors whose infamy has been made preeminently conspicuous by their station, their abilities, and their great public services ; with Godolphin, the great object of whose life was to be in favour with both the rival Kings at once, and to keep, through all revolutions and counterrevolutions, his head, his estate, and a place at the Board of Treasury ; with Shrewsbury, who, having once in a fatal moment entangled himself in criminal and dishonourable engagements, had not had the resolution to break through them ; with Marlborough, who continued to profess the deepest repentance for the past and the best intentions for the future ; and with Russell, who declared that he was still what he had been before the day of La Hogue, and renewed his promise to do what Monk had done, on condition that a general pardon should be granted to all political offenders, and that the royal power should be placed under strong constitutional restraints.

Before Middleton left England he had collected the sense of all the leading Compounders. They were of opinion that there was one expedient which would reconcile contending factions at home, and lead to the speedy pacification of Europe. This expedient was that James should resign the Crown in favour of the Prince of Wales, and that the Prince of Wales should be bred a Protestant. If, as was but too probable, His Majesty should refuse to listen to this suggestion, he must at least consent to put forth a Declaration which might do away the unfavourable impression made by his Declaration of the preceding spring. A paper such as it was thought expedient that he should publish was carefully drawn up, and, after much discussion, approved.

Early in the year 1693, Middleton, having been put in full possession of the views of the principal English Jacobites, stole across the Channel, and made his appearance at the Court of James. There was at that Court no want of slanderers and sneerers, whose malignity was only the more dangerous because it wore a meek and sanctimonious air. Middleton found, on his arrival, that numerous lies, fabricated by

CHARLES, SECOND EARL OF MIDDLETON

From a painting by J. Greenhill, belonging to Mr. J. M. Paton. Plate in the possession of
Mr. Martin Secker

the priests who feared and hated him, were already in circulation. Some Noncompounders too had written from London that he was at heart a Presbyterian and a Republican. He was however graciously received, and was appointed Secretary of State conjointly with Melfort.[1]

It very soon appeared that James was fully resolved never to resign the Crown, or to suffer the Prince of Wales to be bred a heretic ; and it **New** long seemed doubtful whether any arguments or entreaties **Declaration** **put forth** would induce him to sign the Declaration which his friends **by James** in England had prepared. It was indeed a document very different from any that had yet appeared under his Great Seal. He was made to promise that he would grant a free pardon to all his sub-jects who should not oppose him after he should land in the island ; that, as soon as he was restored, he would call a Parliament ; that he would confirm all such laws, passed during the usurpation, as the Houses should tender to him for confirmation ; that he would waive his right to the chimney money ; that he would protect and defend the Established Church in the enjoyment of all her possessions and privileges ; that he would not again violate the Test Act ; that he would leave it to the legislature to define the extent of his dispensing power ; and that he would maintain the Act of Settlement in Ireland.

He struggled long and hard. He pleaded his conscience. Could a son of the Holy Roman Catholic and Apostolic Church bind himself to protect and defend heresy, and to enforce a law which excluded true believers from office ? Some of the ecclesiastics who swarmed in his household told him that he could not without sin give any such pledge as his undutiful subjects demanded. On this point the opinion of Middleton, who was a Protestant, could be of no weight. But Middleton found an ally in one whom he regarded as a rival and an enemy. Mel-fort, scared by the universal hatred of which he knew himself to be the object, and afraid that he should be held accountable, both in England and in France, for his master's wrongheadedness, submitted the case to several eminent Doctors of the Sorbonne. These learned casuists pro-nounced the Declaration unobjectionable in a religious point of view. The great Bossuet, Bishop of Meaux, who was regarded by the Gallican Church as a father scarcely inferior in authority to Cyprian or Augustin, showed, by powerful arguments, both theological and political, that the scruple which tormented James was precisely of that sort against which a much wiser King had given a caution in the words, " Be not righteous overmuch."[2] The authority of the French divines was supported by the

---

[1] As to this change of ministry at Saint Germains see the very curious but very confused nar-rative in the Life of James, ii. 498-515. ; Burnet, ii. 219. ; Mémoires de Saint Simon ; A French Conquest neither desirable nor practicable, 1693 ; and the Letters from the Nairne MSS. printed by Macpherson.

[2] Life of James, ii. 509. Bossuet's opinion will be found in the Appendix to M. Mazure's history. The Bishop sums up his arguments thus : " Je dirai donc volontiers aux Catholiques,

JAMES, PRINCE OF WALES

From an engraving by G. Edelinck, after a painting by N. de Largillière

authority of the French government. The language held at Versailles was so strong that James began to be alarmed. What if Lewis should take serious offence, should think his hospitality ungratefully requited, should conclude a peace with the usurpers, and should request his unfortunate guests to seek another asylum? It was necessary to submit. On the seventeenth of April 1693 the Declaration was signed and sealed. The concluding sentence was a prayer. "We come to vindicate our own right, and to establish the liberties of our people ; and may God give us success in the prosecution of the one as we sincerely intend the confirmation of the other !" [1] The prayer was heard. The success of James was strictly proportioned to his sincerity. What his sincerity was we know on the best evidence. Scarcely had he called on heaven to witness the truth of his professions, when he directed Melfort to send a copy of the Declaration to Rome with such explanations as might satisfy the Pope. Melfort's letter ends thus : "After all, the object of this Declaration is only to get us back to England. We shall fight the battle of the Catholics with much greater advantage at Whitehall than at Saint Germains." [2]

Meanwhile the document from which so much was expected had been despatched to London. There it was printed at a secret press in the house of a Quaker : for there was among the Quakers a party, small in number, but zealous and active, which had imbibed the politics of William Penn. [3] To circulate such a work was a service of some danger : but agents were found. Several persons were taken up while distributing copies in the streets of the city. A hundred packets were stopped in one day at the Post Office on their way to the fleet. But, after a short time, the government wisely gave up the endeavour to suppress what could not be suppressed, and published the Declaration at full length, accompanied by a severe commentary. [4]

The commentary, however, was hardly needed. The Declaration altogether failed to produce the effect which Middleton had anticipated.

s'il y en a qui n'approuvent point la déclaration dont il s'agit ; Noli esse justus multum ; neque plus sapias quam necesse est, ne obstupescas." In the Life of James it is asserted that the French Doctors changed their opinion, and that Bossuet, though he held out longer than the rest, saw at last that he had been in error, but did not choose formally to retract. I think much too highly of Bossuet's understanding to believe this.

[1] Life of James, ii. 505.

[2] "En fin celle cy—j'entends la déclaration—n'est que pour rentrer ; et l'on peut beaucoup mieux disputer des affaires des Catholiques à Whythall qu'à Saint Germain."—Mazure, Appendix.

[3] Baden to the States General, June $\frac{2}{12}$. 1693. Four thousand copies, wet from the press, were found in this house.

[4] Baden's Letters to the States General of May and June 1693 ; An Answer to the Late King James's Declaration published at Saint Germains, 1693.

JACQUES BENIGNE BOSSUET, BISHOP OF MEAUX

From an engraving by P. Drevet, after a painting by H. Rigaud

The truth is that his advice had not been asked till it mattered not what advice he gave.   If James had put forth such a manifesto in
Effect of January 1689, the throne would probably not have been
the new declared vacant.   If he had put forth such a manifesto
Declaration when he was on the coast of Normandy at the head
of an army, he would have conciliated a large part of the nation, and he might possibly have been joined by a large part of the fleet.   But both in 1689 and in 1692 he had held the language of an implacable tyrant ; and it was now too late to affect tenderness of heart and reverence for the constitution of the realm.   The contrast between the new Declaration and the preceding Declaration excited, not without reason, general suspicion and contempt.   What confidence could be placed in the word of a Prince so unstable, of a Prince who veered from extreme to extreme?   In 1692, nothing would satisfy him but the heads and quarters of hundreds of poor ploughmen and boatmen who had, several years before, taken some rustic liberties with him at which his grandfather Henry the Fourth would have had a hearty laugh. In 1693, the foulest and most ungrateful treasons were to be covered with oblivion.   Caermarthen expressed the general sentiment.   " I do not," he said, "understand all this.   Last April I was to be hanged. This April I am to have a free pardon.   I cannot imagine what I have done during the past year to deserve such goodness."   The general opinion was that a snare was hidden under this unwonted clemency, this unwonted respect for law.   The Declaration, it was said, was excellent; and so was the Coronation oath.   Every body knew how King James had observed his Coronation oath ; and every body might guess how he would observe his Declaration.   While grave men reasoned thus, the Whig jesters were not sparing of their pasquinades.   Some of the Non-compounders, meantime, uttered indignant murmurs.   The King was in bad hands, in the hands of men who hated monarchy.   His mercy was cruelty of the worst sort.   The general pardon which he had granted to his enemies was in truth a general proscription of his friends.   Hitherto the Judges appointed by the usurper had been under a restraint, imperfect indeed, yet not absolutely nugatory.   They had known that a day of reckoning might come, and had therefore in general dealt tenderly with the persecuted adherents of the rightful King.   That restraint His Majesty had now taken away.   He had told Holt and Treby that, till he should land in England, they might hang royalists without the smallest fear of being called to account.[1]

But by no class of people was the Declaration read with so much disgust and indignation as by the native aristocracy of Ireland.   This

[1] Life of James, ii. 514.   I am unwilling to believe that Ken was among those who blamed the Declaration of 1693 as too merciful.

The True and Genuine Explanation

Of One King James's *Declaration.*

J. R.

Hereas by mifreprefentation
(Of which Our felf was the occafion)
We loft our Royal Reputation,
And much againft Our Expectation,
Laid the moft Tragical Foundation
Of vacant Throne, and Abdication:
After Mature Deliberation
We now Refolve to Sham the Nation
Into another Reftauration;
Promifing, in Our wonted Fafhion,
Without the leaft Equivocation,
To make an ample Reparation.
And for Our Reinauguration
We chufe to owe the Obligation
To Our kind Subjects Inclination;
For whom We always fhew'd a Pafhon.
And when again they take occafion
To want a King of Our perfwafion,
We'll foon appear to take Our Station,
With the enfuing Declaration.
All fhall be fafe from Rope and Fire,
Or never more believe in J. R.

J. R.

When We Reflect what Defolation
Our Abfence caufes to the Nation,
We would not hold Our felf exempted
From any thing to be Attempted,
Whereby Our Subjects, well Beguil'd,
May to Our Yoke be Reconcil'd.

Be all Affur'd, both Whigg and Tory,
If for paft Faults you can be forry,
You ne're fhall know what we'll do for you.
For 'tis Our noble Refolution
To do more for your Conftitution,
Than e're we'll put in Execution.
Tho fome before us made a pother,
England had never fuch another,
No not Our own Renown'd, Dear, Brother.

We have it fet before Our Eyes,
That our main Intereft wholly lies
In managing with fuch Difguife,
As leaves no room for Jealoufies.

And to Encourage Foes and Friends
With Hearts and Hands to ferve our Ends,
We hereby Publifh and Declare
(And this We do becaufe We Dare)
That to Evince We are not fullen,
We'll bury all paft Faults in Woollen;
By which you may perceive We draw
Our wife Refolves from Statute-Law:
And therefore by this Declaration
We promife Pardon to the Nation,
Excepting only whom We pleafe,
Whether they be on Land or Seas.

And farther Bloodfhed to prevent,
We here Declare Our felf content
To heap as large Rewards on all
That help to bring us to *Whitehall,*
As ever did Our Brother Dear
At his Return on Cavalier:
Or We, to Our immortal Glory,
Conferr'd on non-refifting Tory.

Then be affur'd the firft fair Weather
We'll call a Parliament together,
(Chufe right or wrong no matter whether)
Where with united Inclination
We'll bring the Intereft of the Nation
Under our own Adjudication:
With their Concurrence we'll Redrefs
What We Our felf think Grievances,
All fhall be firm as Words can make it,
And if We promife, what can fhake it?

As for the Church, we'll ftill Defend it,
Or if you pleafe, the Pope fhall mend it:
Your Chappels, Colleges, and Schools
Shall be fupply'd with your own Fools:
But if We live another Summer,
We'll then relieve them from St. *Omers.*

Next

A PARODY OF THE DECLARATION OF KING JAMES

From a broadside in the possession of the Editor

then was the reward of their loyalty. This was the faith of kings. When England had cast James out, when Scotland had rejected him, the Irish had still been true to him ; and he had, in return, solemnly given his sanction to a law which restored to them an immense domain of which they had been despoiled. Nothing that had happened since that time had diminished their claim to his favour. They had defended his cause to the last : they had fought for him long after he had deserted them : many of them, when unable to contend longer against superior force, had followed him into banishment ; and now it appeared that he was desirous to make peace with his deadliest enemies at the expense of his most faithful friends. There was much discontent in the Irish regiments which were dispersed through the Netherlands and along the frontiers of Germany and Italy. Even the Whigs allowed that, for once, the O's and Macs were in the right, and asked triumphantly whether a prince who had broken his word to his devoted servants could be expected to keep it to his foes ?[1]

While the Declaration was the subject of general conversation in England, military operations recommenced on the Continent. The
French pre- preparations of France had been such as amazed even
parations
for the those who estimated most highly her resources and the
campaign abilities of her rulers. Both her agriculture and her commerce were suffering. The vineyards of Burgundy, the interminable cornfields of the Beauce, had failed to yield their increase : the looms of Lyons were silent ; and the merchant ships were rotting in the harbour of Marseilles. Yet the monarchy presented to its numerous enemies a front more haughty and more menacing than ever. Lewis had determined not to make any advance towards a reconciliation with the new government of England till the whole strength of his realm had been put forth in

[1] Among the Nairne Papers is a letter sent on this occasion by Middleton to Macarthy, who was then serving in Germany. Middleton tries to sooth Macarthy and to induce Macarthy to sooth others. Nothing more disingenuous was ever written by a Minister of State. "The King," says the Secretary, "promises in the foresaid Declaration to restore the Settlement, but, at the same time, declares that he will recompense all those who may suffer by it by giving them equivalents." Now James did not declare that he would recompense any body, but merely that he would advise with his Parliament on the subject. He did not declare that he would even advise with his Parliament about recompensing all who might suffer, but merely about re. compensing such as had followed him to the last. Finally he said nothing about equivalents. Indeed the notion of giving an equivalent to every body who suffered by the Act of Settlement, in other words, of giving an equivalent for the fee simple of half the soil of Ireland, was obviously absurd. Middleton's letter will be found in Macpherson's collection. I will give a sample of the language held by the Whigs on this occasion. "The Roman Catholics of Ireland," says one writer, "although in point of interest and profession different from us, yet, to do them right, have deserved well from the late King, though ill from us ; and for the late King to leave them and exclude them is such an instance of uncommon ingratitude that Protestants have no reason to stand by a Prince that deserts his own party, and a people that have been faithful to him and his interest to the very last."—A Short and True Relation of the Intrigues, &c., 1694.

one more effort. A mighty effort in truth it was, but too exhausting to be repeated. He made an immense display of force at once on the Pyrenees and on the Alps, on the Rhine and on the Meuse, in the Atlantic and in the Mediterranean. That nothing might be wanting which could excite the martial ardour of a nation eminently highspirited, he *Institution* instituted, a few days before he left his palace for the camp, *of the Order of Saint* a new military order of knighthood, and placed it under the *Lewis* protection of his own sainted ancestor and patron. The cross of Saint Lewis shone on the breasts of the gentlemen who had been conspicuous in the trenches before Mons and Namur, and on the fields of Fleurus and Steinkirk ; and the sight raised a generous emulation among those who had still to win an honourable fame in arms.[1]

In the week in which this celebrated order began to exist Middleton visited Versailles. A letter in which he gave his friends in England an account of his visit has come down to us.[2] He was presented *Middleton's* to Lewis, was most kindly received, and was overpowered by *account of* gratitude and admiration. Of all the wonders of the Court, *Versailles* —so Middleton wrote,—its master was the greatest. The splendour of the great King's personal merit threw even the splendour of his fortunes into the shade. The language which His Most Christian Majesty held about English politics was, on the whole, highly satisfactory. Yet in one thing this accomplished prince and his able and experienced ministers were strangely mistaken. They were all possessed with the absurd notion that the Prince of Orange was a great man. No pains had been spared to undeceive them : but they were under an incurable delusion. They saw through a magnifying glass of such power that the leech appeared to them a leviathan. It ought to have occurred to Middleton that possibly the delusion might be in his own vision and not in theirs. Lewis and the counsellors who surrounded him were far indeed from loving William. But they did not hate him with that mad hatred which raged in the breasts of his English enemies. Middleton was one of the wisest and most moderate of the Jacobites. Yet even Middleton's judgment was so much darkened by malice that, on this subject, he talked nonsense unworthy of his capacity. He, like the rest of his party, could see in the usurper nothing but what was odious and contemptible, the heart of a fiend, the understanding and manners of a stupid, brutal, Dutch boor, who generally observed a sulky silence, and, when forced to speak, gave short testy answers in bad English. The French statesmen, on the other hand, judged of William's faculties from an intimate knowledge of the way in which he had, during twenty years, conducted affairs of the

---

[1] The edict of creation was registered by the Parliament of Paris on the 10th of April 1693.

[2] The letter is dated the 19th of April 1693. It is among the Nairne MSS., and was printed by Macpherson.

greatest moment and of the greatest difficulty. He had, ever since 1673, been playing against themselves a most complicated game of mixed chance and skill for an immense stake : they were proud, and with reason, of their own dexterity at that game; yet they were conscious that in him they had found more than their match. At the commencement of the long contest every advantage had been on their side. They had at their absolute command all the resources of the greatest kingdom in Europe ; and he was merely the servant of a commonwealth, of which the whole territory was inferior in extent to Normandy or Guienne. A succession of generals and diplomatists of eminent ability had been opposed to him. A powerful faction in his native country had pertinaciously crossed his designs. He had undergone defeats in the field and defeats in the senate : but his wisdom and firmness had turned defeats into victories. Notwithstanding all that could be done to keep him down, his influence and fame had been almost constantly rising and spreading. The most important and arduous enterprise in the history of modern Europe had been planned and had been conducted to a prosperous termination by him alone. The most extensive coalition that the world had seen for ages had been formed by him, and would be instantly dissolved if his superintending care were withdrawn. He had gained two kingdoms by statecraft, and a third by conquest ; and he was still maintaining himself in the possession of all three in spite of both foreign and domestic foes. That these things had been effected by a poor creature, a man of the most ordinary capacity, was an assertion which might easily find credence among the nonjuring parsons who congregated at Sam's Coffeehouse, but which moved the laughter of the veteran politicians of Versailles.

While Middleton was in vain trying to convince the French that William was a greatly overrated man, William, who did full justice to Middleton's merit, felt much uneasiness at learning that the Court of Saint Germains had called in the help of so able a counsellor.[1] But this was only one of a thousand causes of anxiety which during that spring pressed on the King's mind. He was preparing for the opening of the campaign, imploring his allies to be early in the field, rousing the sluggish, haggling with the greedy, making up quarrels, adjusting points of precedence. He had to prevail on the Imperial Cabinet to send timely succours into Piedmont. He had to keep a vigilant eye on those Northern potentates who were trying to form a third party in Europe. He had to act as tutor to the Elector of Bavaria

William's preparations for the campaign

[1] " Il ne me plait nullement que M. Middleton est allé en France. Ce n'est pas un homme qui voudroit faire un tel pas sans quelque chose d'importance, et de bien concerté, sur quoy j'ay fait beaucoup de reflections que je reserve à vous dire à vostre heureuse arrivée."—William to Portland from Loo, April 18/28. 1693.

CHARLES LANDGRAVE OF HESSE

From a mezzotint by J. Gole

in the Netherlands. He had to provide for the defence of Liege, a matter which the authorities of Liege coolly declared to be not at all their business, but the business of England and Holland. He had to prevent the House of Brunswick Wolfenbuttel from going to blows with the House of Brunswick Lunenburg : he had to accommodate a dispute between the Prince of Baden and the Elector of Saxony, each of whom wished to be at the head of an army on the Rhine ; and he had to manage the Landgrave of Hesse, who omitted to furnish his own contingent, and yet wanted to command the contingents furnished by other princes. But of all the quarrels which at this time distracted the coalition the most serious was one which had sprung up between the Courts of Vienna and Dresden. Schœning, the first minister of Saxony, had put himself up to auction. In the summer of 1691 he had been the tool of France. Early in 1692 the Allies had bid high for him, and had, it was thought, secured him : but, during the campaign which followed, they had found good reason to suspect that France had again outbid them. While their resentment was at the height, the perfidious statesman was rash enough to visit a watering place in the territories of the House of Austria. He was arrested, conveyed to a fortress in Moravia, and kept close prisoner. His master, the Elector, complained loudly : the Emperor maintained that the arrest and the detention were in strict conformity with the law of nations, and with the constitution of the Germanic body ; and it was, during some time, apprehended that the controversy might end in a violent rupture.[1]

Meanwhile the time for action had arrived. On the eighteenth of May Lewis left Versailles. Early in June he was under the walls of Namur.

Lewis takes the field The Princesses, who had accompanied him, held their court within the fortress. He took under his immediate command the army of Boufflers, which was encamped at Gembloux. Little more than a mile off lay the army of Luxemburg. The force collected in that neighbourhood under the French lilies did not amount to less than a hundred and twenty thousand men. Lewis had flattered himself that he should be able to repeat in 1693 the stratagem by which Mons had been taken in 1691 and Namur in 1692 ; and he had determined that either Liege or Brussels should be his prey. But William had this year been able to assemble in good time a force, inferior indeed to that which was opposed to him, but still formidable. With this force he took his post near Louvain, on the road between the two threatened cities, and watched every movement of the enemy.

Lewis was disappointed. He found that it would not be possible for him to gratify his vanity so safely and so easily as in the two

---

[1] The best account of William's labours and anxieties at this time is contained in his letters to Heinsius from November 1692 to May 1693.

Monseigneur

THE DAUPHIN OF FRANCE

From a mezzotint by E. Bernard

preceding years, to sit down before a great town, to enter the gates in triumph, and to receive the keys, without exposing himself to any risk greater than that of a staghunt at Fontainebleau. Before he could lay siege either to Liege or to Brussels he must fight and win a battle. The chances were indeed greatly in his favour: for his army was more numerous, better officered, and better disciplined than that of the allies. Luxemburg strongly advised him to march against William. The aristocracy of France anticipated with intrepid gaiety a bloody but a glorious day, followed by a large distribution of the crosses of the new order. William himself was perfectly aware of his danger, and prepared to meet it with calm but mournful fortitude.[1] Just at this conjuncture Lewis announced his intention to return instantly to Versailles, and to send the Dauphin and Boufflers, with part of the army which was assembled near Namur, to join Marshal Lorges who commanded in the Palatinate. Luxemburg was thunderstruck. He expostulated boldly and earnestly. Never, he said, was such an opportunity thrown away. If His Majesty would march against the Prince of Orange, victory was almost certain. Could any advantage which it was possible to obtain on the Rhine be set against the advantage of a victory gained in the heart of Brabant over the principal army and the principal captain of the coalition? The Marshal reasoned: he implored: he went on his knees: but all was vain; and he quitted the royal presence in the deepest dejection. Lewis left the camp a week after he had joined it, and never afterwards made war in person.

The astonishment was great throughout his army. All the awe which he inspired could not prevent his old generals from grumbling and looking sullen, his young nobles from venting their spleen, sometimes in curses, and sometimes in sarcasms, and even his common soldiers from holding irreverent language round their watchfires. His enemies rejoiced with vindictive and insulting joy. Was it not strange, they asked, that this great prince should have gone in state to the theatre of war, and then in a week have gone in the same state back again? Was it necessary that all that vast retinue, princesses, dames of honour, tirewomen, equerries and gentlemen of the bedchamber, cooks, confectioners and musicians, long trains of waggons, droves of led horses and sumpter mules, piles of plate, bales of tapestry, should travel four hundred miles merely in order that the Most Christian King might look at his soldiers and might then return? The ignominious truth was too evident to be concealed. He had gone to the Netherlands in the hope that he might again be able to snatch some military glory without any hazard to his

Lewis returns to Versailles

---

[1] He speaks very despondingly in his letter to Heinsius of the 30th of May. Saint Simon says: "On a su depuis que le Prince d'Orange écrivit plusieurs fois au prince de Vaudmont, son ami intime, qu'il était perdu et qu'il n'y avait que par un miracle qu'il pût échapper"

THE RETREAT OF LEWIS XIV AND HIS SERAGLIO

Number 1287 in the British Museum Catalogue of Satirical Prints

person, and had hastened back rather than expose himself to the chances of a pitched field.[1] This was not the first time that His Most Christian Majesty had shown the same kind of prudence. Seventeen years before he had been opposed under the walls of Bouchain to the same antagonist. William, with the ardour of a very young commander, had most imprudently offered battle. The opinion of the ablest generals was that, if Lewis had seized the opportunity, the war might have been ended in a day. The French army had eagerly demanded to be led to the onset. The King had called his lieutenants round him and had collected their opinions. Some courtly officers, to whom a hint of his wishes had been dexterously conveyed, had, blushing and stammering with shame, voted against fighting. It was to no purpose that bold and honest men, who prized his honour more than his life, had proved to him that, on all principles of the military art, he ought to accept the challenge rashly given by the enemy. His Majesty had gravely expressed his sorrow that he could not, consistently with his public duty, obey the impetuous movement of his blood, had turned his rein, and had galloped back to his quarters.[2] Was it not frightful to think what rivers of the best blood of France, of Spain, of Germany, and of England, had flowed, and were destined still to flow, for the gratification of a man who wanted the vulgar courage which was found in the meanest of the hundreds of thousands whom he had sacrificed to his vainglorious ambition?

Though the French army in the Netherlands had been weakened by the departure of the forces commanded by the Dauphin and Boufflers, and though the allied army was daily strengthened by the arrival of fresh troops, Luxemburg still had a superiority of force; and that superiority he increased by an adroit stratagem. He marched towards Liege, and made as if he were about to form the siege of that city. William was uneasy, and the more uneasy because he knew that there was a French party among the inhabitants. He quitted his position near Louvain, advanced to Nether Hespen, and encamped there with the river Gette in his rear. On his march he learned that Huy had opened its gates to the French. The news increased his anxiety about Liege, and determined him to send thither a force sufficient to overawe malecontents within the city, and to repel any attack from without.[3] This was exactly what Luxemburg had expected and desired. His feint had served its purpose. He turned his back on the fortress which had hitherto seemed to be his object, and hastened towards the Gette. William, who had detached more than twenty thousand men, and who had but fifty thousand left in his camp, was alarmed by learning from his scouts, on the eighteenth

Manœuvres of Luxemburg

---

[1] Saint Simon; Monthly Mercury, June 1693; Burnet, ii. 111.
[2] Mémoires de Saint Simon; Burnet, i. 404.   [3] William to Heinsius, July $\frac{7}{17}$. 1693.

of July, that the French General, with near eighty thousand, was close at hand.

It was still in the King's power, by a hasty retreat, to put between his army and the enemy the narrow, but deep, waters of the Gette, which had lately been swollen by rains. But the site which he occupied was strong ; and it could easily be made still stronger. **Battle of Landen** He set all his troops to work. Ditches were dug, mounds thrown up, palisades fixed in the earth. In a few hours the ground wore a new aspect ; and the King trusted that he should be able to repel the attack even of a force greatly outnumbering his own. Nor was it without much appearance of reason that he felt this confidence. When the morning of the nineteenth of July broke, the bravest men of Lewis's army looked gravely and anxiously on the fortress which had suddenly sprung up to arrest their progress. The allies were protected by a breastwork. Here and there along the entrenchments were formed little redoubts and half moons. A hundred pieces of cannon were disposed on the ramparts. On the left flank, the village of Romsdorff rose close to the little stream of Landen, from which the English have named the disastrous day. On the right was the village of Neerwinden. Both villages were, after the fashion of the Low Countries, surrounded by moats and fences ; and, within these enclosures, the little plots of ground occupied by different families were separated by mud walls five feet in height and a foot in thickness. All these barricades William had repaired and strengthened. Saint Simon, who, after the battle, surveyed the ground, could hardly, he tells us, believe that defences so extensive and so formidable could have been created with such rapidity.

Luxemburg, however, was determined to try whether even this position could be maintained against the superior numbers and the impetuous valour of his soldiers. Soon after sunrise the roar of the cannon began to be heard. William's batteries did much execution before the French artillery could be so placed as to return the fire. It was eight o'clock before the close fighting began. The village of Neerwinden was regarded by both commanders as the point on which every thing depended. There an attack was made by the French left wing commanded by Montchevreuil, a veteran officer of high reputation, and by Berwick, who, though young, was fast rising to an eminent place among the captains of his time. Berwick led the onset, and forced his way into the village, but was soon driven out again with a terrible carnage. His followers fled or perished : he, while trying to rally them, and cursing them for not doing their duty better, was surrounded by foes. He concealed his white cockade, and hoped to be able, by the help of his native tongue, to pass himself off as an officer of the English army. But his face was recognised by one of his mother's brothers, George Churchill,

H.E. V　　　　　　　　　s

who held on that day the command of a brigade. A hurried embrace was exchanged between the kinsmen ; and the uncle conducted the nephew to William, who, as long as every thing seemed to be going well, remained in the rear. The meeting of the King and the captive, united by such close domestic ties, and divided by such inexpiable injuries, was a strange sight. Both behaved as became them. William uncovered, and addressed to his prisoner a few words of courteous greeting. Berwick's only reply was a solemn bow. The King put on his hat : the Duke put on his hat ; and the cousins parted for ever.

By this time the French, who had been driven in confusion out of Neerwinden, had been reinforced by a division under the command of the Duke of Bourbon, and came gallantly back to the attack. William, well aware of the importance of this post, gave orders that troops should move thither from other parts of his line. This second conflict was long and bloody. The assailants again forced an entrance into the village. They were again driven out with immense slaughter, and showed little inclination to return to the charge.

Meanwhile the battle had been raging all along the entrenchments of the allied army. Again and again Luxemburg brought up his troops within pistolshot of the breastwork : but he could bring them no nearer. Again and again they recoiled from the heavy fire which was poured on their front and on their flanks. It seemed that all was over. Luxemburg retired to a spot which was out of gunshot, and summoned a few of his chief officers to a consultation. They talked together during some time ; and their animated gestures were observed with deep interest by all who were within sight.

At length Luxemburg formed his decision. A last attempt must be made to carry Neerwinden ; and the invincible household troops, the conquerors of Steinkirk, must lead the way.

The household troops came on in a manner worthy of their long and terrible renown. A third time Neerwinden was taken. A third time William tried to retake it. At the head of some English regiments he charged the guards of Lewis with such fury that, for the first time in the memory of the oldest warrior, that far famed band was driven back.[1] It was only by the strenuous exertions of Luxemburg, of the Duke of Chartres, and of the Duke of Bourbon, that the broken ranks were rallied. But by this time the centre and left of the allied army had been so much thinned for the purpose of supporting the conflict at Neerwinden that the entrenchments could no longer be defended on other points. A little after four in the afternoon the whole line gave way. All was havoc

---

[1] Saint Simon's words are remarkable. " Leur cavalerie," he says, "y fit d'abord plier des troupes d'élite jusqu'alors invincibles." He adds, " Les gardes du Prince d'Orange, ceux de M. de Vaudemont, et deux régimens Anglais en eurent l'honneur."

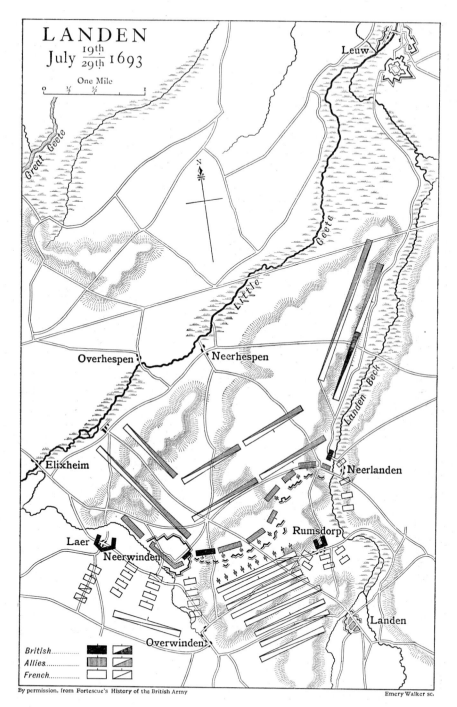

LANDEN
July $\frac{19th}{29th}$ 1693

One Mile

0   ¼   ½   1

Great Geete

Leuw

Little Geete

Geete

Overhespen   Neerhespen

Landen Beck

Elixheim

Neerlanden

Rumsdorp

Laer

Neerwinden

Landen

Overwinden

British............
Allies.............
French............

By permission, from Fortescue's History of the British Army

Emery Walker sc.

PLAN OF THE BATTLE OF LANDEN OR NEERWINDEN

From a plan in Mr. John Fortescue's History of the British Army

and confusion. Solmes had received a mortal wound, and fell, still alive, into the hands of the enemy. The English soldiers, to whom his name was hateful, accused him of having in his sufferings shown pusillanimity unworthy of a soldier. The Duke of Ormond was struck down in the press ; and in another moment he would have been a corpse, had not a rich diamond on his finger caught the eye of one of the French guards, who justly thought that the owner of such a jewel would be a valuable prisoner. The Duke's life was saved ; and he was speedily exchanged for Berwick. Ruvigny, animated by the true refugee hatred of the country which had cast him out, was taken fighting in the thickest of the battle. Those into whose hands he had fallen knew him well, and knew that, if they carried him to their camp, his head would pay for that treason to which persecution had driven him. With admirable generosity they pretended not to recognise him, and suffered him to make his escape in the tumult.

It was only on such occasions as this that the whole greatness of William's character appeared. Amidst the rout and uproar, while arms and standards were flung away, while multitudes of fugitives were choking up the bridges and fords of the Gette or perishing in its waters, the King, having directed Talmash to superintend the retreat, put himself at the head of a few brave regiments, and by desperate efforts arrested the progress of the enemy. His risk was greater than that which others ran. For he could not be persuaded either to encumber his feeble frame with a cuirass, or to hide the ensigns of the garter. He thought his star a good rallying point for his own troops, and only smiled when he was told that it was a good mark for the enemy. Many fell on his right hand and on his left. Two led horses, which in the field always closely followed his person, were struck dead by cannon shots. One musket ball passed through the curls of his wig, another through his coat : a third bruised his side and tore his blue riband to tatters. Many years later greyheaded old pensioners who crept about the arcades and alleys of Chelsea Hospital used to relate how he charged at the head of Galway's horse, how he dismounted four times to put heart into the infantry, how he rallied one corps which seemed to be shrink-ing : " That is not the way to fight, gentlemen. You must stand close up to them. Thus, gentlemen, thus." " You might have seen him,"—thus an eyewitness wrote, only four days after the battle,—" with his sword in his hand, throwing himself upon the enemy. It is certain that, one time among the rest, he was seen at the head of two English regiments, and that he fought seven with these two in sight of the whole army, driving them before him above a quarter of an hour. Thanks be to God that preserved him." The enemy pressed on him so close that it was with difficulty that he at length made his way over

Wilhelmus III D.G. Anglia Rex &

KING WILLIAM III

From a mezzotint by J. Gole

the Gette. A small body of brave men, who shared his peril to the last, could hardly keep off the pursuers as he crossed the bridge.[1]

Never, perhaps, was the change which the progress of civilisation has produced in the art of war more strikingly illustrated than on that day. Ajax beating down the Trojan leader with a rock which two ordinary men could scarcely lift, Horatius defending the bridge against an army, Richard the Lionhearted spurring along the whole Saracen line without finding an enemy to stand his assault, Robert Bruce crushing with one blow the helmet and head of Sir Henry Bohun in sight of the whole array of England and Scotland, such are the heroes of a dark age. In such an age bodily vigour is the most indispensable qualification of a warrior. At Landen two poor sickly beings, who, in a rude state of society, would have been regarded as too puny to bear any part in combats, were the souls of two great armies. In some heathen countries they would have been exposed while infants. In Christendom they would, six hundred years earlier, have been sent to some quiet cloister. But their lot had fallen on a time when men had discovered that the strength of the muscles is far inferior in value to the strength of the mind. It is probable that, among the hundred and twenty thousand soldiers who were marshalled round Neerwinden under all the standards of Western Europe, the two feeblest in body were the hunchbacked dwarf who urged forward the fiery onset of France, and the asthmatic skeleton who covered the slow retreat of England.

The French were victorious : but they had bought their victory dear. More than ten thousand of the best troops of Lewis had fallen. Neerwinden was a spectacle at which the oldest soldiers stood aghast. The streets were piled breast high with corpses. Among the slain were some great lords and some renowned warriors. Montchevreuil was there, and the mutilated trunk of the Duke of Uzes, first in order of precedence among the whole aristocracy of France. Thence too Sarsfield was borne desperately wounded to a pallet from which he never rose again. The Court of Saint Germains had conferred on him the empty title of Earl of Lucan ; but history knows him by the name

---

[1] Berwick ; Saint Simon ; Burnet, i. 112, 113.; Feuquières ; London Gazette, July 27. 31., Aug. 3. 1693 ; French Official Relation ; Relation sent by the King of Great Britain to their High Mightinesses, Aug. 2. 1693 ; Extract of a Letter from the Adjutant of the King of England's Dragoon Guards, Aug. 1.; Dykvelt's Letter to the States General, dated July 30. at noon. The last four papers will be found in the Monthly Mercuries of July and August 1693. See also the History of the Last Campaign in the Spanish Netherlands by Edward D'Auvergne, dedicated to the Duke of Ormond, 1693. The French did justice to William. "Le Prince d'Orange," Racine wrote to Boileau, "pensa être pris, après avoir fait des merveilles." See also the glowing description of Sterne, who, no doubt, had many times heard the battle fought over by old soldiers. It was on this occasion that Corporal Trim was left wounded on the field, and was nursed by the Beguine.

MEDALS ON THE BATTLE OF LANDEN OR NEERWINDEN

which is still dear to the most unfortunate of nations. The region, renowned as the battlefield, through many ages, of the greatest powers of Europe, has seen only two more terrible days, the day of Malplaquet and the day of Waterloo. During many months the ground was strewn with skulls and bones of men and horses, and with fragments of hats and shoes, saddles and holsters. The next summer the soil, fertilised by twenty thousand corpses, broke forth into millions of poppies. The traveller who, on the road from Saint Tron to Tirlemont, saw that vast sheet of rich scarlet spreading from Landen to Neerwinden, could hardly help fancying that the figurative prediction of the Hebrew prophet was literally accomplished, that the earth was disclosing her blood, and refusing to cover the slain.[1]

There was no pursuit, though the sun was still high in the heaven when William crossed the Gette. The conquerors were so much exhausted by marching and fighting that they could scarcely move ; and the horses were in even worse condition than the men. The Marshal thought it necessary to allow some time for rest and refreshment. The French nobles unloaded their sumpter horses, supped gaily, and pledged one another in Champagne amidst the heaps of dead ; and, when night fell, whole brigades gladly lay down to sleep in their ranks on the field of battle. The inactivity of Luxemburg did not escape censure. None could deny that he had in the action shown great skill and energy. But some complained that he wanted patience and perseverance. Others whispered that he had no wish to bring to an end a war which made him necessary to a Court where he had never, in time of peace, found favour or even justice.[2] Lewis, who on this occasion was perhaps not altogether free from some emotions of jealousy, contrived, it was reported, to mingle with the praise which he bestowed on his lieutenant blame which, though delicately expressed, was perfectly intelligible. " In the battle," he said, " the Duke of Luxemburg behaved like Condé ; and since the battle the Prince of Orange has behaved like Turenne."

In truth the ability and vigour with which William repaired his terrible defeat might well excite admiration. " In one respect," said the Admiral Coligni, " I may claim superiority over Alexander, over Scipio, over Cæsar. They won great battles, it is true. I have lost four great battles ; and yet I show to the enemy a more formidable front than ever." The blood of Coligni ran in the veins of William ; and with the blood had descended the unconquerable spirit which could derive

---

[1] Letter from Lord Perth to his sister, June 17. 1694.

[2] Saint Simon mentions the reflections thrown on the Marshal. Feuquières, a very good judge, tells us that Luxemburg was unjustly blamed, and that the French army was really too much crippled by its losses to improve the victory.

from failure as much glory as happier commanders owed to success. The defeat of Landen was indeed a heavy blow. The King had a few days of cruel anxiety. If Luxemburg pushed on, all was lost. Louvain must fall, and Mechlin, and Nieuport, and Ostend. The Batavian frontier would be in danger. The cry for peace throughout Holland might be such as neither States General nor Stadtholder would be able to resist.[1] But there was delay; and a very short delay was enough for William. From the field of battle he made his way through the multitude of fugitives to the neighbourhood of Louvain, and there began to collect his scattered forces. His character is not lowered by the anxiety which, at that moment, the most disastrous of his life, he felt for the two persons who were dearest to him. As soon as he was safe, he wrote to assure his wife of his safety.[2] In the confusion of the flight he had lost sight of Portland, who was then in very feeble health, and had therefore run more than the ordinary risks of war. A short note which the King sent to his friend a few hours later is still extant.[3] "Though I hope to see you this evening, I cannot help writing to tell you how rejoiced I am that you got off so well. God grant that your health may soon be quite restored. These are great trials, which He has been pleased to send me in quick succession. I must try to submit to His pleasure without murmuring, and to deserve His anger less."

William's forces rallied fast. Large bodies of troops which he had, perhaps imprudently, detached from his army while he supposed that Liege was the object of the enemy, rejoined him by forced marches. Three weeks after his defeat he held a review a few miles from Brussels. The number of men under arms was greater than on the morning of the bloody day of Landen: their appearance was soldierlike; and their spirit seemed unbroken. William now wrote to Heinsius that the worst was over. "The crisis," he said, "has been a terrible one. Thank God that it has ended thus." He did not, however, think it prudent to try at that time the event of another pitched field. He therefore suffered the French to besiege and take Charleroy; and this was the only advantage which they derived from the most sanguinary battle fought in Europe during the seventeenth century.

The melancholy tidings of the defeat of Landen found England agitated by tidings not less melancholy from a different quarter. During many months the trade with the Mediterranean Sea had been almost entirely interrupted by the war. There was no chance that a merchantman

---

[1] This account of what would have happened, if Luxemburg had been able and willing to improve his victory, I have taken from what seems to have been a very manly and sensible speech made by Talmash in the House of Commons on the 11th of December following. See Grey's Debates.

[2] William to Heinsius, July ²⁹⁄₃₀. 1693.   [3] William to Portland, July ³¹⁄₂₁. 1693.

from London or from Amsterdam would, if unprotected, reach the Pillars of Hercules without being boarded by a French privateer ; and Miscarriage the protection of armed vessels was not easily to be obtained.

Miscarriage of the Smyrna fleet During the year 1692, great fleets, richly laden for Spanish, Italian, and Turkish markets, had been gathering in the Thames and the Texel. In February 1693, near four hundred ships were ready to start. The value of the cargoes was estimated at several millions sterling. Those galleons which had long been the wonder and envy of the world had never conveyed so precious a freight from the West Indies to Seville. The English government undertook, in concert with the Dutch government, to escort the vessels which were laden with this great mass of wealth. The French government was bent on intercepting them.

The plan of the allies was that seventy ships of the line and about thirty frigates and brigantines should assemble in the Channel under the command of Killegrew and Delaval, the two new Lords of the English Admiralty, and should convoy the Smyrna fleet, as it was popularly called, beyond the limits within which any danger could be apprehended from the Brest squadron. The greater part of the armament might then return to guard the Channel, while Rooke, with twenty sail, might accompany the trading vessels and might protect them against the squadron which lay at Toulon.

The plan of the French government was that the Brest squadron under Tourville, and the Toulon squadron under Estrees should meet in the neighbourhood of the Straits of Gibraltar, and should there lie in wait for the booty.

Which plan was the better conceived may be doubted. Which was the better executed is a question which admits of no doubt. The whole French navy, whether in the Atlantic or in the Mediterranean, was moved by one will. The navy of England and the navy of the United Provinces were subject to different authorities ; and, both in England and in the United Provinces, the power was divided and subdivided to such an extent that no single person was pressed by a heavy responsibility. The spring came. The merchants loudly complained that they had already lost more by delay than they could hope to gain by the most successful voyage ; and still the ships of war were not half manned or half provisioned. The Amsterdam squadron did not arrive on our coast till late in April ; the Zealand squadron not till the middle of May.[1] It was June before the immense fleet, near five hundred sail, lost sight of the cliffs of England.

Tourville was already on the sea, and was steering southward. But Killegrew and Delaval were so negligent or so unfortunate that they had no intelligence of his movements. They at first took it for granted that

[1] London Gazette, April 24., May 15. 1693.

Sᵣ Ralph Delaval, 1691.
From an Original picture.

SIR RALPH DELAVAL

From a drawing by T. Athow, in the Sutherland Collection

he was still lying in the port of Brest. Then they heard a rumour that some shipping had been seen to the northward ; and they supposed that he was taking advantage of their absence to threaten the coast of Devonshire. It never seems to have occurred to them as possible that he might have effected a junction with the Toulon squadron, and might be impatiently waiting for his prey in the neighbourhood of Gibraltar. They therefore, on the sixth of June, having convoyed the Smyrna fleet about two hundred miles beyond Ushant, announced their intention to part company with Rooke. Rooke expostulated, but to no purpose. It was necessary for him to submit, and to proceed with his twenty men of war to the Mediterranean, while his superiors, with the rest of the armament, returned to the Channel.

It was by this time known in England that Tourville had stolen out of Brest, and was hastening to join Estrees. The return of Killegrew and Delaval therefore excited great alarm. A swift vessel was instantly despatched to warn Rooke of his danger ; but the warning never reached him. He ran before a fair wind to Cape Saint Vincent ; and there he learned that some French ships were lying in the neighbouring Bay of Lagos. The first information which he received led him to believe that they were few in number ; and so dexterously did they conceal their strength that, till they were within half an hour's sail, he had no suspicion that he was opposed to the whole maritime strength of a great kingdom. To contend against fourfold odds would have been madness. It was much that he was able to save his squadron from utter destruction. He exerted all his skill. Two or three Dutch men of war, which were in the rear, courageously sacrificed themselves to save the fleet. With the rest of the armament, and with about sixty merchant ships, Rooke got safe to Madeira and thence to Cork. But more than three hundred of the vessels which he had convoyed were scattered over the ocean. Some escaped to Ireland ; some to Corunna ; some to Lisbon ; some to Cadiz : some were captured, and more destroyed. A few which had taken shelter under the rock of Gibraltar, and were pursued thither by the enemy, were sunk when it was found that they could not be defended. Others perished in the same manner under the batteries of Malaga. The gain to the French seems not to have been great : but the loss to England and Holland was immense.[1]

Never within the memory of man had there been in the City a day of more gloom and agitation than that on which the news of the encounter in the Bay of Lagos arrived. Many traders, an **Excitement in London** eyewitness said, went away from the Royal Exchange, as pale as if they had received sentence of death. A deputation from the

---

[1] Burchett's Memoirs of Transactions at Sea ; Burnet, ii. 114, 115, 116. ; London Gazette, July 17. 1693 ; Monthly Mercury of July ; Letter from Cadiz, dated July 4.

merchants who had been sufferers by this great disaster went up to the Queen with an address representing their grievances. They were admitted to the Council Chamber, where she was seated at the head of the Board. She directed Somers to reply to them in her name; and he addressed to them a speech well calculated to sooth their irritation. Her Majesty, he said, felt for them from her heart; and she had already appointed a Committee of the Privy Council to enquire into the cause of the late misfortune, and to consider of the best means of preventing similar misfortunes in time to come.[1] This answer gave so much satisfaction that the Lord Mayor soon came to the palace to thank the

FRENCH MEDAL CELEBRATING THE VICTORY IN LAGOS BAY

Queen for her goodness, to assure her that, through all vicissitudes, London would be true to her and her consort, and to inform her that, severely as the late calamity had been felt by many great commercial houses, the Common Council had unanimously resolved to advance whatever might be necessary for the support of the government.[2]

[1] Narcissus Luttrell's Diary; Baden to the States General, July $\frac{14}{24}$. $\frac{July\ 25.}{Aug.\ 4.}$ Among the Tanner MSS. in the Bodleian Library are letters describing the agitation in the City. " I wish," says one of Sancroft's Jacobite correspondents, " it may open our eyes and change our minds. But by the accounts I have seen, the Turkey Company went from the Queen and Council full of satisfaction and good humour."

[2] London Gazette, August 21. 1693; L'Hermitage to the States General, $\frac{July\ 28.}{Aug.\ 7.}$ As I shall, in this and the following chapters, make large use of the despatches of L'Hermitage, it may be proper to say something about him. He was a French refugee, and resided in London as agent for the Waldenses. One of his employments had been to send newsletters to Heinsius. Some interesting extracts from those newsletters will be found in the work of the Baron Sirtema de

The ill humour which the public calamities naturally produced was inflamed by every factious artifice. Never had the Jacobite pamphleteers been so savagely scurrilous as during this unfortunate summer. The police was consequently more active than ever in seeking for the dens from which so much treason proceeded. With great difficulty and after long search the most important of all the unlicensed presses was discovered. This press belonged to a Jacobite named William Anderton, whose intrepidity and fanaticism marked him out as fit to be employed on services from which prudent men and scrupulous men shrink. During two years he had been watched by the agents of the government : but where he exercised his craft was an impenetrable mystery. At length he was tracked to a house near Saint James's Street, where he was known by a feigned name, and where he passed for a working jeweller. A messenger of the press went thither with several assistants, and found Anderton's wife and mother posted as sentinels at the door. The women knew the messenger, rushed on him, tore his hair, and cried out " Thieves " and " Murder." The alarm was thus given to Anderton. He concealed the instruments of his calling, came forth with an assured air, and bade defiance to the messenger, the Censor, the Secretary, and Little Hooknose himself. After a struggle he was secured. His room was searched ; and at first sight no evidence of his guilt appeared. But behind the bed was soon found a door which opened into a dark closet. The closet contained a press, types, and heaps of newly printed papers. One of these papers, entitled Remarks on the Present Confederacy and the Late Revolution, is perhaps the most frantic of all the Jacobite libels. In this tract the Prince of Orange is gravely accused of having ordered fifty of his wounded English soldiers to be burned alive. The governing principle of his whole conduct, it is said, is not vainglory, or ambition, or avarice, but a deadly hatred of Englishmen and a desire to make them miserable. The nation is vehemently adjured, on peril of incurring the severest judgments, to rise up and free itself from this plague, this curse, this tyrant whose depravity

Grovestins. It was probably in consequence of the Pensionary's recommendation that the States General, by a resolution dated $\frac{\text{July 24.}}{\text{Aug. 3.}}$ 1693, desired L'Hermitage to collect and transmit to them intelligence of what was passing in England. His letters abound with curious and valuable information which is nowhere else to be found. His accounts of parliamentary proceedings are of peculiar value, and seem to have been so considered by his employers.

Copies of the despatches of L'Hermitage, and, indeed, of the despatches of all the ministers and agents employed by the States General in England from the time of Elizabeth downward, now are, or will soon be, in the library of the British Museum. For this valuable addition to the great national storehouse of knowledge, the country is chiefly indebted to Lord Palmerston. But it would be unjust not to add that his instructions were most zealously carried into effect by the late Sir Edward Disbrowe, with the cordial cooperation of the enlightened men who have charge of the noble collection of Archives at the Hague.

makes it difficult to believe that he can have been procreated by a human pair. Many copies were also found of another paper, somewhat less ferocious, but perhaps more dangerous, entitled A French Conquest neither Desirable nor Practicable. In this tract also the people are exhorted to rise in insurrection. They are assured that a great part of the army is with them. The forces of the Prince of Orange will melt away: he will be glad to make his escape; and a charitable hope is sneeringly expressed that it may not be necessary to do him any harm beyond sending him back to Loo, where he may live surrounded by luxuries for which the English have paid dear.

The government, provoked and alarmed by the virulence of the Jacobite pamphleteers, determined to make Anderton an example. He was indicted for high treason, and brought to the bar of the Old Bailey. Treby, now Chief Justice of the Common Pleas, and Powell, who had honourably distinguished himself on the day of the trial of the Bishops, were on the Bench. It is unfortunate that no detailed report of the evidence has come down to us, and that we are forced to content ourselves with such fragments of information as can be collected from the contradictory narratives of writers evidently partial, intemperate, and dishonest. The indictment, however, is extant; and the overt acts which it imputes to the prisoner undoubtedly amount to high treason.[1] To exhort the people of the realm to rise up and depose the King by force, and to add to that exhortation the expression, evidently ironical, of a hope that it may not be necessary to inflict on him any evil worse than banishment, is surely an offence which the least courtly lawyer will admit to be within the scope of the statute of Edward the Third. On this point indeed there seems to have been no dispute, either at the trial or subsequently.

The prisoner denied that he had printed the libels. On this point it seems reasonable that, since the evidence has not come down to us, we should give credit to the judges and the jury who heard what the witnesses had to say.

One argument with which Anderton had been furnished by his advisers, and which, in the Jacobite pasquinades of that time, is represented as unanswerable, was that, as the art of printing had been unknown in the reign of Edward the Third, printing could not be an overt act of treason under a statute of that reign. The Judges treated this argument very lightly; and they were surely justified in so treating it. For it is an argument which would lead to the conclusion that it could not be an overt act of treason to behead a King with a guillotine or to shoot him with a Minie rifle.

[1] It is strange that the indictment should not have been printed in Howell's State Trials. The copy which is before me was made for Sir James Mackintosh.

It was also urged in Anderton's favour,—and this was undoubtedly an argument well entitled to consideration,—that a distinction ought to be made between the author of a treasonable paper and the man who merely printed it. The former could not pretend that he had not understood the meaning of the words which he had himself selected. But to the latter those words might convey no idea whatever. The metaphors, the allusions, the sarcasms, might be far beyond his comprehension ; and, while his hands were busy among the types, his thoughts might be wandering to things altogether unconnected with the manuscript which was before him. It is undoubtedly true that it may be no crime to print what it would be a great crime to write. But this is evidently a matter concerning which no general rule can be laid down. Whether Anderton had, as a mere mechanic, contributed to spread a work the tendency of which he did not suspect, or had knowingly lent his help to raise a rebellion, was a question for the jury; and the jury might reasonably infer, from the change of his name, from the secret manner in which he worked, from the strict watch kept by his wife and mother, and from the fury with which, even in the grasp of the messengers, he railed at the government, that he was not the unconscious tool, but the intelligent and zealous accomplice of traitors. The twelve, after passing a considerable time in deliberation, informed the Court that one of them entertained doubts. Those doubts were removed by the arguments of Treby and Powell ; and a verdict of Guilty was found.

The fate of the prisoner remained during some time in suspense. The Ministers hoped that he might be induced to save his own neck at the expense of the necks of the pamphleteers who had employed him. But his natural courage was kept up by spiritual stimulants which the nonjuring divines well understood how to administer. He suffered death with fortitude, and continued to revile the government to the last. The Jacobites clamoured loudly against the cruelty of the Judges who had tried him, and of the Queen who had left him for execution, and, not very consistently, represented him at once as a poor uneducated artisan who was ignorant of the nature and tendency of the act for which he suffered, and as a martyr who had heroically laid down his life for the banished King and the persecuted Church.[1]

The Ministers were much mistaken if they flattered themselves that the fate of Anderton would deter others from imitating his example. **Writings and artifices of the Jacobites** His execution produced several pamphlets scarcely less virulent than those for which he had suffered. Collier, in what he called Remarks on the London Gazette, exulted with cruel joy over the carnage of Landen, and the vast destruction of English

[1] Most of the information which has come down to us about Anderton's case will be found in Howell's State Trials.

The Right Hon:ble Sr George Treby Knt.
Lord Chief Justice of his Ma:ties Court of Comon Pleas.
1700.

CHIEF-JUSTICE SIR GEORGE TREBY

From an engraving by R. White

property on the coast of Spain.[1] Other writers did their best to raise riots among the labouring people. For the doctrine of the Jacobites was that disorder, in whatever place or in whatever way it might begin, was likely to end in a Restoration. A phrase, which, without a commentary, may seem to be mere nonsense, but which was really full of meaning, was in their mouths at this time, and was indeed a password by which the members of the party recognised each other : " Box it about : it will come to my father." The hidden sense of this gibberish was, " Throw the country into confusion : it will be necessary at last to have recourse to King James."[2] Trade was not prosperous ; and many industrious men were out of work. Accordingly songs addressed to the distressed classes were composed by the malecontent street poets. Numerous copies of a ballad exhorting the weavers to rise against the government were discovered in the house of the Quaker who had printed James's Declaration.[3] Every art was used for the purpose of exciting discontent in a much more formidable body of men, the sailors ; and unhappily the vices of the naval administration furnished the enemies of the State with but too good a choice of inflammatory topics. Some seamen deserted : some mutinied : then came executions ; and then came more ballads and broadsides representing those executions as barbarous murders. Reports that the government had determined to defraud its defenders of their hard earned pay were circulated with so much effect that a great crowd of women from Wapping and Rotherhithe besieged Whitehall, clamouring for what was due to their husbands. Mary had the good sense and good nature to order four of those importunate petitioners to be admitted into the room where she was holding a Council. She heard their complaints, and herself assured them that the rumour which had alarmed them was unfounded.[4] By this time Saint Bartholomew's day drew near ; and the great annual fair, the delight of idle apprentices and the horror of Puritanical Aldermen, was opened in Smithfield with the usual display of dwarfs, giants, and dancing dogs, the man that ate fire, and the elephant that loaded and discharged a musket. But of all the shows none proved so attractive as a dramatic performance which, in conception, though doubtless not in

[1] The Remarks are extant, and deserve to be read.

[2] Narcissus Luttrell's Diary.   [3] Ibid.

[4] There are still extant a handbill addressed to All Gentlemen Seamen that are weary of their Lives, and a ballad accusing the King and Queen of cruelty to the sailors.

> " To robbers, thieves, and felons, they
> Freely grant pardons every day.
> Only poor seamen, who alone
> Do keep them in their father's throne,
> Must have at all no mercy shown."

Narcissus Luttrell gives an account of the scene at Whitehall.

execution, seems to have borne much resemblance to those immortal
masterpieces of humour in which Aristophanes held up Cleon and

A Merry new Song
Les Chanteurs de Chansons
Cantarine & Strada

Maurer delin   P.Tempist exc.
                                                    Cum privilegio

A BALLAD SINGER

From Tempest s Cries of London

Lamachus to derision.   Two strollers personated Killegrew and Dalaval.
The Admirals were represented as flying with their whole fleet before a

few French privateers, and taking shelter under the guns of the Tower. The office of Chorus was performed by a Jackpudding who expressed very freely his opinion of the naval administration. Immense crowds flocked to see this strange farce. The applauses were loud : the receipts were great ; and the mountebanks, who had at first ventured to attack only the unlucky and unpopular Board of Admiralty, now, emboldened by impunity and success, and probably prompted and rewarded by persons of much higher station than their own, began to cast reflections on other departments of the government. This attempt to revive the license of the Attic Stage was soon brought to a close by the appearance of a strong body of constables who carried off the actors to prison.[1] Meanwhile the streets of London were every night strewn with seditious handbills. At the taverns the zealots of hereditary right were limping about with glasses of wine and punch at their lips. This fashion had just come in ; and the uninitiated wondered much that so great a number of jolly gentlemen should have suddenly become lame. But those who were in the secret knew that the word Limp was a consecrated word, that every one of the four letters which composed it was the initial of an august name, and that the loyal subject who limped while he drank was taking off his bumper to Lewis, James, Mary of Modena, and the Prince. It was not only in the capital that the Jacobites, at this time, made a great display of this kind of wit. An alderman of Exeter taught his fellow townsmen to drink to the mysterious Tetragrammaton ; and their orgies excited so much alarm that a regiment was quartered in the city.[2] The malecontents mustered strong at Bath, where the Lord President Caermarthen was trying to recruit his feeble health. In the evenings they met, as they phrased it, to serenade the Marquess. In other words they assembled under the sick man's window, and there sang doggrel lampoons on him.[3]

It is remarkable that the Lord President, at the very time at which he was insulted as a Williamite at Bath, was considered as a stanch Conduct of Jacobite at Saint Germains. How he came to be so con-Caermarthen sidered is a most perplexing question. Some writers are of opinion that he, like Shrewsbury, Russell, Godolphin, and Marlborough, entered into engagements with one king while eating the bread of the other. But this opinion does not rest on sufficient proofs.

[1] L'Hermitage, Sept. $\frac{5}{15}$. 1693 ; Narcissus Luttrell's Diary.

[2] Observator, Jan. 2. 170$\frac{2}{3}$; Narcissus Luttrell's Diary.

[3] Narcissus Luttrell's Diary. In a pamphlet published at this time, and entitled A Dialogue between Whig and Tory, the Whig alludes to " the public insolences at the Bath upon the late defeat in Flanders." The Tory answers, " I know not what some hotheaded drunken men may have said and done at the Bath or elsewhere." In the folio Collection of State Tracts, this Dialogue is erroneously said to have been printed about November 1692.

VIEW OF BARTHOLOMEW FAIR

From a fan in the British Museum

About the treasons of Shrewsbury, of Russell, of Godolphin, and of Marlborough, we have a great mass of evidence, derived from various sources, and extending over several years. But all the information which we possess about Caermarthen's dealings with James is contained in a single short paper written by Melfort on the sixteenth of October 1693. From that paper it is quite clear that some intelligence had reached the banished King and his Ministers which led them to regard Caermarthen as a friend. But there is no proof that they ever so regarded him, either before that day or after that day.[1] On the whole, the most probable explanation of this mystery seems to be that Caermarthen had been sounded by some Jacobite emissary much less artful than himself, and had, for the purpose of getting at the bottom of the new scheme of policy devised by Middleton, pretended to be well disposed to the cause of the banished King, that an exaggerated account of what had passed had been sent to Saint Germains, and that there had been much rejoicing there at a conversion which soon proved to have been feigned. It seems strange that such a conversion, should even for a moment have been thought sincere. It was plainly Caermarthen's interest to stand by the sovereigns in possession. He was their chief minister. He could not hope to be the chief minister of James. It can indeed hardly be supposed that the political conduct of a cunning old man, insatiably ambitious and covetous, was much influenced by personal partiality. But, if there were any person to whom Caermarthen was partial, that person was undoubtedly Mary. That he had seriously engaged in a plot to depose her, with great risk of losing his head if he failed, and with the certainty of losing immense power and wealth if he succeeded, was a story too absurd for any credulity but the credulity of exiles.

Caermarthen had indeed at that moment peculiarly strong reasons for being satisfied with the place which he held in the counsels of

---

[1] The Paper to which I refer is among the Nairne MSS., and will be found in Macpherson's collection That excellent writer Mr. Hallam has, on this subject, fallen into an error of a kind very rare with him. He says that the name of Caermarthen is perpetually mentioned among those whom James reckoned as his friends. I believe that the evidence against Caermarthen will be found to begin and to end with the letter of Melfort which I have mentioned. There is indeed, among the Nairne MSS., which Macpherson printed, an undated and anonymous letter in which Caermarthen is reckoned among the friends of James. But this letter is altogether undeserving of consideration. The writer was evidently a silly hotheaded Jacobite, who knew nothing about the situation or character of any of the public men whom he mentioned. He blunders grossly about Marlborough, Godolphin, Russell, Shrewsbury, and the Beaufort family. Indeed the whole composition is a tissue of absurdities.

It ought to be remarked that, in those parts of the Life of James which are of high historical authority, the assurances of support which he received from Marlborough, Russell, Godolphin, Shrewsbury, and other men of note are mentioned with very copious details. But there is not in any part of the Life a word indicating that any such assurances were ever received from Caermarthen.

THOMAS OSBORNE, 1st DUKE OF LEEDS, K.G., 1631-1712.

From the painting in the National Portrait Gallery.

School of Kneller.

William and Mary. There is but too good ground to believe that he was then accumulating unlawful gain with a rapidity unexampled even in his experience.

The contest between the two East India Companies was, during the autumn of 1693, fiercer than ever. The House of Commons, finding the Old Company obstinately averse to all compromise, had, New charter a little before the close of the late session, requested the King granted to give the three years' warning prescribed by the Charter. East India Child and his fellows now began to be seriously alarmed. Company They expected every day to receive the dreaded notice. Nay, they were not sure that their exclusive privilege might not be taken away without any notice at all : for they found that they had, by inadvertently omitting to pay, at the precise time fixed by law, the tax lately imposed on their stock, forfeited their Charter ; and though it would, in ordinary circumstances, have been thought cruel in the government to take advantage of such a slip, the public was not inclined to allow the Old Company anything more than the strict letter of the covenant. All was lost if the Charter were not renewed before the meeting of Parliament. There can be little doubt that the proceedings of the corporation were still really directed by Child. But he had, it should seem, perceived that his unpopularity had injuriously affected the interests which were under his care, and therefore did not obtrude himself on the public notice. His place was ostensibly filled by his near kinsman Sir Thomas Cook, one of the greatest merchants of London, and Member of Parliament for the borough of Colchester. The Directors placed at Cook's absolute disposal all the immense wealth which lay in their treasury; and in a short time near a hundred thousand pounds were expended in corruption on a gigantic scale. In what proportions this enormous sum was distributed among the great men at Whitehall, and how much of it was embezzled by intermediate agents, is still a mystery. We know with certainty however that thousands went to Seymour and thousands to Caermarthen.

The effect of these bribes was that the Attorney General received orders to draw up a charter regranting the old privileges to the Old Company. No minister, however, could, after what had passed in Parliament, venture to advise the Crown to renew the monopoly without conditions. The Directors were sensible that they had no choice, and reluctantly consented to accept the new Charter on terms substantially the same with those which the House of Commons had sanctioned.

It is probable that, two years earlier, such a compromise would have quieted the feud which distracted the City. But a long conflict, in which satire and calumny had not been spared, had heated the minds of men. The cry of Dowgate against Leadenhall Street was louder than ever. Caveats were entered: petitions were signed; and in those petitions a doctrine which had hitherto been studiously kept in the background was boldly affirmed. While it was doubtful on which side the royal prerogative would be used, that prerogative had not been questioned. But as soon as it appeared that the Old Company was likely to obtain a regrant of the monopoly under the Great Seal, the New Company began to assert with vehemence that no monopoly could be created except by Act of Parliament. The Privy Council, over which Caermarthen presided, after hearing the matter fully argued by counsel on both sides, decided in favour of the Old Company, and ordered the Charter to be sealed.[1]

The autumn was by this time far advanced, and the armies in the Netherlands had gone into quarters for the winter. On the last day of October William landed in England. The Parliament was about to meet ; and he had every reason to expect a session even more stormy than the last. The people were discontented, and not without cause. The year had been every where disastrous to the allies, not only on the sea and in the Low Countries, but also in Servia, in Spain, in Italy, and in Germany. The Turks had compelled the generals of the Empire to raise the siege of Belgrade. A newly created Marshal of France, the Duke of Noailles, had invaded Catalonia and taken the fortress of Rosas. Another newly created Marshal, the skilful and valiant Catinat, had descended from the Alps on Piedmont, and had, at Marsiglia, gained a complete victory over the forces of the Duke of Savoy. This battle is memorable as the first of a long series of battles in which the Irish troops retrieved the honour lost by misfortune and misconduct in domestic war. Some of the exiles of Limerick showed, on that day, under the standard of France, a valour which distinguished them among many thousands of brave men. It is a remarkable fact that, on the same day, a battalion of the persecuted and expatriated Huguenots stood firm amidst the general disorder round the standard of Savoy, and fell fighting desperately to the last.

Return of William to England : military successes of France

The Duke of Lorges had marched into the Palatinate, already twice devastated, and had found that Turenne and Duras had left him something to destroy. Heidelberg, just beginning to rise again from its ruins, was again sacked, the peaceable citizens butchered, their wives and daughters foully outraged. The very choirs of the churches were stained with blood : the pyxes and crucifixes were torn from the altars : the tombs of the ancient Electors were broken open ; the corpses, stripped of their cerecloths and ornaments, were dragged about the streets. The skull of the father of the Duchess of Orleans was beaten to fragments by the soldiers of a prince among the ladies of whose splendid Court she held the foremost place.

[1] A Journal of several Remarkable Passages relating to the East India Trade, 1693.

And yet a discerning eye might have perceived that, unfortunate as the confederates seemed to have been, the advantage had really been on their side. The contest was quite as much a financial as **Distress of** a military contest. The French King had, some months **France** before, said that the last piece of gold would carry the day ; and he now

GUY DE DURASFORT, DUKE DE LORGES, MARSHAL OF FRANCE

From an engraving by P. Simon

began painfully to feel the truth of the saying. England was undoubtedly hard pressed by public burdens : but still she stood up erect. France meanwhile was fast sinking. Her recent efforts had been too much for her strength, and had left her spent and unstrung. Never had her rulers shown more ingenuity in devising taxes, or more severity in exacting them : but by no ingenuity, by no severity, was it possible to raise the sums necessary for another such campaign as that of 1693. In England the harvest had been abundant. In France the corn and the wine had again failed. The people, as usual, railed at the government. The government, with shameful ignorance or more shameful dishonesty, tried to direct the public indignation against the dealers in grain. Decrees appeared which seemed to have been elaborately framed for the purpose of turning dearth into famine. The nation was assured that there was no reason for uneasiness, that there was more than a sufficient supply of food, and that the scarcity had been produced by the villanous arts of misers who locked up their stores in the hope of making enormous gains. Commissioners were appointed to inspect the granaries, and were empowered to send to market all the corn that was not necessary for the consumption of the proprietors. Such interference of course increased the suffering which it was meant to relieve. But in the midst of the general distress there was an artificial plenty in one favoured spot. The most arbitrary prince must always stand in some awe of an immense mass of human beings collected in the neighbourhood of his own palace. Apprehensions similar to those which had induced the Cæsars to extort from Africa and Egypt the means of pampering the rabble of Rome induced Lewis to aggravate the misery of twenty provinces for the purpose of keeping one huge city in good humour. He ordered bread to be distributed in all the parishes of the capital at less than half the market price. The English Jacobites were stupid enough to extol the wisdom and humanity of this arrangement. The harvest, they said, had been good in England and bad in France ; and yet the loaf was cheaper at Paris than in London ; and the explanation was simple. The French had a sovereign whose heart was French, and who watched over his people with the solicitude of a father, while the English were cursed with a Dutch tyrant, who sent their corn to Holland. The truth was that a week of such fatherly government as that of Lewis would have raised all England in arms from Northumberland to Cornwall. That there might be abundance at Paris, the people of Normandy and Anjou were stuffing themselves with nettles. That there might be tranquillity at Paris, the peasantry were fighting with the bargemen and the troops all along the Loire and the Seine. Multitudes fled from those rural districts where bread cost five sous a pound to the happy place where bread was to be had for two sous a pound. It was necessary to drive the famished crowd back by force from the barriers, and to denounce the most terrible punishments against all who should not go home and starve quietly.[1]

[1] See the Monthly Mercuries and London Gazettes of September, October, November, and December, 1693 ; Dangeau, Sept. 5. 27., Oct. 21., Nov. 21. ; the Price of the Abdication, 1693

Elizabeth Charlotte Palatine du Rhin Duchesse d'Orleans.

ELIZABETH CHARLOTTE, DUCHESS OF ORLEANS

From an engraving by C. Simonneau, after a painting by H. Rigaud

Lewis was sensible that the nerves of France had been overstrained by the exertions of the last campaign. Even if her harvests and her vintage had been abundant, she would not have been able to do in 1694 what she had done in 1693 ; and it was utterly impossible that, in a season of extreme distress, she should again send into the field armies superior in number on every point to the armies of the coalition. New conquests were not to be expected. It would be much if the harassed and exhausted land, beset on all sides by enemies, should be able to sustain a defensive war without any disaster. So able a politician as the French King could not but feel that it would be for his advantage to treat with the allies while they were still awed by the remembrance of the gigantic efforts which his kingdom had just made, and before the collapse which had followed those efforts should become visible.

He had long been communicating through various channels with some members of the confederacy, and trying to induce them to separate themselves from the rest. But he had as yet made no overture tending to a general pacification. For he knew that there could be no general pacification unless he was prepared to abandon the cause of James, and to acknowledge the Prince and Princess of Orange as King and Queen of England. This was in truth the point on which everything turned. What should be done with those great fortresses which Lewis had unjustly seized and annexed to his empire in time of peace, Luxemburg which overawed the Moselle, and Strasburg which domineered over the Upper Rhine ; what should be done with the places which he had recently won in open war, Philipsburg, Mons, and Namur, Huy and Charleroy; what barrier should be given to the States General ; on what terms Lorraine should be restored to its hereditary Dukes ; these were assuredly not unimportant questions. But the allimportant question was whether England was to be, as she had been under James, a dependency of France, or, as she was under William and Mary, a power of the first rank. If Lewis really wished for peace, he must bring himself to recognise the Sovereigns whom he had so often designated as usurpers. Could he bring himself to recognise them ? His superstition, his pride, his regard for the unhappy exiles who were pining at Saint Germains, his personal dislike of the indefatigable and unconquerable adversary who had been constantly crossing his path during twenty years, were on one side : his interests and those of his people were on the other. He must have been sensible that it was not in his power to subjugate the English, that he must at last leave them to choose their government for themselves, and that what he must do at last it would be best to do soon. Yet he could not at once make up his mind to what was so disagreeable to him. He however opened a negotiation with the States General through the intervention of Sweden and Denmark, and sent a confidential emissary to confer in secret at Brussels with Dykvelt, who possessed the entire confidence of William.   There was much discussion about matters of secondary importance : but the great question remained unsettled.   The French agent used, in private conversation, expressions plainly implying that the government which he represented was prepared to recognise William and Mary : but no formal assurance could be obtained from him.   Just at the same time the King of Denmark informed the allies that he was endeavouring to prevail on France not to insist on the restoration of James as an indispensable condition of peace, but did not say that his endeavours had as yet been successful.   Meanwhile Avaux, who was now Ambassador at Stockholm, informed the King of Sweden, that, as the dignity of all crowned heads had been outraged in the person of James, the Most Christian King felt assured that not only neutral powers, but even the Emperor, would try to find some expedient which might remove so grave a cause of quarrel.   The expedient at which Avaux hinted doubtless was that James should waive his rights, and that the Prince of Wales should be sent to England, bred a Protestant, adopted by William and Mary, and declared their heir.   To such an arrangement William would probably have had no strong personal objection.   But we may be assured that he neither would nor could have made it a condition of peace with France.   Who should reign in England was a question to be decided by England alone.[1]

It might well be suspected that a negotiation conducted in this manner was merely meant to divide the confederates.   William understood the whole importance of the conjuncture.   He had not, it may be, the eye of a great captain for all the turns of a battle.   But he had, in the highest perfection, the eye of a great statesman for all the turns of a war.   That France had at length made overtures to him was a sufficient proof that she felt herself spent and sinking.   That those overtures were made with extreme reluctance and hesitation proved that she had not yet come to a temper in which it was possible to have peace with her on fair terms.   He saw that the enemy was beginning to give ground, and that this was the time to assume the offensive, to push forward, to bring up every reserve.   But whether the opportunity should be seized or lost it did not belong to him to decide.   The King of France might levy troops and exact taxes without any limit save that which the laws of nature impose on despotism.   But the King of England could do nothing without the support of the House of Commons ; and the House of Commons, though it had hitherto supported him zealously and liberally, was not a body on which he

[1] Correspondence of William and Heinsius ; Danish Note, dated Dec. $\frac{11}{21}$. 1693.   The note delivered by Avaux to the Swedish government at this time will be found in Lamberty's Collection and in the Actes et Mémoires des Négociations de la Paix de Ryswick.

could rely. It had indeed got into a state which perplexed and alarmed all the most sagacious politicians of that age. There was something appalling in the union of such boundless power and such boundless caprice. The fate of the whole civilised world depended on the votes of the representatives of the English people ; and there was no public man who could venture to say with confidence what those representatives might not be induced to vote within twenty four hours.[1] William painfully felt that it was scarcely possible for a prince dependent on an assembly so violent at one time, so languid at another, to effect anything great. Indeed, though no sovereign did so much to secure and to extend the power of the House of Commons, no sovereign loved the House of Commons less. Nor is this strange : for he saw that House at the very worst. He saw it when it had just acquired the power, and had not yet acquired the gravity, of a senate. In his letters to Heinsius he perpetually complains of the endless talking, the factious squabbling, the inconstancy, the dilatoriness of the body which his situation made it necessary for him to treat with deference. His complaints were by no means unfounded : but he had not discovered either the cause or the cure of the evil.

The truth was that the change which the Revolution had made in the situation of the House of Commons had made another

A ministry necessary to parliamentary government

change necessary ; and that other change had not yet taken place. There was parliamentary government : but there was no Ministry ; and, without a Ministry, the working of a parliamentary government, such as ours, must always be unsteady and unsafe.

It is essential to our liberties that the House of Commons should exercise a control over all the departments of the executive administration. And yet it is evident that a crowd of five or six hundred people, even if they were intellectually much above the average of the members of the best Parliament, even if every one of them were a Burleigh or a Sully, would be unfit for executive functions. It has been truly said that every large collection of human beings, however well educated, has a strong tendency to become a mob ; and a country of which the Supreme Executive Council is a mob is surely in a perilous situation.

Happily a way has been found out in which the House of Commons can exercise a paramount influence over the executive government, without assuming functions such as can never be well discharged by a body so numerous and so variously composed. An institution which

[1] " Sir John Lowther says, nobody can know one day what a House of Commons would do the next ; in which all agreed with him." These remarkable words were written by Caermarthen on the margin of a paper drawn up by Rochester in August 1692. Dalrymple, Appendix to part ii. chap. 7.

did not exist in the times of the Plantagenets, of the Tudors, or of the Stuarts, an institution not known to the law, an institution not mentioned in any statute, an institution of which such writers as De Lolme and Blackstone take no notice, began to exist a few years after the Revolution, grew rapidly into importance, became firmly established, and is now almost as essential a part of our polity as the Parliament itself. This institution is the Ministry.

The Ministry is, in fact, a committee of leading members of the two Houses. It is nominated by the Crown: but it consists exclusively of statesmen whose opinions on the pressing questions of the time agree, in the main, with the opinions of the majority of the House of Commons. Among the members of this committee are distributed the great departments of the administration. Each Minister conducts the ordinary business of his own office without reference to his colleagues. But the most important business of every office, and especially such business as is likely to be the subject of discussion in Parliament, is brought under the consideration of the whole Ministry. In Parliament the Ministers are bound to act as one man on all questions relating to the executive government. If one of them dissents from the rest on a question too important to admit of compromise, it is his duty to retire. While the Ministers retain the confidence of the parliamentary majority, that majority supports them against opposition, and rejects every motion which reflects on them or is likely to embarrass them. If they forfeit that confidence, if the parliamentary majority is dissatisfied with the way in which patronage is distributed, with the way in which the prerogative of mercy is used, with the conduct of foreign affairs, with the conduct of a war, the remedy is simple. It is not necessary that the Commons should take on themselves the business of administration, that they should request the Crown to make this man a bishop and that man a judge, to pardon one criminal and to execute another, to negotiate a treaty on a particular basis or to send an expedition to a particular place. They have merely to declare that they have ceased to trust the Ministry, and to ask for a Ministry which they can trust.

It is by means of Ministries thus constituted, and thus changed, that the English government has long been conducted in general conformity with the deliberate sense of the House of Commons, and yet has been wonderfully free from the vices which are characteristic of governments administered by large, tumultuous and divided assemblies. A few distinguished persons, agreeing in their general opinions, are the confidential advisers at once of the Sovereign and of the Estates of the Realm. In the closet they speak with the authority of men who stand high in the estimation of the representatives of the people. In Parliament they speak with the authority of men versed in great affairs and acquainted with all the secrets of the State.   Thus the Cabinet has something of the popular character of a representative body ; and the representative body has something of the gravity of a Cabinet.

Sometimes the state of parties is such that no set of men who can be brought together possesses the full confidence and steady support of a majority of the House of Commons.   When this is the case, there must be a weak Ministry; and there will probably be a rapid succession of weak Ministries.   At such times the House of Commons never fails to get into a state which no person friendly to representative government can contemplate without uneasiness, into a state which may enable us to form some faint notion of the state of that House during the earlier years of the reign of William.   The notion is indeed but faint : for the weakest Ministry has great power as a regulator of parlia-mentary proceedings ; and in the earlier years of the reign of William there was no Ministry at all.

No writer has yet attempted to trace the progress of this institution, an institution indispensable to the harmonious working of our other institutions.   The first Ministry was the work, partly of mere chance, and partly of wisdom ; not however of that highest wisdom which is conversant with great principles of political philosophy, but of that lower wisdom which meets daily exigencies by daily expedients.   Neither William nor the most enlightened of his advisers fully understood the nature and importance of that noiseless revolution,—for it was no less,—which began about the close of 1693, and was completed about the close of 1696.   But every body could perceive that, at the close of 1693, the chief offices in the government were distributed not unequally between the two great parties, that the men who held those offices were perpetually caballing against each other, haranguing against each other, moving votes of censure on each other, exhibiting articles of impeachment against each other, and that the temper of the House of Commons was wild, ungovernable and uncertain.   Every body could perceive that at the close of 1696, all the principal servants of the Crown were Whigs, closely bound together by public and private ties, and prompt to defend one another against every attack, and that the majority of the House of Commons was arrayed in good order under those leaders, and had learned to move, like one man, at the word of command. The history of the period of transition and of the steps by which the change was effected is in a high degree curious and interesting.

The statesman who had the chief share in forming the first English Ministry had once been but too well known, but had long hidden himself from the public gaze, and had but recently emerged from the obscurity in which it had been expected that he would pass the remains of an ignominious and disastrous life.   During that

The first Ministry gradually formed

Sunderland

period of general terror and confusion which followed the flight of James, Sunderland disappeared. It was high time : for of all the agents of the fallen government he was, with the single exception of Jeffreys, the most odious to the nation. Few knew that Sunderland's voice had in secret been given against the spoliation of Magdalene College and the prosecution of the Bishops : but all knew that he had signed numerous instruments dispensing with statutes, that he had sate in the High Commission, that he had turned or pretended to turn Papist, that he had, a few days after his apostasy, appeared in Westminster Hall as a witness against the oppressed fathers of the Church. He had indeed atoned for many crimes by one crime baser than all the rest. As soon as he had reason to believe that the day of deliverance and retribution was at hand, he had, by a most dexterous and season-able treason, earned his pardon. During the three months which preceded the arrival of the Dutch armament in Torbay, he had rendered to the cause of liberty and of the Protestant religion services of which it is difficult to overrate either the wickedness or the utility. To him chiefly it was owing that, at the most critical moment in our history, a French army was not menacing the Batavian frontier, and a French fleet hovering about the English coast. William could not, without staining his own honour, refuse to protect one whom he had not scrupled to employ. Yet it was no easy task even for William to save that guilty head from the first outbreak of public fury. For even those extreme politicians of both sides who agreed in nothing else agreed in calling for vengeance on the renegade. The Whigs hated him as the vilest of the slaves by whom the late government had been served, and the Jacobites as the vilest of the traitors by whom it had been over-thrown. Had he remained in England, he would probably have died by the hand of the executioner, if indeed the executioner had not been anticipated by the populace. But in Holland a political refugee, favoured by the Stadtholder, might hope to live unmolested. To Holland Sunderland fled, disguised, it is said, as a woman ; and his wife accom-panied him. At Rotterdam, a town devoted to the House of Orange, he thought himself secure. But the magistrates were not in all the secrets of the Prince, and were assured by some busy Englishmen that His Highness would be delighted to hear of the arrest of the Popish dog, the Judas, whose appearance on Tower Hill was impatiently expected by all London. Sunderland was thrown into prison, and remained there till an order for his release arrived from Whitehall. He then proceeded to Amsterdam, and there changed his religion again. His second apostasy edified his wife as much as his first apostasy had edified his master. The Countess wrote to assure her pious friends in England that her poor dear lord's heart had at last been really touched by divine grace, and that, in spite of all her afflictions, she was comforted by seeing him so true a convert. We may, however, without any violation of Christian charity, suspect that he was still the same false, callous, Sunderland who, a few months before, had made Bonrepaux shudder by denying the existence of a God, and had, at the same time, won the heart of James by pretending to believe in transubstantiation. In a short time the banished man put forth an apology for his conduct. This apology, when examined, will be found to amount merely to a confession that he had committed one series of crimes in order to gain James's favour, and another series in order to avoid being involved in James's ruin. The writer concluded by announcing his intention to pass all the rest of his life in penitence and prayer. He soon retired from Amsterdam to Utrecht, and at Utrecht made himself conspicuous by his regular and devout attendance on the ministrations of Huguenot preachers. If his letters and those of his wife were to be trusted, he had done for ever with ambition. He longed indeed to be permitted to return from exile, not that he might again enjoy and dispense the favours of the Crown, not that his antechambers might again be filled by the daily swarm of suitors, but that he might see again the turf, the trees, and the family pictures of his country seat. His only wish was to be suffered to end his troubled life at Althorpe ; and he would be content to forfeit his head if ever he went beyond the palings of his park.[1]

While the House of Commons, which had been elected during the vacancy of the throne, was busily engaged in the work of proscription, he could not venture to show himself in England. But when that assembly had ceased to exist, he thought himself safe. He returned a few days after the Act of Grace had been laid on the table of the Lords. From the benefit of that Act he was by name excluded : but he well knew that he had now nothing to fear. He went privately to Kensington, was admitted into the closet, had an audience which lasted two hours, and then retired to his country house.[2]

During many months he led a secluded life, and had no residence in London. Once in the spring of 1691, to the great astonishment of the public, he showed his face in the circle at Court, and was graciously received.[3] He seems to have been afraid that he might, on his re-appearance in Parliament, receive some marked affront. He therefore, very prudently, stole down to Westminster, in the dead time of the year, on a day to which the Houses stood adjourned by the royal command, and on which they met merely for the purpose of adjourning again. He had just time to present himself, to take the oaths, to sign the

---

[1] See Sunderland's celebrated Narrative, which has often been printed, and his wife's letters, which are among the Sidney Papers, published by Mr. Blencowe.

[2] Van Citters, May $\frac{6}{16}$. 1690.　　　　[3] Evelyn, April 24. 1691.

VIEW OF ALTHORPE

From a drawing in the Travels of Cosmo III of Tuscany

declaration against transubstantiation, and to resume his seat. None of the few peers who were present had an opportunity of making any remark.[1] It was not till the year 1692 that he began to attend regularly. He was silent : but silent he had always been in large assemblies, even when he was at the zenith of power. His talents were not those of a public speaker. The art in which he surpassed all men was the art of whispering. His tact, his quick eye for the foibles of individuals, his caressing manners, his power of insinuation, and, above all, his apparent frankness, made him irresistible in private conversation. By means of these qualities he had governed James, and now aspired to govern William.

To govern William, indeed, was not easy. But Sunderland succeeded in obtaining such a measure of favour and influence as excited much surprise and some indignation. In truth, scarcely any mind was strong enough to resist the witchery of his talk and of his manners. Every man is prone to believe in the gratitude and attachment even of the most worthless persons on whom he has conferred great benefits. It can therefore hardly be thought strange that the most skilful of all flatterers should have been heard with favour, when he, with every outward sign of strong emotion, implored permission to dedicate all his faculties to the service of the generous protector to whom he owed property, liberty, life. It is not necessary, however, to suppose that the King was deceived. He may have thought, with good reason, that, though little confidence could be placed in Sunderland's professions, much confidence might be placed in Sunderland's situation ; and the truth is that Sunderland proved, on the whole, a more faithful servant than a less depraved man might have been. He did indeed make, in profound secresy, some timid overtures towards a reconciliation with James. But it may be confidently affirmed that, even had those overtures been graciously received,—and they appear to have been received very ungraciously,—the twice turned renegade would never have rendered any real service to the Jacobite cause. He well knew that he had done that which at Saint Germains must be regarded as inexpiable. It was not merely that he had been treacherous and ungrateful. Marlborough had been as treacherous and as ungrateful ; and Marlborough had been pardoned. But Marlborough had not been guilty of the impious hypocrisy of counterfeiting the signs of conversion. Marlborough had not pretended to be convinced by the arguments of the Jesuits, to be touched by divine grace, to pine for union with the only true Church. Marlborough had not, when Popery was in the ascendant, crossed himself, shrived himself, done penance, taken the communion in one kind, and, as soon as a turn of fortune came, apostatised back again, and proclaimed to all the world that, when he knelt at the confessional and received the

---

[1] Lords' Journals, April 28. 1691.

host, he was merely laughing at the King and the priests. The crime of Sunderland was one which could never be forgiven by James; and a crime which could never be forgiven by James was, in some sense, a recommendation to William. The Court, nay, the Council, was full of men who might hope to prosper if the banished King were restored. But Sunderland had left himself no retreat. He had broken down all the bridges behind him. He had been so false to one side that he must of necessity be true to the other. That he was in the main true to the government which now protected him there is no reason to doubt; and, being true, he could not but be useful. He was, in some respects, eminently qualified to be at that time an adviser of the Crown. He had exactly the talents and the knowledge which William wanted. The two together would have made up a consummate statesman. The master was capable of forming and executing large designs, but was negligent of those small arts in which the servant excelled. The master saw farther off than other men : but what was near no man saw so clearly as the servant. The master, though profoundly versed in the politics of the great community of nations, never thoroughly understood the politics of his own kingdom. The servant was perfectly well informed as to the temper and the organisation of the English factions, and as to the strong and weak parts of the character of every Englishman of note.

Early in 1693, it was rumoured that Sunderland was consulted on all important questions relating to the internal administration of the realm; and the rumour became stronger when it was known that he had come up to London in the autumn, and that he had taken a large mansion near Whitehall. The coffeehouse politicians were confident that he was about to hold some high office. As yet, however, he had the wisdom to be content with the reality of power, and to leave the show to others.[1]

His opinion was that, so long as the King tried to balance the two great parties against each other, and to divide his favour equally between them, both would think themselves ill used, and neither would lend to the government that hearty and steady support which was now greatly needed. His Majesty must make up his mind to give a marked preference to one or the other ; and there were three weighty reasons for giving the preference to the Whigs. *Sunderland advises the King to give the preference to the Whigs*

In the first place, the Whigs were on principle attached to the reigning dynasty. In their view the Revolution had been, not merely necessary, not merely justifiable, but happy and glorious. It had been the triumph of their political theory. When they swore allegiance to William, they swore without scruple or reservation ; and they were so far from having any doubt about his *Reasons for preferring the Whigs*

[1] L'Hermitage, Sept. $\frac{18}{28}$., Oct. $\frac{2}{12}$. 1693

title that they thought it the best of all titles. The Tories, on the other hand, very generally disapproved of that vote of the Convention which had placed him on the throne. Some of them were at heart Jacobites, and had taken the oath of allegiance to him only that they might be better able to injure him. Others, though they thought it their duty to obey him as King in fact, denied that he was King by right, and, if they were loyal to him, were loyal without enthusiasm. There could, therefore, be little doubt on which of the two parties it would be safer for him to rely.

In the second place, as to the particular matter on which his heart was at present set, the Whigs were, as a body, prepared to support him strenuously, and the Tories were, as a body, inclined to thwart him. The minds of men were at this time much occupied by the question, in what way the war ought to be carried on. To that question the two parties returned very different answers. An opinion had during many months been growing among the Tories that the policy of England ought to be strictly insular; that she ought to leave the defence of Flanders and the Rhine to the States General, the House of Austria, and the Princes of the Empire; that she ought to carry on hostilities with vigour by sea, but to keep up only such an army as might, with the help of the militia, be sufficient to repel an invasion. It was plain that, if such a system were adopted, there might be an immediate reduction of the taxes which pressed most heavily on the nation. But the Whigs maintained that this relief would be dearly purchased. Many thousands of brave English soldiers were now in Flanders. Yet the allies had not been able to prevent the French from taking Mons in 1691, Namur in 1692, Charleroy in 1693. If the English troops were withdrawn, it was all but certain that Ostend, Ghent, Liege, Brussels would fall. The German Princes would hasten to make peace, each for himself. The Spanish Netherlands would probably be annexed to the French monarchy. The United Provinces would be again as hard pressed as in 1672, and would accept whatever terms Lewis might be pleased to dictate. In a few months, he would be at liberty to put forth his whole strength against our island. Then would come a struggle for life and death. It might well be hoped that we should be able to defend our soil even against such a general and such an army as had won the battle of Landen. But the fight must be long and hard. How many fertile counties would be turned into deserts, how many flourishing towns would be laid in ashes, before the invaders were destroyed or driven out! One triumphant campaign in Kent and Middlesex would do more to impoverish the nation than ten disastrous campaigns in Brabant. Those Belgian fortresses, in the fate of which shallow politicians imagined that we had no interest, were in truth the outworks of London. It is remarkable that this dispute between the two great factions was, during seventy years, regularly revived as often as our country was at war with France. That England ought never to attempt great military operations on the Continent continued to be a fundamental article of the creed of the Tories till the French Revolution produced a complete change in their feelings.[1] As the chief object of William was to open the campaign of 1694 in Flanders with an immense display of force, it was sufficiently clear to whom he must look for assistance.

In the third place, the Whigs were the stronger party in Parliament. The general election of 1690, indeed, had not been favourable to them. They had been, for a time, a minority : but they had ever since been constantly gaining ground : they were now in number a full half of the Lower House ; and their effective strength was more than proportioned to their number : for in energy, alertness, and discipline, they were decidedly superior to their opponents. Their organisation was not indeed so perfect as it afterwards became : but they had already begun to look for guidance to a small knot of distinguished men, which was long afterwards widely known by the name of the Junto. There is, perhaps, no parallel in history, ancient or modern, to the authority exercised by this council, during twenty troubled years, over the Whig body. The men who acquired that authority in the days of William and Mary continued to possess it, without interruption, in office and out of office, till George the First was on the throne.

Chiefs of the Whig party

One of these men was Russell. Of his shameful dealings with the Court of Saint Germains we possess proofs which leave no room for doubt. But no such proofs were laid before the world till he had been many years dead. If rumours of his guilt got abroad, they were vague and improbable : they rested on no evidence : they could be traced to no trustworthy author ; and they might well be regarded by his contemporaries as Jacobite calumnies. What was quite certain was that he sprang from an illustrious house which had done and suffered great things for liberty and for the Protestant religion, that he had signed the invitation of the thirtieth of June, that he had landed with the Deliverer at Torbay, that he had in Parliament, on all occasions, spoken and voted as a zealous Whig, that he had won a

Russell

---

[1] It is amusing to see how Johnson's Toryism breaks out where we should hardly expect to find it. Hastings says, in the Third Part of Henry the Sixth,

    "Let us be backed with God and with the seas
    Which He hath given for fence impregnable,
    And with their helps alone defend ourselves."

"This," says Johnson in a note, "has been the advice of every man who, in any age, understood and favoured the interest of England."

great victory, that he had saved his country from an invasion, and that, since he had left the Admiralty, every thing had gone wrong. We cannot therefore wonder that his influence over his party should have been considerable.

But the greatest man among the members of the Junto, and, in some respects, the greatest man of that age, was the Lord Keeper Somers. He was equally eminent as a jurist and as a politician, as an orator and as a writer. His speeches have perished : but his State papers remain, and are models of terse, luminous, and dignified eloquence. He had left a great reputation in the House of Commons, where he had, during four years, been always heard with delight ; and the Whig members still looked up to him as their leader, and still held their meetings under his roof. In the great place to which he had recently been promoted, he had so borne himself that, after a very few months, even faction and envy had ceased to murmur at his elevation. In truth, he united all the qualities of a great judge, an intellect comprehensive, quick and acute, diligence, integrity, patience, suavity. In council, the calm wisdom, which he possessed in a measure rarely found among men of parts so quick and of opinions so decided as his, acquired for him the authority of an oracle. The superiority of his powers appeared not less clearly in private circles. The charm of his conversation was heightened by the frankness with which he poured out his thoughts.[1] His good temper and his good breeding never failed. His gesture, his look, his tones were expressive of benevolence. His humanity was the more remarkable, because he had received from nature a body such as is generally found united with a peevish and irritable mind. His life was one long malady : his nerves were weak : his complexion was livid : his face was prematurely wrinkled. Yet his enemies could not pretend that he had ever once, during a long and troubled public life, been goaded, even by sudden provocation, into vehemence inconsistent with the mild dignity of his character. All that was left to them was to assert that his disposition was very far

Somers

---

[1] Swift, in his Inquiry into the Behaviour of the Queen's last Ministry, mentions Somers as a person of great abilities, who used to talk in so frank a manner that he seemed to discover the bottom of his heart. In the Memoirs relating to the change in the Queen's Ministry, Swift says that Somers had one, and only one unconversable fault, formality. It is not very easy to understand how the same man can be the most unreserved of companions, and yet err on the side of formality. Yet there may be truth in both descriptions. It is well known that Swift loved to take rude liberties with men of high rank, and fancied that, by doing so, he asserted his own independence. He has been justly blamed for this fault by his two illustrious biographers, both of them men of spirit at least as independent as his, Samuel Johnson and Walter Scott. I suspect that he showed a disposition to behave with offensive familiarity to Somers, and that Somers, not choosing to submit to impertinence, and not wishing to be forced to resent it, resorted, in self-defence, to a ceremonious politeness which he never would have practised towards Locke or Addison.

The R.^t Hono.^{ble} John Lord Sommers
Baron of Evesham

G. Kneller Eques pinxit.

Geo: Vertue Sculpsit.

JOHN, LORD SOMERS

From an engraving by G. Vertue, after a painting by Sir G. Kneller

from being so gentle as the world believed, that he was really prone to the angry passions, and that sometimes, while his voice was soft, and his words kind and courteous, his delicate frame was almost convulsed by suppressed emotion. It will perhaps be thought that this reproach is the highest of all eulogies.

The most accomplished men of those times have told us that there was scarcely any subject on which Somers was not competent to instruct and to delight. He had never travelled ; and, in that age, an Englishman who had not travelled was generally thought unqualified to give an opinion on works of art. But connoisseurs familiar with the masterpieces of the Vatican and of the Florentine gallery allowed that the taste of Somers in painting and sculpture was exquisite. Philology was one of his favourite pursuits. He had traversed the whole vast range of polite literature, ancient and modern. He was at once a munificent and a severely judicious patron of genius and learning. Locke owed opulence to Somers. By Somers Addison was drawn forth from a cell in a college. In distant countries the name of Somers was mentioned with respect and gratitude by great scholars and poets who had never seen his face. He was the benefactor of Leclerc. He was the friend of Filicaja. Neither political nor religious differences prevented him from extending his powerful protection to merit. Hickes, the fiercest and most intolerant of all the nonjurors, obtained, by the influence of Somers, permission to study Teutonic antiquities in freedom and safety. Vertue, a strict Roman Catholic, was raised by the discriminating and liberal patronage of Somers from poverty and obscurity to the first rank among the engravers of the age.

The generosity with which Somers treated his opponents was the more honourable to him because he was no waverer in politics. From the beginning to the end of his public life he was a steady Whig. His voice was indeed always raised, when his party was dominant in the State, against violent and vindictive counsels : but he never forsook his friends, even when their perverse neglect of his advice had brought them to the verge of ruin.

His powers of mind and his acquirements were not denied even by his detractors. The most acrimonious Tories were forced to admit, with an ungracious snarl which increased the value of their praise, that he had all the intellectual qualities of a great man, and that in him alone among his contemporaries brilliant eloquence and wit were to be found associated with the quiet and steady prudence which ensures success in life. It is a remarkable fact that, in the foulest of all the many libels which were published against him, he was slandered under the name of Cicero. As his abilities could not be questioned, he was charged with irreligion and immorality. That he was heterodox all the country vicars and foxhunting squires firmly believed : but as to the nature and extent of his heterodoxy there were many different opinions. He seems to have been a Low Churchman of the school of Tillotson, whom he always loved and honoured ; and he was, like Tillotson, called by bigots a Presbyterian, an Arian, a Socinian, a Deist, and an Atheist.

The private life of this great statesman and magistrate was malignantly scrutinised ; and tales were told about his libertinism which went on growing till they became too absurd for the credulity even of party spirit. At last, long after he had been condemned to flannel and chicken broth, a wretched courtesan, who had probably never seen him except in the stage box at the theatre, when she was following her vocation below in a mask, published a lampoon in which she described him as the master of a haram more costly than the Great Turk's. There is, however, reason to believe that there was a small nucleus of truth round which this great mass of fiction gathered, and that the wisdom and selfcommand which Somers never wanted in the senate, on the judgment seat, at the council board, or in the society of wits, scholars, and philosophers, were not always proof against female attractions.[1]

Another director of the Whig party was Charles Montague. He was often, when he had risen to power, honours, and riches, called an upstart by those who envied his success. That they should have called him so may seem strange ; for few of the statesmen of his time could show such a pedigree as his. He sprang from a family as old as the Conquest : he was in the succession to an earldom ; and he was, by the paternal side, cousin of three earls. But he was the younger son of a younger brother ; and that phrase had, ever since the time of Shakspeare and Raleigh, and perhaps before their time, been proverbially used to designate a person so poor as to be broken to the most abject servitude or ready for the most desperate adventure.

Montague

Charles Montague was early destined for the Church, was entered on the foundation of Westminster, and, after distinguishing himself there by skill in Latin versification, was sent up to Trinity College, Cambridge. At Cambridge the philosophy of Des Cartes was still dominant in the

---

[1] The eulogies on Somers and the invectives against him are innumerable. Perhaps the best way to come to a just judgment would be to collect all that has been said about him by Swift and by Addison. They were the two keenest observers of their time ; and they both knew him well. But it ought to be remarked that, till Swift turned Tory, he always extolled Somers, not only as the most accomplished, but as the most virtuous of men. In the dedication of the Tale of a Tub are these words, " There is no virtue, either of a public or private life, which some circumstances of your own have not often produced upon the stage of the world ; " and again, " I should be very loth the bright example of your Lordship's virtues should be lost to other eyes, both for their sake and your own." In the Discourse of the Contests and Dissensions at Athens and Rome, Somers is the just Aristides. After Swift had ratted, he described Somers as a man who " possessed all excellent qualifications except virtue."

schools.   But a few select spirits had separated from the crowd, and formed a fit audience round a far greater teacher.[1]   Conspicuous among the youths of high promise who were proud to sit at the feet of Newton was the quick and versatile Montague.   Under such guidance the young student made considerable proficiency in the severe sciences : but poetry was his favourite pursuit ; and when the University invited her sons to celebrate royal marriages and funerals, he was generally allowed to have surpassed his competitors.   His fame travelled to London : he was thought a clever lad by the wits who met at Will's ; and the lively parody which he wrote, in concert with his friend and fellow student Prior, on Dryden's Hind and Panther, was received with great applause.

At this time all Montague's wishes pointed towards the Church.   At a later period, when he was a peer with twelve thousand a year, when his villa on the Thames was regarded as the most delightful of all suburban retreats, when he was said to revel in Tokay from the Imperial cellar, and in soups made out of birds' nests brought from the Indian Ocean, and costing three guineas a piece, his enemies were fond of reminding him that there had been a time when he had eked out by his wits an income of barely fifty pounds, when he had been happy with a trencher of mutton chops and a flagon of ale from the College buttery, and when a tithe pig was the rarest luxury for which he had dared to hope.   The Revolution came, and changed his whole scheme of life. He obtained, by the influence of Dorset, who took a peculiar pleasure in befriending young men of promise, a seat in the House of Commons. Still, during a few months, the needy scholar hesitated between politics and divinity.   But it soon became clear that, in the new order of things, parliamentary ability must fetch a higher price than any other kind of ability ; and he felt that in parliamentary ability he had no superior. He was in the very situation for which he was peculiarly fitted by nature ; and, during some years, his life was a series of triumphs.

Of him, as of several of his contemporaries, especially of Mulgrave and of Sprat, it may be said that his fame has suffered from the folly of those editors who, down to our own time, have persisted in reprinting his rhymes among the works of the British poets.   There is not a year in which hundreds of verses as good as any that he ever wrote are not sent in for the Newdigate prize at Oxford and for the Chancellor's medal at Cambridge.   His mind had indeed great quickness and vigour, but not that kind of quickness and vigour which produces great dramas or odes ; and it is most unjust to him that his Man of Honour and his Epistle on the Battle of the Boyne should be placed side by side with the master-pieces of Milton and Dryden.   Other eminent statesmen and orators, Walpole, Pulteney, Chatham, Fox, wrote poetry not better than his.

[1] See Whiston's Autobiography.

But fortunately for them, their metrical compositions were never thought worthy to be admitted into any collection of our national classics.

It has long been usual to represent the imagination under the figure of a wing, and to call the successful exertions of the imagination flights. One poet is the eagle : another is the swan : a third modestly likens himself to the bee. But none of these types would have suited Montague. His genius may be compared to that pinion which, though it is too weak to lift the ostrich into the air, enables her, while she remains on the earth, to outrun hound, horse and dromedary. If the man who possesses this kind of genius attempts to ascend the heaven of invention, his awkward and unsuccessful efforts expose him to derision. But, if he will be content to stay in the terrestrial region of business, he will find that the faculties which would not enable him to soar into a higher sphere will enable him to distance all his competitors in the lower. As a poet Montague could never have risen above the crowd. But in the House of Commons, now fast becoming supreme in the State, and extending its control over one executive department after another, the young adventurer soon obtained a place very different from the place which he occupies among men of letters. At thirty, he would gladly have given all his chances in life for a comfortable vicarage and a chaplain's scarf. At thirty seven, he was First Lord of the Treasury, Chancellor of the Exchequer, and a Regent of the kingdom ; and this elevation he owed not at all to favour, but solely to the unquestionable superiority of his talents for administration and debate.

The extraordinary ability with which, at the beginning of the year 1692, he managed the conference on the Bill for regulating Trials in cases of Treason, placed him at once in the first rank of parliamentary orators. On that occasion he was opposed to a crowd of veteran senators renowned for their eloquence, Halifax, Rochester, Nottingham, Mulgrave, and proved himself a match for them all. He was speedily seated at the Board of Treasury ; and there the clearheaded and experienced Godolphin soon found that his young colleague was his master. When Somers had quitted the House of Commons, Montague had no rival there. To this day we may discern in many parts of our financial and commercial system the marks of that vigorous intellect and daring spirit. The bitterest enemies of Montague were unable to deny that some of the expedients which he had proposed had proved highly beneficial to the nation. But it was said that these expedients were not devised by himself. He was represented, in a hundred pamphlets, as the daw in borrowed plumes. He had taken, it was affirmed, the hint of every one of his great plans from the writings or the conversation of some ingenious speculator. This reproach was, in truth, no reproach. We can scarcely expect to find in the same human being the talents which are necessary for the making of new discoveries in political science, and the talents which obtain the assent of divided and tumultuous assemblies to great practical reforms.   To be at once Adam Smith and William Pitt is scarcely possible.   It is surely praise enough for a busy politician that he knows how to use the theories of others, that he discerns, among the schemes of innumerable theorists, the precise scheme which is wanted and which is practicable, that he shapes it to suit pressing circumstances and popular humours, that he proposes it just when it is most likely to be favourably received, that he triumphantly defends it against all objectors, and that he carries it into execution with prudence and energy ; and to this praise no English statesman has a fairer claim than Montague.

It is a remarkable proof of his selfknowledge that, from the moment at which he began to distinguish himself in public life, he ceased to be a versifier.   It does not appear that, after he became a Lord of the Treasury, he ever wrote a couplet, with the exception of a few neatly turned lines inscribed on a set of toasting glasses which were sacred to the most renowned Whig beauties of his time.   He wisely determined to derive from the poetry of others a glory which he never would have derived from his own.   As a patron of genius and learning he ranks with his two illustrious friends, Dorset and Somers.   His munificence fully equalled theirs ; and, though he was inferior to them in delicacy of taste, he succeeded in associating his name inseparably with some names which will last as long as our language.

Yet it must be acknowledged that Montague, with admirable parts, and with many claims on the gratitude of his country, had great faults, and unhappily faults not of the noblest kind.   His head was not strong enough to bear without giddiness the speed of his ascent and the height of his position.   He became offensively arrogant and vain.   He was too often cold to his old friends, and ostentatious in displaying his new riches.   Above all, he was insatiably greedy of praise, and liked it best when it was of the coarsest and rankest quality.   But, in 1693, these faults were less offensive than they became a few years later.

With Russell, Somers, and Montague, was closely connected, during a quarter of a century, a fourth Whig, who in character bore little resemblance to any of them.   This was Thomas Wharton, **Wharton** eldest son of Philip Lord Wharton.   Thomas Wharton has been repeatedly mentioned in the course of this narrative.   But it is now time to describe him more fully.   He was in his forty seventh year, but was still a young man in constitution, in appearance, and in manners.   Those who hated him most heartily,—and no man was hated more heartily,—admitted that his natural parts were excellent, and that he was equally qualified for debate and for action.   The history of his

G. Kneller Bart Pinx.   I. Faber fecit 1711

Thomas Wharton   *Marquiss of Wharton*

APLAISIR EN FAITS D'ARMES

THOMAS WHARTON, AFTERWARDS MARQUIS OF WHARTON

From a mezzotint by J. Faber, after a painting by Sir G. Kneller

mind deserves notice : for it was the history of many thousands of minds. His rank and abilities made him so conspicuous that in him we are able to trace distinctly the origin and progress of a moral taint which was epidemic among his contemporaries.

He was born in the days of the Covenant, and was the heir of a covenanted house. His father was renowned as a distributor of Calvinistic tracts, and a patron of Calvinistic divines. The boy's first years were passed amidst Geneva bands, heads of lank hair, upturned eyes, nasal psalmody, and sermons three hours long. Plays and poems, hunting and dancing, were proscribed by the austere discipline of his saintly family. The fruits of this education became visible, when, from the sullen mansion of Puritan parents, the hotblooded, quickwitted, young patrician emerged into the gay and voluptuous London of the Restoration. The most dissolute cavaliers stood aghast at the dissoluteness of the emancipated precisian. He early acquired and retained to the last the reputation of being the greatest rake in England. Of wine indeed he never became the slave ; and he used it chiefly for the purpose of making himself the master of his associates. But to the end of his long life the wives and daughters of his nearest friends were not safe from his licentious plots. The ribaldry of his conversation moved astonishment even in that age. To the religion of his country he offered, in the mere wantonness of impiety, insults too foul to be described. His mendacity and his effrontery passed into proverbs. Of all the liars of his time he was the most deliberate, the most inventive, and the most circumstantial. What shame meant he did not seem to understand. No reproaches, even when pointed and barbed with the sharpest wit, appeared to give him pain. Great satirists, animated by a deadly personal aversion, exhausted all their strength in attacks upon him. They assailed him with keen invective : they assailed him with still keener irony: but they found that neither invective nor irony could move him to any thing but an unforced smile and a goodhumoured curse ; and they at length threw down the lash, acknowledging that it was impossible to make him feel. That, with such vices, he should have played a great part in life, should have carried numerous elections against the most formidable opposition by his personal popularity, should have had a large following in Parliament, should have risen to the highest offices in the State, seems extraordinary. But he lived in times when faction was almost a madness ; and he possessed in an eminent degree the qualities of the leader of a faction. There was a single tie which he respected. The falsest of mankind in all relations but one, he was the truest of Whigs. The religious tenets of his family he had early renounced with contempt : but to the politics of his family he stedfastly adhered through all the temptations and dangers of half a century. In small things and in

great his devotion to his party constantly appeared.   He had the finest
stud in England ; and his delight was to win plates from Tories.
Sometimes when, in a distant county, it was fully expected that the
horse of a High Church squire would be first on the course, down came,
on the very eve of the race, Wharton's Careless, who had ceased to run
at Newmarket merely for want of competitors, or Wharton's Gelding,
for whom Lewis the Fourteenth had in vain offered a thousand pistoles.
A man whose mere sport was of this description was not likely to be
easily beaten in any serious contest.   Such a master of the whole art of
electioneering England had never seen.   Buckinghamshire was his own
especial province ; and there he ruled without a rival.   But he extended
his care over the Whig interest in Yorkshire, Cumberland, Westmoreland,
Wiltshire.   Sometimes twenty, sometimes thirty, members of Parliament
were named by him.   As a canvasser he was irresistible.   He never
forgot a face that he had once seen.   Nay, in the towns in which he
wished to establish an interest, he remembered, not only the voters, but
their families.   His opponents were confounded by the strength of his
memory and the affability of his deportment, and owned that it was
impossible to contend against a great man who called the shoemaker
by his Christian name, who was sure that the butcher's daughter must
be growing a fine girl, and who was anxious to know whether the
blacksmith's youngest boy was breeched.   By such arts as these he made
himself so popular that his journeys to the Buckinghamshire Quarter
Sessions resembled royal progresses.   The bells of every parish through
which he passed were rung, and flowers were strewed along the road.
It was commonly believed that, in the course of his life, he expended on
his parliamentary interest not less than eighty thousand pounds, a sum
which, when compared with the value of estates, must be considered as
equivalent to more than three hundred thousand pounds in our time.

But the chief service which Wharton rendered to the Whig party
was that of bringing in recruits from the young aristocracy.   He was
quite as dexterous a canvasser among the embroidered coats at the
Saint James's Coffeehouse as among the leathern aprons at Wycombe
and Ailesbury.   He had his eye on every boy of quality who came of
age ; and it was not easy for such a boy to resist the arts of a noble,
eloquent, and wealthy flatterer, who united juvenile vivacity to profound
art and long experience of the gay world.   It mattered not what the
novice preferred, gallantry or field sports, the dicebox or the bottle.
Wharton soon found out the master passion, offered sympathy, advice,
and assistance, and, while seeming to be only the minister of his
disciple's pleasures, made sure of his disciple's vote.

The party to whose interests Wharton, with such spirit and constancy, devoted his time, his fortune, his talents, his very vices, judged

him, as was natural, far too leniently. He was widely known by the very undeserved appellation of Honest Tom. Some pious men, Burnet, for example, and Addison, averted their eyes from the scandal which he gave, and spoke of him, not indeed with esteem, yet with goodwill. A most ingenious and accomplished Whig, the third Earl of Shaftesbury, author of the Characteristics, described Wharton as the most mysterious of human beings, as a strange compound of best and worst, of private depravity and public virtue, and owned himself unable to understand how a man utterly without principle in every thing but politics should in politics be as true as steel. But that which, in the judgment of one faction, more than half redeemed all Wharton's faults, seemed to the other faction to aggravate them all. The opinion which the Tories entertained of him is expressed in a single line written after his death by the ablest man of that party, Jonathan Swift; " He was the most universal villain that ever I knew." [1] Wharton's political adversaries thirsted for his blood, and repeatedly tried to shed it. Had he not been a man of imperturbable temper, dauntless courage, and consummate skill in fence, his life would have been a short one. But neither anger nor danger ever deprived him of his presence of mind : he was an incomparable swordsman ; and he had a peculiar way of disarming opponents which moved the envy of all the duellists of his time. His friends said that he had never given a challenge, that he had never refused one, that he had never taken a life, and yet that he had never fought without having his antagonist's life at his mercy. [2]

The four men who have been described resembled each other so little that it may be thought strange that they should ever have been able to act in concert. They did, however, act in the closest concert during many years. They more than once rose and more than once fell together. But their union lasted till it was dissolved by death. Little as some of them may have deserved esteem, none of them can be accused of having been false to his brethren of the Junto.

While the great body of the Whig members of Parliament was, under these able chiefs, arraying itself in order resembling that of a **Chiefs of the Tory party** regular army, the Tories were in the state of a tumultuary militia, undrilled and unofficered. They were numerous ; and they were zealous : but they had no discipline and no chief. The name of Seymour had once been great among them, and had not quite lost its influence. But, since he had been at the Board of Treasury, he had disgusted them by vehemently defending all that he

---

[1] Swift's note on Mackay's Character of Wharton.

[2] This account of Montague and Wharton I have collected from innumerable sources. I ought, however, to mention particularly the very curious Life of Wharton published immediately after his death.

had himself, when out of place, vehemently attacked. They had once looked up to the Speaker, Trevor: but his greediness, impudence, and venality were now so notorious that all respectable gentlemen, of all shades of opinion, were ashamed to see him in the chair. Of the old Tory members Sir Christopher Musgrave alone had much weight. Indeed the real leaders of the party, as far as it can be said to have had leaders, were men bred in principles diametrically opposed to Toryism, men who had carried Whiggism to the verge of republicanism, and who had long been considered not merely as Low Churchmen, but as more than half Presbyterians. Of these men the most eminent were two great Herefordshire squires, Robert Harley and Paul Foley.

The space which Robert Harley fills in the history of three reigns, his elevation, his fall, the influence which, at a great crisis, he exercised on the politics of all Europe, the close intimacy in which he lived with some of the greatest wits and poets of his time,   Harley and the frequent recurrence of his name in the works of Swift, Pope, Arbuthnot, and Prior, must always make him an object of interest. Yet the man himself was of all men the least interesting. There is indeed a whimsical contrast between the very ordinary qualities of his mind and the very extraordinary vicissitudes of his fortune.

He was the heir of a Puritan family. His father, Sir Edward Harley, had been conspicuous among the patriots of the Long Parliament, had commanded a regiment under Essex, had, after the Restoration, been an active opponent of the Court, had supported the Exclusion Bill, had harboured dissenting preachers, had frequented meetinghouses, and had made himself so obnoxious to the ruling powers that, at the time of the Western Insurrection, he had been placed under arrest, and his house had been searched for arms. When the Dutch army was marching from Torbay towards London, he and his eldest son Robert declared for the Prince of Orange and a free Parliament, raised a large body of horse, took possession of Worcester, and evinced their zeal against Popery by publicly breaking to pieces, in the High Street of that city, a piece of sculpture which to rigid precisians seemed idolatrous. Soon after the Convention had become a Parliament, Robert Harley was sent up to Westminster as member for a Cornish borough. His conduct was such as might have been expected from his birth and education. He was a Whig, and indeed an intolerant and vindictive Whig. Nothing would satisfy him but a general proscription of the Tories. His name appears in the list of those members who voted for the Sacheverell clause; and, at the general election which took place in the spring of 1690, the party which he had persecuted made great exertions to keep him out of the House of Commons. A cry was raised that the Harleys were mortal enemies of the Church; and this cry produced so much effect that it was with difficulty that any of them could obtain a seat. Such was the commencement of the public life of a man whose name, a quarter of a century later, was inseparably coupled with High Church in the acclamations of Jacobite mobs.[1]

Soon, however, it began to be observed that in every division Harley was found among those gentlemen who held his political opinions in abhorrence; nor was this strange; for he affected the character of a Whig of the old pattern; and before the Revolution it had always been supposed that a Whig was a person who watched with jealousy every exertion of the prerogative, who was slow to loose the strings of the public purse, and who was extreme to mark the faults of the ministers of the Crown. Such a Whig Harley still professed to be. He did not admit that the recent change of dynasty had made any change in the duties of a representative of the people. The new government ought to be observed as suspiciously, checked as severely, and supplied as sparingly, as the old one. Acting on these principles, he necessarily found himself acting with men whose principles were diametrically opposed to his. He liked to thwart the King: they liked to thwart the usurper: the consequence was that, whenever there was an opportunity of thwarting William, the Roundhead staid in the House or went into the lobby in company with the whole crowd of Cavaliers.

Soon Harley acquired the authority of a leader among those with whom, notwithstanding wide differences of opinion, he ordinarily voted. His influence in Parliament was indeed altogether out of proportion to his abilities. His intellect was both small and slow. He was unable to take a large view of any subject. He never acquired the art of expressing himself in public with fluency and perspicuity. To the end of his life he remained a tedious, hesitating and confused speaker.[2] He had none of the external graces of an orator. His countenance was heavy, his figure mean and somewhat deformed, and his gestures uncouth. Yet he was heard with respect. For, such as his mind was, it had been assiduously cultivated. His youth had been studious; and to the last he continued to love books and the society of men of genius and learning. Indeed he aspired to the character of a wit and a poet, and occasionally employed hours which should have

---

[1] Much of my information about the Harleys I have derived from unpublished memoirs written by Edward Harley, younger brother of Robert. A copy of these memoirs is among the Mackintosh MSS.

[2] The only writer who has praised Harley's oratory, as far as I remember, is Mackay, who calls him eloquent. Swift scribbled in the margin, "A great lie." And certainly Swift was inclined to do more than justice to Harley. "That lord," said Pope, "talked of business in so confused a manner that you did not know what he was about; and every thing he went to tell you was in the epic way; for he always began in the middle."—Spence's Anecdotes.

ROBERT HARLEY, EARL OF OXFORD

From the painting in the National Portrait Gallery, after Sir Godfrey Kneller

been very differently spent in composing verses more execrable than the bellman's.[1] His time however was not always so absurdly wasted. He had that sort of industry and that sort of exactness which would have made him a respectable antiquary or King at Arms. His taste led him to plod among old records ; and, in that age, it was only by plodding among old records that any man could obtain an accurate and extensive knowledge of the law of Parliament. Having few rivals in this laborious and unattractive pursuit, he soon began to be regarded as an oracle on questions of form and privilege. His moral character added not a little to his influence. He had indeed great vices : but they were not of a scandalous kind. He was not to be corrupted by money. His private life was regular. No illicit amour was imputed to him even by satirists. Gambling he held in aversion ; and it was said that he never passed White's, then the favourite haunt of noble sharpers and dupes, without an exclamation of anger. His practice of flustering himself daily with claret was hardly considered as a fault by his contemporaries. His knowledge, his gravity, and his independent position gained for him the ear of the House ; and even his bad speaking was, in some sense, an advantage to him. For people are very loth to admit that the same man can unite very different kinds of excellence. It is soothing to envy to believe that what is splendid cannot be solid, that what is clear cannot be profound. Very slowly was the public brought to acknowledge that Mansfield was a great jurist, and that Burke was a great master of political science. Montague was a brilliant rhetorician, and, therefore, though he had ten times

[1] " He used," said Pope, " to send trifling verses from Court to the Scriblerus Club almost every day, and would come and talk idly with them almost every night even when his all was at stake." Some specimens of Harley's poetry are in print. The best, I think, is a stanza which he made on his own fall in 1714 ; and bad is the best.

> " To serve with love,
> And shed your blood,
> Approved is above ;
> But here below
> The examples show
> 'Tis fatal to be good."

(1855.)

Since the first edition of this part of my history appeared, I have discovered that these lines, poor as they are, were not Harley's own. He took them, with slight alterations, from Dryden's Albion and Albanius. The following stanza I can, I think, warrant as a genuine production of Harley's Muse :

> " I honour the men, Sir,
> Who are ready to answer,
> When I ask them to stand by the Queen,
> In spite of orators
> And bloodthirsty praters,
> Whose hatred I highly esteem."

(1857.)

Harley's capacity for the driest parts of business, was represented by detractors as a superficial, prating, pretender.   But from the absence of show in Harley's discourses many people inferred that there must be much substance ; and he was pronounced to be a deep read, deep thinking gentleman, not a fine talker, but fitter to direct affairs of state than all the fine talkers in the world.   This character he long supported with that cunning which is frequently found in company with ambitious and unquiet mediocrity.   He constantly had, even with his best friends, an air of mystery and reserve which seemed to indicate that he knew some momentous secret, and that his mind was labouring with some vast design.   In this way he got and long kept a high reputation for wisdom.   It was not till that reputation had made him an Earl, a Knight of the Garter, Lord High Treasurer of England, and master of the fate of Europe, that his admirers began to find out that he was really a dull puzzleheaded man.[1]

Soon after the general election of 1690, Harley, generally voting with the Tories, began to turn Tory.   The change was so gradual as to be almost imperceptible, but was not the less real.   He early began to hold the Tory doctrine that England ought to confine herself to a maritime war.   He early felt the true Tory antipathy to Dutchmen and to moneyed men.   The antipathy to Dissenters, which was necessary to the completeness of the character, came much later.   At length the transformation was complete; and the old haunter of conventicles became an intolerant High Churchman.   Yet to the last the traces of his early breeding would now and then show themselves ; and, while he acted after the fashion of Laud, he sometimes wrote in the style of Praise God Barebone.[2]

Of Paul Foley we know comparatively little.   His history, up to a certain point, greatly resembles that of Harley : but he appears to have been superior to Harley both in parts and in elevation of character.   He was the son of Thomas Foley, a new man, but **Foley** a man of great merit, who, having begun life with nothing, had created a noble estate by ironworks, and who was renowned for his spotless integrity and his munificent charity.   The Foleys were, like their neighbours the Harleys, Whigs and Puritans.   Thomas Foley lived on terms

[1] The character of Harley is to be collected from innumerable panegyrics and lampoons, from the works and the private correspondence of Swift, Pope, Arbuthnot, Prior and Bolingbroke, and from multitudes of such works as Ox and Bull, the High German Doctor, and The History of Robert Powell the Puppet Showman.

[2] In a letter dated Sept. 12. 1709, a short time before he was brought into power on the shoulders of the High Church mob, he says : "My soul has been among lyons, even the sons of men, whose teeth are spears and arrows, and their tongues sharp swords.   But I learn how good it is to wait on the Lord, and to possess one's soul in peace."   The letter was to Carstairs.   I doubt whether Harley would have canted thus if he had been writing to Atterbury.

of close intimacy with Baxter, in whose writings he is mentioned with warm eulogy. The opinions and the attachments of Paul Foley were at first those of his family. But he, like Harley, became, merely from the vehemence of his Whiggism, an ally of the Tories, and might, perhaps, like Harley, have been completely metamorphosed into a Tory, if the process of transmutation had not been interrupted by death. Foley's abilities were highly respectable, and had been improved by education. He was so wealthy that it was unnecessary for him to follow the law as a profession ; but he had studied it carefully as a science. His morals were without stain ; and the greatest fault which could be imputed to him was that he paraded his independence and disinterestedness too ostentatiously, and was so much afraid of being thought to fawn that he was almost always growling.

Another convert ought to be mentioned. Howe, lately the most virulent of the Whigs, had been, by the loss of his place, turned into one of the most virulent of the Tories. The deserter brought

Howe

to the party which he had joined no weight of character, no capacity or semblance of capacity for great affairs, but much parliamentary ability of a low kind, much spite, and much impudence. No speaker of that time seems to have had, in such large measure, both the power and the inclination to give pain.

The assistance of these men was most welcome to the Tory party : but it was impossible that they could, as yet, exercise over that party the entire authority of leaders. For they still called themselves Whigs, and generally vindicated their Tory votes by arguments grounded on Whig principles.[1]

From this view of the state of parties in the House of Commons, it seems clear that Sunderland had good reason for recommending that the administration should be entrusted to the Whigs. The King, however, hesitated long before he could bring himself to quit that neutral position which he had long occupied between the contending parties. If one of those parties was disposed to question his title, the other was on principle hostile to his prerogative. He still remembered with bitterness the unreasonable and vindictive conduct of his first Parliament at the close of 1689 and the beginning of 1690; and he shrank from the thought of being entirely in the hands of the men who had obstructed the Bill of Indemnity, who had voted for the Sacheverell clause, who had tried to prevent him from taking the command of his army in Ireland, and who

---

[1] The anomalous position which Harley and Foley at this time occupied is noticed in the Dialogue between a Whig and a Tory, 1693. " Your great P. Fo—y," says the Tory, " turns cadet, and carries arms under the General of the West Saxons. The two Har—ys, father and son, are engineers under the late Lieutenant of the Ordnance, and bomb any bill which he hath once resolv'd to reduce to ashes." Seymour is the General of the West Saxons. Musgrave had been Lieutenant of the Ordnance in the reign of Charles the Second.

had called him an ungrateful tyrant merely because he would not be their
slave and hangman.   He had once, by a bold and unexpected effort, freed

Paul Foley Esq.
From an Original picture at Coldham.

From a drawing by T. Athow, in the Sutherland Collection

himself from their yoke; and he was not inclined to put it on his neck
again. He personally disliked Wharton and Russell. He thought highly

of the capacity of Caermarthen, of the integrity of Nottingham, of the diligence and financial skill of Godolphin. It was only by slow degrees that the arguments of Sunderland, backed by the force of circumstances, overcame all objections.

On the seventh of November 1693 the Parliament met ; and the conflict of parties instantly began. William from the throne pressed on the **Meeting of Parliament** Houses the necessity of making a great exertion to arrest the progress of France on the Continent. During the last campaign, he said, she had, on every point, had a superiority of force ; and it had therefore been found impossible to cope with her. His allies had promised to increase their armies; and he trusted that the Commons would enable him to do the same.[1]

The Commons at their next sitting took the King's speech into consideration. The miscarriage of the Smyrna fleet was the chief **Debates about the naval miscarriages** subject of discussion. The cry for inquiry was universal : but it was evident that the two parties raised that cry for very different reasons. Montague spoke the sense of the Whigs. He declared that the disasters of the summer could not, in his opinion, be explained by the ignorance and imbecility of those who had charge of the naval administration. There must have been treason. It was impossible to believe that Lewis, when he sent his Brest squadron to the Straits of Gibraltar, and left the whole coast of his kingdom from Dunkirk to Bayonne unprotected, had trusted merely to chance. He must have been well assured that his fleet would meet with a vast booty under a feeble convoy. As there had been treachery in some quarters, there had been incapacity in others. The State was ill served. And then the orator pronounced a warm panegyric on his friend Somers. "Would that all men in power would follow the example of my Lord Keeper! If all patronage were bestowed as judiciously and disinterestedly as his, we should not see the public offices filled with men who draw salaries and perform no duties." It was moved and carried unanimously, that the Commons would support their Majesties, and would forthwith proceed to investigate the causes of the disaster in the Bay of Lagos.[2] The Lords of the Admiralty were directed to produce a great mass of documentary evidence. The King sent down copies of the examinations taken before the Committee of Council which Mary had appointed to inquire into the grievances of the Turkey merchants. The Turkey merchants themselves were called in and interrogated. Rooke, though too ill to stand or speak, was brought in a chair to the bar, and there delivered in a narrative of his proceedings. The Whigs soon thought that sufficient ground had been laid for a vote

[1] Lords' and Commons' Journals, Nov. 7. 1693.
[2] Commons' Journals, Nov. 13. 1693 ; Grey's Debates.

condemning the naval administration, and moved a resolution attributing the miscarriage of the Smyrna fleet to notorious and treacherous mismanagement. That there had been mismanagement could not be disputed; but that there had been foul play had certainly not been proved. The Tories proposed that the word "treacherous" should be omitted. A division took place; and the Whigs carried their point by a hundred and forty votes to a hundred and three. Wharton was a teller for the majority.[1]

It was now decided that there had been treason, but not who was the traitor. Several keen debates followed. The Whigs tried to throw the blame on Killegrew and Delaval, who were Tories: the Tories did their best to make out that the fault lay with the Victualling Department, which was under the direction of Whigs. But the House of Commons has always been much more ready to pass votes of censure drawn in general terms than to brand individuals by name. A resolution clearing the Victualling Office was proposed by Montague, and carried by a hundred and eighty eight votes to a hundred and fifty two.[2] But when the victorious party brought forward a motion inculpating the admirals, the Tories came up in great numbers from the country, and, after a debate which lasted from nine in the morning till near eleven at night, succeeded in saving their friends. The Noes were a hundred and seventy, and the Ayes only a hundred and sixty one. Another attack was made a few days later with no better success. The Noes were a hundred and eighty five, the Ayes only a hundred and seventy five. The indefatigable and implacable Wharton was on both occasions teller for the minority.[3]

In spite of this check the advantage was decidedly with the Whigs. The Tories who were at the head of the naval administration had indeed escaped impeachment: but the escape had been so **Russell** narrow that it was impossible for the King to employ them **First Lord** **of the** any longer. The advice of Sunderland prevailed. A new **Admiralty** Commission of Admiralty was prepared: and Russell was named First Lord. He had already been appointed to the command of the Channel fleet.

His elevation made it necessary that Nottingham should retire. For, though it was not then unusual to see men who were personally and politically hostile to each other holding high offices at **Retirement** the same time, the relation between the First Lord of the **of Notting-** **ham** Admiralty and the Secretary of State, who had charge of what would now be called the War Department, was of so peculiar a nature that the public service could not be well conducted without

[1] Commons' Journals, Nov. 17. 1693.   [2] Ibid. Nov. 22. 27. 1693; Grey's Debates.
[3] Commons' Journals, Nov. 29. Dec. 6. 1693; L'Hermitage, Dec. $\frac{1}{11}$. 1693.

cordial cooperation between them ; and between Nottingham and Russell such cooperation was not to be expected. " I thank you," William said to Nottingham, " for your services. I have nothing to complain of in your conduct. It is only from necessity that I part with you." Nottingham retired with dignity. Though a very honest man, he went out of office much richer than he had come in five years before. What were then considered as the legitimate emoluments of his place were great : he had sold Kensington House to the Crown for a large sum ; and he had probably, after the fashion of that time, obtained for himself some lucrative grants. He laid out all his gains in purchasing land. He heard, he said, that his enemies meant to accuse him of having acquired wealth by illicit means. He was perfectly ready to abide the issue of an enquiry. He would not, as some ministers had done, place his fortune beyond the reach of the justice of his country. He would have no secret hoard. He would invest nothing in foreign funds. His property should all be such as could be readily discovered and seized.[1]

During some weeks the seals which Nottingham had delivered up remained in the royal closet. To dispose of them proved no easy **Shrewsbury** matter. They were offered to Shrewsbury, who of all the **refuses** Whig leaders stood highest in the King's favour : but Shrews-**office** bury excused himself, and, in order to avoid further importunity, retired into the country. There he soon received a pressing letter from Elizabeth Villiers. This lady had, when a girl, inspired William with a passion which had caused much scandal and much unhappiness in the little Court of the Hague. Her influence over him she owed not to her personal charms,—for it tasked all the art of Kneller to make her look tolerably on canvass,—not to those talents which peculiarly belong to her sex,—for she did not excel in playful talk, and her letters are remarkably deficient in feminine ease and grace,—but to powers of mind which qualified her to partake the cares and guide the counsels of statesmen. To the end of her life great politicians sought her advice. Even Swift, the shrewdest and most cynical of her contemporaries, pronounced her the wisest of women, and more than once sate, fascinated by her conversation, from two in the afternoon till near midnight.[2] By degrees the virtues and charms of Mary conquered the first place in her husband's affection. But he still, in difficult conjunctures, frequently applied to Elizabeth Villiers for advice and assistance. She now implored Shrewsbury to reconsider his determination, and not to throw away the opportunity of uniting the Whig party for ever. Wharton and Russell wrote to the same

---

[1] L'Hermitage, Sept. $\frac{1}{11}$., Nov. $\frac{7}{17}$. 1693.
[2] See the Journal to Stella, lii. liii. lix. lxi.; and Lady Orkney's Letters to Swift.

effect. In reply came flimsy and unmeaning excuses : " I am not qualified for a court life : I am unequal to a place which requires much exertion : I do not quite agree with any party in the State : in short,

ELIZABETH VILLIERS, COUNTESS OF ORKNEY
From a painting in the possession of the Earl of Cork

I am unfit for the world : I want to travel : I want to see Spain." [1] These were mere pretences. Had Shrewsbury spoken the whole truth,

[1] See the letters written at this time by Elizabeth Villiers, Wharton, Russell and Shrewsbury, in the Shrewsbury Correspondence.

he would have said that he had, in an evil hour, been false to the cause of that Revolution in which he had borne so great a part, that he had entered into engagements of which he repented, but from which he knew not how to extricate himself, and that, while he remained under those engagements, he was unwilling to enter into the service of the existing government. Marlborough, Godolphin, and Russell, indeed, had no scruple about corresponding with one King while holding office under the other. But Shrewsbury had, what was wanting to Marlborough, Godolphin, and Russell, a conscience, a conscience which indeed too often failed to restrain him from doing wrong, but which never failed to punish him.

In consequence of his refusal to accept the Seals, the ministerial arrangements which the King had planned were not carried into entire effect till the end of the session. Meanwhile the proceedings of the two Houses had been highly interesting and important.

Soon after the Parliament met, the attention of the Commons was again called to the state of the trade with India ; and the charter which
Debates about the trade with India had just been granted to the Old Company was laid before them. They would probably have been disposed to sanction the new arrangement, which, in truth, differed little from that which they had themselves suggested not many months before, if the Directors had acted with prudence. But the Directors, from the day on which they had obtained their charter, had persecuted the interlopers without mercy, and had quite forgotten that it was one thing to persecute interlopers in the Eastern Seas, and another to persecute them in the port of London. Hitherto the war of the monopolists against the private trade had been carried on at the distance of fifteen thousand miles from England. If harsh things were done, the English public did not see them done, and did not hear of them till long after they had been done ; nor was it by any means easy to ascertain at Westminster who had been right and who had been wrong in a dispute which had arisen three or four years before at Moorshedabad or Canton. With incredible rashness the Directors determined, at the very moment when the fate of their Company was in the balance, to give the people of this country a near view of the most odious features of the monopoly. Some wealthy merchants of London had equipped a fine ship named the Redbridge. Her crew was numerous, her cargo of immense value. Her papers had been made out for Alicant : but there was some reason to suspect that she was really bound for the countries lying beyond the Cape of Good Hope. She was stopped by the Admiralty, in obedience to an order which the Company obtained from the Privy Council, doubtless by the help of the Lord President. Every day that she lay in the Thames caused a heavy expense to the owners. The indignation in

the City was great and general. The Company maintained that from the legality of the monopoly the legality of the detention necessarily followed. The public turned the argument round, and, being firmly convinced that the detention was illegal, drew the inference that the monopoly must be illegal too. The dispute was at the height when the Parliament met. Petitions on both sides were speedily laid on the table of the Commons ; and it was resolved that these petitions should be taken into consideration by a Committee of the whole House. The first question on which the conflicting parties tried their strength was the choice of a chairman. The enemies of the Old Company proposed Papillon, once the closest ally and subsequently the keenest opponent of Child, and carried their point by a hundred and thirty eight votes to a hundred and six. The Committee proceeded to inquire by what authority the Redbridge had been stopped. One of her owners, Gilbert Heathcote, a rich merchant and a stanch Whig, appeared at the bar as a witness. He was asked whether he would venture to deny that the ship had really been fitted out for the Indian trade. " It is no sin that I know of," he answered, " to trade with India ; and I shall trade with India till I am restrained by Act of Parliament." Papillon reported that, in the opinion of the Committee, the detention of the Redbridge was illegal. The question was then put, that the House would agree with the Committee. The friends of the Old Company ventured on a second division, and were defeated by a hundred and seventy one votes to a hundred and twenty five.[1]

The blow was quickly followed up. A few days later it was moved that all subjects of England had equal right to trade to the East Indies unless prohibited by Act of Parliament ; and the supporters of the Old Company, sensible that they were in a minority, suffered the motion to pass without a division.[2]

This memorable vote settled the most important of those constitutional questions which had been left unsettled by the Bill of Rights. It has ever since been held to be the sound doctrine that no power but that of the whole legislature can give to any person or to any society an exclusive privilege of trading to any part of the world.

The opinion of the great majority of the House of Commons was that the Indian trade could be advantageously carried on only by means of a joint stock and a monopoly. It might therefore have been expected that the resolution which destroyed the monopoly of the Old Company would have been immediately followed by a law granting a monopoly to the New Company. No such law, however, was passed. The Old Company, though not strong enough to defend its own privileges, was able, with the help of its Tory friends, to prevent the rival association

[1] Commons' Journals, Jan. 6. 8. 169¾.　　　[2] Ibid. Jan. 11. 169¾.

from obtaining similar privileges. The consequence was that, during some years, there was nominally a free trade with India. In fact, the trade still lay under severe restrictions. The private adventurer found indeed no difficulty in sailing from England : but his situation was as perilous as ever when he had turned the Cape of Good Hope. Whatever respect might be paid to a vote of the House of Commons by public functionaries in London, such a vote was, at Bombay or Calcutta, much less regarded than a private letter from Child ; and Child still continued to fight the battle with unbroken spirit. He sent out to the factories of the Company orders that no indulgence should be shown to the intruders. For the House of Commons and for its resolutions he expressed the bitterest contempt. " Be guided by my instructions," he wrote, " and not by the nonsense of a few ignorant country gentlemen who have hardly wit enough to manage their own private affairs, and who know nothing at all about questions of trade." It appears that his directions were obeyed. Every where in the East, during this period of anarchy, the servant of the Company and the independent merchant waged war on each other, accused each other of piracy, and tried by every artifice to exasperate the Mogul government against each other.[1]

The three great constitutional questions of the preceding year were, in this year, again brought under the consideration of Parliament. In the first week of the session, a Bill for the Regulation of Trials in cases of High Treason, a Triennial Bill, and a Place Bill were laid on the table of the House of Commons.

None of these bills became a law. The first passed the Commons, but was unfavourably received by the Peers. William took so much
Bill for the Regulation of Trials in cases of Treason interest in the question that he came down to the House of Lords, not in his crown and robes, but in the ordinary dress of a gentleman, and sate through the whole debate on the second reading. Caermarthen spoke of the dangers to which the State was at that time exposed, and entreated his brethren not to give, at such a moment, impunity to traitors. He was powerfully supported by two eminent orators, who had, during some years, been on the uncourtly side of every question, but who, in this session, showed a disposition to strengthen the hands of the government, Halifax and Mulgrave. Marlborough, Rochester, and Nottingham spoke for the bill : but the general feeling was so clearly against them that they did not venture to divide. It is probable, however, that the reasons urged by Caermarthen were not the reasons which chiefly swayed his hearers. The Peers were fully determined that the bill should not pass without a clause altering the constitution of the Court of the Lord High Steward :

[1] Hamilton's New Account.

Wilhelmus III. D. G. Angliæ, Scotiæ, Franciæ, et Hiberniæ, Rex &c

KING WILLIAM III .

From a mezzotint by N. Visscher

they knew that the Lower House was as fully determined not to pass such a clause ; and they thought it better that what must happen at last should happen speedily, and without a quarrel.[1]

The fate of the Triennial Bill confounded all the calculations of the best informed politicians of that time, and may therefore well seem

Triennial Bill
 extraordinary to us. During the recess, that bill had been described in numerous pamphlets, written for the most part by persons zealous for the Revolution and for popular principles of government, as the one thing needful, as the universal cure for the distempers of the State. On the first, second, and third readings in the House of Commons, no division took place. The Whigs were enthusiastic. The Tories seemed to be acquiescent. It was understood that the King, though he had used his Veto for the purpose of giving the Houses an opportunity of reconsidering the subject, had no intention of offering a pertinacious opposition to their wishes. But Seymour, with a cunning which long experience had matured, after deferring the conflict to the last moment, snatched the victory from his adversaries, when they were most secure. When the Speaker held up the bill in his hands, and put the question whether it should pass, the Noes were a hundred and forty six, the Ayes only a hundred and thirty six.[2] Some eager Whigs flattered themselves that their defeat was the effect of a surprise, and might be retrieved. Within three days, therefore, Monmouth, the most ardent and restless man in the whole party, brought into the Upper House a bill substantially the same with that which had so strangely miscarried in the Lower. The Peers passed this bill very expeditiously, and sent it down to the Commons. But in the Commons it found no favour. Many members, who professed to wish that the duration of parliaments should be limited, resented the interference of the hereditary branch of the legislature in a matter which peculiarly concerned the elective branch. The subject, they said, is one which especially belongs to us : we have considered it : we have come to a decision ; and it is scarcely parliamentary, it is certainly most indelicate, in their Lordships, to call upon us to reverse that

---

[1] The bill I found in the Archives of the Lords. Its history I learned from the Journals of the two Houses, from a passage in the Diary of Narcissus Luttrell, and from two letters to the States General, both dated on $\frac{\text{Feb. 27}}{\text{March 9.}}$ 1694, the day after the debate in the Lords. One of these letters is from Van Citters ; the other, which contains fuller information, is from L'Hermitage.

[2] Commons' Journals, Nov. 28. 1693 ; Grey's Debates. L'Hermitage fully expected that the bill would pass, and that the royal assent would not be withheld. On November $\frac{17}{27}$. he wrote to the States General, " Il paroist dans toute la chambre beaucoup de passion à faire passer ce bil." On $\frac{\text{Nov. 28.}}{\text{Dec. 8.}}$ he says that the division on the passing "n'a pas causé une pétite surprise. Il est difficile d'avoir un point fixe sur les idées qu'on peut se former des émotions du parlement, car il paroist quelquefois de grandes chaleurs qui semblent devoir tout enflammer, et qui, peu de tems après, s'évaporent." That Seymour was the chief manager of the opposition to the bill is asserted in the once celebrated Hush Money Pamphlet of that year.

decision. The question now is, not whether the duration of parliaments ought to be limited, but whether we ought to submit our judgment to the authority of the Peers, and to undo, at their bidding, what we did only a fortnight ago. The animosity with which the patrician order was regarded was inflamed by the arts and the eloquence of Seymour. The bill contained a definition of the words, " to hold a Parliament." This definition was scrutinised with extreme jealousy, and was thought by many, with very little reason, to have been framed for the purpose of extending the privileges, already invidiously great, of the nobility. It appears, from the scanty and obscure fragments of the debates which have come down to us, that bitter reflections were thrown on the general conduct, both political and judicial, of the Peers. Old Titus, though zealous for triennial parliaments, owned that he was not surprised at the ill humour which many gentlemen showed. " It is true," he said, "that we ought to be dissolved : but it is rather hard, I must own, that the Lords are to prescribe the time of our dissolution. The Apostle Paul wished to be dissolved : but, I doubt, if his friends had set him a day, he would not have taken it kindly of them." The bill was rejected by a hundred and ninety seven votes to a hundred and twenty seven.[1]

The Place Bill, differing very little from the Place Bill which had been brought in twelve months before, passed easily through the Commons. Most of the Tories supported it warmly ; and the Whigs did not venture to oppose it. It went up to the **Place Bill** Lords, and soon came back completely changed. As it had been originally drawn, it provided that no member of the House of Commons, elected after the first of January 1694, should accept any place of profit under the Crown, on pain of forfeiting his seat, and of being incapable of sitting again in the same Parliament. The Lords had added the words, " unless he be afterwards again chosen to serve in the same Parliament." These words, few as they were, sufficed to deprive the bill of nine tenths of its efficacy, both for good and for evil. It was most desirable that the crowd of subordinate public functionaries should be kept out of the House of Commons. It was most undesirable that the heads of the great executive departments should be kept out of that House. The bill, as altered, left that House open both to those who ought and to those who ought not to have been admitted. It very properly let in the Secretaries of State and the Chancellor of the Exchequer ; but it let in with them Commissioners of Wine

---

[1] Commons' Journals ; Grey's Debates. The engrossed copy of this Bill went down to the House of Commons and is lost. The original draught on paper is among the Archives of the Lords. That Monmouth brought in the bill I learned from a letter of L'Hermitage to the States General, Dec. $\frac{1}{11}$. 1693. As to the numbers on the division, I have, with some hesitation, followed the Journals. In Grey's Debates, and in the letters of Van Citters and L'Hermitage, the minority is said to have been 172.

Licenses and Commissioners of the Navy, Receivers, Surveyors, Store-keepers, Clerks of the Acts and Clerks of the Cheque, Clerks of the Green Cloth and Clerks of the Great Wardrobe.   So little did the Commons understand what they were about that, after framing a law, in one view most mischievous, and in another view most beneficial, they were perfectly willing that it should be transformed into a law quite harmless and almost useless.   They agreed to the amendment ; and nothing was now wanting but the royal sanction.

That sanction certainly ought not to have been withheld, and probably would not have been withheld, if William had known how unimportant the bill now was.   But he understood the question as little as the Commons themselves.   He knew that they imagined that they had devised a most stringent limitation of the royal power ; and he was determined not to submit, without a struggle, to any such limitation. He was encouraged by the success with which he had hitherto resisted the attempts of the two Houses to encroach on his prerogative.   He had refused to pass the bill which quartered the Judges on his hereditary revenue ; and the Parliament had silently acquiesced in the justice of the refusal.   He had refused to pass the Triennial Bill ; and the Commons had since, by rejecting two Triennial Bills, acknow-ledged that he had done well.   He ought, however, to have considered that, on both these occasions, the announcement of his refusal was immediately followed by the announcement that the Parliament was prorogued.   On both these occasions, therefore, the members had half a year to think and to grow cool before the next sitting.   The case was now very different.   The principal business of the session was hardly begun : estimates were still under consideration : bills of supply were still depending ; and, if the Houses should take a fit of ill humour, the consequences might be serious indeed.

He resolved, however, to run the risk.   Whether he had any adviser is not known.   His determination seems to have taken both the leading Whigs and the leading Tories by surprise.   When the Clerk had proclaimed that the King and Queen would consider of the bill touching free and impartial proceedings in Parliament, the Commons retired from the bar of the Lords in a resentful and ungovernable mood.   As soon as the Speaker was again in his chair there was a long and tempestuous debate.   All other business was postponed.   All committees were adjourned.   It was resolved that the House would, early the next morning, take into consideration the state of the nation. When the morning came, the excitement did not appear to have abated.   The mace was sent into Westminster Hall and into the Court of Requests.   All members who could be found were brought into the House.   That none might be able to steal away unnoticed,

the back door was locked, and the key laid on the table.   All strangers
were ordered to retire.   With these solemn preparations began a sitting
which reminded a few old men of some of the first sittings of the Long
Parliament.   High words were uttered by the enemies of the government.   Its friends, afraid of being accused of abandoning the cause of
the Commons of England for the sake of royal favour, hardly ventured
to raise their voices.   Montague alone seems to have defended the
King.   Lowther, though high in office and a member of the cabinet,
owned that there were evil influences at work, and expressed a wish
to see the Sovereign surrounded by counsellors in whom the representatives of the people could confide.   Harley, Foley and Howe
carried every thing before them.   A resolution, affirming that those
who had advised the Crown on this occasion were public enemies, was
carried with only two or three Noes.   Harley, after reminding his hearers
that they had their negative voice as the King had his, and that, if His
Majesty refused them redress, they could refuse him money, moved that
they should go up to the Throne, not, as usual, with a Humble Address,
but with a Representation.   Some members proposed to substitute the
more respectful word Address : but they were overruled ; and a committee was appointed to draw up the Representation.

Another night passed ; and, when the House met again, it appeared
that the storm had greatly subsided.   The malignant joy and the wild
hopes which the Jacobites had, during the last forty eight hours, expressed
with their usual imprudence, had incensed and alarmed the Whigs and
the moderate Tories.   Many members too were frightened by hearing
that William was fully determined not to yield without an appeal to the
nation.   Such an appeal might have been successful : for a dissolution,
on any ground whatever, would, at that moment, have been a highly
popular exercise of the prerogative.   The constituent bodies, it was well
known, were generally zealous for the Triennial Bill, and cared comparatively little about the Place Bill.   Many Tory members, therefore,
who had recently voted against the Triennial Bill, were by no means
desirous to run the risks of a general election.   When the Representation
which Harley and his friends had prepared was read, it was thought
offensively strong.   After being recommitted, shortened, and softened,
it was presented by the whole House.   William's answer was kind and
gentle : but he conceded nothing.   He assured the Commons that he
remembered with gratitude the support which he had on many occasions
received from them, that he should always consider their advice as most
valuable, and that he should look on counsellors who might attempt to raise
dissension between him and his Parliament as his enemies : but he uttered
not a word which could be construed into an acknowledgment that he had
used his Veto ill, or into a promise that he would not use it again.

The Commons on the morrow took his speech into consideration. Harley and his allies complained that the King's answer was no answer at all, threatened to tack the Place Bill to a money bill, and proposed to make a second representation pressing His Majesty to explain himself more distinctly. But by this time there was a strong reflux of feeling in the assembly. The Whigs had not only recovered from their dismay, but were in high spirits and eager for conflict. Wharton and Russell maintained that the House ought to be satisfied with what the King had said. Sir Thomas Littleton, the son of that Sir Thomas who had been distinguished among the chiefs of the country party in the days of Charles the Second, showed that he had inherited his father's eloquence. " Do you wish," said he, " to make sport for your enemies ? There is no want of them. They besiege our very doors. We read, as we come through the lobby, in the face and gestures of every nonjuror whom we pass, delight at the momentary coolness which has arisen between us and the King. That should be enough for us. We may be sure that we are voting rightly when we give a vote which tends to confound the hopes of traitors." The House divided. Harley was a teller on one side, Wharton on the other. Only eighty eight voted with Harley, two hundred and twenty nine with Wharton. The Whigs were so much elated by their victory that some of them wished to move a vote of thanks to William for his gracious answer : but they were restrained by wiser men. " We have lost time enough already in these unhappy debates," said a leader of the party. "Let us get to Ways and Means as fast as we can. The best form which our thanks can take is that of a money bill."

Thus ended, more happily than William had a right to expect, one of the most dangerous contests in which he ever engaged with his Parliament. At the Dutch Embassy the rising and going down of this tempest had been watched with intense interest ; and the opinion there seems to have been that the King had on the whole lost neither power nor popularity by his conduct.[1]

Another question, which excited scarcely less angry feeling in Parliament and in the country, was, about the same time, under consideration. **Bill for the Naturalisation of Foreign Protestants** On the sixth of December, a Whig member of the House of Commons obtained leave to bring in a bill for the Naturalisation of Foreign Protestants. Plausible arguments in favour of such a bill were not wanting. Great numbers of people, eminently industrious and intelligent, firmly attached to our faith, and deadly enemies of our deadly enemies, were at that time without a

---

[1] The bill is in the Archives of the Lords. Its history I have collected from the Journals, from Grey's Debates, and from the highly interesting letters of Van Citters and L'Hermitage. I think it clear from Grey's Debates that a speech which L'Hermitage attributes to a nameless "quelq'un" was made by Sir Thomas Littleton.

country. Among the Huguenots who had fled from the tyranny of the French King were many persons of great fame in war, in letters, in arts, and in sciences ; and even the humblest refugees were intellectually and morally above the average of the common people of any kingdom in Europe. With French Protestants who had been driven into exile by the edicts of Lewis were now mingled German Protestants who had been driven into exile by his arms. Vienna, Berlin, Basle, Hamburg, Amsterdam, London, swarmed with honest laborious men who had once been thriving burghers of Heidelberg or Manheim, or who had cultivated vineyards on the banks of the Neckar or the Rhine. A statesman might well think that it would be at once generous and politic to invite to the English shores and to incorporate with the English people emigrants so unfortunate and so respectable. Their ingenuity and their diligence could not fail to enrich any land which should afford them an asylum ; nor could it be doubted that they would manfully defend the country of their adoption against him whose cruelty had driven them from the country of their birth.

The first two readings passed without a division. But, on the motion that the bill should be committed, there was a debate in which the right of free speech was most liberally used by the opponents of the government. It was idle, they said, to talk about the poor Huguenots or the poor Palatines. The bill was evidently meant for the benefit, not of French Protestants or German Protestants, but of Dutchmen, who would be Protestants, Papists, or Pagans for a guilder a head, and who would, no doubt, be as ready to sign the Declaration against Transubstantiation in England as to trample on the Cross in Japan. They would come over in multitudes. They would swarm in every public office. They would collect the customs, and gauge the beer barrels. Our Navigation Laws would be virtually repealed. Every merchant ship that cleared out from the Thames or the Severn would be manned by Zealanders, and Hollanders, and Frieslanders. To our own sailors would be left the hard and perilous service of the royal navy. For Hans, after filling the pockets of his huge trunk hose with our money by assuming the character of a native, would, as soon as a pressgang appeared, lay claim to the privileges of an alien. The intruders would soon rule every corporation. They would elbow our own Aldermen off the Royal Exchange. They would buy the hereditary woods and halls of our country gentlemen. Already one of the most noisome of the plagues of Egypt was among us. Frogs had made their appearance even in the royal chambers. Nobody could go to Saint James's without being disgusted by hearing the reptiles of the Batavian marshes croaking all round him ; and if this bill should pass, the whole country would be as much infested by the loathsome brood as the palace already was.

The orator who indulged himself most freely in this sort of rhetoric was Sir John Knight, member for Bristol, a coarseminded and spiteful Jacobite, who, if he had been an honest man, would have been a non-juror. Two years before, when Mayor of Bristol, he had acquired a discreditable notoriety by treating with gross disrespect a commission sealed with the great seal of the Sovereigns to whom he had repeatedly sworn allegiance, and by setting on the rabble of his city to hoot and pelt the Judges.[1] He now concluded a savage invective by desiring that the Serjeant at Arms would open the doors, in order that the odious roll of parchment, which was nothing less than a surrender of the birthright of the English people, might be treated with proper contumely. "Let us first," he said, "kick the bill out of the House ; and then let us kick the foreigners out of the kingdom."

On a division the motion for committing the bill was carried by a hundred and sixty three votes to a hundred and twenty eight.[2] But the minority was zealous and pertinacious ; and the majority speedily began to waver. Knight's speech, retouched and made more offensive, soon appeared in print without a license. Tens of thousands of copies were circulated by the post, or dropped in the streets ; and such was the strength of national prejudice that too many persons read this ribaldry with assent and admiration. But, when a copy was produced in the House, there was such an outbreak of indignation and disgust, as cowed even the impudent and savage nature of the orator. Finding himself in imminent danger of being expelled and sent to prison, he apologised, and disclaimed all knowledge of the paper which purported to be a report of what he had said. He escaped with impunity : but his speech was voted false, scandalous and seditious, and was burned by the hangman in Palace Yard. The bill which had caused all this ferment was prudently suffered to drop.[3]

Meanwhile the Commons were busied with financial questions of grave importance. The estimates for the year 1694 were enormous.

Supply The King proposed to add to the regular army, already the greatest regular army that England had ever supported, four regiments of dragoons, eight of horse, and twenty five of infantry. The whole number of men, officers included, would thus be increased to about ninety four thousand.[4] Cromwell, while holding down three

[1] Narcissus Luttrell's Diary, August 1691.   [2] Commons' Journals, Jan. 4. 169¾.

[3] Of the Naturalisation Bill no copy, I believe, exists. The history of that bill will be found in the Journals. From Van Citters and L'Hermitage we learn less than might have been expected on a subject which must have been interesting to Dutch statesmen. Knight's speech will be found among the Somers Papers. He is described by his brother Jacobite, Roger North, as "a gentleman of as eminent integrity and loyalty as ever the city of Bristol was honoured with."

[4] Commons' Journals, Dec. 5. 169¾.

reluctant kingdoms, and making vigorous war on Spain in Europe and America, had never had two thirds of the military force which William now thought necessary. The great body of the Tories, headed by three Whig chiefs, Harley, Foley, and Howe, opposed any augmentation. The great body of the Whigs, headed by Montague and Wharton, would have granted all that was asked. After many long discussions, and probably many close divisions, in the Committee of Supply, the King obtained the greater part of what he demanded. The House allowed him four new regiments of dragoons, six of horse, and fifteen of infantry. The whole number of troops voted for the year amounted to eighty three thousand, the charge to more than two millions and a half, including about two hundred thousand pounds for the ordnance.[1]

The naval estimates passed much more rapidly; for Whigs and Tories agreed in thinking that the maritime ascendency of England ought to be maintained at any cost. Five hundred thousand pounds were voted for paying the arrears due to seamen, and two millions for the expenses of the year 1694.[2]

The Commons then proceeded to consider the Ways and Means. The land tax was renewed at four shillings in the pound; and by this simple but powerful machinery about two millions were raised with certainty and despatch.[3] A poll tax was imposed.[4] Stamp duties had long been among the fiscal resources of Holland and France, and had existed here during part of the reign of Charles the Second, but had been suffered to expire. They were now revived; and they have ever since formed an important part of the revenue of the State.[5] The hackney coaches of the capital were taxed, and were placed under the government of commissioners, in spite of the resistance of the wives of the coachmen, who assembled round Westminster Hall and mobbed the members.[6] But, notwithstanding all these expedients, there was still a large deficiency; and it was again necessary to borrow. A new duty on salt and some other imposts of less importance were set apart to form a fund for a loan. On the security of this fund a million was to be raised by a lottery, but by a lottery which had scarcely any thing but the name in common with the lotteries of a later period.

Ways and Means: lottery loan

[1] Commons' Journals, Dec. 20. and 22. 169¾. The Journals did not then contain any notice of the divisions which took place when the House was in committee. There was only one division on the army estimates of this year, when the mace was on the table. That division was on the question whether 60,000*l.* or 147,000*l.* should be granted for hospitals and contingencies. The Whigs carried the larger sum by 184 votes to 120. Wharton was a teller for the majority, Foley for the minority.

[2] Commons' Journals, Nov. 25. 169¾.   [3] Stat. 5 W. & M. c. 1.

[4] Stat. 5 & 6 W. & M. c. 14.   [5] Stat. 5 & 6 W. & M. c. 21.; Narcissus Luttrell's Diary.

[6] Stat. 5 & 6 W. & M. c. 22.; Narcissus Luttrell's Diary.

The sum to be contributed was divided into a hundred thousand shares of ten pounds each. The interest on each share was to be twenty shillings annually or, in other words, ten per cent, during sixteen years. But ten per cent for sixteen years was not a bait which was likely to attract lenders. An additional lure was therefore held out to capitalists. Some of the shares were to be prizes ; and the holders of the prizes were not only to receive the ordinary ten per cent, but were also to divide among them the sum of forty thousand pounds annually, during sixteen years. Which of the shares should be prizes was to be determined by lot. The arrangements for the drawing of the tickets were made by an adventurer of the name of Neale, who, after squandering away two fortunes, had been glad to become groom porter at the palace. His duties were to call the odds when the Court played at hazard, to provide cards and dice, and to decide any dispute which might arise on the bowling green or at the gaming table. He was eminently skilled in the business of this not very exalted post, and had made such sums by raffles that he was able to engage in very costly speculations, and was then covering the ground round the Seven Dials with buildings. He was probably the best adviser that could have been consulted about the details of a lottery. Yet there were not wanting persons who thought it hardly decent in the Treasury to call in the aid of a gambler by profession.[1]

By the lottery loan, as it was called, one million was obtained. But another million was wanted to bring the estimated revenue for the year 1694 up to a level with the estimated expenditure. The ingenious and enterprising Montague had a plan ready, a plan to which, except under the pressure of extreme pecuniary difficulties, he might not easily have induced the Commons to assent, but which, to his large and vigorous mind, appeared to have advantages, both commercial and political, more important than the immediate relief to the finances. He succeeded, not only in supplying the wants of the State for twelve months, but in creating a great institution, which, after the lapse of more than a century and a half, continues to flourish, and which he lived to see the stronghold, through all vicissitudes, of the Whig party, and the bulwark, in dangerous times, of the Protestant succession.

1694

The Bank of England

In the reign of William old men were still living who could remember the days when there was not a single banking house in the city of London. So late as the time of the Restoration every trader had his own strong box in his own house, and, when an acceptance was

---

[1] Stat. 5 W. & M. c. 7. ; Evelyn's Diary, Oct. 5. Nov. 22. 1694 ; A Poem on Squire Neale's Projects ; Malcolm's History of London. Neale's functions are described in several editions of Chamberlayne's State of England. His name frequently appears in the London Gazette, as, for example, on July 28. 1684.

presented to him, told down the crowns and Caroluses on his own counter. But the increase of wealth had produced its natural effect, the subdivision of labour. Before the end of the reign of Charles the Second, a new mode of paying and receiving money had come into fashion among the merchants of the capital. A class of agents arose, whose office was to keep the cash of the commercial houses. This new branch of business naturally fell into the hands of the goldsmiths, who were accustomed to traffic largely in the precious metals, and who had vaults in which great masses of bullion could lie secure from fire and from robbers. It was at the shops of the goldsmiths of Lombard Street that all the payments in coin were made. Other traders gave and received nothing but paper.

This great change did not take place without much opposition and clamour. Oldfashioned merchants complained bitterly that a class of men, who, thirty years before, had confined themselves to their proper functions, and had made a fair profit by embossing silver bowls and chargers, by setting jewels for fine ladies, and by selling pistoles and dollars to gentlemen setting out for the Continent, had become the treasurers, and were fast becoming the masters, of the whole City. These usurers, it was said, played at hazard with what had been earned by the industry and hoarded by the thrift of other men. If the dice turned up well, the knave who kept the cash became an alderman : if they turned up ill, the dupe who furnished the cash became a bankrupt. On the other side the conveniences of the modern practice were set forth in animated language. The new system, it was said, saved both labour and money. Two clerks, seated in one counting house, did what, under the old system, must have been done by twenty clerks in twenty different establishments. A goldsmith's note might be transferred ten times in a morning ; and thus a hundred guineas, locked in his safe close to the Exchange, did what would formerly have required a thousand guineas, dispersed through many tills, some on Ludgate Hill, some in Austin Friars, and some in Tower Street.[1]

Gradually even those who had been loudest in murmuring against the innovation gave way, and conformed to the prevailing usage. The last person who held out, strange to say, was Sir Dudley North. When, in 1680, after residing many years abroad, he returned to London, nothing astonished or displeased him more than the practice of making payments by drawing bills on bankers. He found that he could not go on Change without being followed round the piazza by goldsmiths, who, with low bows, begged to have the honour of serving

[1] See, for example, the Mystery of the Newfashioned Goldsmiths or Brokers, 1676 ; Is not the Hand of Joab in all this? 1676 ; and an answer published in the same year. See also England's Glory in the great Improvement by Banking and Trade, 1694.

him. He lost his temper when his friends asked where he kept his cash. "Where should I keep it," he asked, "but in my own house?" With difficulty he was induced to put his money into the hands of one of the Lombard Street men, as they were called.   Unhappily, the Lombard Street man broke; and some of his customers suffered severely.   Dudley North lost only fifty pounds: but this loss confirmed him in his dislike of the whole mystery of banking.   It was in vain, however, that he exhorted his fellow citizens to return to the good old practice, and not to expose themselves to utter ruin in order to spare themselves a little trouble.   He stood alone against the whole community.   The advantages of the modern system were felt every hour of every day in every part of London; and people were no more disposed to relinquish those advantages for fear of calamities which occurred at long intervals than to refrain from building houses for fear of fires, or from building ships for fear of hurricanes.   It is a curious circumstance that a man, who, as a theorist, was distinguished from all the merchants of his time by the largeness of his views and by his superiority to vulgar prejudices, should, in practice, have been distinguished from all the merchants of his time by the obstinacy with which he adhered to an ancient mode of doing business, long after the dullest and most ignorant plodders had abandoned that mode for one better suited to a great commercial society.[1]

No sooner had banking become a separate and important trade, than men began to discuss with earnestness the question whether it would be expedient to erect a national bank.   The general opinion seems to have been decidedly in favour of a national bank: nor can we wonder at this: for few were then aware that trade is in general carried on to much more advantage by individuals than by great societies; and banking really is one of those few trades which can be carried on to as much advantage by a great society as by an individual.   Two public banks had long been renowned throughout Europe, the Bank of Saint George at Genoa, and the Bank of Amsterdam.   The immense wealth which was in the keeping of those establishments, the confidence which they inspired, the prosperity which they had created, their stability, tried by panics, by wars, by revolutions, and found proof against all, were favourite topics.   The Bank of Saint George had nearly completed its third century.   It had begun to receive deposits and to make loans before Columbus had crossed the Atlantic, before Gama had turned the Cape, when a Christian Emperor was reigning at Constantinople, when a Mahomedan Sultan was reigning at Granada, when Florence was a Republic, when Holland obeyed a hereditary Prince.   All these things had been changed.   New con-

[1] See the Life of Dudley North by his brother Roger.

tinents and new oceans had been discovered. The Turk was at Constantinople : the Castilian was at Granada : Florence had its hereditary Prince : Holland was a Republic : but the Bank of Saint George was still receiving deposits and making loans. The Bank of Amsterdam was little more than eighty years old : but its solvency had stood severe tests. Even in the terrible crisis of 1672, when the whole Delta of the Rhine was overrun by the French armies, when the white flags were seen from the top of the Stadthouse, there was one place where, amidst the general consternation and confusion, tranquillity and security were still to be found ; and that place was the Bank. Why should not the Bank of London be as great and as durable as the Banks of Genoa and of Amsterdam ? Before the end of the reign of Charles the Second several plans were proposed, examined, attacked, and defended. Some pamphleteers maintained that a national bank ought to be under the direction of the King. Others thought that the management ought to be entrusted to the Lord Mayor, Aldermen, and Common Council of the capital.[1] After the Revolution the subject was discussed with an animation before unknown. For, under the influence of liberty, the breed of political projectors multiplied exceedingly. A crowd of plans, some of which resemble the fancies of a child or the dreams of a man in a fever, were pressed on the government. Pre-eminently conspicuous among the political mountebanks, whose busy faces were seen every day in the lobby of the House of Commons, were John Briscoe and Hugh Chamberlayne, two projectors worthy to have been members of that Academy which Gulliver found at Lagado. These men affirmed that the one cure for every distemper of the State was a Land Bank. A Land Bank would work for England miracles such as had never been wrought for Israel, miracles exceeding the heaps of quails and the daily shower of manna. There would be no taxes ; and yet the Exchequer would be full to overflowing. There would be no poor rates : for there would be no poor. The income of every landowner would be doubled. The profits of every merchant would be increased. In short, the island would, to use Briscoe's words, be the paradise of the world. The only losers would be the moneyed men, those worst enemies of the nation, who had done more injury to the gentry and yeomanry than an invading army from France would have had the heart to do.[2]

[1] See a pamphlet entitled Corporation Credit ; or a Bank of Credit, made Current by Common Consent in London, more Useful and Safe than Money.

[2] A proposal by Dr. Hugh Chamberlayne, in Essex Street, for a Bank of Secure Current Credit to be founded upon Land, in order to the General Good of Landed Men, to the great Increase of the Value of Land, and the no less Benefit of Trade and Commerce, 1695 ; Proposals for the supplying their Majesties with Money on Easy Terms, exempting the Nobility, Gentry, &c., from Taxes, enlarging their Yearly Estates, and enriching all the Subjects of the Kingdom by a National Land Bank ; by John Briscoe. " O fortunatos nimium bona si sua norint

These blessed effects the Land Bank was to produce simply by issuing enormous quantities of notes on landed security. The doctrine of the projectors was that every person who had real property ought to have, besides that property, paper money to the full value of that property. Thus, if his estate was worth two thousand pounds, he ought to have his estate and two thousand pounds in paper money.[1] Both Briscoe and Chamberlayne treated with the greatest contempt the notion that there could be an overissue of paper as long as there was, for every ten pound note, a piece of land in the country worth ten pounds. Nobody, they said, would accuse a goldsmith of overissuing as long as his vaults contained guineas and crowns to the full value of all the notes which bore his signature. Indeed no goldsmith had in his vaults guineas and crowns to the full value of all his paper. And was not a square mile of rich land in Taunton Dean at least as well entitled to be called wealth as a bag of gold or silver? The projectors could not deny that many people had a prejudice in favour of the precious metals, and that therefore, if the Land Bank were bound to cash its notes, it would very soon stop payment. This difficulty they got over by proposing that the notes should be inconvertible, and that every body should be forced to take them.

The speculations of Chamberlayne on the subject of the currency may possibly find admirers even in our own time. But to his other errors he added an error which began and ended with him. He was fool enough to take it for granted, in all his reasonings, that the value of an estate varied directly as the duration. He maintained that, if the annual income derived from a manor were a thousand pounds, a grant of that manor for twenty years must be worth twenty thousand pounds, and a grant for a hundred years worth a hundred thousand pounds. If, therefore, the lord of such a manor would pledge it for a hundred years to the Land Bank, the Land Bank might, on that security, instantly issue notes for a hundred thousand pounds. On this subject

Anglicanos." Third Edition, 1696. Briscoe seems to have been as much versed in Latin literature as in political economy.

[1] In confirmation of what is said in the text, I extract a single paragraph from Briscoe's proposals. " Admit a gentleman hath barely 100l. per annum estate to live on, and hath a wife and four children to provide for; this person, supposing no taxes were upon his estates, must be a great husband to be able to keep his charge, but cannot think of laying up anything to place out his children in the world : but according to this proposed method he may give his children 500l. a piece and have 90l. per annum left for himself and his wife to live upon, the which he may also leave to such of his children as he pleases after his and his wife's decease. For first having settled his estate of 100l. per annum, as in proposals 1. 3., he may have bills of credit for 2000l. for his own proper use, for 10s. per cent per annum, as in proposal 22., which is but 10l. per annum for the 2000l., which being deducted out of his estate of 100l. per annum, there remains 90l. per annum clear to himself." It ought to be observed that this nonsense reached a third edition.

Chamberlayne was proof even to arithmetical demonstration. He was reminded that the fee simple of land would not sell for more than twenty years' purchase. To say, therefore, that a term of a hundred years was worth five times as much as a term of twenty years, was to say that a term of a hundred years was worth five times the fee simple, in other words, that a hundred was five times infinity. Those who reasoned thus were refuted by being told that they were usurers ; and it should seem that a large number of country gentlemen thought the refutation complete.[1]

In December 1693 Chamberlayne laid his plan, in all its naked absurdity, before the Commons, and petitioned to be heard. He confidently undertook to raise eight thousand pounds on every freehold estate of a hundred and fifty pounds a year which should be brought, as he expressed it, into his Land Bank, and this without dispossessing the freeholder.[2] All the squires in the House must have known that the fee simple of such an estate would hardly fetch three thousand pounds in the market. That less than the fee simple of such an estate could, by any device, be made to produce eight thousand pounds, would, it might have been thought, have seemed incredible to the most illiterate clown that could be found on the benches. Distress, however, and animosity had made the landed gentlemen credulous. They insisted on referring Chamberlayne's plan to a committee ; and the committee reported that the plan was practicable, and would tend to the benefit of the nation.[3] But by this time the united force of demonstration and derision had begun to produce an effect even on the most ignorant rustics in the House. The report lay unnoticed on the table ; and the country was saved from a calamity compared with which the defeat of Landen and the loss of the Smyrna fleet would have been blessings.

All the projectors of this busy time, however, were not so absurd as Chamberlayne. One among them, William Paterson, was an ingenious,

[1] See Chamberlayne's Proposal, his Positions supported by the Reasons explaining the Office of Land Credit, and his Bank Dialogue. See also an excellent little tract on the other side entitled " A Bank Dialogue between Dr. H. C. and a Country Gentleman, 1696," and " Some Remarks upon a nameless and scurrilous Libel entitled a Bank Dialogue between Dr. H. C. and a Country Gentleman, in a Letter to a Person of Quality."

[2] Commons' Journals, Dec. 7. 1693. I am afraid that I may be suspected of exaggerating the absurdity of this scheme. I therefore transcribe the most important part of the petition. " In consideration of the freeholders bringing their lands into this bank, for a fund of current credit, to be established by Act of Parliament, it is now proposed that, for every 150*l.* per annum, secured for 150 years, for but one hundred yearly payments of 100*l.* per annum, free from all manner of taxes and deductions whatsoever, every such freeholder shall receive 4000*l.* in the said current credit, and shall have 2000*l.* more put into the fishery stock for his proper benefit ; and there may be further 2000*l.* reserved at the Parliament's disposal towards the carrying on this present war. . . . The freeholder is never to quit the possession of his said estate unless the yearly rent happens to be in arrear."

[3] Commons' Journals, Feb. 5. 169¾.

though not always a judicious, speculator. Of his early life little is known except that he was a native of Scotland, and that he had been in the West Indies. In what character he had visited the West Indies was a matter about which his contemporaries differed. His friends said that he had been a missionary ; his enemies that he had been a buccaneer. He seems to have been gifted by nature with fertile invention, an ardent temperament, and great powers of persuasion, and to have acquired somewhere in the course of his vagrant life a perfect knowledge of accounts.

This man submitted to the government, in 1691, a plan of a national bank ; and his plan was favourably received both by statesmen and by merchants. But years passed away ; and nothing was done, till, in the spring of 1694, it became absolutely necessary to find some new mode of defraying the charges of the war. Then at length the scheme devised by the poor and obscure Scottish adventurer was taken up in earnest by Montague. With Montague was closely allied Michael Godfrey, the brother of that Sir Edmondsbury Godfrey whose sad and mysterious death had, fifteen years before, produced a terrible outbreak of popular feeling. Michael was one of the ablest, most upright, and most opulent of the merchant princes of London. He was, as might have been expected from his near connection with the martyr of the Protestant faith, a zealous Whig. Some of his writings are still extant, and prove him to have had a strong and clear mind.

By these two distinguished men Paterson's scheme was fathered. Montague undertook to manage the House of Commons, Godfrey to manage the City. An approving vote was obtained from the Committee of Ways and Means ; and a bill, the title of which gave occasion to many sarcasms, was laid on the table. It was indeed not easy to guess that a bill, which purported only to impose a new duty on tonnage for the benefit of such persons as should advance money towards carrying on the war, was really a bill creating the greatest commercial institution that the world had ever seen.

The plan was that twelve hundred thousand pounds should be borrowed by the government on what was then considered as the moderate interest of eight per cent. In order to induce capitalists to advance the money promptly on terms so favourable to the public, the subscribers were to be incorporated by the name of the Governor and Company of the Bank of England. The corporation was to have no exclusive privilege, and was to be restricted from trading in any thing but bills of exchange, bullion, and forfeited pledges.

As soon as the plan became generally known, a paper war broke out as furious as that between the swearers and the nonswearers, or as that between the Old East India Company and the New East India Company.

The projectors who had failed to gain the ear of the government fell like madmen on their more fortunate brother. All the goldsmiths and pawn-brokers set up a howl of rage. Some discontented Tories predicted ruin to the monarchy. It was remarkable, they said, that Banks and Kings had never existed together. Banks were republican institutions. There were flourishing banks at Venice, at Genoa, at Amsterdam and at Hamburg. But who had ever heard of a Bank of France or a Bank of Spain.[1] Some discontented Whigs, on the other hand, predicted ruin to our liberties. Here, they said, is an instrument of tyranny more formidable than the High Commission, than the Star Chamber, than even the fifty thousand soldiers of Oliver. The whole wealth of the nation will be in the hands of the Tonnage Bank,—such was the nick-name then in use ;—and the Tonnage Bank will be in the hands of the Sovereign. The power of the purse, the one great security for all the rights of Englishmen, will be transferred from the House of Commons to the Governor and Directors of the new Company. This last con-sideration was really of some weight, and was allowed to be so by the authors of the bill. A clause was therefore most properly inserted which inhibited the Bank from advancing money to the Crown without authority from Parliament. Every infraction of this salutary rule was to be punished by forfeiture of three times the sum advanced; and it was provided that the King should not have power to remit any part of the penalty.

The plan, thus amended, received the sanction of the Commons more easily than might have been expected from the violence of the adverse clamour. In truth, the Parliament was under duress. Money must be had, and could in no other way be had so easily. What passed when the House had resolved itself into a committee cannot be dis-covered : but, while the Speaker was in the chair, no division took place.

The bill, however, was not safe when it had reached the Upper House. Some Lords suspected that the plan of a national bank had been devised for the purpose of exalting the moneyed interest at the expense of the landed interest. Others thought that this plan, whether good or bad, ought not to have been submitted to them in such a form. Whether it would be safe to call into existence a body which might one day rule the whole commercial world, and how such a body should be constituted, were questions which ought not to be decided by one branch of the Legislature. The Peers ought to be at perfect liberty to examine all the details of the proposed scheme, to suggest amendments, to ask for conferences. It was therefore most unfair that the law establishing the Bank should be sent up as part of a law granting supplies to the Crown. The Jacobites entertained some hope that the session would end with a quarrel between the Houses, that the Tonnage Bill would

---

[1] Account of the Intended Bank of England, 1694.

be lost, and that William would enter on the campaign without money. It was already May, according to the New Style. The London season was over; and many noble families had left Covent Garden and Soho Square for their woods and hayfields. But summonses were sent out. There was a violent rush of Earls and Barons back to town. The benches which had lately been deserted were crowded. The sittings began at an hour unusually early, and were prolonged to an hour unusually late. On the day on which the bill was committed the contest lasted without intermission from nine in the morning till six in the evening. Godolphin was in the chair. Nottingham and Rochester proposed to strike out all the clauses which related to the Bank. Something was said about the danger of setting up a gigantic corporation which might soon give law to the King and the three Estates of the Realm. But the Peers seemed to be most moved by the appeal which was made to them as landlords. The whole scheme, it was asserted, was intended to enrich usurers at the expense of the nobility and gentry. Persons who had laid by money would rather put it into the Bank than lend it on mortgage at moderate interest. Caermarthen said little or nothing in defence of what was, in truth, the work of his rivals and enemies. He owned that there were grave objections to the mode in which the Commons had provided for the public service of the year. But would their Lordships amend a money bill? Would they engage in a contest of which the end must be that they must either yield, or incur the grave responsibility of leaving the Channel without a fleet during the summer? This argument prevailed; and, on a division, the amendment was rejected by forty three votes to thirty one. A few hours later the bill received the royal assent, and the Parliament was prorogued.[1]

In the City the success of Montague's plan was complete. It was then at least as difficult to raise a million at eight per cent as it would now be to raise forty millions at four per cent. It had been supposed that contributions would drop in very slowly: and a considerable time had therefore been allowed by the Act. This indulgence was not needed. So popular was the new investment that on the day on which the books were opened three hundred thousand pounds were subscribed: three hundred thousand more were subscribed during the next forty eight hours; and, in ten days, to the delight of all the friends of the government, it was announced that the list was full. The whole sum which the Corporation was bound to lend to the State was paid into the Exchequer before the first instalment was due.[2] Somers gladly put the Great Seal to a charter framed in conformity with the terms

---

[1] See the Lords' Journals of April 23, 24, 25. 1694, and the letter of L'Hermitage to the States General dated $\frac{\text{April 24.}}{\text{May 4.}}$

[2] Narcissus Luttrell's Diary, June 1694.

The Bank of England, in y.e Poultry.

VIEW OF GROCERS' HALL, OCCUPIED BY THE BANK OF ENGLAND FROM 1694 TO 1734

From an engraving in the British Museum

prescribed by Parliament; and the Bank of England commenced its operations in the house of the Company of Grocers. There, during many years, directors, secretaries, and clerks might be seen labouring in different parts of one spacious hall. The persons employed by the Bank were originally only fifty four. They are now nine hundred. The sum paid yearly in salaries amounted at first to only four thousand three hundred and fifty pounds. It now exceeds two hundred and ten thousand pounds. We may therefore fairly infer that the incomes of commercial clerks are, on an average, about three times as large in the reign of Victoria as they were in the reign of William the Third.[1]

It soon appeared that Montague had, by skilfully availing himself of the financial difficulties of the country, rendered an inestimable service to his party. During several generations the Bank of England was emphatically a Whig body. It was Whig, not accidentally, but necessarily. It must have instantly stopped payment if it had ceased to receive the interest on the sum which it had advanced to the government; and of that interest James would not have paid one farthing. Seventeen years after the passing of the Tonnage Bill, Addison, in one of his most ingenious and graceful little allegories, described the situation of the great Company through which the immense wealth of London was constantly circulating. He saw Public Credit on her throne in Grocers' Hall, the Great Charter over her head, the Act of Settlement full in her view. Her touch turned every thing to gold. Behind her seat, bags filled with coin were piled up to the ceiling. On her right and on her left the floor was hidden by pyramids of guineas. On a sudden the door flies open. The Pretender rushes in, a sponge in one hand, in the other a sword which he shakes at the Act of Settlement. The beautiful Queen sinks down fainting. The spell by which she has turned all things around her into treasure is broken. The money bags shrink like pricked bladders. The piles of gold pieces are turned into bundles of rags or faggots of wooden tallies.[2] The truth which this parable was meant to convey was constantly present to the minds of the rulers of the Bank. So closely was their interest bound up with the interest of the government that the greater the public danger, the more ready were they to come to the rescue. Formerly, when the Treasury was empty, when the taxes came in slowly, and when the pay of the soldiers and sailors was in arrear, it had been necessary for the Chancellor of the Exchequer to go, hat in hand, up and down Cheapside and Cornhill, attended by the Lord Mayor and by the Aldermen, and to make up a sum by borrowing

[1] Heath's Account of the Worshipful Company of Grocers; Francis's History of the Bank of England.

[2] Spectator, No. 3.

a hundred pounds from this hosier, and two hundred pounds from that ironmonger.[1] Those times were over. The government, instead of laboriously scooping up supplies from numerous petty sources, could now draw whatever it required from one immense reservoir, which all those petty sources kept constantly replenished. It is hardly too much to say that, during many years, the weight of the Bank, which was constantly in the scale of the Whigs, almost counterbalanced the weight of the Church, which was as constantly in the scale of the Tories.

A few minutes after the bill which established the Bank of England had received the royal assent, the Parliament was prorogued by the King with a speech in which he warmly thanked the Commons for their liberality. Montague was immediately rewarded for his services with the place of Chancellor of the Exchequer.[2]

Proroga-tion of Parliament: ministerial arrange-ments

Shrewsbury had a few weeks before consented to accept the seals. He had held out resolutely from November to March. While he was trying to find excuses which might satisfy his political friends, Sir James Montgomery visited him. Montgomery was now the most miserable of human beings. Having borne a great part in a great revolution, having been charged with the august office of presenting the Crown of Scotland to the Sovereigns whom the Estates had chosen, having domineered without a rival, during several months, in the Parliament at Edinburgh, having seen before him in near prospect the seals of Secretary, the coronet of an Earl, ample wealth, supreme power, he had on a sudden sunk into obscurity and abject penury. His fine parts still remained; and he was therefore used by the Jacobites: but, though used, he was despised, distrusted, and starved. He passed his life in wandering from England to France and from France back to England, without finding a resting place in either country. Sometimes he waited in the antechamber at Saint Germains, where the priests scowled at him as a Calvinist, and where even the Protestant Jacobites cautioned one another in whispers against the old Republican. Sometimes he lay hid in the garrets of London, imagining that every footstep which he heard on the stairs was that of a bailiff with a writ, or that of a King's messenger with a warrant. He now obtained access to Shrewsbury, and ventured to talk as a Jacobite to a brother Jacobite. Shrewsbury, who was not at all inclined to put his estate and his neck in the power of a man whom he knew to be both rash and perfidious, returned very guarded answers. Through some channel which is not known to us, William obtained full intelligence of what had passed on this occasion. He sent for Shrewsbury,

Shrewsbury Secretary of State

---

[1] Proceedings of the Wednesday Club in Friday Street.

[2] Lords' Journals, April 25. 1694; London Gazette, May 7, 1694.

and again spoke earnestly about the secretaryship. Shrewsbury again excused himself. His health, he said, was bad. " That," said William, " is not your only reason." " No, Sir," said Shrewsbury, " it is not." And he began to speak of public grievances, and alluded to the fate of the Triennial Bill, which he had himself introduced. But William cut him short. " There is another reason behind. When did you see Montgomery last ?" Shrewsbury was thunderstruck. The King proceeded to repeat some things which Montgomery had said. By this time Shrewsbury had recovered from his dismay, and had recollected that, in the conversation which had been so accurately reported to the government, he had fortunately uttered no treason, though he had heard much. " Sir," said he, " since Your Majesty has been so correctly informed, you must be aware that I gave no encouragement to that man's attempts to seduce me from my allegiance." William did not deny this, but intimated that such secret dealings with noted Jacobites raised suspicions which Shrewsbury could remove only by accepting the seals. " That," he said, " will put me quite at ease. I know that you are a man of honour, and that, if you undertake to serve me, you will serve me faithfully." So pressed, Shrewsbury complied, to the great joy of his whole party ; and was immediately rewarded for his compliance with a dukedom and a garter.[1]

Thus a Whig ministry was gradually forming. There were now two Whig Secretaries of State, a Whig Keeper of the Great Seal, a Whig First Lord of the Admiralty, a Whig Chancellor of the Exchequer. The Lord Privy Seal, Pembroke, might also be called a Whig : for his mind was one which readily took the impress of any stronger mind with which it was brought into contact. Seymour, having been long enough a Commissioner of the Treasury to lose much of his influence with the Tory country gentlemen who had once listened to him as to an oracle, was dismissed ; and his place was filled by John Smith, a zealous and able Whig, who had taken an active part in the debates of the late session.[2] The only Tories who still held great offices in the executive government were the Lord President, Caermarthen, who, though he began to feel that power was slipping from his grasp, still clutched it desperately, and the First Lord of the Treasury, Godolphin, who meddled little out of his own department, and performed the duties of that department with skill and assiduity.

William, however, still tried to divide his favours between the two parties. Though the Whigs were fast drawing to themselves the

[1] Life of James, ii. 520.; Floyd's (Lloyd's) Account in the Nairne Papers, under the date of May 1. 1694; London Gazette, April 26. 30. 1694.

[2] London Gazette, May 3. 1694.

John Smith Esq.ʳ Speaker, 1705.
From an Original picture at the Speakers house.

JOHN SMITH, SUBSEQUENTLY SPEAKER OF THE HOUSE OF COMMONS

From a drawing by T. Athow, in the Sutherland Collection

substance of power, the Tories obtained their share of honorary distinctions. Mulgrave, who had, during the late session, exerted his great **New titles bestowed** parliamentary talents in favour of the King's policy, was created Marquess of Normanby, and named a Cabinet Councillor, but was never consulted. He obtained at the same time a pension of three thousand pounds a year. Caermarthen, whom the late changes had deeply mortified, was in some degree consoled by a signal mark of royal approbation. He became Duke of Leeds. It had taken him little more than twenty years to climb from the station of a Yorkshire country gentleman to the highest rank in the peerage. Two great Whig Earls were at the same time created Dukes, Bedford and Devonshire. It ought to be mentioned that Bedford had repeatedly refused the dignity which he now somewhat reluctantly accepted. He declared that he preferred his Earldom to a Dukedom, and gave a very sensible reason for the preference. An Earl who had a numerous family might send one son to the Temple and another to a counting house in the city. But the sons of a Duke were all lords ; and a lord could not make his bread either at the bar or on Change. The old man's objections, however, were overcome ; and the two great houses of Russell and Cavendish, which had long been closely connected by friendship and by marriage, by common opinions, common sufferings, and common triumphs, received on the same day the highest honour which it is in the power of the Crown to confer.[1]

The Gazette which announced these creations announced also that the King had set out for the Continent. He had, before his departure, consulted with his ministers about the means of counteracting a plan of naval operations which had been formed by the French government. Hitherto the maritime war had been carried on chiefly in the Channel **French plan of war** and the Atlantic. But Lewis had now determined to concentrate his maritime forces in the Mediterranean. He hoped that, with their help, the army of Marshal Noailles would be able to take Barcelona, to subdue the whole of Catalonia, and to compel Spain to sue for peace. Accordingly, Tourville's squadron, consisting of fifty three men of war, set sail from Brest on the twenty fifth of April and passed the Straits of Gibraltar on the fourth of May.

William, in order to cross the designs of the enemy, determined to send Russell to the Mediterranean with the greater part of the com- **English plan of war** bined fleet of England and Holland. A squadron was to remain in the British seas under the command of the Earl of Berkeley. Talmash was to embark on board of this squadron with a large body of troops, and was to attack Brest, which would, it was

---

[1] London Gazette, April 30. May 7. 1694 ; Shrewsbury to William, May $\frac{11}{21}$. ; William to Shrewsbury, $\frac{\text{May 22.}}{\text{June 1.}}$; L'Hermitage, $\frac{\text{April 27.}}{\text{May 7.}}$

WILLIAM RUSSELL, FIRST DUKE OF BEDFORD

From the painting in the National Portrait Gallery by Sir G. Kneller

supposed, in the absence of Tourville and his fifty three vessels, be an easy conquest.

That preparations were making at Portsmouth for an expedition, in which the land forces were to bear a part, could not be kept a secret. There was much speculation at the Rose and at Garraway's touching the destination of the armament. Some talked of Rhe, some of Oleron, some of Rochelle, some of Rochefort. Many, till the fleet actually began to move westward, believed that it was bound for Dunkirk. Many guessed that Brest would be the point of attack ; but they only guessed this : for the secret was much better kept than most of the secrets of that age.[1] Russell, till he was ready to weigh anchor, persisted in assuring his Jacobite friends that he knew nothing. His discretion was proof even against all the arts of Marlborough. Marlborough, however, had other sources of intelligence. To those sources he applied himself ; and he at length succeeded in discovering the whole plan of the government. He instantly wrote to James. He had, he said, but that moment ascertained that twelve regiments of infantry and two regiments of marines were about to embark, under the command of Talmash, for the purpose of destroying the harbour of Brest and the shipping which lay there. "This," he added, "would be a great advantage to England. But no consideration can, or ever shall, hinder me from letting you know what I think may be for your service." He then proceeded to caution James against Russell. "I endeavoured to learn this some time ago from him : but he always denied it to me, though I am very sure that he knew the design for more than six weeks. This gives me a bad sign of this man's intentions."[2]

The intelligence sent by Marlborough to James was communicated by James to the French government. That government took its measures with characteristic promptitude. Promptitude was indeed necessary ; for, when Marlborough's letter was written, the preparations at Portsmouth were all but complete ; and, if the wind had been favourable to the English, the objects of the expedition might have been attained without a struggle. But adverse gales detained our fleet in the Channel during another month. Meanwhile a large body of troops

---

[1] L'Hermitage, May $\frac{15}{25}$. After mentioning the various reports, he says, "De tous ces divers projets qu'on s'imagine aucun n'est venu à la cognoissance du public." This is important : for it has often been said, in excuse for Marlborough, that he communicated to the Court of Saint Germains only what was the talk of all the coffeehouses, and must have been known without his instrumentality.

[2] Life of James, ii. 522. ; Macpherson, i. 487. The letter of Marlborough is dated May 4. It was inclosed in one from Sackville to Melfort, which would alone suffice to prove that those who represent the intelligence as unimportant are entirely mistaken. "I send it," says Sackville, "by an express, judging it to be of the utmost consequence for the service of the King, my master, and consequently for the service of his Most Christian Majesty." Would Sackville have written thus if the destination of the expedition had been already known to all the world?

was collected at Brest. Vauban was charged with the duty of putting the defences in order; and, under his skilful direction, batteries were

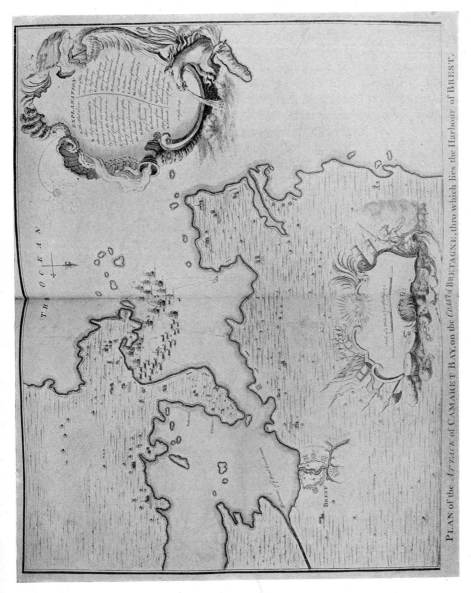

PLAN of the *ATTACK* of CAMARET BAY, on the *Coast of* BRETAGNE, thro which lies the Harbour of BREST.

From a plan in Tindal's continuation of Rapin's History of England

planted which commanded every spot where it seemed likely that an invader would attempt to land. Eight large rafts, each carrying many mortars, were moored in the harbour, and, some days before the English arrived, all was ready for their reception.

On the sixth of June the whole allied fleet was about fifteen leagues west of Cape Finisterre. There Russell and Berkeley parted company. Russell proceeded towards the Mediterranean. Berkeley's squadron, with the troops on board, steered for the coast of Britanny, and anchored just without Camaret Bay, close to the mouth of the harbour of Brest. Talmash proposed to land in Camaret Bay. It was therefore desirable to ascertain with accuracy the state of the coast. The eldest son of the Duke of Leeds, now called Marquess of Caermarthen, undertook to enter the basin and to obtain the necessary information. The passion of this brave and eccentric young man for maritime adventure was unconquerable. He had solicited and obtained the rank of Rear Admiral, and had accompanied the expedition in his own yacht, the Peregrine, renowned as the masterpiece of shipbuilding. Cutts, who had distinguished himself by his intrepidity in the Irish war, and had been rewarded with an Irish peerage, offered to accompany Caermarthen. Lord Mohun, who, desirous, it may be hoped, to efface by honourable exploits the stain which a shameful and disastrous brawl had left on his name, was serving with the troops as a volunteer, insisted on being of the party. The Peregrine went into the bay with its gallant crew, and came out safe, but not without having run great risks. Caermarthen reported that the defences, of which however he had seen only a small part, were formidable. But Berkeley and Talmash suspected that he overrated the danger. They were not aware that their design had long been known at Versailles, that an army had been collected to oppose them, and that the greatest engineer in the world had been employed to fortify the coast against them. They therefore did not doubt that their troops might easily be put on shore under the protection of a fire from the ships. On the following morning Caermarthen was ordered to enter the bay with eight vessels and to batter the French works. Talmash was to follow with about a hundred boats full of soldiers. It soon appeared that the enterprise was even more perilous than it had on the preceding day appeared to be. Batteries which had then escaped notice opened on the ships a fire so murderous that several decks were soon cleared. Great bodies of foot and horse were discernible ; and, by their uniforms, they appeared to be regular troops. The young Rear Admiral sent an officer in all haste to warn Talmash. But Talmash was so completely possessed by the notion that the French were not prepared to repel an attack that he disregarded all cautions, and would not even trust his own eyes. He felt sure that the force which he saw assembled on the coast was a mere rabble of peasants, who had been brought together in haste from the surrounding country. Confident that these mock soldiers would run like sheep before real soldiers, he ordered his men to pull for the land.

PEREGRINE OSBORNE, SECOND DUKE OF LEEDS

From an engraving in the Sutherland Collection, after a painting by Petitot

He was soon undeceived. A terrible fire mowed down his troops faster than they could get on shore. He had himself scarcely sprung on dry ground when he received a wound in the thigh from a cannon ball, and was carried back to his skiff. His men reembarked in confusion. Ships and boats made haste to get out of the bay, but did not succeed till four hundred sailors and seven hundred soldiers had fallen. During many days the waves continued to throw up pierced and shattered corpses on the beach of Britanny. The battery from which Talmash received his wound is called, to this day, the Englishman's Death.

The unhappy general was laid on his couch ; and a council of war was held in his cabin. He was for going straight into the harbour

MEDAL COMMEMORATING THE REPULSE OF THE ENGLISH AT CAMARET BAY

of Brest and bombarding the town. But this suggestion, which indicated but too clearly that his judgment had been affected by the irritation of a wounded body and a wounded mind, was wisely rejected by the naval officers. The armament returned to Portsmouth. There Talmash died, exclaiming with his last breath that he had been lured into a snare by treachery. The public grief and indignation were loudly expressed. The nation remembered the services of the unfortunate general, forgave his rashness, pitied his sufferings, and execrated the unknown traitors whose machinations had been fatal to him. There were many conjectures and many rumours. Some sturdy Englishmen, misled by national prejudice, swore that none of our plans would ever be kept a secret from the enemy while French refugees were in high military command. Some zealous Whigs, misled by party spirit,

The Valiant Souldiers Lamentation,

FOR

The Loss of their Noble General *TALMARSH*,

Who headed the Froces at the Decent on *France*, where he received
his fatal Wound, of which he soon after Died, to the unspeakable Grief of his Friends and Followers.

To the Tune of, *The Fortune of War*, &c.

COme all you brave Heroes of Fame and Renown,
Let a Tribute of Tears now run trickling down
For the Loss of a Souldier that's lately deceas'd,
You will find by these Lines he was none of the least:
Therefore have we just reason, alas! to complain,
For the Valiant brave General *Talmarsh* is slain.

He did a true Souldier of Courage apper,
For his Heart was an absolute stranger to Fear,
In the greatest of Danger his Life he'd expose,
Thorough Fire and Smoak in the face of his Foes,
That he might the rich Trophies of Victory gain,
But, alas! this brave General *Talmarsh* is slain.

In *Flanders* his Valour has often been try'd,
When as conquering Death in full triumph did ride
Through the Hosts of the *French* and Confederates too,
With a courage undaunted he still did pursue
That he might the rich Trophies of Victory gain,
But, alas! this brave General *Talmarsh* is slain.

In *Ireland* likewise his Valour was known
At the Storming the City of famous *Athlone*,
He in passing that River was one of the first,
As a Souldier couragious and true to his Trust, [tain;
That the Rights of three Kingdoms he then might main
But, alas! this brave General *Talmarsh* in slain.

So great was his Soul in the Action of Fight
That it was his Ambition and chiefest Delight
To press on where the greatest of Danger appear'd:
For the Coast of fair *France* with an Army he stear'd,
That he there might true Honour and Victory gain;
But, alas! this brave General *Talmarsh* is slain.

Chear up, my brave Souldiers, he often reply'd,
By the Blessing of God we may pull down the Pride
Of the huffing proud Frenchmen and make them to fly;
You shall none of you venture, Boys, further then I.
And with this Resolution he crossed the Main,
But, alas! this brave General *Talmarsh* is slain.

With courage undaunted they then did advance
To the pleasant fair Bancks of the Kingdom of *France*
And altho' the loud Cannons like Thunder did roar,
Yet he was the first Man that set foot on the shoar,
That he might the lost Honour of *Britain* regain,
But, alas! this brave General *Talmarsh* is slain.

Tho' in this great Action small was his Success,
Yet his Courage and Valour was never the less,
He behaved himself like a General bold,
While a Sword in his hand he was able to hold,
That he might the rich Trophies of Honour obtain;
But, alas! this brave General *Talmarsh* is slain.

He's free'd from the Tumults and Noise of this Life,
Which is nothing but War with Contention and Strife
For we hope that in Regents of Joy he's at rest,
Where no Warlike Alarms can his Quiet molest;
Tho' our Loss, it may be his unspeakable Gain,
Yet we needs must lament that Great *Talmarsh* is slain

F I N I S.

London: Printed for *Eben. Tracy*, on *London bridge*.

THE VALIANT SOLDIER'S LAMENTATION

From a ballad in the Pepysian Collection

muttered that the Court of Saint Germains would never want good intelligence while a single Tory remained in the Cabinet Council. The real criminal was not named; nor, till the archives of the House of Stuart were explored, was it known to the public that Talmash had perished by the basest of all the hundred villanies of Marlborough.[1]

Yet never had Marlborough been less a Jacobite than at the moment when he rendered this wicked and shameful service to the Jacobite cause. It may be confidently affirmed that to serve the banished family was not his object, and that to ingratiate himself with the banished family was only his secondary object. His primary object was to force himself into the service of the existing government, and to regain possession of those important and lucrative places from which he had been dismissed more than two years before. He knew that the country and the Parliament would not patiently bear to see the English army commanded by foreign generals. Two Englishmen only had shown themselves fit for high military posts, himself and Talmash. If Talmash were defeated and disgraced, William would scarcely have a choice. In fact, as soon as it was known that the expedition had failed, and that Talmash was no more, the general cry was that the King ought to receive into his favour the accomplished Captain who had done such good service at Walcourt, at Cork, and at Kinsale. Nor can we blame the multitude for raising this cry. For every body knew that Marlborough was an eminently brave, skilful, and successful officer: but very few persons knew that he had, while commanding William's troops, while sitting in William's council, while waiting in William's bedchamber, formed a most artful and dangerous plot for the subversion of William's throne; and still fewer suspected the real author of the recent calamity, of the slaughter in the Bay of Camaret, of the melancholy fate of Talmash. The effect therefore of the foulest of all treasons was to raise the traitor in the public estimation. Nor was he wanting to himself at this conjuncture. While the Royal Exchange was in consternation at the disaster of which he was the cause, while many families were clothing themselves in mourning for the brave men of whom he was the murderer, he repaired to Whitehall; and there, doubtless with all that grace, that nobleness, that suavity, under which lay, hidden from all common observers, a seared conscience and a remorseless heart, he professed himself the most devoted, the most loyal, of all the subjects of William and Mary, and expressed a hope that he might, in this emergency, be permitted to offer his sword to their Majesties. Shrewsbury was very desirous that the offer should be accepted: but a short and dry answer from William, who was then in the Netherlands, put an

[1] London Gazette, June 14. 18. 1694; Paris Gazette, June 16./July 3.; Burchett; Journal of Lord Caermarthen; Baden. June 15/25.; L'Hermitage, June 15/25. 19/29.

THE BOMBARDMENT OF DIEPPE

From a mezzotint by R. Robinson, in the Sutherland Collection

end for the present to all negotiation.   About Talmash the King expressed himself with generous tenderness.   " The poor fellow's fate," he wrote, " has affected me much.   I do not indeed think that he managed well : but it was his ardent desire to distinguish himself that impelled him to attempt impossibilities."[1]

The armament which had returned to Portsmouth soon sailed again for the coast of France, but achieved only exploits worse than inglorious. An attempt was made to blow up the pier at Dunkirk.   Some towns inhabited by quiet tradesmen and fishermen were bombarded.   In Dieppe scarcely a house was left standing : a third part of Havre was laid in ashes ; and shells were thrown into Calais which destroyed thirty private dwellings.   The French and the Jacobites loudly exclaimed against the cowardice and barbarity of making war on an unwarlike population.   The English government vindicated itself by reminding the world of the sufferings of the thrice wasted Palatinate ; and, as against Lewis and the flatterers of Lewis, the vindication was complete.   But whether it were consistent with humanity and with sound policy to visit the crimes which an absolute Prince and a ferocious soldiery had committed in the Palatinate on shopkeepers and labourers, women and children, who did not know that the Palatinate existed, may perhaps be doubted.

Meanwhile Russell's fleet was rendering good service to the common cause.   Adverse winds had impeded his progress through the Straits of Gibraltar so long that he did not reach Carthagena till the middle of July.   By that time the progress of the French arms had spread terror even to the Escurial.   Noailles had, on the banks of the Tar, routed an army commanded by the Viceroy of Catalonia : and, on the day on which this victory was won, the Brest squadron had joined the Toulon squadron in the Bay of Rosas. Palamos, attacked at once by land and sea, was taken by storm.   Gerona capitulated after a faint show of resistance.   Ostalric surrendered at the first summons.   Barcelona would in all probability have fallen, had not the French Admirals learned that the conqueror of La Hogue was approaching.   They instantly quitted the coast of Catalonia, and never thought themselves safe till they had taken shelter under the batteries of Toulon.

Naval operations in the Mediterranean

The Spanish government expressed warm gratitude for this seasonable assistance, and presented to the English Admiral a jewel which was popularly said to be worth near twenty thousand pounds sterling. There was no difficulty in finding such a jewel among the hoards of gorgeous trinkets which had been left by Charles the Fifth and

---

[1] Shrewsbury to William, June $\frac{15}{25}$. 1694.   William to Shrewsbury, July 1.; Shrewsbury to William, $\frac{\text{June 22.}}{\text{July 2.}}$

ANNE JULES, DUKE DE NOAILLES, MARSHAL OF FRANCE

From an engraving by G. Edelinck, after a painting by H. Rigaud

Philip the Second to a degenerate race. But, in all that constitutes the true wealth of states, Spain was poor indeed. Her treasury was empty : her arsenals were unfurnished : her ships were so rotten that they seemed likely to fly asunder at the discharge of their own guns. Her ragged and starving soldiers often mingled with the crowd of beggars at the doors of convents, and battled there for a mess of pottage and a crust of bread. Russell underwent those trials which no English commander whose hard fate it has been to cooperate with Spaniards has escaped. The Viceroy of Catalonia promised much, did nothing, and expected every thing. He declared that three hundred and fifty thousand rations were ready to be served out to the fleet at Carthagena. It turned out that there were not in all the stores of that port provisions sufficient to victual a single frigate for a single week. Yet His Excellency thought himself entitled to complain because England had not sent an army as well as a fleet, and because the heretic Admiral did not choose to expose the fleet to utter destruction by attacking the French under the guns of Toulon. Russell implored the Spanish authorities to look well to their dockyards, and to try to have, by the next spring, a small squadron which might at least be able to float ; but he could not prevail on them to careen a single ship. He could with difficulty obtain, on hard conditions, permission to send a few of his sick men to marine hospitals on shore. Yet, in spite of all the trouble given him by the imbecility and ingratitude of a government which has generally caused more annoyance to its allies than to its enemies, he acquitted himself well. It is but just to him to say that, from the time at which he became First Lord of the Admiralty, there was a decided improvement in the naval administration. Though he lay with his fleet many months near an inhospitable shore, and at a great distance from England, there were no complaints about the quality or the quantity of provisions. The crews had better food and drink than they had ever had before : comforts which Spain did not afford were supplied from home ; and yet the charge was not greater than when, in Torrington's time, the sailor was poisoned with mouldy biscuit and nauseous beer.

As almost the whole maritime force of France was in the Mediterranean, and as it seemed likely that an attempt would be made on Barcelona in the following year, Russell received orders to winter at Cadiz. In October he sailed to that port ; and there he employed himself in refitting his ships with an activity unintelligible to the Spanish functionaries, who calmly suffered the miserable remains of what had once been the greatest navy in the world to rot under their eyes.[1]

[1] This account of Russell's expedition to the Mediterranean I have taken chiefly from Burchett.

Along the eastern frontier of France the war during this year seemed to languish. In Piedmont and on the Rhine the most important events of the campaign were petty skirmishes and predatory incursions. **War by land** Lewis remained at Versailles, and sent his son, the Dauphin, to represent him in the Netherlands: but the Dauphin was placed under the tutelage of Luxemburg, and proved a most submissive

MEDALS COMMEMORATING THE BOMBARDMENT OF THE FRENCH
SEAPORTS BY THE ENGLISH AND DUTCH FLEETS

pupil. During several months the hostile armies observed each other. The allies made one bold push with the intention of carrying the war into the French territory: but Luxemburg, by a forced march, which excited the admiration of persons versed in the military art, frustrated the design. William on the other hand succeeded in taking Huy, then a fortress of the third rank. No battle was fought: no important town was besieged: but the confederates were satisfied with their campaign.   Of the four previous years every one had been marked by some great disaster.   In 1690 Waldeck had been defeated at Fleurus. In 1691 Mons had fallen.   In 1692 Namur had been taken in sight of the allied army ; and this calamity had been speedily followed by the defeat of Steinkirk.   In 1693 the battle of Landen had been lost ; and Charleroy had submitted to the conqueror.   At length in 1694 the tide had begun to turn.   The French arms had made no progress. What had been gained by the allies was indeed not much : but the smallest gain was welcome to those whom a long run of evil fortune had discouraged.

In England, the general opinion was that, notwithstanding the disaster in Camaret Bay, the war was on the whole proceeding satisfactorily both by land and by sea.   But some parts of the internal administration excited, during this autumn, much discontent.

Since Trenchard had been appointed Secretary of State, the Jacobite agitators had found their situation much more unpleasant than before. Complaints Sidney had been too indulgent and too fond of pleasure to of Trenchard's ad- give them much trouble.   Nottingham was a diligent and ministration honest minister : but he was as high a Tory as a faithful subject of William and Mary could be : he loved and esteemed many of the nonjurors ; and, though he might force himself to be severe when nothing but severity could save the State, he was not extreme to mark the transgressions of his old friends ; nor did he encourage talebearers to come to Whitehall with reports of conspiracies.   But Trenchard was both an active public servant and an earnest Whig.   Even if he had himself been inclined to lenity, he would have been urged to severity by those who surrounded him.   He had constantly at his side Hugh Speke and Aaron Smith, men to whom a hunt after a Jacobite was the most exciting of all sports.   The cry of the malecontents was that Nottingham had kept his bloodhounds in the leash, but that Trenchard had let them slip.   Every honest gentleman who loved the Church and hated the Dutch went in danger of his life.   There was a constant bustle at the Secretary's Office, a constant stream of informers coming in, and of messengers with warrants going out.   It was said, too, that the warrants were often irregularly drawn, that they did not specify the person, that they did not specify the crime, and yet that, under the authority of such instruments as these, houses were entered, desks and cabinets searched, valuable papers carried away, and men of good birth and breeding flung into gaol among felons.[1]   The minister and his agents answered that Westminster Hall was open ; that, if any man had been illegally imprisoned, he had only to bring his action ; that juries were quite sufficiently disposed to listen to any person who

[1] Letter to Trenchard, 1694.

pretended to have been oppressed by cruel and griping men in power ; and that, as none of the prisoners whose wrongs were so pathetically described had ventured to resort to this obvious and easy mode of obtaining redress, it might fairly be inferred that nothing had been done which could not be justified. The clamour of the malecontents, however, made a considerable impression on the public mind ; and, at length, a transaction, in which Trenchard was more unlucky than culpable, brought on him and on the government with which he was connected much temporary obloquy.

MEDAL COMMEMORATING THE CAPTURE OF HUY BY WILLIAM III

Among the informers who haunted his office was an Irish vagabond who had borne more than one name and had professed more than one religion. He now called himself Taaffe. He had been a priest of the Roman Catholic Church, and secretary to Adda the Papal Nuncio, but had, since the Revolution, turned **The Lancashire prosecutions** Protestant, had taken a wife, and had distinguished himself by his activity in discovering the concealed property of those Jesuits and Benedictines who, during the late reign, had been quartered in London. The ministers despised him : but they trusted him. They thought that he had, by his apostasy, and by the part which he had borne in the spoliation of the religious orders, cut himself off from all retreat, and that, having nothing but a halter to expect from King James, he must be true to King William.[1]

This man fell in with a Jacobite agent named Lunt, who had, since the Revolution, been repeatedly employed among the discontented gentry of Cheshire and Lancashire, and who had been privy to those

[1] Burnet, ii. 141, 142. ; and Onslow's Note ; Kingston's True History, 1697.

plans of insurrection which had been disconcerted by the battle of the Boyne in 1690, and by the battle of La Hogue in 1692. Lunt had once been arrested on suspicion of treason, but had been discharged for want of legal proof of his guilt. He was a mere hireling, and was, without much difficulty, induced by Taaffe to turn approver. The pair went to Trenchard. Lunt told his story, mentioned the names of some Cheshire and Lancashire squires to whom he had, as he affirmed, carried commissions from Saint Germains, and of others, who had, to his knowledge, formed secret hoards of arms and ammunition. His single oath would not have been sufficient to support a charge of high treason : but he produced another witness whose evidence seemed to make the case complete. The narrative was plausible and coherent ; and indeed, though it may have been embellished by fictions, there can be little doubt that it was in substance true.[1] Messengers and search warrants were sent down to Lancashire. Aaron Smith himself went thither ; and Taaffe went with him. The alarm had been given by some of the numerous traitors who ate the bread of William. Many of the accused persons had fled ; and others had buried their sabres and muskets, and burned their papers. Nevertheless, discoveries were made which confirmed Lunt's depositions. Behind the wainscot of the old mansion of one Roman Catholic family was discovered a commission signed by James. Another house, of which the master had absconded, was strictly searched, in spite of the solemn asseverations of his wife and his servants that no arms were concealed there. While the lady, with her hand on her heart, was protesting on her honour that her husband was falsely accused, the messengers observed that the back of the chimney did not seem to be firmly fixed. It was removed, and a heap of blades such as were used by horse soldiers tumbled out. In one of the garrets were found, carefully bricked up, thirty saddles for troopers, as many breastplates, and sixty cavalry swords. Trenchard and Aaron Smith thought the case complete ; and it was determined that those culprits who had been apprehended should be tried by a special commission.[2]

Taaffe now confidently expected to be recompensed for his services : but he found a cold reception at the Treasury. He had gone down to Lancashire chiefly in order that he might, under the protection of a search warrant, pilfer trinkets and broad pieces from secret drawers. His sleight of hand however had not altogether escaped the observation of his companions. They discovered that he had made free with the communion plate of the Popish families, whose private hoards he had assisted in ransacking. When therefore he applied for reward, he was dismissed, not merely with a refusal, but with a stern reprimand. He went away mad with greediness and spite. There was yet one way in which he

[1] See the Life of James, ii. 524.　　　[2] Kingston ; Burnet, ii. 142.

might obtain both money and revenge ; and that way he took. He made overtures to the friends of the prisoners. He and he alone could undo what he had done, could save the accused from the gallows, could cover the accusers with infamy, could drive from office the Secretary and the Solicitor who were the dread of all the friends of King James. Loathsome as Taaffe was to the Jacobites, his offer was not to be slighted. He received a sum in hand: he was assured that a comfortable annuity for life should be settled on him when the business was done ; and he was sent down into the country, and kept in strict seclusion against the day of trial.[1]

Meanwhile unlicensed pamphlets, in which the Lancashire plot was classed with Oates's plot, with Dangerfield's plot, with Fuller's plot, with Young's plot, with Whitney's plot, were circulated all over the kingdom, and especially in the county which was to furnish the jury. Of these pamphlets the longest, the ablest, and the bitterest, entitled a Letter to Secretary Trenchard, was commonly ascribed to Ferguson. It is not improbable that Ferguson may have furnished some of the materials, and may have conveyed the manuscript to the press. But many passages are written with an art and a vigour which assuredly did not belong to him. Those who judge by internal evidence may perhaps think that, in some parts of this remarkable tract, they can discern the last gleam of the malignant genius of Montgomery. A few weeks after the appearance of the Letter he sank, unhonoured and unlamented, into the grave.[2]

There were then no printed newspapers except the London Gazette. But since the Revolution the newsletter had become a more important political engine than it had previously been. The newsletters of one writer named Dyer were widely circulated in manuscript. He affected to be a Tory and a High Churchman, and was consequently regarded by the foxhunting lords of manors, all over the kingdom, as an oracle. He had already been twice in prison : but his gains had more than compensated for his sufferings, and he still persisted in seasoning his intelligence to suit the taste of the country gentlemen. He now turned the Lancashire plot into ridicule, declared that the guns which had been found were old fowling pieces, that the saddles were meant only for hunting, and that the swords were rusty reliques of Edge Hill and Marston Moor.[3] The effect produced by all this invective and sarcasm on the public mind seems to have been great. Even at the Dutch

[1] Kingston. For the fact that a bribe was given to Taaffe, Kingston cites the evidence, not now extant, which was taken on oath by the Lords.

[2] Narcissus Luttrell's Diary, Oct. 6. 1694.

[3] As to Dyer's newsletter, see Narcissus Luttrell's Diary for June and August 1693, and September 1694.

Embassy, where assuredly there was no leaning towards Jacobitism, there was a strong impression that it would be unwise to bring the prisoners to trial. In Lancashire and Cheshire the prevailing sentiments were pity for the accused and hatred of the prosecutors. The government however persevered. In October four Judges went down to Manchester. At present the population of that town is made up of persons born in every part of the British Isles, and consequently has no especial sympathy with the landowners, the farmers and the agricultural labourers of the neighbouring districts. But in the seventeenth century the Manchester man was a Lancashire man. His politics were those of his county. For the old Cavalier families of his county he felt a great respect ; and he was furious when he thought that some of the best blood of his county was about to be shed by a knot of Roundhead pettifoggers from London. Multitudes of people from the neighbouring villages filled the streets of the town, and saw with grief and indignation the array of drawn swords and loaded carbines which surrounded the culprits. Aaron Smith's arrangements do not seem to have been skilful. The chief counsel for the Crown was Sir William Williams, who, though now well stricken in years and possessed of a great estate, still continued to practise. One fault had thrown a dark shade over the latter part of his life. The recollection of that day on which he had stood up in Westminster Hall, amidst laughter and hooting, to defend the dispensing power and to attack the right of petition, had, ever since the Revolution, kept him back from honour. He was an angry and disappointed man, and was by no means disposed to incur unpopularity in the cause of a government to which he owed nothing, and from which he expected nothing.

Of the trial no detailed report has come down to us ; but we have both a Whig narrative and a Jacobite narrative.[1] It seems that the prisoners who were first arraigned did not sever in their challenges, and were consequently tried together. Williams examined, or rather cross-examined, his own witnesses with a severity which confused them. The crowd which filled the court laughed and clamoured. Lunt in particular became completely bewildered, mistook one person for another, and did not recover himself till the Judges took him out of the hands of the counsel for the Crown. For some of the prisoners an alibi was set up. Evidence was also produced to show, what was undoubtedly true, that Lunt was a man of abandoned character. The result however seemed doubtful till, to the dismay of the prosecutors, Taaffe entered the box. He swore with unblushing forehead that the whole story of

---

[1] The Whig narrative is Kingston's ; the Jacobite narrative, by an anonymous author, has lately been printed by the Chetham Society. See also a Letter out of Lancashire to a Friend in London, giving some Account of the late Trials, 1694.

VIEW OF MANCHESTER

From an engraving by S. and N. Buck

the plot was a circumstantial lie devised by himself and Lunt. Williams threw down his brief; and, in truth, a more honest advocate might well have done the same. The prisoners who were at the bar were instantly acquitted : those who had not yet been tried were set at liberty: the witnesses for the prosecution were pelted out of Manchester : the Clerk of the Crown narrowly escaped with life ; and the Judges took their departure amidst hisses and execrations.

A few days after the close of the trials at Manchester William returned to England. On the twelfth of November, only forty eight hours after his arrival at Kensington, the Houses met. He congratulated them on the improved aspect of affairs. Both by land and by sea the events of the year which was about to close had been, on the whole, favourable to the allies : the French armies had made no progress : the French fleets had not ventured to show themselves : nevertheless, a safe and honourable peace could be obtained only by a vigorous prosecution of the war ; and the war could not be vigorously prosecuted without large supplies. William then reminded the Commons that the Act by which they had settled the Customs on the Crown for four years was about to expire, and expressed his hope that it would be renewed.

Meeting of the Parliament

After the King had spoken, the Commons, for some reason which no writer has explained, adjourned for a week. Before they met again, an event took place which caused great sorrow at the palace, and through all the ranks of the Low Church party. Tillotson was taken suddenly ill while attending public worship in the chapel of Whitehall. Prompt remedies might perhaps have saved him : but he would not interrupt the prayers ; and, before the service was over, his malady was beyond the reach of medicine. He was almost speechless : but his friends long remembered with pleasure a few broken ejaculations which showed that he enjoyed peace of mind to the last. He was buried in the church of Saint Lawrence Jewry, near Guildhall. It was there that he had won his immense oratorical reputation. He had preached there during the thirty years which preceded his elevation to the throne of Canterbury. His eloquence had attracted to the heart of the City crowds of the learned and polite, from the Inns of Court and from the lordly mansions of Saint James's and Soho. A considerable part of his congregation had generally consisted of young clergymen, who came to learn the art of preaching at the feet of him who was universally considered as the first of preachers. To this church his remains were now carried through a mourning population. The hearse was followed by an endless train of splendid equipages from Lambeth through Southwark and over London Bridge. Burnet preached the funeral sermon. His kind and honest heart was overcome by so many

Death of Tillotson

MONUMENT TO ARCHBISHOP TILLOTSON IN THE CHURCH OF
ST. LAWRENCE, JEWRY

tender recollections that, in the midst of his discourse, he paused and burst into tears, while a loud moan of sorrow rose from the whole auditory. The Queen could not speak of her favourite instructor without weeping. Even William was visibly moved. "I have lost," he said, "the best friend that I ever had, and the best man that I ever knew." The only Englishman who is mentioned with tenderness in any part of the great mass of letters which the King wrote to Heinsius is Tillotson. The Archbishop had left a widow. To her William granted a pension of four hundred a year, which he afterwards increased to six hundred. His anxiety that she should receive her income regularly and without stoppages was honourable to him. Every quarterday he ordered the money, without any deduction, to be brought to himself, and immediately sent it to her. Tillotson had bequeathed to her no property, except a great number of manuscript sermons. Such was his fame among his contemporaries that those sermons were purchased by the booksellers for the almost incredible sum of two thousand five hundred guineas, equivalent, in the wretched state in which the silver coin then was, to at least three thousand six hundred pounds. Such a price had never before been given in England for any copyright. About the same time Dryden, whose reputation was then in the zenith, received thirteen hundred pounds for his translation of all the works of Virgil, and was thought to have been splendidly remunerated.[1]

It was not easy to fill satisfactorily the high place which Tillotson had left vacant. Mary gave her voice for Stillingfleet, and pressed his

Tenison Archbishop of Canterbury

claims as earnestly as she ever ventured to press any thing. In abilities and attainments he had few superiors among the clergy. But, though he would probably have been considered as a Low Churchman by Jane and South, he was too high a Churchman for William ; and Tenison was appointed. The new primate was not eminently distinguished by eloquence or learning : but he was honest, prudent, laborious, and benevolent : he had been a good rector of a large parish, and a good bishop of a large diocese : detraction had not yet been busy with his name ; and it might well be thought that a man of plain sense, moderation, and integrity, was more likely than a man of brilliant genius and lofty spirit to succeed in the arduous task of quieting a discontented and distracted Church.

Meanwhile the Commons had entered upon business. They cheerfully voted about two million four hundred thousand pounds for the army, and as much for the navy. The land tax for the year was again fixed at four shillings in the pound : the Act which settled the Customs on the Crown was renewed for a term of five years ; and a fund was

[1] Birch's Life of Tillotson ; the Funeral Sermon preached by Burnet ; William to Heinsius, $\frac{\text{Nov. 23.}}{\text{Dec. 3.}}$ 1694.

established on which the government was authorised to borrow two millions and a half.

Some time was spent by both Houses in discussing the Manchester trials. If the malecontents had been wise, they would have been satisfied with the advantage which they had already gained. Their friends had been set free. The prosecutors had with difficulty escaped from the hands of an enraged multitude. The character of the government had been seriously damaged. The ministers were accused, in prose and in verse, sometimes in earnest and sometimes in jest, of having hired a gang of ruffians to swear away the lives of honest gentlemen. Even moderate politicians, who gave no credit to these foul imputations, owned that Trenchard ought to have remembered the villanies of Fuller and Young, and to have been on his guard against such wretches as Taaffe and Lunt. The unfortunate Secretary's health and spirits had given way. It was said that he was dying; and it was certain that he would not long continue to hold the seals. The Tories had won a great victory; but, in their eagerness to improve it, they turned it into a defeat.

Debates on the Lancashire prosecutions

Early in the session Howe complained, with his usual vehemence and asperity, of the indignities to which innocent and honourable men, highly descended and highly esteemed, had been subjected by Aaron Smith and the wretches who were in his pay. The leading Whigs, with great judgment, demanded an inquiry. Then the Tories began to flinch. They well knew that an inquiry could not strengthen their case, and might weaken it. The issue, they said, had been tried: a jury had pronounced: the verdict was definitive; and it would be monstrous to give the false witnesses who had been stoned out of Manchester an opportunity of repeating their lesson. To this argument the answer was obvious. The verdict was definitive as respected the defendants, but not as respected the prosecutors. The prosecutors were now in their turn defendants, and were entitled to all the privileges of defendants. It did not follow, because the Lancashire gentlemen had been found, and very properly found, not guilty of treason, that the Secretary of State and the Solicitor of the Treasury had been guilty of unfairness, or even of rashness. The House, by one hundred and nineteen votes to one hundred and two, resolved that Aaron Smith and the witnesses on both sides should be ordered to attend. Several days were passed in examination and crossexamination; and sometimes the sittings extended far into the night. It soon became clear that the prosecution had not been lightly instituted, and that some of the persons who had been acquitted had been concerned in treasonable schemes. The Tories would now have been content with a drawn battle: but the Whigs were not disposed to forego their advantage. It was moved that there had been a sufficient ground for the proceedings before the Special Commission ; and this motion was carried without a division. The opposition proposed to add some words implying that the witnesses for the Crown had forsworn themselves : but these words were rejected by one hundred and thirty six votes to one hundred and nine ; and it was resolved by one hundred and thirty three votes to ninety seven that there had been a dangerous conspiracy. The Lords had meanwhile been deliberating on the same subject, and had come to the same conclusion. They sent Taaffe to prison for prevarication ; and they passed resolutions acquitting both the government and the judges of all blame. The public however continued to think that the gentlemen who had been tried at Manchester had been unjustifiably persecuted, till a Jacobite plot of singular atrocity, brought home to the plotters by decisive evidence, produced a violent revulsion of feeling.[1]

Meanwhile three bills, which had been repeatedly discussed in preceding years, and two of which had been carried in vain to the foot of the throne, had been again brought in ; the Place Bill, the Bill for the Regulation of Trials in cases of Treason, and the Triennial Bill.

The Place Bill did not reach the Lords. It was thrice read in the Lower House, but was not passed. At the very last moment it was
Place Bill rejected by a hundred and seventy five votes to a hundred and forty two. Howe and Harley were the tellers for the minority.[2]

The Bill for the Regulation of Trials in cases of Treason went up again to the Peers. Their Lordships again added to it the clause
Bill for the Regulation of Trials in cases of Treason which had formerly been fatal to it. The Commons again refused to grant any new privilege to the hereditary aristocracy. Conferences were again held : reasons were again exchanged : both Houses were again obstinate ; and the bill was again lost.[3]

The Triennial Bill was more fortunate. It was brought in on the first day of the session, and went easily and rapidly through both
The Triennial Bill passed Houses. The only question about which there was any serious contention was, how long the existing Parliament should be suffered to continue. After several sharp debates November in the year 1696 was fixed as the extreme term. The Bill

---

[1] See the Journals of the two Houses. The only account that we have of the debates is in the letters of L'Hermitage.

[2] Commons' Journals, Feb. 20. 169¾. As this bill never reached the Lords, it is not to be found among their archives. I have therefore no means of discovering whether it differed in any respect from the bill of the preceding year.

[3] The history of this bill may be read in the Journals of the Houses. The contest, not a very vehement one, lasted till the 20th of April.

settling the Customs on the Crown and the Triennial Bill proceeded almost side by side. Both were, on the twenty-second of December, ready for the royal assent. William came in state on that day to Westminster. The attendance of members of both Houses was large.

DR. JOHN RADCLIFFE

From a painting by Sir G. Kneller in 1712, in the possession of the Radcliffe Trustees

When the Clerk of the Crown read the words, " A Bill for the frequent Calling and Meeting of Parliaments," the anxiety was great. When the Clerk of the Parliament made answer, " Le roy et la royne le veulent," a loud and long hum of delight and exultation rose from the benches and the bar.[1] William had resolved many months before not to refuse his assent a second time to so popular a law.[2] There were some however who thought that he would not have made so great a concession if he had on that day been quite himself. It was plain indeed that he was strangely agitated and unnerved. It had been announced that he would dine in public at Whitehall. But he disappointed the curiosity of the multitude which on such occasions flocked to the Court, and hurried back to Kensington.[3]

He had but too good reason to be uneasy. His wife had, during two or three days, been poorly ; and on the preceding evening grave **Death of Mary** symptoms had appeared. Sir Thomas Millington, who was physician in ordinary to the King, thought that she had the measles. But Radcliffe, who, with coarse manners and little book learning, had raised himself to the first practice in London chiefly by his rare skill in diagnostics, uttered the more alarming words, small pox. That disease, over which science has since achieved a succession of glorious and beneficent victories, was then the most terrible of all the ministers of death. The havoc of the plague had been far more rapid : but the plague had visited our shores only once or twice within living memory ; and the small pox was always present, filling the churchyards with corpses, tormenting with constant fears all whom it had not yet stricken, leaving on those whose lives it spared the hideous traces of its power, turning the babe into a changeling at which the mother shuddered, and making the eyes and cheeks of the betrothed maiden objects of horror to the lover. Towards the end of the year 1694, this pestilence was more than usually severe. At length the infection spread to the palace, and reached the young and blooming Queen. She received the intimation of her danger with true greatness of soul. She gave orders that every lady of her bedchamber, every maid of honour, nay, every menial servant, who had not had the small pox, should instantly leave Kensington House. She locked herself up during a short time in her closet, burned some papers, arranged others, and then calmly awaited her fate.

During two or three days there were many alternations of hope and fear. The physicians contradicted each other and themselves in a way which sufficiently indicates the state of medical science in that age. The disease was measles : it was scarlet fever : it was spotted fever : it was erysipelas. At one moment some symptoms, which in truth showed

---

[1] "The Commons," says Narcissus Luttrell, "gave a great hum." "Le murmure qui est la marque d'applaudissement fut si grand qu'on peut dire qu'il estoit universel."—L'Hermitage, $\frac{\text{Dec. 25.}}{\text{Jan. 4.}}$

[2] L'Hermitage says this in his despatch of Nov. $\frac{20}{30}$.

[3] Burnet, ii. 137. ; Van Citters, $\frac{\text{Dec. 25.}}{\text{Jan. 4.}}$

that the case was almost hopeless, were hailed as indications of returning health.   At length all doubt was over.   Radcliffe's opinion proved to be right.   It was plain that the Queen was sinking under small pox of the most malignant type.

QUEEN MARY LYING IN STATE

From a Dutch engraving in the Sutherland Collection

All this time William remained night and day near her bedside. The little couch on which he slept when he was in camp was spread for him in the antechamber : but he scarcely lay down on it.   The sight of his misery, the Dutch Envoy wrote, was enough to melt the hardest heart.   Nothing seemed to be left of the man whose serene fortitude had been the wonder of old soldiers on the disastrous day of Landen, and of old sailors through that fearful night among the sheets of ice and banks of sand on the coast of Goree. The very domestics saw the tears running unchecked down that face, of which the stern composure had seldom been disturbed by any triumph or by any defeat. Several of the prelates were in attendance. The King drew Burnet aside, and gave way to an agony of grief. "There is no hope," he cried. "I was the happiest man on earth; and I am the most miserable. She had no fault; none: you knew her well: but you could not know, nobody but myself could know, her goodness." Tenison undertook to tell her that she was dying. He was afraid that such a communication, abruptly made, might agitate her violently, and began with much management. But she soon caught his meaning, and, with that meek womanly courage which so often puts our bravery to shame, submitted herself to the will of God. She called for a small cabinet in which her most important papers were locked up, gave orders that, as soon as she was no more, it should be delivered to the King, and then dismissed worldly cares from her mind. She received the Eucharist, and repeated her part of the office with unimpaired memory and intelligence, though in a feeble voice. She observed that Tenison had been long standing at her bedside, and, with that sweet courtesy which was habitual to her, faltered out her commands that he would sit down, and repeated them till he obeyed. After she had received the sacrament she sank rapidly, and uttered only a few broken words. Twice she tried to take a last farewell of him whom she had loved so truly and entirely: but she was unable to speak. He had a succession of fits so alarming that his Privy Councillors, who were assembled in a neighbouring room, were apprehensive for his reason and his life. The Duke of Leeds, at the request of his colleagues, ventured to assume the friendly guardianship of which minds deranged by sorrow stand in need. A few minutes before the Queen expired, William was removed, almost insensible, from the sick room.

Mary died in peace with Anne. Before the physicians had pronounced the case hopeless, the Princess, who was then in very delicate health, had sent a kind message; and Mary had returned a kind answer. The Princess had then proposed to come herself: but William had, in very gracious terms, declined the offer. The excitement of an interview, he said, would be too much for both sisters. If a favourable turn took place, Her Royal Highness should be most welcome to Kensington. A few hours later all was over.[1]

---

[1] Burnet, ii. 136. 138.; Narcissus Luttrell's Diary; Van Citters, $\frac{\text{Dec. 28.}}{\text{Jan. 7.}}$ 169$\frac{4}{8}$; L'Hermitage, $\frac{\text{Dec. 25.}}{\text{Jan. 4.}}$ $\frac{\text{Dec. 28.}}{\text{Jan. 7.}}$ Jan. $\frac{1}{11}$.; Vernon to Lord Lexington, Dec. 21. 25. 28., Jan. 1.; Tenison's Funeral Sermon.

The Court and Kingdom in Tears:

OR, THE

Sorrowful Subject's Lamentation for the DEATH

OF

Her Royal Majesty Queen Mary,

Who departed this Life the 28th of this instant *December*, 1694; to the Unspeakable Grief of his Majesty, and all his Loyal and Loving Subjects.

To the Tune of, *If Love's a sweet Passion*, &c.

THE COURT AND KINGDOM IN TEARS

From a ballad in the Pepysian Collection

The public sorrow was great and general. For Mary's blameless life, her large charities, and her winning manners had conquered the hearts of her people. When the Commons next met they sate for a time in profound silence. At length it was moved and resolved that an Address of Condolence should be presented to the King; and then the House broke up without proceeding to other business. The Dutch Envoy informed the States General that many of the members had handkerchiefs at their eyes. The number of sad faces in the street struck every observer. The mourning was more general than even the mourning for Charles the Second had been. On the Sunday which followed the Queen's death her virtues were celebrated in almost every parish church of the Capital, and in almost every great meeting of non-conformists.[1]

The most estimable Jacobites respected the sorrow of William and the memory of Mary. But to the fiercer zealots of the party neither the house of mourning nor the grave was sacred. At Bristol the adherents of Sir John Knight rang the bells as if for a victory.[2] It has often been repeated, and is not at all improbable, that a nonjuring divine, in the midst of the general lamentation, preached on the text, "Go: see now this cursed woman and bury her: for she is a King's daughter." It is certain that some of the ejected priests pursued her to the grave with invectives. Her death, they said, was evidently a judgment for her crime. God had, from the top of Sinai, in thunder and lightning, promised length of days to children who should honour their parents; and in this promise was plainly implied a menace. What father had ever been worse treated by his daughters than James by Mary and Anne? Mary was gone, cut off in the prime of life, in the glow of beauty, in the height of prosperity; and Anne would do well to profit by the warning. Wagstaffe went further, and dwelt much on certain wonderful coincidences of time. James had been driven from his palace and country in Christmas week. Mary had died in Christmas week. There could be no doubt that, if the secrets of Providence were disclosed to us, we should find that the turns of the daughter's complaint in December 1694 bore an exact analogy to the turns of the father's fortune in December 1688. It was at midnight that the father ran away from Rochester: it was at midnight that the daughter expired. Such was the profundity and such the ingenuity of a writer whom the Jacobite schismatics justly regarded as one of their ablest chiefs.[3]

[1] Evelyn's Diary; Narcissus Luttrell's Diary; Commons' Journals, Dec. 28. 1694; Shrewsbury to Lexington, of the same date; Van Citters, of the same date; L'Hermitage, Jan. $\frac{11}{21}$. 1695. Among the sermons on Mary's death, that of Sherlock, preached in the Temple Church, and those of Howe and Bates, preached to great Presbyterian congregations, deserve notice.

[2] Narcissus Luttrell's Diary.

[3] Remarks on some late Sermons, 1695; A Defence of the Archbishop's Sermon, 1695.

THE FUNERAL OF QUEEN MARY

From a Dutch engraving in the Sutherland Collection

The Whigs soon had an opportunity of retaliating. They triumph-antly related that a scrivener in the Borough, a stanch friend of hereditary right, while exulting in the judgment which had overtaken the Queen, had himself fallen down dead in a fit.[1]

The funeral was long remembered as the saddest and most august that Westminster had ever seen. While the Queen's remains lay in **Funeral of Mary** state at Whitehall, the neighbouring streets were filled every day, from sunrise to sunset, by crowds which made all traffic impossible. The two Houses with their maces followed the hearse, the Lords robed in scarlet and ermine, the Commons in long black mantles. No preceding Sovereign had ever been attended to the grave by a Parlia-ment : for, till then, the Parliament had always expired with the Sovereign. A paper had indeed been circulated, in which the logic of a small sharp pettifogger was employed to prove that writs, issued in the joint names of William and Mary, ceased to be of force as soon as William reigned alone. But this paltry cavil had completely failed. It had not even been mentioned in the Lower House, and had been men-tioned in the Upper only to be contemptuously overruled. The whole Magistracy of the City swelled the procession. The banners of England and France, Scotland and Ireland, were carried by great nobles before the corpse. The pall was borne by the chiefs of the illustrious houses of Howard, Seymour, Grey, and Stanley. On the gorgeous coffin of purple and gold were laid the crown and sceptre of the realm. The day was well suited to such a ceremony. The sky was dark and troubled; and a few ghastly flakes of snow fell on the black plumes of the funeral car. Within the Abbey, nave, choir and transept were in a blaze with innumerable wax-lights. The body was deposited under a sumptuous canopy in the centre of the church while the Primate preached. The earlier part of his discourse was deformed by pedantic divisions and subdivisions : but towards the close he told what he had himself seen and heard with a simplicity and earnest-ness more affecting than the most skilful rhetoric. Through the whole ceremony the distant booming of cannon was heard every minute from the batteries of the Tower. The gentle Queen sleeps among her illus-trious kindred in the southern aisle of the Chapel of Henry the Seventh.[2]

The affection with which her husband cherished her memory was soon attested by a monument the most superb that was ever erected to **Greenwich Hospital founded** any sovereign. No scheme had been so much her own, none had been so near her heart, as that of converting the palace at Greenwich into a retreat for seamen. It had occurred to her when she had found it difficult to provide good shelter and good

---

[1] Luttrell's Diary.

[2] L'Hermitage, March $\frac{1}{11}$. $\frac{6}{16}$. 1695; London Gazette, March 7. ; Tenison's Funeral Sermon; Evelyn's Diary.

attendance for the thousands of brave men who had come back to England wounded after the battle of La Hogue. While she lived scarcely any step was taken towards the accomplishing of her favourite design. But

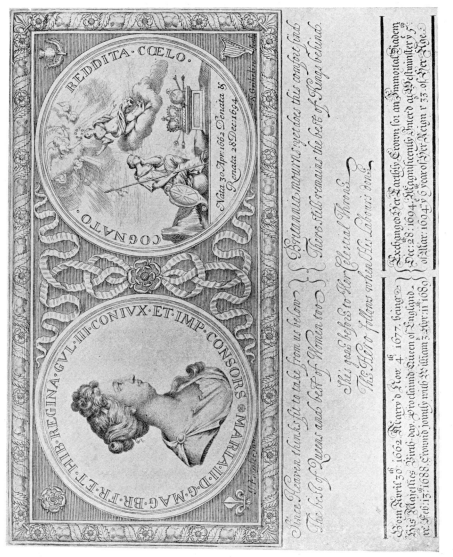

EMBLEMATIC DESIGN ON THE DEATH OF QUEEN MARY

From an engraving by S. Gribelin, in the Sutherland Collection

it should seem that, as soon as her husband had lost her, he began to reproach himself for having neglected her wishes. No time was lost. A plan was furnished by Wren ; and soon an edifice, surpassing that asylum which the magnificent Lewis had provided for his soldiers, rose on the

margin of the Thames. Whoever reads the inscription which runs round
the frieze of the hall will observe that William claims no part of the
merit of the design, and that the praise is ascribed to Mary alone. Had
the King's life been prolonged till the works were completed, a statue of
her who was the real foundress of the institution would have had a

MEDALS COMMEMORATING THE DEATH OF QUEEN MARY

conspicuous place in that court which presents two lofty domes and two
graceful colonnades to the multitudes who are perpetually passing up and
down the imperial river. But that part of the plan was never carried into
effect; and few of those who now gaze on the noblest of European
hospitals are aware that it is a memorial of the virtues of the good Queen
Mary, of the love and sorrow of William, and of the great victory of
La Hogue.

QUEEN MARY II., 1662-1694.

From the painting by William Wissin, in the National Portrait Gallery.

CHAPTER XXI

On the Continent the news of Mary's death excited various emotions. The Huguenots, in every part of Europe to which they had wandered, bewailed the Elect Lady, who had retrenched from her own royal state in order to furnish bread and shelter to the persecuted people of God.[1] In the United Provinces, where she was well known and had always been popular, she was tenderly lamented. Matthew Prior, whose parts and accomplishments had obtained for him the patronage of the munificent Dorset, and who was now attached to the Embassy at the Hague, wrote that the coldest and most passionless of nations was touched. The very marble, he said, wept.[2] The lamentations of Cambridge and Oxford were echoed by Leyden and Utrecht. The States General put on mourning. The bells of all the steeples of Holland tolled dolefully day after day.[3] James, meanwhile, strictly prohibited all mourning at Saint Germains, and prevailed on Lewis to issue a similar prohibition at Versailles. Some of the most illustrious nobles of France, and among them the Dukes of Bouillon and of Duras, were related to the House of Nassau, and had always, when death visited that House, punctiliously observed the decent ceremonial of sorrow. They were now forbidden to wear black ; and they submitted : but it was beyond the power of the great King to prevent his highbred and sharpwitted courtiers from whispering to each other that there was something pitiful in this revenge taken by the living on the dead, by a parent on a child.[4]

1695.
Effect of
Mary's
death on the
Continent

[1] See Claude's Sermon on Mary's death.

[2] Prior to Lord and Lady Lexington, Jan. $\frac{14}{24}$. 1695. The letter is among the Lexington papers, a valuable collection, and well edited.

[3] Monthly Mercury for January 1695. An orator who pronounced an eulogium on the Queen at Utrecht was so absurd as to say that she spent her last breath in prayers for the prosperity of the United Provinces :—" Valeant et Batavi ;"—these are her last words—" sint incolumes ; sint florentes ; sint beati ; stet in æternum, stet immota præclarissima illorum civitas, hospitium aliquando mihi gratissimum, optime de me meritum." See also the orations of Peter Francius of Amsterdam, and of John Ortwinius of Delft.

[4] Journal de Dangeau ; Mémoires de Saint Simon.

The hopes of James and of his companions in exile were now higher than they had been since the day of La Hogue. Indeed the general opinion of politicians, both here and on the Continent, was that William would find it impossible to sustain himself much longer on the throne. He would not, it was said, have sustained himself so long but

GREAT SEAL OF WILLIAM III

for the help of his wife. Her affability had conciliated many who had been repelled by his freezing looks and short answers. Her English tones, sentiments, and tastes had charmed many who were disgusted by his Dutch accent and Dutch habits. Though she did not belong to the High Church party, she loved that ritual to which she had been accustomed from infancy, and complied willingly and reverently with some ceremonies which he considered, not indeed as sinful, but as childish, and in which he could hardly bring himself to take part. While the war lasted, it would be necessary that he should pass nearly half the year out of England. Hitherto she had, when he was absent, supplied his place, and had supplied it well. Who was to supply it now? In what vicegerent could he place equal confidence? To what

GREAT SEAL OF WILLIAM III

vicegerent would the nation look up with equal respect? All the statesmen of Europe therefore agreed in thinking that his position, difficult and dangerous at best, had been made far more difficult and more dangerous by the death of the Queen. But all the statesmen of Europe were deceived; and, strange to say, his reign was decidedly more prosperous and more tranquil after the decease of Mary than during her life.

A few hours after William had lost the most tender and beloved of all his friends, he was delivered from the most formidable of all his **Death of** enemies.   Death had been busy at Paris as well as in London.
Luxemburg While Tenison was praying by the bed of Mary, Bourdaloue was administering the last unction to Luxemburg.   The great French general had never been a favourite at the French Court: but when it was known that his feeble frame, exhausted by war and pleasure, was sinking under a dangerous disease, the value of his services was, for the first time, fully appreciated : the royal physicians were sent to prescribe for him : the sisters of Saint Cyr were ordered to pray for him : but prayers and prescriptions were vain.   "How glad the Prince of Orange will be," said Lewis, "when the news of our loss reaches him."   He was mistaken. That news found William unable to think of any loss but his own.[1]

During the month which followed the death of Mary the King was incapable of exertion.   Even to the addresses of the two Houses of **Distress of** Parliament he replied only by a few inarticulate sounds.
William   The answers which appear in the Journals were not uttered by him, but were delivered in writing.   Such business as could not be deferred was transacted by the intervention of Portland, who was himself oppressed with sorrow.   During some weeks the important and confidential correspondence between the King and Heinsius was suspended. At length William forced himself to resume that correspondence : but his first letter was the letter of a heartbroken man.   Even his martial ardour had been tamed by misery.   "I tell you in confidence," he wrote, "that I feel myself to be no longer fit for military command.   Yet I will try to do my duty; and I hope that God will strengthen me."   So despondingly did he look forward to the most brilliant and successful of his many campaigns.[2]

There was no interruption of parliamentary business.   While the Abbey was hanging with black for the funeral of the Queen, the **Parliamentary** Commons came to a vote, which at the time attracted little **proceedings:** attention, which produced no excitement, which has been **emancipation** **of the press** left unnoticed by voluminous annalists, and of which the history can be but imperfectly traced in the Journals of the House, but which has done more for liberty and for civilisation than the Great Charter or the Bill of Rights.   Early in the session a select committee had been appointed to ascertain what temporary statutes were about to expire, and to consider which of those statutes it might be expedient to continue.   The report was made ; and all the recommendations contained in that report were adopted, with one exception.   Among the

[1] Saint Simon ; Dangeau ; Monthly Mercury for January 1695.

[2] L'Hermitage, Jan. $\frac{1}{11}$. 1695 ; Vernon to Lord Lexington, Jan. 1. 4. ; Portland to Lord Lexington, Jan. $\frac{15}{25}$. ; William to Heinsius, $\frac{\text{Jan. 22.}}{\text{Feb. 1.}}$

laws which the Committee thought that it would be advisable to renew was the law which subjected the press to a censorship. The question was put, "that the House do agree with the Committee on the Resolution

THE FUNERAL OF THE MARECHAL DE LUXEMBOURG

From a Dutch caricature. Number 1293 in the British Museum Catalogue of Satirical Prints

that the Act entitled an Act for preventing Abuses in printing seditious, treasonable, and unlicensed Pamphlets, and for regulating of Printing and Printing Presses, be continued." The Speaker pronounced that the Noes had it; and the Ayes did not think fit to divide.

A bill for continuing all the other temporary Acts, which, in the opinion of the committee, could not properly be suffered to expire, was brought in, passed, and sent to the Lords. In a short time this bill came back with an important amendment. The Lords had inserted in the list of Acts to be continued the Act which placed the press under the control of licensers. The Commons resolved not to agree to the amendment, demanded a conference, and appointed a committee of managers. The leading manager was Edward Clarke, a stanch Whig, who represented Taunton, the stronghold, during fifty troubled years, of civil and religious freedom.

Clarke delivered to the Lords in the Painted Chamber a paper containing the reasons which had determined the Lower House not to renew the Licensing Act. This paper completely vindicates the resolution to which the Commons had come. But it proves at the same time that they knew not what they were doing, what a revolution they were making, what a power they were calling into existence. They pointed out concisely, clearly, forcibly, and sometimes with a grave irony which is not unbecoming, the absurdities and iniquities of the statute which was about to expire. But all their objections will be found to relate to matters of detail. On the great question of principle, on the question whether the liberty of unlicensed printing be, on the whole, a blessing or a curse to society, not a word is said. The Licensing Act is condemned, not as a thing essentially evil, but on account of the petty grievances, the exactions, the jobs, the commercial restrictions, the domiciliary visits, which were incidental to it. It is pronounced mischievous because it enables the Company of Stationers to extort money from publishers, because it empowers the agents of the government to search houses under the authority of general warrants, because it confines the foreign book trade to the port of London, because it detains valuable packages of books at the Custom House till the pages are mildewed. The Commons complain that the amount of the fee which the licenser may demand is not fixed. They complain that it is made penal in an officer of the Customs to open a box of books from abroad, except in the presence of one of the censors of the press. How, it is very sensibly asked, is the officer to know that there are books in the box till he has opened it? Such were the arguments which did what Milton's Areopagitica had failed to do.[1]

[1] In the Craftsman of November 20. 1731, it is said that Locke drew up the paper in which the Commons gave their reasons for refusing to renew the Licensing Act. If this were so, it must be remembered that Locke wrote, not in his own name, but in the name of a multitude of plain country gentlemen and merchants, to whom his opinions touching the liberty of the press would probably have seemed strange and dangerous. We must suppose, therefore, that, with his usual prudence, he refrained from giving an exposition of his own views, and contented himself with putting into a neat and perspicuous form arguments suited to the capacity of the parliamentary majority.

The Lords yielded without a contest. They probably expected that some less objectionable bill for the regulation of the press would soon be sent up to them ; and in fact such a bill was brought into the House of Commons, read twice, and referred to a select committee. But the session closed before the committee had reported ; and English literature was emancipated, and emancipated for ever, from the control of the government.[1]

This great event passed almost unnoticed. Evelyn and Luttrell did not think it worth mentioning in their diaries. The Dutch minister did not think it worth mentioning in his despatches. No allusion to it is to be found in the Monthly Mercuries. The public attention was occupied by other and far more exciting subjects.

One of those subjects was the death of the most accomplished, the most enlightened, and, in spite of great faults, the most estimable of the statesmen who were formed in the corrupt and licentious   Death of Whitehall of the Restoration. About a month after the   Halifax splendid obsequies of Mary, a funeral procession of almost ostentatious simplicity passed round the shrine of Edward the Confessor to the Chapel of Henry the Seventh. There, at the distance of a few feet from her coffin, lies the coffin of George Savile, Marquess of Halifax.

Halifax and Nottingham had long been friends : and Lord Eland, now Halifax's only son, had been affianced to the Lady Mary Finch, Nottingham's daughter. The day of the nuptials was fixed : a joyous company assembled at Burley on the Hill, the mansion of the bride's father, which, from one of the noblest terraces in the island, looks down on magnificent woods of beech and oak, on the rich valley of Catmos, and on the spire of Oakham. The father of the bridegroom was detained in London by indisposition, which was not supposed to be dangerous. On a sudden his malady took an alarming form. He was told that he had but a few hours to live. He received the intimation with tranquil fortitude. It was proposed to send off an express to summon his son to town. But Halifax, good natured to the last, would not disturb the felicity of the wedding day. He gave strict orders that his interment should be private, prepared himself for the great change by devotions which astonished those who had called him an atheist, and died with the serenity of a philosopher and of a Christian, while his friends and kindred, not suspecting his danger, were tasting the sack posset and drawing the curtain.[2] His legitimate male

---

[1] See the Commons' Journals of Feb. 11., April 12. and April 17., and the Lords' Journals of April 8. and April 18. 1695. Unfortunately there is a hiatus in the Commons' Journal of the 12th of April, so that it is now impossible to discover whether there was a division on the amendment made by the Lords.

[2] L'Hermitage, April $\frac{16}{26}$. 1695 ; Evelyn's Diary ; Burnet, ii. 149.

posterity and his titles soon became extinct. No small portion, however, of his wit and eloquence descended to his daughter's son, Philip Stanhope, fourth Earl of Chesterfield. But it is perhaps not generally known that some adventurers, who, without advantages of fortune or position, made themselves conspicuous by the mere force of ability, inherited the blood of Halifax. He left a natural son, Henry Carey, whose dramas once drew crowded audiences to the theatres, and some of whose gay and spirited verses still live in the memory of hundreds of thousands. From Henry Carey descended that Edmund Kean, who, in our own time, transformed himself so marvellously into Shylock, Iago, and Othello.

More than one historian has been charged with partiality to Halifax. The truth is that the memory of Halifax is entitled in an especial manner to the protection of history. For what distinguishes him from all other English statesmen is this, that, through a long public life, and through frequent and violent revolutions of public feeling, he almost invariably took that view of the great questions of his time which history has finally adopted. He was called inconstant, because the relative position in which he stood to the contending factions was perpetually varying. As well might the pole star be called inconstant because it is sometimes to the east and sometimes to the west of the pointers. To have defended the ancient and legal constitution of the realm against a seditious populace at one conjuncture, and against a tyrannical government at another; to have been the foremost champion of order in the turbulent Parliament of 1680, and the foremost champion of liberty in the servile Parliament of 1685; to have been just and merciful to Roman Catholics in the days of the Popish plot, and to Exclusionists in the days of the Rye House Plot; to have done all in his power to save both the head of Stafford and the head of Russell; this was a course which contemporaries, heated by passion, and deluded by names and badges, might not unnaturally call fickle, but which deserves a very different name from the late justice of posterity.

There is one and only one deep stain on the memory of this eminent man. It is melancholy to think that he, who had acted so great a part in the Convention, could have afterwards stooped to hold communication with Saint Germains. The fact cannot be disputed: yet for him there are excuses which cannot be pleaded for others who were guilty of the same crime. He did not, like Marlborough, Russell, and Godolphin, betray a master by whom he was trusted, and with whose benefits he was loaded. It was by the ingratitude and malice of the Whigs that he was driven to take shelter for a moment among the Jacobites. It may be added that he soon repented of the error into which he had been hurried by passion, that, though never reconciled

to the Court, he distinguished himself by his zeal for the vigorous prosecution of the war, and that his last work was a tract in which he
exhorted his countrymen to remember that the public burdens, heavy
as they might seem, were light when compared with the yoke of
France and of Rome.[1]

About a fortnight after the death of Halifax, a fate far more cruel
than death befell his old rival and enemy, the Lord President. That
able, ambitious and daring statesman was again hurled down from
power. In his first fall, terrible as it was, there had been something of
dignity ; and he had, by availing himself with rare skill of an extraordinary crisis in public affairs, risen once more to the most elevated
position among English subjects. The second ruin was indeed less
violent than the first : but it was ignominious and irretrievable.

The peculation and venality by which the official men of that age
were in the habit of enriching themselves had excited in the public mind
a feeling such as could not but vent itself, sooner or later, in Parliament-
some formidable explosion. But the gains were immediate : ary enquiries
the day of retribution was uncertain ; and the plunderers of into the corruption of the
the public were as greedy and as audacious as ever, when the public offices
vengeance, long threatened and long delayed, suddenly overtook the
proudest and most powerful among them.

The first mutterings of the coming storm did not at all indicate the
direction which it would take, or the fury with which it would burst. An
infantry regiment, which was quartered at Royston, had levied contributions on the people of that town and of the neighbourhood. The sum
exacted was not large. In France or Brabant the moderation of the
demand would have been thought wonderful. But to English shopkeepers and farmers military extortion was happily quite new and quite
insupportable. A petition was sent up to the Commons. The Commons
summoned the accusers and the accused to the bar. It soon appeared
that a grave offence had been committed, but that the offenders were
not altogether without excuse. The public money which had been
issued from the Exchequer for their pay and subsistence had been
fraudulently detained by their colonel and by his agent. It was not
strange that men who had arms, and who had not necessaries, should
trouble themselves little about the Petition of Right and the Declaration
of Right. But it was monstrous that, while the citizen was heavily taxed
for the purpose of paying to the soldier the largest military stipend
known in Europe, the soldier should be driven by absolute want to
plunder the citizen. This was strongly set forth in a representation
which the Commons laid before William. William, who had been long
struggling against abuses which grievously impaired the efficiency of his

[1] An Essay upon Taxes, calculated for the present Juncture of Affairs, 1693.

army, was glad to have his hands thus strengthened. He promised ample redress, cashiered the offending colonel, gave strict orders that the troops should receive their due regularly, and established a military board for the purpose of detecting and punishing such malpractices as had taken place at Royston.[1]

But the whole administration was in such a state that it was hardly possible to track one offender without discovering ten others. In the course of the enquiry into the conduct of the troops at Royston, it was discovered that a bribe of two hundred guineas had been received by Henry Guy, member of Parliament for Heydon and Secretary of the Treasury. Guy was instantly sent to the Tower, not without much exultation on the part of the Whigs : for he was one of those tools who had passed, together with the buildings and furniture of the public offices, from James to William : he affected the character of a High Churchman ; and he was known to be closely connected with some of the heads of the Tory party, and especially with Trevor.[2]

Another name, which was afterwards but too widely celebrated, first became known to the public at this time. James Craggs had begun life as a barber. He had then been a footman. His abilities, eminently vigorous, though not improved by education, had raised him in the world ; and he was now entering on a career which was destined to end, after many years of prosperity, in unutterable misery and despair. He had become an army clothier. He was examined as to his dealings with the colonels of regiments ; and, as he obstinately refused to produce his books, he was sent to keep Guy company in the Tower.[3]

A few hours after Craggs had been thrown into prison, a committee, which had been appointed to enquire into the truth of a petition signed by some of the hackney coachmen of London, laid on the table of the House a report which excited universal disgust and indignation. It appeared that these poor hardworking men had been cruelly wronged by the board under the authority of which an Act of the preceding session had placed them. They had been pillaged and insulted, not only by the commissioners, but by one commissioner's lacquey and by another

---

[1] Commons' Journals, Jan. 12., Feb. 26., Mar. 6. ; A Collection of the Debates and Proceedings in Parliament in 1694 and 1695 upon the Inquiry into the late Briberies and Corrupt Practices, 1695 ; L'Hermitage to the States General, March $\frac{8}{18}$. ; Van Citters, Mar. $\frac{15}{25}$. ; L'Hermitage says : " Si par cette recherche la chambre pouvoit remédier au désordre qui règne, elle rendroit un service très utile et très agréable au Roy."

[2] Commons' Journals, Feb. 16. 1695 ; Collection of the Debates and Proceedings in Parliament in 1694 and 1695 ; Life of Wharton ; Burnet, ii. 144.

[3] Speaker Onslow's note on Burnet, ii. 583. ; Commons' Journals, Mar. 6, 7. 1695. The history of the terrible end of this man will be found in the pamphlets of the South Sea year.

JAMES CRAGGS

From an engraving by G. Vertue, after a painting by Sir G. Kneller

commissioner's harlot. The Commons addressed the King ; and the King turned the delinquents out of their places.[1]

But by this time delinquents far higher in power and rank were beginning to be uneasy. At every new detection, the excitement, both within and without the walls of Parliament, became more intense. The frightful prevalence of bribery, corruption, and extortion was every where the subject of conversation. A contemporary pamphleteer compares the state of the political world at this conjuncture to the state of a city in which the plague has just been discovered, and in which the terrible words, "Lord have mercy on us," are already seen on some doors.[2] Whispers, which at another time would have speedily died away and been forgotten, now swelled, first into murmurs, and then into clamours. A rumour rose and spread that the funds of the two wealthiest corporations in the kingdom, the City of London and the East India Company, had been largely employed for the purpose of corrupting great men ; and the names of Trevor, Seymour, and Leeds were mentioned.

The mention of these names produced a stir in the Whig ranks. Trevor, Seymour, and Leeds were all three Tories, and had, in different ways, greater influence than perhaps any other three Tories in the kingdom. If they could all be driven at once from public life with blasted characters, the Whigs would be completely predominant both in the Parliament and in the Cabinet.

Wharton was not the man to let such an opportunity escape him. At White's, no doubt, among those lads of quality who were his pupils in politics and in debauchery, he would have laughed heartily at the fury with which the nation had on a sudden begun to persecute men for doing what every body had always done and was always trying to do. But, if people would be fools, it was the business of a statesman to make use of their folly. The cant of political purity was not so familiar to the lips of Wharton as blasphemy and ribaldry : but his abilities were so versatile, and his impudence so consummate, that he ventured to appear before the world as an austere patriot mourning over the venality and perfidy of a degenerate age. While he, animated by that fierce party spirit, which in honest men would be thought a vice, but which in him was almost a virtue, was eagerly stirring up his friends to demand an enquiry into the truth of the evil reports which were in circulation, the subject was suddenly and strangely forced forward. It chanced that, while a bill of little interest was under discussion in the Commons, the postman arrived with numerous letters directed to members ; and the distribution took place at the bar with a buzz of conversation which

---

[1] Commons' Journals, March 8, 1695 ; Exact Collection of Debates and Proceedings in Parliament in 1694 and 1695 ; L'Hermitage, March $\frac{8}{18}$.

[2] Exact Collection of Debates.

drowned the voices of the orators. Seymour, whose imperious temper always prompted him to dictate and to chide, lectured the talkers on the scandalous irregularity of their conduct, and called on the Speaker to reprimand them. An angry discussion followed; and one of the offenders was provoked into making an allusion to the stories which were current about both Seymour and the Speaker. " It is undoubtedly improper to talk while a bill is under discussion : but it is much worse to take money for getting a bill passed. If we are extreme to mark a slight breach of form, how severely ought we to deal with that corruption which is eating away the very substance of our institutions !" That was enough : the spark had fallen : the train was ready : the explosion was immediate and terrible. After a tumultuous debate, in which the cry of " the Tower" was repeatedly heard, Wharton managed to carry his point. Before the House rose a committee was appointed to examine the books of the City of London and of the East India Company.[1]

Foley was placed in the chair of the committee. Within a week he reported that the Speaker, Sir John Trevor, had, in the preceding session, received from the City a thousand guineas for expediting a local bill. This discovery gave great satisfaction to the Whigs, who had always hated Trevor, and was not unpleasing to many of the Tories. During six busy sessions his sordid rapacity had made him an object of general aversion. The legitimate emoluments of his post amounted to about four thousand a year : but it was believed that he had pocketed at least ten thousand a year.[2] His profligacy and insolence united had been too much even for the angelic temper of Tillotson. It was said that the gentle Archbishop had been heard to mutter something about a knave as the Speaker passed by him.[3] Yet, great as were the offences of this bad man, his punishment was fully proportioned to them. As soon as the report of the committee had been read, it was moved that he had been guilty of a high crime and misdemeanour. He had to stand up and to put the question. There was a loud cry of Aye. He called on the Noes ; and scarcely a voice was heard. He was forced to declare that the Ayes had it. A man of spirit would have given up the ghost with remorse and shame ; and the unutterable ignominy of that moment left its mark even on the callous heart and brazen forehead of Trevor. Had he returned to the House on the following day, he would have had to put the question on a motion for his own expulsion. He therefore pleaded illness, and shut himself up in his bedroom. Wharton soon

Vote of censure on the Speaker

---

[1] Life of Wharton, 1715 ; L'Hermitage, March ⁸⁄₁₈. 1695. L'Hermitage's narrative is confirmed by the Journals, March 7. 169⁴⁄₅, from which it appears that, just before the committee was appointed, the House resolved that letters should not be delivered out to members during a sitting.

[2] L'Hermitage, Mar. ¹⁹⁄₂₈. 1695.   [3] Birch's Life of Tillotson.

brought down a royal message authorising the Commons to elect another Speaker.

The Whig chiefs wished to place Sir Thomas Littleton in the chair : but they were unable to accomplish their object. Foley was chosen, presented, and approved. Though he had of late generally voted with the Tories, he still called himself a Whig, and was not unacceptable to many of the Whigs. He had both the abilities and the knowledge which were necessary to enable him to preside over the debates with dignity ; but what, in the peculiar circumstances in which the House then found itself placed, was not unnaturally considered as his principal recommendation, was that implacable hatred of jobbery and corruption which he somewhat ostentatiously professed, and doubtless sincerely felt. On the day after he entered on his functions, his predecessor was expelled.[1]

Foley elected Speaker

The indiscretion of Trevor had been equal to his baseness ; and his guilt had been apparent on the first inspection of the accounts of the City. The accounts of the East India Company were more obscure. The committee reported that they had sate in Leadenhall Street, had examined documents, had interrogated directors and clerks, but had been unable to arrive at the bottom of the mystery of iniquity. Some most suspicious entries had been discovered, under the head of special service. The expenditure on this account had, in the year 1693, exceeded eighty thousand pounds. It was proved that, as to the outlay of this money, the directors had placed implicit confidence in the governor, Sir Thomas Cook. He had merely told them in general terms that he had been at a charge of twenty three thousand, of twenty five thousand, of thirty thousand pounds, in the matter of the Charter ; and his colleagues had, without calling on him for any detailed explanation, thanked him for his care, and ordered warrants for these great sums to be instantly made out. It appeared that a few mutinous directors had murmured at this immense outlay, and had called for a detailed statement. But the only answer which they had been able to extract from Cook was that there were some great persons whom it was necessary to gratify.

Enquiry into the accounts of the East India Company

The committee also reported that they had lighted on an agreement by which the Company had covenanted to furnish a person named Colston with two hundred tons of saltpetre. At the first glance, this transaction seemed merchantlike and fair. But it was soon discovered that Colston was merely an agent for Seymour. Suspicion was excited. The complicated terms of the

Suspicious dealings of Seymour

---

[1] Commons' Journals, March 12, 13, 14, 15, 16., 169⁴⁄₅ ; Vernon to Lexington, March 15. ; L'Hermitage, March ¹⁶⁄₂₆.

bargain were severely examined, and were found to be framed in such a manner that, in every possible event, Seymour must be a gainer and the Company a loser to the extent of ten or twelve thousand pounds. The opinion of all who understood the matter was that the contract was merely a disguise intended to cover a bribe.   But the disguise was so skilfully managed that the country gentlemen were perplexed, and that even the lawyers doubted whether there were such evidence of corruption as would be held sufficient by a court of justice.   Seymour escaped without a vote of censure, and still continued to take a leading part in the debates of the Commons.[1]   But the authority which he had long exercised in the House and in the western counties of England, though not destroyed, was visibly diminished ; and, to the end of his life, his traffic in saltpetre was a favourite theme of Whig pamphleteers and poets.[2]

The escape of Seymour only inflamed the ardour of Wharton and of Wharton's confederates.   They were determined to discover what had been done with the eighty or ninety thousand pounds of secret service money which had been entrusted to Cook by the East India Company.   Cook, who was member for Colchester, was questioned in his place : he refused to answer : he was sent to the Tower ; and a bill was brought in providing that if, before a certain day, he should not acknowledge the whole truth, he should be incapable of ever holding any office, should refund to the Company the whole of the immense sum which had been confided to him, and should pay a fine of twenty thousand pounds to the Crown.   Rich as he was, these penalties would have reduced him to penury.   The Commons were in such a temper that they passed the bill without a single division.[3]   Seymour, indeed, though his saltpetre contract was the talk of the whole town, came forward with unabashed forehead to plead for his accomplice: but his effrontery only injured the cause which he defended.[4] In the Upper House the bill was condemned in the strongest terms by the Duke of Leeds.   Pressing his hand on his heart, he declared, on his faith, on his honour, that he had no personal interest in the question, and that he was actuated by no motive but a pure love of justice.   His

Bill against Sir Thomas Cook

---

[1] On vit qu'il étoit impossible de le poursuivre en justice, chacun toutefois démeurant convaincu que c'étoit un marché fait à la main pour lui faire présent de la somme de 10,000l., et qu'il avoit été plus habile que les autres novices que n'avoient pas su faire si finement leurs affaires.—L'Hermitage, $\frac{\text{March 29.}}{\text{April 8.}}$.   Commons' Journals, March 12. ; Vernon to Lexington, April 26. ; Burnet, ii. 145.

[2] In a poem called the Prophecy (1703), is the line
                "When Seymour scorns saltpetre pence."
In another satire is the line
                " Bribed Seymour bribes accuses."

[3] Commons' Journals from March 26. to April 8. 1695.   [4] L'Hermitage, April $\frac{19}{29}$. 1695.

eloquence was powerfully seconded by the tears and lamentations of Cook, who, from the bar, implored the Peers not to subject him to a species of torture unknown to the mild laws of England. "Instead of this cruel bill," he said, " pass a bill of indemnity ; and I will tell you all." The Lords thought his request not altogether unreasonable. After some communication with the Commons, it was determined that a joint committee of the two Houses should be appointed to enquire into the manner in which the secret service money of the East India Company had been expended ; and an Act was rapidly passed providing that, if Cook would make to this committee a true and full discovery, he should be indemnified for the crimes which he might confess, and that, till he made such a discovery, he should remain in the Tower. To this arrangement Leeds gave in public all the opposition that he could with decency give. In private those who were conscious of guilt employed numerous artifices for the purpose of averting enquiry. It was whispered that things might come out which every good Englishman would wish to hide, and that the greater part of the enormous sums which had passed through Cook's hands had been paid to Portland for His Majesty's use. But the Parliament and the nation were determined to know the truth, whoever might suffer by the disclosure.[1]

As soon as the Bill of Indemnity had received the royal assent, the joint committee, consisting of twelve lords and twenty four members of the House of Commons, met in the Exchequer Chamber. Wharton was placed in the chair ; and in a few hours great discoveries were made.

Enquiry by a joint committee of Lords and Commons

The King and Portland came out of the enquiry with unblemished honour. Not only had not the King taken any part of the secret service money dispensed by Cook ; but he had not, during some years, received even the ordinary present which the Company had, in former reigns, laid annually at the foot of the throne. It appeared that not less than fifty thousand pounds had been offered to Portland, and rejected. The money lay during a whole year ready to be paid to him if he should change his mind. He at length told those who pressed this immense bribe on him, that, if they persisted in insulting him by such an offer, they would make him an enemy of their Company. Many people wondered at the probity which he showed on this occasion, for he was generally thought interested and grasping. The truth seems to be that he loved money, but that he was a man of strict integrity and honour. He took, without scruple, whatever he thought that he could honestly take, but was incapable of stooping to an act of baseness. Indeed, he resented as affronts the compliments which were paid him on this occasion.[2]

[1] Exact Collection of Debates and proceedings.

[2] L'Hermitage, $\frac{\text{Apr'l 30.}}{\text{May 10.}}$ 1695 ; Portland to Lexington, $\frac{\text{April 23.}}{\text{May 3.}}$

The integrity of Nottingham could excite no surprise. Ten thousand pounds had been offered to him, and had been refused. The number of cases in which bribery was fully made out was small. A large part of the sum which Cook had drawn from the Company's treasury had probably been embezzled by the brokers whom he had employed in the work of corruption; and what had become of the rest it was not easy to learn from the reluctant witnesses who were brought before the committee. One glimpse of light however was caught: it was followed; and it led to a discovery of the highest moment. A large sum was traced from Cook to an agent named Firebrace, and from Firebrace to another agent named Bates, who was well known to be closely connected with the High Church party and especially with Leeds. Bates was summoned: but he absconded: messengers were sent in pursuit of him: he was caught, brought into the Exchequer Chamber and sworn. The story which he told showed that he was distracted between the fear of losing his ears and the fear of injuring his patron. He owned that he had undertaken to bribe Leeds, had been for that purpose furnished with five thousand five hundred guineas, which were then worth at least eight thousand pounds, had offered those guineas to His Grace, and had, by His Grace's permission, left them long at His Grace's house in the care of a Swiss named Robart, who was His Grace's confidential man of business. It should seem that these facts admitted of only one interpretation. Bates however swore that the Duke had refused to accept a farthing. "Why then," it was asked, "was the gold left, by his permission, at his house and in the hands of his servant?" "Because," answered Bates, "I am bad at telling coin. I therefore begged His Grace to let me leave the pieces, in order that Robart might count them for me; and His Grace was so good as to consent." It was evident that, if this strange story had been true, the guineas would, in a few hours, have been taken away. But Bates was forced to confess that they had remained half a year where he had left them. The money had indeed at last,—and this was one of the most suspicious circumstances in the case,—been paid back by Robart on the very morning on which the committee first met in the Exchequer Chamber. Who could believe that, if the transaction had been free from all taint of corruption, the money would have been detained as long as Cook was able to remain silent, and would have been refunded on the very first day on which he was under the necessity of speaking out?[1]

A few hours after the examination of Bates, Wharton reported to the Commons what had passed in the Exchequer Chamber. The

---

[1] L'Hermitage ($\frac{\text{April 30.}}{\text{May 10.}}$ 1695) justly remarks, that the way in which the money was sent back strengthened the case against Leeds.

indignation was general and vehement. "You now understand," said Wharton, "why obstructions have been thrown in our way at every step,

Impeach-
ment of
Leeds

why we have had to wring out truth drop by drop, why His Majesty's name has been artfully used to prevent us from going into an enquiry which has brought nothing to light but what is to His Majesty's honour. Can we think it strange that our difficulties should have been great, when we consider the power, the dexterity, the experience of him who was secretly thwarting us? It is time for us to prove signally to the world that it is impossible for any criminal to double so cunningly that we cannot track him, or to climb so high that we cannot reach him. Never was there a more flagitious instance of corruption. Never was there an offender who had less claim to indulgence. The obligations which the Duke of Leeds has to his country are of no common kind. One great debt we generously cancelled : but the manner in which our generosity has been requited forces us to remember that he was long ago impeached for receiving money from France. How can we be safe while a man proved to be venal has access to the royal ear? Our best laid enterprises have been defeated. Our inmost counsels have been betrayed. And what wonder is it? Can we doubt that, together with this home trade in charters, a profitable foreign trade in secrets is carried on? Can we doubt that he who sells us to one another will, for a good price, sell us all to the common enemy?" Wharton concluded by moving that Leeds should be impeached of high crimes and misdemeanours.[1]

Leeds had many friends and dependents in the House of Commons : but they could say little. Wharton's motion was carried without a division ; and he was ordered to go to the bar of the Lords, and there, in the name of the Commons of England, to impeach the Duke. But, before this order could be obeyed, it was announced that His Grace was at the door and requested an audience.

While Wharton had been making his report to the Commons, Leeds had been haranguing the Lords. He denied with the most solemn asseverations that he had taken any money for himself. But he acknowledged, and indeed almost boasted, that he had abetted Bates in getting money from the Company, and seemed to think that this was a service which any man in power might be reasonably expected to render to a friend. Too many persons, indeed, in that age, made a most absurd and pernicious distinction between a minister who used his influence to obtain presents for himself and a minister who used his influence to obtain presents for his dependents. The former was corrupt : the latter was merely goodnatured. Leeds proceeded to tell,

---

[1] There can, I think, be no doubt, that the member who is called D in the Exact Collection was Wharton.

The most Noble and Mighty Prince
THOMAS, DUKE OF LEEDS, MARQUIS OF CARMARTHEN, EARLE OF DANBY,
Viscount Latimer, Baron Osborne of Kiveton, L.ᵈ President of His Ma.ᵗⁱᵉˢ most Hon.ᵇˡᵉ Privy Councel
L.ᵈ Leiutenant of the three Rideings of Yorkshire, Govern.ʳ of the Town & Fort of Kingston upon Hull
And Knight of the most Noble Order of the Garter.

THOMAS OSBORNE, DUKE OF LEEDS

From an engraving by R. White

with great complacency, a story about himself, which would, in our days, drive a public man, not only out of office, but out of the society of gentlemen. "When I was Treasurer, in King Charles's time, my Lords, the excise was to be farmed. There were several bidders. Harry Savile, for whom I had a great value, informed me that they had asked for his interest with me, and begged me to tell them that he had done his best for them. 'What!' said I: 'tell them all so, when only one can have the farm?' 'No matter;' said Harry: 'tell them all so; and the one who gets the farm will think that he owes it to me.' The gentlemen came. I said to every one of them separately, 'Sir, you are much obliged to Mr. Savile:' 'Sir, Mr. Savile has been much your friend.' In the end Harry got a handsome present; and I wished him good luck with it. I was his shadow then. I am Mr. Bates's shadow now."

The Duke had hardly related this anecdote, so strikingly illustrative of the state of political morality in that generation, when it was whispered to him that a motion to impeach him had been made in the House of Commons. He hastened thither: but, before he arrived, the question had been put and carried. Nevertheless he pressed for admittance; and he was admitted. A chair, according to ancient usage, was placed for him within the bar; and he was informed that the House was ready to hear him.

He spoke, but with less tact and judgment than usual. He magnified his own public services. But for him, he said, there would have been no House of Commons to impeach him; a boast so extravagant that it naturally made his hearers unwilling to allow him the praise which his conduct at the time of the Revolution really deserved. As to the charge against him he said little more than that he was innocent, that there had long been a malicious design to ruin him, that he would not go into particulars, that the facts which had been proved would bear two constructions, and that of the two constructions the more favourable ought in candour to be adopted. He withdrew, after praying the House to reconsider the vote which had just been passed, or, if that could not be, to let him have speedy justice.

His friends felt that his speech was no defence: they therefore did not attempt to rescind the resolution which had been carried just before he was heard. Wharton, with a large following, went up to the Lords, and informed them that the Commons had resolved to impeach the Duke. A committee of managers was appointed to draw up the articles and to prepare the evidence.[1]

[1] As to the proceedings of this eventful day, April 27. 1695, see the Journals of the two Houses, and the Exact Collection.

The articles were speedily drawn : but to the chain of evidence one link appeared to be wanting. That link Robart, if he had been severely examined and confronted with other witnesses, would in all probability have been forced to supply. He was summoned to the bar of the Commons. A messenger went with the summons to the house of the Duke of Leeds, and was there informed that the Swiss was not within, that he had been three days absent, and that where he was the porter could not tell. The Lords immediately presented an address to the King, requesting him to give orders that the ports might be stopped and the fugitive arrested. But Robart was already in Holland on his way to his native mountains.

The flight of this man made it impossible for the Commons to proceed. They vehemently accused Leeds of having sent away the witness who alone could furnish legal proof of that which was already established by moral proof. Leeds, now at ease as to the event of the impeachment, gave himself the airs of an injured man. "My Lords," he said, " the conduct of the Commons is without precedent. They impeach me of a high crime : they promise to prove it : then they find that they have not the means of proving it ; and they revile me for not supplying them with the means. Surely they ought not to have brought a charge like this, without well considering whether they had or had not evidence sufficient to support it. If Robart's testimony be, as they now say, indispensable, why did they not send for him and hear his story before they made up their minds ? They may thank their own intemperance, their own precipitancy, for his disappearance. He is a foreigner : he is timid : he hears that a transaction in which he has been concerned has been pronounced by the House of Commons to be highly criminal, that his master is impeached, that his friend Bates is in prison, that his own turn is coming. He naturally takes fright : he escapes to his own country ; and, from what I know of him, I will venture to predict that it will be long before he trusts himself again within reach of the Speaker's warrant. But what is that to me ? Am I to lie all my life under the stigma of an accusation like this, merely because the violence of my accusers has scared their own witness out of England ? I demand an immediate trial. I move your Lordships to resolve that, unless the Commons shall proceed before the end of the session, the impeachment shall be dismissed." A few friendly voices cried out " Well moved." But the Peers were generally unwilling to take a step which would have been in the highest degree offensive to the Lower House, and to the great body of those whom that House represented. The Duke's motion fell to the ground ; and a few hours later the Parliament was prorogued.[1]

[1] Exact Collection ; Lords' Journals, May 3. 1695 ; Commons' Journals, May 2, 3. L'Hermitage, May $\frac{3}{13}$.; London Gazette, May 13.

The impeachment was never revived.   The evidence which would warrant a formal verdict of guilty was not forthcoming ; and a formal

Disgrace of Leeds

verdict of guilty would hardly have answered Wharton's purpose better than the informal verdict of guilty which the whole nation had already pronounced.   The work was done.   The Whigs were dominant.   Leeds was no longer chief minister, was indeed no longer a minister at all.   William, from respect probably for the memory of the beloved wife whom he had lately lost, and to whom Leeds had shown peculiar attachment, avoided every thing that could look like harshness.   The fallen statesman was suffered to retain during a considerable time the title of Lord President, and to walk on public occasions between the Great Seal and the Privy Seal.   But he was told that he would do well not to show himself at Council : the business and the patronage even of the department of which he was the nominal head passed into other hands ; and the place which he ostensibly filled was considered in political circles as really vacant.[1]

He hastened into the country, and hid himself there, during some months, from the public eye.   When the Parliament met again, however, he emerged from his retreat.   Though he was well stricken in years and cruelly tortured by disease, his ambition was still as ardent as ever. With indefatigable energy he began a third time to climb, as he flattered himself, towards that dizzy pinnacle which he had twice reached, and from which he had twice fallen.   He took a prominent part in debate : but, though his eloquence and knowledge always secured to him the attention of his hearers, he was never again, even when the Tory party was in power, admitted to the smallest share in the direction of affairs.

There was one great humiliation which he could not be spared. William was about to take the command of the army in the Netherlands : and it was necessary that, before he sailed, he should determine by whom the government should be administered during his absence.   Hitherto Mary had acted as his vicegerent when he was out of England : but she was gone.   He therefore delegated his authority to seven Lords Justices,

Lords Justices appointed

Tenison, Archbishop of Canterbury, Somers, Keeper of the Great Seal, Pembroke, Keeper of the Privy Seal, Devonshire, Lord Steward, Dorset, Lord Chamberlain, Shrewsbury, Secretary of State, and Godolphin, First Commissioner of the Treasury.   It is easy to judge from this list of names which way the balance of power was now leaning.   Godolphin alone of the seven was a Tory.   The Lord President, still second in rank, and a few days before first in power, of the great lay dignitaries of the realm, was passed over ; and the omission was universally regarded as an official announcement of his disgrace.[2]

[1] L'Hermitage, May $\frac{10}{20}$. 1695 ; Vernon to Shrewsbury, June 22. 1697.
[2] London Gazette, May 6. 1695.

THE SEVEN LORDS JUSTICES

From an engraving by R. White

There were some who wondered that the Princess of Denmark was not appointed Regent.   The reconciliation, which had been begun while Mary was dying, had since her death been, in external show at least, completed.   This was one of those occasions on which Sunderland was peculiarly qualified to be useful.   He was admirably fitted to manage personal negotiations, to soften resentment, to sooth wounded pride, to select, among all the objects of human desire, the very bait which was most likely to allure the mind with which he was dealing.   On this occasion his task was not difficult.   He had two excellent assistants, Marlborough in the household of Anne, and Somers in the cabinet of William.

Marlborough was now as desirous to support the government as he had once been to subvert it.   The death of Mary had produced a complete change in all his schemes.   There was one event to which he looked forward with the most intense longing, the accession of the Princess to the English throne.   It was certain that, from the day on which she began to reign, he would be in her Court all that Buckingham had been in the Court of James the First.   Marlborough too must have been conscious of powers of a very different order from those which Buckingham had possessed, of a genius for politics not inferior to that of Richelieu, of a genius for war not inferior to that of Turenne. Perhaps the disgraced General, in obscurity and inaction, anticipated the day when his power to help and hurt in Europe would be equal to that of her mightiest princes, when he would be servilely flattered and courted by Cæsar on one side and by Lewis the Great on the other, and when every year would add another hundred thousand pounds to the largest fortune that had ever been accumulated by any English subject. All this might be if Mrs. Morley were Queen.   But that Mr. Freeman should ever see Mrs. Morley Queen had till lately been not very probable. Mary's life was a much better life than his, and quite as good a life as her sister's.   That William would have issue seemed unlikely.   But it was generally expected that he would soon die.   His widow might marry again, and might leave children who would succeed her.   In these circumstances, Marlborough might well think that he had very little interest in maintaining that settlement of the Crown which had been made by the Convention.   Nothing was so likely to serve his purpose as confusion, civil war, another revolution, another abdication, another vacancy of the throne.   Perhaps the nation, incensed against William, yet not reconciled to James, and distracted between hatred of foreigners and hatred of Jesuits, might prefer to the Dutch King and to the Popish King one who was at once a native of our country and a member of our Church.   That this was the real explanation of Marlborough's dark and complicated plots was, as we have seen, firmly

His Excellency John Duke of Marlborough, Prince of the Holy Empire, Marquis of Blanford, Earl of Marlborough, Baron Churchill, of Sandridge and Baron Churchill, of Aumouth, Captain General of all Her Majesty's Forces, Master General of the Ordnance, One of the Lords of Her Majesty's most Honourable Privy Council and Knight of the most Noble Order of the Garter, Her Majesty's Ambassador Extraordinary and Plenipotentiary to the States General of the United Provinces & General of the Confederate Armies.

J. Closterman pinxit Ano. 1706   J. Simon fecit   Cum Privilegio   Sold by E. Cooper at the 3 Pigeons in Bedford Street Covent Garden.

JOHN CHURCHILL, DUKE OF MARLBOROUGH

From a mezzotint by J. Simon, after a painting by J. Closterman

believed by some of the most zealous Jacobites, and is in the highest degree probable. It is certain that during several years he had spared no efforts to inflame the army and the nation against the government. But all was now changed. Mary was no more. By the Bill of Rights the crown was entailed on Anne after the death of William. The death of William could not be far distant. Indeed all the physicians who attended him wondered that he was still alive; and, when the risks of war were added to the risks of disease, the probability seemed to be that in a few months he would be in his grave. Marlborough saw that it would now be madness to throw every thing into disorder and to put every thing to hazard. He had done his best to shake the throne while it seemed unlikely that Anne would ever mount it except by violent means. But he did his best to fix it firmly, as soon as it became highly probable that she would soon be called to fill it in the regular course of nature and of law.

The Princess was easily induced by the Churchills to write to the King a submissive and affectionate letter of condolence. The King, who was never much inclined to engage in a commerce of insincere compliments, and who was still in the first agonies of his grief, showed little disposition to meet her advances. But Somers, who felt that every thing was at stake, went to Kensington, and made his way into the royal closet. William was sitting there, so deeply sunk in melancholy that he did not seem to perceive that any person had entered the room. The Lord Keeper, after a respectful pause, broke silence, and, doubtless with all that cautious delicacy which was characteristic of him, and which eminently qualified him to touch the sore places of the mind without hurting them, implored His Majesty to be reconciled to the Princess. "Do what you will," said William: "I can think of no business." Thus authorised, the mediators speedily concluded a treaty.[1] Anne came to Kensington, and was graciously received: she was lodged in Saint James's Palace: a guard of honour was again placed at her door; and the Gazettes again, after a long interval, announced that foreign ministers had had the honour of being presented to her.[2] The Churchills were again permitted to dwell under the royal roof. But William did not at first include them in the peace which he had made with their mistress. Marlborough remained excluded from military and political employment; and it was not without much difficulty that he was admitted into the circle at Kensington, and permitted to kiss the royal hand.[3] The feeling with which he was regarded

---

[1] Letter from Mrs. Burnet to the Duchess of Marlborough, 1704, quoted by Coxe; Shrewsbury to Russell, January 24. 1695; Burnet, ii. 149.

[2] London Gazette, April 8. 15. 29. 1695.

[3] Shrewsbury to Russell, January 24. 1695; Narcissus Luttrell's Diary.

by the King explains why Anne was not appointed Regent. The Regency of Anne would have been the Regency of Marlborough ; and it is not strange that a man whom it was not thought safe to entrust with any office in the State or the army should not have been entrusted with the whole government of the kingdom.

Had Marlborough been of a proud and vindictive nature, he might have been provoked into raising another quarrel in the royal family, and into forming new cabals in the army. But all his passions, except ambition and avarice, were under strict regulation. He was destitute alike of the sentiment of gratitude and of the sentiment of revenge. He had conspired against the government while it was loading him with favours. He now supported it, though it requited his support with contumely. He perfectly understood his own interest : he had perfect command of his temper : he endured decorously the hardships of his present situation, and contented himself by looking forward to a reversion which would amply repay him for a few years of patience. He did not indeed immediately cease to correspond with the Court of Saint Germains : but the correspondence gradually became more and more slack, and seems, on his part, to have been made up of vague professions and trifling excuses.

The event which had changed all Marlborough's views had filled the minds of fiercer and more pertinacious politicians with wild hopes and atrocious projects.

During the two years and a half which followed the execution of Grandval, no serious design had been formed against the life of William. Some hotheaded malecontents indeed laid schemes for kidnapping or murdering him : but those schemes were not, while his wife lived, countenanced by her father. James did not feel, and, to do him justice, was not such a hypocrite as to pretend to feel, any scruple about removing his enemies by those means which he had justly thought base and wicked when employed by his enemies against himself. If any such scruple had arisen in his mind, there was no want, under his roof, of casuists willing and competent to sooth his conscience with sophisms such as had corrupted the far nobler natures of Anthony Babington and Everard Digby. To question the lawfulness of assassination, in cases where assassination might promote the interests of the Church, was to question the authority of the most illustrious Jesuits, of Bellarmine and Suarez, of Molina and Mariana : nay, it was to rebel against the Chair of Saint Peter. One Pope had walked in procession at the head of his cardinals, had proclaimed a jubilee, had ordered the guns of Saint Angelo to be fired, in honour of the perfidious butchery in which Coligni had perished. Another Pope had in a solemn allocution

Jacobite plots against William's person

applied to the murder of Henry the Third of France rapturous language borrowed from the ode of the prophet Habakkuk, and had extolled the murderer above Eleazar and Judith.[1] William was regarded at Saint Germains as a monster compared with whom Coligni and Henry the Third were saints. Nevertheless James, during some years, refused to sanction any attempt on his nephew's person. The reasons which he assigned for his refusal have come down to us, as he wrote them with his own hand. He did not affect to think that assassination was a sin which ought to be held in horror by a Christian, or a villany unworthy of a gentleman : he merely said that the difficulties were great, and that he would not push his friends on extreme danger when it would not be in his power to second them effectually.[2] In truth, while Mary lived, it might well be doubted whether the murder of her husband would really be a service to the Jacobite cause. By his death the government would lose indeed the strength derived from his eminent personal qualities, but would at the same time be relieved from the load of his personal unpopularity. His whole power would at once devolve on his widow ; and the nation would probably rally round her with enthusiasm. If her political abilities were not equal to his, she had not his repulsive manners, his foreign pronunciation, his partiality for every thing Dutch and for every thing Calvinistic. Many, who had thought her culpably wanting in filial piety, would be of opinion that now at least she was absolved from all duty to a father stained with the blood of her husband. The whole machinery of the administration would continue to work without that interruption which ordinarily followed a demise of the Crown. There would be no dissolution of the Parliament, no suspension of any tax : commissions would retain their force ; and all that James would have gained by the fall of his enemy would have been a barren revenge.

The death of the Queen changed every thing. If a dagger or a bullet should now reach the heart of William, it was probable that there would instantly be general anarchy. The Parliament and the Privy Council would cease to exist. The authority of ministers and judges would expire with him from whom it was derived. It seemed not improbable that at such a moment a restoration might be effected without a blow.

Scarcely therefore had Mary been laid in the grave when restless and unprincipled men began to plot in earnest against the life of William.

Charnock

Foremost among these men in parts, in courage, and in energy, was Robert Charnock. He had been liberally educated, and had, in the late reign, been a fellow of Magdalene College, Oxford.

---

[1] De Thou, liii. xcvi.

[2] Life of James, ii. 545., Orig. Mem. Of course James does not use the word assassination. He talks of the seizing and carrying away of the Prince of Orange.

Alone in that great society he had betrayed the common cause, had consented to be the tool of the High Commission, had publicly apostatised from the Church of England, and, while his college was a Popish seminary, had held the office of Vice President. The Revolution came, and altered at once the whole course of his life. Driven from the quiet cloister and the old grove of oaks on the bank of the Cherwell, he sought haunts of a very different kind. During several years he led the perilous and agitated life of a conspirator, passed and repassed on secret errands between England and France, changed his lodgings in London often, and was known at different coffeehouses by different names. His services had been requited with a captain's commission signed by the banished King.

With Charnock was closely connected George Porter, an adventurer who called himself a Roman Catholic and a Royalist, but who was in truth destitute of all religious and of all political principle. **Porter** Porter's friends could not deny that he was a rake and a coxcomb, that he drank, that he swore, that he told extravagant lies about his amours, and that he had been convicted of manslaughter for a stab given in a brawl at the playhouse. His enemies affirmed that he was addicted to nauseous and horrible kinds of debauchery, and that he procured the means of indulging his infamous tastes by cheating and marauding; that he was one of a gang of clippers; that he sometimes got on horseback late in the evening and stole out in disguise, and that, when he returned from these mysterious excursions, his appearance justified the suspicion that he had been doing business on Hounslow Heath or Finchley Common.[1]

Cardell Goodman, popularly called Scum Goodman, a knave more abandoned, if possible, than Porter, was in the plot. Goodman had been on the stage, had been kept, like some much greater men, by **Goodman** the Duchess of Cleveland, had been taken into her house, had been loaded by her with gifts, and had requited her by bribing an Italian quack to poison two of her children. As the poison had not been administered, Goodman could be prosecuted only for a misdemeanour. He was tried, convicted, and sentenced to a ruinous fine. He had since distinguished himself as one of the first forgers of bank notes.[2]

Sir William Parkyns, a wealthy knight bred to the law, who had been conspicuous among the Tories in the days of the **Parkyns** Exclusion Bill, was one of the most important members of the confederacy. He bore a much fairer character than most of his

[1] Every thing bad that was known or rumoured about Porter came out in the course of the State Trials of 1696.

[2] As to Goodman see the evidence on the trial of Peter Cook; Van Cleverskirke, $\frac{Feb. 28.}{March 9.}$ 1696; L'Hermitage, April $\frac{19}{29}$. 1696; and a pasquinade entitled the Duchess of Cleveland's Memorial.

accomplices : but in one respect he was more culpable than any of them.   For he had, in order to retain a lucrative office which he held in the Court of Chancery, sworn allegiance to the Prince against whose life he now conspired.

The design was imparted to Sir John Fenwick, celebrated on account of the cowardly insult which he had offered to the deceased Queen. **Fenwick** Fenwick, if his own assertion is to be trusted, was willing to join in an insurrection, but recoiled from the thought of assassination, and showed so much of what was in his mind as sufficed to make him an object of suspicion to his less scrupulous associates. He kept their secret, however, as strictly as if he had wished them success.

It should seem that, at first, a natural feeling restrained the conspirators from calling their design by the proper name.   Even in their private consultations they did not as yet talk of killing the Prince of Orange.   They would try to seize him and to carry him alive into France.   If there were any resistance they might be forced to use their swords and pistols, and nobody could be answerable for what a thrust or a shot might do.   In the spring of 1695, the scheme of assassination, thus thinly veiled, was communicated to James, and his sanction was earnestly requested.   But week followed week ; and no answer arrived from him.   He doubtless remained silent in the hope that his adherents would, after a short delay, venture to act on their own responsibility, and that he might thus have the advantage without the scandal of their crime. They seem indeed to have so understood him.   He had not, they said, authorised the attempt : but he had not prohibited it ; and, apprised as he was of their plan, the absence of prohibition was a sufficient warrant. They therefore determined to strike : but before they could make the necessary arrangements William set out for Flanders ; and the plot against his life was necessarily suspended till his return.

It was on the twelfth of May that the King left Kensington for Gravesend, where he proposed to embark for the Continent.   Three days **Session of the Scottish Parliament** before his departure the Parliament of Scotland had, after a recess of about two years, met again at Edinburgh.   Hamilton, who had, in the preceding session, sate on the throne and held the sceptre, was dead ; and it was necessary to find a new Lord High Commissioner.   The person selected was John Hay, Marquess of Tweeddale, Chancellor of the Realm, a man grown old in business, well informed, prudent, humane, blameless in private life, and, on the whole, as respectable as any Scottish peer who had been long and deeply concerned in the politics of those troubled times.

His task was not without difficulty.   It was indeed well known that the Estates were generally inclined to support the government.   But it

JOHN HAY, MARQUIS OF TWEEDDALE

From a mezzotint by J. Smith, after a painting by Sir G. Kneller

was also well known that there was one matter which would require the most dexterous and cautious management.　The cry of the blood shed

more than three years before in Glencoe had at length made itself heard.　Towards the close of the year 1693, the reports, which had at first been contemptuously derided as factious calumnies, began to be thought deserving of serious attention.　Many people, who were little disposed to place confidence in any thing that came forth from the secret presses of the Jacobites, owned that, for the honour of the government, some enquiry ought to be instituted.　The amiable Mary had been much shocked by what she had heard.　William had, at her request, empowered the Duke of Hamilton and several other Scotchmen of note to investigate the whole matter.　But the Duke died: his colleagues were slack in the performance of their duty; and the King, who knew little and cared little about Scotland, forgot to urge them.[1]

It now appeared that the government would have done wisely as well as rightly by anticipating the wishes of the country.　The horrible story repeated by the nonjurors pertinaciously, confidently, and with so many circumstances as almost enforced belief, had at length roused all Scotland.　The sensibility of a people eminently patriotic was galled by the taunts of southern pamphleteers, who asked whether there was on the north of the Tweed no law, no justice, no humanity, no spirit to demand redress even for the foulest wrongs.　Each of the two extreme parties, which were diametrically opposed to each other in general politics, was impelled by a peculiar feeling to call for enquiry.　The Jacobites were delighted by the prospect of being able to make out a case which would bring discredit on the usurper, and which might be set off against the many offences imputed by the Whigs to Dundee and Mackenzie.　The zealous Presbyterians were not less delighted at the prospect of being able to ruin the Master of Stair.　They had never forgotten or forgiven the service which he had rendered to the House of Stuart in the time of the persecution.　They knew that, though he had cordially concurred in the political revolution which had freed them from the hated dynasty, he had seen with displeasure that ecclesiastical revolution which was, in their view, even more important.　They knew that church government was with him merely an affair of State, and that, looking at it as an affair of State, he preferred the episcopal to the synodical model.　They could not without uneasiness see so adroit and eloquent an enemy of pure religion constantly attending the royal steps, and constantly breathing counsel in the royal ear.　They were therefore impatient for an investigation, which, if one half of what was rumoured were true, must produce revelations fatal to the power and fame of the

[1] See the preamble to the Commission of 1695.

minister whom they distrusted. Nor could that minister rely on the cordial support of all who held office under the Crown. His genius and influence had excited the jealousy of many less successful courtiers, and especially of his fellow secretary, Johnstone.

Thus, on the eve of the meeting of the Scottish Parliament, Glencoe was in the mouths of Scotchmen of all factions and of all sects. William, who was just about to start for the Continent, learned that, on this subject, the Estates must have their way, and that the best thing that he could do would be to put himself at the head of a movement which it was impossible for him to resist. A Commission authorising Tweeddale and several other privy councillors to examine fully into the matter about which the public mind was so strongly excited was signed by the King at Kensington, was sent down to Edinburgh, and was there sealed with the Great Seal of the realm. This was accomplished just in time.[1] The Parliament had scarcely entered on business when a member rose to move for an enquiry into the circumstances of the slaughter of Glencoe. Tweeddale was able to inform the Estates that His Majesty's goodness had prevented their desires, that a Commission of Precognition had, a few hours before, passed in all the forms, and that the lords and gentlemen named in that instrument would hold their first meeting before night.[2] The Parliament unanimously voted thanks to the King for this instance of his paternal care : but some of those who joined in the vote of thanks expressed a very natural apprehension that the second investigation might end as unsatisfactorily as the first investigation had ended. The honour of the country, they said, was at stake ; and the Commissioners were bound to proceed with such diligence that the result of the inquest might be known before the end of the session. Tweeddale gave assurances which, for a time, silenced the murmurers.[3] But, when three weeks had passed away, many members became mutinous and suspicious. On the fourteenth of June it was moved that the Commissioners should be ordered to report. The motion was not carried : but it was renewed day after day. In three successive sittings Tweeddale was able to restrain the eagerness of the assembly. But, when he at length announced that the report had been completed, and added that it would not be laid before the Estates till it had been submitted to the King, there was a violent outcry. The public curiosity was intense : for the examination had been conducted with closed doors ; and both Commissioners and clerks had been sworn to secrecy. The King was in the Netherlands. Weeks must elapse before his pleasure could be

[1] The Commission will be found in the Minutes of the Parliament.
[2] Act. Parl. Scot., May 21. 1695 ; London Gazette, May 30.
[3] Act. Parl. Scot., May 23. 1695.

taken; and the session could not last much longer. In a fourth debate there were signs which convinced the Lord High Commissioner that it was expedient to yield; and the report was produced.[1]

It is a paper highly creditable to those who framed it, an excellent digest of evidence, clear, passionless, and austerely just. No source from which valuable information was likely to be derived had been neglected. Glengarry and Keppoch, though notoriously disaffected to the government, had been permitted to conduct the case on behalf of their unhappy kinsmen. Several of the Macdonalds who had escaped from the havoc of that night had been examined, and among them the reigning Mac Ian, the eldest son of the murdered Chief. The correspondence of the Master of Stair with the military men who commanded in the Highlands had been subjected to a strict but not unfair scrutiny. The conclusion to which the Commissioners came, and in which every intelligent and candid enquirer will concur, was that the slaughter of Glencoe was a barbarous murder, and that of this murder the letters of the Master of Stair were the sole warrant and cause.

That Breadalbane was an accomplice in the crime was not proved: but he did not come off quite clear. In the course of the investigation it was incidentally discovered that he had, while distributing the money of William among the Highland Chiefs, professed to them the warmest zeal for the interest of James, and advised them to take what they could get from the usurper, but to be constantly on the watch for a favourable opportunity of bringing back the rightful King. Breadalbane's defence was that he was a greater villain than his accusers imagined, and that he had pretended to be a Jacobite only in order to get at the bottom of the Jacobite plans. In truth the depths of this man's knavery were unfathomable. It was impossible to say which of his treasons were, to borrow the Italian classification, single treasons, and which double treasons. On this occasion the Parliament supposed him to have been guilty only of a single treason, and sent him to the Castle of Edinburgh. The government, on full consideration, gave credit to his assertion that he had been guilty of a double treason, and let him out again.[2]

The Report of the Commission was taken into immediate consideration by the Estates. They resolved, without one dissentient voice, that the order signed by William did not authorise the slaughter of Glencoe. They next resolved, but, it should seem, not unanimously, that the slaughter was a murder.[3] They proceeded to pass several votes, the sense of which was finally summed up in an address to the

[1] Act. Parl. Scot., June 14. 18. 20. 1695.; London Gazette, June 27.

[2] Burnet, ii. 157.; Act. Parl., June 10. 1695.

[3] Act. Parl., June 26. 1695; London Gazette, July 4.

King. How that part of the address which related to the Master of Stair should be framed was a question about which there was much debate. Several of his letters were called for and read ; and several amendments were put to the vote. The Jacobites and the extreme Presbyterians were, with but too good cause, on the side of severity. The majority, however, under the skilful management of the Lord High Commissioner, acquiesced in words which made it impossible for the guilty minister to retain his office, but which did not impute to him such criminality as would have affected his life or his estate. They censured him, but censured him in terms far too soft. They blamed his immoderate zeal against the unfortunate clan, and his warm directions about performing the execution by surprise. His excess in his letters they pronounced to have been the original cause of the massacre : but, instead of demanding that he should be brought to trial as a murderer, they declared that, in consideration of his absence and of his great place, they left it to the royal wisdom to deal with him in such a manner as might vindicate the honour of the government.

The indulgence which was shown to the principal offender was not extended to his subordinates. Hamilton, who had fled, and had been vainly cited by proclamation at the City Cross to appear before the Estates, was pronounced not to be clear of the blood of the Glencoe men. Glenlyon, Captain Drummond, Lieutenant Lindsay, and Serjeant Barbour, were still more distinctly designated as murderers ; and the King was requested to command the Lord Advocate to prosecute them.

The Parliament of Scotland was undoubtedly, on this occasion, severe in the wrong place and lenient in the wrong place. The cruelty and baseness of Glenlyon and his comrades excite, even after the lapse of a hundred and sixty years, emotions which make it difficult to reason calmly. Yet whoever can bring himself to look at the conduct of these men with judicial impartiality will probably be of opinion that they could not, without great detriment to the commonwealth, have been treated as assassins. They had slain nobody whom they had not been positively directed by their commanding officer to slay. That subordination without which an army is the worst of all rabbles would be at an end, if every soldier were to be held answerable for the justice of every order in obedience to which he pulls his trigger. The case of Glencoe was doubtless an extreme case : but it cannot easily be distinguished in principle from cases which, in war, are of ordinary occurrence. Very terrible military executions are sometimes indispensable. Humanity itself may require them. Who then is to decide whether there be an emergency such as makes severity the truest mercy ? Who is to determine whether it be or be not necessary to lay a thriving town in ashes, to decimate a large body of mutineers, to shoot a whole gang of banditti? Is the responsibility with the commanding officer, or with the rank and file whom he orders to make ready, present, and fire? And if the general rule be that the responsibility is with the commanding officer, and not with those who obey him, is it possible to find any reason for pronouncing the case of Glencoe an exception to that rule? It is remarkable that no member of the Scottish Parliament proposed that any of the private men of Argyle's regiment should be prosecuted for murder. Absolute impunity was granted to every body below the rank of Serjeant. Yet on what principle? Surely, if military obedience was not a valid plea, every man who shot a Macdonald on that horrible night was a murderer. And, if military obedience was a valid plea for the musketeer who acted by order of Serjeant Barbour, why not for Barbour who acted by order of Glenlyon? And why not for Glenlyon who acted by order of Hamilton? It can scarcely be maintained that more deference is due from a private to a noncommissioned officer than from a noncommissioned officer to his captain, or from a captain to his colonel.

It may be said that the orders given to Glenlyon were of so peculiar a nature that, if he had been a virtuous man, he would have thrown up his commission, would have braved the displeasure of colonel, general, and Secretary of State, would have incurred the heaviest penalty which a Court Martial could inflict, rather than have performed the part assigned to him; and this is perfectly true: but the question is not whether he acted like a virtuous man, but whether he did that for which the government could, without infringing a rule essential to the discipline of camps and to the security of nations, hang him as a murderer. In this case, disobedience was assuredly a moral duty: but it does not follow that obedience was a legal crime.

It seems therefore that the guilt of Glenlyon and his fellows was not within the scope of the penal law. The only punishment which could properly be inflicted on them was that which made Cain cry out that it was greater than he could bear; to be vagabonds on the face of the earth, and to carry wherever they went a mark from which even bad men should turn away sick with horror.

It was not so with the Master of Stair. He had been solemnly pronounced, both by the Commission of Precognition and by the Estates of the Realm in full Parliament, to be the original author of the massacre. That it was not advisable to make examples of his tools was the strongest reason for making an example of him. Every argument which can be urged against punishing the soldier who executes the unjust and inhuman orders of his superior is an argument for punishing with the utmost rigour of the law the superior with whom the unjust and inhuman orders originate. Where there can be no responsibility

below, there should be double responsibility above.   What the Parliament of Scotland ought with one voice to have demanded was, not that
a poor illiterate serjeant, who was hardly more accountable than his own
halbert for the bloody work which he had done, should be hanged in
the Grassmarket, but that the real murderer, the most politic, the most
eloquent, the most powerful, of Scottish statesmen, should be brought to
a public trial, and should, if found guilty, die the death of a felon.
Nothing less than such a sacrifice could expiate such a crime.   Unhappily the Estates, by extenuating the guilt of the chief offender, and,
at the same time, demanding that his humble agents should be treated
with a severity beyond the law, made the stain which the massacre had
left on the honour of the nation broader and deeper than before.

    Nor is it possible to acquit the King of a great breach of duty.   It
is, indeed, highly probable that, till he received the report of his Commissioners, he had been very imperfectly informed as to the circumstances of the slaughter.   We can hardly suppose that he was much in
the habit of reading Jacobite pamphlets; and, if he did read them,
he would have found in them such a quantity of absurd and rancorous
invective against himself that he would have been very little inclined to
credit any imputation which they might throw on his servants.   He
would have seen himself accused, in one tract, of being a concealed
Papist, in another of having poisoned Jeffreys in the Tower, in a third
of having contrived to have Talmash taken off at Brest.   He would
have seen it asserted that, in Ireland, he once ordered fifty of his
wounded English soldiers to be burned alive.   He would have seen that
the unalterable affection which he felt from his boyhood to his death for
three or four of the bravest and most trusty friends that ever prince had
the happiness to possess was made a ground for imputing to him abomina-
tions as foul as those which are buried under the waters of the Dead Sea.
He might naturally be slow to believe frightful imputations thrown by
writers whom he knew to be habitual liars on a statesman whose abilities
he valued highly, and to whose exertions he had, on some great occasions, owed much.   But he could not, after he had read the documents
transmitted to him from Edinburgh by Tweeddale, entertain the slightest
doubt of the guilt of the Master of Stair.   To visit that guilt with
exemplary punishment was the sacred duty of a Sovereign who had
sworn, with his hand lifted up towards heaven, that he would, in his
kingdom of Scotland, repress, in all estates and degrees, all oppression,
and would do justice, without acceptance of persons, as he hoped for
mercy from the Father of all mercies.   William contented himself with
dismissing the Master from office.   For this great fault, a fault amounting
to a crime, Burnet tried to frame, not a defence, but an excuse.   He
would have us believe that the King, alarmed by finding how many

persons had borne a part in the slaughter of Glencoe, thought it better to grant a general amnesty than to punish one massacre by another. But this representation is the very reverse of the truth. Numerous instruments had doubtless been employed in the work of death : but they had all received their impulse, directly or indirectly, from a single mind. High above the crowd of offenders towered one offender, preeminent in parts, knowledge, rank, and power. In return for many victims immolated by treachery, only one victim was demanded by justice ; and it must ever be considered as a blemish on the fame of William that the demand was refused.

On the seventeenth of July the session of the Parliament of Scotland closed. The Estates had liberally voted such a supply as the poor country which they represented could afford. They had indeed been put into high good humour by the notion that they had found out a way of speedily making that poor country rich. Their attention had been divided between the enquiry into the slaughter of Glencoe and some specious commercial projects of which the nature will be explained and the fate related in a future chapter.

Meanwhile all Europe was looking anxiously towards the Low Countries. The great warrior, who had been victorious at Fleurus, at Steinkirk, and at Landen, had not left his equal behind him. But France still possessed Marshals well qualified for high command. Already Catinat and Boufflers had given proofs of skill, of resolution, and of zeal for the interests of the state. Either of those distinguished officers would have been a successor worthy of Luxemburg and an antagonist worthy of William : but their master, unfortunately for himself, preferred to both the Duke of Villeroy. The new general had been Lewis's playmate when they were both children, had then become a favourite, and had never ceased to be so. In those superficial graces for which the French aristocracy was then renowned throughout Europe, Villeroy was preeminent among the French aristocracy. His stature was tall, his countenance handsome, his manners nobly and somewhat haughtily polite, his dress, his furniture, his equipages, his table, magnificent. No man told a story with more vivacity: no man sate his horse better in a hunting party : no man made love with more success : no man staked and lost heaps of gold with more agreeable unconcern : no man was more intimately acquainted with the adventures, the attachments, the enmities of the lords and ladies who daily filled the halls of Versailles. There were two characters especially which this fine gentleman had studied during many years, and of which he knew all the plaits and windings, the character of the King, and the character of her who was Queen in every thing but name. But there ended Villeroy's acquirements. He was profoundly ignorant both of

War in the Netherlands: Marshal Villeroy

Monsieur le Mareschal de Villeroy

G. Valck. excud.   Cum Privil. Ord. Holl. et West-frisiæ

FRANÇOIS DE NEUVILLE, DUKE DE VILLEROY AND MARSHAL OF FRANCE

From a mezzotint by G. Valck

books and of business.   At the Council Board he never opened his
mouth without exposing himself.   For war he had not a single qualification except that personal courage which was common to him with the
whole class of which he was a member.   At every great crisis of his
political and of his military life he was alternately drunk with arrogance
and sunk in dejection.   Just before he took a momentous step his self-
confidence was boundless : he would listen to no suggestion : he would
not admit into his mind the thought that failure was possible.   On the
first check he gave up every thing for lost, became incapable of directing,
and ran up and down in helpless despair.   Lewis however loved him;
and he, to do him justice, loved Lewis.   The kindness of the master
was proof against all the disasters which were brought on his kingdom
by the rashness and weakness of the servant ; and the gratitude of the
servant was honourably, though not judiciously, manifested on more
than one occasion after the death of the master.[1]

Such was the general to whom the direction of the campaign in the
Netherlands was confided.   The Duke of Maine was sent to learn the
art of war under this preceptor.   Maine, the natural son of
Lewis by the Marchioness of Montespan, had been brought
up from childhood by Madame de Maintenon, and was loved by Lewis
with the love of a father, by Madame de Maintenon with the not less
tender love of a foster mother.   Grave men were scandalised by the
ostentatious manner in which the King, while making a high profession
of piety, exhibited his partiality for this offspring of a double adultery.
Kindness, they said, was doubtless due from a parent to a child : but
decency was also due from a Sovereign to his people.   In spite of these
murmurs the youth had been publicly acknowledged, loaded with wealth
and dignities, created a Duke and Peer, placed, by an extraordinary
act of royal power, above Dukes and Peers of older creation, married
to a Princess of the blood royal, and appointed Grand Master of the
Artillery of the realm.   With abilities and courage he might have
played a great part in the world.   But his intellect was small : his
nerves were weak ; and the women and priests who had educated him
had effectually assisted nature.   He was orthodox in belief, correct in
morals, insinuating in address, a hypocrite, a mischiefmaker, and a
coward.

It was expected at Versailles that Flanders would, during this year,
be the chief theatre of war.   Here, therefore, a great army was collected.
Strong lines were formed from the Lys to the Scheld, and Villeroy
fixed his headquarters near Tournay.   Boufflers, with about twelve
thousand men, guarded the banks of the Sambre.

The Duke
of Maine

---

[1] There is an excellent, though perhaps overcharged, portrait of Villeroy in Saint Simon's
Memoirs.

On the other side the British and Dutch troops, who were under William's immediate command, mustered in the neighbourhood of Ghent. The Elector of Bavaria, at the head of a great force, lay near Brussels. A smaller army, consisting chiefly of Brandenburghers, was encamped not far from Huy.

Early in June military operations commenced. The first movements of William were mere feints intended to prevent the French generals from suspecting his real purpose. He had set his heart on retaking Namur. The loss of Namur had been the most mortifying of all the disasters of a disastrous war. The importance of Namur in a military point of view had always been great, and had become greater than ever during the three years which had elapsed since the last siege. New works, the masterpieces of Vauban, had been added to the old defences which had been constructed with the utmost skill of Cohorn. So ably had the two illustrious engineers vied with each other and cooperated with nature that the fortress was esteemed the strongest in Europe. Over one of the gates had been placed a vaunting inscription which defied the allies to wrench the prize from the grasp of France.

William kept his own counsel so well that not a hint of his intention got abroad. Some thought that Dunkirk, some that Ypres was his object. The marches and skirmishes by which he disguised his design were compared by Saint Simon to the moves of a skilful chess player. Feuquieres, much more deeply versed in military science than Saint Simon, informs us that some of these moves were hazardous, and that such a game could not have been safely played against Luxemburg; and this is probably true: but Luxemburg was gone; and what Luxemburg had been to William, William now was to Villeroy.

While the King was thus employed, the Jacobites at home, being unable, in his absence, to prosecute their design against his person, contented themselves with plotting against his government. Jacobite plots against the government during William's absence They were somewhat less closely watched than during the preceding year: for the event of the trials at Manchester had discouraged Aaron Smith and his agents. Trenchard, whose vigilance and severity had made him an object of terror and hatred, was no more, and had been succeeded, in what may be called the subordinate Secretaryship of State, by Sir William Trumball, a learned civilian and an experienced diplomatist, of moderate opinions, and of temper cautious to timidity.[1] The malecontents were emboldened by the lenity of the administration. William had scarcely sailed for the Continent when they held a great meeting at one of their favourite haunts, the Old King's Head in Leadenhall Street. Charnock, Porter, Goodman, Parkyns, and Fenwick were present. The

[1] Some curious traits of Trumball's character will be found in Pepys's Tangier Diary.

Louis Auguste de Bourbon Duc du Maine

se vend a Paris chez A. Trouvain rue S.t Jacques au grand Monarque attenant les Mathurins auec priuil. du Roy.

LOUIS AUGUSTE DE BOURBON, DUC DU MAINE

From an engraving by Trouvain

LOUIS ALEXANDRE DE BOURBON, COMTE DE TOULOUSE

From an engraving by Trouvain

Earl of Ailesbury was there, a man whose attachment to the exiled house was notorious, but who always denied that he had ever thought of effecting a restoration by immoral means.   His denial would be entitled to more credit if he had not, by taking the oaths to the government against which he was constantly intriguing, forfeited the right to be considered as a man of conscience and honour.   In the assembly was Sir John Friend, a nonjuror, who had indeed a very slender wit, but who had made a very large fortune by brewing, and who spent it freely in sedition.   After dinner,—for the plans of the Jacobite party were generally laid over wine, and generally bore some trace of the conviviality in which they had originated,—it was resolved that the time was come for an insurrection and a French invasion, and that a special messenger should carry the sense of the meeting to Saint Germains.   Charnock was selected.   He undertook the commission, crossed the Channel, saw James, and had interviews with the ministers of Lewis, but could arrange nothing.   The English malecontents would not stir till ten thousand French troops were in the island ; and ten thousand French troops could not, without great risk, be withdrawn from the army which was contending against William in the Low Countries.   When Charnock returned to report that his embassy had been unsuccessful, he found some of his confederates in gaol.   They had during his absence amused themselves, after their fashion, by trying to raise a riot in London on the tenth of June, the birthday of the unfortunate Prince of Wales.   They met at a tavern in Drury Lane, and, when hot with wine, sallied forth sword in hand, headed by Porter and Goodman, beat kettledrums, unfurled banners, and began to light bonfires.   But the watch, supported by the populace, was too strong for the revellers.   They were put to rout : the tavern where they had feasted was sacked by the mob : the ringleaders were apprehended, tried, fined, and imprisoned, but regained their liberty in time to bear a part in a far more criminal design.[1]

All was now ready for the execution of the plan which William had formed.   That plan had been communicated to the other chiefs of the allied forces, and had been warmly approved.   Vaudemont was left in Flanders with a considerable force to watch Villeroy.   The King, with the rest of his army, marched straight on Namur.   At the same moment the Elector of Bavaria advanced towards the same point on one side, and the Brandenburghers on another. So well had these movements been concerted, and so rapidly were they performed, that the skilful and energetic Boufflers had but just time to throw himself into the fortress.   He was accompanied by seven

Siege of Namur

[1] Postboy, June 13., July 9. 11., 1695 ; Intelligence Domestic and Foreign, June 14. ; Pacquet Boat from Holland and Flanders, July 9.

regiments of dragoons, by a strong body of gunners, sappers and miners, and by an officer named Megrigny, who was esteemed the

REDUCED FACSIMILE OF A LETTER FROM WILLIAM III TO THE PRINCE
DE VAUDEMONT, 11 JULY, 1695

From the British Museum. Add. MS. 21493, f. 5

best engineer in the French service with the exception of Vauban. A few hours after Boufflers had entered the place the besieging forces closed round it on every side ; and the lines of circumvallation were rapidly formed.

The news excited no alarm at the French Court. There it was not doubted that William would soon be compelled to abandon his enterprise with grievous loss and ignominy. The town was strong : the castle was believed to be impregnable : the magazines were filled with provisions and ammunition sufficient to last till the time at which the armies of that age were expected to retire into winter quarters : the garrison consisted of sixteen thousand of the best troops in the world : they were commanded by an excellent general : he was assisted by an excellent engineer ; nor was it doubted that Villeroy would march with his great army to the assistance of Boufflers, and that the besiegers would then be in much more danger than the besieged.

These hopes were kept up by the despatches of Villeroy. He proposed, he said, first to annihilate the army of Vaudemont, and then to drive William from Namur. Vaudemont might try to avoid an action ; but he could not escape. The Marshal went so far as to promise his master news of a complete victory within twenty four hours. Lewis passed a whole day in impatient expectation. At last, instead of an officer of high rank laden with English and Dutch standards, arrived a courier bringing news that Vaudemont had effected a retreat with scarcely any loss, and was safe under the walls of Ghent. William extolled the generalship of his lieutenant in the warmest terms. " My cousin," he wrote, " you have shown yourself a greater master of your art than if you had won a pitched battle." [1] In the French camp, however, and at the French Court, it was universally held that Vaudemont had been saved less by his own skill than by the misconduct of those to whom he was opposed. Some threw the whole blame on Villeroy ; and Villeroy made no attempt to vindicate himself. But it was generally believed that he might, at least to a great extent, have vindicated himself, had he not preferred royal favour to military renown. His plan, it was said, might have succeeded, had not the execution been entrusted to the Duke of Maine. At the first glimpse of danger the dastard's heart had died within him. He had not been able to conceal his poltroonery. He had stood trembling, stuttering, calling for his confessor, while the old officers round him, with tears in their eyes, urged him to advance. During a short time the disgrace of the son was concealed from the father. But the silence of Villeroy showed that there was a secret : the pleasantries of the Dutch gazettes soon elucidated the mystery ; and Lewis learned, if not the whole truth, yet enough to make him miserable. Never during his long reign had he been so moved. During some hours his gloomy irritability kept his

---

[1] Vaudemont's Despatch and William's Answer are in the Monthly Mercury for July 1695.

MENNO, BARON VON COEHORN

From a Dutch engraving in the Sutherland Collection

servants, his courtiers, even his priests, in terror.   He so far forgot the grace and dignity for which he was renowned throughout the world that, in the sight of all the splendid crowd of gentlemen and ladies who came to see him dine at Marli, he broke a cane on the shoulders of a lacquey, and pursued the poor man with the handle.[1]

The siege of Namur meanwhile was vigorously pressed by the allies. The scientific part of their operations was under the direction of Cohorn, who was spurred by emulation to exert his utmost skill.   He had suffered, three years before, the mortification of seeing the town, as he had fortified it, taken by his great master Vauban.   To retake it, now that the fortifications had received Vauban's last improvements, would be a noble revenge.

On the second of July the trenches were opened.   On the eighth a gallant sally of French dragoons was gallantly beaten back ; and, late on the same evening, a strong body of infantry, the English footguards leading the way, stormed, after a bloody conflict, the outworks on the Brussels side.   The King in person directed the attack ; and his subjects were delighted to learn that, when the fight was hottest, he laid his hand on the shoulder of the Elector of Bavaria, and exclaimed, " Look, look at my brave English ! "   Conspicuous in bravery even among those brave English was Cutts.   In that bulldog courage which flinches from no danger, however terrible, he was unrivalled.   There was no difficulty in finding hardy volunteers, German, Dutch and British, to go on a forlorn hope : but Cutts was the only man who appeared to consider such an expedition as a party of pleasure.   He was so much at his ease in the hottest fire of the French batteries that his soldiers gave him the honourable nickname of the Salamander.[2]

On the seventeenth the first counterscarp of the town was attacked. The English and Dutch were thrice repulsed with great slaughter, and returned thrice to the charge.   At length, in spite of the exertions of the French officers, who fought valiantly sword in hand on the glacis, the assailants remained in possession of the disputed works.   While the conflict was raging, William, who was giving his orders under a shower of bullets, saw with surprise and anger, among the officers of his staff, Michael Godfrey, the Deputy Governor of the Bank of England.   This gentleman had come to the King's headquarters in order to make some arrangements for the speedy and safe remittance of money from England to the army in the Netherlands, and was curious to see real war.   Such curiosity William could not endure.   " Mr. Godfrey," he said, " you ought

[1] See Saint Simon's Memoirs, and his note upon Dangeau.

[2] London Gazette, July 22. 1695 ; Monthly Mercury of August, 1695.   Swift, ten years later, wrote a lampoon on Cutts, so dull and so nauseously scurrilous that Ward or Gildon would have been ashamed of it, entitled the Description of a Salamander.

not to run these hazards : you are not a soldier : you can be of no use to us here." "Sir," answered Godfrey, "I run no more hazard than Your Majesty." "Not so," said William : "I am where it is my duty to be ; and I may without presumption commit my life to God's keeping : but you——" While they were talking a cannon ball from the ramparts laid Godfrey dead at the King's feet. It was not found however that the fear of being Godfreyed,—such was during some time the cant phrase,—sufficed to prevent idle gazers from coming to the trenches.[1] Though William .forbade his coachmen, footmen, and cooks to expose themselves, he repeatedly saw them skulking near the most dangerous spots and trying to get a peep at the fighting. He was sometimes, it is

MEDALS ON THE RECAPTURE OF NAMUR

said, provoked into horsewhipping them out of the range of the French guns ; and the story, whether true or false, is very characteristic.

On the twentieth of July the Bavarians and Brandenburghers, under the direction of Cohorn, made themselves masters, after a hard fight, of a line of works which Vauban had cut in the solid rock from the Sambre to the Meuse. Three days later, the English and Dutch, Cutts, as usual, in the front, lodged themselves on the second counterscarp. All was ready for a general assault, when a white flag was hung out from the ramparts. The effective strength of the garrison was now little more than one half of what it had been when the trenches were opened. Boufflers apprehended that it would be impossible for eight thousand men to defend the whole circuit of the walls much longer ; but he felt confident that such a force would be

Surrender of the town of Namur

---

[1] London Gazette, July 29. 1695 ; Monthly Mercury for August 1695 ; Stepney to Lord Lexington, Aug. $\frac{16}{26}$.; Robert Fleming's Character of King William, 1702. It was in the attack of July $\frac{17}{27}$. that Captain Shandy received the memorable wound in his groin.

sufficient to keep the stronghold on the summit of the rock. Terms of capitulation were speedily adjusted. A gate was delivered up to the allies. The French were allowed forty eight hours to retire into the castle, and were assured that the wounded men whom they left below about fifteen hundred in number, should be well treated. On the sixth the allies marched in. The contest for the possession of the town was over ; and a second and more terrible contest began for the possession of the citadel.[1]

Villeroy had in the meantime made some petty conquests. Dixmuyde, which might have offered some resistance, had opened its gates to him, not without grave suspicion of treachery on the part of the governor. Deynse, which was less able to make any defence, had followed the example. The garrisons of both towns were, in violation of a convention which had been made for the exchange of prisoners, sent into France. The Marshal then advanced towards Brussels in the hope, as it should seem, that, by menacing that beautiful capital, he might induce the allies to raise the siege of the castle of Namur. During thirty six hours he rained shells and redhot bullets on the city. The Electress of Bavaria, who was within the walls, miscarried from terror. Six convents perished. Fifteen hundred houses were at once in flames. The whole lower town would have been burned to the ground, had not the inhabitants stopped the conflagration by blowing up numerous buildings. Immense quantities of the finest lace and tapestry were destroyed : for the industry and trade which made Brussels famous throughout the world had hitherto been little affected by the war. Several of the stately piles which looked down on the market place were laid in ruins. The Town Hall itself, the noblest of the many noble senate houses reared by the burghers of the Netherlands, was in imminent peril. All this devastation, however, produced no effect except much private misery. William was not to be intimidated or provoked into relaxing the firm grasp with which he held Namur. The fire which his batteries kept up round the castle was such as had never been known in war. The French gunners were fairly driven from their pieces by the hail of balls, and forced to take refuge in vaulted galleries under the ground. Cohorn exultingly betted the Elector of Bavaria four hundred pistoles that the place would fall by the thirty-first of August, New Style. The great engineer lost his wager indeed, but lost it only by a few hours.[2]

Boufflers began to feel that his only hope was in Villeroy. Villeroy had proceeded from Brussels to Enghien : he had there collected all the

[1] London Gazette, Aug. 1. 5. 1695 ; Monthly Mercury of August 1695, containing the Letters of William and Dykvelt to the States General.

[2] Monthly Mercury for August 1695 ; Stepney to Lord Lexington, Aug. $\frac{13}{23}$.

French troops that could be spared from the remotest fortresses of the Netherlands; and he now, at the head of more than eighty thousand

THE EXECUTION OF THE GOVERNOR OF DIXMUYDE

From an engraving in the possession of the Editor

men, marched towards Namur. Vaudemont meanwhile joined the besiegers. William therefore thought himself strong enough to offer battle to Villeroy, without intermitting for a moment the operations against the castle. The Elector of Bavaria was entrusted with the immediate direction of the siege. The King of England took up, on the west of the town, a strong position strongly intrenched, and there awaited the French, who were advancing from Enghien. Every thing seemed to indicate that a great day was at hand. Two of the most numerous and best ordered armies that Europe had ever seen were brought face to face. On the fifteenth of August the defenders of the citadel saw from their watchtowers the mighty host of their countrymen. But between that host and Namur was drawn up in battle order the not less mighty host of William. Villeroy, by a salute of ninety guns, conveyed to Boufflers the promise of a speedy rescue; and at night Boufflers, by fire signals which were seen far over the vast plain of the Meuse and Sambre, urged Villeroy to fulfil that promise without delay. In the capitals both of France and England the anxiety was intense. Lewis shut himself up in his oratory, confessed, received the Eucharist, and gave orders that the host should be exposed in his chapel. His wife ordered all her nuns to their knees.[1] London was kept in a state of distraction by a succession of rumours, which sprang, some from the malice of Jacobites, and some from the avidity of stockjobbers. Early one morning it was confidently averred that there had been a battle, that the allies had been beaten, that the King had been killed, that the siege had been raised. The Exchange, as soon as it was opened, was filled to overflowing by people who came to learn whether the bad news was true. The streets were stopped up all day by groups of talkers and listeners. In the afternoon the Gazette, which had been impatiently expected, and which was eagerly read by thousands, calmed the excitement, but not completely: for it was known that the Jacobites sometimes received, by the agency of privateers and smugglers who put to sea in all weathers, intelligence earlier than that which came through regular channels to the Secretary of State at Whitehall. Before night, however, the agitation had altogether subsided: but it was suddenly revived by a bold imposture. A horseman in the uniform of the Guards spurred through the City, announcing that the King had been killed. He would probably have raised a serious tumult, had not some apprentices, zealous for the Revolution and the Protestant religion, knocked him down and carried him to Newgate. The confidential correspondent of the States General informed them that, in spite of all the stories which the disaffected party invented and circulated, the general persuasion was that the allies would be successful. The touchstone of sincerity in England, he said, was the betting. The Jacobites were ready enough to prove that William must be defeated, or to assert that he had been defeated: but

---

[1] Monthly Mercury for August 1695; Letter from Paris, $\frac{\text{Aug. 26.}}{\text{Sept. 5.}}$ 1695; among the Lexington Papers.

THE TOWN HALL OF BRUSSELS

From a photograph

they would not give the odds, and could hardly be induced to take any moderate odds. The Whigs, on the other hand, were ready to stake thousands of guineas on the conduct and good fortune of the King.[1]

The event justified the confidence of the Whigs and the backwardness of the Jacobites. On the sixteenth, seventeenth, and eighteenth of August the army of Villeroy and the army of William confronted each other. It was fully expected that the nineteenth would be the decisive day. The allies were under arms before dawn. At four William mounted, and continued till eight at night to ride from post to post, disposing his own troops and watching the movements of the enemy. The enemy approached his lines, in several places, near enough to see that it would not be easy to dislodge him : but there was no fighting. He lay down to rest, expecting to be attacked when the sun rose. But when the sun rose he found that the French had fallen back some miles. He immediately sent to request that the Elector would storm the castle without delay. While the preparations were making, Portland was sent to summon the garrison for the last time. It was plain, he said to Boufflers, that Villeroy had given up all hope of being able to raise the siege. It would therefore be an useless waste of life to prolong the contest. Boufflers however thought that another day of slaughter was necessary to the honour of the French arms ; and Portland returned unsuccessful.[2]

Early in the afternoon the assault was made in four places at once by four divisions of the confederate army. One point was assigned to the Brandenburghers, another to the Dutch, a third to the Bavarians, and a fourth to the English. The English were at first less fortunate than they had hitherto been. The truth is that most of the regiments which had seen service had marched with William to encounter Villeroy. As soon as the signal was given by the blowing up of two barrels of powder, Cutts, at the head of a small body of grenadiers, marched first out of the trenches with drums beating and colours flying. This gallant band was to be supported by four battalions which had never been in action, and which, though full of spirit, wanted the steadiness which so terrible a service required. The officers fell fast. Every Colonel, every Lieutenant Colonel, was killed or severely wounded. Cutts received a shot in the head which for a time disabled him. The raw recruits, left almost without direction, rushed forward impetuously till they found themselves in disorder and out of breath, with a precipice before them, under a terrible fire, and under a shower, scarcely less terrible, of fragments of rock and wall. They lost heart, and rolled

[1] L'Hermitage, Aug. 13/23. 1695.
[2] London Gazette, Aug. 26. 1695 ; Monthly Mercury ; Stepney to Lexington, Aug. 20/30.

FRANÇOIS DE NEUVILLE, DUKE DE VILLEROY AND MARSHAL OF FRANCE

From an engraving by G. Edelinck

back in confusion, till Cutts, whose wound had by this time been dressed, succeeded in rallying them. He then led them, not to the place from which they had been driven back, but to another spot where a fearful battle was raging. The Bavarians had made their onset gallantly but unsuccessfully : their general had fallen ; and they were beginning to waver, when the arrival of the Salamander and his men changed the fate of the day. Two hundred English volunteers, bent on retrieving at all hazards the disgrace of the recent repulse, were the first to force a way, sword in hand, through the palisades, to storm a battery which had made great havoc among the Bavarians, and to turn the guns against the garrison. Meanwhile the Brandenburghers, excellently disciplined and excellently commanded, had performed, with no great loss, the duty assigned to them. The Dutch had been equally successful. When the evening closed in the allies had made a lodgment of a mile in extent on the outworks of the castle. The advantage had been purchased by the loss of two thousand men.[1]

And now Boufflers thought that he had done all that his duty required. On the morrow he asked for a truce of forty eight hours in order that the hundreds of corpses, which choked the ditches, and which would soon have spread pestilence among both the besiegers and the besieged, might be removed and interred. His request was granted ; and, before the time expired, he intimated that he was disposed to capitulate. He would, he said, deliver up the castle in ten days, if he were not relieved sooner. He was informed that the allies would not treat with him on such terms, and that he must either consent to an immediate surrender, or prepare for an immediate assault. He yielded ; and it was agreed that he and his men should be suffered to depart, leaving the citadel, the artillery, and the stores to the conquerors. Three peals from all the guns of the confederate army notified to Villeroy the fall of the stronghold which he had vainly attempted to succour. He instantly retreated towards Mons, leaving William to enjoy undisturbed a triumph which was made more delightful by the recollection of many misfortunes.

The twenty-sixth of August was fixed for an exhibition such as the oldest soldier in Europe had never seen, and such as, a few weeks before,

Surrender of the castle of Namur

the youngest had scarcely hoped to see. From the first battle of Condé to the last battle of Luxemburg, the tide of military success had run, without any serious interruption, in one direction. That tide had turned. For the first time, men said, since France had Marshals, a Marshal of France was to deliver up a fortress to a victorious enemy.

[1] Boyer's History of King William III., 1703 ; London Gazette, Aug. 29. 1695 ; Stepney to Lexington, Aug. $\frac{29}{30}$. ; Blathwayt to Lexington, Sept. 2.

JOHN, LORD CUTTS

From a mezzotint by P. Schenck

The allied forces, foot and horse, drawn up in two lines, formed a magnificent avenue from the breach which had lately been so desperately contested to the bank of the Meuse. The Elector of Bavaria, the Landgrave of Hesse, and many distinguished officers were on horseback in the vicinity of the castle. William was near them in his coach. The garrison, reduced to about five thousand men, came forth with drums beating and ensigns flying. Boufflers and his staff closed the procession. There had been some difficulty about the form of the greeting which was to be exchanged between him and the allied Sovereigns. An Elector of Bavaria was hardly entitled to be saluted by the Marshal with the sword. A King of England was undoubtedly entitled to such a mark of respect : but France did not recognise William as King of England. At last Boufflers consented to perform the salute without

MEDALS ON THE RECAPTURE OF NAMUR AND THE BOMBARDMENT OF BRUSSELS

marking for which of the two princes it was intended. He lowered his sword. William alone acknowledged the compliment. A short conversation followed. The Marshal, in order to avoid the use of the words Sire and Majesty, addressed himself only to the Elector. The Elector, with every mark of deference, reported to William what had been said ; and William gravely touched his hat. The officers of the garrison carried back to their country the news that the upstart, who at Paris was designated only as Prince of Orange, was treated by the proudest potentates of the Germanic body with a respect as profound as that which Lewis exacted from the gentlemen of his bedchamber.[1]

The ceremonial was now over ; and Boufflers passed on : but he had proceeded but a short way when he was stopped by Dykvelt who accompanied the allied army as deputy from the States General.

Arrest of Boufflers "You must return to the town, Sir," said Dykvelt. "The King of England has ordered me to inform you that you are his prisoner." Boufflers was in transports of rage. His officers crowded round him,

[1] Postscript to the Monthly Mercury for August 1695 ; London Gazette, Sept. 9.; Saint Simon ; Dangeau.

and vowed to die in his defence.   But resistance was out of the question: a strong body of Dutch cavalry came up ; and the Brigadier who com-

WILLIAM III RECEIVING THE SURRENDER OF NAMUR

From a painting by J. Van Wyck, in the possession of Sir James H. Stronge, Bart.

manded them demanded the Marshal's sword.   The Marshal uttered indignant exclamations : " This is an infamous breach of faith.   Look at the terms of the capitulation.   What have I done to deserve such an affront ?   Have I not behaved like a man of honour ?   Ought I not to be treated as such ?   But beware what you do, gentlemen.   I serve a master who can and will avenge me."   " I am a soldier, Sir," answered the Brigadier ; " and my business is to obey orders without troubling myself about consequences."   Dykvelt calmly and courteously replied to the Marshal's indignant exclamations.   " The King of England has reluctantly followed the example set by your master.   The soldiers who garrisoned Dixmuyde and Deynse have, in defiance of plighted faith, been sent prisoners into France.   The Prince whom they serve would be wanting in his duty to them if he did not retaliate.   His Majesty might with perfect justice have detained all the French who were in Namur.   But he will not follow to such a length a precedent which he disapproves.   He has determined to arrest you and you alone ; and, Sir, you must not regard as an affront what is in truth a mark of his very particular esteem.   How can he pay you a higher compliment than by showing that he considers you as fully equivalent to the five or six thousand men whom your sovereign wrongfully holds in captivity ? Nay, you shall even now be permitted to proceed if you will give me your word of honour to return hither unless the garrisons of Dixmuyde and Deynse are released within a fortnight."   " I do not at all know," answered Boufflers, " why the King my master detains those men ; and therefore I cannot hold out any hope that he will liberate them.   You have an army at your back : I am alone ; and you must do your pleasure."   He gave up his sword, returned to Namur, and was sent thence to Huy, where he passed a few days in luxurious repose, was allowed to choose his own walks and rides, and was treated with marked respect by those who guarded him.   In the shortest time in which it was possible to post from the place where he was confined to the French Court and back again, he received full powers to promise that the garrisons of Dixmuyde and Deynse should be released.   He was instantly liberated ; and he set off for Fontainebleau, where an honourable reception awaited him.   He was created a Duke and a Peer.   That he might be able to support his new dignities a considerable sum of money was bestowed on him ; and, in the presence of the whole aristocracy of France, he was welcomed home by Lewis with an affectionate embrace.[1]

In all the countries which were united against France the news of the fall of Namur was received with joy : but here the exultation was greatest.   During several generations our ancestors had achieved nothing considerable by land against foreign enemies.   We had indeed occasionally furnished to our allies small bands of auxiliaries who had well

[1] Boyer, History of King William III., 1703 ; Postscript to the Monthly Mercury, Aug. 1695; London Gazette, Sept. 9. 12.; Blathwayt to Lexington, Sept. 6.; Saint Simon ; Dangeau.

maintained the honour of the nation.   But from the day on which the
two brave Talbots, father and son, had perished in the vain attempt to
reconquer Guienne, till the Revolution, there had been on the Continent

LOUIS, DUKE DE BOUFFLERS, AND MARSHAL OF FRANCE

From an engraving by C. Duflos

no campaign in which Englishmen had borne a principal part.   At
length our ancestors had again, after an interval of near two centuries
and a half, begun to dispute with the warriors of France the palm of

military prowess. The struggle had been hard. The genius of Luxemburg and the consummate discipline of the household troops of Lewis had prevailed in two great battles : but the event of those battles had been long doubtful : the victory had been dearly purchased ; and the victor had gained little more than the honour of remaining master of the field of slaughter. Meanwhile he was himself training his adversaries. The recruits who survived that severe tuition speedily became veterans. Steinkirk and Landen had formed the volunteers who followed Cutts through the palisades of Namur. The judgment of all the great warriors whom all the nations of Western Europe had sent to the confluence of the Sambre and the Meuse was that the English subaltern was inferior to no subaltern and the English private soldier to no private soldier in Christendom. The English officers of higher rank were thought hardly worthy to command such an army. Cutts, indeed, had distinguished himself by his intrepidity. But those who most admired him acknowledged that he had neither the capacity nor the science necessary to a general.

The joy of the conquerors was heightened by the recollection of the discomfiture which they had suffered, three years before, on the same spot, and of the insolence with which their enemy had then triumphed over them. They now triumphed in their turn. The Dutch struck medals. The Spaniards sang Te Deums. Many poems, serious and sportive, appeared, of which one only has lived. Prior burlesqued, with admirable spirit and pleasantry, the bombastic verses in which Boileau had celebrated the first taking of Namur. The two odes, printed side by side, were read with delight in London ; and the critics at Will's pronounced that, in wit as in arms, England had been victorious.

The fall of Namur was the great military event of this year. The Turkish war still kept a large part of the forces of the Emperor employed in indecisive operations on the Danube. Nothing deserving to be mentioned took place either in Piedmont or on the Rhine. In Catalonia the Spaniards obtained some slight advantages, advantages due to their English and Dutch allies, who seem to have done all that could be done to help a nation never much disposed to help itself. The maritime superiority of England and Holland was now fully established. During the whole summer Russell was the undisputed master of the Mediterranean, passed and repassed between Spain and Italy, bombarded Palamos, spread terror along the whole shore of Provence, and kept the French fleet imprisoned in the harbour of Toulon. Meanwhile Berkeley was the undisputed master of the Channel, sailed to and fro in sight of the coasts of Artois, Picardy, Normandy, and Britanny, threw shells into Saint Maloes, Calais, and Dunkirk, and burned Granville to the ground. The navy of Lewis, which, five years before, had been the most formidable in Europe, which had ranged the British seas unopposed from the Downs to the Land's End, which had anchored in Torbay, and had laid Teignmouth in ashes, now gave no sign of existence except by

ENGRAVED BROADSIDE CELEBRATING THE RECAPTURE OF NAMUR

From the Sutherland Collection

pillaging merchantmen which were unprovided with convoy. In this lucrative war the French privateers were, towards the close of the summer, very successful. Several vessels laden with sugar from Barbadoes were captured. The losses of the unfortunate East India Company, already surrounded by difficulties, and impoverished by boundless prodigality in corruption, were enormous. Five large ships returning from the Eastern seas, with cargoes of which the value was popularly estimated at a million, fell into the hands of the enemy. These misfortunes produced some murmuring on the Royal Exchange. But, on the whole, the temper of the capital and of the nation was better than it had been during some years.

Meanwhile events which no preceding historian has condescended to mention, but which were of far greater importance than the achievements of William's army or of Russell's fleet, were taking place in London. A great experiment was making. A great revolution was in progress. Newspapers had made their appearance.

While the Licensing Act was in force there was no newspaper in England except the London Gazette, which was edited by a clerk in the office of the Secretary of State, and which contained nothing but what the Secretary of State wished the nation to know. There were indeed many periodical papers : but none of those papers could be called a newspaper. Welwood, a zealous Whig, published a journal called the Observator : but his Observator, like the Observator which Lestrange had formerly edited, contained, not the news, but merely dissertations on politics. A crazy bookseller, named John Dunton, published the Athenian Mercury : but the Athenian Mercury merely discussed questions of natural philosophy, of casuistry and of gallantry. A fellow of the Royal Society, named John Houghton, published what he called a Collection for the Improvement of Industry and Trade : but his Collection contained little more than the prices of stocks, explanations of the modes of doing business in the City, puffs of new projects, and advertisements of books, quack medicines, chocolate, Spa water, civet cats, surgeons wanting ships, valets wanting masters, and ladies wanting husbands. If ever he printed any political news, he transcribed it from the Gazette. The Gazette was so partial and so meagre a chronicle of events that, though it had no competitors, it had but a small circulation. Only eight thousand copies were printed, much less than one to each parish in the kingdom. In truth a person who had studied the history of his own time only in the Gazette would have been ignorant of many events of the highest importance. He would, for example, have known nothing about the Court Martial on Torrington, the Lancashire Trials, the burning of the Bishop of Salisbury's Pastoral Letter, or the impeachment of the Duke of Leeds. But the deficiencies of the Gazette were to a certain extent supplied in London by the coffeehouses, and in the country by the newsletters.

On the third of May 1695 the law which had subjected the press to a censorship expired. Within a fortnight, a stanch old Whig, named

Effect of the emancipation of the English press

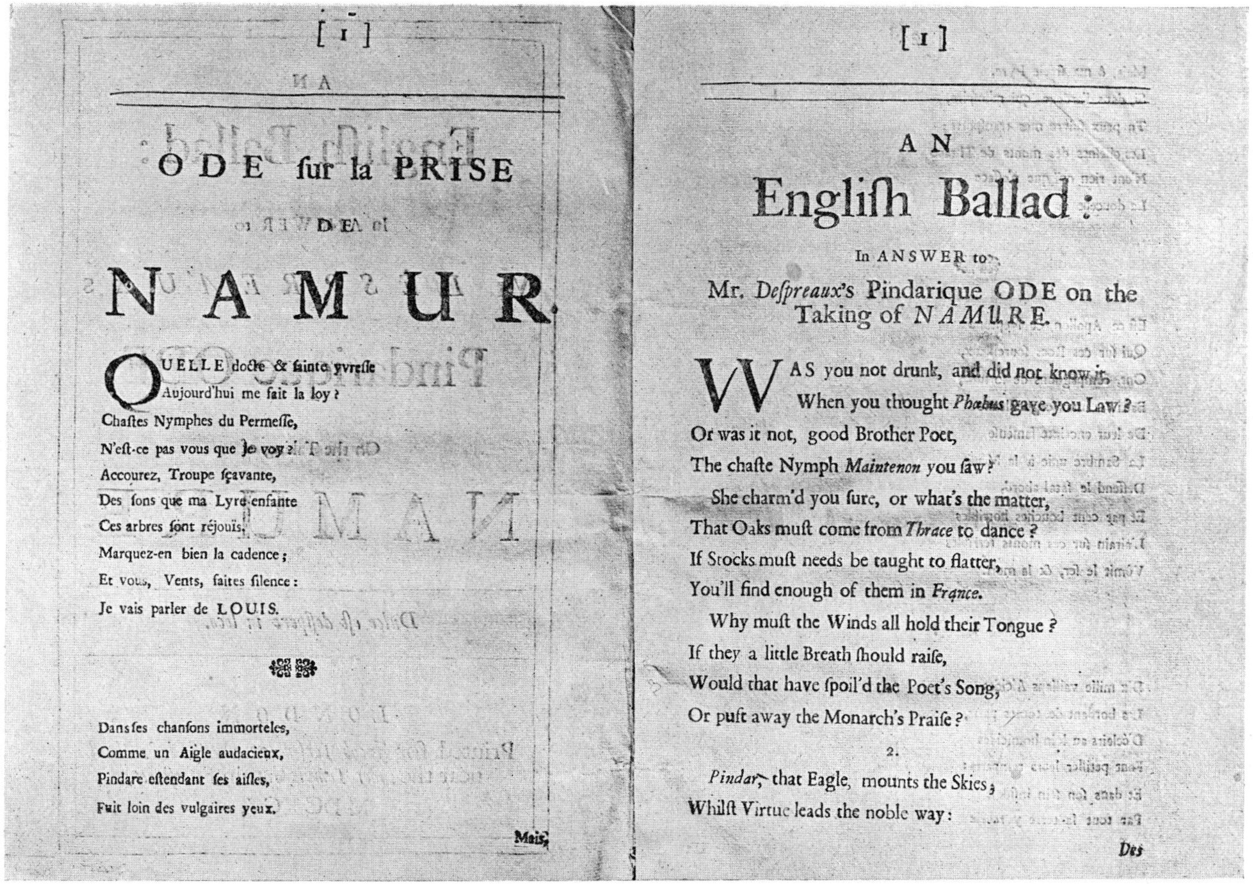

AN

Engliſh Ballad:

In ANSWER to

Mr. *Deſpreaux's* Pindarique ODE on the
Taking of *NAMURE.*

W AS you not drunk, and did not know it,
   When you thought *Phœbus* gave you Law?
Or was it not, good Brother Poet,
   The chaſte Nymph *Maintenon* you ſaw?
She charm'd you ſure, or what's the matter,
   That Oaks muſt come from *Thrace* to dance?
If Stocks muſt needs be taught to flatter,
   You'll find enough of them in *France.*

Why muſt the Winds all hold their Tongue?
   If they a little Breath ſhould raiſe,
Would that have ſpoil'd the Poet's Song,
   Or puff away the Monarch's Praiſe?

2.

Pindar, that Eagle, mounts the Skies;
   Whilſt Virtue leads the noble way:

Des

A N

ODE ſur la PRISE
de NAMUR.

QUELLE docte & ſainte yvreſſe
   Aujourd'hui me fait la loy?
Chaſtes Nymphes du Parneſſe,
   N'eſt-ce pas vous que Je voy?
Accourez, Troupe ſçavante,
Des ſons que ma Lyre enfante
   Ces arbres ſont réjouis;
Marquez-en bien la cadence,
Et vous, Vents, faites ſilence:
   Je vais parler de LOUIS.

Dans ſes chanſons immortelles,
Comme un Aigle audacieux,
Pindare eſtendant ſes aiſles,
Fuit loin des vulgaires yeux.

Mais

REDUCED FACSIMILE OF THE FIRST PAGE OF PRIOR'S ANSWER TO BOILEAU'S
ODE ON THE CAPTURE OF NAMUR

Harris, who had, in the days of the Exclusion Bill, attempted to set up a newspaper entitled Intelligence Domestic and Foreign, and who had been speedily forced to relinquish that design, announced that the Intelligence Domestic and Foreign, suppressed fourteen years before by tyranny, would again appear.   Ten days later was printed the first number of the English Courant.   Then came the Packet Boat from Holland and Flanders, the Pegasus, the London Newsletter, the London Post, the Flying Post, the Old Postmaster, the Postboy, and the Postman.   The history of the newspapers of England from that time to the present day is a most interesting and instructive part of the history of the country.   At first they were small and meanlooking.   Even the Postboy and the Postman, which seem to have been the best conducted and the most prosperous, were wretchedly printed on scraps of dingy

FRENCH MEDALS ON THE NAVAL OPERATIONS OF 1695

paper such as would not now be thought good enough for street ballads. Only two numbers came out in a week ; and a number contained little more matter than may be found in a single column of a daily paper of our time.   What is now called a leading article seldom appeared, except when there was a scarcity of intelligence, when the Dutch mails were detained by the west wind, when the Rapparees were quiet in the Bog of Allen, when no stage coach had been stopped by highwaymen, when no nonjuring congregation had been dispersed by constables, when no ambassador had made his entry with a long train of coaches and six, when no lord or poet had been buried in the Abbey, and when consequently it was difficult to fill up two pages.   Yet the leading articles, though inserted, as it should seem, only in the absence of more attractive matter, are by no means contemptibly written.

It is a remarkable fact that the infant newspapers were all on the side of King William and the Revolution.   This fact may be partly explained by the circumstance that the editors were, at first, on their good behaviour.   It was by no means clear that their trade was not in

itself illegal.   The printing of newspapers was certainly not prohibited
by any statute.   But, towards the close of the reign of Charles the Second,

London's Gazette here
Nouvelle Gazette
Che Compra gl'anisi di Londra

A GAZETTE SELLER

From an engraving in Tempest's Cries of London

the judges had pronounced that it was a misdemeanour at common law
to publish political intelligence without the King's license.   It is true that

the judges who had laid down this doctrine were removable at the royal pleasure and were eager on all occasions to exalt the royal prerogative. How the question, if it were again raised, would be decided by Holt and Treby was doubtful; and the effect of the doubt was to make the ministers of the Crown indulgent, and to make the journalists cautious. On neither side was there a wish to bring the question of right to issue. The government therefore connived at the publication of the newspapers ; and the conductors of the newspapers carefully abstained from publishing any thing that could provoke or alarm the government. It is true that, in one of the earliest numbers of one of the new journals, a paragraph appeared which seemed intended to convey an insinuation that the Princess Anne did not sincerely rejoice at the fall of Namur. But the printer made haste to atone for his fault by the most submissive apologies. During a considerable time the unofficial gazettes, though much more garrulous and amusing than the official gazette, were scarcely less courtly. Whoever examines them will find that the King is always mentioned with profound respect. About the debates and divisions of the two Houses a reverential silence is preserved. There is much invective : but it is almost all directed against the Jacobites and the French. It seems certain that the government of William gained not a little by the substitution of these printed newspapers, composed under constant dread of the Attorney General, for the old newsletters, which were written with unbounded license.[1]

The pamphleteers were under less restraint than the journalists : yet no person who has studied with attention the political controversies of that time can have failed to perceive that the libels on William's person and government were decidedly less coarse and rancorous during the latter half of his reign than during the earlier half. And the reason evidently is that the press, which had been fettered during the earlier half of his reign, was free during the latter half. While the censorship existed, no tract blaming, even in the most temperate and decorous language, the conduct of any public department, was likely to be printed with the approbation of the licenser. To print such a tract without the approbation of the licenser was illegal. In general, therefore, the

[1] There is a noble, and, I suppose, unique Collection of the newspapers of William's reign in the British Museum. I have turned over every page of that Collection. It is strange that neither Luttrell nor Evelyn should have noticed the first appearance of the new journals. The earliest mention of those journals which I have found is in a despatch of L'Hermitage, dated July $\frac{12}{22}$. 1695. I will transcribe his words :—" Depuis quelque tems on imprime ici plusieurs feuilles volantes en forme de gazette, qui sont remplies de toutes sortes de nouvelles. Cette licence est venue de ce que le parlement n'a pas achévé le bill ou projet d'acte qui avoit été porté dans la Chambre des Communes pour régler l'imprimerie et empêcher que ces sortes de choses n'arrivassent. Il n'y avoit ci-devant qu'un des commis des Secrétaires d'Etat qui eût le pouvoir de faire des gazettes : mais aujourdhui il s'en fait plusieurs sous d'autres noms." L'Hermitage mentions the paragraph reflecting on the Princess, and the submission of the libeller.

REMEMBER TO DIE

The *Mercury Hawkers* in Mourning.

AN
ELEGY

On the much Lamented Death of
Edward Jones, the famous *Gazette* Printer of the *Savoy*;
Who departed this Life at his House at Kensington, *on* Saturday *the* 16th *Day of*
February, 170⅚, *in the* 54 *Year of his Age.*

ASift ye *Mufes* (all in number) Nine,
  And lend your Aid to this frail Pen of mine:
Not lofty Lines, but humble Strains infuse,
While I relate the fudden fatal Newes:
Great *Jones* ; is Dead, we had it by Exprefs,
Which brings us Grief and Sorrow to excefs,
That famous Printer, whofe renowned Name,
Will ftill furvive, with never Dying Fame,
In ev'ry Corner of this Nation round,
The Name of *Jones* did other News confound ;
The *London* Poft, with *Flying Men or Boys*,
Compar'd to his, were only Shams and Toys,
When they related difmal News from far,
By his *Exprefs* we gain'd by Forreign War,
In former Reigns, when Fortune prov'd fo Crofs,
His kind *Exprefs*, made up our fatal Lofs;
When other Printers dreadful News did tell,
The *Savoy* Paper made all things go well,
Nay, fo obliging was he, or'e and or'e
He told us News we knew a *Month* before,
In every Alley Lane and fpacious Street,
His Name declar'd fuccefs by Land and Fleet :
Tho *B——d* and fome others did devife,
To fet his Name to many hundred Lies ;
And confequently him did much Abufe,
Yet ftill more famous was great *Jones's* Newes,
Great Numbers of poor People have been Fed,
And daily by his News have earn'd their Bread ;
Old *Bennet* from mean Fortune did advance,
To Wealth and Plenty by the fmiles of chance ;
Brave News he cry'd, what e'er came by the Poft,
How many Thoufand Men the *French* had loft :
I need not tell yóu how he rais'd his Fame
Becaufe it was by Famous *Jones's* Name.
There's *Ward* and *Sawyer* with their new Exprefs,
Confirm'd by *Jones* ; had mighty good Succefs,
There's *Kempton* too, when Bloody News came o're
With pleafant Voice his Name aloud did roar,

This was the Aim, and only Confequence,
By which he daily gather'd up the Pence ;
And *Robert Sheers*, who gift of Runing had,
At this dull Newes became extreamly fad ;
Befides fwift *Tuffin, Cummins* and the reft,
For this great Lofs, their Sorrow have exprest ;
There's many others of the Female throng,
As can't be Nam'd in this my mournful Song ;
Whofe Greif exceeds the bounds of common Woe,
And Tears in fhowers from their Eyes do flow :
How will the Nation be amaz'd to hear
Another Name Proclaimed in their Ear :
No News but *Jones's*, will be counted true,
Nor Forreign Actions Credited by few,
All Printed News, will be efteem'd but fhams
And pafs for Nothing, but invented flams ;
The very Gazette hardly now will pafs,
To be the Paper which before it was,
For by his Death fuch Changes will enfue.
As mortal Hawkers feldom ever knew ;
Let Printers Mourn for they can do no lefs,
Since *Jones* has Printed now his laft Exprefs.

The EPITAPH.

HEre Liet a Printer Famous in his Time,
  Whofe Life by Lingering Sicknefs did Decline :
He Liv'd in Credit, and in Peace he Dy'd,
And often had the Chance of Fortune Try'd ;
Whofe Smiles by various Methods did Promote
Him to the Favour of the Senates Vote :
And fo became by National confent,
The only Printer for the Parliament ;
Thus by degrees, (fo Profperous was his Fate,)
He left his Heirs, a very good Eftate.

LONDON, Printed for *T. Sawyer,* near *Ludgate-hill,* 1706.

AN ELEGY ON A JOURNALIST

From a broadside in the British Museum

respectable and moderate opponents of the Court, not being able to publish in the manner prescribed by law, and not thinking it right or safe
to publish in a manner prohibited by law, held their peace, and left the
business of criticising the administration to two classes of men, fanatical
nonjurors who hated the ruling powers with an insane hatred, and Grub
Street hacks, coarseminded, badhearted, and foulmouthed.   Thus there
was scarcely a single man of judgment, temper, and integrity among
the many who were in the habit of writing against the government.
Indeed the habit of writing against the government had, of itself, an
unfavourable effect on the character.   For whoever was in the habit of
writing against the government was in the habit of breaking the law ;
and the habit of breaking even an unreasonable law tends to make men
altogether lawless.   However absurd a tariff may be, a smuggler is but
too likely to be a knave and a ruffian.   However oppressive a game law
may be, the transition is but too easy from poaching to assault and battery,
and from assault and battery to murder.   And so, though little indeed can
be said in favour of the statutes which imposed restraints on literature,
there was much risk that a man who was constantly violating those
statutes would not be a man of rigid uprightness and stainless honour.
An author who was determined to print, and could not obtain a license,
must employ the services of needy and desperate outcasts, who, hunted
by the peace officers, and forced to assume every week new aliases and
new disguises, hid their paper and their types in those dens of vice
which are the pest and the shame of great capitals.   Such wretches as
these he must bribe to keep his secret, and to run the chance of having
their backs flayed and their ears clipped in his stead.   A man stooping
to such companions and to such expedients could hardly retain unimpaired the delicacy of his sense of what was right and becoming.   The
emancipation of the press produced a great and salutary change.   The
best and wisest men in the ranks of the opposition now assumed an
office which had hitherto been abandoned to the unprincipled or the
hotheaded.   Tracts against the government were written in a style not
misbecoming statesmen and gentlemen ; and even the compositions of
the lower and fiercer class of malecontents became somewhat less brutal
and less ribald than formerly.

Some weak men had imagined that religion and morality stood in
need of the protection of the licenser.   The event signally proved that
they were in error.   In truth the censorship had scarcely put any
restraint on licentiousness or profaneness.   The Paradise Lost had
narrowly escaped mutilation : for the Paradise Lost was the work of a
man whose politics were hateful to the government.   But Etherege's
She Would If She Could, Wycherley's Country Wife, Dryden's Trans-
lations from the Fourth Book of Lucretius, obtained the Imprimatur

His Highneſs The Duke of Gloceſter

G. Kneller Eques pinx:

J. Smith fec: et exc:

THE DUKE OF GLOUCESTER

From a mezzotint by J. Smith, after a painting by Sir G. Kneller

without difficulty: for Etherege, Wycherley, and Dryden were courtiers. From the day on which the emancipation of our literature was accomplished, the purification of our literature began.   That purification was effected, not by the intervention of senates or magistrates, but by the opinion of the great body of educated Englishmen, before whom good and evil were set, and who were left free to make their choice.   During a hundred and sixty years the liberty of our press has been constantly becoming more and more entire ; and during those hundred and sixty years the restraint imposed on writers by the general feeling of readers has been constantly becoming more and more strict.   At length even that class of works in which it was formerly thought that a voluptuous imagination was privileged to disport itself, love songs, comedies, novels, have become more decorous than the sermons of the seventeenth century.   At this day foreigners, who dare not print a word reflecting on the government under which they live, are at a loss to understand how it happens that the freest press in Europe is the most prudish.

On the tenth of October, the King, leaving his army in winter quarters, arrived in England, and was received with unwonted enthusiasm.

Return of William to England : dissolution of the Parliament During his passage through the capital to his palace, the bells of every church were ringing, and every street was lighted up. It was late before he made his way through the shouting crowds to Kensington.   But, late as it was, a council was instantly held.   An important point was to be decided.   Should the House of Commons be permitted to sit again, or should there be an immediate dissolution ?   The King would probably have been willing to keep that House to the end of his reign.   But this was not in his power.   The Triennial Act had fixed the first of November, 1696, as the latest day of the existence of the Parliament.   If therefore there were not a general election in 1695, there must be a general election in 1696 ; and who could say what might be the state of the country in 1696 ?   There might be an unfortunate campaign.   There might be, indeed there was but too good reason to believe that there would be, a terrible commercial crisis.   In either case, it was probable that there would be much ill humour.   The campaign of 1695 had been brilliant : the nation was in an excellent temper ; and William wisely determined to seize the fortunate moment.   Two proclamations were immediately published.   One of them announced, in the ordinary form, that His Majesty had determined to dissolve the old Parliament, and that he had ordered writs to be issued for a new Parliament. The other signified the royal pleasure to be that every regiment quartered in a place where an election was to be held should march out of that place the day before the nomination, and should not return till the people had made their choice.   From this order, which was generally

His Highness William Duke of Glocester & Mr. Benj. Bathurst

T. Murrey pinx   1697.   I. Smith fe. et ex.

THE DUKE OF GLOUCESTER IN THE ROBES OF THE GARTER

From a mezzotint by J. Smith, after a painting by T. Murray

considered as indicating a laudable respect for popular rights, the garrisons of fortified towns and castles were necessarily excepted

But, though William carefully abstained from disgusting the constituent bodies by any thing that could look like coercion or intimidation, he did not disdain to influence their votes by milder means. He resolved to spend the six weeks of the general election in showing himself to the people of many districts which he had never yet visited. He hoped to acquire in this way a popularity which might have a considerable effect on the returns. He therefore forced himself to behave with a graciousness and affability in which he was too often deficient ; and the consequence was that he received, at every stage of his progress, marks of the good will of his subjects. Before he set out he paid a visit in form to his sister in law, and was much pleased with his reception. The Duke of Gloucester, only six years old, with a little musket on his shoulder, came to meet his uncle, and presented arms. "I am learning my drill," the child said, "that I may help you to beat the French." The King laughed much, and, a few days later, rewarded the young soldier with the Garter.[1]

On the seventeenth of October William went to Newmarket, now a place rather of business than of pleasure, but, in the autumns of that age, the gayest and most luxurious spot in the island. It was not unusual for the whole Court and Cabinet to go down to the meetings. Jewellers and milliners, players and fiddlers, venal wits and venal beauties followed in crowds. The streets were made impassable by coaches and six. In the places of public resort peers flirted with maids of honour ; and officers of the Life Guards, all plumes and gold lace, jostled professors in trencher caps and black gowns. For, on such occasions, the neighbouring University of Cambridge always sent her highest functionaries with loyal addresses, and selected her ablest theologians to preach before the Sovereign and his splendid retinue. In the wild days of the Restoration, indeed, the most learned and eloquent divine might fail to draw a fashionable audience, particularly if Buckingham announced his intention of holding forth : for sometimes His Grace would enliven the dulness of a Sunday morning by addressing to the bevy of fine gentlemen and fine ladies a ribald exhortation which he called a sermon. But the Court of William was more decent ; and the Academic dignitaries were treated with marked respect. With lords and ladies from Saint James's and Soho, and with doctors from Trinity College and King's College, were mingled the provincial aristocracy, foxhunting squires and their rosy-cheeked daughters, who had come in queerlooking family coaches drawn by carthorses from the remotest parishes of three or four counties to see

William makes a progress through the country

[1] L'Hermitage, Oct. $\frac{15}{25}$., Nov. $\frac{1}{11}$. 1695.

VIEW OF LINCOLN

From an engraving by J. Kip

their Sovereign.   The heath was fringed by a wild gipsylike camp of
vast extent.   For the hope of being able to feed on the leavings of
many sumptuous tables, and to pick up some of the guineas and crowns
which the spendthrifts of London were throwing about, attracted
thousands of peasants from a circle of many miles.[1]

William, after holding his court a few days at this joyous place, and
receiving the homage of Cambridgeshire, Huntingdonshire, and Suffolk,
proceeded to Althorpe.   It seems strange that he should, in the course
of what was really a canvassing tour, have honoured with such a mark
of favour a man so generally distrusted and hated as Sunderland.   But
the people were determined to be pleased.   All Northamptonshire
crowded to kiss the royal hand in that fine gallery which had been
embellished by the pencil of Vandyke and made classical by the muse
of Waller ; and the Earl tried to conciliate his neighbours by feasting
them at eight tables, all blazing with plate.   From Althorpe the King
proceeded to Stamford.   The Earl of Exeter, whose princely seat was,
and still is, one of the great sights of England, had never taken the
oaths, and had, in order to avoid an interview which must have been
disagreeable, found some pretext for going up to London, but had left
directions that the illustrious guest should be received with fitting
hospitality.   William was fond of architecture and of gardening ; and
his nobles could not flatter him more than by asking his opinion about
the improvement of their country seats.   At a time when he had many
cares pressing on his mind he took a great interest in the building of
Castle Howard ; and a wooden model of that edifice, the finest specimen of a vicious style, was sent to Kensington for his inspection.   We
cannot therefore wonder that he should have seen Burleigh with delight.
He was indeed not content with one view, but rose early on the following morning for the purpose of examining the house a second time.
From Stamford he went on to Lincoln, where he was greeted by the
clergy in full canonicals, by the magistrates in scarlet robes, and by a
multitude of baronets, knights, and esquires, from all parts of the
immense plain which lies between the Trent and the German Ocean.
After attending divine service in the magnificent cathedral, he took his
departure, and journeyed westward.   On the frontier of Nottinghamshire
the Lord Lieutenant of that county, John Holles, Duke of Newcastle,
with a great following, met the royal carriages and escorted them to his
seat at Welbeck, a mansion surrounded by gigantic oaks which scarcely
seem older now than on the day when that splendid procession passed

[1] London Gazette, Oct. 24. 1695.   See Evelyn's Account of Newmarket in 1671, and Pepys,
July 18. 1668.   From Tallard's despatches written after the Peace of Ryswick, it appears that
the autumn meetings were not less numerous or splendid in the days of William than in those
of his uncles.

The West View of Welbeck Abbey, near Mansfield, in the County of Nottingham.

To the Right Honble EDWARD Earl of Oxford and Mortimer, & Baron Harley of Wigmore, Owner of this Abbey. This Prospect is Humbly Inscribed by My Lord. Your Lordships most Obedt & Obliged Servt Saml Buck.

THIS Monastry of Premonstratensians, was the Gift of Ralph de Bellfour, to the Church of St James at Welbek, and performed in King Stephen, in whose reign it was begun and afterwards finished in the Reign of King Henry 2, by Tho: de Cuckeney, who directed his Charter of Foundation, to Roger Arch Bpp of York.

WELBECK ABBEY

From an engraving by S. Buck

under their shade.   The house, in which William was then, during a few hours, a guest, was transferred, long after his death, by female descents, from the Holleses to the Harleys, and from the Harleys to the Bentincks, and now contains the originals of those singularly interesting letters which were exchanged between him and his trusty friend and servant Portland.   At Welbeck the grandees of the north were assembled.   The Lord Mayor of York came thither with a train of magistrates, and the Archbishop of York with a train of divines. William hunted several times in that forest, the finest in the kingdom, which in old times gave shelter to Robin Hood and Little John, and which is now portioned out into the lordly domains of Welbeck, Thoresby, Clumber, and Worksop.   Four hundred gentlemen on horse-back partook of his sport.   The Nottinghamshire squires were charmed to hear him say at table, after a noble stag chase, that he hoped that this was not the last run which he should have with them, and that he must hire a hunting box among their delightful woods.   He then turned southward.   He was entertained during one day by the Earl of Stamford at Bradgate, the place where Lady Jane Grey sate alone reading the last words of Socrates while the deer was flying through the park followed by the whirlwind of hounds and hunters.   On the morrow the Lord Brook welcomed his Sovereign to Warwick Castle, the finest of those fortresses of the middle ages which have been turned into peaceful dwellings.   Guy's Tower was illuminated.   A cistern containing a hundred and twenty gallons of punch was emptied to his Majesty's health ; and a mighty pile of faggots blazed in the middle of that spacious court which is overhung by ruins green with the ivy of centuries.   The next morning the King, accompanied by a multitude of Warwickshire gentlemen on horseback, proceeded towards the borders of Gloucestershire.   He deviated from his route to dine with Shrews-bury at a secluded mansion in the Wolds, and in the evening went on to Burford.   The whole population of Burford met him, and entreated him to accept a small token of their love.   Burford was then renowned for its saddles.   One inhabitant of the town, in particular, was said by the English to be the best saddler in Europe.   Two of his masterpieces were respectfully offered to William, who received them with much grace, and ordered them to be especially reserved for his own use.[1]

At Oxford he was received with great pomp, complimented in a Latin oration, presented with some of the most beautiful productions of the Academic press, entertained with music, and invited to a sumptuous feast in the Sheldonian theatre.   He departed in a few hours, pleading

---

[1] I have taken this account of William's progress chiefly from the London Gazettes, from the despatches of L'Hermitage, from Narcissus Luttrell's Diary, and from the letters of Vernon, Yard, and Cartwright among the Lexington Papers.

as an excuse for the shortness of his stay that he had seen the colleges before, and that this was a visit, not of curiosity, but of kindness.　As it was well known that he did not love the Oxonians and was not loved

WARWICK CASTLE IN 1710

From an engraving by J. Collins, after a drawing by J. Fish

by them, his haste gave occasion to some idle rumours which found credit with the vulgar.　It was said that he hurried away without tasting the costly banquet which had been provided for him, because he had been warned by an anonymous letter that, if he ate or drank in the theatre, he was a dead man.　But it is difficult to believe that a prince, who could scarcely be induced, by the most earnest entreaties of his friends, to take the most common precautions against assassins of whose designs he had trustworthy evidence, would have been scared by so silly a hoax ; and it is quite certain that the stages of his progress had been marked, and that he remained at Oxford as long as was compatible with arrangements previously made.[1]

He was welcomed back to his capital by a splendid show, which had been prepared at great cost during his absence. Sidney, now Earl of Romney and Master of the Ordnance, had determined to astonish London by an exhibition of a kind which had never been seen in England on so large a scale. The whole skill of the pyrotechnists of his department was employed to produce a display of fireworks which might vie with any that had been seen in the gardens of Versailles or on the great tank at the Hague. Saint James's Square was selected as the place for the spectacle. All the stately mansions on the northern, eastern and western sides were crowded with people of fashion. The King appeared at a window of Romney's drawing room. The Princess of Denmark, her husband, and her court occupied a neighbouring house. The whole diplomatic body assembled at the dwelling of the minister of the United Provinces. A huge pyramid of flame in the centre of the area threw out brilliant cascades which were seen by hundreds of thousands who crowded the neighbouring streets and parks. The States General were informed by their correspondent that, great as the multitude was, the night had passed without the slightest disturbance.[2]

By this time the elections were almost completed. In every part of the country it had been manifest that the constituent bodies were generally zealous for the King and for the war. The City of London, which had returned four Tories in 1690, returned four Whigs in 1695. Of the proceedings at Westminster an account more than usually circumstantial has come down to us. In 1690 the electors, disgusted by the Sacheverell Clause, had returned two Tories. In 1695, as soon as it was known that a new Parliament was likely to be called, a meeting was held, at which it was resolved that a deputation should be sent with an invitation to two Commissioners of the Treasury, Charles Montague and Sir Stephen Fox. Sir Walter Clarges stood on the Tory interest. On the day of nomination near five thousand electors paraded the streets on horseback. They were divided into three bands ; and at the head of each band rode one of the candidates. It was easy to estimate at a glance the comparative strength of the parties. For the cavalcade which followed Clarges was the least numerous

The elections

[1] See the letter of Yard to Lexington, Nov. 8. 1695, and the note by the editor of the Lexington Papers.

[2] L'Hermitage, Nov. $\frac{15}{25}$. 1695.

CCCXXX

Advertisements from the Delegates of Convocation for his Majesties Reception, for the Heads of Houses to deliver with great charge unto their Companies.

1. THAT they Admonish all such as are under their Charge, that they appear no where during the Kings abode in the University, without their Caps and Gowns suitable to their Degree and condition.

2. That no Scholar of what condition soever, shall presume to go out to meet the King, either on foot or on Horseback, or to be at, or upon the way where the King is to come; but shall attend in that place and posture wherein he shall be required to be, upon notice from his Superiors.

3. That on Saturday Morning *Novemb.* the 9th. immediately upon the ringing of St. Maries great Bell, all Persons, Graduats and others, (that do not ride out with Mr. Vice-Chancellor) forthwith repair to the Schools Quadrangle, there to remain till they have further orders, where to dispose of themselves for the more convenient and better reception of his Majesty.

4. That at what time his Majesty shall be pleased to accept of a Banquet in the Theater, the Masters, who have Procuratorial power, repair unto the Apodyterium, to assist the Curators in providing that all things may be performed with decency and order.

5. That during his Majesty's stay in the Theater, the Area will be the place for his Majesty and his Retinue; and that no Person whatever presume to press or go into the said Area, but such Persons only as are of his Majesties Retinue, or otherwise appointed.

It is strictly required, that during the time of this Solemnity, all Persons observe the aforesaid orders, and comport themselves with that sobriety and modesty, as may tend to the Honour and Reputation of the University.

Doctors in all Faculties appointed to meet the KING.

Dr. *Fitzherbert Adams* Vice-Can.
Dr. *Finch* è Coll. Omn. An.
Dr. *Mill* ex Aula S. Edm.
Dr. *Edwards* è Coll. Jesu.
Dr. *Meare* è Coll. Æn. Nasi.
Dr. *Pudsey* è Coll. Magd.

Dr. *Mander* è Coll. Baliol.
Dr. *Sykes* Marg. Prof.
Dr. *Dunster* è Coll. Wadh.
Dr. *Charlett* è Coll. Univers.
Dr. *Painter* è Coll. Exon.
Dr. *Royse* è Coll. Oriel.

Dr. *Luffe* R. P. Med.
Dr. *King* è Coll. Mert.
Dr. *Bouchier* R. P. Jur. Civil.
Dr. *Irish* è Coll. Om. An.
Dr. *Aldworth* è Coll. D. J. Bapt.
Dr. *Gibbs* è Coll. Om. An.

Dr. *Traffles* è Coll. Nov.
Dr. *Martin* è Coll. Mert.
Dr. *Hanns* ex Æde Christi.
Dr. *Helier* } è C. C. C.
Dr. *Creed* }
Dr. *Aldworth* Hist. Camd. Prof.

Masters of Arts appointed to meet the KING.

Mr. *Bagwell* } Proctors.
Mr. *Waugh* }
Mr. *Codrington* è Coll. Om. An.
Mr. *Almont* è Coll. Trin.
Mr. *Bertie* è Coll. Univers.
Mr. *Bourne* ex Æde Christi.

Mr. *Watkins* ex Æde Christi.
Mr. *Walker* è Coll. Oriel.
Mr. *White* è Coll. Bal.
Mr. *Holland* è Coll Merton.
Mr. *Whiting* è Coll. Wadh.
Mr. *Wase* è C. C. C.

Mr. *Greenway* } è Coll. Nov.
Mr. *Bisse* }
Mr. *Bernard* è Coll. D. J. Bapt.
Mr. *Bartholomew* è Coll. Linc.
Mr. *Brown* è Coll. Æn. Nasi.

Mr. *Tho. Holt.* } è Coll. Magd.
Mr. *Sam. Adams* }
Mr. *Davies* è Coll. Jesu.
Mr. *Sloper* è Coll. Pemb.
Mr. *Whitehall* ex Aula B. M. V.

The Names of the Masters of Arts that have a Procuratorial Power given them during his MAJESTY'S abode in the University.

Mr. *Freind* } ex Æde Christi.
Mr. *Wells* }
Mr. *Kenton* } è Coll. Mag.
Mr. *Bagshaw* }
Mr. *Barker* è Coll. Nov.
Mr. *Creech* è Coll. Om. An.

Mr. *Offley* è Coll. Om. An.
Mr. *Tasser* è Coll. Mert.
Mr. *Buckeridge* è C C C.
Mr. *Smith* è Coll. D. J. Bapt.
Mr. *Norris* è Coll. Æn. Nasi.
Mr. *Allen* è Coll. Univers.

Mr. *Wise* è Coll. Exon.
Mr. *Atkinson* è Coll. Reg.
Mr. *Fifield* è Coll. Trin.
Mr. *Theed* è Coll. Lincoln.
Mr. *Gerard* è Coll. Wadh.

Mr. *Baron* è Coll. Baliol.
Mr. *Winne* è Coll. Jesu.
Mr. *Goddard* è Coll. Pembr.
Mr. *Randall* ex Aula Magd.
Mr. *Martin* ex Aula Cerv.

Fitzherbert Adams Vice-Can.

OXFORD, Printed at the THEATER, M. DC. XCV.

published Nov 8 1695

ADVERTISEMENTS FOR HIS MAJESTY'S RECEPTION AT OXFORD

From a broadside in the Bodleian Library

of the three ; and it was well known that the followers of Montague would vote for Fox, and the followers of Fox for Montague. The business of the day was interrupted by loud clamours. The Whigs cried shame on the Jacobite candidate who wished to make the English go to mass, eat frogs, and wear wooden shoes. The Tories hooted the two placemen who were raising great estates out of the plunder of the poor overburdened nation. From words the incensed factions proceeded to blows : and there was a riot which was with some difficulty quelled. The High Bailiff then walked round the three companies of horsemen, and pronounced, on the view, that Montague and Fox were duly elected. A poll was demanded. The Tories exerted themselves strenuously. Neither money nor ink was spared. Clarges disbursed two thousand pounds in a few hours, a great outlay in times when the average estate of a member of Parliament was not estimated at more than eight hundred a year. In the course of the night which followed the nomination, broadsides filled with invectives against the two courtly upstarts who had raised themselves by knavery from poverty and obscurity to opulence and power were scattered all over the capital. The Bishop of London canvassed openly against the government ; for the interference of peers in elections had not yet been declared by the Commons to be a breach of privilege. But all was vain. Clarges was at the bottom of the poll without hope of rising. He withdrew ; and Montague was carried on the shoulders of an immense multitude from the hustings in Palace Yard to his office at Whitehall.[1]

The same feeling exhibited itself in many other places. The free-holders of Cumberland instructed their representatives to support the King, and to vote whatever supplies might be necessary for the purpose of carrying on the war with vigour ; and this example was followed by several counties and towns.[2] Russell did not arrive in England till after the writs had gone out. But he had only to choose for what place he would sit. His popularity was immense : for his villanies were secret, and his public services were universally known. He had won the battle of La Hogue. He had commanded two years in the Mediterranean. He had there shut up the French fleets in the harbour of Toulon, and had stopped and turned back the French armies in Catalonia. He had taken many men of war, and among them two ships of the line ; and he had not, during his long absence in a remote sea, lost a single vessel either by war or by weather. He had made the red cross of Saint George an object of terror to all the princes and commonwealths of Italy. The effect of these successes was that embassies were on their way from Florence, Genoa, and Venice, with tardy congratulations to William on

---

[1] L'Hermitage, $\frac{\text{Oct. 25.}}{\text{Nov. 4.}}$, $\frac{\text{Oct. 29.}}{\text{Nov. 8.}}$ 1695.   [2] Ibid. Nov. $\frac{5}{15}$. 1695.

G. Kneller pinx   I. Becket exc

WRIOTHESLEY LORD RUSSELL, AFTERWARDS SECOND DUKE OF BEDFORD

From a mezzotint by I. Becket, after a painting by Sir G. Kneller

his accession.   Russell's merits, artfully magnified by the Whigs, made such an impression that he was returned to Parliament, not only by Portsmouth where his official situation gave him great influence, and by Cambridgeshire where his private property was considerable, but also by Middlesex.   This last distinction, indeed, he owed chiefly to the name which he bore.   Before his arrival in England, it had been generally thought that two Tories would be returned for the metropolitan county. Somers and Shrewsbury were of opinion that the only way to avert such a misfortune was to conjure with the name of the most virtuous of all the martyrs of English liberty.   As there was then no law excluding minors from the House of Commons, they entreated Lady Russell to suffer her eldest son, a boy of fifteen, who was about to commence his studies at Cambridge, to be put in nomination.   He must, they said, drop, for one day, his new title of Marquess of Tavistock, and call himself by his father's honoured name, Lord Russell.   There will be no expense. There will be no contest.   Thousands of gentlemen on horseback will escort him to the hustings : nobody will dare to stand against him ; and he will not only come in himself, but bring in another Whig.   The widowed mother, in a letter written with all the excellent sense and feeling which distinguished her, refused to sacrifice her son to her party. His education, she said, would be interrupted : his head would be turned: his triumph would be his undoing.   Just at this conjuncture the Admiral arrived.   He made his appearance before the freeholders of Middlesex assembled on the top of Hampstead Hill, and was returned without opposition.[1]

Meanwhile several noted malecontents received marks of public disapprobation.   Sir John Knight, the most factious and insolent of those Jacobites who had dishonestly sworn fealty to King William in order to qualify themselves to sit in Parliament, ceased to represent the great city of Bristol.   Exeter, the capital of the west, was violently agitated. It had been long supposed that the ability, the eloquence, the experience, the ample fortune, the noble descent of Seymour would make it impossible to unseat him.   But his moral character, which had never stood very high, had, during the last three or four years, been constantly sinking.   He had been virulent in opposition till he had got a place. While he had a place he had defended the most unpopular acts of the government.   As soon as he was again out of place, he had again been virulent in opposition.   His saltpetre contract had left a deep stain on his personal honour.   Two candidates were therefore brought forward against him ; and a contest, the longest and fiercest of that age, fixed the attention of the whole kingdom, and was watched with interest even

[1] L'Hermitage, Nov. $\frac{6}{15}$. $\frac{15}{25}$. 1695 ; Sir James Forbes to Lady Russell, Oct. 3. 1695 ; Lady Russell to Lord Edward Russell ; The Postman, Nov. 16. 1695.

by foreign governments. The poll was open five weeks. The expense on both sides was enormous. The freemen of Exeter, who, while the election lasted, fared sumptuously every day, were by no means impatient for the termination of their luxurious carnival. They ate and drank heartily: they turned out every evening with good cudgels to fight for Mother Church or for King William : but the votes came in very slowly. It was not till the eve of the meeting of Parliament that the return was made. Seymour was defeated, to his bitter mortification, and was forced to take refuge in the small borough of Totness.[1]

It is remarkable that, at this election as at the preceding election, John Hampden failed to obtain a seat. He had, since he ceased to be a member of Parliament, been brooding over his evil fate and his indelible shame, and occasionally venting his spleen in bitter pamphlets against the government. When the Whigs had become predominant at the Court and in the House of Commons, when Nottingham had retired, when Caermarthen had been impeached, Hampden, it should seem, again conceived the hope that he might play a great part in public life. But the leaders of his party, apparently, did not wish for an ally of so acrimonious and turbulent a spirit. He found himself still excluded from the House of Commons. He led, during a few months, a miserable life, sometimes trying to forget his cares among the wellbred gamblers and frail beauties who filled the drawing room of the Duchess of Mazarin, and sometimes sunk in religious melancholy. The thought of suicide often rose in his mind. Soon there was a vacancy in the representation of Buckinghamshire, the county which had repeatedly sent himself and his progenitors to Parliament ; and he expected that he should, by the help of Wharton, whose dominion over the Buckinghamshire Whigs was absolute, be returned without difficulty. Wharton, however, gave his interest to another candidate. This was a final blow. The town was agitated by the news that John Hampden had cut his throat, that he had survived his wound a few hours, that he had professed deep penitence for his sins, had requested the prayers of Burnet, and had sent a solemn warning to the Duchess of Mazarin. A coroner's jury found a verdict of insanity. The wretched man had entered on life with the fairest prospects. He bore a name which was more than noble. He was heir to an ample estate, and to a patrimony much more precious, the confidence and attachment of hundreds of thousands of his countrymen. His own abilities were considerable, and had been carefully cultivated. Unhappily ambition and party spirit impelled him to place himself in a situation full of danger. To that danger his fortitude proved unequal. He stooped to supplications which saved him and dishonoured him. From that moment, he never knew peace of mind. His temper became

---

[1] There is a highly curious account of this contest in the despatches of L'Hermitage.

perverse ; and his understanding was perverted by his temper.　He tried to find relief in devotion and in revenge, in fashionable dissipation and in political turmoil.　But the dark shade never passed away from his mind, till, in the twelfth year of his humiliation, his unhappy life was terminated by an unhappy death.[1]

The result of the general election proved that William had chosen a fortunate moment for dissolving.　The number of new members was about a hundred and sixty ; and·most of these were known to be thoroughly well affected to the government.[2]

It was of the highest importance that the House of Commons should, at that moment, be disposed to cooperate cordially with the King.　For it was absolutely necessary to apply a remedy to an internal evil which had by slow degrees grown to a fearful magnitude.　The silver coin, which was then the standard coin of the realm, was in a state at which the boldest and most enlightened statesmen stood aghast.[3]

Alarming state of the currency

Till the reign of Charles the Second our coin had been struck by a process as old as the thirteenth century.　Edward the First had invited hither skilful artists from Florence, which, in his time, was to London what London, in the time of William the Third, was to Moscow.　During many generations, the instruments which were then introduced into our mint continued to be employed with little alteration.　The metal was divided with shears, and afterwards shaped and stamped by the hammer. In these operations much was left to the hand and eye of the workman. It necessarily happened that some pieces contained a little more and some a little less than the just quantity of silver : few pieces were exactly round ; and the rims were not marked.　It was therefore in the course of years discovered that to clip the coin was one of the easiest and most profitable kinds of fraud.　In the reign of Elizabeth it had been thought necessary to enact that the clipper should be, as the coiner had long been, liable to the penalties of high treason.[4]　The practice of paring down money, however, was far too lucrative to be so checked ; and, about the time of the Restoration, people began to observe that a large proportion of the crowns, halfcrowns and shillings which were passing from hand to hand had undergone some slight mutilation.

[1] Postman, Dec. 15. 17. 1696 ; Vernon to Shrewsbury, Dec. 13. 15. ; Narcissus Luttrell's Diary ; Burnet, i. 647. ; Saint Evremond's Verses to Hampden.

[2] L'Hermitage, Nov. $\frac{18}{28}$. 1695.

[3] I have derived much valuable information on this subject from a MS. in the British Museum, Lansdowne Collection, No. 801.　It is entitled Brief Memoires relating to the Silver and Gold Coins of England, with an Account of the Corruption of the Hammered Money, and of the Reform by the late Grand Coinage at the Tower and the Country Mints, by Hopton Haynes, Assay Master of the Mint.

[4] Stat. 5 Eliz. c. 11., and 18 Eliz. c. 1.

That was a time fruitful of experiments and inventions in all the departments of science. A great improvement in the mode of shaping and striking the coin was suggested. A mill, which to a great extent superseded the human hand, was set up in the Tower of London. This mill was worked by horses, and would doubtless be considered by modern engineers as a rude and feeble machine. The pieces which it produced, however, were among the best in Europe. It was not easy to counterfeit them ; and, as their shape was exactly circular, and their edges were inscribed with a legend, clipping was not to be apprehended.[1] The hammered coins and the milled coins were current together. They were received without distinction in public, and consequently in private, payments. The financiers of that age seem to have expected that the new money, which was excellent, would soon displace the old money which was much impaired. Yet any man of plain understanding might have known that, when the State treats perfect coin and light coin as of equal value, the perfect coin will not drive the light coin out of circulation, but will itself be driven out. A clipped crown, on English ground, went as far in the payment of a tax or a debt as a milled crown. But the milled crown, as soon as it had been flung into the crucible or carried across the Channel, became much more valuable than the clipped crown. It might therefore have been predicted, as confidently as any thing can be predicted which depends on the human will, that the inferior pieces would remain in the only market in which they could fetch the same price as the superior pieces, and that the superior pieces would take some form or fly to some place in which some advantage could be derived from their superiority.[2]

[1] Pepys's Diary, November 23. 1663.

[2] The first writer who noticed the fact that, where good money and bad money are thrown into circulation together, the bad money drives out the good money, was Aristophanes He seems to have thought that the preference which his fellow citizens gave to light coins was to be attributed to a depraved taste, such as led them to entrust men like Cleon and Hyperbolus with the conduct of great affairs. But, though his political economy will not bear examination, his verses are excellent :—

> πολλάκις γ' ἡμῖν ἔδοξεν ἡ πόλις πεπονθέναι
> ταὐτὸν ἔς τε τῶν πολιτῶν τοὺς καλούς τε κἀγαθούς
> ἔς τε τἀρχαῖον νόμισμα καὶ τὸ καινὸν χρυσίον.
> οὔτε γὰρ τούτοισιν οὖσιν οὐ κεκιβδηλευμένοις
> ἀλλὰ καλλίστοις ἁπάντων, ὡς δοκεῖ, νομισμάτων,
> καὶ μόνοις ὀρθῶς κοπεῖσι, καὶ κεκωδωνισμένοις
> ἔν τε τοῖς Ἕλλησι καὶ τοῖς βαρβάροισι πανταχοῦ,
> χρώμεθ' οὐδέν, ἀλλὰ τούτοις τοῖς πονηροῖς χαλκίοις,
> χθές τε καὶ πρώην κοπεῖσι τῷ κακίστῳ κόμματι.
> τῶν πολιτῶν θ' οὓς μὲν ἴσμεν εὐγενεῖς καὶ σώφρονας
> ἄνδρας ὄντας, καὶ δικαίους, καὶ καλούς τε κἀγαθούς,
> καὶ τραφέντας ἐν παλαίστραις καὶ χοροῖς καὶ μουσικῇ,
> προυσελοῦμεν· τοῖς δὲ χαλκοῖς, καὶ ξένοις, καὶ πυρρίαις,
> καὶ πονηροῖς, κἀκ πονηρῶν, εἰς ἅπαντα χρώμεθα.

The politicians of that age, however, generally overlooked these very obvious considerations. They marvelled exceedingly that every body should be so perverse as to use light money in preference to good money. In other words, they marvelled that nobody chose to pay twelve ounces of silver when ten would serve the turn. The horse in the Tower still paced his rounds. Fresh waggonloads of choice money still came forth from the mill; and still they vanished as fast as they appeared. Great masses were melted down; great masses exported; great masses hoarded: but scarcely one new piece was to be found in the till of a shop, or in the leathern bag which the farmer carried home after the cattle fair. In the receipts and payments of the Exchequer the milled money did not exceed ten shillings in a hundred pounds. A writer of that age mentions the case of a merchant who, in a sum of thirty five pounds, received only a single halfcrown in milled silver. Meanwhile the shears of the clippers were constantly at work. The coiners too multiplied and prospered: for the worse the current money became the more easily it was imitated. During many years this evil went on increasing. At first it was disregarded: but it at length became an insupportable curse to the country. It was to no purpose that the rigorous laws against coining and clipping were rigorously executed. At every session that was held at the Old Bailey terrible examples were made. Hurdles, with four, five, six wretches convicted of counterfeiting or mutilating the money of the realm, were dragged month after month up Holborn Hill. One morning seven men were hanged and a woman burned for clipping. But all was vain. The gains were such as to lawless spirits seemed more than proportioned to the risks. Some clippers were said to have made great fortunes. One in particular offered six thousand pounds for a pardon. His bribe was indeed rejected: but the fame of his riches did much to counteract the effect which the spectacle of his death was designed to produce.[1] Nay, the severity of the punishment gave encouragement to the crime. For the practice of clipping, pernicious as it was, did not excite in the common mind a detestation resembling that with which men regard murder, arson, robbery, even theft. The injury done by the whole body of clippers to the whole society was indeed immense: but each particular act of clipping was a trifle. To pass a halfcrown, after paring a pennyworth of silver from it, seemed a minute, an almost imperceptible, fault. Even while the nation was crying out most loudly under the distress which the state of the currency had produced, every individual who was capitally punished for contributing to bring the currency into

---

[1] Narcissus Luttrell's Diary is filled with accounts of these executions. "Le métier de rogneur de monnoye," says L'Hermitage, "est si lucratif et paroît si facile que, quelque chose qu'on fasse pour les détruire, il s'en trouve toujours d'autres pour prendre leur place. Oct. $\frac{1}{11}$. 1695."

that state had the general sympathy on his side.   Constables were
unwilling to arrest the offenders.   Justices were unwilling to commit.
Witnesses were unwilling to tell the whole truth.   Juries were unwilling
to pronounce the word Guilty.   The convictions, therefore, numerous as
they might seem, were few indeed when compared with the offences ;
and the offenders who were convicted looked on themselves as mur-

THE DESTRUCTION OF PLAIN DEALING

From the Bagford Ballads

dered men, and were firm in the belief that their sin, if sin it were, was
as venial as that of a schoolboy who goes nutting in the wood of a
neighbour.   All the eloquence of the ordinary could seldom induce
them to conform to the wholesome usage of acknowledging in their
dying speeches the enormity of their wickedness.[1]

[1] As to the sympathy of the public with the clippers, see the very curious sermon which
Fleetwood, afterwards Bishop of Ely, preached before the Lord Mayor in December 1694.

The evil proceeded with constantly accelerating velocity. At length in the autumn of 1695 it could hardly be said that the country possessed, for practical purposes, any measure of the value of commodities. It was a mere chance whether what was called a shilling was really tenpence, sixpence, or a groat. The results of some experiments which were tried at that time deserve to be mentioned. The officers of the Exchequer weighed fifty seven thousand two hundred pounds of hammered money which had recently been paid in. The weight ought to have been above two hundred and twenty thousand ounces. It proved to be under one hundred and fourteen thousand ounces.[1] Three eminent London goldsmiths were invited to send a hundred pounds each in current silver to be tried by the balance. Three hundred pounds ought to have weighed about twelve hundred ounces. The actual weight proved to be six hundred and twenty four ounces. The same test was applied in various parts of the kingdom. It was found that a hundred pounds, which should have weighed about four hundred ounces, did actually weigh at Bristol two hundred and forty ounces, at Cambridge two hundred and three, at Exeter one hundred and eighty, and at Oxford only one hundred and sixteen.[2] There were, indeed, some northern districts into which the clipped money had only begun to find its way. An honest Quaker, who lived in one of these districts, recorded, in some notes which are still extant, the amazement with which, when he travelled southward, shopkeepers and innkeepers stared at the broad and heavy halfcrowns with which he paid his way. They asked whence he came, and where such money was to be found. The guinea which he purchased for twenty two shillings at Lancaster bore a different value at every stage of his journey. When he reached London it was worth thirty shillings, and would indeed have been worth more had not the government fixed that rate as the highest at which gold should be received in the payment of taxes.[3]

Fleetwood says that "a soft pernicious tenderness slackened the care of magistrates, kept back the under officers, corrupted the juries, and withheld the evidence." He mentions the difficulty of convincing the criminals themselves that they had done wrong. See also a Sermon preached at York Castle by George Halley, a clergyman of the Cathedral, to some clippers who were to be hanged the next day. He mentions the impenitent ends which clippers generally made, and does his best to awaken the consciences of his hearers. He dwells on one aggravation of their crime which I should not have thought of. "If," says he, "the same question were to be put in this age, as of old, 'Whose is this image and superscription?' we could not answer the whole. We may guess at the image: but we cannot tell whose it is by the superscription: for that is all gone." The testimony of these two divines is confirmed by that of Tom Brown, who tells a facetious story, which I do not venture to quote, about a conversation between the ordinary of Newgate and a clipper.

[1] Lowndes's Essay for the Amendment of the Silver Coins, 1695.

[2] L'Hermitage, $\frac{\text{Nov. 29.}}{\text{Dec. 9.}}$ 1695.

[3] The Memoirs of this Lancashire Quaker were printed a few years ago in a most respectable newspaper, the Manchester Guardian.

The evils produced by this state of the currency were not such as have generally been thought worthy to occupy a prominent place in history. Yet it may well be doubted whether all the misery which had been inflicted on the English nation in a quarter of a century by bad Kings, bad Ministers, bad Parliaments, and bad Judges, was equal to the misery caused in a single year by bad crowns and bad shillings.   Those events which furnish the best themes for pathetic or indignant eloquence are not always those which most affect the happiness of the great body of the people.   The misgovernment of Charles and James, gross as it had been, had not prevented the common business of life from going steadily and prosperously on.   While the honour and independence of the State were sold to a foreign power, while chartered rights were invaded, while fundamental laws were violated, hundreds of thousands of quiet, honest, and industrious families laboured and traded, ate their meals and lay down to rest, in comfort and security.   Whether Whigs or Tories, Protestants or Jesuits were uppermost, the grazier drove his beasts to market : the grocer weighed out his currants : the draper measured out his broadcloth : the hum of buyers and sellers was as loud as ever in the towns : the harvest home was celebrated as joyously as ever in the hamlets : the cream overflowed the pails of Cheshire : the apple juice foamed in the presses of Herefordshire : the piles of crockery glowed in the furnaces of the Trent ; and the barrows of coal rolled fast along the timber railways of the Tyne.   But when the great instrument of exchange became thoroughly deranged, all trade, all industry, were smitten as with a palsy.   The evil was felt daily and hourly in almost every place and by almost every class, in the dairy and on the threshing floor, by the anvil and by the loom, on the billows of the ocean and in the depths of the mine.   Nothing could be purchased without a dispute. Over every counter there was wrangling from morning to night.   The workman and his employer had a quarrel as regularly as the Saturday came round.   On a fair day or a market day the clamours, the reproaches, the taunts, the curses, were incessant : and it was well if no booth was overturned and no head broken.[1]   No merchant would contract to deliver goods without making some stipulation about the quality of the coin in which he was to be paid.   Even men of business were often bewildered by the confusion into which all pecuniary transactions were thrown.   The simple and the careless were pillaged without mercy by extortioners whose demands grew even more rapidly than the money shrank.   The price of the necessaries of life, of shoes, of ale, of oatmeal rose fast.   The labourer found that the bit of metal, which, when he received it, was called a shilling, would hardly, when he wanted to purchase a pot of beer or a loaf of rye bread, go as far as sixpence.

[1] Lowndes's Essay.

Where artisans of more than usual intelligence were collected in great numbers, as in the dockyard at Chatham, they were able to make their complaints heard and to obtain some redress.[1]   But the ignorant and helpless peasant was cruelly ground between one class which would give money only by tale and another which would take it only by weight.   Yet his sufferings hardly exceeded those of the unfortunate race of authors.   Of the way in which obscure writers were treated we may easily form a judgment from the letters, still extant, of Dryden to his bookseller Tonson.   One day Tonson sends forty brass shillings, to say nothing of clipped money.   Another day he pays a debt with pieces so bad that none of them will go.   The great poet sends them all back, and demands in their place guineas at twenty nine shillings each.   " I expect," he says in one letter, "good silver, not such as I have had formerly."   " If you have any silver that will go," he says in another letter, " my wife will be glad of it.   I lost thirty shillings or more by the last payment of fifty pounds."   These complaints and demands, which have been preserved from destruction only by the eminence of the writer, are doubtless merely a fair sample of the correspondence which filled all the mail bags of England during several months.[2]

In the midst of the public distress one class prospered greatly, the bankers ; and among the bankers none could in skill or in luck bear a comparison with Charles Duncombe.   He had been, not many years before, a goldsmith of very moderate wealth.   He had probably, after the fashion of his craft, plied for customers under the arcades of the Royal Exchange, had saluted merchants with profound bows, and had begged to be allowed the honour of keeping their cash.   But so dexterously did he now avail himself of the opportunities of profit which the general confusion of prices gave to a moneychanger that, at the moment when the trade of the kingdom was depressed to the lowest point, he laid down near ninety thousand pounds for the estate of Helmsley in the North Riding of Yorkshire.   That great property had, in a troubled time, been bestowed by the Commons of England on their victorious general Fairfax, and had been part of the dower

----

[1] L'Hermitage, $\frac{\text{Dec. 24.}}{\text{Jan. 3.}}$ 1695.

[2] Allusions to the state of the currency abound in the essays, plays, and poems, which appeared about this time.   I will give two or three specimens.   Dryden, in the dedication of his translation of the Æneid, complains that he had completely exhausted his vocabulary in order to meet the demands of the original.   " What," he says, " had become of me, if Virgil had taxed me with another book ?   I had certainly been reduced to pay the public in hammered money, for want of milled."   In Cibber's Comedy, entitled " Love's Last Shift, or the Fool in Fashion," a gay young gentleman says : " Virtue is as much debased as our money ; and, faith, *Dei Gratia* is as hard to be found in a girl of sixteen as round the brim of an old shilling."   Blackmore's Satire on Wit is nothing but a clumsy allegory, in which our literature is typified by coin so much impaired that it must be called in, thrown into the melting pot, and restamped.

JACOB TONSON

From a mezzotint by J. Faber, after a painting by Sir G. Kneller

which Fairfax's daughter had brought to the brilliant and dissolute Buckingham. Thither Buckingham, having wasted in mad intemperance, sensual and intellectual, all the choicest bounties of nature and of fortune, had carried the feeble ruins of his fine person and of his fine mind; and there he had closed his chequered life under that humble roof and on that coarse pallet which the great satirist of the succeeding generation described in immortal verse. The spacious domain passed to a new race; and in a few years a palace more splendid and costly than had ever been inhabited by the magnificent Villiers rose amidst the beautiful woods and waters which had been his, and was called by the once humble name of Duncombe.

Since the Revolution the state of the currency had been repeatedly discussed in Parliament. In 1689 a committee of the Commons had been appointed to investigate the subject, but had made no report. In 1690 another committee had reported that immense quantities of silver were carried out of the country by Jews, who, it was said, would do any thing for profit. Schemes were formed for encouraging the importation and discouraging the exportation of the precious metals. One foolish bill after another was brought in and dropped. At length, in the beginning of the year 1695, the question assumed so serious an aspect that the Houses applied themselves to it in earnest. The only practical result of their deliberations, however, was a new penal law which, it was hoped, would prevent the clipping of the hammered coin and the melting and exporting of the milled coin. It was enacted that every person who informed against a clipper should be entitled to a reward of forty pounds, that every clipper who informed against two clippers should be entitled to a pardon, and that whoever should be found in possession of silver filings or parings should be burned in the cheek with a redhot iron. Certain officers were empowered to search for bullion. If bullion were found in a house or on board of a ship, the burden of proving that it had never been part of the money of the realm was thrown on the owner. If he failed in making out a satisfactory history of every ingot he was liable to severe penalties. This Act was, as might have been expected, altogether ineffective. During the following summer and autumn, the coins went on dwindling, and the cry of distress from every county in the realm became louder and more piercing.

But happily for England there were among her rulers some who clearly perceived that it was not by halters and branding irons that her decaying industry and commerce could be restored to health. The state of the currency had during some time occupied the serious attention of four eminent men closely connected by public and private ties. Two of them were politicians who had never, in the midst of official and parliamentary business, ceased to love and honour philosophy ; and two were philosophers, in whom habits of abstruse meditation had not impaired the homely good sense without which even genius is mischievous in politics. Never had there been an occasion which more urgently required both practical and speculative abilities ; and never had the world seen the highest practical and the highest speculative abilities united in an alliance so close, so harmonious, and so honourable as that which bound Somers and Montague to Locke and Newton.

It is much to be lamented that we have not a minute history of the conferences of the men to whom England owed the restoration of her currency and the long series of prosperous years which dates from that restoration. It would be interesting to see how the pure gold of scientific truth found by the two philosophers was mingled by the two statesmen with just that quantity of alloy which was necessary for the working. It would be curious to study the many plans which were propounded, discussed, and rejected, some as inefficacious, some as unjust, some as too costly, some as too hazardous, till at length a plan was devised of which the wisdom was proved by the best evidence, complete success.

Newton has left to posterity no exposition of his opinions touching the currency. But the tracts of Locke on this subject are happily still extant ; and it may be doubted whether in any of his writings, even in those ingenious and deeply meditated chapters on language which form perhaps the most valuable part of the Essay on the Human Understanding, the force of his mind appears more conspicuously. Whether he had ever been acquainted with Dudley North is not known. In moral character the two men bore little resemblance to each other. They belonged to different parties. Indeed, had not Locke taken shelter from tyranny in Holland, it is by no means impossible that he might have been sent to Tyburn by a jury which Dudley North had packed. Intellectually, however, there was much in common between the Tory and the Whig. They had laboriously thought out, each for himself, a theory of political economy, substantially the same with that which Adam Smith afterwards expounded. Nay, in some respects the theory of Locke and North was more complete and symmetrical than that of their illustrious successor. Adam Smith has often been justly blamed for maintaining, in direct opposition to all his own principles, that the rate of interest ought to be regulated by the State ; and he is the more blamable because, long before he was born, both Locke and North had taught that it was as absurd to make laws fixing the price of money as to make laws fixing the price of cutlery or of broadcloth.[1]

---

[1] It ought always to be remembered, to Adam Smith's honour, that he was entirely converted by Bentham's Defence of Usury, and that he acknowledged, with candour worthy of a true philosopher, that the doctrine laid down in the Wealth of Nations was erroneous.

Dudley North died in 1693. A short time before his death he published, without his name, a small tract which contains a concise sketch of a plan for the restoration of the currency. This plan appears to have been substantially the same with that which was afterwards fully developed and ably defended by Locke.

One question, which was doubtless the subject of many anxious deliberations, was whether any thing should be done while the war lasted. In whatever way the restoration of the coin might be effected, great sacrifices must be made, either by the whole community or by a part of the community. And to call for such sacrifices at a time when the nation was already paying taxes such as, ten years before, no financier would have thought it possible to raise, was undoubtedly a course full of danger. Timorous politicians were for delay : but the deliberate conviction of the great Whig leaders was that something must be hazarded, or that every thing was lost. Montague, in particular, is said to have expressed in strong language his determination to kill or cure. If indeed there had been any hope that the evil would merely continue to be what it was, it might have been wise to defer till the return of peace an experiment which must severely try the strength of the body politic. But the evil was one which daily made progress almost visible to the eye. There might have been a recoinage in 1694 with half the risk which must be run in 1696 ; and, great as would be the risk in 1696, that risk would be doubled if the recoinage were postponed till 1698.

Those politicians whose voice was for delay gave less trouble than another set of politicians, who were for a general and immediate re-coinage, but who insisted that the new shilling should be worth only ninepence or ninepence halfpenny. At the head of this party was William Lowndes, Secretary of the Treasury, and member of Parliament for the borough of Seaford, a most respectable and industrious public servant, but much more versed in the details of his office than in the higher parts of political philosophy. He was not in the least aware that a piece of metal with the King's head on it was a commodity of which the price was governed by the same laws which govern the price of a piece of metal fashioned into a spoon or a buckle, and that it was no more in the power of Parliament to make the kingdom richer by calling a crown a pound than to make the kingdom larger by calling a furlong a mile. He seriously believed, incredible as it may seem, that, if the ounce of silver were divided into seven shillings instead of five, foreign nations would sell us their wines and their silks for a smaller number of ounces. He had a considerable following, composed partly of dull men who really believed what he told them, and partly of shrewd men who were perfectly willing to be authorised by law to pay

JOHN LOCKE, 1632-1704.

From the painting by T. Brownover, in the National Portrait Gallery.

a hundred pounds with eighty. Had his arguments prevailed, the evils of a vast confiscation would have been added to all the other evils which afflicted the nation : public credit, still in its tender and sickly infancy, would have been destroyed ; and there would have been much risk of a general mutiny of the fleet and army. Happily Lowndes was completely refuted by Locke in a paper drawn up for the use of Somers. Somers was delighted with this little treatise, and desired that it might be printed. It speedily became the text book of all the most enlightened politicians in the kingdom, and may still be read with pleasure and profit. The effect of Locke's forcible and perspicuous reasoning is greatly heightened by his evident anxiety to get at the truth, and by the singularly generous and graceful courtesy with which he treats an antagonist of powers far inferior to his own. Flamsteed, the Astronomer Royal, described the controversy well by saying that the point in dispute was whether five was six or only five.[1]

Thus far Somers and Montague entirely agreed with Locke : but as to the manner in which the restoration of the currency ought to be effected there was some difference of opinion. Locke recommended, as Dudley North had recommended, that the King should by proclamation fix a near day after which the hammered money should in all payments pass only by weight. The advantages of this plan were doubtless great and obvious. It was most simple, and, at the same time, most efficient. What searching, fining, branding, hanging, burning, had failed to do would be done in an instant. The clipping of the hammered pieces, the melting of the milled pieces, would cease. Great quantities of good coin would come forth from secret drawers and from behind the panels of wainscots. The mutilated silver would gradually flow into the mint, and would come forth again in a form which would make mutilation impossible. In a short time the whole currency of the realm would be in a sound state ; and, during the progress of this great change, there would never at any moment be any scarcity of money.

These were weighty considerations ; and to the joint authority of North and Locke on such a question great respect is due. Yet it must be owned that their plan was open to one serious objection, which did not indeed altogether escape their notice, but of which they seem to have thought too lightly. The restoration of the currency was a benefit to the whole community. On what principle then was the expense of restoring the currency to be borne by a part of the community? It was most desirable doubtless that the words pound and shilling should again have a fixed signification, that every man should know what his contracts

[1] Lowndes's Essay for the Amendment of the Silver Coins ; Locke's Further Considerations concerning raising the Value of Money ; Locke to Molyneux, Nov. 20. 1695 ; Molyneux to Locke, Dec. 24. 1695.

meant and what his property was worth.   But was it just to attain this excellent end by means of which the effect would be that every farmer who had put by a hundred pounds to pay his rent, every trader who had scraped together a hundred pounds to meet his acceptances, would find his hundred pounds reduced in a moment to fifty or sixty?   It was not the fault of such a farmer or of such a trader that his crowns and half-crowns were not of full weight.   The government itself was to blame. The evil which the State had caused the State was bound to repair ; and it would evidently have been wrong to throw the charge of the repara-tion on a particular class, merely because that class was so situated that it could conveniently be pillaged.   It would have been as reasonable to require the timber merchants to bear the whole cost of fitting out the Channel fleet, or the gunsmiths to bear the whole cost of supplying arms to the regiments in Flanders, as to restore the currency of the kingdom at the expense of those individuals in whose hands the clipped silver happened at a particular moment to be.

Locke declared that he lamented the loss which, if his advice were taken, would fall on the holders of the short money.   But it appeared to him that the nation must make a choice between evils.   And in truth it was much easier to lay down the general proposition that the expenses of restoring the currency ought to be borne by the public than to devise any mode in which they could without extreme inconvenience and danger be so borne.   Was it to be announced that every person who should, within a term of a year or half a year, carry to the mint a clipped crown should receive in exchange for it a milled crown, and that the difference between the value of the two pieces should be made good out of the public purse?   That would be to offer a premium for clipping.   The shears would be more busy than ever.   The short money would every day become shorter.   The difference which the taxpayers would have to make good would probably be greater by a million at the end of the term than at the beginning : and the whole of this million would go to reward malefactors.   If only a very short time were allowed for the bringing in of the hammered coin, the danger of further clipping would be reduced to little or nothing : but another danger would be incurred. The silver would flow into the mint so much faster than it could possibly flow out, that there must during some months be a grievous scarcity of money.

A singularly bold and ingenious expedient occurred to Somers and was approved by William.   It was that a proclamation should be pre-pared with great secresy, and published at once in all parts of the kingdom.   This proclamation was to announce that hammered coins would thenceforth pass only by weight.   But every possessor of such coins was to be invited to deliver them up within three days, in a sealed packet, to the public authorities. The coins were to be examined, numbered, weighed, and returned to the owner with a promissory note entitling him to receive from the Treasury at a future time the difference between the actual quantity of silver in his pieces and the quantity of silver which, according to the standard, those pieces ought to have contained.[1] Had this plan been adopted, an immediate stop would have been put to the clipping, the melting, and the exporting ; and the expense of the restoration of the currency would have been borne, as was right, by the public. The inconvenience arising from a scarcity of money would have been of very short duration : for the mutilated pieces would have been detained only till they could be told and weighed : they would then have been sent back into circulation ; and the recoinage would have

A DUTCH MEDAL ON THE CAMPAIGN OF 1695

taken place gradually and without any perceptible suspension or disturbance of trade. But against these great advantages were to be set off great hazards. The mutilated pieces would indeed not have been long detained. But they must all have been detained at once : or the same coin would have been presented in several places ; and the public would thus have been cheated to an immense extent. During three or four days the country would have been absolutely in a state of barter. And what tumults, what rebellions, might not three or four such days produce ? To incur such danger without the previous sanction of Parliament was to run the risk of censure, impeachment, imprisonment, ruin. The King and the Lord Keeper were alone in the Council. Even Montague quailed ; and it was determined to do nothing without the authority of the legislature. Montague undertook to submit to the Commons a scheme, which was not indeed without dangers and inconveniences, but which was probably the best which he could hope to carry.

On the twenty-second of November the Houses met. Foley was on that day again chosen Speaker. On the following day he was

[1] Burnet, ii. 147.

presented and approved. The King opened the session with a speech very skilfully framed. He congratulated his hearers on the success of

Meeting of the Parliament: loyalty of the House of Commons the campaign on the Continent. That success he attributed, in language which must have gratified their feelings, to the bravery of the English army. He spoke of the evils which had arisen from the deplorable state of the coin, and of the necessity of applying a speedy remedy. He intimated very plainly his opinion that the expense of restoring the currency ought to be borne by the State: but he declared that he referred the whole matter to the wisdom of his Great Council. Before he concluded he addressed himself particularly to the newly elected House of Commons, and warmly expressed his approbation of the excellent choice which his people had made. The speech was received with a low but very significant hum of assent both from above and from below the bar, and was as favourably received by the public as by the Parliament.[1] In the Commons an address of thanks was moved by Wharton, faintly opposed by Musgrave, adopted without a division, and carried up by the whole House to Kensington. At the palace the loyalty of the crowd of gentlemen showed itself in a way which would now be thought hardly consistent with senatorial gravity. When refreshments were handed round in the antechamber, the Speaker filled his glass, and proposed two toasts, the health of King William, and confusion to King Lewis; and both were drunk with loud acclamations. Yet near observers could perceive that, though the representatives of the nation were as a body zealous for civil liberty and for the Protestant religion, and though they were prepared to endure every thing rather than see their country again reduced to vassalage, they were anxious and dispirited. All were thinking of the state of the coin: all were saying that something must be done; and all acknowledged that they did not know what could be done. " I am afraid," said a member who expressed what many felt, " that the nation can bear neither the disease nor the cure."[2]

There was indeed a minority by which the difficulties and dangers of the country were seen with malignant delight; and of that minority the keenest, boldest, and most factious leader was Howe, whom poverty had made more acrimonious than ever. He moved that the House should resolve itself into a Committee on the State of the Nation; and the Ministry,—for that word may now with propriety be used,—readily consented. Indeed the great question touching the currency could not be brought forward more conveniently than in such a Committee. When the Speaker had left the chair, Howe harangued against the war

---

[1] Commons' Journals, Nov. 22, 23. 26. 1695; L'Hermitage, $\frac{Nov.\ 26.}{Dec.\ 6.}$

[2] Commons' Journals, Nov. 26, 27, 28, 29. 1695; L'Hermitage, $\frac{Nov.\ 26.}{Dec.\ 6.}$, $\frac{Nov.\ 29.}{Dec.\ 9.}$, $\frac{Dec.\ 3.}{13.}$

as vehemently as he had in former years harangued for it. He called for peace, peace on any terms. The nation, he said, resembled a wounded man, fighting desperately on, with blood flowing in torrents. During a short time the spirit might bear up the frame : but faintness must soon come on. No moral energy could long hold out against physical exhaustion. He found very little support. The great majority of his hearers were fully determined to put every thing to hazard rather than submit to France. It was sneeringly remarked that the state of his own finances had suggested to him the image of a man bleeding to death, and that, if a cordial were administered to him in the form of a salary, he would trouble himself little about the drained veins of the commonwealth. " We did not," said the Whig orators, " degrade our-selves by suing for peace when our flag was chased out of our own Channel, when Tourville's fleet lay at anchor in Torbay, when the Irish nation was in arms against us, when every post from the Netherlands brought news of some disaster, when we had to contend against the genius of Louvois in the cabinet and of Luxemburg in the field. And are we to turn suppliants now, when no hostile squadron dares to show itself even in the Mediterranean, when our arms are victorious on the Continent, when God has removed the great statesman and the great soldier whose abilities long frustrated our efforts, and when the weak-ness of the French administration indicates, in a manner not to be mistaken, the ascendency of a female favourite ? " Howe's suggestion was contemptuously rejected ; and the Committee proceeded to take into consideration the state of the currency.[1]

Meanwhile the newly liberated presses of the capital never rested a moment. Innumerable pamphlets and broadsides about the coin lay on the counters of the booksellers, and were thrust into the hands of members of Parliament in the lobby. In one of the most curious and amusing of these pieces Lewis and his ministers are introduced, expressing the greatest alarm lest England should make herself the richest country in the world by the simple expedient of calling ninepence a shilling, and confidently predicting that, if the old standard were maintained, there would be another revolution. Some writers vehemently objected to the proposition that the public should bear the expense of restoring the currency : some urged the government to take this opportunity of assimilating the money of England to the money of neighbouring nations : one projector was for coining guilders ; another for coining dollars.[2]

Controversy touching the currency

---

[1] Commons' Journals, Nov. 28, 29. 1695 ; L'Hermitage, Dec. $\frac{9}{15}$.

[2] L'Hermitage, $\frac{Nov. 22.}{Dec. 2.}$, Dec. $\frac{6}{16}$. 1695 ; An Abstract of the Consultations and Debates between the French King and his Council concerning the new Coin that is intended to be made in Eng-land, privately sent by a Friend of the Confederates from the French Court to his Brother at

Within the walls of Parliament the debates continued during several anxious days. At length Montague, after defeating, first those who **Parliamentary proceedings touching the currency** were for letting things remain unaltered till the peace, and then those who were for the little shilling, carried eleven resolutions in which the outlines of his own plan were set forth. It was resolved that the money of the kingdom should be recoined according to the old standard both of weight and of fineness; that all the new pieces should be milled; that the loss on the clipped pieces should be borne by the public; that a time should be fixed after which no clipped money should pass, except in payments to the government; and that a later time should be fixed, after which no clipped money should pass at all. What divisions took place in the Committee cannot be ascertained. When the resolutions were reported there was one division. It was on the question whether the old standard of weight should be maintained. The Noes were a hundred and fourteen; the Ayes two hundred and twenty five.[1]

It was ordered that a bill founded on the resolutions should be brought in. A few days later the Chancellor of the Exchequer explained to the Commons, in a Committee of Ways and Means, the plan by which he proposed to meet the expense of the recoinage. It was impossible to estimate with precision the charge of making good the deficiencies of the clipped money. But it was certain that at least twelve hundred thousand pounds would be required. Twelve hundred thousand pounds the Bank of England undertook to advance on good security. It was a maxim received among financiers that no security which the government could offer was so good as the old hearth money had been. That tax, odious as it was to the great majority of those who paid it, was remembered with regret at the Treasury and in the City. It occurred to the Chancellor of the Exchequer that it might be possible to devise an impost on houses, which might be not less productive nor less certain than the hearth money, but which might press less heavily on the poor, and might be collected by a less vexatious process. The number of hearths in a house could not be ascertained without domiciliary visits. The windows a collector might count without passing the threshold. Montague proposed that the inhabitants of cottages, who had been cruelly harassed by the chimney men, should be altogether exempted from the new duty. His plan was approved

Brussels, Dec. 12. 1695; A Discourse of the General Notions of Money, Trade, and Exchanges, by Mr. Clement of Bristol; A Letter from an English Merchant at Amsterdam to his Friend in London; A Fund for preserving and supplying our Coin; An Essay for regulating the Coin, by A. V.; A Proposal for supplying His Majesty with 1,200,000*l*., by mending the Coin, and yet preserving the ancient Standard of the Kingdom. These are a few of the tracts which were distributed among members of Parliament at this conjuncture.

[1] Commons' Journals, Dec. 10. 1695; L'Hermitage, Dec. $\frac{3}{13}$. $\frac{6}{16}$. $\frac{10}{20}$.

by the Committee of Ways and Means, and was sanctioned by the House without a division. Such was the origin of the window tax, a tax which, though doubtless a great evil, must be considered as a blessing when compared with the curse from which it was the means of rescuing the nation.[1]

Thus far things had gone smoothly. But now came a crisis which required the most skilful steering. The news that the Parliament and the government were determined on a reform of the currency produced an ignorant panic among the common people. Every man wished to get rid of his clipped crowns and halfcrowns. No man liked to take them. There were brawls approaching to riots in half the streets of London. The Jacobites, always full of joy and hope in a day of adversity and public danger, ran about with eager looks and noisy tongues. The health of King James was publicly drunk in taverns and on ale benches. Many members of Parliament, who had hitherto supported the government, began to waver ; and, that nothing might be wanting to the difficulties of the conjuncture, a dispute on a point of privilege arose between the Houses. The Recoinage Bill, framed in conformity with Montague's resolutions, had gone up to the Peers and had come back with amendments, some of which, in the opinion of the Commons, their Lordships had no right to make. The emergency was too serious to admit of delay. Montague brought in a new bill, which was in fact his former bill modified in some points to meet the wishes of the Lords : the Lords, though not perfectly contented with the new bill, passed it without any alteration ; and the royal assent was immediately given. The fourth of May, a date long remembered over the whole kingdom and especially in the capital, was fixed as the day on which the government would cease to receive the clipped money in payment of taxes.[2]

The principles of the Recoinage Act are excellent. But some of the details, both of that Act and of a supplementary Act which was passed at a later period of the session, seem to prove that Montague had not fully considered what legislation can, and what it cannot, effect. For example, he persuaded the Parliament to enact that it should be penal to give or take more than twenty two shillings for a guinea. It may be confidently affirmed that this enactment was not suggested or approved by Locke. He well knew that the high price of gold was not the evil which afflicted the State, but merely a symptom of that evil, and that

---

[1] Commons' Journals, Dec. 13. 1695.

[2] Stat. 7 Gul. 3. c. 1. ; Lords' and Commons' Journals ; L'Hermitage, $\frac{\text{Dec. 31.}}{\text{Jan. 10.}}$, Jan. $\frac{7}{17}$. $\frac{10}{20}$. $\frac{14}{24}$. 1696. L'Hermitage describes in strong language the extreme inconvenience caused by the dispute between the Houses :—"La longueur qu'il y a dans cette affaire est d'autant plus désagréable qu'il n'y a point de sujet sur lequel le peuple en général puisse souffrir plus d'incommodité, puis qu'il n'y a personne qui, à tous moments, n'aye occasion de l'esprouver."

a fall in the price of gold would inevitably follow, and could by no human power or ingenuity be made to precede, the recoinage of the silver. In fact, the penalty seems to have produced no effect whatever. Till the milled silver was in circulation, the guinea continued, in spite of the law, to pass for thirty shillings. When the milled silver became plentiful, the price of the guinea fell ; and the fall did not stop at twenty two shillings, but continued till it reached twenty one shillings and sixpence.[1]

Early in February the panic which had been caused by the first debates on the currency subsided ; and, from that time till the fourth of May, the want of money was not very severely felt. The recoinage began. Ten furnaces were erected in a garden behind the Treasury, which was then a part of Whitehall, and which lay between the Banqueting House and the river. Every day huge heaps of pared and defaced crowns and shillings were here turned into massy ingots which were instantly sent off to the mint in the Tower.[2]

With the fate of the law which restored the currency was closely connected the fate of another law, which had been several years under

Passing of the Act regulating Trials in cases of High Treason

the consideration of Parliament, and had caused several warm disputes between the hereditary and the elective branch of the legislature. The session had scarcely commenced when the Bill for regulating Trials in cases of High Treason was again laid on the table of the Commons. Of the debates which followed nothing is known except one interesting circumstance which has been preserved by tradition. Among those who supported the bill appeared conspicuous a young Whig of high rank, of ample fortune, and of great abilities which had been assiduously improved by study. This was Anthony Ashley Cooper, Lord Ashley, eldest son of the second Earl of Shaftesbury, and grandson of that renowned politician who had, in the days of Charles the Second, been at one time the most unprincipled of ministers, and at another the most unprincipled of demagogues. Ashley had just been returned to Parliament for the borough of Poole, and was in his twenty-fifth year. In the course of his speech he faltered, stammered, and seemed to lose the thread of his reasoning. The House, then, as now, indulgent to novices, and then, as now, well aware that, on a first appearance, the hesitation which is

[1] That Locke was not a party to the attempt to make gold cheaper by penal laws, I infer from a passage in which he notices Lowndes's complaints about the high price of guineas. "The only remedy," says Locke, "for that mischief, as well as a great many others, is the putting an end to the passing of clipp'd money by tale."—Locke's Further Considerations. That the penalty proved, as might have been expected, inefficacious, appears from several passages in the despatches of L'Hermitage, and even from Haynes's Brief Memoires, though Haynes was a devoted adherent of Montague.

[2] L'Hermitage, Jan. $\frac{14}{24}$. 1696.

The Right Honorable Anthony Ashley Cooper Earl of Shaftesbury, Baron Ashley of Winbourn S^t. Giles, & Lord Cooper of Pawlett.

J. Closterman Pinx.   Sim: Gribelin Sculp.

ANTHONY ASHLEY COOPER, THIRD EARL OF SHAFTESBURY

From an engraving by S. Gribelin, after a painting by J. Closterman

the effect of modesty and sensibility is quite as promising a sign as volubility of utterance and ease of manner, encouraged him to proceed. " How can I, Sir," said the young orator, recovering himself, " produce a stronger argument in favour of this bill than my own failure? My fortune, my character, my life, are not at stake. I am speaking to an audience whose kindness might well inspire me with courage. And yet, from mere nervousness, from mere want of practice in addressing large assemblies, I have lost my recollection : I am unable to go on with my argument. How helpless, then, must be a poor man who, never having opened his lips in public, is called upon to reply, without a moment's preparation, to the ablest and most experienced advocates in the kingdom, and whose faculties are paralysed by the thought that, if he fails to convince his hearers, he will in a few hours die on a gallows, and leave beggary and infamy to those who are dearest to him ! " It may reasonably be suspected that Ashley's confusion and the ingenious use which he made of it had been carefully premeditated. His speech, however, made a great impression, and probably raised expectations which were not fulfilled. His health was delicate : his taste was refined even to fastidiousness : he soon left politics to men whose bodies and minds were of coarser texture than his own, gave himself up to mere intellectual luxury, lost himself in the mazes of the old Academic philosophy, and aspired to the glory of reviving the old Academic eloquence. His diction, affected and florid, but often singularly beautiful and melodious, fascinated many young enthusiasts. He had not merely disciples, but worshippers. His life was short : but he lived long enough to become the founder of a new sect of English freethinkers, diametrically opposed in opinions and feelings to that sect of freethinkers of which Hobbes was the oracle. During many years the Characteristics continued to be the Gospel of romantic and sentimental unbelievers, while the Gospel of coldblooded and hardheaded unbelievers was the Leviathan.[1]

The bill, so often brought in and so often lost, went through the Commons without a division, and was carried up to the Lords. It soon came back with the long disputed clause altering the constitution of the Court of the Lord High Steward. A strong party among the representatives of the people was still unwilling to grant any new privilege to the nobility : but the moment was critical. The misunderstanding which had arisen between the Houses touching the Recoinage Bill had produced inconveniences which might well alarm even a bold politician. It was necessary to purchase concession by concession. The Commons,

---

[1] A remarkable instance of the fascinating effect which Shaftesbury's eloquence produced on young and ardent minds will be found in the autobiography of Cowper's friend and spiritual guide. John Newton.

by a hundred and ninety two votes to a hundred and fifty, agreed to the amendment on which the Lords had, during four years, so obstinately insisted ; and the Lords in return immediately passed the Recoinage Bill without any amendment.

There had been much contention as to the time at which the new system of procedure in cases of high treason should come into operation; and the bill had once been lost in consequence of a dispute on this point. Many persons were of opinion that the change ought not to take place till the close of the war. It was notorious, they said, that the foreign enemy was abetted by many traitors at home ; and, at such a time, the severity of the laws which protected the commonwealth against the machinations of bad citizens ought not to be relaxed. It was at last determined that the new regulations should take effect on the twenty-fifth of March, the first day, according to the old Calendar, of the year 1696.

On the twenty-first of January the Recoinage Bill and the Bill for regulating Trials in cases of High Treason received the royal assent. On the following day the Commons repaired to Kensington on an errand by no means agreeable either to themselves or to the King. They were, as a body, fully resolved to support him, at whatever cost and at whatever hazard, against every foreign and domestic foe. But they were, as indeed every assembly of five hundred and thirteen English gentlemen that could by Parliamentary proceedings touching the grant of Crown lands in Wales to Portland any process have been brought together must have been, jealous of the favour which he showed to the friends of his youth. He had set his heart on placing the house of Bentinck on a level in wealth and dignity with the houses of Howard and Seymour, of Russell and Cavendish. Some of the fairest hereditary domains of the Crown had been granted to Portland, not without murmuring on the part both of Whigs and Tories. Nothing had been done, it is true, which was not in conformity with the letter of the law and with a long series of precedents. Every English sovereign had, from time immemorial, considered the lands to which he had succeeded in virtue of his office as his private property. Every family that had been great in England, from the De Veres down to the Hydes, had been enriched by royal deeds of gift. Charles the Second had carved ducal estates for his bastards out of his hereditary domain. Nor did the Bill of Rights contain a word which could be construed to mean that the King was not at perfect liberty to alienate the manors and forests of the Crown. At first, therefore, William's liberality to his countrymen, though it caused much discontent, called forth no remonstrance from the Parliament. But he at length went too far. In 1695 he ordered the Lords of the Treasury to make out a warrant granting to Portland a magnificent estate in Denbighshire. This estate was said to be worth more than a hundred thousand pounds. The annual income, therefore, can hardly have been less than six thousand pounds ; and the annual rent which was reserved to the Crown was only six and eightpence. This, however, was not the worst. With the property were inseparably connected extensive royalties, which the people of North Wales could not patiently see in the hands of any subject. More than a century before Elizabeth had bestowed a part of the same territory on her favourite Leicester. On that occasion the population of Denbighshire had risen in arms ; and, after much tumult and several executions, Leicester had thought it advisable to resign his mistress's gift back to her. The opposition to Portland was less violent, but not less effective. Some of the chief gentlemen of the principality made strong representations to the ministers through whose offices the warrant had to pass, and at length brought the subject under the consideration of the Lower House. An address was unanimously voted requesting the King to stop the grant : Portland begged that he might not be the cause of a dispute between his master and the Parliament ; and the King, though much mortified, yielded to the general wish of the nation.[1]

This unfortunate affair, though it terminated without an open quarrel, left much sore feeling. The King was angry with the Commons, and still more angry with the Whig ministers who had not ventured to defend his grant. The loyal affection which the Parliament had testified to him during the first days of the session had perceptibly cooled ; and he was almost as unpopular as he had ever been when an event took place which suddenly brought back to him the hearts of millions, and made him for a time as much the idol of the nation as he had been at the end of 1688.[2]

The plan of assassination which had been formed in the preceding spring had been given up in consequence of William's departure for the Continent. The plan of insurrection which had been formed in the summer had been given up for want of help from France. But before the end of the autumn both plans were resumed. William had returned to England ; and the possibility of getting rid of him by a lucky shot or stab was again seriously discussed. The French troops had gone into winter quarters ; and the force, which

Two Jacobite plots formed

---

[1] Commons' Journals, Jan. 14. 17. 23. 1696 ; L'Hermitage, Jan. $\frac{14}{24}$.; Gloria Cambriæ, or Speech of a Bold Briton against a Dutch Prince of Wales, 1702 ; Life of the late Honourable Robert Price, &c. 1734. Price was the bold Briton whose speech—never, I believe, spoken— was printed in 1702. He would have better deserved to be called bold, if he had published his impertinence while William was living. The Life of Price is a miserable performance, full of blunders and anachronisms.

[2] L'Hermitage mentions the unfavourable change in the temper of the Commons ; and William alludes to it repeatedly in his letters to Heinsius, Jan. $\frac{21}{31}$. 1696, $\frac{\text{Jan. 28.}}{\text{Feb. 7.}}$

The Honourable ROBERT PRICE, Esqr. one of the BARONS of his Majesties Court of EXCHEQUER 1714.

ROBERT PRICE

From an engraving by G. Vertue, after a painting by Sir G. Kneller

Charnock had in vain demanded while war was raging round Namur, might now be spared without inconvenience. Now, therefore, a plot was laid, more formidable than any that had yet threatened the throne and the life of William : or rather, as has more than once happened in our history, two plots were laid, one within the other. The object of the greater plot was an open insurrection, an insurrection which was to be supported by a foreign army. In this plot almost all the Jacobites of note were more or less concerned. Some laid in arms : some bought horses : some made lists of the servants and tenants in whom they could place firm reliance. The less warlike members of the party could at least take off bumpers to the King over the water, and intimate by significant shrugs and whispers that he would not be over the water long. It was universally remarked that the malecontents looked wiser than usual when they were sober, and bragged more loudly than usual when they were drunk.[1] To the smaller plot, of which the object was the murder of William, only a few select traitors were privy.

Each of these plots was under the direction of a leader specially sent from Saint Germains. The more honourable mission was entrusted **Berwick's plot** to Berwick. He was charged to communicate with the Jacobite nobility and gentry, to ascertain what force they could bring into the field, and to fix a time for the rising. He was authorised to assure them that the French government was collecting troops and transports at Calais, and that, as soon as it was known there that a rebellion had broken out in England, his father would embark with twelve thousand veteran soldiers, and would be among them in a few hours.

A more hazardous part was assigned to an emissary of lower rank, but of great address, activity, and courage. This was Sir George **The Assassination Plot. Sir George Barclay** Barclay, a Scotch gentleman who had served with credit under Dundee, and who, when the war in the Highlands had ended, had retired to Saint Germains. Barclay was called into the royal closet, and received his orders from the royal lips. He was directed to steal across the Channel and to repair to London. He was told that a few select officers and soldiers should speedily follow him by twos and threes. That they might have no difficulty in finding him, he was to walk, on Mondays and Thursdays, in the Piazza of Covent Garden after nightfall, with a white handkerchief hanging from his coat pocket. He was furnished with a considerable sum of money, and with a commission, which was not only signed, but written from beginning to end, by James himself. This commission authorised the bearer to do from time to time such acts of hostility against the Prince of Orange and that Prince's adherents as should most

---

[1] The gaiety of the Jacobites is said by Van Cleverskirke to have been noticed during some time ; $\frac{\text{Feb. 25.}}{\text{March 6.}}$ 1696.

conduce to the service of the King. What explanation of these very comprehensive words was orally given by James we are not informed.

Lest Barclay's absence from Saint Germains should cause any suspicion, it was given out that his loose way of life had made it necessary for him to put himself under the care of a surgeon at Paris.[1] He set out with eight hundred pounds in his portmanteau, hastened to the coast, and embarked on board of a privateer which was employed by the Jacobites as a regular packet boat between France and England. This vessel conveyed him to a desolate spot in Romney Marsh. About half a mile from the landing place a smuggler named Hunt lived on a dreary and unwholesome fen where he had no neighbours but a few rude fishermen and shepherds. His dwelling was singularly well situated for a contraband traffic in French wares. Cargoes of Lyons silk and Valenciennes lace sufficient to load thirty packhorses had repeatedly been landed in that dismal solitude without attracting notice. But, since the Revolution, Hunt had discovered that of all cargoes a cargo of traitors paid best. His lonely abode became the resort of men of high consideration, Earls and Barons, Knights and Doctors of Divinity. Some of them lodged many days under his roof while waiting for a passage. A clandestine post was established between his house and London. The couriers were constantly going and returning : they performed their journeys up and down on foot : but they appeared to be gentlemen ; and it was whispered that one of them was the son of a titled man. The letters from Saint Germains were few and small. Those directed to Saint Germains were numerous and bulky : they were made up like parcels of millinery, and were buried in the morass till they were called for by the privateer.

Here Barclay landed in January 1696 ; and hence he took the road to London. He was followed, a few days later, by a tall young man, who concealed his name, but who produced credentials of the highest authority. This stranger too proceeded to London. Hunt afterwards discovered that his humble roof had had the honour of sheltering the Duke of Berwick.[2]

The part which Barclay had to perform was difficult and hazardous ; and he omitted no precaution. He had been little in London ; and his face was consequently unknown to the agents of the government. Nevertheless he had several lodgings : he disguised himself so well that his oldest friends would not have known him by broad daylight ; and yet he seldom ventured into the streets except in the dark. His chief agent was a monk who, under several names, heard confessions and said masses at the risk of his neck. This man intimated to some of the zealots with whom he consorted that a special agent of the royal family was to be

---

[1] Harris's deposition, March 28. 1696.   [2] Hunt's deposition.

spoken with in Covent Garden, on certain nights, at a certain hour, and might be known by certain signs.[1]   In this way Barclay became acquainted with several men fit for his purpose.

The first persons to whom he fully opened himself were Charnock and Parkyns.   He talked with them about the plot which they and some of their friends had formed in the preceding spring against the life of William.   Both Charnock and Parkyns declared that the plan then laid might easily be executed, that there was no want of resolute hearts among the Royalists, and that all that was wanting was some sign of His Majesty's approbation.

Then Barclay produced his commission.   He showed his two accomplices that James had expressly commanded all good Englishmen, not only to rise in arms, not only to make war on the usurping government, not only to seize forts and towns, but also to do from time to time such other acts of hostility against the Prince of Orange as might be for the royal service.   These words, Barclay said, plainly authorised an attack on the Prince's person.   Charnock and Parkyns were satisfied.   How in truth was it possible for them to doubt that James's confidential agent correctly interpreted James's expressions?   Nay, how was it possible for them to understand the large words of the commission in any sense but one, even if Barclay had not been there to act as commentator?   If indeed the subject had never been brought under James's consideration, it might perhaps have been thought that those words had dropped from his pen without any definite meaning.   But he had been repeatedly apprised that some of his friends in England meditated a deed of blood, and that they were waiting only for his approbation.   They had importuned him to speak one word, to give one sign.   He had long kept silence ; and, now that he broke silence, he merely told them to do whatever might be beneficial to himself and prejudicial to the usurper.   They had his authority as plainly given as they could reasonably expect to have it given in such a case.[2]

All that remained was to find a sufficient number of courageous and trustworthy assistants, to provide horses and weapons, and to fix the hour and the place of the slaughter.   Forty men, it was thought, would be sufficient.   Those troopers of James's guard who had already followed Barclay across the Channel made up nearly half that number.   James had himself seen some of these men before their departure from Saint Germains, had given them money for their journey, had told them by what name each of them was to pass in England, had commanded them to act as they should be directed by Barclay, and had informed them

[1] Fisher's and Harris's depositions.

[2] Barclay's narrative, in the Life of James, ii. 548.; Paper by Charnock among the Nairne MSS. in the Bodleian Library.

COVENT GARDEN

THE PIAZZA, COVENT GARDEN, ABOUT 1720

From an engraving by Sutton Nicholls

where Barclay was to be found and by what tokens he was to be known.[1] They were ordered to depart in small parties, and to assign different reasons for going. Some were ill: some were weary of the service: Cassels, one of the most noisy and profane among them, announced that, since he could not get military promotion, he should enter at the Scotch college, and study for a learned profession. Under such pretexts about twenty picked men left the palace of James, made their way by Romney Marsh to London, and found their captain walking in the dim lamplight of the Piazza with the handkerchief hanging from his pocket. One of these men was Ambrose Rookwood, who held the rank of Brigadier, and who had a high reputation for courage and honour: another was Major John Bernardi, an adventurer of Genoese extraction, whose name has derived a melancholy celebrity from a punishment so strangely prolonged that it at length shocked a generation which could not remember his crime.[2]

It was in these adventurers from France that Barclay placed his chief trust. In a moment of elation he once called them his Janissaries, and expressed a hope that they would get him the George and Garter. But twenty more assassins at least were wanted. The conspirators probably expected valuable help from Sir John Friend, who had received a Colonel's commission signed by James, and had been most active in enlisting men and providing arms against the day when the French should appear on the coast of Kent. The design was imparted to him: but he thought it so rash, and so likely to bring reproach and disaster on the good cause, that he would lend no assistance to his friends, though he kept their secret religiously.[3] Charnock undertook to find eight brave and trusty fellows. He communicated the design to Porter, not with Barclay's entire approbation; for Barclay appears to have thought that a tavern brawler, who had recently been in prison for swaggering drunk about the streets and huzzaing in honour of the Prince of Wales, was hardly to be trusted with a secret of such fearful import. Porter entered into the plot with enthusiasm, and promised to bring in others who would be useful. Among those whose help he engaged was his servant Thomas Keyes. Keyes was a far more formidable conspirator than might have been expected from his station in life. The household troops generally were devoted to William: but there was a taint of disaffection among the Blues. The chief conspirators had already been tampering with some Roman Catholics who were in that regiment; and Keyes was excellently qualified to bear a part in this work: for he had

[1] Harris's deposition.

[2] Harris's deposition. Bernardi's autobiography is not at all to be trusted. It contains some absurd mistakes, and some deliberate falsehoods.

[3] See his trial.

Quo Fata Trahunt.

Major JOHN BERNARDI Anno ætatis 83. primum die Junii Æ Dni 1738.

W. Cooper pinx.   Ger. Vander Gucht sculp.

*Libertate privatus et Carcere inclusus Aliquis,
triginta et tres penè Annos, inauditus, absque
aliquâ certâ Liberationis Spe, Criminis
Suspectus allegati tantùm, sed non probati
miseram equidem vitam agit, morte multò
deteriorem, puniri verùm haud justè videtur
Talis in Angliâ Quæ dicitur et jactatur plurimis,
fore Patria libera.*

MAJOR JOHN BERNARDI

From an engraving by G. Vander Gucht, prefixed to Bernardi's Memoirs

formerly been trumpeter of the corps, and, though he had quitted the service, he still kept up an acquaintance with some of the old soldiers in whose company he had lived at free quarter on the Somersetshire farmers after the battle of Sedgemoor.

Parkyns, who was old and gouty, could not himself take a share in the work of death. But he employed himself in providing horses, saddles, and weapons for his younger and more active accomplices. In this department of business he was assisted by Charles Cranburne, a person who had long acted as a broker between Jacobite plotters and people who dealt in cutlery and firearms. Special orders were given by Barclay that the swords should be made rather for stabbing than for slashing. Barclay himself enlisted Edward Lowick, who had been a Major in the Irish army, and who had, since the capitulation of Limerick, been living obscurely in London. The monk who had been Barclay's first confidant recommended two busy Papists, Richard Fisher and Christopher Knightley; and this recommendation was thought sufficient. Knightley drew in Edward King, a Roman Catholic gentleman of hot and restless temper; and King procured the assistance of a French gambler and bully named De la Rue.[1]

Meanwhile the heads of the conspiracy held frequent meetings at treason taverns, for the purpose of settling a plan of operations. Several schemes were proposed, applauded, and, on full consideration, abandoned. At one time it was thought that an attack on Kensington House at dead of night might probably be successful. The outer wall might easily be scaled. If once forty armed men were in the garden, the palace would soon be stormed or set on fire. Some were of opinion that it would be best to strike the blow on a Sunday as William went from Kensington to attend divine service at the chapel of Saint James's Palace. The murderers might assemble on the ground where Apsley House and Hamilton Place now stand. Just as the royal coach passed out of Hyde Park, and was about to enter what has since been called the Green Park, thirty of the conspirators, well mounted, might fall on the guards. The guards were ordinarily only five and twenty. They would be taken completely by surprise; and probably half of them would be shot or cut down before they could strike a blow. Meanwhile ten or twelve resolute men on foot would stop the carriage by shooting the horses, and would then without difficulty despatch the King. At last the preference was given to a plan originally sketched by Fisher and put into shape by Porter. William was in the habit of going every Saturday from Kensington to hunt in Richmond Park. There was then no bridge over the Thames between London and Kingston. The King therefore went, in a coach escorted by some of his body guards,

[1] Fisher's deposition ; Knightley's deposition ; Cranburne's trial ; De la Rue's deposition.

God Preſerve from all his **KING** *Willm* Enemies.

The Villanous Plot,

Being a contrivance of ſeveral villanous Papiſts

To kill King Willam.

To the Tune of, *Liggan Water.*

What means this grumbletonian crew,
Oh what is it they fain would do,
Sure miſchief on themſelves *they bring*,
Who Plots againſt our gracious King.

What is it more theſe Men would have,
Then what there is a Prince moſt brave,
Who for this Nation thinks it good,
To venture ſtill his deareſt blood.

To *Flanders* yearly he does go,
To fight brave *England's* greateſt Foe,
And yet the Jacobites they ſay,
Are plotting miſchief ery day.

For Knights and Majors, Captains too,
And others of this helliſh crew,
Who all did plot upon one day,
To take the King's dear life away.

Forty or Fifty were the gang,
In time at *Tybourn* they may hang,
And then their Quarters ſeparate,
For to be ſet upon each Gate.

For wickedly thus to combine,
In this ſame Helliſh baſe deſign,
That is to give the fatal blow
When th' King ſhould to his Chappel go.

But thanks to Heaven which ore rules,
Theſe Jacobites and plotting fouls,
And put it in the Heart of one,
For to diſcover the whole gang.

Who did a Letter ſend away,
For to prevent this bloody day,
Which notice gave of ev'ry thing,
And who they were to kill the King.

Oh Traytors, Traytors, full of blood,
You nere can Act for *England's* good,
Who ſtrives for to deſtrey our King,
And in his room a Papiſt bring.

Beſides the bloody French muſt come,
Oh where are we then cry one,
For Father, Mother, Son and Wench
Muſt all be ſlaves unto the French.

Our Liberty, Religion, and
All that's dear to us in this Land,
Muſt by a Papiſt power be,
Inſlaved then in miſery.

But Heaven who does power give,
Does ſtill preſerve our King alive,
Inſpite of Plotters wicked hand,
Who would deſtroy our King and Land.

As by this wicked bloody Plot,
Of Papiſts who together got,
Some *Iriſh French* and *Engliſh*, who
Would hands in Royal blood imbrew.

At *Richmond* they deſign'd to act
This villanous and bloody fact,
But by a Letter that was ſent,
It did, thank God, the ſame prevent.

Another time they had pitch'd on,
When the King was a Hunting gone,
Two or three hundred had agree'd
To make our Royal King to bleed.

But now comes all their diſcont;
For ſev'ral are to *Newgate* ſent;
And muſt remain in Goal each one
Till try'd; then *Tybourn* is their Doom.

London, Printed for *T. M.* 1696.

THE VILLANOUS PLOT TO KILL KING WILLIAM

From the Pepysian Collection of Ballads

through Turnham Green to the river. There he took boat, crossed the water, and found another coach and another set of guards ready to receive him on the Surrey side. The first coach and the first set of guards awaited his return on the northern bank. The conspirators ascertained with great precision the whole order of these journeys, and carefully examined the ground on both sides of the Thames. They thought that they should attack the King with more advantage on the Middlesex than on the Surrey bank, and when he was returning than when he was going. For, when he was going, he was often attended to the water side by a great retinue of lords and gentlemen; but on his return he had only his guards about him. The place and time were fixed. The place was to be a narrow and winding lane leading from the landingplace on the north of the river to Turnham Green. The spot may still be easily found. The ground has since been drained by trenches. But in the seventeenth century it was a quagmire, through which the royal coach was with difficulty tugged at a foot's pace. The time was to be the afternoon of Saturday the fifteenth of February. On that day the Forty were to assemble in small parties at public houses near the Green. When the signal was given that the coach was approaching, they were to take horse and repair to their posts. As the cavalcade came up the lane, Charnock was to attack the guards in the rear, Rookwood on one flank, Porter on the other. Meanwhile Barclay, with eight trusty men, was to stop the coach and to do the deed. That no movement of the King might escape notice, two orderlies were appointed to watch the palace. One of these men, a bold and active Fleming, named Durant, was especially charged to keep Barclay well informed. The other, whose business was to communicate with Charnock, was a ruffian named Chambers, who had served in the Irish army, had received a severe wound in the breast at the Boyne, and, on account of that wound, bore a savage personal hatred to William.[1]

While Barclay was making all his arrangements for the assassination, Berwick was endeavouring to persuade the Jacobite aristocracy to rise

Failure of Berwick's plot   in arms. But this was no easy task. Several consultations were held; and there was one great muster of the party under the pretence of a masquerade, for which tickets were distributed among the initiated at one guinea each.[2] All ended however in talking, singing, and drinking. Many men of rank and fortune indeed declared that they would draw their swords for their rightful Sovereign as soon as their rightful Sovereign was in the island with a French army; and Berwick had been empowered to assure them that a French army should be sent as soon as they had drawn the sword.

[1] See the trials and depositions.   [2] L'Hermitage, March $\frac{3}{13}$. 1696.

But between what they asked and what he was authorised to grant there was a difference which admitted of no compromise. Lewis, situated as he was, would not risk ten or twelve thousand excellent soldiers on the mere faith of promises. Similar promises had been made in 1690; and yet, when the fleet of Tourville had appeared on the coast of Devonshire, the western counties had risen as one man in defence of the government, and not a single malecontent had dared to utter a whisper in favour of the invaders. Similar promises had been made in 1692; and to the confidence which had been placed in those promises was to be attributed the great disaster of La Hogue. The French King would not be deceived a third time. He would gladly help the English royalists; but he must first see them help themselves. There was much reason in this; and there was reason also in what the Jacobites urged on the other side. If, they said, they were to rise, without a single disciplined regiment to back them, against an usurper supported by a regular army, they should all be cut to pieces before the news that they were up could reach France. As Berwick could hold out no hope that there would be an invasion before there was an insurrection, and as his English friends were immovable in their determination that there should be no insurrection till there was an invasion, he had nothing more to do here, and became impatient to depart.

He was the more impatient to depart because the fifteenth of February drew near. For he was in constant communication with the assassins, and was perfectly apprised of all the details of the crime which was to be perpetrated on that day. He was generally considered as a man of sturdy and even ungracious integrity. But to such a degree had his sense of right and wrong been perverted by his zeal for the interests of his family, and by his respect for the lessons of his priests, that he did not, as he has himself ingenuously confessed, think that he lay under any obligation to dissuade the murderers from the execution of their purpose. He had indeed only one objection to their design; and that objection he kept to himself. It was simply this, that all who were concerned were very likely to be hanged. That, however, was their affair; and, if they chose to run such a risk in the good cause, it was not his business to discourage them. His mission was quite distinct from theirs: he was not to act with them; and he had no inclination to suffer with them. He therefore hastened down to Romney Marsh, and crossed to Calais.[1]

At Calais he found preparations making for a descent on Kent. Troops filled the town : transports filled the port. Boufflers had been ordered to repair thither from Flanders, and to take the command. James himself was daily expected. In fact he had already left Saint

---

[1] See Berwick's Memoirs.

Germains.   Berwick, however, would not wait.   He took the road to Paris, met his father at Clermont, and made a full report of the state of things in England.   His embassy had failed: the Royalist nobility and gentry seemed resolved not to rise till a French army was in the island: but there was still a hope : news would probably come within a few days that the usurper was no more ; and such news would change the whole aspect of affairs.   James determined to go on to Calais, and there to await the event of Barclay's plot.   Berwick hastened to Versailles for the purpose of giving explanations to Lewis.   What the nature of the explanations was we know from Berwick's own narrative.   He plainly told the French King that a small band of loyal men would in a short time make an attempt on the life of the great enemy of France. The next courier might bring tidings of an event which would probably subvert the English government and dissolve the European coalition. It might have been thought that a prince who ostentatiously affected the character of a devout Christian and of a courteous knight would instantly have taken measures for conveying to his rival a caution which perhaps might still arrive in time, and would have severely reprimanded the guests who had so grossly abused his hospitality.   Such, however, was not the conduct of Lewis.   Had he been asked to give his sanction to a murder he would probably have refused with indignation.   But he was not moved to indignation by learning that, without his sanction, a crime was likely to be committed which would be far more beneficial to his interests than ten such victories as that of Landen.   He sent down orders to Calais that his fleet should be in readiness to take advantage of the great crisis which he anticipated.   At Calais James waited with still more impatience for the signal that his nephew was no more. That signal was to be given by a fire, of which the fuel was already prepared on the cliffs of Kent, and which would be visible across the straits.[1]

But a peculiar fate has, in our country, always attended such conspiracies as that of Barclay and Charnock.   The English regard assassination, and have during some ages regarded it, with a loathing peculiar to themselves.   So English indeed is this sentiment that it cannot even now be called Irish, and that, till a recent period, it was not Scotch.   In Ireland to this day the villain who shoots at his enemy from behind a hedge is too often protected from justice by public sympathy.   In Scotland plans of assassination were often, during the sixteenth and seventeenth centuries,

Detection of the Assassination Plot

---

[1] Van Cleverskirke, $\frac{\text{Feb. 25.}}{\text{March 6.}}$ 1696.   I am confident that no sensible and impartial person, after attentively reading Berwick's narrative of these transactions, and comparing it with the narrative in the Life of James, (ii. 544.) which is taken, word for word, from the Original Memoirs, can doubt that James was accessory to the design of assassination.

successfully executed, though known to great numbers of persons. The murders of Beaton, of Rizzio, of Darnley, of Murray, of Sharpe, are conspicuous instances. The royalists who murdered Lisle in Switzerland were Irishmen: the royalists who murdered Ascham at Madrid were Irishmen: the royalists who murdered Dorislaus at the Hague were Scotchmen. In England, as soon as such a design ceases to be a secret hidden in the recesses of one gloomy and ulcerated heart, the risk of detection and failure becomes extreme. Felton and Bellingham reposed trust in no human being; and they were therefore able to accomplish their evil purposes. But Babington's conspiracy against Elizabeth, Fawkes's conspiracy against James, Gerard's conspiracy against Cromwell, the Rye House conspiracy, Despard's conspiracy, the Cato Street conspiracy, were all discovered, frustrated, and punished. In truth such a conspiracy is here exposed to equal danger from the good and from the bad qualities of the conspirators. Scarcely any Englishman, not utterly destitute of conscience and honour, will engage in a plot for slaying an unsuspecting fellow creature; and a wretch who has neither conscience nor honour is likely to think much on the danger which he incurs by being true to his associates, and on the rewards which he may obtain by betraying them. There are, it is true, persons in whom religious or political fanaticism has destroyed all moral sensibility on one particular point, and yet has left that sensibility generally unimpaired. Such a person was Digby. He had no scruple about blowing King, Lords and Commons into the air. Yet to his accomplices he was religiously and chivalrously faithful; nor could even the fear of the rack extort from him one word to their prejudice. But this union of depravity and heroism is very rare. The vast majority of men are either not vicious enough or not virtuous enough to be loyal and devoted members of treacherous and cruel confederacies; and, if a single member should want either the necessary vice or the necessary virtue, the whole confederacy is in danger. To bring together in one body forty Englishmen, all hardened cutthroats, and yet all so upright and generous that neither the hope of opulence nor the dread of the gallows can tempt any one of them to be false to the rest, has hitherto been found, and will, it is to be hoped, always be found impossible.

There were among Barclay's followers both men too bad and men too good to be trusted with such a secret as his. The first whose heart failed him was Fisher. Even before the time and place of the crime had been fixed, he obtained an audience of Portland, and told that lord that a design was forming against the King's life. Some days later Fisher came again with more precise intelligence. But his character was not such as entitled him to much credit; and the knavery of Fuller, of Young, of Whitney, and of Taaffe, had made men of sense slow to believe stories of plots.   Portland, therefore, though in general very easily alarmed where the safety of his master and friend was concerned, seems to have thought little about the matter.   But, on the evening of the fourteenth of February, he received a visit from a person whose testimony he could not treat lightly.   This was a Roman Catholic gentleman of known courage and honour, named Pendergrass.   He had, on the preceding day, come up to town from Hampshire, in consequence of a pressing summons from Porter, who, dissolute and unprincipled as he was, had to Pendergrass been a most kind friend, indeed almost a father.   In a Jacobite insurrection Pendergrass would probably have been one of the foremost.   But he learned with horror that he was expected to bear a part in a wicked and shameful deed.   He found himself in one of those situations which most cruelly torture noble and sensitive natures.   What was he to do?   Was he to commit a murder?   Was he to suffer a murder which he could prevent to be committed?   Yet was he to betray one who, however culpable, had loaded him with benefits?   Perhaps it might be possible to save William without harming Porter.   Pendergrass determined to make the attempt.   " My lord," he said to Portland, "as you value King William's life, do not let him hunt tomorrow.   He is the enemy of my religion : yet my religion constrains me to give him this caution.   But the names of the conspirators I am resolved to conceal : some of them are my friends : one of them especially is my benefactor ; and I will not betray them."

Portland went instantly to the King : but the King received the intelligence very coolly, and seemed determined not to be frightened out of a good day's sport by such an idle story.   Portland argued and implored in vain.   He was at last forced to threaten that he would immediately make the whole matter public, unless His Majesty would consent to remain within doors during the next day ; and this threat was successful.[1]

Saturday the fifteenth came.   The Forty were all ready to mount, when they received intelligence from the orderlies who watched Kensington House that the King did not mean to hunt that morning. " The fox," said Chambers, with vindictive bitterness, " keeps his earth." Then he opened his shirt, showed the great scar on his breast, and vowed revenge on William.

The first thought of the conspirators was that their design had been detected.   But they were soon reassured.   It was given out that the weather had kept the King at home ; and indeed the day was cold and stormy.   There was no sign of agitation at the palace.   No extraordinary precaution was taken.   No arrest was made.   No ominous whisper was

[1] L'Hermitage, Feb. 25. / March 6.

THE TRIUMPHS OF PROVIDENCE

A broadside on the failure of the Plot. Number 1296 in the British Museum Catalogue Satirical Prints

heard at the coffeehouses.   The delay was vexatious : but Saturday the twenty-second would do as well.

But, before Saturday the twenty-second arrived, a third informer, De la Rue, had presented himself at the palace.   His way of life did not entitle him to much respect : but his story agreed so exactly with what had been said by Fisher and Pendergrass that even William began to believe that there was real danger.

Very late in the evening of Friday the twenty-first, Pendergrass, who had as yet disclosed much less than either of the other informers, but whose single word was worth much more than their joint oath, was sent for to the royal closet.   The faithful Portland and the gallant Cutts were the only persons who witnessed the singular interview between the King and his generous enemy.   William, with courtesy and animation which he rarely showed, but which he never showed without making a deep impression, urged Pendergrass to speak out. " You are a man of true probity and honour : I am deeply obliged to you : but you must feel that the same considerations which have induced you to tell us so much ought to induce you to tell us something more.   The cautions which you have as yet given can only make me suspect every body that comes near me.   They are sufficient to embitter my life, but not sufficient to preserve it.   You must let me know the names of these men."   During more than half an hour the King continued to entreat and Pendergrass to refuse.   At last Pendergrass said that he would give the information which was required, if he could be assured that it would be used only for the prevention of the crime, and not for the destruction of the criminals.   " I give you my word of honour," said William, " that your evidence shall not be used against any person without your own free consent."   It was long past midnight when Pendergrass wrote down the names of the chief conspirators.

While these things were passing at Kensington, a large party of the assassins were revelling at a Jacobite tavern in Maiden Lane.   Here they received their final orders for the morrow.   " Tomorrow or never," said King.   " Tomorrow, boys," cried Cassels with a curse, " we shall have the plunder of the field."   The morrow came.   All was ready : the horses were saddled : the pistols were loaded : the swords were sharpened : the orderlies were on the alert : they early sent intelligence from the palace that the King was certainly going a hunting : all the usual preparations had been made : a party of guards had been sent round by Kingston Bridge to Richmond : the royal coaches, each with six horses, had gone from the stables at Charing Cross to Kensington. The chief murderers assembled in high glee at Porter's lodgings.   Pendergrass, who, by the King's command, appeared among them, was greeted with ferocious mirth. "Pendergrass," said Porter, "you are named one of the eight who are to do his business. I have a musquetoon for you that will carry eight balls." "Mr. Pendergrass," said King, "pray do not be afraid of smashing the glass windows." From Porter's lodgings the party adjourned to the Blue Posts in Spring Gardens, where they meant to take some refreshment before they started for Turnham Green. They were at table when a message came from an orderly that the King had changed his mind and would not hunt; and scarcely had they recovered from their first surprise at this ominous news, when Keyes, who had been out scouting among his old comrades, arrived with news more ominous still. "The coaches have returned to Charing Cross. The guards that were sent round to Richmond have just come back to Kensington at full gallop, the flanks of the horses all white with foam. I have had a word with one of the Blues. He told me that strange things are muttered." Then the countenances of the assassins fell; and their hearts died within them. Porter made a feeble attempt to disguise his uneasiness. He took up an orange and squeezed it. "What cannot be done one day may be done another. Come, gentlemen, before we part let us have one glass to the squeezing of the rotten orange." The squeezing of the rotten orange was drunk; and the company dispersed.[1]

A few hours elapsed before all the conspirators abandoned all hope. Some of them derived comfort from a report that the King had taken physic, and that this was his only reason for not going to Richmond. If it were so, the blow might still be struck. Two Saturdays had been unpropitious. But Sunday was at hand. One of the plans which had formerly been discussed and abandoned might be resumed. The usurper might be set upon at Hyde Park Corner on his way to his chapel. Charnock was ready for the most desperate enterprise. However great the risk, however small the chance of success, it was better to die biting and scratching to the last than to be worried without resistance or revenge. He assembled some of his accomplices at one of the numerous houses at which he had lodgings, and plied them hard with healths to the King, to the Queen, to the Prince, and to the Grand Monarch, as they called Lewis. But the terror and dejection of the gang were beyond the power of wine; and so many had stolen away that those who were left could effect nothing. In the course of the afternoon it was known that the guards had been doubled at the palace; and soon after nightfall messengers from the Secretary of State's office were hurrying to and fro with torches through the streets, accompanied by files of

[1] My account of these events is taken chiefly from the trials and depositions. See also Burnet, ii. 165, 166, 167., Blackmore's True and Impartial History, compiled under the direction of Shrewsbury and Somers, and Boyer's History of King William III., 1703.

musketeers.　Before the dawn of Sunday Charnock was in custody.　A little later, Rookwood and Bernardi were found in bed at a Jacobite alehouse on Tower Hill.　Seventeen more traitors were seized before noon; and three of the Blues were put under arrest.　That morning a Council was held; and, as soon as it rose, an express was sent off to call home some regiments from Flanders: Dorset set out for Sussex, of which he was Lord Lieutenant: Romney, who was Warden of the Cinque Ports, started for the coast of Kent; and Russell hastened down the Thames to take the command of the fleet.　In the evening the Council sate again.　Some of the prisoners were examined and committed.　The Lord Mayor was in attendance, was informed of what had been discovered, and was specially charged to look well to the peace of the capital.[1]

On Monday morning all the trainbands of the City were under arms.　The King went in state to the House of Lords, sent for the

Parliamentary proceedings touching the Assassination Plot Commons, and from the throne told the Parliament that, but for the protection of a gracious Providence, he should at that moment have been a corpse, and the kingdom would have been invaded by a French army.　The danger of invasion, he added, was still great: but he had already given such orders as would, he hoped, suffice for the protection of the realm.　Some traitors were in custody: warrants were out against others: he should do his part in this emergency; and he relied on the Houses to do theirs.[2]

The Houses instantly voted a joint address in which they thankfully acknowledged the divine goodness which had preserved him to his people, and implored him to take more than ordinary care of his person.　They concluded by exhorting him to seize and secure all whom he regarded as dangerous.　On the same day two important bills were brought into the Commons.　By one the Habeas Corpus Act was suspended.　The other provided that the Parliament should not be dissolved by the death of William.　Sir Rowland Gwyn, an honest country gentleman, made a motion of which he did not at all foresee the important consequences.　He proposed that the members should enter into an association for the defence of their Sovereign and their country.　Montague, who of all men was the quickest at taking and improving a hint, saw how much such an association would strengthen the government and the Whig party.[3]　An instrument was immediately drawn up, by which the representatives of the people, each for himself, solemnly recognised William as rightful and lawful King, and bound themselves to stand by him and by each other against James and

---

[1] Portland to Lexington, March $\frac{3}{13}$. 1696; Van Cleverskirke, $\frac{\text{Feb. 25.}}{\text{Mar. 6.}}$; L'Hermitage, of the same date.

[2] Commons' Journals, Feb. 24. 1695.　　　[3] England's Enemies Exposed, 1701.

James's adherents.   Lastly they vowed that, if His Majesty's life should be shortened by violence, they would avenge him signally on his murderers, and would, with one heart, strenuously support the order

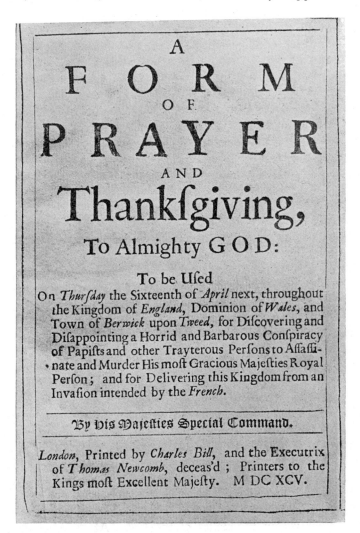

A
FORM
OF
PRAYER
AND
Thankſgiving,
To Almighty GOD:

To be Uſed
On *Thurſday* the Sixteenth of *April* next, throughout the Kingdom of *England*, Dominion of *Wales*, and Town of *Berwick* upon *Tweed*, for Diſcovering and Diſappointing a Horrid and Barbarous Conſpiracy of Papiſts and other Trayterous Perſons to Aſſaſſi-・nate and Murder His moſt Gracious Majeſties Royal Perſon; and for Delivering this Kingdom from an Invaſion intended by the *French*.

By His Majeſties Special Command.

London, Printed by *Charles Bill*, and the Executrix of *Thomas Newcomb*, deceas'd ; Printers to the Kings moſt Excellent Majeſty.   M DC XCV.

FACSIMILE OF THE TITLE PAGE OF THE THANKSGIVING SERVICE

From a copy in the possession of the Editor

of succession settled by the Bill of Rights.   It was ordered that the House should be called over the next morning.[1]   The attendance was consequently great : the Association, engrossed on parchment, was on

[1] Commons' Journals, Feb. 24. 169⅝.

the table ; and the members went up, county by county, to sign their names.[1]

The King's speech, the joint address of both Houses, the Association framed by the Commons, and a proclamation, containing a list of the conspirators, and offering a reward of a thousand pounds for the apprehension of any one of them, were soon cried in all the streets of the capital and carried out by all the postbags.

State of public feeling

Wherever the news came it raised the whole country. Those two hateful words, assassination and invasion, acted like a spell. No impressment was necessary. The seamen came forth from their hiding places by thousands to man the fleet. Only three days after the King had appealed to the nation, Russell sailed out of the Thames with one great squadron. Another was ready for action at Spithead. The militia of all the maritime counties from the Wash to the Land's End was under arms. For persons accused of offences merely political there was generally much sympathy. But Barclay's assassins were hunted like wolves by the whole population. The abhorrence which the English have, through many generations, felt for domiciliary visits, and for all those impediments which the police of continental states throws in the way of travellers, was for a time suspended. The gates of the City of London were kept many hours closed while a strict search was made within. The magistrates of almost every walled town in the kingdom followed the example of the capital. On every highway parties of armed men were posted with orders to stop passengers of suspicious appearance. During a few days it was hardly possible to perform a journey without a passport, or to procure posthorses without the authority of a justice of the peace. Nor was any voice raised against these precautions. The common people indeed were, if possible, more eager than the public functionaries to bring the traitor to justice. This eagerness may perhaps be in part ascribed to the great rewards promised by the royal proclamation. The hatred which every good Protestant felt for Popish cutthroats was not a little strengthened by the songs in which the street poets celebrated the lucky hackney coachman who had caught his traitor, had received the promised thousand pounds, and had set up as a gentleman.[2] The zeal of the populace could in some places hardly be kept within the limits of the law. At the country seat of Parkyns in Warwickshire, arms and accoutrements sufficient to equip a troop of cavalry were found. As soon as this was known, a furious

---

[1] Commons' Journals, Feb. 25. 169$\frac{5}{6}$. ; Van Cleverskirke, $\frac{\text{Feb. 28.}}{\text{Mar. 9.}}$; L'Hermitage, of the same date.

[2] According to L'Hermitage, $\frac{\text{Feb. 28.}}{\text{Mar. 9.}}$, there were two of these fortunate hackney coachmen. A shrewd and vigilant hackney coachman indeed was, from the nature of his calling, very likely to be successful in this sort of chase. The newspapers abound with proofs of the general enthusiasm.

mob assembled, pulled down the house, and laid the gardens utterly waste.[1] Parkyns himself was tracked to a garret in the Temple. Porter and Keyes, who had fled into Surrey, were pursued by the hue and cry, stopped by the country people near Leatherhead, and, after some show of resistance, secured and sent to prison. Friend was found hidden in the house of a Quaker. Knightley was caught in the dress of a fine lady, and recognised in spite of his patches and paint. In a few days all the chief conspirators were in custody except Barclay, who succeeded in making his escape to France.

At the same time some notorious malecontents were arrested, and were detained for a time on suspicion. Old Roger Lestrange, now in his eightieth year, was taken up. Ferguson was found hidden under a bed in Gray's Inn Lane, and was, to the general joy, locked up in Newgate.[2] Meanwhile a special commission was issued for the trial of the traitors. There was no want of evidence. For, of the conspirators who had been seized, ten or twelve were ready to save themselves by bearing witness against their associates. None had been deeper in guilt, and none shrank with more abject terror from death, than Porter. The government consented to spare him, and thus obtained, not only his evidence, but the much more respectable evidence of Pendergrass. Pendergrass was in no danger : he had committed no offence : his character was fair ; and his testimony would have far greater weight with a jury than the testimony of a crowd of approvers swearing for their necks. But he had the royal word of honour that he should not be a witness without his own consent ; and he was fully determined not to be a witness unless he were assured of Porter's safety. Porter was now safe ; and Pendergrass had no longer any scruple about relating the whole truth.

Charnock, King, and Keyes were set first to the bar. The Chiefs of the three Courts of Common Law and several other Judges were on the bench ; and among the audience were many members of both Houses of Parliament.

Trial of Charnock, King and Keyes

It was the eleventh of March. The new Act for regulating the procedure in cases of high treason was not to come into force till the twenty-fifth. The culprits urged that, as the Legislature had, by passing that Act, recognised the justice of allowing them to see their indictment, and to avail themselves of the assistance of an advocate, the tribunal ought either to grant them what the highest authority had declared to be a reasonable indulgence, or to defer the trial for a fortnight. The Judges, however, would consent to no delay. They have therefore been accused by some writers of using the mere letter of the law in order

[1] Postman, March 5. 169⅚.
[2] The Postman, Feb. 29., March 2., March 12., March 14. 169⅚.

to destroy men who, if the law had been construed according to its spirit, might have had some chance of escape. This accusation is unjust. The Judges undoubtedly carried the real intention of the legislature into effect; and, for whatever injustice was committed, the legislature, and not the Judges, ought to be held accountable. The words, "twenty-fifth of March," had not slipped into the Act by mere inadvertence. All parties in Parliament had long been agreed as to the principle of the new regulations. The only matter about which there was any dispute was the time at which those regulations should take effect. After debates extending through several sessions, after repeated divisions with various results, a compromise had been made; and it was surely not for the Courts to alter the terms of that compromise. It may indeed be confidently affirmed that, if the Houses had foreseen that a plot against the person of William would be detected in the course of that year, they would have fixed, not an earlier, but a later day for the commencement of the new system. Undoubtedly the Parliament, and especially the Whig party, deserved serious blame. For, if the old rules of procedure gave no unfair advantage to the Crown, there was no reason for altering them; and if, as was generally admitted, they did give an unfair advantage to the Crown, and that against a defendant on trial for his life, they ought not to have been suffered to continue in force a single day. But no blame is due to the tribunals for not acting in direct opposition both to the letter and to the spirit of the law.

The government might indeed have postponed the trials till the new Act came into force; and it would have been wise, as well as right, to do so; for the prisoners would have gained nothing by the delay. The case against them was one on which all the ingenuity of the Inns of Court could have made no impression. Porter, Pendergrass, De la Rue, and others gave evidence which admitted of no answer. Charnock said the very little that he had to say with readiness and presence of mind. The jury found all the defendants guilty. It is not much to the honour of that age that the announcement of the verdict was received with loud huzzas by the crowd which surrounded the Courthouse. Those huzzas were renewed when the three unhappy men, having heard their doom, were brought forth under a guard.[1]

Charnock had hitherto shown no sign of flinching: but when he was again in his cell his fortitude gave way. He begged hard for mercy. He would be content, he said, to pass the rest of his days in an easy confinement. He asked only for his life. In return for his life, he promised to discover all that he knew of the schemes of the Jacobites against the government. If it should appear that he prevaricated or

[1] Postman, March 12. 1696; Vernon to Lexington, March 13.; Van Cleverskirke, March 13/23. The proceedings are fully reported in the Collection of State Trials.

that he suppressed any thing, he was willing to undergo the utmost rigour of the law. This offer produced much excitement, and some difference of opinion, among the councillors of William. But the King decided, as in such cases he seldom failed to decide, wisely and magnanimously. He saw that the discovery of the Assassination Plot had changed the whole posture of affairs. His throne, lately tottering, was fixed on an immovable basis. His popularity had risen impetuously to as great a height as when he was on his march from Torbay to London. Many who had been out of humour with his administration, and who had, in their spleen, held some communication with Saint Germains, were shocked to find that they had been, in some sense, leagued with murderers. He would not drive such persons to despair. He would not even put them to the blush. Not only should they not be punished: they should not undergo the humiliation of being pardoned. He would not know that they had offended. Charnock was left to his fate.[1] When he found that he had no chance of being received as a deserter, he assumed the dignity of a martyr, and played his part resolutely to the close. That he might bid farewell to the world with a better grace, he ordered a fine new coat to be hanged in, and was very particular on his last day about the powdering and curling of his wig.[2] Just before he was turned off, he delivered to the Sheriffs a paper in which he avowed that he had conspired against the life of the Prince of Orange, but solemnly denied that James had given any commission authorising assassination. The denial was doubtless literally correct: but Charnock did not deny, and assuredly could not with truth have denied, that he had seen a commission written and signed by James, and containing words which might without any violence be construed, and which were, by all to whom they were shown, actually construed, to authorise the murderous ambuscade of Turnham Green.

Indeed Charnock, in another paper, which is still in existence, but has never been printed, held very different language. He plainly said that, for reasons too obvious to be mentioned, he could not tell the whole truth in the paper which he had delivered to the Sheriffs. He acknowledged that the plot in which he had been engaged seemed, even to many loyal subjects, highly criminal. They called him assassin and murderer. Yet what had he done more than had been done by Mucius Scævola? Nay, what had he done more than had been done by every body who had borne arms against the Prince of Orange? If an army of twenty thousand men had suddenly landed in England and surprised the usurper, this

---

[1] Burnet, ii. 171.; The Present Disposition of England considered, 1701 ; England's Enemies Exposed, 1701 ; L'Hermitage, March ⅟₇. 1696. L'Hermitage says, "Charnock a fait des grandes instances pour avoir sa grace, et a offert de tout déclarer : mais elle lui a esté refusée."

[2] L'Hermitage, March ⅟₇.

would have been called legitimate war. Did the difference between war and assassination depend merely on the number of persons engaged? What then was the smallest number which could lawfully surprise an enemy? Was it five thousand, or a thousand, or a hundred? Jonathan and his armourbearer were only two. Yet they made a great slaughter of the Philistines. Was that assassination? It cannot, said Charnock, be the mere act, it must be the cause, that makes killing assassination. It followed that it was not assassination to kill one,—and here the dying man gave a loose to all his hatred,—who had declared a war of extermination against loyal subjects, who hung, drew, and quartered every man who stood up for the right, and who had laid waste England to enrich the Dutch. Charnock admitted that his enterprise would have been unjustifiable if it had not been authorised by James: but he maintained that it had been authorised, not indeed expressly, but by implication. His Majesty had indeed formerly prohibited similar attempts: but he had prohibited them, not as in themselves criminal, but merely as inexpedient at this or that conjuncture of affairs. Circumstances had changed. The prohibition might therefore reasonably be considered as withdrawn. His Majesty's faithful subjects had then only to look to the words of his commission; and those words, beyond all doubt, fully warranted an attack on the person of the usurper.[1]

King and Keyes suffered with Charnock. King behaved with firmness and decency. He acknowledged his crime, and said that he **Execution of Charnock, King, and Keyes** repented of it. He thought it due to the Church of which he was a member, and on which his conduct had brought reproach, to declare that he had been misled, not by any casuistry about tyrannicide, but merely by the violence of his own evil passions. Poor Keyes was in an agony of terror. His tears and lamentations moved the pity of some of the spectators. It was said at the time, and it has often since been repeated, that a servant drawn into crime by a master, and then betrayed by that master, was a proper object of royal clemency. But those who have blamed the severity with which Keyes was treated have altogether omitted to notice the important circumstance which distinguished his case from that of every other

[1] This most curious paper is among the Nairne MSS. in the Bodleian Library. A short, and not perfectly ingenuous, abstract of it will be found in the Life of James, ii. 555. Why Macpherson, who has printed many less interesting documents, did not choose to print this document, it is easy to guess. I will transcribe two or three important sentences. " It may reasonably be presumed that what, in one juncture, His Majesty had rejected he might in another accept, when his own and the public good necessarily required it. For I could not understand it in such a manner as if he had given a general prohibition that at no time the Prince of Orange should be touched . . . . . . Nobody that believes His Majesty to be lawful King of England can doubt but that in virtue of his commission to levy war against the Prince of Orange and his adherents, the setting upon his person is justifiable, as well by the laws of the land duly interpreted and explained as by the law of God."

NINE JACOBITE PLOTTERS

From a German engraving in the Sutherland Collection

conspirator.　He had been one of the Blues.　He had kept up to the last an intercourse with his old comrades.　On the very day fixed for the murder he had contrived to mingle with them and to pick up intelligence from them.　The regiment had been so deeply infected with disloyalty that it had been found necessary to confine some men and to dismiss many more.　Surely, if any example was to be made, it was proper to make an example of the agent by whose instrumentality the men who meant to shoot the King communicated with the men whose business was to guard him.

Friend was tried next.　His crime was not of so black a dye as that of the three conspirators who had just suffered.　He had indeed **Trial of Friend** invited foreign enemies to invade the realm, and had made preparations for joining them.　But, though he had been privy to the design of assassination, he had not been a party to it.　His large fortune however, and the use which he was well known to have made of it, marked him out as a fit object for punishment.　He, like Charnock, asked for counsel, and, like Charnock, asked in vain.　The Judges could not relax the law ; and the Attorney General would not postpone the trial.　The proceedings of that day furnish a strong argument in favour of the Act from the benefit of which Friend was excluded.　It is impossible to read them over at this distance of time without feeling compassion for a silly ill educated man, unnerved by extreme danger, and opposed to cool, astute, and experienced antagonists.　Charnock had defended himself and those who were tried with him as well as any professional advocate could have done.　But poor Friend was as helpless as a child.　He could do little more than exclaim that he was a Protestant, and that the witnesses against him were Papists, who had dispensations from their priests for perjury, and who believed that to swear away the lives of heretics was a meritorious work.　He was so grossly ignorant of law and history as to imagine that the Statute of Treasons, passed in the reign of Edward the Third, at a time when there was only one religion in the kingdom, contained a clause providing that no Papist should be a witness, and actually forced the Clerk of the Court to read the whole Act from beginning to end.　About Friend's guilt it was impossible that there could be a doubt in any rational mind.　He was convicted ; and he would have been convicted if he had been allowed the privileges for which he asked.

Parkyns came next.　He had been deeply concerned in the worst part of the plot, and was, in one respect, less excusable than any of his **Trial of Parkyns** accomplices : for they were all nonjurors ; and he had taken the oaths to the existing government.　He too insisted that he ought to be tried according to the provisions of the new Act.　But the counsel for the Crown stood on their extreme right ; and his request

was denied.   As he was a man of considerable abilities, and had been
bred to the bar, he probably said for himself all that counsel could have
said for him ; and that all amounted to very little.   He was found guilty,
and received sentence of death on the evening of the twenty-fourth of
March, within six hours of the time when the law of which he had vainly
demanded the benefit was to come into force.[1]

The execution of the two knights was eagerly expected by the population of London.   The States General were informed by their correspondent that, of all sights, that in which the English most delighted was a
hanging, and that, of all hangings within the memory of the oldest man,
that of Friend and Parkyns had excited the greatest interest.   The multitude had been incensed against Friend by reports touching the exceeding
badness of the beer which he brewed.   It was even rumoured that he had,
in his zeal for the Jacobite cause, poisoned all the casks which he had
furnished to the navy.   An innumerable crowd accordingly assembled
at Tyburn.   Scaffolding had been put up which formed an immense
amphitheatre round the gallows.   On this scaffolding the wealthier
spectators stood, row above row ; and expectation was at the height when
it was announced that the show was deferred.   The mob broke up in bad
humour, and not without many fights between those who had given
money for their places and those who refused to return it.[2]

The cause of this severe disappointment was a resolution suddenly
passed by the Commons.   A member had proposed that a Committee
should be sent to the Tower with authority to examine the prisoners,
and to hold out to them the hope that they might, by a full and ingenuous confession, obtain the intercession of the House.   The debate
appears, from the scanty information which has come down to us, to
have been a very curious one.   Parties seemed to have changed characters.   It might have been expected that the Whigs would have been
inexorably severe, and that, if there was any tenderness for the unhappy
men, that tenderness would have been found among the Tories.   But
in truth many of the Whigs hoped that they might, by sparing two
criminals who had no power to do mischief, be able to detect and
destroy numerous criminals high in rank and office.   On the other
hand, every man who had ever had any dealings direct or indirect with
Saint Germains, or who took an interest in any person likely to have
had such dealings, looked forward with dread to the disclosures which
the captives might, under the strong terrors of death, be induced to
make.   Seymour, simply because he had gone further in treason than
almost any other member of the House, was louder than any other
member of the House in exclaiming against all indulgence to his brother

---

[1] The trials of Friend and Parkyns will be found, excellently reported, among the State Trials.
[2] L'Hermitage, April $\frac{3}{13}$. 1696.

traitors. Would the Commons usurp the most sacred prerogative of the Crown? It was for His Majesty, and not for them, to judge whether lives justly forfeited could be without danger spared. The Whigs however carried their point. A Committee, consisting of all the Privy Councillors in the House, set off instantly for Newgate. Friend and Parkyns were interrogated, but to no purpose. They had, after sentence had been passed on them, shown at first some symptoms of weakness : but their courage had been fortified by the exhortations of nonjuring divines who had been admitted to the prison. The rumour was that Parkyns would have given way but for the entreaties of his daughter, who adjured him to suffer like a man for the good cause. The criminals acknowledged that they had done the acts of which they had been convicted, but, with a resolution which is the more respectable because it seems to have sprung, not from constitutional hardihood, but from sentiments of honour and religion, refused to say any thing which could compromise others.[1]

In a few hours the crowd again assembled at Tyburn ; and this time the sightseers were not defrauded of their amusement. They saw indeed one sight which they had not expected, and which pro-

Execution of Friend and Parkyns duced a greater sensation than the execution itself. Jeremy Collier and two other nonjuring divines of less celebrity, named Cook and Snatt, had attended the prisoners in Newgate, and were in the cart under the gallows. When the prayers were over, and just before the hangman did his office, the three schismatical priests stood up, and laid their hands on the heads of the dying men who continued to kneel. Collier pronounced a form of absolution taken from the service for the Visitation of the Sick, and his brethren exclaimed " Amen ! "

This ceremony raised a great outcry ; and the outcry became louder when, a few hours after the execution, the papers delivered by the two traitors to the Sheriffs were made public. It had been supposed that Parkyns at least would express some repentance for the crime which had brought him to the gallows. Indeed he had, before the Committee of the Commons, owned that the Assassination Plot could not be justified. But, in his last declaration, he avowed his share in that plot, not only without a word indicating remorse, but with something which resembled exultation. Was this a man to be absolved by Christian divines, absolved before the eyes of tens of thousands, absolved with rites evidently intended to attract public attention, with rites of which there was no trace in the Book of Common Prayer or in the practice of the Church of England ?

[1] Commons' Journals, April 1, 2. 1696 ; L'Hermitage, April $\frac{3}{13}$. 1696 ; Van Cleverskirke, of the same date.

In journals, pamphlets, and broadsides, the insolence of the three Levites, as they were called, was sharply reprehended. Warrants were

SOME SMALL REMARKS ON THE LATE PLOT.

From a broadside in the Sutherland Collection

soon out. Cook and Snatt were taken and imprisoned: but Collier was able to conceal himself, and, by the help of one of the presses which were at the service of his party, sent forth from his hiding place a defence of his conduct. He declared that he abhorred assassination as much as any of those who railed against him ; and his general character warrants us in believing that this declaration was perfectly sincere. But the rash act into which he had been hurried by party spirit furnished his adversaries with very plausible reasons for questioning his sincerity. A crowd of answers to his defence appeared. Preeminent among them in importance was a solemn manifesto, signed by the two Archbishops, and by all the Bishops who were then in London, twelve in number. Even Crewe of Durham and Sprat of Rochester set their names to this document. They condemned the proceedings of the three nonjuring divines, as in form irregular, and in substance impious. To remit the sins of impenitent sinners was a profane abuse of the power which Christ had delegated to his ministers. It was not denied that Parkyns had planned an assassination. It was not pretended that he had professed any repentance for planning an assassination. The plain inference was that the divines who absolved him did not think it sinful to assassinate King William. Collier rejoined : but, though a pugnacious controversialist, he on this occasion shrank from close conflict, and made his escape as well as he could under a cloud of quotations from Tertullian, Cyprian, and Jerome, Albaspinæus and Hammond, the Council of Carthage and the Council of Toledo. The public feeling was strongly against the three absolvers. The government however wisely determined not to confer on them the honour of martyrdom. A bill was found against them by the grand jury of Middlesex : but they were not brought to trial. Cook and Snatt were set at liberty after a short detention ; and Collier would have been treated with equal lenity if he would have consented to put in bail. But he was determined to do no act which could be construed into a recognition of the usurping government. He was therefore outlawed ; and when he died, more than thirty years later, his outlawry had not been reversed.[1]

Parkyns was the last Englishman who was tried for high treason under the old system of procedure. The first who was tried under the new system was Rookwood. He was defended by Sir Bar-

Trials of Rookwood, Cranburne and Lowick tholomew Shower, who in the preceding reign had made himself unenviably conspicuous as a servile and cruel sycophant, had obtained from James the Recordership of London when Holt honourably resigned it, had, as Recorder, sent soldiers to the gibbet for breaches of military discipline, and had justly earned the nickname of the Manhunter. Shower had deserved, if any offender had deserved, to be excepted from the Act of Indemnity, and left to the utmost rigour of those laws which he had shamelessly perverted. But

---

[1] L'Hermitage, April $\frac{7}{17}$. 1696. The Declaration of the Bishops, Collier's Defence, and Further Defence, and a long legal argument for Cook and Snatt will be found in the Collection of State Trials.

he had been saved by the clemency of William, and had requited that clemency by pertinacious and malignant opposition.[1] It was doubtless on account of Shower's known leaning towards Jacobitism that he was employed on this occasion. He raised some technical objections which the Court overruled. On the merits of the case he could make no defence. The jury returned a verdict of guilty. Cranburne and Lowick were then tried and convicted. They suffered with Rookwood ; and there the executions stopped.[2]

 The temper of the nation was such that the government might have shed much more blood without incurring the reproach of cruelty. The feeling which had been called forth by the discovery of the The plot continued during several weeks to increase day by day. Association Of that feeling the able men who were at the head of the Whig party made a singularly skilful use. They saw that the public enthusiasm, if left without guidance, would exhaust itself in huzzas, healths, and bonfires, but might, if wisely guided, be the means of producing a great and lasting effect. The Association, into which the Commons had entered while the King's speech was still in their ears, furnished the means of combining four fifths of the nation in one vast club for the defence of the order of succession with which were inseparably combined the dearest liberties of the English people, and of establishing a test which would distinguish those who were zealous for that order of succession from those who sullenly and reluctantly acquiesced in it. Of the five hundred and thirteen members of the Lower House about four hundred and twenty voluntarily subscribed the instrument which recognised William as rightful and lawful King of England. It was moved in the Upper House that the same form should be adopted : but objections were raised by the Tories. Nottingham, ever conscientious, honourable, and narrowminded, declared that he could not assent to the words "rightful and lawful." He still held, as he had held from the first, that a prince who had taken the Crown, not by birthright, but by the gift of the Convention, could not properly be so described. William was doubtless King in fact, and, as King in fact, was entitled to the obedience of Christians. "No man," said Nottingham, "has served or will serve His Majesty more faithfully than I. But to this document I cannot set my hand." Rochester and Normanby held similar language. Monmouth, in a speech of two hours and a half, earnestly exhorted the Lords to agree with the Commons. Burnet was vehement on the same side. Wharton, whose father had lately died, and who was now Lord Wharton, appeared in the foremost rank of the Whig peers. But no man distinguished himself more in the debate than one whose life, both public and private, had been a long series of faults and disasters, the incestuous

[1] See the Manhunter, 1690.   [2] State Trials.

lover of Henrietta Berkeley, the unfortunate lieutenant of Monmouth. He had recently ceased to be called by the tarnished name of Grey of Wark, and was now Earl of Tankerville. He spoke on that day with great force and eloquence for the words, " rightful and lawful." Leeds, after expressing his regret that a question about a mere phrase should have produced dissension among noble persons who were all equally attached to the reigning Sovereign, undertook the office of mediator. He proposed that their Lordships, instead of recognising William as rightful and lawful King, should declare that William had the right by law to the English Crown, and that no other person had any right whatever to that Crown. Strange to say, almost all the Tory peers were perfectly satisfied with what Leeds had suggested. Among the Whigs there was some unwillingness to consent to a change which, slight as it was, might be thought to indicate a difference of opinion between the two Houses on a subject of grave importance. But Devonshire and Portland declared themselves content : their authority prevailed ; and the alteration was made. How a rightful and lawful possessor is to be distinguished from a possessor who has the exclusive right by law, is a question which a Whig may, without any painful sense of shame, acknowledge to be beyond the reach of his faculties, and leave to be discussed by High Churchmen. Eighty three peers immediately affixed their names to the amended form of association ; and Rochester was among them. Nottingham, not yet quite satisfied, asked time for consideration.[1]

Beyond the walls of Parliament there was none of this verbal quibbling. The language of the House of Commons was adopted by the whole country. The City of London led the way. Within thirty six hours after the Association had been published under the direction of the Speaker, it was subscribed by the Lord Mayor, by the Aldermen, and by almost all the members of the Common Council. The municipal corporations all over the kingdom followed the example. The spring assizes were just beginning ; and at every county town the grand jurors and the justices of the peace put down their names. Soon shopkeepers, artisans, yeomen, farmers, husbandmen, came by thousands to the tables where the parchments were laid out. In Westminster there were thirty seven thousand associators, in the Tower Hamlets eight thousand, in Southwark eighteen thousand. The rural parts of Surrey furnished seventeen thousand. At Ipswich all the freemen signed except two. At Warwick all the male inhabitants who had attained the age of sixteen signed, except two Papists and two Quakers. At Taunton, where the memory of the Bloody Circuit was fresh, every man who could write

---

[1] The best, indeed the only good, account of these debates is given by L'Hermitage, Feb. 28. Mar. 9. 1696. He says, very truly : " La différence n'est qu'une dispute de mots, le droit qu'on a à une chose selon les loix estant aussy bon qu'il puisse estre."

gave in his adhesion to the government. All the churches and all the meeting houses in the town were crowded, as they had never been crowded before, with people who came to thank God for having preserved him whom they fondly called William the Deliverer. Of all the counties of England Lancashire was the most Jacobitical. Yet Lancashire furnished fifty thousand signatures. Of all the great towns of

MEDALS ON THE ASSASSINATION PLOT

England Norwich was the most Jacobitical. The magistrates of that city were supposed to be in the interest of the exiled dynasty. The nonjurors were numerous, and had, just before the discovery of the plot, seemed to be in unusual spirits and ventured to take unusual liberties. One of the chief divines of the schism had preached a sermon there which gave rise to strange suspicions. He had taken for his text the verse in which the Prophet Jeremiah announced that the day of vengeance was come, that the sword would be drunk with blood, that the Lord God of Hosts had a sacrifice in the north country by the river Euphrates. Very soon it was known that, at the time when this discourse was delivered, swords had actually been sharpening, under the direction of Barclay and Parkyns, for a bloody sacrifice on the north bank of the river Thames. The indignation of the common people of Norwich was not to be restrained. They came in multitudes, though discouraged by the municipal authorities, to plight faith to William, rightful and lawful King. In Norfolk the number of signatures amounted to forty eight thousand, in Suffolk to seventy thousand. Upwards of five hundred rolls went up to London from every part of England. The number of names attached to twenty seven of those rolls appears from the London Gazette to have been three hundred and fourteen thousand. After making the largest allowance for fraud, it seems certain that the Association included the great majority of the adult male inhabitants of England who were able to sign their names. The tide of popular feeling was so strong that a man who was known not to have signed ran considerable risk of being publicly affronted. In many places nobody appeared without wearing in his hat a red riband on which were embroidered the words, " General Association for King William." Once a party of Jacobites had the courage to parade a street in London with an emblematic device which seemed to indicate their contempt for what they called the new Solemn League and Covenant. They were instantly put to rout by the mob, and their leader was well ducked. The enthusiasm spread to secluded isles, to factories in foreign countries, to remote colonies. The Association was signed by the rude fishermen of the Scilly Rocks, by the English merchants of Malaga, by the English merchants of Genoa, by the citizens of New York, by the tobacco planters of Virginia, and by the sugar planters of Barbadoes.[1]

Emboldened by success, the Whig leaders ventured to proceed a step further. They brought into the Lower House a bill for the securing of the King's person and government. By this bill it was provided that whoever, while the war lasted, should come from France into England without the royal license should incur the penalties of treason, that the suspension of the Habeas Corpus Act should continue to the end of the year 1696, and that all functionaries appointed by William should retain their offices, notwithstanding his death, till his successor should be pleased to dismiss them. The form of Association which the House of Commons had adopted was solemnly ratified ; and it was provided that no person should sit in that House or should hold

[1] See the London Gazettes during several weeks, L'Hermitage, March $\frac{17}{27}$., $\frac{\text{March 24.}}{\text{April 3.}}$, April $\frac{11}{21}$. 1696 ; Postman, April 9. 25. 30.

any office, civil or military, without signing. The Lords were indulged in the use of their own form ; and nothing was said about the clergy.

The Tories, headed by Finch and Seymour, complained bitterly of this new test, and ventured once to divide, but were defeated. Finch seems to have been heard patiently : but, notwithstanding all Seymour's eloquence, the contemptuous manner in which he spoke of the Association raised a storm against which he could not stand. Loud cries of "the Tower, the Tower," were heard. Haughty and imperious as he was, he was forced to explain away his words, and could scarcely, by apologising in a manner to which he was little accustomed, save himself from the humiliation of being called to the bar and reprimanded on his knees. The bill went up to the Lords, and passed with great speed in spite of the opposition of Rochester and Nottingham.[1]

ASSOCIATION MEDALS

The nature and extent of the change which the discovery of the Assassination Plot had produced in the temper of the House of Commons and of the nation is strikingly illustrated by the history of a bill entitled a Bill for the further Regulation of Elections of Members of Parliament.

Bill for the Regulation of Elections

The moneyed interest was almost entirely Whig, and was therefore an object of dislike to the Tories. The rapidly growing power of that interest was generally regarded with jealousy by landowners whether they were Whigs or Tories. It was something new and monstrous to see a trader from Lombard Street, who had no tie to the soil of our island, and whose wealth was entirely personal and movable, post down to Devonshire or Sussex with a portmanteau full of guineas, offer himself as candidate for a borough in opposition to a neighbouring gentleman whose ancestors had been regularly returned ever since the Wars of the Roses, and come in at the head of the poll. Yet even this was not the worst. More than one seat in Parliament, it was said, had been bought and sold over a dish of coffee at Garraway's. The purchaser had not been required even to go through the form of showing himself to the electors. Without leaving his counting house in Cheapside, he

[1] Journals of the Commons and Lords ; L'Hermitage, April $\frac{7}{17}$. $\frac{10}{20}$. 1696.

had been chosen to represent a place which he had never seen. Such things were intolerable. No man, it was said, ought to sit in the English legislature who was not master of some hundreds of acres of English ground.[1] A bill was accordingly brought in for excluding from the House of Commons every person who had not a certain estate in land. For a knight of a shire the qualification was fixed at five hundred a year; for a burgess at two hundred a year. Early in February this bill was read a second time and referred to a Select Committee. A motion was made that the Committee should be instructed to add a clause enacting that all elections should be by ballot. Whether this motion proceeded from a Whig or from a Tory, by what arguments it was supported, and on what grounds it was opposed, we have now no means of discovering. We know only that it was rejected without a division.

Before the bill came back from the Committee, some of the most respectable constituent bodies in the kingdom had raised their voices against the new restriction to which it was proposed to subject them. There had in general been little sympathy between the commercial towns and the Universities. For the commercial towns were the chief seats of Whiggism and Nonconformity; and the Universities were zealous for the Crown and the Church. Now, however, Oxford and Cambridge made common cause with London and Bristol. It was hard, said the Academics, that a grave and learned man, sent by a large body of grave and learned men to the Great Council of the nation, should be thought less fit to sit in that Council than a boozing clown who had scarcely literature enough to entitle him to the benefit of clergy. It was hard, said the traders, that a merchant prince, who had been the first magistrate of the first city in the world, whose name on the back of a bill commanded entire confidence at Smyrna and at Genoa, at Hamburg and at Amsterdam, who had at sea ships every one of which was worth a manor, and who had repeatedly, when the liberty and religion of the kingdom were in peril, advanced to the government, at an hour's notice, five or ten thousand pounds, should be supposed to have a less stake in the prosperity of the commonwealth than a squire who sold his own bullocks and hops over a pot of ale at the nearest market town. On the report, it was moved that the Universities should be excepted: but the motion was lost by a hundred and fifty one votes to a hundred and forty three. On the third reading it was moved that the City of London should be excepted: but it was not thought advisable to divide. The final question, that the bill do pass, was carried by a hundred and seventy three votes to a hundred and fifty, on the day

[1] See the Freeholder's Plea against Stockjobbing Elections of Parliament Men, and the Considerations upon Corrupt Elections of Members to serve in Parliament. Both these pamphlets were published in 1701.

which preceded the discovery of the Assassination Plot. The Lords agreed to the bill without any amendment.

William had to consider whether he would give or withhold his assent. The commercial towns of the kingdom, and among them the City of London, which had always stood firmly by him, and which had extricated him many times from great embarrassments, implored his protection. It was represented to him that the Commons were far indeed from being unanimous on this subject ; that, in the last stage, the majority had been only twenty three in a full House ; that the motion to except the Universities had been lost by a majority of only eight. On full consideration he resolved not to pass the bill. Nobody, he said, could accuse him of acting selfishly on this occasion : his prerogative was not concerned in the matter ; and he could have no objection to the proposed law except that it would be mischievous to his people.

On the tenth of April 1696, therefore, the Clerk of the Parliament was commanded to inform the Houses that His Majesty would consider of the Bill for the further Regulation of Elections. Some violent Tories in the House of Commons flattered themselves that they might be able to carry a resolution reflecting on the King. They moved that whoever had advised him to refuse his assent to their bill was an enemy to him and to the nation. Never was a greater blunder committed. The temper of the House was very different from what it had been on the day when the address against Portland's grant had been voted by acclamation. The detection of a murderous conspiracy, the apprehension of a French invasion, had changed every thing. William was popular. Every day ten or twelve bales of parchment covered with the signatures of associators were laid at his feet. Nothing could be more imprudent than to propose, at such a time, a thinly disguised vote of censure on him. The moderate Tories accordingly separated themselves from their angry and unreasonable brethren. The motion was rejected by two hundred and nineteen votes to seventy ; and the House ordered the question and the numbers on both sides to be published, in order that the world might know how completely the attempt to produce a quarrel between the King and his Parliament had failed.[1]

The country gentlemen might perhaps have been more inclined to resent the loss of their bill, had they not been put into high good humour by the passing of another bill which they considered as even more important. The project of a Land Bank had been revived, in a form less shocking to common sense and less open to ridicule than that which had, two years before, been under the

Act establishing a Land Bank

---

[1] The history of this bill will be found in the Journals of the Commons, and in a very interesting despatch of L'Hermitage, April $\frac{14}{24}$. 1696. The bill itself is among the Archives of the House of Lords.

consideration of the House of Commons. Chamberlayne indeed protested loudly against all modifications of his plan, and proclaimed, with undiminished confidence, that he would make all his countrymen rich if they would only let him. He was not, he said, the first great discoverer whom princes and statesmen had regarded as a dreamer. Henry the Seventh had, in an evil hour, refused to listen to Christopher Columbus ; and the consequence had been that England had lost the mines of Mexico and Peru. But what were the mines of Mexico and Peru to the riches of a nation blessed with an unlimited paper currency ? By this time, however, the united force of reason and ridicule had reduced the once numerous sect which followed Chamberlayne to a small and select company of incorrigible fools. Few even of the squires now believed in his two great doctrines ; the doctrine that the State can, by merely calling a bundle of old rags ten millions sterling, add ten millions sterling to the riches of the nation ; and the doctrine that a lease of land for a term of years may be worth many times the fee simple. But it was still the general opinion of the country gentlemen that a bank, of which it should be the special business to advance money on the security of land, might be a great blessing to the nation. Harley and the Speaker Foley now proposed that such a bank should be established by Act of Parliament, and promised that, if their plan was adopted, the King should be amply supplied with money for the next campaign.

The Whig leaders, and especially Montague, saw that the scheme was a delusion, that it must speedily fail, and that, before it failed, it might not improbably ruin their own favourite institution, the Bank of England. But on this point they had against them, not only the whole Tory party, but also their master and many of their followers. The necessities of the State were pressing. The offers of the projectors were tempting. The Bank of England had, in return for its charter, advanced to the State only one million at eight per cent. The Land Bank would advance more than two millions and a half at seven per cent. William, whose chief object was to procure money for the service of the year, was little inclined to find fault with any source from which two millions and a half could be obtained. Sunderland, who generally exerted his influence in favour of the Whig leaders, failed them on this occasion. The Whig country gentlemen were delighted by the prospect of being able to repair their stables, replenish their cellars, and give portions to their daughters. It was impossible to contend against such a combination of force. A bill was passed which authorised the government to borrow two million five hundred and sixty four thousand pounds at seven per cent. A fund, arising chiefly from a new tax on salt, was set apart for the payment of the interest. If, before the first of August, the subscription for one half of this loan should have been filled, and if one half of the sum subscribed should have been paid into the Exchequer, the subscribers were to become a corporate body, under the name of the National Land Bank. As this bank was expressly intended to accommodate country gentlemen, it was strictly interdicted from lending money on any private security other than a mortgage of land, and was bound to lend on mortgage at least half a million annually. The interest on this half million was not to exceed three and a half per cent, if the payments were quarterly, or four per cent, if the payments were half yearly. At that time the market rate of interest on the best mortgages was full six per cent. The shrewd observers at the Dutch Embassy therefore thought that the subscription would never be half filled up ; and it seems strange that any sane person should have thought otherwise.[1]

It was vain however to reason against the general infatuation. The Tories exultingly predicted that the Bank of Robert Harley would completely eclipse the Bank of Charles Montague. The bill passed both Houses. On the twenty-seventh of April it received the royal assent ; and the Parliament was immediately afterwards prorogued.

[1] The Act is 7 and 8 Will. 3. c. 31. Its history may be traced in the Journals.

END OF VOLUME V

GLASGOW : PRINTED AT THE UNIVERSITY PRESS BY ROBERT MACLEHOSE AND CO. LTD.